Mississippian
Political Economy

INTERDISCIPLINARY CONTRIBUTIONS TO ARCHAEOLOGY

Series Editor: Michael Jochim, *University of California, Santa Barbara*
Founding Editor: Roy S. Dickens, Jr., *Late of University of North Carolina, Chapel Hill*

A Chronological Listing of Volumes in this series appears at the back of this volume.

A Continuation Order Plan is available for this series. A continuation order will bring delivery
of each new volume immediately upon publication. Volumes are billed only upon actual
shipment. For further information please contact the publisher.

Mississippian Political Economy

JON MULLER

Southern Illinois University
Carbondale, Illinois

PLENUM PRESS • NEW YORK AND LONDON

Library of Congress Cataloging in Publication Data

Muller, Jon.
 Mississippian political economy / Jon Muller.
  p.   cm.—(Interdisciplinary contributions to archaeology)
 Includes bibliographical references and index.
 ISBN 0-306-45529-3 (Hardbound)—ISBN 0-306-45675-3 (Paperback)
  1. Mississippian culture—Southern States. 2. Indians of North America—Southern
 States—Economic conditions. 3. Indians of North America—Southern States—Social condi-
 tions. 4. Indians of North America—Industries—Southern States. I. Title. II. Series.
 E99.M6815M85 1997
 975—dc21   97-16721
                                                                                CIP

ISBN 0-306-45529-3 (Hardbound)
ISBN 0-306-45675-3 (Paperback)

© 1997 Plenum Press, New York
A Division of Plenum Publishing Corporation
233 Spring Street, New York, N. Y. 10013

http://www.plenum.com

10 9 8 7 6 5 4 3 2 1

Printed in the United States of America

To Jean, Karen, and Edith with thanks

Preface

This book is written from a particular theoretical and practical position. The first chapter outlines some of these issues, but a few issues require emphasis.

The first is what is meant by "political economy." The concept of political economy used here derives from common economic and social science usage. Sometimes, however, a few individuals seem to consider political economy to consist only of power relationships, especially in regard to distribution and consumption, often excluding or ignoring social reproduction or production. Although power and its uses *are* important issues, this is a very incomplete view of political economy from my perspective, one that ignores arguably central issues.

Another issue is that of historical comparisons. Some of the chapters that follow have much historical data. The historical comparisons are not the point of this volume, however. Testing of historical "models" is important, but the reader should not be distracted by them. I have long preached against misuse of historical analogy. I do argue that the historic and prehistoric Southeastern societies have been misunderstood so as to make an artificial gap between them, but this is a secondary issue. In any case, the thesis of similarity is being *tested* against empirical evidence. The historical data are absolutely not being used to *interpret* the prehistoric data. My emphasis throughout is strongly on the archaeological rather than the historical data, although correction of some misconceptions, as I believe, of historical data requires more lengthy exegesis than I anticipated when I began writing this volume.

The volume is explicitly materialist. The very reason for a political economy is to treat economics and politics together within a materialist frame of interpretation. As will become quite clear, I hope, I find idealist emphases on individual political choices to be unsatisfying as theory or practice. Modes of production are at the heart of the concept of political economy, and the entire volume is built around this framework as broken down into its components, although not in this order:

1. Direct production technology
2. The means of production, including social organization of production
3. The development of elite groups—managing, appropriating, or even supported by surplus-labor

  4. The characteristics of social reproduction

These are the leitmotifs of this volume.

I have tried to take an overview of Mississippian in general. This volume is not intended to be the survey of everything known about Mississippian phases that might be appropriate for an areal textbook. I suspect that many researchers may find my treatment of their own research area to lack the detail they might wish. However, *Mississippian Political Economy* is not intended to be a phase-by-phase survey of Mississippian. Its goal is to present an areawide synthetic approach in contrast to the analytical and regional focus of many other books on Mississippian.

As everyone does, I often start from the material I know best, that of the Lower Ohio Valley, but the discussion is not limited to the Lower Ohio Valley. I want to explain why I am using these Lower Ohio data. One reason is that these are the data developed by our own project, and I have more detailed information available to me than I can obtain on settlement and site character from other regions. In addition, much of the Lower Ohio region has escaped heavy urban development. We have nearly complete survey data on the Black Bottom locality surrounding the Kincaid mound site and very substantial regional survey at high resolution that allows us to detect small farmsteads and even smaller sites (e.g., Butler 1977, 1991; Muller 1978b, 1986b) from the Wabash to the Mississippi (Ahler et al. 1980; Butler et al. 1979; Muller 1984a, 1986b). In addition to our own work, there are many surveys and excavations covering areas up the Tennessee and Cumberland, as well as down-stream in the confluence area (e.g., Boisvert 1977; Clay 1976, 1979; Kreisa 1991; Lewis 1986; Nance 1980; Stephens 1995; Wesler 1991; and many, many more). In short, this all adds up to Mississippian complexes that can be placed in regional, not just local, perspective. There is a depth of research information here that spans over 60 years of intensive archaeological research in this well-defined region (Black 1967; Cole et al. 1951). I believe this region presents us with data on Mississippian organi-zation that will prove to be "typical" of many more Mississippian complexes, once comparable data are available. This has already proved to be the case in the Ameri-can Bottom FAI-270 project, where "large" sites have become more like those of the Black Bottom, once each temporal phase is considered separately (e.g., Mehrer 1995).

In current Mississippian archaeology, there are no less than three "schools" of interpretation. There are the persons, who often began as culture-historians, who are inclined to exaggerated estimates of population, social, and political complexity. These are the people, for example, who see Cahokia as the "City of the Sun" and tend to interpret Mississippian using constructs such as *core* and *periphery* derived from industrial societies. A second school of so-called "minimalists" originally stemmed from the processualism of the 1960s. These argued that the scale of complexes such as Moundville or Cahokia have been exaggerated by the culture historians and their large site-focused descendants. A third school of "postmodern" interpretation has recruits from both the older schools, but grades into the first and is often preoccupied with concepts such as *power*. This idealist approach is one "current" trend in Missis-sippian archaeology, but not the only one—this late 1970s theory has been around long enough to make its "currency" questionable. I hope that *Mississippian Political*

Economy will help to return discussion of Mississippian to a consideration of empirical evidence in contrast to "just-so" or "might-have-been" stories.

We have more than 100 years of archaeological research on Mississippian. As a whole, this is a remarkable data set allowing us to investigate the issues that intrigue all of us who study this complex. Overall, I want *Mississippian Political Economy* to be an opening argument in a broader debate than would be possible if discussion continues to be confined largely to analyses of single regions.

I have spent much of my 30-year professional career discussing and arguing for regional and economic diversity of different Mississippian complexes (see Muller and Stephens in the *Cahokia and the Hinterlands* volume, for example), so I hope no one will think—because *this* volume is general—that I believe that Mississippian societies were all the same. Local differences in so-called Mississippian societies were very important, but neither is each such society unique and amenable only to local, particularistic analysis. I do ask the question of what common features in Mississippian and related societies reflect areawide similarities in production and social structure. I do not start from a conclusion that they are unitary, but I try to consider their similarities while not forgetting their differences.

ACKNOWLEDGMENTS

I worked on this book for a number of years during a period when I was taking my turn at being Chair of my department. During that time, I gave a series of public presentations at professional meetings that were based on this research program. Some of the data employed in the discussion that follows has been used by me in other papers presented or published during this period as noted in footnotes in particular sections.

The Lower Ohio Valley research discussed in this volume was funded by Southern Illinois University, with grants from the National Science Foundation, the National Forest Service, the National Science Foundation Undergraduate Research Program, the United States Geological Survey, the Illinois Historic Preservation Agency, the Illinois Department of Conservation, the Soil Conservation Service, and the Louisville District Corps of Engineers. I especially want to thank Dan Haas and Mary McCorvie of the Shawnee National Forest for their support. I want to thank again what are now several generations of graduate and undergraduate students who worked with me on the Lower Ohio Valley project since 1966. I also want to thank the landowners who have been so generous in allowing us to work on their property. I want to acknowledge invaluable and considerable help from many colleagues, including William Baden, James Brown, Brian Butler, Charles Cobb, Ann Early, Mark Mehrer, George Milner, Lee Newsom, Timothy Pauketat, Dean Saitta, Mark Schurr, Jeanette Stephens, and Vincas Steponaitis—all of whom commented on or assisted with various sections of this volume in manuscript or in other forms without, of course, incurring any responsibility for my errors. I want very especially to acknowledge the great assistance given me by Paul Welch in going over the entire near-final manuscript. I know that he does not agree with everything that I have proposed, but he has helped make the volume better than it would have been without his help. A work of this kind inevitably owes a debt to some persons whose discussions and papers may have escaped formal citation by me in this book. I hope those authors will accept my apologies and thanks. Finally, but not least, I have to thank my family for their patience and assistance.

Contents

Chapter **1**

An Introduction to Political Economy and Mississippian Political Economy

First grub, then ethics.
Bert Brecht

1. ECONOMY AND POLITICAL ECONOMY

Brecht's observation has crystal clarity. Starving people do not worry about table manners. Yet somewhere between starvation and prosperity, people do begin to concern themselves not only with table manners, but also all manner of ethical and moral issues. This book is about the relationships of "eating" and "politics" for various late prehistoric peoples, loosely called Mississippian, who lived in what is now the Southeastern United States.

Unfortunately, before that task can be begun, it is necessary to outline what a political economy really is and how it can be studied. The bulk of this chapter deals with these issues in a summary fashion. I try to define basic terms and clarify some related issues, but that is all. Since I hope that this book will be read by more than just a few Mississippian specialists, I have necessarily to deal with a rather broad range of topics. I shall do so by presenting capsule accounts of major theories and issues, together with references to relevant literature for those who wish to go more deeply into the minutiae. This chapter is also a position paper, however. Readers of earlier versions of this chapter have indicated that they found some sections to be "old hat," whereas other sections were "tough sledding." Unfortunately, different readers did not identify the *same* sections as belonging to either of these two classes. Although I expect that most readers will scan through those sections that are "old

1

hat" to them, I ask that the reader remember that the terminology I use in later chapters is special to the approaches summarized in this first chapter.

At the end of this chapter, I also present a sketch of Mississippian political economy, but this section is only a preview of what follows in constructing such an analysis in the following chapters.

The concept of political economy emerged during the Enlightenment, and some background is necessary to understand what its terms mean. Political economy is the "theory of social wealth," that is, the "science of the production, distribution, and consumption of wealth" (Ingram 1885). The "political economy" of the 19th century has largely become the simple "economics" of the 20th century. The original term, however, survives as a marker of approaches that emphasize the social, political, and even environmental contexts of economy. Originally, the term *economy* meant only what we would today call "domestic economy." *Economy* comes from the Greek οικονομος, a "steward", from οικος, a "house", plus νεμειν, "to manage". As we shall see, Mississippian economy is rather closer to the original sense than to the micro- and macroeconomics of our own time. Nonetheless, Mississippian economies and Mississippian social formations have a political content, being neither "states" nor "tribes," that makes them important to understand.

Since the 18th-century works of Locke, Rousseau, and others, social theory has linked the development of features such as hierarchies, classes, and specialization. Nineteenth-century economic theories utilized such features as the labor theory of value and placed emphasis on class relationships that linked the social phenomena to the means of production (e.g., Engels 1891; Morgan 1877).

I want to emphasize that I do not suggest any necessary priority in causation to the technical means of production. Indeed, one of the chief reasons for using such concepts as *political economy* and *mode of production* in the following discussion is to break away from the perception of economic and political structures as determined solely by technique, demography, or ideas. I will roughly define *mode of production* below, but it includes the social organization of production and the organization of distribution, exchange, and consumption, as well as the means of production. Although I feel material conditions of everyday life are more important in some ultimate sense than other social and cultural factors, I explicitly affirm my belief in the importance of forces that are not purely economic or material. At the same time, recognition of the political and ideological roles played by rational human beings in their social systems does not mean that we must conclude that their actions have the effects, meaning, or consequences that they intended or planned.

Cultural materialist theory has introduced some of the concepts used here into Americanist theoretical discussion (e.g., Harris 1979; Sahlins 1972), but the alternative theoretical tradition of historical materialism can now be considered directly. A new synthesis is now possible that casts out the debris resulting from the isolation caused by ideology and doctrinaire social theories. A political economy grounded in historical materialism can now be assessed on its own merits, without the baggage of opposing world systems. Past misapplication in practice of some historical materialist theory does not mean that it has no value historically, theoretically, or practically.

Economics Background

It is amazing today that the famous, late-19th-century "encyclopedic" ninth edition of the *Encylopædia Britannica* had no entry under "economics." Instead, the field was discussed under the heading of "Political Economy." The author commented that "there prevails wide-spread dissatisfaction with the existing state of economic science, and much difference of opinion both as to its method and as to its doctrines" (Ingram 1885:346). Some things seem not to have changed so much!

Early Economics

The first economists were involved with aristocratically dominated governments that had mercantilist policies and were often obsessed with precious metals as measures of value. On the other side, the free-market philosophy of Adam Smith, still much revered by free-market economists, argued for free trade and governmental noninterference. The "invisible hand" of the market economy meant that the best choice for each individual producer or consumer was the best choice for all (Smith 1776).

Benjamin Franklin is among the early theorists to recognize the utility of labor as central to the concept of value of goods (Franklin 1729; see Marx 1859 [1977:55–56]). Franklin may well have been acquainted with William Petty's (1631) earlier formulation of labor value, which is expressed by both men in terms of the cost of raising corn in relation to silver. For Franklin, it was surely to be expected that an understanding of economic theory in terms of precious metals was not particularly useful, given the shortage of coinage and money in the colonies, and given the fact that substantial portions of the trade of the colonies was still exchange in kind with Native Americans.

An underlying concept of labor value was Adam Smith's starting point as well. For Smith, and for many who followed, labor was the true measure of the exchangeable value of all commodities. Smith believed that in the simplest economies labor was the only important determinant of value, but that as private property and money arose, "profit" (capital) and rent (land) became the other two major components in determining the "price" of a commodity. Rent might well be considered "overhead" regarding the physical facilities necessary for production (*infrastructure*, *sensu* NATO). For Smith, the productivity of labor was increased by virtue of "division of labor," that is to say, specialization. Exchange in the broadest sense was seen as underlying the development of specialization. Finally, as each specialist became dependent upon goods produced by others, the importance of having a medium of exchange increased, leading to money and to "value" as expressed either in terms of other commodities or money.

David Ricardo (1821) also expounded the labor basis of value, and he also emphasized the importance of free competition. Ricardo also argued that rent was based on productivity of land. Ricardo pioneered the awareness of diminishing returns in this context of land and agricultural production.

Classical economists in the tradition of Smith, Ricardo, and John Stuart Mill were all bourgeois and free market in their orientation. Classical economic science developed in the context of economies (especially colonial economies) that were not entirely based on money, and economists struggled with the issue of value and price in a way that led to concern with labor–value theories. However, as the 19th century dragged on, the almost-universal adoption of pecuniary economies made it possible, even convenient, to focus on "price" rather than value. At the same time, it became increasingly difficult to argue that the "invisible hand" produced nothing but social good out of the individual choices made by unregulated capitalists.

Social Economics

The abuses of industrial society led to a number of utopian alternatives in the early to mid-19th century. Of many such schemes, a few were put to practical test, such as Robert Owen's settlement at New Harmony, Indiana, and a number of small-scale efforts to implement Fourier's concept of industrial communes (called *pha-lanxes*; see Nordhoff 1875; Noyes 1870). Engels critiqued these developments and contrasted them with "scientific" socialism (1878, 1882).

Karl Marx and Friedrich Engels developed socialist theories based on a combi-nation of the dialectical method of Hegel and a materialist, not idealist, viewpoint. The dialectic is often treated as a theory of knowledge, concerning the internally contradictory elements within each unitary set of conditions. Adopting and refining the labor theory of value, Marx and Engels built a detailed critique of economic theory and of capitalism itself from this basis. It is important to remember that the focus of almost all of Marx's work was in the analysis of what were seen as contradic-tions implicit in the structure of 19th-century capitalist economies. The economic theory that was developed in the Marxist framework of dialectical and historical materialism is one that was tightly delimited by the practical need to understand and negate contemporary (19th-century) capitalism. The theory was not abstract, but was concerned with practical application in political action (*praxis*).

In developing their theories, however, Marx and Engels, discovering Lewis Henry Morgan's parallel work, became interested in the broader scope of human history and prehistory. In seeking the origins of capitalism, Marx and Engels applied historical materialist analysis to medieval and even more remote social systems. Although this was rarely the main interest of either man, both used dialectical and materialist analysis to examine these other kinds of social systems. In fact, historical materialist analysis on this level was remarkably successful in providing a theoretically motivated approach to non-Western political economies, especially given the ethnographic facts available to them. This was true not least because the labor–value theory was easily adaptable to situations in which modern European economic "facts" such as market systems and money were absent. It may be arguable whether pecuniary capital can be explained only in terms of labor value (failing to give capital and rents sufficient roles in economic structures, according to classical and neoclassical economists), but efforts to define equivalents of these variables in nonmonetary economies seem strained. So it is that a rereading of Engels's *The Origin of the Family, Private Property, and the State* (original publication 1884, rev. 4th ed., 1891) has a currency and freshness of approach, allowing for terminological changes, that will not be found in E. B. Tylor (1865) or in other 19th-century anthropological writing. The issues raised in *Origin* are still of concern to social scientists today—including issues such as the role of exploitation in the origins of more complex social systems. Elements of the analysis are still viable, even if *praxis* proved to be difficult. One of the key reasons for anthropologists to be interested in this kind of economic theory is that it defines concepts and analytical tools that work well in nonpecuniary economies.

One of Marx's contributions was the recognition that "rent," "interest," and "profit" shared a common basis in what he called *surplus value*. As Ernest Mandel put it, this may have "made it possible for the first time to base moral indignation on firm scientific foundations" (1968:706). The concern in this volume, however, is not with the morality or social costs of such "alienation," but rather to explore the theoretical and empirical question of how this process of extraction of "surplus value" comes about—and how much of this kind of process occurred in Mississippian societies. Mississippian presents a specific example of societies that had not moved to strong social differentiation and may be expected to help in the investigation of the relationships among such variables as social differentiation and labor specialization.

Following a discussion of other economic schools and principles, we shall return to the issue of mode of production and how this relates to overall social theory.

Neoclassical Economics

Classical economics was concerned mostly with scarcity, and Marxian economics was concerned with the contradictions of the extraction of surplus value in an industrial setting. After the 1870s, however, there arose what is called "neoclassical economics," which emphasized consumer and producer choice in the marketplace. Neoclassical economists saw *price* as defined by consumer demand within the context of "marginal" costs rather than by labor. Neoclassical economics makes capital a central input, and although labor and land are also seen as inputs in production, they are still transformed into commodities with prices set by demand. Such an economics does not concern itself with the evolution or origins of wealth or the social aspects of production, distribution, and consumption, as examination of neoclassical economics textbooks will quickly reveal (e.g., Case and Fair 1989). With this in mind, let us briefly examine a few neoclassical economic concepts.

Marginal Cost, etc. Marginal cost is the cost of producing just one more item. Demand is similarly defined in terms of marginal utility (the additional satisfaction of demand by consuming one more unit of something). These, with related concepts, are central to neoclassical economics. Among the useful aspects of "marginality" is that it recognizes the variable nature of costs, as opposed to assuming fixed costs. This alteration in costs as volume increases is a kind of reverse logistic feedback. However, it is hard to see how marginal cost would be usefully determined in non-money-based societies, and at best it can probably only be approximated in terms of some kind of return to the concept of labor value and *costs* of raw material (again in terms of labor value). In addition, the economies of scale characteristic of industrial production are less easily achieved in handwork kinds of simple production, so that the n + 1 item produced tends to cost the same as each of the first *n* objects. Even though many features of supply and demand curves in nonpecuniary economies might be similar to those of neoclassical economics, the mechanisms for "price" determination are dependent upon exchange mechanisms in which markets, *per se*, are either lacking or poorly developed. Goods may be given in relationships that are not directly related to supply or demand. So it is that there are major difficulties in applying this "marginal" approach to non-Western, nonpecuniary economies where neither *price* nor *money* nor *market* has any meaning. Similar problems apply to all of the "marginal" concepts, such as marginal utility, marginal revenue, and so on.

Money and Economics. "Choice" and "scarcity" are also key concepts in the neoclassical model, but their use is within the framework of a market, pecuniary economic system. In a market system, these two aspects of economic behavior are transformed into "demand" and "supply. " As shown in Figure 1.1, demand curves show choice for reduced numbers of a commodity as price increases. In a real sense, this kind of microeconomic phenomenon is seen as psychological. In the same figure, scarcity (and abundance) are matters of the "law of supply" and ultimately to the principle that "price will rise or fall until the quantity of a commodity demanded and the quantity supplied are equal" (see Marshall 1890, still in print in 1982). Of course, the amount produced will also rise or fall as a function of price.

The chart in Figure 1.1a shows different demand and supply curves at two different levels of income and two different levels of production costs. The chart in Figure 1.1b shows the values at the intersection of the supply and demand curves for a particular set of circumstances that determine the market equilibrium. Rather than surplus and shortage, one has "excess supply" and "excess demand." "Excess demand" for resources such as food and housing seems, according to these theorists, to be best solved by "price rationing"—those who can afford to eat will presumably do so without the wasted time (cost) of waiting in line that occurs with efforts to otherwise ration resources (e.g., Case and Fair 1989: 108–111 and fn. 109). It is especially striking to anyone not committed to this ideology to see how textbook examples are chosen for such matters as fancier and poorer restaurants, rather than in terms of the real economic choices faced by too many of our species—if you eat, you may have no money left for shelter or clothes (1989).

Modern economic theorists see most, and some radical, free market theorists see *all*, economic choices as resulting from price. In practice, astonishingly to an anthropologist or to anyone that remembers the Edsel automobile, surveys of demand are sometimes based on questionnaire surveys of stated intent to buy at given price. Although such data may not be entirely garbage, neither are they likely to be good predictors of actual human *behavior*. Empirically determined demand and supply curves based on past responses are more useful, but these are still limited to the cases and circumstances in which they originate. The curves connect points of choice, but only *ceteris paribus*. In the absence of a more general theory of "choice," it is no simple matter to construct demand and supply curves for historical, much less prehistoric, economies. Of course, efforts have been made (e.g., Keegan and Butler 1987). I would, however, point to Allen's interesting conclusions that a supply and demand curve in the context of self-organizing social systems is "fundamentally misleading, because it can only be constructed in retrospect" (1982:362–364). Similar problems

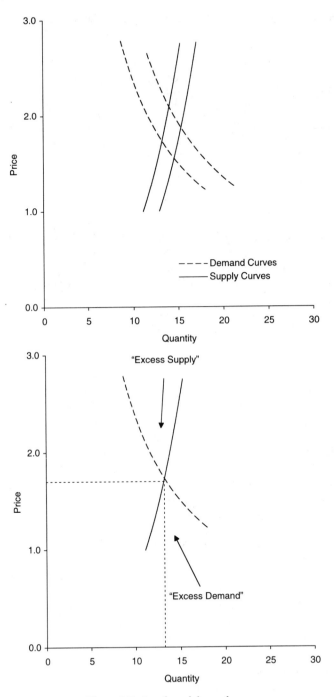

Figure 1.1. Supply and demand curves.

exist for the special analytical methods of input–output relations in economics (Leontief 1936, 1986; Miernyk 1965).

Micro- and Macroeconomics. The distinction between microeconomics and macroeconomics is the difference between the economics of individuals and the economics of aggregates. Much of macroeconomics has evolved from the concerns of Keynesian economic theory (discussed briefly below).

Overall, microeconomics is the study of the process of allocation of goods and services. Microeconomics is concerned with individual production and consumption decisions and with such matters as the pricing of individual goods. Another concern of microeconomic theory is the distribution of wealth and income. On the employment side, there is also interest in questions of differentiation of labor in specific production systems.

Macroeconomic theory and studies are social, rather than individual. They are concerned with production in the aggregate in terms of overall inputs and outputs. Surplus and shortages in relation to total social demand and the aggregate income, as expressed in such measures as Gross National Product, are concerns of macroeconomic studies. Employment is studied through overall unemployment figures and numbers of specialized professions.

Keynesian Economics. John Maynard Keynes's *The General Theory of Employment, Interest, and Money* (1936) had a revolutionary effect on neoclassical and classical models in arguing that price and wage levels did not predict unemployment, but that "aggregate demand"—total spending by all purchasers of goods and services—determined unemployment. The implication was that large investors and government, not private families, were the only economic players with sufficient purchasing power to effect changes in aggregate demand. Thus the government, in times of economic stress, is seen as taking a major role in encouraging business investment by means such as lowering interest rates and, in harder times, even by direct intervention, such as public works. Despite sectarian differences with neoclassical theory, and its emphasis on macroeconomic aspects, the basic framework of Keynesian economics is less "revolutionary" than evolutionary. Like neoclassical economics proper, it shares a concern with money rather than production.

Relevance of Economics for Pre- and Noncapitalist Economies? However powerful (or not) neoclassical and Keynesian theory may be for well-developed industrial societies, the economics taught in college classes is a hothouse species that does not survive transplantation to other climates. Anthropologists and others interested in human societies in general really must seek some more nearly universal principles behind the special cases involving money. At the same time, we must not simply *assume* that *all* economic principles are or should be universal in scope. For example, can we assume that maximization of return for investment makes the same sense in a nonpecuniary environment as it does in modern Wall Street?

Although I think it can be overplayed in both directions, one central difference between neoclassical and historical materialist positions lies in a tendency to reductionism in the former and attention to a broad range of multiple causation in the latter (so-called "overdetermination," or "dialectical" reasoning; see Wolff and Resnick 1987:20ff.). Of course, it is stupid to assert that all attention to testing against empirical facts is necessarily reductionist, or that dialectical thinking can deal with all variables simultaneously.

There is a debate between what are called "formalists" and "substantivists" in the anthropological study of economics. Formalists seek to apply Western economic principles to non-Western economic systems, arguing that such conditions as scarcity and choice are universal. The substantivists have argued that different economic systems require different assumptions and models. For what it is worth, I believe in underlying universal principles in economics, but I do not believe the neoclassical models provide us with much more than a series of corollaries of those principles as they apply to one particular, historically unique case. Ironically, this is also a criticism aimed at widespread application of the analytical methods of Marx, who was equally concerned with Capitalism but for somewhat different reasons. In the same kind of discussion, others have seen the need not to merely "apply" Marxian concepts, but to duplicate the kind of study done in *Capital* for noncapitalist social formations (Meillassoux 1972). The difficulty of shoehorning non-Western economies into Western categories is manifest in formalist works and, indeed, is often referred to at least obliquely in them (e.g., Herskovits 1952:332). But neither do I find many of the particularistic economic arguments of substantivists to be very useful (e.g., Dalton 1968). A more attractive (to me) kind of substantivism is that of Sahlins (1972, see his introduction). This debate will not be resolved soon and, particularly, will not be resolved here. There is an extensive literature comparing neoclassical theory with others to which those interested in the discussion can turn (e.g., Wolff and Resnick 1987).

Dialectical Theory and "Western Marxism"

In addition to the political economics of traditional Marxist theory, there are Western European theories that draw less on the materialism of Marxism than on its dialectical traditions. These theories place considerable emphasis on social relationships of power rather than upon economics, as such (e.g., Anderson 1976; Ollman 1971; Sayer 1987; I have discussed the latter two of these in Muller 1991).

A recent work, *Marxist Archaeology* by Randall McGuire (1992, see also 1993), provides a sympathetic history of these "Western Marxists," including the dialectical, "internal relations" theories upon which McGuire's own theory is grounded. Although a critical discussion of these theories is out of place here, the approach seems to me to be more Hegelian than Marxist (see Marx's discussion of Proudhon in his letter of December 28, 1846 to Pavel Annenkov; Engels 1886; also compare Kahn and Llobera 1981:304 and elsewhere). For example, labor–value theory (along with most other materialist considerations) is virtually abandoned in favor of a theory of ideas, symbols, and power relations.

Ideas, symbols, and power are hardly unimportant, but in this book, at any rate, my concern is how such structures may emerge in the context of the material conditions of everyday life. I especially profess myself to be unable to see just how the proposition that forces of production, relations of production, and superstructure are "facets of the same social totality" leads to the "realist"[1] conclusions reached by Sayer and McGuire. McGuire, following Ollman, chooses to call the analysis of material dimensions reification or fetishization (1992:50), terms that have a considerable Marxist tradition behind them, but I believe that Ollman and McGuire's usage is actually at odds with that tradition. The word used in this discussion by Marx was not *reification*, but rather *personification* (*Personifikation*, Marx 1867 [1962:16, 100, 128]; see Muller 1991:253–5). It refers to treating these dimensions too much as relations and forgetting their material basis that imposes capitalist modes of thought on precapitalist systems, not the other way around. In the end, only a few people really care whether Marx (or Engels) was a "realist" or a materialist, but the issue of whether causes are to be sought *primarily* in the realm of ideas *is* important (see also Trigger 1993). However, I suppose I will be forgiven if I do not seek or claim to resolve this fundamental, age-old debate. While I am not quite as pessimistic as Kahn and Llobera are that careful, contextual study of Marx's writing could never resolve the issues of what *he* meant to do, they are certainly correct that this is not the central issue of a historical materialist anthropology (1981:305ff.).

Others have made interesting efforts to extend the issues surrounding Marxian "class" theory to "precapitalist" societies (e.g., for such a discussion with a useful bibliography, see Saitta 1994). Of course, the term *precapitalist* is unfortunate in many ways. Many "precapitalist" systems are contemporary with capitalist societies. Even the term *noncapitalist*, which I use on occasion in this book, still retains the unfortunate implication that the world is either capitalist or not, when there are many different social formations and modes of production. However, If we create a neologism for every term that has some baggage, we shall not communicate at all.

I would also mention that without being necessarily "Marxist" in any traditional sense, a substantial number of studies of Mississippian societies have taken power relationships as fundamental (most notably, papers in Barker and Pauketat 1992). Power relationships are necessarily part of the discussion of state formation (e.g., Patterson and Gailey 1987). Emphases on power as a key factor have commonly been found among certain flavors of postprocessualist archaeology from its beginnings (e.g., some papers in Hodder 1982).

Economic Dimensions and Definitions

Before proceeding, it is necessary to examine briefly the nature of political economic behavior. This is not an economics textbook, but some of the terminology employed in later chapters needs explanation. One problem with analyses of economic behavior has been a tendency to classify behavior into a convenient series of typological pigeonholes. What we need instead, is to look not at the *types*, but at the

---

[1]*Realism* here refers to the "the attribution of objective existence to a subjective conception" (*Oxford English Dictionary*[OED]). This *realism* has much in common with Platonic realism and does *not* refer to "naive" or even "critical" realism—the belief that *things* are real independently of perception. Platonic, or at least neo-Hegelian, *realism* underlies much postprocessual archaeology and is also developed in *Anthropological Archaeology* by Guy Gibbon, 1984, a largely unrecognized herald of this kind of realist theory.

dimensions of activity. These are universal dimensions—the reporters' "who, what, when, where, how, and why." We have to be concerned with such matters as agency, voluntariness, the nature of the goods produced, how "value" is determined, the timing of production, the place where the behavior takes place, the organization of the activities, and measurement of success.

Agency

The simplest kinds of activities are individual, and all activities begin at the individual level. Single producers, the "economic man" of classical theory, expend labor to acquire or produce an object for their own consumption. Such a Robinson Crusoe–type figure has no problems with distribution or consumption so long as his or her own labor is sufficient unto needs. Human beings, of course, are social animals, and only deprivation such as that suffered by Crusoe or the real-life Ishi result in a individual producer and consumer. To be sure, choices of what, when, and where to produce something do have a strong individual component. It is at this level that the simplest kinds of decisions about the relative value of goods and effort are made. The individual organism must ensure at least as much input of calories as is expended. Every being has to have a balanced economic budget over the intermediate term. Evolutionary selection will ensure that many "noneconomic" choices about activities will disappear *in the long term*, insofar as deficits in energy expenditure are not made up socially or by other means. The discussion about maximization and satisficing behaviors rests largely on choices made by individuals.

This aspect of individual choice presents a kind of evolutionary contradiction however, just as it does in the biological question of sexual selection (for a discussion of this problem in biology, see Andersson 1994). In sexual selection, the aspect of choice adds a potential for "runaway" selection that may not produce optimal survival. The importance of choice in cultural evolution in general is another reason for caution in accepting direct analogies to biological evolution. There is also the possibility that the simple choices made by individuals may show what are called "emergent properties" as they are combined on a mass level—which is to say that there is a leap in structural terms that creates new behavior *in mass* that is not easily predictable from the "laws" of individual choices (for a popular treatment of *emergence* and *complexity*, see Waldrop 1992; for detailed studies of complexity and economics, see Anderson et al. 1988 or Barnett et al. 1989; for emergence, see Forrest 1991).

There is considerable evidence, some of it even scientific, that persons will try to maximize, to get as much for their effort as they can. But there is also considerable evidence that individuals may cease their efforts not far past the point at which their needs have been satisfied (e.g., Chaianov 1923, 1925; Zipf 1949). There is no inconsistency here between optimization and the principle of least effort, merely a difference in what *optimum* means in different situations. This problem in defining *maximum* is what is behind the economic term, *marginal utility*. There is a gradation from maximizing to satisficing that reflects the social and natural conditions in which the behavior is taking place.

At the simplest level, decisions of how much and when to produce are made by producers themselves in relation to their own immediate and short-term needs. These are the "decisions" that any organism has to make to survive. However, as storage is used to buffer seasonal and other perturbations of availability of necessities, the amount of labor invested becomes a matter of risk management (see Jochim 1981). The ant and the squirrel both illustrate the production of short-term surplus and subsequent storage as one kind of solution to "expected" shortages. In nontropical environments, especially, the variability of climate can selectively favor the development of storage "strategies" of "surplus" production. We generally do not feel that we have to understand much about the *motivations* of squirrels or ants to understand how such patterns of behavior emerge and become established. However, as cultural animals, humans can *decide* to take courses of actions and plan how to meet longer-term goals. It would be clearly wrong to ignore this human capability, but it is just as wrong to be overwhelmed by it. We cannot, and should not, assume that humans are somehow immune to evolutionary and natural processes.

In nearly all cases, the focus of economic production remains the domestic unit, loosely called the "family." Even in complex societies, the family lies at the heart of the "needs" that motivate the producer to produce and reproduce (e.g., see, Solo's discussion of American domestic economy, 1967:337–342). The family is, of course, the basis of reproduction, both biologically and socially. Thus the "domestic" economy is a fundamental part of all economies, however buried it may be under elaboration.

The domestic unit also incorporates the simplest kind of division of labor. The individual choices about production and consumption take place within this context in which distribution is very much "from each according to their[2] ability to each according to their need." Only in the most deprived or pathological social circumstances does individual choice ignore the needs of the reproducing unit. Even in conditions of extreme deprivation, the last social tie to break is that of the mother and offspring. In this sense, the mother–child connection is the most fundamental human social relation.

Biology thus provides a basis for a sexual division of labor. Sexual dimorphism in our species is slight, but not trivial, so potential gender differences must be taken into account in models of labor and consumption. Practically, infant care is usually in the hands and arms of the mother, so there are implications for conflicts between external and domestic activities. However, one advantage to "tribal"-scale societies may be the degree to which the entire community and older children can lift this burden from the mothers directly (see the labor–time observations in Grossman 1984, also Figure 1.2).

Of course, the reproducing "family" is only the simplest of a series of different kinds of social units. Such social entities as lineages, clans, and moieties may play important economic roles, especially in allocation of land resources in agricultural societies. Among the most important economic roles of kinship units are those involved with marriage regulation, since marriage is as much an economic as a social fact. Beyond these "consanguineal" organizations are sodalities of many different kinds that constitute intermediate levels of political economy even in large-scale societies (see Meillassoux 1972, 1981).

---

[2] *Their*: "often used for 'him' or 'her,' referring to a singular person whose sex is not stated," and "often used in relation to a singular sb. or pronoun denoting a person, after *each*"(*OED*). This usage is recorded as early as A.D. 1420, and is used by everyone except the overeducated.

Residential groups, sometimes also being kinship or interest based, also play important roles in political economic terms. Indeed, the community forms a biological and economic unit that can even replace ties of kinship as the scale of integration of a society increases. As the economic interactions of the community come to be more important than those of the nonnuclear family, then a qualitative change in social organization may take place that transforms the relation, replacing kin with class relations.

It is clear that there is an emergent character to economic organization. An economy, any economy, is made up of a series of individual actors, each making choices. These choices, however, are made in line with social values that are highly conditioned by interaction with other individuals and by patterns of behavior that are learned through being embedded in large social groups. Thus, choices, paradoxically, are not only, perhaps not even primarily, *individual*.

Groups of people form communities, and different kinds of communities have a variety of organizations. Political structures vary with the kinds of economic and social conditions. In each form of community, there are regional and social limits and social relationships among the members of the community. As differences in access to goods and services emerge, some subgroups within a community come to take on the character of elites. It is important to understand that differences in status are constituted out of many kinds of relationships, and that the final form of these differences will reflect their historical derivation as nonranked social relations are transformed into hierarchical ones. Some differences are, as we might say, horizontal—they represent differences that do not have a hierarchical dimension. Hierarchical differences, where they do exist, may be of many different kinds. One useful distinction made by Fried (1960, 1967) was that between ranked societies and stratified societies. Ranked societies have hierarchical structure, but without major differences in access to the necessities of life (Fried 1967:185–186). There was already a good term available for Fried's stratified societies—*class societies*. While the idea is not new that hierarchical social structures can exist, indeed do exist, in nonclass, nonstate social formations, the term *rank* is a convenient and useful label. As we shall see in Chapter 2, the early colonial commentators did not appreciate the difference between rank and stratification, so their accounts either "grandify" reality by use of terms such as *king* and *tribute*, or else dismiss the power of chiefs and elites as inconsequential when they sometimes realized that stratification in the European sense was absent (note the discussion on Powhatan's power in Rountree 1993:19).

One special and critical form of social groups is that known as *classes*. In Marxian theory of modern social formations, the notion of class is central, since struggle between classes is seen as the motive force of historical development. In the strictest sense, history begins and ends with the formation and disappearance of classes. *Classes* are usually defined as being large groups with a distinctive position in a historically determined system of social production, largely determined by their relation to the means of production, and their ability to acquire social wealth—especially in the ability of one such group to appropriate the labor of another. Such a definition does not quite presuppose production differentiation, but it comes close to doing so. When I say that Mississippian social formations are "nonclass," it is in this sense. Class structures of this kind have nothing to do with the arbitrary groupings by material wealth or self-recognition used in Western sociology.

Another question of agency relates to the roles of specialists in production and in trade. As discussed elsewhere, definitions of chiefly societies in the 1960s laid great emphasis on the role of redistribution—referring to production by geographically dispersed specialists, combined with rationing by elite economic managers (e.g., Service 1962). The beginning of my research on political economy had its distant origins in efforts to test this model in the Mississippian societies of the lower Ohio Valley (see Muller 1978b, 1986b, 1993a). As it happens, *redistribution* is, at best, a rather poor term to describe a system of accumulation of surplus use values by elites in some areas of Polynesia (see Johnson and Earle 1987:235), although the long-term effect may not be so different from the rationing system envisioned by Service (1975). Contrary to the model of Service, there seems to be little, if any, specialization of production (in the sense discussed in later chapters) on either occupational or spatial bases in societies with rank but not classes. The following chapters on production deal with this issue in Mississippian political economy at some length.

Although we shall consider the internal movement of goods in these societies in detail in the chapter on exchange, it would be as well to deal with the use of the term *tribute* to apply to payments in kind made by the members of society to their chief. Such usage is not advisable for a number of reasons. First, properly, the term *tribute* most often refers to "a tax or impost paid by one prince or state to another in acknowledgment of submission" (*OED*). *Tribute* can also mean "rent or homage paid in money or an equivalent by a subject to his sovereign or a vassal to his lord" (*OED*); and this sense could, perhaps, be taken to apply to Southeastern examples. However, *tribute* has a definite implication of state structure, much less class asymmetry, that needs to be proved, not assumed for the Southeast. A slightly preferable term, if only because it is less familiar and therefore less likely to have undesirable implications, is *prestation*, "the act of paying, in money or service, what is due by law or custom, or in recognition of feudal superiority" (*OED*). Although this feudal term may be fairly appropriate in the Southeast, we have to remember that the basis of feudal relations was in allocation of land—in its most developed forms, in conjunction with conquest.[3] In the Southeast, we have at best only a very loose kind of vassalage. Such "warrior power" as existed, appears to have been in the hands of war chiefs rather than the chiefs *per se*. In Blitz's discussion of Tombigbee Mississippian, he notes that "tribute is often used as a catchall term of the mobilization of material goods or labor by the elite" (1993:14), but unfortunately, I think, he chooses to use the term anyway, while quite correctly questioning how similar the Southeastern systems of goods movement really were to the feudal systems of the European describers.

Voluntariness

The individual is a member of, is reared within, a social group. As a result. there are patterns to economic and political behavior that reflect values that are themselves a matrix of interests at many different levels. In this sense, neither the

---

[3] Although there are some interesting similarities to Japanese feudalism (see Asakawa 1931). Perhaps "Shoguns of the Southeast" is as good as "Lords."

individual nor the issue of choice is separate from the influence of the social and environmental setting.

The choices made are neither entirely free nor voluntary. No market is entirely "free," as questions of utility and value are intensely interwoven with social practice and biological necessities. "Letting the market set the price"—that is to say, rationing by price—is, for better or worse, profoundly conservative, since the values that determine price in this context are essentially historically derived. However, "market" mechanisms, even if we accept them as the "best" economic system for industrial states, are so foreign to nonpecuniary societies that it is difficult to see how such models can usefully be applied to such kin or community systems of production, exchange, and consumption.

This raises the issue of whether markets, with all their features of voluntary exchange, exist outside state-level political systems. The answer at first glance is "Of course they do." On closer examination, the answer may not be so obvious. The problem is that "markets" are easily confused with *places* of exchange. A market "in economic parlance is the area within which the forces of demand and supply converge to establish a single price" (Hardy 1933:131). A "market" can be an organized group of people who buy and sell, *or* it can be a place. The problem is that many nonmarket kinds of exchange still occur in physical places (see discussion, p.). The essential feature of a market, in the strict economic sense, is the feature of *price*. It is *not* a system of barter, but a system in which money plays a critical role. This kind of market should not be confused with events that are closer to fairs, rendezvous, or corroborees. True markets imply not only money, but also commodities. Markets do develop out of nonmarket exchanges, just as specialist commodity production and exchange may grow from excess production of use values. However, when production shifts from exchange of surplus use value to production for exchange value, the producer exchanges a condition of independence for one of potential dependence. This affects the "freedom" of market exchange. The question of what *surplus* means is not trivial and will be discussed in a little more detail later.

One must also mention the distinction between "command" and "market" economies. In the former, centralized planning and control extend to all levels of the economy. These economic systems may be superficially like communal economies, but on a massive scale. Command economies are often instituted by "capitalist" economies in times of stress such as war, but real economic situations are so complex that command economies tend to work well only for short periods of time, after which increasing disparities between plans and reality create chaos. This issue would be irrelevant for our purposes, but needs to be noted since "command-economy" features are sometimes confused either with communal systems or with elite "management" in developing hierarchical systems.

Goods and Commodities

A central concern of any economic study has to be what goods are being manufactured and how they work their way through the economy. Later chapters deal with these issues in the context of Mississippian society, but we note here merely that there are well-defined usages for such terms as *commodity*, and that archaeologists need to be more cautious not to willfully misuse these terms.

In this book, as in economics, a *commodity* is an item produced not for its use, but for exchange. This brings in a whole set of complex issues relating to control of the economy and money that are not particularly useful in the study of nonpecuniary economies. The identification of commodities, as such, is best left to be proved in a particular case, rather than assumed or implied. For this reason and many others, the more neutral term *goods* seems more appropriate when we cannot know beforehand what and how items were produced, exchanged, and used (e.g., Douglas and Isherwood 1979).

It is important to recognize that the kinds of goods that can constitute commodities in market situations were present long before they were commoditized by becoming primarily an object of exchange. There may be aspects of their morphology that reflect this change in their "social" character, but there are more likely to be changes in association—at least at the beginning—than differences in form. When exchange becomes a central part of an economic system, it is common for some highly desired commodities to become standards by which other goods are valued. So *money* arises, first as an intermediate exchange value and then as an object of desire in its own right in which money buys commodities that are then sold for money. As money and standard units of exchange emerge, so does the potential for a possessor of money (capital) to alienate the difference between the amount of labor necessary to support a producer and the amount of labor that can be extracted before he or she is paid for that labor. To take the now-classic example, in even "marginal" environments like the Kalahari, the amount of labor necessary on the average for subsistence (and reproduction) by hunters and gatherers seems to be about 15 hours per week (Lee 1968:38)![4] It would be unrealistic to suppose that all work in excess of such a minimal level is *surplus* value, but the differences between labor value and other measures of value, especially price, can be large. It should be no surprise that a labor-value theory is unattractive to those who see capital as the driving force of Economy.

The emergence of private property seems to be associated with this process of commoditizing production and exchange. As the means of production come to be owned by moneyed interests, then labor itself becomes another commodity. Labor, goods, and the material nature of production may change very little in the course of this process—what does change is the social nature of production, from being embedded in community relations (*Gemeindeschaft*) to being property (*Eigentum*).

It has long been recognized that there are divisions between exchange of utilitarian goods and those goods that are "more or less reserved for the State" (e.g., Mandel

---

[4] After a long period of ethnographic belief that hunters and gatherers had to work all the time to survive, studies such as those of Lee rediscovered what Malthus had indicated in his *Essay on the Principle of Population* (1798-1960:57): "I cannot conclude this general review of that department of human society which has been classed under the name of savage life without observing that the only advantage in it above civilised life that I can discover is the possession of a greater degree of leisure by the mass of the people. There is less work to be done, and consequently there is less labour." Malthus, however, does go on to say that civilized men may hope to enjoy, while "the savage expects only to suffer."

1968:58–59; also see Frankenstein and Rowlands 1978; Johnson and Earle 1987). Earle and many of his associates have found the "prestige economy" model attractive for explaining the extension of "self-interest" beyond the local group to larger social entities (see Johnson and Earle 1987:322–325). Prestige economy is one means of enhancing solidarity, and there is no reason to doubt that this and other mechanisms ensuring "social solidarity" are important in the operation of many social systems. In the end, however, the "prestige goods" argument turns out not be so much about *why* social solidarity is needed as it is about *how* it is achieved—an essentially functionalist explanation. The real question for many of us is how it is possible for status differences to develop that *require* either symbolization or mobilization. There is much to be learned from the examination of different classes of goods, so long as the definition of "prestige goods" does not become circular or *a priori*. In general, I will discuss these items in the following chapters in terms of *display* goods, a slightly more neutral term. In addition, the production and use of "prestige goods" does not necessarily imply all aspects of the model as proposed by Earle.

Value

The concept of labor value has already been introduced historically above (also see Dobb 1973). In short, it is a measurement of value by the amount of labor expended in production of goods. However, the labor value is not the individual producer's time, but rather the "socially necessary labor" expended in a given society and at a given form of production.[5] *Value* and *socially necessary* are general, not necessarily universal, principles; and they must be specifically defined for particular social formations.

"Use value" refers to the value of an item as determined by its ability to satisfy some need of the consumer. Use value has no existence, aside from the goods themselves, and becomes a reality only by virtue of consumption. It is independent of the labor required to appropriate its useful qualities. "Exchange values" emerge from the exchange of one kind of use value in one commodity for another kind in a different commodity. Marginal values, as discussed earlier, enter into the exchange value of goods, but the labor expended in their production is seen as the determinant of the exchangeability of commodities.

The definition of surplus value was an important part of Marx's contribution to economic analysis (e.g., Marx 1867: Chapters I and II). Surplus-value theory refers to his conclusion that the difference, in the form of money, between what was necessary to support the producer and the amount of labor extracted by the capitalist was the origin of the wealth of the capitalist. This is a substantially different way of looking at

---

[5] There is an enormous literature on the utility of the "labor–value theory," from both neoclassical and various Marxist and Marxian sources. For example, Roemer (1981) sees exploitation theory as replacing labor–value theory in many circumstances. This, of course, makes little sense in societies in which the presence of exploitation is debatable, at best. Can anyone suggest that there can be no concept of value at all in the absence of exploitation or even classes? Other discussion may be found in Wolff and Resnick (1987).

profit, primarily in *class* terms, than the views characteristic of neoclassical economics (discussed earlier). However, as important as this theory may be for the study of bourgeois societies—and whether it is right or wrong at that level—it is largely irrelevant to our purposes here. The appropriation of surplus value in the classic form presupposes the existence of money and a market economy. In many small-scale societies, it would also be useful to distinguish between goods that are in excess of needs, and goods extracted by force. For the leader to obtain the former—as prestations, for example—is quite different from appropriation, although one can imagine how a transition from one to the other could easily have occurred. Marx saw the appropriation of surplus value as a defining issue in *bourgeois* societies, although he recognized other kinds of appropriation and exploitation in noncapitalist societies. The nature of these methods of appropriation are related to an issue called *primitive accumulation*.

An associated issue in the analysis of the origins of capitalism is that economic studies have found it difficult to document voluntary abstinence and "saving" as a means of accumulation of wealth in nonpecuniary social formations (according to Mandel 1968:88–89). The "ant" capitalists, much-beloved of economists, who accumulate wealth through thrift while their more profligate "grasshopper" neighbors become workers, seem to be largely a fable. As a result, there is a historical problem of what has been called "primitive accumulation"—the problem of explaining what starts the accumulation of "surplus" wealth that can lead to the rise of systems of exploitation. As discussed, the so-called surplus can accumulate as a by-product, as it were, of the normal process of risk management (for discussion of "normal surplus," see Allan 1965; another example may be found in Sebastian 1992). The instability of conditions through time "encourages" prudent producers to accumulate sufficient resources for the worst-case, to the extent that they are able, with the labor and resources available to them. Even squirrels bury more nuts than they need in the "average" year, just as the trees seem to "plan" a surplus of nuts so that the squirrels will plant their seeds for them.

In situations in which it may prove difficult to store surpluses, systems of "delayed exchange" (Heider 1969; Jochim 1981:177) often develop. If the distribution of the resources in nature is not even, then long-term asymmetries often result.

There many related answers to how surplus finds its way out of the hands of the producers, but two ways perhaps represent the range: Surplus can be appropriated purely through force, and surplus may be given up for community purposes. In the latter case, some portions may find their way into the hands of "managers." The use of force—theft, in social terms, or predation, in biological terms—is the forcible alienation of the product from the producer. As in any predator–prey relationship, the predator is defined by virtue of its removal of the prey target from the population in order to gain its resources. As a result, the number of predators has to be low relative to the number of prey in order to allow the reproduction of the prey species or else both may become extinct. As in ecology, this kind of relationship is more likely to occur in relation to other populations than within a single population. This internal–external dichotomy makes a difference in the kinds of expected behavior on the part of both the exploiter and the exploited. Although the gradations of ecological definitions are subtle, human relationships tend to settle into relations more like those of parasites and hosts (see McNaughton and Wolf 1973: Chapter 10; Pielou 1977:88–99 for formal ecological models of these relationships).

In human societies, there are typically many different mechanisms for the consumption of these "surpluses" in years when they are not needed for survival—various festivals and ritually sponsored events are examples of these that are common in smaller societies. The ability to control such short-term surpluses and to act as sponsors of these ritual events typically confers "prestige" and social standing (see Johnson and Earle's discussion of this in "Big Men" social formations; 1987). However, as such sponsors find themselves in control of what, in this context, begins to be "wealth," the temptation to enhance one's own fitness at the expense of the commune seems to be very great. This is an inevitable and universal contradiction for social animals: the conflict between the reproductive interest of the population and the interest of the individual organism. Long-term evolutionary processes allow the survival of appropriation only up to the level at which it does not impinge on the reproduction of the society as a whole.

Timing

Human economic activities, like the behavior of all organisms, take place within the flow of time. Time separates actions and their consequences, and it also conjoins independent events in apparent connection. Time and its measure in terms of cultural phases or stages has long been a near-obsession in archaeology. At one time, it seemed that if only time could be measured accurately, all archaeological problems would be solved. Despite great improvements and some revolutionary reinterpretations, even radiocarbon dating has not resolved our struggles with time in the abstract and concrete.

Despite the difficulty that archaeological research has in controlling temporal placement in increments smaller than 50 to 100 years, much of our actual *evidence* is the result of behavior that played out on the scale from seconds to weeks, rather than years. The ashes and charcoal in a hearth are the remains of the last fire, which may have burned for only a few hours. A utilized flake tool is the result of a manufacturing process that lasted for only a few minutes, and its use and discard may have consumed no more than a few hours. A house was, perhaps, built in a matter of days; and, although its occupation may have spanned a few years, much of the remains found in its ruins reflect only the later *days* of its occupation. This contradiction is somewhat abated by continuation and consistency of activity through time, and also by the ability of archaeology to make a kind of "meta"-analysis from such scraps of evidence.

So time and timing are complex metaphysical issues for archaeology that deserve careful deliberation. Constructing an account of a sequence of behaviors is, as some have pointed out in excruciating detail, narrative art, but unlike just-so storytelling, the scraps of evidence do provide us with a means of testing such narratives against a dim, but not invisible, objective reality. From the overlaying of lines on painted jars, for example, we can reject some sequences of painting as impossible. In the same way, we can use the innumerable evidences of economic activity as a touchstone against which to test the possibilities of behavior in time.

One temporal dimension of great importance is that of scheduling. Some economic activities are controlled rigidly by natural, temporal limitations—harvest must occur within a narrow range of days. Often, perturbations in resources are predictable, such as those associated with the seasons; and many organisms store food against less productive times. Other perturbations, such as flood or drought, are less predictable but still occur on a sufficiently short-term scale that humans are able to remember the results of past failures to provide sufficient resources. The worst kinds of events, from an evolutionary perspective, are those that are so rare, or so long between, that neither rational plans or natural processes could take them into account.

Another temporal problem is that of only being able to be at one place at one time. A choice to harvest a resource at one location prevents an individual from harvesting another resource elsewhere. These scheduling conflicts limit alternatives and often commit producers to one set of activities rather than another. Agricultural production, for example, places severe restraints on the ability to exploit wild plant resources that ripen at the same time. Behavior is by no means *entirely* Markovian in character, but *much* of it is.

Time is also a matter of concern in terms of the duration of activities. Indeed the amount of time—on the average for a level of production—taken to produce something is at the basis of the concept of labor–value and also plays an important part in economic theories of all flavors. As noted, this duration of labor is *not* the time spent by an individual, who may be a slow or fast worker. In fact, aside from the few Stakhanovites, enthusiastically overproducing, the difference between talented and untalented labor is buried in the overall production of a small social group and translates, at most, into more or less social time aside from production. Studies such as those of Grossman (1984; Figure 1.2) and others (e.g., Richards 1961) have shown how much time is spent on social activities as opposed to what we would think of as "work." It would be unwise to treat, *a priori*, this social time as being unproductive. In the figure, there has already been imposed a state labor requirement, and cash crops are grown, but the economy is still mostly at a subsistence level. Remember that Lee's study of the Dobe Bushmen (1968:37) showed only about 15 hours of "work," and other studies in the same volume (Lee and DeVore) suggest about the same level of effort. As an aside, it is interesting to see how little time is spent in overt child care.

Temporal dimensions of economic behavior also involve the issues of supply, raw materials, and distribution. The problem of scheduling access to the raw materials for unspecialized producers is not trivial, but neither is it of overwhelming importance. A single, generalized producer can obtain a raw material directly from its sources or go to other producers engaged in similar tasks. The timing of acquisition is usually not crucial to the nonspecialist producer. Acquisition is part of a cycle of events, or is undertaken within the temporal framework of other activities; that is, if hunting takes one past a chert source, a few nodules may be gathered for later use. In such a context, the individual labor "cost" of some item may be minimal in being "charged off" to other activities.

For specialists, timing of supply is another matter. As I will discuss in the chapters on production, it may be misleading to believe in "degrees" of specialization, since there are real qualitative transformations that can be seen under closer analysis

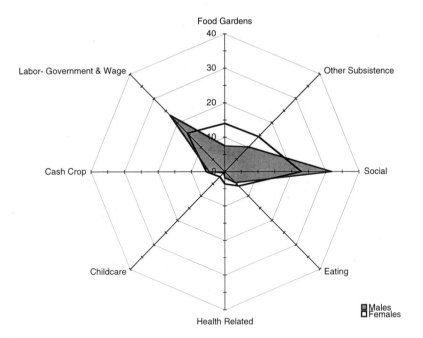

Figure 1.2. Average hours per week spent by adults and teens in activities in Kapanara (Papua New Guinea). (Data from Grossman 1984, with food preparation included in subsistence tasks.)

(see also Cobb 1993d). Jacobs (1967) gives many examples of the revolutionary impacts of the development of specialization in even modern economies).

"Real" specialist producers produce in greater quantity, usually within some kinds of "deadlines" for delivery of a product to "market." Specialists without the raw materials they need are without a livelihood. Raw materials access may be carried out by the specialist producer, but this often involves some kind of seasonal schedule—that is, a kind of sequential specialization. As production becomes still larger-scale, acquisition and supply of raw materials, like the distribution of the end product itself, become the purview of *other* specialists.

Finally, work, in the physicists' sense, is movement, and it is this kind of work that defines time. *Work* is defined as the product of the force and the distance though which it produces movement.

Place

Behavior, including economic behavior, takes place—literally. Production, distribution, and consumption tend to "take place" according to a kind of law of convenience—the principle of least effort (see Zipf 1949). For example, if two sources of chert are of roughly equal quality for some use, then the source closest to the user will be chosen for exploitation. However, geographic, straight-line distance is not the important variable, and "closeness" has to be determined in terms of the time and effort required for access to a source. "Effort" in this context can also include social variables. If a chert source, for example, were controlled by an enemy group, then sources farther away, but under one's own control, might be chosen. In fact, distributions that show unusual sources of raw or finished materials may be one line for investigating "control" of resource locations, although many other variables such as knowledge of the source's existence, special requirements not appreciated by the archaeologist, and so on, have to be considered as well. In short, geographical location is an important part of economic behavior, and there are many volumes dealing with the topic at length (e.g., Hietala 1984, and the classic geographical survey by Haggett 1965—both have extensive bibliographies). Some of these geographical methods will be used in later chapters to look at economic behavior in spatial terms.

It is, however, worth noting here that the various levels already discussed under the heading "Agency" also have decided spatial dimensions. A household production unit is not only a social, but also a spatial unit. Similarly, occupationally defined barrios and communities engaged in particular kinds of economic activities have to be considered at a series of scales from local to regional. Land plays a role as either *subject* of labor or as an *instrument* of labor in which social relations become intertwined with production (Meillassoux 1972).

However, there is another vexing question of what "place" means in terms of "property." One of the forms of surplus extraction by "owners" of land is in the form of "rents" for land use, often in the form of unpaid labor or payment in kind. What is not always clear in specific historical cases is how kin unit or other community control of land use rights became mutated into private ownership by "land-lords." That such a transformation commonly occurred is not in question, but there seem to have been many different paths to that end. Arguably, one of the key events in the development of state-level economic systems is the commoditization of agricultural production, and the transformation, at the same time, of agricultural producers into specialists—into peasants. The introduction of a money economy into this setting, as into others, further transforms the social and economic relationships. Payments of rents in kind allow the accumulation of use values, but money historically allowed the development of capital in ways that led to profound alteration in production in capitalist societies (e.g., Case and Fair 1989:272ff., 318ff.; Mandel 1968:95–100). However, these changes, in this specific historical form, are not particularly relevant for the issues discussed in this book. We do need to remember that there are historically specific spatial dimensions such as questions of usufruct that have to be investigated empirically for social formations such as Mississippian. In addition, the limited, circumscribed character of land makes it a peculiar phenomenon as compared to produced items.

How

As always, *how* involves several kinds of issues. How do we know something—what tools do we use to analyze the objective facts? An equally interesting *how* refers to the physical and social tools used by the people being studied to achieve their ends.

Adaptation, selection, critical theory, and dialectics are some of the conceptual tools that can be used to attempt to understand *how* events interact in time and space to produce new results and new combinations, and how archaeologists can deal with these issues. Each of these tools has been characterized as associated with one or another school of archaeology in the period following the emergence in the 1960s of alternatives to the then dominant culture-historical school of archaeology (Willey and Sabloff, 1980, present a history of archaeology that describes some of the schools in detail). Adaptation, typically not always completely correctly, has been attributed to the scientistic and positivist "New Archaeology," a.k.a. "processual archaeology" (e.g., Binford and Binford 1968). Selection, and a broader range of neo-Darwinian theory, of course, are typical of "selectionist" archaeology (e.g., Dunnell 1980). Both critical theory and dialectical analysis have most often been associated with the postprocessual school (Hodder 1982).

There is much that we can know about how people did things. Traditionally popularizers have listed technology among the "easiest" areas for archaeologists to investigate, and such matters as religion and beliefs as the most inaccessible to archaeological investigation. As Binford pointed out at the beginning of the New Archaeology, however, the "accessibility" of past behavior depends upon the kinds of material remains associated with any particular behavior. Some aspects of technology can, in fact, be difficult to investigate, whereas religious behavior involving massive public works can be fairly easy to study.

For all that, there is *some* truth to the generalization that economic activities are somewhat more likely than others to leave archaeological traces. But perhaps this is just as well, for these are the activities that lie at the roots of human survival. Without biological survival of the population, no culture endures. However, the debate between idealism and materialism cannot be resolved here—suffice it to say that this book tries to provide a materialist theory of Mississippian social formations. At the least, I hope that a careful study of what we do know about Mississippian economic systems will reveal much about their political and ideological behavior as well.

Notwithstanding postmodern attacks on knowledge, we do have ways, then, of studying how people in the past achieved their ends. We can, with some chance of success, approach an objective past through a method of refutation and testing against material evidence. Although we may never find Truth in some metaphysical sense, we clearly can reject as being impossible many theories and stories about the past. We may find many possible "right" answers that are consistent with objective data, but some answers can be logically and empirically rejected as just plain false (see my polemic in Muller 1991).

My greatest concern with "process," however, lies with the past events, not present analysis. How do people affect each other in their behavior? What kinds of economic relationships occur at the simplest levels of social interaction, for example? Marshall Sahlins has outlined a "sociology of primitive exchange" (e.g., 1972: Chapter 5, originally published in 1965) that has become fairly standard for discussion of various patterns of reciprocity. These range from the relatively altruistic relations known as "generalized reciprocity" through "balanced reciprocity" to the exploitative relations characterized as "negative reciprocity." These largely figure in discussions of distribution and exchange and will be dealt with in Chapter 8 in a general discussion of archaeological evidence for internal and external distribution in Mississippian period societies.

As noted, another issue is the question of how resources come to be distributed unevenly. When this happens, what kinds of concentration of resources occur, in whose hands, and how intensive is the concentration? Concentrations of resources may be held, perhaps first on a temporary basis, by each of the kinds of social entities discussed under "Agency." As "holding" becomes ownership, there are possibilities that the new social relationships involving property can destroy expectations of reciprocity, for example, and transform social relationships into those characteristic of state-level systems. There is considerable evidence that this process occurred, in the Southeast, during the Historic period in the course of establishment of trading relationships with the European invaders (see Chapter 2). There is, however, little evidence supporting similar transformations in the distribution of wealth in prehistoric times, as we shall see in Chapter 8.

Measures

In addition, a few words need to be said about measurement of these various variables. *Efficiency* is a relationship of input in some measure such as labor time, and of output per unit of input. The higher the ratio of output to input, the more "efficient" the activity is. However, although efficiency might seem to be rewarded by evolutionary processes, there are a number of reasons why this may not be so in any obvious way. First of all, there is the question of what the "output" and "input" really are. Input *can* always be measured in terms of labor time or some other kinds of energy units. However, the ability to be so measured does not necessarily mean that this is always useful or meaningful. In any situation, the absolutely most efficient way of accomplishing some end by some measures may not be the form that survives. Survival of one technology or behavior may be linked behaviorally with others so that the "package" of behaviors is the object of selection, rather than the individual traits.

Another measure of an economic system is its ability to provide its actors with sufficient resources for survival and reproduction. On a broader scale, it is possible to use various kinds of measures to deal with the degree of inequality in distribution of goods, resources, and services. This latter kind of measure is important in assessing the hierarchical development of a social formation, expecting that lack of equity implies the intrusion of "power" relationships into distribution.

The question of economic growth is difficult to deal with in the absence of money. How are we to define economic growth? Is population increase a sign of economic success? Or is the true measure of success more calories per capita? Economic systems that have money to count thereby have statistical measures of success or failure; but although other measures could be used—such as amount of food or other goods in storage—these do not provide the same scope for "bean" counting. Archaeologically, we could expect to see economic success translated into reproductive success, and vice versa.

This raises the vexing question of stability. Not the least of the often criticized failures of functionalist explanation in archaeology has been the naive assumption of stability. Social systems contain the seeds of their own change into something else. A few socioeconomic systems are relatively successful, but many are not. We have to ask whether a particular political economy could maintain itself through time, in the long term. We also have to examine social and economic change to understand whether changes in the system are likely to be gradual and smooth, or disruptive of previously existing forms.

Why?

There is an empirical "why" and an analytical "why." Causation should not be confused with motivation on the part of the actor, as noted earlier. We seem to be able to understand much about the evolution of animal behavior without worrying overmuch about individual, psychological motivations. Human culture and society are much more complex, and there are many additional ways for behaviors to become established than among other animals. Nevertheless, although we need to account for the impact of human conscious desires in our models, we cannot ignore the basic selective forces that affect humans, as part of nature.

A culture's developmental trajectory is *created* in historical and dialectical analysis as much as it is discovered. At any particular time, any *necessary* outcomes of growth or decline are determined by a given set of social, natural, and historical environments; but not *all* outcomes are *necessary!* Human action in the framework of historical development is affected by the conditions in which the "tradition of all the dead generations weighs like a nightmare on the brain of the living" (Marx 1852 [1975:96]). Indeed, much change results from conscious efforts to stand still. Movements seeking to restructure societies are often revitalistic—they seek to restore a fantastic golden age. Most of the time, most places, the motives of many individuals are conservative. They try to preserve or improve their own positions relative to other persons. This is especially so in those social formations loosely called "tribes," where generally egalitarian attitudes are accompanied by achieved status based on merit in one or another realm of achievement.

The problems faced by each generation are the result of their own actions and the actions of their predecessors. The interplay of selective pressures resulting from new productive and *social* technology is as important as the changes in the physical and technological environment around people. This is why emphasis on the evolution of physical tools alone is rarely adequate. "Survival of the fittest among tools" (e.g., Gorodzov 1933) is only part of the evolutionary process. Insofar as we can, we have to place tools into a behavioral, especially social, context. The tools themselves are only parts of behaviors, social as well as technological. The complete behavioral context (a kind of inclusive fitness)—not the technology, *per se*—is the level at which natural or cultural selection normally operates. An especially interesting, if highly polemical, example of an effort to assess various models of these processes is to be found in Bettinger's study of hunter–gatherer "theory," in which he settles on a kind of "neo-Darwinian" approach in preference to Marxian or other analytical models (1991). I would not imagine that all neo-Darwinists will be particularly attracted to the specific kind of analysis Bettinger proposes, but I can say that his "analysis" of Marxism deals with only a narrow range of Marxist theory. Given his statement that "Marxist literature is so easy to ignore—polemics, epithets, and all" (1991:135), one might perhaps be excused some surprise at his tone in calling various concepts of Hodder, Shanks, and Tilley "dangerous nonsense" (1991:147). In any case, perhaps theories might best be judged on somewhat broader bases than their existing body of hunter–atherer literature? Selection is certainly an important *process*. However, reducing biology to a study of only "differential persistence of variability" would satisfy few evolutionary biologists (e.g., see Gould 1977: Chapter 4). It is one thing to criticize those who proceed from "generalizations about consequences to inferences about processes" (Bettinger 1991:219); but it is disappointing when the alternatives offered are particularistic in terms of the subjects studied *and* are largely metaphorical in the treatment of central concepts such as *selection* and *reproduction* (e.g., Bettinger 1991:182–209; Diener 1980). When one compares the scientifically based mechanisms of transmission in biological evolutionary theory with those proposed for transmission in cultural selection, it is apparent that there are many details to be worked out in the latter cases.

Questions about "why" do involve us in questions of consequences as well as process. The hard facts of consequences are not so much the inferential basis of process models as they are the basis on which to test different models of both particulars and process. The biological sciences have often been criticized for their mushiness in this regard by "hard" scientists, and there are many better models for science than those of 19th-century practice in evolutionary biology. As mentioned in the discussion entitled Agency, sexual selection and other elements of modern evolutionary biology show processes that seem to involve "complexity" and emergent properties that are not like the explanations offered by most neo-Darwinist archaeologists.

The analytical "why" relates to the kinds of explanations that a particular school or theory allows as causal. The empirical "why" discussed earlier refers to the particular explanations of specific historical events. These are not exclusive, of course. Some are inclined to see cause in terms of prime movers. For example, Johnson and Earle take a straightforward position with refreshing lack of equivocation: "The primary motor for cultural evolution is population growth" (1987:16). There is a long tradition behind this viewpoint, going well back into the last century (e.g., Marx 1857–1859 [1979:99], but *only* for nonclass societies, 1859 [1970:205]). Some postprocessualists argue for a dialectical (in the Hegelian sense) process of "knowing" that argues that both "hard science" and "relativism" are wrong (e.g., Hodder 1991). In fact, archaeology today has wide diversity of opinion about what constitutes explanation at all (see the range of the papers in Preucel 1991). I explicitly reject both "vulgar"[6] and "effete"[7] materialism. I must leave it to the "critical critics" to decide where this book belongs; my "vulgarity" or "effeteness," will, I suspect, be dependent upon the standpoint of the critic. I can only express my conviction that there is a real and objectively knowable world, that, though *data* are contingent upon theory, *facts* are not, or at least not so severely that there is no hope of seeing through the veil. The trick is to know how to meaningfully convert *fact* into

---

[6] *Vulgar* here is a term that refers to a nondialectical approach that, according to Marxist–Leninist dogma, places too much emphasis on the material conditions of life and too little on the dialectical process.

[7] So-called in Johnson and Earle 1987:8–10.

data. The framework in this book is materialist, and materialist in a way that gives priority (please note, not a *monopoly*) in explanation to "the material conditions of everyday life." I agree that population growth is often important, but it is important not as an *only* cause so much as it is one of many possible factors that affect the ability of humans to reproduce themselves biologically and socially. Beyond the material basis, the mechanisms of change are, for me, at any rate, clearly evolutionary in a broad sense. However, the view of evolutionary theory taken here has little theoretical ground in common with selectionism. Most particularly, I am concerned with selection in the context of past human *behavior*, not in the sense of studying those "struggling artifacts" of Gorodzov.

Dialectics and "Why"

I will reiterate that my purpose in this book is to develop a materialist view of the late prehistoric Southeast that incorporates the evolutionary, dialectical, and social features of these social formations. My goal is the practical one of presenting a series of models and suggestions for understanding Mississippian in this context, not a doctrinaire demonstration of the theory. Moreover, I want to emphasize that I, unlike many others, do not see the approach taken here as existing in opposition to ecological, selectionist, or processual views of archaeology. Historical materialism provides a framework for understanding how each of these approaches can contribute to a materialist view of human development.

A dialectical approach to knowledge seems to provide considerable analytical benefits. Following a realist perspective (from Ollman's work 1971), McGuire (1992) has essentially rejected a natural dialectic and relegated the dialectic to the realm of ideas. Sartre presented much the same view in his *Critique de la Raison Dialectique* (see Desan 1966). Trigger has a somewhat different interpretation of *realism* in Marx (1993). Saitta takes an Althusserian view of the same issues (e.g., 1988, 1991, 1994). Indeed, emphasis on the dialectic as an *analytical tool* is not restricted to the West. Even in the Soviet Union, the official handbook on Marxism stated, "Materialist dialectics provides us with a scientific method of cognition," emphasizing the dialectic as *method* (Kuusinen et al. 1963:87).

Although it seems that something like dialectical processes are built into human cognition, there is still doubt on the issue of a "natural" dialectic in the sense advocated long ago by Engels in *Anti-Dühring* (1878) and in the manuscripts of the *Dialectics of Nature* (1873–1886). However, the dialectics of nature cannot simply be dismissed. For just one example, the major challenge to Darwinist gradualism draws on a dialectical tradition in the natural sciences (see Gould and Eldredge 1977, Levins and Lewontin 1985). Punctuated equilibrium is the dialectical leap, as expressed in natural science. In any event, we do not need either to claim the dialectic as a universal characteristic of nature or to accept the realist position of Ollman and McGuire to acknowledge that the dialectic is an extremely useful tool in working around the excesses of extreme relativism or extreme positivism. The practical position taken in this book is close in many ways to that of Philip Kohl (1985, without agreeing completely with his views on the usefulness of certain other concepts, e.g., Kohl 1987). This book takes a kind of objective dialectical approach, then, but really fits into none of McGuire's categories of dialectical approaches (1992:92–93). Lee comments on the similar terminological issues in hunter–gatherer studies (1992).

Persons interested in Marxian epistemology can follow a long and detailed course of study. On the one side are the realist, even idealist, traditions of the Western Marxists such as Sayer and Ollman; on the other is the "party line" defined by Kuusinen and his colleagues (1963). Such debates can be all too "obscurely engaging," in the words of Christopher Chippindale (1993), but it is enough to simply define the basic concepts here. The purpose in this section is not to make some contribution to theory, but rather to outline the concepts used in this book, directly or indirectly, to analyze specific, historical social formations. Several points are critical:

1. As a didactic and analytical tool, dialectical analysis, particularly dialectical materialist analysis, focuses on the study of change within the universal connections of phenomena. It accepts, particularly in "objective dialectics," the idea of cause and effect. It sees mechanisms of change such as natural selection as showing *how* causes operate. However, cause and effect do not exhaust the relationships of phenomena and are part of relationships that may be called *interaction*. For example, in the course of development, cause and effect in the first instance may be reversed in the second. That is to say, the relationship of cause and effect is dialectical. Dialectical materialism sees some events as *necessary*, given the nature of the relations among phenomena. *Laws* are regularities in necessary connections that are "independent of human will." Not all events are the result of development according to laws, however, and these are accidental. Accidental phenomena, however, may themselves have regularities such as those of statistical generalizations.

2. Contrary to gradualist ideas of change, dialectical materialism sees that quantitative changes can cause *qualitative* changes, or "leaps." *Quality*, in this context, refers to the essential features of a thing or phenomenon that distinguish it from others and does not imply value of any sort. Examples of this may be found in the logistics equation in population ecology, in which different ranges of reproductive rate produce dramatic changes in population structure. For dialectical materialism, changes that are purely quantitative are evolutionary, whereas changes in quality, in *structure,* in effect, are revolutionary. This terminology is not new to archaeology (e.g., the "Neolithic Revolution," etc.), but its dialectical underpinnings are not often appreciated. Hence many social phenomena that are seen by some as merely a matter of degree, such as specialization, may be empirically analyzed from a dialectical viewpoint as potentially showing *structural* differences.

3. From a dialectical viewpoint, the motive force pushing old quantitative changes into new qualitative changes is the contradictory nature of all reality—or, in our case, of social formations. This dialectical contradiction is "the presence in a phenomenon or process of opposite, mutually exclusive aspects which, at the same time, presuppose each other and within the

framework of the given phenomenon exist only in mutual contradiction" (Kuusinen et al. 1963:77). As indicated, there can be considerable arguments about whether contradiction is a fundamental property of nature; one may especially be uncertain whether natural contradictions are fundamentally *dualist* in character. All the same, the great power of dialectical analysis is that it focuses attention on dynamic oppositions of mutually opposing forces that are "built-in" to the very nature of phenomena, at the least in the realm of human development. Understanding social developments, then, involves identification of the principal, "determining" contradictions from all the many contradictions. This is the problem, as the identification of key contradictions in contemporary practice, for ongoing events, proved, shall we say, difficult. Even so, once events are past, a dialectical materialist method can work from events back to determining contradictions, using *empirical testing*, as repeatedly advocated by Engels. For example, in the historical analysis of the origin of capitalism, specific historical analyses such as Marx's "18th Brumaire" (1852), and Engels' *Origin of the Family...* (1878) illustrate the extraordinary power of dialectical materialism as analytical tool.

4. The last part of the fundamental principles of dialectical materialism are those enchantingly known as "Dialectical Negation" and the "Negation of the Negation." In Hegelian dialectical terms, the combination of negation and contradiction form the dialectical triad of thesis, antithesis, and synthesis. The negation of a phenomenon is implicit in itself; it is *not* an external intrusion. *Dialectical* development builds upon and incorporates the elements of the old phenomenon into the new. In turn, any new "negation" contains its own internal contradictions. These contradictions of a new negation of the negation would be less obvious after a structural shift to a new form, but as the implications of these increase quantitatively through time, the dialectical process continues, spiraling away from the original forms.

In addition, traditional Marxists see the dialectic as universal, but its operation is different in each case according to the conditions of the phenomena being studied. In the words of Kuusinen et al., "Mastery of dialectics is not enough, a profound knowledge of concrete facts and circumstances is required" (1963:89). In Marxism–Leninism, and for most other flavors of Marxian discussion such as Trotskyism, the dialectical method is necessarily concerned with what is called "practice". Although this term does apply to the actual "practice" of dialectical analysis in specific cases (as in McGuire 1992:252ff.), it also refers to the use of dialectical materialist analysis to change reality in revolutionary ways. One has to acknowledge a certain ironic truth to Bettinger's bitter challenge (1991:148) that archaeologists who seek to change the world through archaeology "are in the wrong field." All the same, it is easy for such a polemic to ignore the fact that an understanding of the past is extremely important in understanding the present. We can be equally certain that those who seek to use Social Darwinist or Spencerian archaeology to justify injustice are also in the wrong field. More particularly, we can suspect that those who want to trivialize archaeology by restricting its horizon to tiny details will form just as severe an impediment to public support of archaeology as those who seek to radicalize it politically.

In the end, few of the great historical developments predicted by Marx and Engels happened in anything like the manner suggested by them. Their practice, as extended by Lenin, concerning the nature of political and economic control of a non-Capitalist world, contained contradictions that proved even more fundamental than those of post-Industrial societies as they actually developed out of 19th-century capitalism. Overly extended central economic control proved unworkable in practice. Far from being the end of history, the end of dialectical processes, the fall of East Bloc communism illustrates quite well the very processes it claimed to be based upon. The causes of that failure will be debated for generations by the old revolutionaries, but the record of success for *any* economic theory in actual practice has proved, shall we say, less than stellar when all factors and costs are taken into account.

Marx himself saw the overall direction of change as being progressive, a 19th-century conviction that has not withstood the horrors of the 20th century very well. To understand the contemporary world, we still need analytical methods that embrace analysis of the whole range of human behavior, including social forms, as well as technology. And we need an archaeology that tries, within our human limits, to investigate what really happened, rather than what we might wish had happened. This book is my effort at providing a broader kind of analysis of the specific case of the Mississippian societies of the Southeast.

2. MODE OF PRODUCTION

Early political economists employed the term *mode of production (Produktionsweise)* in the context of separating analytical stages of economic development (e.g., Marx 1859 [1977:21]). Marx named a series of "modes of production"—so-called primitive, Asiatic, ancient, feudal, and bourgeois or capitalist. As often pointed out (e.g., Hindess and Hirst 1977; Hobsbawm 1965:11; Service 1975:35), the initial usage was as "epochs." Later usage inclined more toward these modes as analytical types rather than historical stages. Nineteenth-century revolutionaries had their own agenda and were embedded in their own cultural milieu, of course.

Since the 19th century, the topic of modes of production has received much attention. A few of the many discussions include Krader (1975), Bailey and Llobera (1981), Foster-Carter (1978), and Hindess and Hirst (1975, 1977), who may be referred to for summaries of still other sources and discussions. For another example, Dunn (1982) summarizes Russian discussion of the Asiatic mode of production. For our purposes, however, a quick summary will suffice. Efforts have been made to refine the concepts of mode of production. For example, Althusser and Balibar (1970), and especially Balibar in that work, reconstitute mode of production in a structuralist form. Balibar summarizes the key elements in the concept, as they interpret it:

1. Laborer (direct producer)
2. Means of production

      a. Object of labor
      b. Means of labor
   3. Nonlaborer, appropriating surplus-labor

as well as property "connections" (Balibar in Althusser and Balibar 1970:213–215; but see also Foster-Carter 1978; Rudra 1988).

The conceptual basis of Althusser and Balibar's structuralist approach has been seriously questioned (e.g., Hindess and Hirst 1977), but fortunately these issues make little difference in what we are doing here. These mode-of-production characteristics are difficult to reconcile with non-Western economies, despite efforts to analyze "Asiatic" and other non-Western modes of production. Even more problems emerge when the traditional modes (Asiatic, Ancient, Feudal, and Capitalist) are forced into an evolutionary series of "epochs" (e.g., see Stalin 1938; cf. Hindess and Hirst 1975, and especially their "autocritique," 1977).

It is difficult to approach the problems of mode of production from new directions. An effort has to be made to avoid the Scylla of ignorance of various special definitions, on one side, and the Charybdis of arguments from authority, on the other. Although this is not the place for a detailed discussion, most Marxist production theorists have not sufficiently considered anthropological data and theories (as concluded also by Dunn 1982). Separating the pure from the dross in mode-of-production theory is not easy, so why bother at all? Precisely because the concept of mode of production emphasizes the social conditions of production in ways that are much more consistent with anthropological concerns than are theories emphasizing either prime causes of social development or those based solely on one kind of evolutionary process. Mode-of-production studies emphasize the social organization not only of production, in the narrow sense, but also distribution, exchange, and consumption. Epistemological matters are important in this discussion (see Hindess and Hirst 1977: Chapter 1), but the practical problem is to characterize economies, as well as to develop a general theory of hierarchical development. These problems call for more concern with the heuristic value of the approach than its philosophical grounding. I specifically eschew ideological purity in any particular school, although acknowledging a certain tendency to see economic systems as "ultimately" determinant (Engels 1890).

I want to avoid efforts to force my discussion away from the problems of Mississippian social formations and into definitions and epistemology more than I have already done.[8] I would be the first to acknowledge that consistency of terminology is important, and that theory and method have claim to priority, but I structure my argument in my own terms, rather than in terms of a critical theory that is based on umbilicospection rather than on relationships to real problems. In this book, the term *mode of production* will refer to (1) direct production technology; (2) the means of production, including social organization of production; (3) the differentiation of social groups—producing, managing, appropriating, or even supported by surplus-labor; and (4) the characteristics of social reproduction.

---

[8] I presume to take as a model the view presented by Marx (1859 [1970:206]): "The concrete concept is concrete because it is a synthesis of many definitions, thus representing the unity of diverse aspects."

These concepts in turn are incorporated into a broader political economy of the prehistoric Mississippian peoples, even though I do not, perhaps, use the actual words, *mode of production*, very often.

The Classic Modes of Production

Although "property" was once central to the definitions of modes of production, recent discussions have played down its importance and have focused on areas such as social reproduction (e.g., Goody 1976; Hindess and Hirst 1977, Meillassoux 1981; also Rudra 1988:376ff.). Even though our concern is with the utility of these concepts and not their conformity to received theory, summarizing some of the features of various classic modes of production should prove helpful in seeing how such concepts work. The classic "types" of production modes are as follows:

- Communal ("Primitive")
- Asiatic
- Ancient (Classical, Slave)
- Feudal
- Bourgeois (or Capitalist)

To these may be added some additional modes, such as the Germanic, Slavonic, and, more recently, various African modes (e.g., Crummey and Stewart 1981). Contrary to most "histories," 19th-century discussion of modes of production by Marx and Engels described multilinear, rather than unilineal, development. It is true that Stalin came to emphasize a fundamentally unilineal approach (1938).

Communal Organization

It may be argued that communal organization is not a mode of production since, by classic theory, such social formations have no division of classes and, thereby, no "political economy" in the narrow sense. Of course, the grouping of all nonstate societies into categories such as "communal" is inadequate (cf. Hindess and Hirst 1975). Systems such as the so-called communal mode, whether a "mode of production" or not in 19th-century theory, are treated as the evolutionary source for the development of other kinds of production systems, such as Asiatic or Germanic. The difficulty of fitting non-Western (and, especially, nonstate) societies into this analytical framework has resulted in a number of types to bridge the gap between "tribal" and stratified societies ("social formations or orders"). These types included reexamination of Asiatic and Germanic modes. In recent years, there has been some tendency to multiply the number of non-Western modes into many different forms (e.g., see the bibliography in Crummey and Stewart 1981, but also Godelier 1977:87 and elsewhere). A few have argued that there is, indeed, only a single level of communal production (Hindess and Hirst 1975, but also note their later abandonment of the concept of mode of production—and pretty much every thing else—1977:4, 5).

Property is important in the classic schemes of modes, and social problems were seen as forming out of the conditions of nonsedentary societies becoming involved in the cooperative appropriation of land by the "tribe" (Marx 1857–1858 [1965:68]).

What happened in each case was dependent upon the specific natural and social environment. Physical power was limited to human efforts, perhaps supplemented by modest inputs of animal energy. The tools and conditions of production, according to the classical model, required cooperative labor in order to survive. Today, we are more inclined to see production under these conditions in far more positive ways, given relatively low population density in relation to local carrying capacity. The absence of appropriation once seen as resulting from a lack of surplus is now understood to be more a matter of superabundance. When there is enough for all with relatively modest inputs of labor, there is no need for coercion.

Thus, one key feature of so-called communal societies is that they lack social classes. The term *class* has special meanings, but for our purposes, communal societies might be characterized as "nonstratified" (e.g., Fried 1967). The failure to appreciate grades of organization such as the distinction between ranking and stratification is one of the greatest weaknesses of the traditional view of the communal or "primitive" condition. The most famous characterization (and most misleading to naive readers) of these kinds of social formations is their "primitive communism." Marxist economists precisely define their terms involving property (*Eigentum*) as opposed to possession (*Besitz*) so that "communism" in this sense has special, nonobvious, meanings. Suffice it to say that production centers on the community (*Gemeinde*) rather than on individuals. Kinship and community are closely linked, even being the same. The kinds of patterns described for this state of existence are similar to those described for modern San societies in which generalized reciprocity is important. Ideological and economic matters articulate closely (Hindess and Hirst 1975:41). Another feature of so-called primitive economies, but one that is by no means limited to them, is that of "domestic economy" (Chaianov 1923, 1925; Sahlins 1972; but also see Meillassoux 1981). Production centers on domestic units and there is little or no alienation of surplus production from that unit. Communal economies have little nongender division of labor, although individual differences in skill and production do occur. Redistribution of goods based on temporary or longer-term relations was seen as important (Hindess and Hirst 1975:45). Population is small, and the simplest communal societies only rarely (and usually temporarily) exceed 64 persons in size. In all, the many different structures included in so-called communal or "primitive" economies are better known to anthropologists than to ideologues.

Since class struggle is seen as the "engine" of history, how and why did nonclass social formations come to change? The usual Marxist explanation was that the development of productive forces led in turn to division of labor (specialization). Exchange of products of labor developed among larger groups and even within the local group. Families became independent economic units, and private property emerged. These factors produced contradictions between the communal order and the organization of productive relations (Kuusinen et al. 1963:126–127). In fact, both Engels and Marx recognized a series of causal factors for these problems that would be familiar to the most "vulgar" of cultural materialists today. Marx and Engels, unlike the Leninists, had seen that population increase could prevent reproduction of the social forms, thus creating contradictions in communal social formations (Marx 1857–1858 [1965:82–83]; Engels 1881–1882 [1979:346]). Marx even anticipated the

Boserupian emphasis on population growth as one phenomenon driving social evolution in nonclass societies, including the communal form:

> If the community as such is to continue in the old way, the reproduction of its members under the objective conditions already assumed as given, is necessary. Production itself, the advance of population (which also falls under the head of production), in time necessarily eliminates these conditions, destroying instead of reproducing them, etc., and as this occurs the community decays and dies, together with the property relations on which it was based. Marx   1857–1858 [1965:82]

Asiatic Mode of Production

The Asiatic or Oriental mode of production (see Marx 1857–1858 [1965]) has, perhaps, received the most attention of the *non*-Western modes defined in the 19th century (e.g., Bailey 1981; Bailey and Llobera 1981; Dunn 1982; Krader 1975). The Asiatic mode was based on the lack of differentiation between general production and agriculture (Hobsbawm 1965:33; Marx 1857–1858 [1965:70, 83, 91]), but the concept was somewhat modified through time. Leninists and Stalinists opposed the idea of a distinctive Asiatic form of society (see Dunn 1982), but the model has had attraction for Western Marxists (e.g., Godelier 1977:119–122; Hindess and Hirst 1975:206, 218; Wittfogel 1963) and underwent a revival in late Soviet theory (Dunn 1982).

In the classic Asiatic society, the individual community "contains within itself all conditions of production and surplus production" (Marx 1857–1858 [1965:70]). Surplus labor and production are devoted to the community and to the leader of the community, although the form may be more or less "democratic" or "despotic" in form. This form, seen as surviving to the present day, was thought to be a exceptionally stable production mode, despite contradictions involved in the alienation of surplus production from producers to leaders. Asiatic social formations were seen as either classless or at the lowest level of class development. Many aspects of the Asiatic mode are similar to the characteristics defined for "chiefdoms," but these social formations include some clear cases of state-level organization (as per Service 1975). However, Marx saw individual villages as self-sustaining and exchange was therefore supposed to have been at a low level except for "tribute" to the despot (Krader 1975:119, 287; Marx 1857–1858 [1965:69–70]). This feature is distinct from the importance placed on exchange and sharing in Americanist models of chiefdom-level societies (e.g., Muller 1986b; Service 1975). Control of water resources was often important (thus the "heresy" of Wittfogel's "hydraulic" model, 1963).

Another important element of the Asiatic mode was its appropriation of surplus produce through "tax" (rent) paid to the political organization, which owned the land (but see Hindess and Hirst 1975:194, 200; 1977:42). Labor was supposed to be bound to the land in a collective form (Krader 1975:288) and governments provided public works (Marx 1853[1979:71]). There was some division of labor in terms of handicraft, but only on the community level, and "specialists" in any community were supposed to be rare (Krader 1975:122, 287). Each village tended to be much like another. The major social distinction is that between the rulers and the agricultural producers. The emergence of the leader is seen as coming from the need for social insurance, just as in Service's later model:

A certain amount of labour is required for the *common store-for insurance* as it were-on the one hand; and on the other for *defraying the costs of the community as such*, i.e., for war, religious worship, etc. The dominion of lords, in its most primitive sense, arises only at this point, e.g., in the Slavonic and Rumanian communities, etc. Here lies the possibility of a transition to corvée, etc. Marx 1857–1858 [1979:87]

Although classes developed in some Asiatic societies, class struggle was poorly developed, according to Marx. However, Asiatic societies were often state-level, notwithstanding the poor development of social classes.

Germanic Mode of Production

There has been debate about whether there is a merely a Germanic form of property rather than a separate mode of production (Krader 1975:114; cf. Marx 1857–1858 [1965:78–79]). Since the original modes now have mostly heuristic value, it is enough to outline some salient features of the classic German model as another example. The Germanic mode of production was based perhaps more on Tacitus than on ancient German life itself, but has value as a description of nonstate social formations, as understood by contemporary "Ancient" observers. A section in Chapter 2 on classically based biases in ethnohistorical accounts gives some examples of Tacitus and Caesar on these issues. The main feature of the Germanic social formation was its basis in the domestic household. Whereas the community was the unit in the Asiatic mode, in the Germanic mode, "every individual household contains an entire economy, forming as it does an independent centre of production (manufacture merely the domestic subsidiary labour of the women, etc.)" (Marx 1857–1858 [1965:79]). The economy was neither "communal" nor "political," but "domestic." Each family settlement was isolated and independent, but in association with other similar units of the same tribe (Marx 1857–1858[1965:80]). Features of the Germanic mode can be found in "tribal" and "chiefly" societies.

Feudal Production

One essential feature of the Feudal mode is the dependency of peasants upon feudal lords (Marx and Engels 1846, Marx 1857–1858[1965]). The Feudal mode of production reveals some analytical characteristics relevant to our discussion (see also papers in Hilton 1976). Because of the historical accident that Europe passed through a feudal stage, that "mode of production" was treated in more universal terms than these collapsed states reconstituted as chiefdomlike societies may deserve (see Bloch 1961; Postan 1975; also Dunn 1982, on "slaveholding" social orders). In this sense, Feudalism is one example of simplified social organization that follows the collapse of states, rather than a universal stage between "Ancient" and "Capitalist" social formations (cf. Rudra 1988). The European case provides numerous examples of how "state-level institutions" can occur in smaller-scale societies after state collapse (as Yoffee notes in general, 1993). There were "Germanic"-like elements in Feudal social formations that compare to some "feudal" features such as those of chiefdom-level (i.e., nonclass, ranked) social formations in the American East. In the next chapter, I shall briefly comment on these similarities in discussion of the social setting of the

16th- and 17th-century European observers of North American indigenous peoples—and the resulting biases in their interpretations.

Other Modes of Production

Other modes of production are associated with fully developed state and class societies, and so are of less interest here. Foremost among these are the Ancient and Capitalist modes of production. The Ancient mode of production is linked with slave-holding, among other things (Marx and Engels 1846, Marx 1857–1858[1965]). In the Ancient mode, not only the means of production are owned, but also the very producers themselves. The key classes were the slaveholders and the slaves, and specialization of labor was increased. Massive public works were characteristic of this mode of production. One of the central internal contradictions is supposed to be that of the inability of the system to accommodate improvements in the efficiency of the instruments of production as a result of the cheap cost of labor and the disaffection of the laborer. The failure of the Ancient mode of production has always been a sticky problem, especially as the collapse of the Western Roman empire did not seem to resolve the contradictions between the supposed key classes. Considerable effort was expended on a redefinition of the Ancient mode by Hindess and Hirst (1975), but one is inclined to accept their own criticism and rejection of that effort only two years later (1977) without necessarily accepting their overall viewpoints in the latter work.

The Capitalist or Bourgeois mode of production was Marx's central issue, and many of the concepts and analytical tools developed by him and Engels were specifically tailored to the needs of this particular analysis. It seems wise not to use these tools blithely until some reasonable argument has been made for their relevance to non-Capitalist modes of production. As an example, I am reluctant to accept "class"-based analyses of non-Capitalist social history. Regardless, the key dialectical opposition fueling the decline of the Capitalist mode was supposed to be that production was *socialized* (in the form of mass, even monopoly production) as opposed to appropriation that was *private*. Thus, labor does not have the wealth to purchase the goods made, so economic crises occur from overproduction, market and price collapse, followed by curtailment of production, further impoverishment of the customers, and so on and on.

The older literature makes a number of more or less *ad hoc* references to variant modes such as Slavonic (e.g., Engels 1894 [1979:475–481]). Still other modes such as "lineage mode of production" have been defined in particular cases (see Crummey and Stewart 1981; Hindess and Hirst 1975; also cf.e McGuire 1986; Southall 1988). These share a number of characteristics with those already defined and tend to be empirical inductions relevant to particular cases. There is nothing wrong with this, except insofar as the students try to elevate any of these to general relevance independent of the problems that spawned them. The situation almost got to the stage of the "mode of the month club." Many new structuralist or Marxist analyses produced a new set of modes emphasizing just those characteristics of interest to the investigator. For just one example, Dunn (1982:124) has suggested that "I consider it advisable to replace the slaveholding social order with a variable 'prefeudal' stage that can take widely differing forms depending on both natural factors (climate, topography, fertility of the soil, and the like) and particular historical conditions." Again, this is fine, so long as we recognize the particular concerns of the analyst. Although this book will deal with the particular aspects of Mississippian political and domestic economy, I shall not be proposing a formal "Mississippian mode of production," although it is no less justified than many that have been defined.

Some other concepts are closely related to these typologies of modes and social formations, even though they are not really "modes" in the strictest sense of the term. These include the "domestic mode of production" discussed by Sahlins (1972: Chapters 2–3), which is related to household components in production and is a part of other modes, *sensu strictu*. The stages of tribe, chiefdom, and state defined by Service (1962; 1975) also correspond in some ways to the comparable "stagelike" uses of modes such as Communal, Germanic, and Ancient.

Modes of Modes

Americanist approaches such as Sahlins's "domestic mode of production" (1972) have been criticized for confusing different pre-Capitalist modes. The charge of "vulgarity"— too little emphasis on the forces of production, social relations of production, and the dialectical process—is common against Americanist materialist approaches. Many Americanists revel in their vulgarity, but a major lesson to be learned from the European tradition is that it is useful, even essential, to have more detailed and subtle treatments of the interrelationships of production, social relations, and reproduction. On the other hand, despite their sophistication in philosophical discourse, some European sociologists and structuralists have tended to be weak in terms of empirical data and, paradoxically, to have a hard time breaking out of a kind of *ad hoc* empiricism. I suspect the contradiction here arises partly from the idealist, even Hegelian, character of much Western Marxist social theory—their idealist theory finds no place for material, objective fact. The best European approaches have been by those who have developed general theories in a particular context. One such is Meillassoux (1981, 1964), although his work is somewhat less useful as a model for more general theory of how such structures arise by being restricted in its geographic basis, and in being based on societies that are arguably not independent developments of hierarchical organization.

From these double contradictions, we may come to a synthesis of sorts. The "middle range" of explanation deserves a great deal more attention, with concern for the heuristics of social life. It can be expected that every society (i.e., *social formation*) will have its own unique mode of production, in the strict sense. At the same time, general principles apply to the variables involved, and these must surely be more complex in analytical form than a typology of modes. I have commented elsewhere (Muller 1991:255) on the confusion of "particularist" and "empiricist" in assessing past efforts at explanation; but one thing should surely be clear: Testing statements against an objective reality is a necessary step regardless of one's theoretical position. The uniqueness of individual cases does not mean that we can make no generalizations from them.

3. THE POLITICAL ECONOMY OF *CHIEFDOMS?*[9]

The most influential state-origin (and by implication, hierarchical development) theory at the beginning of the "New Archaeology" was the now-classic Service model (1962, 1975) that had considerable impact on archaeological discussions of social development in the 1960s and 1970s (e.g., Peebles and Kus 1977, Sanders and Price 1968). These models, as we shall see, tended to emphasize administrative roles for elites, rather than exploitation.

Since Service, the term *chiefdom* has been widely and loosely used to indicate social formations that are neither states nor tribes, but somehow in between (see Wright 1977, 1984). The lack of good, more or less pristine cases of this residual social category has not been the least of the problems in dealing with the course(s) of hierarchical development. Relatively pristine cases are important, because state and chiefdom formation in the vicinity of already existing, more complex organizations *may* have quite different features than organization without such military and economic pressure. Unfortunately, from the 19th century on, many of the societies chosen to exemplify transitional organizations have been societies in which vertical social differentiation was already relatively well developed. For example, Engels used ancient Greece to typify societies that were posttribal and developing into states (Engels 1891[1975:521–528]). Earle used the Hawaiian kingdom to show problems with Service's concepts relating to that level of development (1978). However useful as examples, these and other societies at these levels do not illustrate the *early* history of elite formation, nor are these cases clearly pristine developments.

By the 1990s, reaction had set in to the extent of many critiques coming to reject *chiefdom* and similar terms as misleading or worse (e.g., Feinman and Neitzel 1984; McGuire 1983; Yoffee 1979; and others; cf. Spencer 1990), not least because some of these critics saw social change in gradualist terms. Many of us suspect that social change is usually not gradual, but shows structural, qualitative changes. For us, the assertion of *gradualism* is no more convincing than some have found an "as-yet-undemonstrated steplike view of change" (Feinman and Neitzel 1984:44). *Either* concept of change requires testing in real, historical cases. The problem, of course, is that the data that seem so obviously punctuated to some seem equally obviously gradual to others.

The excellent and useful ethnographic comparisons made by Feinman and Neitzel show variability in ethnographic societies, however, rather than chronological gradualism in development. In a strange sort of paradox, such efforts come close to repeating the "social fossil" error of the 19th century (that led to so-called neoevolutionary stages in the first place). However, Lee's (1992) summary of the current state of hunter–gatherer studies could apply equally well to "chiefdom studies," (see also Johnson and Earle 1987). That is to say, we need some kind of terminology. This is another of those cases that cannot be resolved in this book, or perhaps ever, but—at the least—surely we need to separate our arguments on this issue from our convictions of either gradualism or punctuation.

---

[9]This section, with some other portions, is also discussed in different form by Muller (1994).

In a recent meeting at the Amerind Foundation (Neitzel, in preparation), efforts were made to discuss the similarities and differences between the Southeast and the Southwest across a number of dimensions. In this context, the term *duck*[10] was jokingly suggested as a "neoevolutionary-free" term, but I suggest that *chiefdom* is a better term to describe the specific, historically documented societies of the Late Prehistoric Southeast. After all is said and done, *chiefdom* was a common description of these social formations when they were directly observed. Whether in specific or general cases, I have often criticized "typological" thinking, but we must have some names, at the end. For example, Yoffee ends up still using terms such as *chiefdom* and *state-level*, even as he criticizes them (1993:73).

An analytical level something like Service's "chiefdom" and Fried's "ranked societies" marks a development, gradual or punctuated, from less to more highly organized. We may ask what the features of Service's concept were, and which of these might still be of value in examining early hierarchical development.

Power

One element of chiefdoms is inheritance of power as a part of a rank hierarchy (Fried 1967; Service 1975:16, 72). Service also saw the economic functions of leadership roles as important in the emergence of chiefdoms, especially as a form of *redistribution* based on localization of natural resources (1975:75). He indicated that "sedentary chiefdoms normally inhabit areas of variegated natural resources with numerous ecological niches requiring local and regional symbiosis" (1975:75). Service saw an imbalance of exchange of goods as leading to increases in status for persons living in fortunate locations. Other features include so-called theocratic government and the *absence* of repressive force (1975:16). Even given the importance of economic redistribution to his definition of *chiefdom*, Service's model concentrates more on power than on production, a point sometimes obscured in archaeological treatments of the theme in Mississippian studies. However, with the beginning of the 1990s, there has come a florescence of political studies of Mississippian societies (e.g., Anderson 1994b; Blitz 1993; Pauketat 1994; Welch 1991; and others).[11] However, in some political studies, the emphasis has become so *political* as to obscure the *economic*. If processual archaeology had overdone economic treatments of redistribution, that was certainly corrected in a spate of studies emphasizing the social aspects of dominance and domination in Mississippian societies. So long as we do not forget where power comes from, studies of the role of power do have the potential of making substantial contributions.

---

[10] Why a *duck*? As I recalled, it had something to do with quacking like one (for a typically trenchant Marxist perspective, see Chico Marx et al. 1929).

[11] And not only in Mississippian studies, of course. Yoffee's suggestion (1993) for a "new social evolutionary" theory to replace "neoevolution" is directly focused on dimensions of power. Also see Patterson and Gailey (1987).

Cooperation and Redistribution

Whereas Service's model emphasized cooperation rather than conflict in discussing the roles of chiefs, other theories of the development of hierarchical systems have tended to emphasize conflict instead (e.g., Carneiro 1970). Still other models have described the relationships of developing chiefs to external networks of exchange as often being significant (e.g., Flannery 1968). Many Western "Marxian" discussions of hierarchical development have commonly emphasized exploitation by emerging elites, often in terms that directly translate into the pre-1848 concept of *alienation*[12] (e.g., Marx 1844, but later not much used; See Ollman 1971 and Sayer 1987; cf. Althusser 1970:10–11, 249; Muller 1991). Critical assessment of the concepts introduced or emphasized by Service have been skeptical of his proposed mechanisms and functions for leadership in chiefly societies (e.g., Peebles and Kus 1977), eventually bringing the arguments toward the alienation view (see Earle 1977, 1987). Much of the discussion ranged along the ancient division between those who see the elites as serving a positive function in society, and those who see elite roles in terms of exploitation. Some theorists see the emerging class interests of the elite as crucial (e.g., Engels 1891), although even Engels acknowledged that elites also may serve positive functions (Engels 1878 [1959:247]; 1891). The recent political studies of Mississippian referred to here have tended to fall between the cooperation and exploitation poles of explanation.

Up to the 1980s in Mississippian archaeology, the simple answer seemed to be that the establishment of political subordination followed from economic subordination, especially in conditions of economic interdependence of local, specialized producers (anticipated in Engels 1891; developed in Service 1975). In the light of much new evidence on chiefdom-level economics, some of it from Mississippian archaeology, it now seems unlikely that the "classic redistribution model," as it is called, has much utility in explaining the origins or continuation of chiefly power. However, the problem still remains how and why the elites develop and survive in the context of "tribal" economic and political systems.

Specific cases have been examined in relation to Service's ideas about redistribution (e.g., Earle 1977; Peebles and Kus 1977). It now seems unlikely that Service's localized and specialized production systems, as characterized in his "sketch" (1975:75–78), were common in nascent hierarchical societies, if they ever existed at all (see Muller, 1987a; Muller and Stephens 1983, 1991 in relation to Mississippian). Even if redistribution were found more generally, the best known Mississippian production systems were clearly not characterized by systems of specialist local surplus production of locally plentiful resources and exchange of these for other goods through redistributive mediators. However, Service also suggests that development of chiefs was related to their location in more productive zones with positive exchange balances (1975:76). In this sense, there is more of an argument for a "leveling" kind of redistribution, but one

---

[12] *Entfremdung—Entäusserung:* For Marx, the confiscation of the producer's labor but used earlier by Feuerbach and Hegel as an idealist concept relating to such things as the externalization of the human essence as a deity (see also Muller 1991).

that levels differential success in production over high-risk zones rather than rationing differential production (see Ford 1974; Isbell 1978; Muller 1978a, 1986b, 1987b, Chapter 8 and elsewhere in this volume). Another issue is the already mentioned role of (re)distribution of display (a.k.a., "prestige") goods in these societies.

Chiefdoms or Ducks, Then?

What about terminology? Can we simply call those societies that we once called *chiefdoms, ducks*? Will that renaming eliminate the adverse effects of the type? We can now all agree that *chiefdom* (or *duck*) is not a coherent "type" that is marked by invariant attributes. We can surely use the term *chiefdom* with this understanding. The absence of true social classes is a key difference between *states* and these not-quite states of chiefdoms, although this is a rule of thumb more often stated in terms of implications than directly. As used here, *chiefdom* loosely describes those societies or social formations with some degree of centralized political and economic authority, especially as expressed across generational boundaries, and lacking an armed "public power." In the most powerfully organized chiefly societies, the distinction between chief and state leader may be slight. Relationships with nearby states strongly affected the forms of chiefdoms, as described in the historical and ethnographic literature (Steward and Faron 1959; Whitecotton and Pailes 1986). On the other hand, archaeological evidence suggests that many of the features of so-called chiefdoms were present before the formation of states, near or far (Stark 1986:274). To avoid awkward circumlocutions, I will use such terms as *tribe, chiefdom,* and *state* in the following chapters as indicating rough **levels** of developmental organization without accepting them as more than convenient analytical labels. To remind the reader of this qualification, I will try to append "-level" to at least the initial use of each term in a particular discussion, or to place the term in quotation marks. Although this is a somewhat unsatisfactory solution, it seems even worse either to go back to 19th-century terminology or to create some new set of potentially confusing terms. The issue here is to avoid the baggage of the terminology (see Yoffee 1979). At the same time it seems no improvement to fall back to a particularistic and empiricist refusal to accept any discussion of commonalties and general similarities. As unsatisfactory as the term *chiefdom* is, as applied to a particular typological construct, it still seems to me to be perfectly acceptable as a label for a kind of political and economic control, however that control may be *particularly* organized.

But what were these polities? How were they organized, and what kinds of internal differentiation existed? In the 1960s, in line with the positivist paradigms then current in archaeology, the functionalist-evolutionary models of Service and Fried were applied to the Southeast, especially in the form of the concept of *chiefdom*. As noted, subsequent changes in archaeological theoretical positions have resonated, if in a somewhat muted way, in Mississippian archaeology. There are a series of paradoxes implicit in the nature of chiefly and—in our cases, Mississippian—societies. They lacked classes but had elites. They lacked true economic differentiation (i.e., specialization) but had production of fancy goods. They had economies that were still largely communal, but they had more and more goods indicating differences in wealth and power. How and why persons that are free give up their freedom and become intermeshed in relations of subordination such as those that seem to have been developing in Mississippian is by no means a simple or easily answered question. It is precisely to deal with these issues, whether *chiefdom* is used or not, that makes a political economic approach so valuable (for an excellent general argument to this effect, see Cobb 1993d).

Finally, I should mention that studies of areas where states later developed have often shown a tendency to see the late, prestate societies from the top down, that is, as somehow directed toward the later state form. This teleological view naturally leads to the problem of imposing the later, historically more developed forms upon the more fragile and less-developed societies.

4. THE POLITICAL ECONOMY OF MISSISSIPPIAN

We now come, at long last, to the specific cases to be studied. After A.D. 800, Native Americans living along the Mississippi River and its tributaries developed new ways of living in their environments through a combination of hierarchical social organization and cultivation of crops. The best known of these groups were located in the river floodplains from modern-day St. Louis to central Louisiana, and from the Mississippi Valley to the falls of the Ohio and the upper reaches of the Tennessee and Cumberland Rivers. Many of these archaeological complexes are now called "Mississippian" by archaeologists; and, although I strongly believe in important differences among these, I will use the term *Mississippian* more loosely than I would prefer simply to avoid circumlocutions such as "hierarchically organized, ranked Late Prehistoric" or, still worse, acronyms such as "HORLP." Each Southeastern locality had its own distinctive course of development, and sometimes either hierarchical development or cultivation came first. Thus, neither food production nor hierarchical organization was the "cause" of Mississippian development; rather, more fundamental pressures impelled efforts to increase production on the one hand, and to control, if not production, the distribution of products on the other. By the beginning of the 11th century, Mississippian societies were present in much of southeastern North America. The cultural landscape during these developments is discussed in Chapter 3.

Some of these Mississippian and related archaeological complexes can be identified as ancestral to historical Native Americans such as the Creek (Muskogee[13]), the Chickasaw, and the Choctaw. In other cases, virtual abandonment of Mississippian centers by historical times makes it difficult to identify what linguistic groups may have been associated with particular archaeological entities. The central portion of the territories occupied by Mississippians was occupied historically by those speaking languages belonging to the Muskhogean group, but other linguistic groups probably were also "Mississippian" in the 13th century. Ethnic groups that participated in similar cultural systems that were not Mississippian—strictly speaking— included the Natchez of Louisiana and some Caddoan-speaking groups to the west of the Mississippi (see Swanton 1946).

---

[13] In most cases, I have used the ethnic names as spelled in Swanton (1946).

Taken altogether, Mississippian and other societies with more or less hereditary chiefs in eastern North America have been treated in terms of specific details of cross-generational power relationships and—to a lesser, but still important, degree—in terms of exchange relationships such as redistribution of goods or information. Among the weaknesses of such approaches are the tendencies toward construction of *ad hoc* functional rationalizations and toward particularism. Perhaps the most serious problem is the confusion of fully developed structures of advanced chiefdoms with the developing features of emergent chiefdom-level societies. In this way, *dominance*—relationships between individuals—and *domination*—relationships among social groups—are confused. Like the evolutionary development of a bird's wing, the "functions" of nascent chiefs cannot have been the same as those of fully developed chiefs. For this reason, the most fruitful models for the early development of hierarchical societies are not to be found in the logic of highly developed hierarchical formations, but rather in less-organized kinds of status (something like McGuire's suggestions in other cases, 1983). As Flannery suggested (1972:413), lower level institutions provide the personnel and even the infrastructure (in the sense of facilities and material support) for "promotion" to higher organizational levels. The character of new chiefly institutions will necessarily reflect their original, prechiefly, structures. Highly distinctive social forms result that cannot be understood simply in terms of specific social *types* such as "conical clans" or even "chiefs," *per se*. The fruitless quest for specific typological criteria to define so-called "chiefdoms" has been a major barrier to understanding the general mechanisms of developments and organization of these societies, notwithstanding my earlier reasons for retaining the terminology.

The Mississippian case is of particular interest for several reasons. First, these societies seem to be relatively pristine cases of development of hierarchical organization. There is some Mesoamerican "influence" on the Southeast in the sense that Mesoamerican crops were somehow introduced, but there is no evidence of direct contact such as manufactured Mesoamerican items. Present archaeological evidence makes it quite clear that Mesoamerican "influence" was even more indirect than in the Southwest (compare Stark's criticism of treatments of the Southwest as a Mesoamerican "periphery," 1986). Second, Mississippian had recent development of "chiefly" organizations in an area where more complex social structures did not develop later to obscure the initial forms. Third, Mississippian is now very well documented by archaeological standards. Fourth, the historical records for the area are reasonably good. I will argue here, as I have done previously (1987a), that the historical and prehistoric societies of the Southeast may have been more alike than is generally credited. Finally, many features of Mississippian economic and social organization do not correspond well to expectations from general theories of hierarchical development that are still embedded in our discussions of these matters.

What follows is an initial outline of a Mississippian political economy. The rest of this volume will explore these issues in more detail. Before beginning, however, I want to emphasize again that this is not a general survey of Mississippian, nor is it an assertion that there are no differences among the various Mississippian societies in the Southeast. Here, however, I am trying to synthesize what I see as similarities, rather than explaining differences.

Mode of Production in Mississippian

One unfortunate "advantage" of Southeastern cases over the Asian and African examples (that formed the basis for the 19th-century theoretical discussion of pre-capitalist modes of production) is that Mississippian development was truncated by European invasion. Thus, Mississippian social and economic structures were not widely reinterpreted and "promoted" into state-level systems—except, probably, in a few cases, in response to the European threat. The negative result of this truncation is that the Mississippians are known primarily archaeologically. Ethnographic and historical information on Southeastern Native Americans can compensate, but our historical records generally describe peoples who had already been affected considerably by European disease and domination, an important, if overemphasized, problem. Partly for these reasons, there is less information on the conditions of social reproduction than there is about the forces of production, for example.

What are the salient features of a generalized Mississippian "political economy"? From the data on the central riverine area, we see that these social formations were classless societies that, nonetheless, had ranked social status. This is not say that there was little or no social and productive differentiation. The question is how important and how pervasive such differentiation was. The following discussion previews issues that are developed more fully in the following chapters.

Forces of Production

Mississippian production of subsistence goods appears to have been firmly based in the domestic level. At the Kincaid site in the Lower Ohio Valley, the amount of available land per household for the largest center is not significantly larger or smaller than for other sites. Although there may have been some communally worked fields or donation of labor or goods to either the elite or other central authority, evidence suggests that the normal productive capacities of the homestead and of the local community were adequate in *most* circumstances (cf. Muller 1978a, 1978b; Peebles and Kus 1977). Nearly all communities and households seem to have engaged in the same round of activities throughout the year. Most household inventories at large Mississippian sites can scarcely be distinguished from those at isolated farmsteads or small hamlets. The production of display goods seems to have taken place at the household or domestic level (e.g., Muller 1987a). Present evidence is strongly supportive of production of other resources such as chert or salt, with domestic, or at most, local control of production.

Under such circumstances, interhousehold or intercommunity interaction would be low were it not for the necessity of managing risk, reproduction, and information, among other things (e.g., Johnson 1978; Muller 1986b, Muller and Stephens 1991). Exchange, as such, seems to have been fairly limited, and most Mississippian exchange relationships seem to have revolved around a relatively restricted number of exotic and/or unevenly distributed raw materials (see Muller 1986a, 1987 and Chapter 8 for more discussion of exchange). The term *trade*, often used for Mississippian exchange, begs the question by implying a more formal and even specialized form of exchange in which specialized agents ("traders") participate under the conditions that Sahlins called "negative reciprocity" (1972:195).

The technology associated with the exploitation of restricted-source raw materials such as salt was relatively straightforward. Salt production consisted of evaporating brine from natural saline springs. Vessel size and the size of auxiliary production components vary in size, although the tool kit for salt production is similar over a large area of production. Although we need more data on the social relations and domestic conditions of, say, salt producers, production areas do not show much evidence of such indications as standardization, normally thought to follow from large-scale specialist production (but see Muller 1984a, 1986a). As I have stressed elsewhere, Mississippian specialist production of some items cannot be completely ruled out, but many efforts to argue for specialization have not given sufficient effort to rejecting more straightforward, nonspecialist hypotheses first. Before concluding that mere concentration of production of some resource indicates a distinct social group of specialists (cf. Yerkes 1986), we have to examine the possibility of nonspecialist production. Highly skilled craftsmen or craftswomen produced some display goods. Skill and artistry, however, are not necessarily signs of *specialist* production in any nontrivial sense.

Most resources exploited by Mississippian producers, however, were not found in just a few localities but were widespread and relatively common. Although some land circumscription probably occurred, an area such as the Black Bottom—located at the junction of the Ohio with the Tennessee and Cumberland Rivers—has many zones of relatively high-fertility soil that had little or no Mississippian occupation. The best soils were filled up with settlement, but soils of only slightly lower fertility were ignored in favor of less fertile terrace soils (Butler 1977; Muller 1978b, 1986b). There are undoubtedly good reasons (such as lower flood risk) to explain these Mississippian settlement patterns, but the fact remains that neither population level nor settlement patterns suggest crowding of the sort that would have forced use of other bottomland areas. I have argued elsewhere that the evening out of local production inequalities and risk was a major factor in Mississippian social organization, but the kinds of local variation that are important are largely unpredictable perturbations of the natural and social environments (Ford 1974; Isbell 1978; Muller 1978a) *rather than geographical differences in the normal distribution of resources*. It would not be entirely realistic to describe Mississippian resources as being superabundant, especially given the clear concentrations of populations around favorable bottomlands. All the same, even though circumscription (see Carneiro 1970) was present, it cannot be described as intense. Normal self-sustenance at the homestead level should not be confused with complete economic or political autonomy (see Meillassoux 1981:37).

Hoe cultivation of maize was typically the basis of horticultural production. In historical times, the female members of the household did most of the horticultural work, and this was probably true prehistorically as well. Male production systems included various hunting activities, including those centered on protection of horticultural fields. Many of the species taken by Mississippian hunters were those most attracted to field margins and maize itself. Mississippians collected many other kinds of wild food resources, and these wild foods provided a significant percentage of the diet, especially in some seasons. Sexual division of labor and some division along age lines appear to have been the only major task distinctions in subsistence production. Little or no evidence has been presented to indicate that Mississippian elite households were in any significant sense "nonproducing" in terms of the subsistence sector, despite common claims to the contrary. Spouses of the elite appear to have undertaken the normal range of production activities.

As we shall see in later chapters, the hoes were made from cherts that were exchanged widely. Although exchange in chert, by weight, probably far exceeded that of any other good, my own assessment of chert production is that this was nonspecialist production (Muller 1995b, but also see Cobb 1988, 1995). Mississippian exchange among localities and regions cannot be characterized as being solely concerned with exotic, display goods. The diversity of Mississippian exchange is important in considering models emphasizing valuables exchange at this social level (see Brumfiel and Earle 1987).

Artifacts apparently intended for display of status or wealth[14] certainly can play a role in rewarding loyal followers through elite patronage. In the Mississippian case, however, the widespread production of valuables and their widespread use does not support great social distinction between a supposed patron and client (Muller 1986a). As we have already seen, the bulk of Mississippian exchange seems to have been in items such as stone hoes. We do not know how much exchange of foodstuffs there may have been, but the surviving data support the idea of nonvaluables exchange as being important. Substantial amounts of "display" items were exchanged, but their production and distribution in Mississippian sites of all sizes and kinds does not support their associations as being restricted to elite contexts. Identification of "elite" objects, and persons by these objects, has too often been circular, as discussed in the next section.

Taken altogether, Mississippian production and organization of production seem to have taken place largely at the domestic level. Mississippian homesteads were often dispersed, but they did maintain some kinds of ritual and economic links to larger centers. I have suggested that the relationship of leaders or elite to the mass of Mississippian producers was not that of exploiters, since there is so little evidence for significant differences in access to the material conditions of everyday life, or even to exotic goods. In this sense, as well as in others, Mississippian society lacked true classes (in the sense of Ste. Croix 1984). The degree of alienation of surplus product or of labor from the individual household appears to have been low. In Americanist terms, this society appears to show ranking, but little evidence exists for stratification in Fried's sense. In this nonstratified society, one germ of specialist production may be found in unevenness in distribution of some natural resources. The sometime diversion of household surplus goods into exchange is also significant (compare Engels 1878[1958:223]) but is not true specialization. Nonetheless, these conditions together clearly provide one possible way for specialization to arise.

---

[14] Display goods are sometimes misleadingly called *sumptuary goods* by extension from sumptuary *law* in Medieval Europe, which was concerned with regulating *expenditure*, which is what *sumptuary* refers to, rather than the display goods so regulated.

Relations of Production and Elites

Social differentiation is normally expected to be reflected archaeologically in differential access to both nonsubsistence and subsistence goods, at least where those goods are not superabundant. Studies of Mississippian burial patterns are available (e.g., Goldstein 1980; Hatch 1976; Milner 1984a; Rothschild 1979), and they suggest persistent, although minor, social differences through time. There may have been differences in access to subsistence goods, but the skeletal data do not support *major* differences. Such differences as those in stature or health between elite and nonelite burials are difficult to interpret (Cook and Buikstra 1979; Hatch 1976; Hill 1986). Are some people taller because they are elite, or are they elite because they are taller? If we do not know that different burials reflect the same environmental history, the effect of ambient conditions on physical development has to be ruled out before we can speak of the biological characteristics of the elite. Elite individuals may have been marginally more cushioned against environmental perturbations, but the lack of extremely fine-grained temporal control makes this a difficult circumstance to determine, especially given the scale and cyclicity of environmental conditions. Studies suggest that "rural" or otherwise peripheral Mississippian cemeteries show a mostly egalitarian structure (e.g., Goldstein 1980:135; Milner 1984a:472). Comparison with supposed elite burials (so determined from their placement and associations) shows a number of differences that are surely significant in indicating some kinds of rank differences. The question that has to be settled is whether the differences are of sufficient scale to indicate developing class differences. Even in the American Bottom, for example, special treatment in burial seems to be mostly associated with adults (Milner 1984a:472). In other regions too, the diet, for example, of elites does not seem very different in terms of adequacy from those of the mass of people (compare Schoeninger and Peebles 1981; Schurr and Schoeninger 1995; Welch 1991:132), notwithstanding possible "provisioning" of elites with specially favored animal parts (e.g., Susan L. Scott's reports summarized in Welch 1991:88–103). As we shall see in the Historic period accounts in Chapter 2, food was a common donation or "prestation" to elites. By all indications that we have, provisioning under force that left the donors starving was a European introduction.

Differences in display goods, both in mortuary and nonmortuary context, are easier to approach than the relatively scanty data on elite versus nonelite diet and health. But (1) we must be cautious of interpreting all finds of exotic or display goods as indicating elite status, or our argument becomes circular[15]; (2) some burials and residential areas are much richer in exotic and expensive (in terms of energy investment) items; and, (3) at the same time, such goods are *not* limited to the largest communities or to associations with individuals who can be identified *on other grounds* as "elites."

Differences in socioeconomic status are marked by behaviors and display artifacts that distinguish one group from other groups (for a general discussion of hierarchical

---

[15] As in "We know these are elite individuals because they have goods with them that we know are elite because they are with elite individuals."

differentiation, see Lenski 1966; Turner 1984; see also Wobst's various discussions of this in archaeological contexts, e.g., 1977). In these terms, some Mississippian societies do not show the degree of differences that would be expected from strong social differentiation. In the Black Bottom society surrounding the Kincaid site (Cole et al. 1951; Muller 1986a, 1987b), some individuals in even small communities appear to have had access to exotic raw materials and finished goods. Similar dispersal of fancy goods may be seen in the objects recovered from smaller Mississippian sites in the American Bottom (FAI-270 project; e.g., Bareis and Porter 1984; Milner 1986; Pauketat 1987b). Although such goods *might* indicate local rank distinctions, they can just as easily reflect a generally low level of differentiation or even local autonomy. These latter hypotheses must be rejected before one can interpret these sites as having elite "lieutenants," especially in light of the low level of differentiation seen in non-mound-center burials. All in all, Griffin's summary still seems to apply to the most developed of the Mississippian social organizations, "Cahokia was probably, ..., the most complex chiefdom in the East, but had not reached the level of a highly structured elite with an organized bureaucracy and the other features required for statehood" (1983:280; cf. Fowler 1969, 1974, 1978; Porter 1969; Sears 1968).

The degree of domination in Mississippian societies also seems to have been fairly low. Several kinds of widely used raw materials occurred in fairly restricted source areas. These include favored chert resources and salt. No hard evidence either at the salt springs (Muller 1984a, 1986a) or at the chert resources (Cobb 1993a,b,c) even weakly supports an interpretation that these sites were garrisoned or controlled by the major Mississippian population centers. Efforts to estimate Mississippian political boundaries (such as Lafferty 1977) have found little indication of strong political control beyond the immediate bottomlands surrounding the larger centers. There can be no doubt of the considerable "influence" of the large centers over their "hinterlands," but those hinterlands were surely smaller than the most exaggerated estimates. The best that can be said for hypotheses of direct invasion or efforts to exert direct control over supposed peripheral groups is that they need much more work before they can be even treated as warranted, much less proved. The archaeological record is quite consistent with the historical social environments described by the European invaders in the Southeast between the 16th and the late 18th centuries (see Chapter 2). That is to say that the archaeological evidence is not consistent with models of areawide domination and powerful control over peripheral societies.

Differentiation of labor seems to have been low (Muller 1984a, 1986a, 1987a), fitting well within models of domestic production (e.g., Sahlins 1972). Surely those fortunate households and communities near localized resources were able to translate some surplus production into commodity exchange, but there is little evidence that the commodities were ever alienated from the local production units. Most producers were working even with exotic raw materials in a way that suggests that they were engaged in supplemental production rather than as true craft or full-time specialists (Meillassoux 1981:37; Muller 1984a, 1986a). A few cases of possible specialization have been proposed for the largest Mississippian sites (shell-working and fine-ware pottery manufacture—Yerkes 1983,1986; Welch 1986; also Prentice 1983, 1985), but I remain unconvinced that *full-time* or true specialization is involved in these circumstances (see Chapter 7; Muller 1986a; Pauketat 1987b). The question is not merely a quibble over terminology, since full-time specialization is a significant step in the development of relations of production.

It is especially notable that even those Mississippian communities that "controlled" rare, localized raw materials were unable to translate control of these resources into political power. The important exception to this statement seems to be that the main determinants of Mississippian site size and complexity appear to have been access to the varied resources of the major floodplains. Each major Mississippian center is located in a site that was the richest collecting and agricultural zone in its region. Just as in the case of households-to-land ratio, the overall area of the main site is at the same ratio to available land as is the case for smaller, more isolated settlements—in those cases where the settlement system has been studied in close detail, such as Kincaid (see Muller 1986b). These data make it difficult to argue in general, and impossible at Kincaid, that the size of the central site reflects its economic support from "rents" or taxes on land beyond its immediate environs. It seems likely that most Mississippian sites were able to feed themselves from their own production in *most* years. The interactions in those years that this was not possible were an important aspect of Mississippian life.

In the Mississippian case, the main source of political power does not seem to have been the alienation of land from the producers. What, then, was the source of the political power represented in the elite mortuary treatments of many Mississippian societies? I have argued elsewhere that this developing elite was controlling some "surplus" products through several mechanisms (Muller 1987a). The first of these may have been through more or less voluntary contributions to the central stores of the political elite that could then be shared in times of shortage (as reported in the historical literature on some of these societies, e.g., Bartram 1791 [1928:401]). This is a kind of redistribution, but not like that postulated by Service (see also Feinman and Neitzel 1984). The persistence of contributions to the central stores is partly an indication of the assessment of risk by the donor, since the central stores in historical times in the East were used to alleviate local shortages in production. The Mississippian producer's essential autonomy in good years is likely, but the power of the elite to mobilize subsistence resources in this manner would be greatest in those environments in which environmental risks were highest, in short, in the floodplains.

Another mechanism for enhancement of the power of the elites was their ability to sponsor community rituals at which both community and domestic stores were mobilized and (re)distributed (Muller 1987a, Seeman 1979). Lawson (1709:176) described the nature of these community events, albeit using European terminology:

> At these feasts, they meet from all the Towns within fifty or sixty miles round, where they buy and sell several Commodities, as we do at Fairs and Markets. Besides they game very much, and often strip one another of all they have in the World...

It is also likely that the elite were also able to stimulate short-term surplus production through community rituals and activities.

Still another mechanism for the elites to control power in these largely undifferentiated communities was their supposed greater access to external goods. Their putative ability to control patronage of exotic, and thereby largely display, goods could have allowed them to enhance their own prestige in relation to the ordinary producers in their societies. As we shall see in later chapters, however, elite control of display goods is often assumed, but not yet demonstrated. In some cases, external exchange and social relations may also have served to provide more basic needs as a kind of social security against really widespread shortfalls in production.

Little in either the archaeological or historical evidence suggests that there was much alienation of even "surplus" goods by the leadership. There is little indication that Mississippian leaders could have been successful in restricting access to raw materials or finished goods. The historical literature does suggest high mobility of individuals in terms of the potential for moving to or interacting with individuals in other polities. Mississippian population was concentrated in the high-productivity zones, but the degree of circumscription for the individual domestic unit was much lower than for the community as a whole. In the event of efforts at domination, individual production units could easily have "voted with their feet," and just such responses are evident in historical sources from the area. Indeed, some of the upland Mississippian farmsteads could represent pioneering settlements of this kind (for other kinds of "pioneering" settlement, see Clay 1976).

Reproduction

We know that Mississippian societies existed for roughly 400 to 500 years in many localities. In some regions in the Southeast, essentially Mississippian peoples survived into the historical period and became the Creek, Choctaw, and other groups known in the historical records. A gap in historical records from the 16th until the late-17th century covers a time when there may have been important shifts in population distribution and social relations under pressure from European diseases. I have suggested that the historical circumstances are not necessarily different in kind, merely in the number of societies, but many feel that there were major social as well as population changes in this period (e.g., M. T. Smith 1987). In either case, the historical record can be used with caution to suggest some of the dimensions of social and biological reproduction. Douglas Davy (1982) has built a simple simulation model of some aspects of the reproductive system in the Black Bottom, although his purpose was to model settlements, not human behavior directly. All the same, his simulation shows a pattern based on a few simple assumptions that corresponds reasonably well to the archaeological data for the Black Bottom. His assumptions (1982:181–182) include the following:

1. Abandonment of household at death of residents at roughly age 50, a figure that implies at least one rebuilding during the use of the homestead
2. Inheritance of the homestead will be limited by postmarital residence rules to one gender on the average
3. Davy assumed only two surviving offspring per couple. This allows four possible combinations of gender (2 male, 1 female–1 male, 1 male–1 female, 2 female)
4. Abandonment of a homestead will occur according to the results of inheritance according to (1) above, giving a 25 percent chance of abandonment for each generation

Despite the simplicity of these assumptions about coresidence and inheritance, Davy's model produced results in 10 runs that are consistent with the observed distribution and character of Mississippian settlement in the Kincaid locality. Although a complete model of Mississippian social and biological reproduction would necessarily be much more complex, Davy did prove his point that "it is possible for a very few people to generate many archaeological sites" (1982:189).

For our purposes, we need to try to look a little deeper into Mississippian social life. Some of the verified data and reasonable inferences from historical and archaeological evidence can be summarized. Lower Ohio Mississippian domestic units were relatively standardized. From data both in small isolated farmsteads and from the central sites themselves, the typical farmstead/homestead unit is rarely more than three contemporary structures. It is unlikely that all of these were used primarily as "residences," and 7 to 8 persons per homestead seems a reasonable modal figure. However, to be on the conservative side, I shall usually treat the household as having had 5 members in the estimates to follow later. Descent was probably unilineal and often matrilineal. New family units, formed by marriage and immigration of spouses might have settled near the parental homestead, but availability of the best soils forced linear dispersal of settlement along the ridges. Formation of homesteads would have depended on the land being available for settlement (through earlier abandonment) when new productive units were formed by alliance. Smaller and more isolated ridge areas would probably have been more likely to see abandonment and reoccupation by new groups than large ridges having many related occupants. Exchange of spouses from one kin group to another would have provided alliance ties of potential importance in meeting the risks of production in this environment. Most of the relatively small Mississippian groups in the immediate vicinity of larger centers would probably have forged alliance ties to chiefly kin groups. Kin unit elders would likely have held important leadership roles in these societies (compare with the African forms described by Meillassoux 1981). Elders on this social level often control marriage, but it would be dangerous to follow models such as Meillassoux's Africa-specific modes too closely (1981:42ff.). The control of subsistence goods may have rested with kin elders, but present evidence could as easily support the control of most foodstuffs by the individual homestead. The structuralist African model seems too specifically tailored to the social formations of Africa, and seems to place too little emphasis on the development and role of hierarchies to be applied to the Mississippian case. Having said this, there are some useful concepts in the "alimentary forms of kinship" presented by Meillassoux (1981).

Reproduction of the entire social group was probably facilitated through festivals sponsored by the elite. There is surprisingly little evidence on the social background of these events in historical times, but surely both social and biological reproduction were symbolized and encouraged.

Much more work is needed. We have to have more data on Mississippian household structure, more information on the size of social groups within a fine-grained chronology. We also need to reanalyze the existing ethnographic information in terms of its potential relationships of reproduction. This chapter has been an outline of some basic features of Mississippian organization and the social context of production. The last step in this chapter is to look quickly at a few of the possible problems faced by developing Mississippian peoples.

The Genesis of Mississippian

In the Late Woodland context in which Mississippian developed—as discussed in Chapter 3—increased production was probably converted directly into reproduction. Having more producers conferred selective advantages over other social groups. Inevitably, a larger population comes to depend absolutely on high levels of production, and fewer alternatives are left open in the event of poor yields. Thus, the very features that seem, at first, to promise greater security to the autonomous domestic production unit will, in the long run, make that unit more dependent on its neighbors *in times of hardship*. Here is part of the answer to why these autonomous units surrendered some of their freedom to support elites.

One of the functions of Mississippian leaders that was mentioned was their ability to use community pressures to stimulate more production than required by the household units. The skill of the leader in accomplishing this end, however, creates other problems in its own right since it is likely that consistent surpluses will be translated into increased reproduction. The power of emergent Mississippian leaders even partially to control surplus production over a larger territory could thus also make their roles in controlling this production more important to the reproduction of the society. Selective pressures could also favor some kind of revocable alienation of surplus production that would help reduce the conversion of surplus into biological reproduction, while maintaining the high levels necessary to avoid poor-year risks. One such program, of course, would be mound construction, which could be sponsored or not as circumstances allowed.

Growing dependence on bottomland resources would also have decreased risk in the earlier stages of transition from Late Woodland to Mississippian. With increased numbers of people, however, the upland, alternative resources of earlier times were no longer sufficient to provide for the larger populations. Thus, actions originally seen as decreasing risk could, in the long run, have had the opposite effect.

Increased dependence on relatively localized resources (as opposed to upland hunting and gathering) could have led to concentration of populations that were almost totally dependent on their bottomland environments. Another implication in the other direction is that dramatic improvement of production capabilities of the household could lead to reduction in the authority of the elites, at least in the short term. Hall has called this the Schmoo Effect after an episode in the Lil' Abner comic strip (1980). I have proposed elsewhere that increased use of the common bean might have made individual household production both more balanced in dietary terms and have increased the dietary independence of the household from centrally controlled stores. The decline of many Mississippian centers does follow relatively shortly on the beginning of heavier bean cultivation, but it is not clear that there is any causal relationship. Whether the bean "killed" Mississippian central organization in the late 13th century or not, the example illustrates how technology, production, and organizational factors must be seen as interrelated. In fact, there is evidence of population declines before the known introduction of the bean (Chapters 4 and 5).

5. CONCLUSION

This chapter has introduced political economy in general, and hinted how the mode-of-production concept may aid in understanding Mississippian political economy. Examples of classical modes of production were briefly discussed in order to show how political and economic features may be seen as related through a social structure concerned with the material conditions of everyday life.

The Mississippian and related societies of the American Southeast are seen as instances of general theoretical interest. As relatively pristine nonstate, hierarchically ordered societies, the Mississippians inform many issues of general theory. A brief summary of forces of production, relations of production, and conditions of social and biological reproduction were introduced and are the topic of the remainder of this book.

Finally, a brief discussion of the political economic origins of Mississippian was begun. One issue is that the role of leaders in the early stages of hierarchical formation may yet have to be understood in terms of the positive forces reinforcing their power rather than in terms of exploitation or domination (compare Engels 1878[1959:246–247], Ostrovitianov and Sterbalova 1977:31–32).

In the next chapter, I shall present a background to the understanding of Historic Southeastern polities and the nature of their political organization—not to allow us to "interpret" Mississippian from these cases, but as a source of information on the actual structures of Eastern groups as opposed to the phantasmagoric models they have sometimes spawned in the historical and archaeological literature.

Chapter 2

Historical Southeastern Chiefs

He will not fail to exaggerate
everything. He speaks more in
keeping with what he wishes than
with what he knows.
LaSalle's comment on Hennepin

1. INTRODUCTION

Historical narratives have often been used in various ways in the discussion of Mississippian economic and political structures. Recently, those especially concerned with "power" and its relationships use these sources to suggest the complexity of prehistoric systems (e.g., Barker and Pauketat 1992). This chapter will introduce the issue of the use of historical sources in a general way. Following that, I shall reexamine the character of chiefly authority in selected historical Eastern societies.

My purpose here is not to do an exhaustive reanalysis of the ethnohistoric literature. Such an effort would be worthwhile, but it is far beyond what is possible here. In this chapter, I want to warrant a view of Historic period political authority that recognizes its complexity without exaggerating it. In later chapters, I discuss other aspects of Historic political economies such as production, distribution, and consumption as I move, in turn, into discussions of these aspects for prehistoric political economies. I want strongly to assure the reader that I am not arguing for "continuity" in some old-fashioned sense of denying differences between historical and prehistoric. Rather, I am arguing that the historic and prehistoric Southeastern societies are *similar* social formations, and that both faced certain problems that are often mistakenly taken to be novel to the Historic period. Although I am using Historic period societies as a check, a counterfoil, to exaggeration of the Prehistoric record, I am also arguing for the complexity of the Historic societies as well. I certainly am *not* using Historic behavior to *interpret* prehistoric social systems. Rather, I see careful study of these societies to be more useful sources of *models* to test in prehistoric societies than are, say, Oceanic or African societies.

A fresh, broad anthropological restudy of the historical literature on the Southeast is needed, but I am happy to say that a reexamination of the original sources is now underway by a number of scholars (see Hudson 1990: 52, n. 1; cf. Sturtevant 1983). Much of this reworking is still being directed to specific social and historical cases, of course. Such reexamination is necessary because of the changes in anthropological and archaeological viewpoints, and knowledge since the great surveys of Swanton and other pioneers. There are better uses for the ethnohistorical literature than merely to address questions of "tribal" government (Sturtevant 1983), and it doesn't make much sense to ignore what evidence we have about the direct descendants of the archaeological cultures.

To be sure, the older, "established" views of many matters, such as kinship, seem still to be correct in broad outline. Even post–World War II summaries of these topics in books such as Hudson's (1976) do not differ dramatically from those of the past, nor, indeed, does there seem to be much reason for them to do so. The greatest changes from the old culture histories may be found in those areas of most importance to this book, namely, political and economic interpretations. Collections such as *The Forgotten Centuries* (Hudson and Tesser 1994) and the *Columbian Consequences* volumes (Thomas 1990, 1991) contain many examples of these new approaches and provide an entrée into this literature. Examples of what needs to be done more generally are the restudies of Historic Middle Atlantic societies exemplified in Potter's (1993) and Rountree's (1993) books. Swanton treated these matters in considerable detail in his various books, perhaps unfortunately, since many archaeologists seemed to feel that there was no point to reading the accounts for themselves.

Because of my particular interests in political economy, I present detailed discussion of issues related to "power" in this chapter. I confess an ambivalence about the emphasis on "power" in reexamination of Mississippian societies. I welcome the studies, many of which are theoretically close to my own positions. At the same time, I am uneasy about what sometimes seem unnecessarily complex interpretations that seem unwarranted by either hard historical or archaeological fact. Frankly, the political systems described, if not understood, by the early travelers seem quite sufficient to explain the prehistoric record, without any real need to postulate overly complex levels of organization (see also Muller 1993a). Both prehistoric and some early Historic societies have been aggrandized, whereas others have been treated as either degenerate or "tribal." Generally I conclude here that there is probably more political continuity between historical and prehistoric societies than is commonly thought.

The Use of Historical Accounts

We do not need to buy the atheoretical nihilism of postmodernism to recognize the truth that sources and texts are documents that require careful analysis of their context, as well as content. For example, historical accounts by male explorers, traders, and missionaries emphasized male activities. They often described Eastern societies as living primarily by hunting, even though we know that the bulk of the food for these aboriginal groups was from domesticated plants and other foods collected by women. Even without gender bias, European travelers' emphasis on meat consumption and hunting was culturally conditioned—18th-century Japanese described Europeans as "stinking of beef" (see Braudel 1981:199–202).

The purposes of the author, the taphonomy of which sources survived and why, and other questions are essential, not just for the colonial records of the Americas, but for any historical documents. Galloway (1991, 1995) presents a more extensive discussion of these important issues, proposing an "archaeology" of historical sources. To get around these problems, we need to emphasize objective human *behaviors* described in the accounts rather than the observer's *understanding* of their meaning. We need to know what was seen and done, before we can even begin to discuss what it meant. It is even better when a datum can be recorded from more than one source. It is particularly important to be very, very cautious in using some sections of a report that are "reasonable" while ignoring the same author's clear errors and exaggerations on other points.

The issue of how ethnohistorical accounts may best be used is complex, but attention to observed detail can go a long way toward making the biases less troublesome. For example, when an observer called the leader of a community an "emperor," we should be skeptical, but we have less reason to doubt the observation that a "leader" was carried upon a litter by others of her community. If an account says the leader was carried by 60 people, we may be skeptical of the number without doubting that some number of people were carrying him or her. It is often the detail that was incidental to the observer that may be most useful in trying to understand the events described. As useful as observer accounts are for model building, they are still a treacherous source for unsophisticated *interpretation* of past social formations.

This is a caution only slightly different in word and purpose than the recent reminders of the need to deal with these historical sources in a rational and skeptical fashion (see Adams 1980; Brain 1985; Galloway 1991; Henige 1993; and many others). The illustrations in Figure 2.1 are representations of Native Americans, but they clearly reflect the taste of the contemporaries who viewed them. If this is so for

Figure 2.1. Illustrations of Southeasterners: left, by John White as engraved by T. de Bry in Hariot 1590; center, Le Page du Pratz 1758; right, Trumbell 1790, in Swanton 1946: plate 26.

pictures that are supposed to be realistic, can we imagine that the written records of the same periods are less reflective of the "views" of both author and reader? And yet, at the same time, there are details in these pictures that we may, with caution, be able to use. Although the details of bow, clothing, and headdress are influenced by their European forms, we can reasonably suppose that bows were present. We may even note that necklaces and gorgets were worn, and so on. As I once said in relation to another matter, to say that there is bias in *all* historical accounts does not mean that there is *nothing but* bias.

The accounts are important in another way. There is what may be called the "feet of the natives are large" phenomenon (see Firth 1963:1–14; also comments by Berliner 1962). That is to say, new observers of a culture will see a chaotic kaleidoscope of actions, not knowing what behavior is significant and what is not. As the observer begins to make patterns of the chaos—and even military explorers must try to do that—there will be an interplay between objective reality and the models being unconsciously built by the observers. There is good evidence that elaboration of explanatory models will only be revised so far as they fail to work "well enough." As we shall see in the de Soto accounts, there were occasions when the models failed and had to be revised. In addition, there are many differences in a new cultural context that will be noticed and remarked on only as they are fresh. Another mound, another this or that, may not be remarked upon in accounts after they have been seen many times, even if they were initially strange to the observer. In any case, these are mostly memoirs, not diaries, so there is great likelihood that common features that were novel to the Europeans became familiar with time and may have escaped explicit notice in the accounts.

Notwithstanding these genuine problems of reliability and accuracy, historical records can tell us a surprising amount about Eastern political economies.

Other Biases in the Accounts

Classicism

National and temporal origins were not the only source of bias in travelers' accounts. Much of the travelers' understanding of "chiefdom" and early states was influenced, to say the least, by Classical literature on "savages" and "barbarians" (as also noted by Galloway 1991:461). For example, Tacitus and Caesar described German and other social groups in terms that were echoed in the historical accounts of the Southeast and have a haunting familiarity for those acquainted with literature on political evolution.

> Private and individual ownership of land does not exist among them, nor is it lawful to work the same farm longer than a year. Caesar, *Gallic War* 4.1 (1957:74)

> German institutions are very different [as compared to the more organized Gauls, JM]. They have no Druids to preside over ritual, and no inclination to sacrifice. As gods they recognize only those they see are directly useful—Sun, Fire-god, Moon; the others they have not even heard of. Their whole life consists of hunting and war; they are inured to toil and deprivation from infancy. Caesar, *Gallic War* 6.21 (1957:138–139)

> For the management of war, aggressive or defensive, they choose supreme commanders who are vested with power of life or death. In time of peace, there is no central authority; the chiefs of districts and cantons administer justice among their own people and settle quarrels. Caesar, *Gallic War* 6.23 (1957:139–140)

> About small matters the chiefs deliberate, about the more important, the whole group. Yet even when the final decision rests with the people, the affair is always first discussed by the chiefs. Tacitus, *Germania* 11

> Whenever they are not fighting, they pass much of their time in the chase, and still more in idleness, giving themselves up to sleep and to feasting, surrendering the management of the household, of the home, of the land, to the women, the old men, and all the weakest members of the family. Tacitus, *Germania* 15

> It is the custom of the states to bestow by voluntary and individual contribution on the chiefs a present of cattle or of grain, which, while accepted as a compliment, supplies their wants. They are particularly delighted by gifts from neighboring tribe, which are sent not simply by individuals but also by the public, such as choice steeds, heavy armour, trappings, and neckchains. Tacitus, *Germania* 15

This is enough to show how similar the descriptions of chiefly societies of the Southeast and the Roman period German tribes are. Caesar and, by later times at least, Tacitus were the mother's milk of historical writing until the onset of modern illiteracy, and it is not surprising that observers chose to describe "chiefly" societies using similar wording. It is more difficult to know how much a traveler's understanding of Southeastern polities was directed consciously or unconsciously by these literary models. This is another reason why actual observations by the travelers have more value than do poorly understood tales told them and their own inevitably biased interpretations of what they saw. We would be foolish to ignore their eyewitness accounts, but even more foolish to accept them uncritically.

Feudalism

The earliest travelers in the Southeast were themselves embedded in barely postfeudal societies that shared some genuine similarities with the chiefdoms they were describing. Native Eastern North America had its similarities to Medieval Europe (Muller 1986b). Some of the conditions of everyday life for Mississippians and their historical descendants *were* similar to those of Medieval and early Renaissance European societies, particularly in rural contexts. Gottfried (1983: 1–2) described the Medieval landscape that was contemporary with Mississippian:

> There were no sprawling urban and industrial complexes and surprisingly few towns of any size. Towns were usually far apart, located next to the sea or astride great rivers. Nine out of ten Europeans lived in still smaller settlements, nucleated villages or hamlets of a few hundred people, fifteen to twenty miles apart. Both town and village were small and cramped, with woefully inadequate sanitation and transportation facilities.

The natural and social conditions of late Medieval to 17th-century Europeans were more similar to the societies of the East than *we* appreciate in looking back on their interactions. Early Western European feudalism itself can be interpreted as "chiefly" organization as it redeveloped in the ruins of collapsed states (e.g., see Johnson and Earle 1987:249; also Bloch 1961; Duby 1988:3–31; Hays 1966). At the same time, the historical connections of feudal societies to the expansion of Germanic groups (such as the Anglo-Saxons and the Franks) in the Dark Ages suggest some of the features of feudalism might have been developments (promotions) of older patterns (cf. Postan 1975:2–14). Many Medieval social conditions, such as size of many polities, were at chiefly levels, but state-level institutions such as the Church also survived in some form. My point is that for all the exaggeration implicit in using terms such as *lord* for the Southeast, there is perhaps a grain of truth in the comparisons, *if we are willing to scale down our views of the European cases as well!* Although it is necessary to be cautious in accepting "feudal" elements in descriptions of the Historic East, we also have to recognize the likelihood that some of the similarities are not only apparent but also real. However, Eastern archaeologists have not been very precise in their indirect use of feudal models—as I have already said in Chapter 1, loose usage of terms such as *tribute* is a serious impediment to communicating with scholars who are working in areas that have *tribute* in the strict meaning of that term.

Spanish feudalism, particularly, was shaped by the brigandage surrounding the reconquest of Spain from the Muslims (Bloch 1961:4–5). Thus, Iberian feudalism was a conquest-induced institution, both in terms of the Muslim conquest itself, which was followed by assertion of local fiscal autonomy (Lybyer 1931) and the later Christian reconquest. In Spain, the reconquest also involved resettlement by Christian peasant producers who were small holders, sometimes very poor, who were nevertheless able to avoid the worst of feudal subordination. However, these circumstances encouraged a general sort of freebootery of just the sort seen in the conquest of the New World (see Bloch 1961:187).

The need for avoiding modern biases in relation to even European Medieval accounts has been cautioned by European historians:

> The traders of the middle ages have been too readily described in modern and indeed twentieth-century terms. The interpretation of the past in the light of the present has on this point proved quite exceptionally dangerous and misleading. quotation from G. von Below in Hasebroek 1928:5.

> What is said here of mediæval history may be said with equal force of ancient history. Hasebroek 1928:5, 1965:6.

To which I would add that this caution doubly applies to the role of exchange in Mississippian society.

Having expressed these cautions, one feature of Gaulish, Germanic, and Medieval social formations that can be noted is the presence of *dependence* even in societies with concerns about natural liberty. The interplay between conditions of dependence and the emergence of classes is far too complex for a simple summary here, but persons interested in these important issues will profit from reading Bloch's seminal account of Feudal society with its emphasis on social relations (1961). An economic history of British Medieval society of special interest is Postan (1975).[1]

---

[1] Postan presents a predominantly demographic model of Medieval society. A critique of this approach has spurred a considerable debate over the relative roles of demography and class (presented in Aston and Philpin 1988). In any case, classes cannot reasonably be postulated in eastern North America before the European invasions.

Just as in eastern North America, northern European simple economies had been affected by the cooling trends of the late 13th century. European populations seem to have expanded, perhaps partly because of new marriage patterns (Gottfried 1983:25) while there seem to have been declines in North America. Increasing population in Europe, combined with less favorable climatic conditions, resulted in famines by the 14th century. Another major factor was the concomitant increase in epidemic disease that followed on the re-establishment of long-distance economic ties and increasing population. These diseases were not a factor in North America until historical times.

Finally, we shall also see that there are differences in the accounts given by each nationality of explorers, each emphasizing elements that were familiar from their own national and cultural background.

In Any Case

All in all, European travelers paid enough attention to what we may call political economy to allow a *general* picture to be built up. On a more specific level, the view is dimmer. What we have is a series of vignettes of different groups at different moments in their history of interaction with the European invaders. Notwithstanding some recognition of differences in language and culture across the East, Europeans tended to assume that "their" Indians were typical of all Native Americans. Local accounts typically glossed over differences in the same area between, say, the Piedmont Siouans and the Algonkian speakers. The Europeans were still less aware of those groups' differences from the Creek or Choctaw confederacies. Most anthropologists believe important differences existed in historical times among these various societies, and we should not expect less diversity in the prehistoric record. Accordingly, the general view can be accepted only with caution—recognizing the existence of areawide similarities, but also local differences.

Those who emphasize a divide between historical and prehistoric societies in the Southeast have a point (e.g., M. T. Smith 1987). Old World diseases often spread in the Southeast ahead of the earliest Western explorers, and the Southeast suffered terrible population losses overall (as proposed by Dobyns 1983; Ramenofsky 1987; Thornton 1987; but also see Chapter 4 and below). Depopulation has been seen by some as creating a near-unbridgeable gap between historical narratives and archaeological realities. Although some have scrutinized the historical accounts for supposed survivals of a larger-scale and grander time, Occam's razor demands that we show that simpler explanations are inadequate before we create overly complex models of either prehistoric or historical societies.

The map (Figure 2.2) shows the approximate locations of some of the more prominent Historic period societies. However, it is important to recognize, as will be discussed in more detail below and in Chapter 4, that movement, amalgamation, and fission were reshaping the Southeastern social landscape in both historical and prehistoric times.

We have to find out what level of control or alienation existed outside "domestic," communal production, before trying to build any general model of historical "Southeastern" economy. Accordingly, the next section of this chapter will examine

Figure 2.2. Locations of some historical Southeastern societies.

the issue of chiefly authority in the classic case of the Natchez of the Mississippi Valley (see also Muller 1994); then the following sections go on to look at political leadership in the broader context of ethnohistorical literature. The Natchez "divine" leader, the Sun, is an appropriate place to begin, since he has been the favorite historical figure for those who argue for strong, centralized, chiefly authority in the prehistoric Southeast. For many, the autocratic Natchez chief was a pale reminder of the great "sun kings" of Mississippian times. What do these accounts *really* say about the behavior of the Sun(s) in the events of the Great Natchez Revolt? How does this view contrast with other historically described societies? What additional characteristics and behaviors were associated with leadership in a broader range of historical accounts from earliest contact to the early 19th century? I am going to argue that prehistoric and historical chiefs alike have been misunderstood by being forced into models drawn from Europe or even Oceania.

2. CHIEFLY POLITICAL AUTHORITY

A "search for survivals" of a formerly more complex Mississippian social order is perhaps most common in dealing with the institutions of political power. Those who wish to see "puissant states" (as put by Adair in 1775) in the prehistoric record have naturally looked to historical accounts emphasizing what have seemed to be kingly or near-kingly power on the part of a few Southeastern leaders. What is said about the differences between the larger Choctaw communities as opposed to the tiny Natchez?

> It is still argued whether the so-called "Mississippian decline" was caused or merely hastened by the Spanish passage, with its probable introduction of disease into the Mississippian heartland and its possible effects upon the balance of power between various Mississippian chiefdoms, but what is certain is that profound changes did occur. Although such changes were not everywhere uniform, and for example the Natchez, Koroa, and Taensa groups of the Mississippian heartland seem to have brought a "Mississippian"-style sociopolitical structure essentially intact into the French period, it seems to be the case that most of the numerically predominant historical tribes—specifically here the Chickasaw and Choctaw are cases in point—were organized as egalitarian societies with autonomous village groups rather than centrally organized chiefdoms, and achieved rather than ascribed status for their leaders. Because this change had taken place, and because its dynamics are still not clear, the documents reporting the first French contact with these tribes have special importance because they report the new situation before the effects of continuous contact and acculturation began to be felt. In other words, the societies they document had changed since contact with the first Europeans to penetrate the area, but they had changed within an environment still dominated by the aboriginal societies themselves. Galloway 1982b:146–147

This view is accepted by a number of other scholars in the same volume (Galloway, editor, 1982c; see also 1995) and elsewhere. The question is whether these conclusions have taken sufficient account of the historical context of these sources (recall Galloway's call for such treatment, 1991; also see 1994). I shall argue that these distinctions exaggerate the complexity of both the historical Natchez and the prehistoric Mississippians, and underestimate the complexity of groups such as the Creek and, especially, the Choctaw. I also feel that insufficient attention has been given to the distinct social and political backgrounds of the European observers.

The Natchez Revolt

Because the Natchez loom so large in many discussions of Mississippian political organization, I shall begin this discussion with an examination of the Natchez revolt as an illustration of the need for caution in interpreting the historical accounts. I shall then move to a general discussion of chiefly authority in mostly chronological order.

By many summaries, one would think that the most "important" polity in the historical Southeast was the Natchez. The historical accounts of the Natchez, rather than their actual social system, have been cited again and again as an example of a remnant of complex government in the interior of North America. Those who have postulated a collapse of complex societies following 16th- and 17th-century depopulation seem to give examples from the Natchez more often than from any other group.

The reported territory *claimed* by the Natchez ran from Bayou Manchac some 50 leagues from the sea to the Ohio—460 leagues[2] upstream (in reality only some 625 km; Bossu 1762 [1968:29]). Despite this huge supposed territory, only 9 to 12 small Natchez villages were reported in the late 17th century (e.g., De Montigny 1699; d'Iberville 1981[1699–1702]; Tonty 1702), and the population was certainly no more than 4000 persons at that time. Thus, the Natchez were only a moderate-sized entity, even by 17th-century standards (see Chapter 4).

The chief himself is described thus: "This chief is a man 5 feet 3 or 4 inches tall, rather thin, of intelligent countenance. To me he seemed the most tyrannical Indian I have beheld," although the French word—*absolu*—seems even stronger than "tyrannical." Does this not sound like an absolutist state leader? Unfortunately, d'Iberville continues, in the same sentence, "as beggarly as the others, just like his subjects—all tall men, well made, quite idle, showing us many marks of friendship" (d'Iberville 1700, in 1981:126). Richebourg Gaillard McWilliams's translation here (1981) is certainly not unreasonable, but the French text is open to other interpretations: "Il m'a paru le Sauvage le plus absolu que j'aye veu, aussi gueux que les autres, aussi bien que ses sujets" (Margry 1880(4):412). This could be "He seems to me the most absolute savage I've seen, just as beggarly as the rest."[3] This, perhaps, implies a little less power and majesty! There are certainly enough claims in the historical accounts for the strong power of the chiefs, but there are also a number of other comments on these leaders that are ignored by those who assert their "puissance."[4]

Le Page du Pratz (1758) and Bossu (1768) are the most commonly cited accounts of the Natchez. These give us illuminating, if hearsay, accounts of Natchez politics before their "destruction" in 1730–1731. In fact, the Natchez continued as individual towns among other groups, especially the Chickasaw and the Creek. Even though written more than 20 years after the disappearance of the Natchez as an

---

[2] A French league was approximately 2 English miles or 3.2 km (*OED*), but leagues are as much an indication of time to a location as of distance. The distance by river is certainly greater than by air, but the number of leagues here would indicate an "empire" some 1500 km long. There is, of course, not the slightest archaeological or historical evidence that the area from the Wickliffe site (near the mouth of the Ohio) to the Fatherland site (at Natchez) was ever united in a single Native American political entity.

[3] I wish to thank Dr. Margaret Winters of SIU's Foreign Languages and Literatures Department for confirming my alternative translation as reasonable for late-17th-century French.

[4] For example, "Les chefs ne sont pas plus maistres de leurs gens, que ne le sont les chefs des autres nations du costé du Canada. J'ay remarqué seulement parmi ceux-cy plus de civilité" (LeMoyne d'Iberville 1700, in Margry 4:184). Bossu speaks of considerable power: "You ask me if the Indians have captains and a king who governs them. Thanks to the time I have spent among them, I can satisfy your curiosity. You know that they are divided into tribes or nations, each of which is governed by a chief or a minor king, who is given his power by the Great Spirit or the Supreme Being. Although these chiefs are despotic rulers, their authority is not resented because they know how to gain love and respect. They have the great satisfaction of knowing that their subjects consider them demigods, born to make them happy in this world. The chiefs consider themselves the fathers of their people and are prouder of this than is the ostentatious Great Mogul of his pompous titles"; but he goes on to talk of elected war chiefs and the functions of the council as well (Bossu 1768[1962:113]). The simple fact is that neither the British nor the French accounts can be read simply as statements of objective reality. In each case, one must analyze the actual behaviors *described* as well as considering the authors' interpretations!

Figure 2.3. The "Transport" of the Great Sun of the Natchez (after Le Page du Pratz, in Swanton 1946: plate 75).

independent group, these accounts relate events as perceived by Frenchmen who were sympathetic to the Natchez who were being abused by French authorities. They are also the sources for most discussion of supposed Natchez power. Earlier accounts that describe the Natchez generally agree with the views presented in du Pratz and Bossu when the same topics are covered (e.g., d'Iberville's 1699–1702 journals [1981]; du Ru 1700 [1935]; and others discussed below). In the following quotations, parallels between Bossu's account and du Pratz's often indicate "borrowings" by Bossu, but the latter author added additional perspectives from his own observations of other indigenous peoples in the French territories, as well as from other sources known to him. Bossu's account is mentioned in Adam's discussion of "travel liars" as a notable example of the tendency to misrepresent Native Americans as "noble savages" (1980:184, 198, 200). Even so, Bossu is not worthless as a record of events, especially if descriptions of behavior rather than of intent are examined. Bossu felt himself a victim of the mistreatment by French governmental authorities, so it is not surprising that he sympathized with the Natchez in their difficulties. The issue here is what the accounts say actually happened as opposed to their interpretation of the beliefs and attitudes of the Natchez:

> The Natchez, who lived here formerly, were a very important people. They had several villages ruled by individual chiefs, who in turn were governed by the great chief of the nation. All of these chiefs were called "Suns," and all five hundred of them were related to the Great Sun, their sovereign, who wore on his chest a picture of the sun from whom he claimed descent. Ouachil, the name under which the sun was worshipped, means "very great fire" or "supreme fire." Bossu 1962 [1762:31]

Thus, the "Suns" made nearly 13 percent of the probable total population! There are also a number of other kinds of leaders at different levels. We are obliged either to accept the idea that the Natchez have so much "administration" because of their former glory (as in post–World War I Austria) or else that, just possibly, these "offi-cials" are not so grand as the French accounts imply. Hudson has placed the Natchez situation into perspective that illustrates their essentially Southeastern character (1976:205, 207–208, 240).

The trouble began with a corrupt French official seeking to profit from his office:

> Monsieur de Chepar [Chépart], who was eager to make a fortune as quickly as possible, ordered the Sun of a village called Pomme to move out with all his people. The land, which Chepar was to turn into a plantation, would bring him a handsome profit. The Chief explained that the bones of his ancestors were buried there, but his arguments were useless. The French commander ordered the Chief Sun to evacuate the village and even threatened to send him to New Orleans in chains if he did not obey promptly. Perhaps the officer thought that he could treat this chief like a slave. It never occurred to him that he was speaking to a man who was accustomed to giving commands and whose authority over his subjects was absolute. Bossu 1768 [1962:37–38]

Here Bossu echoes other accounts in stressing the power of the Natchez chief. In dealing with this local chief, Chépart's manners were improper.

> The Commandant, doubtless, supposed that he was talking to a slave, whom we may com-mand in a tone of absolute authority. But he knew not that the natives of Louisiana are such enemies to a state of slavery, that they prefer death itself thereto; above all, the Suns, accustomed to govern despotically, have still a greater aversion to it. Le Page du Pratz 1758 [1972:74]

But the account does not indicate merely that the Sun alone was jealous of his liberty. Rather it was the "natives of Louisiana," even if the *chief* was "despotic." After receiving these demands, the Sun promptly assembled his council of elders.

> The Sun, without discovering any emotion or passion, withdrew; only saying that he was going to assemble the old men of his village, to hold a council on this affair. Le Page du Pratz 1758 [1972:74]

> The Chief Sun listened to him and went off without becoming angry. He assembled his council, and they decided to inform Monsieur de Chepar that, before Pomme could be abandoned, plans for a new village would have to be drawn up. That would take two moons. Bossu 1768 [1962:37]

The decision about what to do was *made jointly in council*, notwithstanding the expressed emphasis on the "absolute" power of the leader. The council decided to try to stall Chépart, and—when that failed—to bribe him.

> The Sun reported this answer to his council, who debated the question, which was knotty. But the policy of the old men was, that they should be allowed to stay in their village till harvest, and till they had time to dry their corn, and shake out the grain; on condition each hut of the village should pay him in so many moons (months) which they agreed on, a basket of corn and a fowl. Le Page du Pratz 1758 [1972:75]

> The decision was made known to the commander [Chépart], who rebuked the messengers and threatened them with the severest punishment if Pomme were not turned over to him in a very short time. When this answer was returned to the council, the elders concluded that the best policy was to try to gain enough time so they could think of a way to get rid of these disagreeable guests who were becoming tyrannical. Since they knew that Monsieur de Chepar was very greedy, they thought up a scheme whereby he would grant them a delay of

several moons, during which period each cabin would pay him in corn, fowl and skins. The Commander fell into the trap because of his greed. Bossu 1768 [1962:37–38]

Thus it appears that Chépart was bribed by the Natchez *Council*, **not** the Great Sun, and with payments from "*each cabin.*" The bribe did not come from common stores controlled by the Sun or Suns. Chépart agreed to accept these bribes, out of concern for the Natchez—or so he claimed.

The Sun, who was not taken in by this false altruism, assembled his council once more and announced that the time requested had be granted. During this period of grace, they were to think of a way to end the burdensome tribute they were paying, and, especially, to put a stop to the domination of the tyrannical French. ... They were to come back to the council as soon as they had thought of a plan whose success could be assured. Bossu 1768 [1962:38,39]

Again, the "absolute" ruler went back to his council.

The Sun, upon his return, caused the council to be assembled; told the old men, that the French Commandant has acquiesced in the offers which he had made him. Le Page du Pratz 1758 [1972:75]

Far from *ordering* an action to be taken, the Sun and the council were both involved in the decisions:

that this affair required some days to reflection, before they came to a resolution therein, and before it should be proposed to the Grand Sun and his council: that at present they had only to retire; and in a few days he would assemble them again, that they might then determine the part they were to act. Le Page du Pratz 1758 [1972: 76]

Again, the course to be taken was to be planned by the council, and the Great Sun did not himself direct the action. The council reported its decision to the Sun:

In five or six days he brought together the old men, who in that interval were consulting with each other: which was the reason that all the suffrages were unanimous in the same and only means of obtaining the end they proposed to themselves, which was the entire destruction of the French in this province. Le Page du Pratz 1758 [1972:76]

For five or six days the noble elders conferred with each other, and they concluded once again unanimously to destroy all the French. After having greeted his chief, the oldest member of the council reported the decision. Bossu 1768 [1962:39]

After some days, the council reported to the Great Sun who told them that he set the goals, and the council is to tell him the best means.

The Sun, seeing them all assembled, said: "You have had time to reflect on the proposition I made you; and so I imagine you will soon set forth the best means how to get rid of our bad neighbors without hazard." The Sun having done speaking, the oldest rose up, saluted his Chief after his manner. Le Page du Pratz 1758 [1972:76]

The elder said, among other things, "Is not death preferable to slavery?"(Le Page du Pratz 1758 [1972:77]).

I ask if this is the response of a subject of an absolute ruler? Is the behavior of the Sun in relation to the council consistent with an interpretation of Natchez political authority as being absolute or despotic? These accounts *explicitly* assert the chiefs' power, but simultaneously and *implicitly* reveal the Suns' dependence upon their councils. We also learn something about the attitudes of the Natchez about the proper character of political authority.

Of course, these accounts were written at the time of the "noble savage" in European travel literature. It is also not surprising that Enlightenment travelers, themselves still embedded in autocratic governments, used their accounts as a vehicle for veiled political criticism, just as Tacitus did in *Germania*. However, even given biases in the accounts, we can see that the Sun of Pomme did not *order*; he called into session a council of elders to *consider*. Upon the council's reaching a conclusion, he took the results to convince not just the Great Sun, but *also* the Great Sun's council. In short, despite the *terminology* of despotism, what we see here is not an autocratic state ruler in the mold of Louis XIV, but *chiefly* authority almost exactly in the classic sense (e.g., Service 1975). This would not be surprising *except for the effort to interpret the supposed absolutism of the Natchez political system as though it were a survival of a formerly more complex polity*. The historical accounts' explicit statements about the Great Sun's power tell us more about the viewpoint of the narrator than about the Natchez. A careful reading of the descriptions of behavior rather than the opinions of the narrator, as we have seen, reveals a truer picture of political relations among the Natchez. It is also important to remember that this is the leader (together with that of the Taensas) who, as we saw, is often described as the "most absolute" of the various chiefs encountered in the Lower Mississippi Valley (e.g., du Ru 1700; d'Iberville 1700). Recall the earlier discussion (p. 64) on the origin of this phrase in an ambiguous "Il m'a paru le Sauvage le plus absolu que j'aye veu." We should also remember that some of the late-17th-century travelers through this part of the Mississippi Valley thought, or heard, so little of the Natchez that they failed to mention them as separate from the Koroa (Membré 1682; Minet 1685; cf. Tonty 1693, in which the Koroa are left out instead). One possibility is that the Natchez were subordinate to the Koroa at the time of first contact, but too little is known to be sure who was part of whom (cf. Brain 1982; Galloway 1987b:51). The Natchez do not loom large in these accounts either from direct contact by the French or from hearsay from their neighbors.

There *was* disastrous depopulation after contact with Europeans, as discussed later and in Chapter 4, but the implications this had for the character of political and economic organization are less clear than many have inferred. Groups such as the Natchez may have once been parts of larger polities, but this is not to say that the large polities had therefore to be so much more complex. Particularly, it may not simply be assumed that depopulation resulted in the complete or nearly complete collapse of political organizations, as opposed to the undoubted dispersal of individual communities. There is another kind of Natchez paradox here. Were we to take the Natchez accounts at face value, they would themselves be a clear example of continuity despite population loss—since this supposed autocratic kingdom was objectively so small and weak in the late 17th and early 18th century. The point I am making here is that the observational evidence in the very accounts stressing the Great Sun's power indicates that this power was exercised in chiefly ways, not royal. Of course the French subjects of an autocratic king did not write the only available accounts of Native American societies in the 18th century and earlier. What of accounts by other travelers who saw similar peoples from a different national and personal perspectives?

16th-Century Accounts of Chiefly and Other Power

A number of contacts with Eastern Native Americans were made in the 16th century. Although the bulk of these were Spanish, there were a few by English and French explorers, as well. These are the people who saw the Native Americans of the Southeast as close to their uncontacted state as we shall ever get from written records. The de Soto accounts are arguably the most important of all of these, since they were the first Europeans to penetrate deeply into the interior of the Southeast. Earlier expeditions had tended to poke away at the coastal areas of the Southeast. I am not trying to duplicate the more detailed discussion in works such as *The Forgotten Centuries* edited by Hudson and Tesser (1994); rather, I am trying to see what kinds of behaviors were associated with persons perceived by the Europeans to be persons of authority.

Early 16th-Century Accounts of Power

Some coastal peoples were contacted remarkably early. As Scarry notes (1994:26), Juan Ponce de León's early 16th-century landing in Florida, which he named (Oviedo 1547–1549 [1959:II:102]), was probably not the first visit. *Florida* became the term used for all of eastern North America in Spanish and in many other languages during this period. It does not mean the modern state, although these events did take place there. The historical background of these early coastal landings is well summarized in many works (e.g., Milanich and Milbrath 1989), and I shall simply comment here that many of the initial recorded meetings were hostile, probably because of still earlier, undocumented contacts. The famous Calusa chief Carlos was taken prisoner, released to make peace, promised to return, and did so in an attack by 80 canoes that lasted all day (Davis 1935; Lowery 1959 [reprint]). There are too few data to really tell whether the scale of the attack justifies Widmer's conclusion that this "clearly demonstrated the existence of a highly organized and centralized political system" (1988:1). Such a number of attackers might reflect centralization, but one can construct any number of scenarios in which individuals in a relatively populous area could have, in effect, shouted "Hey rube" without much centralization or real authority in the hands of the chief. As Widmer shows, the historical data do indicate that there were at least two levels of subordination in what may be, despite the peculiarities of its economic basis, an otherwise fairly "typical" chiefdom (for an extensive analysis of this situation, see Widmer 1988).

Ponce de León died as a result of an arrow wound received in attacks during a 1521 effort to found a colony in Florida. One of the discoveries he made in the Calusa country, unfortunately for the Southeastern Indians, was gold. Although it seems clear that the metal was entirely the result of scavenging from Spanish shipwrecks (Swanton 1946: 34–35; see especially photographs of the wonderful artifacts made from this salvaged metal in Lyon 1989:162–163), the reports of gold and silver raised hopes in the hearts of many explorers that there must surely be gold somewhere over the next hill or two.

By 1521, Lucas Vázquez de Ayllón explored along the south Atlantic coast (see Hoffman 1994a). Pietro Martire d'Anghiera, "Peter Martyr," described what he was told by Ayllón and published an account of what are probably Siouan and perhaps Muskhogean peoples. Martire d'Anghiera's account (1533) was based on Spanish records and memories of the Lucas Vázquez de Ayllón expeditions of 1521–1526 (also described in Oviedo y Valdés 1547–1549 [1959:IV:322–330]), and the account of a Native American, Francisco Chicorana, who had been with the Spaniards. Hoffman (1994a) has summarized the general outlines of the Ayllón voyages and settlements and discussed the poor level of reliability of these accounts.

A place called Duhare may have been based on Siouan groups (Swanton 1922:42ff.). These were said to have no temples but the homes of their "sovereigns." Altogether as many as 22 provinces were said to be subordinate to Duhare, and their "gigantic kings" received prestations from these:

> All the provinces mentioned pay them tributes and these tributes are paid in kind; for they are free from the pest of money, and trade is carried on by exchanging goods. Martire d'Anghiera [in Swanton 1922:45]

The "king" was carried about:

> In place of horses the king is carried on the shoulders of strong young men who run with him to the different places he wishes to visit. Martire d'Anghiera [in Swanton 1922:42]

and

> It is quite laughable to hear how the people salute the lords and how the king responds, especially to his nobles. As a sign of respect the one who salutes puts his hands to his nostrils and gives a bellow like a bull, after which he extends his hands toward the forehead and in front of the face. The king does not bother to return the salutes of his people, and responds to the nobles by half bending his head toward the left shoulder without saying anything. Martire d'Anghiera [in Swanton 1922:46]

However, the "kings" are said to live in houses of stone, and all of these people were supposed to have domesticated deer that they milked—so there just may be just a little inaccuracy here. Although we can place no reliance on the description of "tribute," the notion that it was paid in kind certainly conforms to what we know from better sources. Swanton cautioned us, "Of course no reliance can be placed upon tales of subjection and the exaction of tribute" (1922:47). These were not "Mississippian" peoples in any meaningful sense, and it is unlikely that their political organization was, in fact, very complex.

Oviedo also included discussion of what was found in the land of Guadelupe, where settlement was dispersed, but "mosques or temples" were on the islands, containing "many bones of their dead, those of the children or babies apart from the adults" (1547–1549 [1959:IV:327–328]). These seemed to be of the "common people," since "those of the principal men were in a chapel or temple separate from the other community, and also on the islands" (1547–1549 [1959:IV:328]). As is the problem with this account, just as it starts to seem reasonable, we are told that the houses were made of stone and mortar, the latter made of oyster shells. (1547–1549 [1959:IV:328]). The description of Guadelupe then comments on large "principal houses" holding 200 people, each essentially a *pueblo*, a village, in its own right. They are, however, made of living pine trees (1547–1549 [1959:IV:328])! The danger of choosing what one wishes from such accounts should be reasonably clear.

For an example of *kings* that surely cannot have been so, we note that Verrazano encountered "kings" of societies that "change their habitations from place to place, as the circumstances of situation and seasons may require. This is easily done, as they have only to take with them their mats, and they have other houses prepared at once" (in roughly the Long Island coastal area; Verrazano 1524 [in Shipp 1881:89]).

In April 1528, Pánfilo de Narváez, in an especially ill-fated effort to colonize in the Taumaulipas area of Mexico, came to Florida, probably because of shortages of supplies (Hoffman 1994b:54). One of the members of the expedition was Alvar Nuñez Cabeça de Vaca, who survived a long overland journey back to New Spain ending in 1536 and wrote an account of his travels (Nuñez Cabeça de Vaca 1542 [1871]). It is not really necessary for our purposes to determine the route taken (see Hoffman 1994b for that), but we can note what was observed of the organization of the Indians encountered along this long path.

The first habitations that they found were a few *buhíos*, one of them large enough to hold hundreds of people (Nuñez Cabeça de Vaca 1542 [1871:21]), but the people had fled at the approach of the Spaniards. Without an interpreter, even when some of the people came in to talk to the Spaniards, they had no hope of understanding. Four Indians were captured. On leading them to a place where the Spaniards hoped to find maize,

> There we saw many cases, such as are used to contain the merchandise of Castilla, in each of them a dead man, and the bodies were covered with painted deer skins. Nuñez Cabeça de Vaca 1542 [1871:24]

This seemed to be idolatry, so the Commissary burned the burials! They continued to scare off people as they moved along:

> We traveled without seeing any natives who would venture to await our coming until the seventeenth day of June, when a chief approached, borne on the back of another Indian, and covered with a painted deer-skin. A great many people attended him, some walking in advance, playing on flutes of reed.
>
> By signs we gave him to understand that we were going to Apalachen, and it appeared to us by those that he made that he was an enemy to the people of Apalachen, and would go to assist us against them. We gave him beads and hawk bells, with other articles of barter; and he having presented the Governor with the skin he wore, went back, when we followed in the road he took. Nuñez Cabeça de Vaca 1542 [1871:31]

They managed to surprise Apalachen and took 9 cavalry and 50 infantry and assailed the town. The town consisted of forty small houses (Nuñez Cabeça de Vaca 1542 [1871:35]), but "in this Province are many maize fields; and the houses are scattered as are those of the Gelves" (1542 [1871:36]).

In these cases, we do get a few bits of data. There were social distinctions, marked by leaders being carried. It is possible that the mortuary complex was for leaders, but it may have been for the whole population. We hear that the core community of Apalachen, later described as "largest town in all the region" (Nuñez Cabeça de Vaca 1542 [1871:37]), was only 40 houses, although much of the population was dispersed—it was considered "thinly peopled" (Nuñez Cabeça de Vaca 1542 [1871:37]). The Spaniards continued to abduct leaders, with the result being continued attacks on them. It is interesting here that the result of these abductions was not peace (as it was for de Soto, as we shall see).

Subsequent events were tragic for the party. After a shipwreck, the survivors found refuge with Indians of Texas. The events there have little to do with chiefly authority, of which there is no mention. Although it is not directly pertinent here, I believe the wording means that Cabeça de Vaca's trading activities among the early Texans were introduced by him rather than his taking on a native role.

Far to the north, early accounts of the Huron provide us with another basis to aid in understanding European interpretations of historic, Mississippian-descended groups. The Huron were, in fact, a surprisingly large-scale society in the 16th century; but we have little reason to believe that their political organization was even chiefly. Nonetheless, the European accounts depicted the Huron in terms of "cities," and "kings." Hochelaga, at what is now Montreal, was a "citie":

> The citie of Hochelaga is round, compassed about with timber with three course of Rampires [rampart]...

> There are in the town about fiftie houses, about fiftie paces long, and twelve, or fifteene broad, built all of wood as broad as any boord, very finely and cunningly joyned togither. Cartier 1535 [1932:59, 1580:50]

> That done, the Lord and King of the countrey was brought upon 9 or 10 mens shoulders, (whom in their tongue they call Agouhanna) sitting upon a great Stagges skin, and they laide him down upon the foresaid mats neere to the Captaine. Cartier 1535 [1932:61, 1580:52]

As we shall see in a following section on how travelers were greeted, some of the behaviors supposedly associated with paramount chiefs are found here among people who are unlikely to have had such political structures. There is no doubt that persons of high status were treated deferentially across the East, and both large tribal and even quite small-scale societies in the Northeast sometimes had persons carried about to mark their status. All the same, we need to understand what 16th-century Europeans meant when they used these terms, and we need to realize that we cannot take terms like *city*, *lord*, and *king* to mean what they do today.

The de Soto Expedition

The first Europeans who penetrated deeply into the interior were the party of Hernando de Soto. This was an invasion force of around 600 soldiers (and one Spanish woman, Francisca Hinestrosa, the wife of one of the soldiers), more than 220 horses, and "many" pigs. These soldiers pillaged and raped their way from Florida to west of the Mississippi in 1539–43 (e.g., Ranjel in Oviedo 1547–1549 [1959:154, 155, 157], Biedma 1544 [1904:3]). Their actions aroused Southeastern hostility and anger against the Spanish party. This animosity virtually meant the ruin of the expedition, and traditions about these events arguably damaged Spanish colonial efforts in the area long afterward. In interpreting the Native American responses to European behavior, these reactions are important evidence about the conditions within which these acts occurred (e.g., see Hoffman's excellent introduction in Clayton et al. 1993:1–17; cf. Smith and Hally 1992). We also need to remember the size and nature of the Spanish force when assessing their descriptions of scale and complexity of the societies they encountered. As Hoffman points out, the rhetoric of de Soto is that of the explorer–treasure seeker, whereas accounts in the later de Luna expedition are those of "settler's rhetoric" (in Clayton et al. 1993:12–13).

Only three more or less participant accounts of the de Soto *entrada* survive. The relation of Luys Hernández de Biedma (1544) is only 20 pages of handwritten text and, accordingly, has value largely in corroboration of the two longer accounts. It is, however, the only true primary source. The longest relation by a participant, or so it seems, is that of the Gentleman of Elvas, an unnamed Portuguese adventurer (1557; hereafter Elvas). However, it is not clear how much of this account is "as told to," as Galloway puts it (Galloway 1995:104). At the same time, its publication was still fairly close in time to the events. The relation of Rodrigo Ranjel [a.k.a. Rangel] only survives in an excerpt or abstract by Oviedo (1547–1549), but it is nonetheless often considered to be the most reliable of the accounts (Worth, in Clayton et al. 1993:249). Most details generally agree with the longer Elvas account, although a small portion of Oviedo's manuscript has been lost. Finally, there is the interview and record-based story, *La Florida del Inca*, by "el Inca," Garcilaso de la Vega (1605). This literary monument is long and detailed but is not necessarily historically dependable. Garcilaso apparently had access to contemporary documents that are now lost, and he *may* have interviewed a participant, possibly Gonzolo Sylvestre. Unfortunately, the passage of more than 40 years, confusion, and misunderstandings meant that Garcilaso's secondhand account is the least reliable of all the accounts, with many errors such as towns switched around, which are obvious from comparison with the other accounts. Nevertheless, it has often been used because of its artistic detail, often with too little caution. Henige (1993:156 *et passim*) argues that *La Florida* is essentially a work of fiction, but Hudson et al. have replied to this and other criticisms by Henige of their own determination of de Soto's route in a strongly worded reply (1993). However, aside from any other criticisms of the utility of *La Florida*, it is almost certain to be least reliable precisely in the areas such as descriptions of power relationships that we are most interested in. It also is reinterpreted into both European and Incan terms. As a result, I shall not use *La Florida* in this discussion, although it is definitely worth reading.

There have been many editions and translations of these accounts (e.g., Buckingham Smith 1866; Bourne 1904; Varner and Varner 1951). A new set of more literal English translations of all of the accounts has now been published by the University of Alabama Press (Clayton et al. 1993). John Worth's new translation of the 1544 de Biedma document has recently been published (in Clayton et al. 1993), and that is the translation cited here for both de Biedma and Elvas. The Ranjel account was translated by Bourne (1904); and a new translation in Clayton et al. (1993) has been made by John Worth. I have used a 1959 Spanish reprint of Oviedo here (volumes 117–121 of the *Biblioteca de Autores Españoles*), with assistance from the Worth and Bourne translations, although I have used the forms of the names given in the Spanish text. The text, as noted, is felt by many to be the most reliable account of distances and times, and it is also marked by a developed sense of concern about the mistreatment of the Indians, probably mostly interjected by Oviedo.

The accounts of the de Soto expedition have been the subject of prolonged and careful study. The emphasis, however, has often been on determination of the route taken rather than the "archaeology" of the texts called for by Galloway (1991). There are obviously toes to be stepped on in the debate on the de Soto route (compare Boyd and Schroedl 1987; Brain 1985; DePratter et al. 1985; Henige 1993, 1994; Hudson 1988, 1994; Hudson et al. 1984, 1987, 1993; Little and Curren 1990). Unfortunately, discussion has gotten to a pitch in which words such as *pretends* and *imprudent* have come to be used freely; and *ad hominem* arguments have been made. One expects amateur historians to be reluctant to see the route shifted away from their own locality, and even professionals can become rigid about issues that necessarily retain some element of doubt. Let me get it over with by stating my impressions and then moving on. The de Soto expedition clearly visited groups that are known from later records. Better, one should say that they encountered peoples whose names may have been retained by some of their descendants—among these were the Chickasaw and the Coosa. There are, however, considerable problems if political entities in the Southeast are treated as static, relatively unchanging entities. As we should see from later historical documentation, and even from the de Soto accounts themselves, Southeastern polities were fluid groups with variable membership. In any case, I am more interested in *what* these societies were like, not *where* they were in the 1539–1543 period. Location is important, but not for all purposes. Searching for the particular site that was called *Chicaça* on December 9, 1540, will no doubt yield some rewards, but is not the end of what can be done with these sources. It is definitely not their most important use. Problems in identification are exacerbated when one can, completely legitimately, choose the length of the league one wishes to use and explain away distances by appealing to the subjective judgment of the chroniclers. In such circumstances, there is room for enough alternative routes to satisfy everyone.

Towns cannot be assumed to have remained in the same place for even 20 years—much less longer. We also know that town names persisted for centuries. An examination of the names of modern eastern Oklahoma towns shows many that are similar to those found in the de Soto accounts (see Swanton 1939:56ff.), which should provide an antidote to any ideas that town names in the aboriginal Southeast were only or even primarily indications of geographic locations rather than of groups of people. There was not one location called Talise, but many. When people moved, so, as a general rule, did the town name (e.g., see the discussion in M. T. Smith 1989:142). This is one reason, I suppose, that Hudson, in his book on Southeastern Indians, used *chiefdom* for what most call *towns* (1976: 202). Moreover, many names are generic—the equivalent of "New Town"—that might be used and reused by different communities, just as they have been in our society. Finally, places once occupied by one political entity sometimes retained that name when reoccupied by other people (as pointed out by Hudson et al. 1987:848).

Many artifacts—such as beads and metal items—associated with earliest European contacts were portable. For example, artifacts from Ayllón's expedition were, within a few years, buried in mortuary temples in Cofitachequi, as much 175 km inland. As Hudson et al. (1987:852) point out, this is the contemporary Spanish interpretation on the origin of the artifacts, but even if these objects were from some *other* European contact, it is entirely clear that they were from the coast and far away

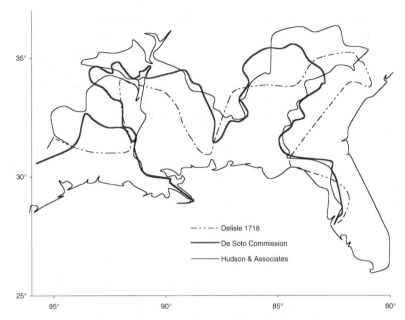

35°

30°

----- Delisle 1718

——— De Soto Commission

——— Hudson & Associates

25°

95° 90° 85° 80°

Figure 2.4. Some proposed routes of the de Soto expedition.

from their point of introduction into Florida! There is no need to postulate an undocumented movement inland by Europeans when we have every reason to conclude that native exchange systems were quite capable of moving these objects just as far as they did coastal shell. The fact that these artifacts were buried so soon after they were introduced augurs well for dating using 16th-century European artifacts but does not reassure us that the places where such objects are found were where a particular explorer visited. Figure 2.4 schematically indicates some alternative routes for de Soto's path across the Southeast merely to show that the differences between one route and another are important, but not vast on a world scale.

Having expressed these cautions, I cannot refrain throwing in my own two cents on another matter. I do not want to join the list of combatants concerning de Soto's route (e.g., Brain 1985; Henige 1993, 1994; Hudson et al. 1984; Little and Curren 1990), but I *have* worked more closely with Southeastern shell gorgets than most of these scholars have. I must say that I am very doubtful about the association (e.g., Hally et al. 1990:133; Hudson et al. 1985; M. T. Smith 1989:138–139) of the gorget style–type that I named *Citico* (Muller 1966a, 1966b, 1979, 1989) with a political unit in general, and particularly with the Coosa chiefdom. Galloway presents a cogent critique of the idea of a Coosa paramount chiefdom (1995:110ff.). The distribution of this and other gorget styles is discussed in Chapter 8.

Leaving the route aside, what do we need from the de Soto accounts? We mainly want to see how persons of authority behaved. What was the power of chiefs and how do the observed greetings and "homages" reveal the character of Mississippian social relations? What were the gifts that were given to the Spaniards, and how did they function? Who were the *principales*, the principal persons, so often mentioned in the de Soto accounts? We also want to get some idea of the political and economic scale of these societies. How big were chiefdoms and towns, and how did they interact with one another? What kinds of labor obligations existed, and what does the reaction to Spanish demands for forced labor tell us? What goods were stored, in what quantity, and under whose control? Finally, we shall look at a few indications of interpretation of the names and ethnicity of the groups encountered by the Spaniards.

The de Soto accounts are important as the first fairly detailed descriptions of the Southeast from a time when, even by the most extreme views, disruption from the European intrusions was minimal. As a result, they form a baseline for comparison to later accounts of social structure and organization. European diseases *had* spread into the Southeast ahead of actual invasion, but it is hard to agree that Southeastern political systems were so fragile that they would have collapsed as soon as de Soto's time. In addition, the effects of epidemics are rarely uniform or universal, as is shown by the late dates of introduction of some diseases into the Plains.

As already discussed, it is important to look at the objective data in the observations, rather than the interpretations of the observers and authors. Although there have been some excellent efforts to examine specific aspects of Southeastern *behavior* from the accounts (e.g., Dye and Cox 1990; Smith and Hally 1992), many discussions of these events have been marred by too-ready acceptance of a European narrator's interpretations. I shall take the main topics in turn, and discuss—as briefly as possible—the implications of what was actually described. I originally prepared a longer, separate discussion of each of the accounts, but that approach meant embedding the key points in a chronological and geographical narrative that obscured the issues. The discussion below is by topics, keeping in mind Galloway's injunction not "to create [a] composite account for the several accounts of it according to ill-defined and ill-documented criteria" (1991:455). Galloway has also presented a summary of features noted in these accounts, as well as a more detailed discussion of each insofar as it relates to her issues (1995:98–109, passim). Although time and place are important, the purpose here is to assess political and economic dimensions of these accounts. Those who wish to place them into a chronological and geographical framework should consult Swanton (1939, especially the tables and lists of names on pp. 56–61), the various papers of Hudson and his associates and critics already cited, and most recently, the summary tables on de Soto in Galloway's book on the Choctaw (1995). In the discussion that follows, I have used the original forms of names as given in each account when quoted. I have otherwise used names as given in Elvas, as a matter of convenience, except in the case of Cofitachequi, or when there are no names for that group in Elvas.

Power of Chiefs. The power of Southeastern chiefs may not have been merely a "hollow sound," as one later commentator put it, but neither can we simply assume that the authority of the chief was necessarily great. In this discussion, I draw first on information relating to chiefs and paramount chiefs, then present some of the evidence on different indicators of rank and authority, and finally have a little discussion of kinship and power.

Chiefs and paramount chiefs. Local terms for leaders varied by language group in the Southeast, but it is significant that the Spanish chroniclers avoided using terms such as *king*. *Señor* and its equivalents are the common terms when cacique was not used. The terms cacique and *cacica* were introduced by the Spanish from the Caribbean. As Garcilaso de la Vega puts it in explaining his use of a Peruvian term: "The title 'curaca' in the common tongue of the Indians of Peru signifies the same as 'cacique' or 'lord of vassals' in the language of Hispañola and its neighboring islands" (1605 [1951:95]). Such usage is in line with the meanings of *señor*, ranging from "master" to "mister." It is also worth noting that there were few, if any, areawide terms for leaders such as the post-Roman European titles reflecting the former glories of Caesar, such as Kaiser or Tsar. It would be expected that any great prehistoric Mississippian "empire" should have left such titles and pretentions behind. Homage, in the feudal sense, is often implied in the Spanish accounts and sometimes explicitly stated (e.g., Elvas 1557 [1993:62, 106, 132]), but this, like the "tribute" paid, is most definitely an instance in which we cannot take the Spanish understanding of the events as truth.

At the start of the de Soto expedition in Florida, they encountered Juan Ortiz, who had been a captive of the caciques of Ucita and Mocoço. Ortiz indicated that the relatively small political units under a single named cacique were grouped together into larger political units under a *Paracoxi*. As it turns out, *Paracoxi* could mean what we call a "paramount chief" (Swanton 1922:327). Cacique Mocoço came to visit, did what the Spaniards considered an act of homage to de Soto, and went home with gifts. The paramount chief's "power" was acknowledged by groups of different languages. However, having the same paramount chief was not, apparently, enough to stop one chief from attacking another! In Ranjel's account, the cacique at Mocoço who had held Juan Ortiz complained that the caciques Orriygua, Neguarete, Zapaloey, and Ecita (Ucita) were all menacing him because of his help in giving Ortiz to the Spaniards (Oviedo 1547–1549[1959:II:155]). Well, these are Timucuans, probably, and perhaps we cannot expect chiefs to be very powerful? Arguably, these first societies contacted may have been less organized than the large societies to the north.

In another case at Piachi (Piache), even though the cacique of Tascaluca was being held hostage, the Spanish crossing of the river was said to have been resisted by a "malicious" cacique whose people managed to kill two of the Spaniards (Oviedo 1547–1549 [1959:II:174]). If this happened, it might suggest that Piache was not subordinate to Tascaluca. However, Elvas only mentions an easy crossing of the river with the help of the cacique, so it is hard to tell if this is a meaningful example of incomplete control over subordinates by paramount chiefs.

There are, however, other examples that suggest that Southeastern chiefly power was sometimes transitory and hard to enforce. The cacique Chicaça "made complaint to him [the governor], that one of his vassals had risen against him, withholding his tribute, and asked the governor to go against him, saying that he was about to go to seek him in his land and punish him as he deserved" (Elvas 1557 [1993:106]; also described in Ranjel, Oviedo 1547–1549 [1959:II:176]). De Soto got involved in this way in various local political situations and, we may suspect, transformed these relationships by his actions and presence. We simply do not know how much these expeditions in aid of particular caciques were inspired by local greed for power and how much by the suggestions of the invaders. I think that offers to guide the Spaniards to somewhere else, much richer, were likely efforts to hurry along these troublesome freeloaders and freebooters (as also noted by Galloway 1995).

Nonetheless, *some* kind of claim of paramountcy was being asserted by Chicaça over Saquechuma. Whether the specific claim was true or not, the assertion suggests that subordination was sometimes enforced by conflict. As it happened, this was later thought by the Iberians to be a ruse to divide their forces in preparation for an attack by Chicaça; but even through the filter of translation and possible deceit, it suggests the subordination of some chiefs to others, while reaffirming the weakness of the bonds.

Evidence can be found of the willingness of chiefs to attempt control through military means. West on the Mississippi, the cacique Casqui offered to deliver the cacique of Pacaha into de Soto's hands, and went back to Casqui, where both canoes and a land force were sent out to search for Pacaha. Because Casqui slipped away, de Soto now determined to make war upon him, seeking to enlist Pacaha's aid against him (Elvas 1557 [1993:119]). Sorting out the Spanish from the native military goals is difficult, but there seemed to be some degree of concurrence on means to achieve dominance. When de Soto held cacique Aguaycaleiquen (Caliquen), many efforts were made to free him. Seven caciques who said they were subjects of Uzachile offered to ally themselves with the Spaniards against Apalache, an enemy of Uzachile and themselves, but this turned out to be a ruse, for which de Soto was prepared, to free the cacique (Oviedo 1547–1549 [1959:II:160]). We do see in these accounts a willingness of the subordinates of a chief to undertake energetic action to rescue him. In some cases, as when Añasco had captured 30 persons, and was tricked into giving them to *un gandul*, a "loafer," [5] someone was sent to pose as the cacique (Oviedo 1547–1549 [1959:II:159]). This was not the only time that a substitute was sent to take the heat from the Spaniards, suggesting that at least some followers were sufficiently motivated to deal with the unpredictable and dangerous foreigners in place of their leaders.

Such military competition could make borders between chiefdoms risky zones. Moving from Altamaha (Altamaca), the Spaniards came to Zamumo (Camumo), a subject of Ocute, who always went about armed because he was on the frontier of another cacique, Cofitachequi (Oviedo 1547–1549 [1959:II:164]).

Not all localities necessarily had either paramount chiefs or even chiefs at all. In Chalaque province, the Spaniards were not only unable to find the town of the seignior (*pueblo del señor*), but also the gifts were brought to them simply by Indians, apparently not even "principal" ones. This is another indication that Chalaque may have had different social and political structures than those found at Cofitachequi. Again, at Guaquili, there was no mention of caciques, señors, or principal men, rather just gifts of turkeys and dogs from Indians (Oviedo 1547–1549 [1959:II:168]). There are other indications of areas without paramount chiefs, at least. For example, the cacique of

---

[5] Worth translates this as "vassal," which is not really implied by this term, and even Bourne's "vagabond" (1904:70) does not quite bring out the sense that person was of low rank.

Chicaça came to the Spanish in January 1541, offering guides and translators to go to Caluza. "Caluza is a province of more than ninety towns (*not subject to anyone*)" [emphasis added, JM] (Oviedo 1547–1549 [1959:II:176]). Who these ferocious, but leaderless, people were is not at all clear, unfortunately (Swanton 1911:302).

Rank and authority. Ranked societies were found by the Iberians throughout much of their journey. At Cofitachequi on the first day of May 1540, the Spaniards were indisputably greeted by persons of rank. According to Ranjel, this was the *cacica señora* of the land who came out carried on a litter borne by "principals" (Oviedo 1547–1549 [1959:II:167]). There are some important points to note about this encounter. The greeting behavior described is typical of Eastern groups over several centuries, as will be discussed. A litter bearing the cacica was a mark of respect by the *principales* who bore her, but it tells us relatively little about the "power" of this chief. The bearers were *"principales con mucha auctoridad"* covered with white cloth (Oviedo 1547–1549 [1959:II:167]). *Auctoridad* can either mean "authority" or, perhaps better here, "pomp." It is not altogether clear whether the "authority" applies here to the principals or to the carrying.

At Coça, as at Cofitachequi, the Spaniards were met by a person carried on a litter (Biedma 1544 [1993:232]). Ranjel says here that they were met by the cacique "on a litter covered with the white blankets of the land, borne ceremoniously by 60 or 70 of his *principales* in turn, with none of them plebeians or commoners" (Oviedo 1547–1549 [1959:II:171]). Those "plebeians" however, stayed hidden for the days that the Spaniards stayed there, leaving the cacique and some other *principales* in the custody of the Spaniards. Many of the Indians were hunted down and imprisoned with iron collars and chains (Oviedo 1547–1549 [1959:II:171]).

Much later on when they reached the residence of the cacique Tascaluca, the Spaniards found Tascaluca outside his house on mats and cushions in plaza. According to Ranjel, the cacique was named Actahachi, but was cacique of Tascaluca. The cacique was wearing a turbanlike headdress, which gave him "authoritativeness." He was wearing a feather mantle that went down to his feet, also very "authoritative." The cacique was seated on high cushions with many *principales* of his Indians with him (Oviedo 1547–9 [1959:II:173]). Elvas thought those of highest rank were nearest to the cacique. In Elvas, one of these held a sort of fan of deerskin that kept the sun from him, round and the size of a shield, quartered with black and white, with a cross [*aspa*[6]] made in the middle. From a distance, it was said to look like "taffeta, for the colors were very perfect. It was set on a small and very long staff. This was the device he bore in his wars" (Elvas 1557 [1993:96]). An umbrella-fan described in de Biedma, is used in a similar manner to that described in Elvas but was said to be made of feathers, not skin (de Biedma 1544 [1993:233]). In Ranjel, the sunshade over the cacique is described in virtually identical terms as in Elvas—a circular black field with a white cross like that

---

[6]Hann's note suggests that *aspa* may mean an "X," rather than a vertical cross (in Clayton et al. 1993:96). Probably this is a white cross on a black field (in heraldic, "sable, a cross argent" or "sable, a saltire argent"). See also the description of Ranjel, below. However, note that in Ranjel's description of a cross made by an arrow piercing a lance, the term *aspa* was also used (Oviedo 1547-1549 [1959:II:175]), and it seems less likely to be a saltire, or St. Andrew's cross, in that case.

carried by the knights of the Order of St. John of Rhodes.[7] When they left, they took Tascaluca, together with many *principales*, and "always the Indian with the sunshade before the *señor*" (Oviedo 1547–1549 [1959:II:174]). This certainly suggests that the fan-umbrella was some kind of emblem of rank and importance.

Tascaluca had a rather more haughty manner than is described for earlier caciques, but de Soto treated him just as he had the others, taking him hostage as he marched on through his territory. De Biedma describes cacique Tascaluza (in Elvas, *Tascaluca*) as being very large. When asked to give bearers to the Spaniards, he said that "he was not accustomed to serving anyone, rather that all served him before" (de Biedma 1544 [1993:232]). The governor sat with him since, "as if he were a king" (*como si fuera un rey*), he would not get up (Oviedo 1547–1549 [1959:II:173]). Whether it is simple disdain for the "savages" or not, it is clear that the Spaniards considered that the power of this chief did not justify such pretensions.

There were also spatial representations of dominance of the sort that occur worldwide. De Soto got the two caciques of Casqui and Pacaha together for a feast, and the "caciques had a quarrel as to who was to sit at his right hand" (Elvas 1557 [1993:120]; confirmed in De Biedma 1544 [1993:241]). According to Elvas's account, this was settled by de Soto saying the side did not matter to Christians.

Another spatial dimension of rank was that of literal elevation of some members of the community. Near Coça, Ranjel mentions mounds: "This Talimeco was a town of great authority, with its oratory on a high mound and very respectable." The house of the cacique was very large, covered with mats (Oviedo 1547–1549 [1959:II:168]).[8] This is slightly puzzling, since this large structure was the house of the cacique, not the *cacica*, yet this was said to be the señora's own town. Similarly, at Casqui, "Having arrived at the town, we found that the caciques there were accustomed to have, next to the houses where they live, some very high mounds (*cerros*), made by hand, and that others have their houses on the mounds themselves" (de Biedma 1544 [1993:239]). These are the most explicit accounts of historic mound use, and one presumes that a cacique on "the mound" is the overall chief, the others presumably being principal men. In Ranjel's account of the first meeting with Tascaluca at *Actahachi* (Athahachi; *hata*, "white," *hatci*, "river," a *pueblo nuevo*, (Oviedo 1547–1549 [1959:II:173]), they found the cacique on a *balcón* made on a mound (*en un cerro*) on one side of the plaza. As in the Elvas account, the term *balcón* makes more sense as a shelter of a square-ground structure type than as a second-story addition.

Kinship and lineage. Not so much was understood by the Spaniards of the kin relations they encountered. At Cofitachequi, the Spaniards were also said to have been greeted by the cacica's sister (or perhaps her niece). We can compare this to the historic Muskogee, whose term for "sister," *wanwa*, would be applied to a number of

---

[7] Although this might be taken to mean the shape of the cross was the eight-pointed cross of the Knights of St. John—like that of Malta—almost certainly what is referred to here is the *tincture* of the heraldic marking, not the form of the cross itself.

[8] Este Talimeco era pueblo de gran auctoridad, y aquel su oratorio en un cerro alto y muy auctorizado; el caney o casa del cacique muy grande y muy alto e ancho, todo esterado, alto y bajo, con muy primas y hermosas esteras, y por tan buen arte asentadas, que parescía que todas las esteras eran una sola estera.

women on the same generation level. The term for "niece," *hakpati*, would apply to the sister's daughter or daughters of anyone called "sister." If Elvas's account is true that the Senhora of Cutifachiqui (otherwise *Cofitachequi*) even encouraged de Soto to pillage graves in nearby abandoned towns, we may suspect lack of direct kinship ties, at least to the Senhora, from which we may guess at distinct kin groups in these towns (1557 [1993:83]). This is, however, a complicated situation, as we shall see further in discussion of prestations. We also should remember the claims and statements made about relative importance, history, and power of kinship groups in the rivalry between Casqui and Pacaha. Other indications were that matrilineal descent of chiefly rank was described to, but not completely understood by, the Spaniards.

Principales. There were certainly other status differences in the accounts than those of cacique and follower. Shortly after landing in Florida, Juan Ortiz—the stranded Spaniard with cacique Mococo— was sent to the de Soto party, together with a dozen or so "principal Indians" (Elvas 1557 [1993:62]).The term *principal* is often used in the de Soto accounts in contexts that make it clear that there are persons whose roles are distinct from those of the caciques. However, the Iberians seem not to have fully understood what these *principales* were doing, and this makes interpretation even more problematical than usual.

We commonly see—standing in the mist of the chroniclers' understanding—these "principal Indians." Were they merely hangers-on, the courts, of these rulers? Or were they what we might expect from our knowledge of later Southeastern political organization: the councils of each of these chiefs? As in the earlier discussion of the Natchez, we see repeated mention of "asking the principal Indians." Even if caciques were merely stalling an outrageous Spanish demand, there is still their expectation that the excuse would be credible—that is, that granting demands such as those for porters or women would not be in the power of a chief, but would require concurrence of the *principales*. From the documents, it seems likely that some of the *principales* would have been community officers, such as the war chief, whereas others were town chiefs, and still others, elders from the councils.

Distinctness from chief and association with the chief. There are many indications of the distinctness of the principal Indians from other members of the society and from the chief. At Coste, where native resistance to Spanish "foraging" (*ranchear*, translated by Worth as "pillage," Clayton et al. 1993:266) occurred, de Soto lured the cacique *and his principal men* to him and took them captive until they provided him with guides and porters (Elvas 1557 [1993:90–91]). Some 3 days out from Coça, the Spaniards came to Ullibahali, where they were met by "principal Indians" (*not* a cacique, Elvas 1557 [1993:94]).

At Quizquiz, "six of the principal Indians came to the camp and said that they were come to see what people they were and that they were about to return to the cacique to tell him to come immediately to render obedience and service to the governor" (Elvas 1557 [1993:111]). The Spaniards usually interpreted both the subordination of the *principales* and various towns in feudal terms such as *vassalage* and *homage*. On arriving at Cofaqui, they were met by the principal men with gifts (Oviedo 1547–1549 [1959:II:165]). Here, again, we see the importance of these principal men, whose roles were often confused with those of subordinate caciques. In a few places, there seem to be neither caciques nor *principales*. As we have seen, in Chalaque province, they were unable to find the town of the seignior (*pueblo del señor*), although gifts were brought to them in the pine woods where they camped, but by Indians, apparently not even "principal" ones. Again, at Guaquili, there were just gifts of turkeys and dogs from Indians, not *principales* (Oviedo 1547–1549 [1959:II:168]).

Although it is not clear that it had much effect, the Spaniards commonly took *principales* captive, either alone or together with their chiefs, as at Tianto, a town subordinate to Nilco (Elvas 1557 [1993:130]). At town of Coste, the Spaniards grabbed the "cacique and 10 or 12 of the principals," put them in chains and collars, and threatened to burn them all (Oviedo 1547–1549 [1959:II:170]). In the territory of Tascaluca, they took the cacique and many *principales* captive (1547–1549 [1959:II:174]). Oviedo comments that the reasons they detained the caciques and *principales* was so their subjects would not hinder the Spanish thefts (1547–1549 [1959:II:172]).

Markers of status. There are many indications that the *principales* shared markers of status with the chiefs. At the town Actahachi of Tascaluca, the cacique was seated on high cushions with many *principales* of his Indians with him (Oviedo 1547–1549 [1959:II:173]). At Toalli, both the houses of the cacique and the principales were larger than ordinary houses (Elvas 1557 [1993:75]). Both had the *balcões*, which appear to have functioned as reception locations for visitors. When the Spaniards passed Quigaltam, the Indians "got together one hundred canoes, some of which held sixty or seventy Indians, and those of the principal men with their awnings, and they with white and colored plumes of feathers as a device" (Elvas 1557 [1993:155–156]).

Service to the chief. The duties of *principales* involved some services to the cacique. At Cofitachequi, the Spaniards were met outside the town by the "principal Indians," bearing gifts. Other *"principales con mucha auctoridad"* carried the *cacica señora* on a litter (Oviedo 1547–1549 [1959:II:167]; also in Elvas 1557 [1993:82]). At Coça (Coosa) as we saw earlier, the *principales* carried the litter and were held captive with the cacica. The Spaniards told the cacique Tascaluca that he must stay with them overnight; and although he was annoyed, he did so, while sending on his *principales* (Oviedo 1547–1549 [1959:II:173]).The *principales* were clearly important, and were seen by the Spaniards as a kind of noble, but we may note that the services to the chief in these accounts were consistent with what we know of the 18th-century Creek councils, for an example.

There are also some indications that principales would try to protect their chief. At Mavila, one of the Spaniards tried to pull the cacique out, and slashed, according to this account, the arm off a *principal* (Oviedo 1547–1549 [1959:II:174]). At the crossing near Piachi (Piache), Ranjel raised the possibility that "the *principales* who were accompanying the cacique,"[9] were attacked and some killed, perhaps just mean-

---

[9] "y el cacique de él malicioso, e púsose en resistirles el paso; pero en efeto pasaron el río con trabajo, e matáronles dos cristianos, e fuéronse los principales que accompañaban al cacique" (Oviedo 1547–1549 [1959:II:174]).

ing the escape of the *principales* (Oviedo 1547–1549 [1959:II:174]), since no conflict was indicated here in Elvas. After some difficulties with various caciques in the west, the cacique of Naguatex took up an offer of pardon by first sending some principal men to test the waters (Elvas 1557 [1993:142]).

Exchange of spouses may have been cemented alliances, not only between caciques, but also may have involved the *principales*—Casqui brought a daughter for de Soto, and Pacaha gave him a wife of his, "fresh and very chaste" as well as a sister and another "*india principal*" (Oviedo 1547–1549 [1959:II:180]).

In Talise, Elvas indicated that one of the "principal Indians," not the cacique, came to de Soto to deliver a message from the cacique Tascaluca (of the Mobile) paying homage and asking when de Soto would come (Elvas 1557 [1993:95]). While this might suggest that Talise was a border land and may have had some autonomy,[10] it is not clear, why a "principal Indian" of Talise would have been delivering messages for Tascaluca, and it seems more likely that this was a messenger from Tascaluca. Ranjel's account makes Talise either an autonomous border town, or subordinate to Tascaluca.

Authority. There are many documented instances of the chief consulting with *principales* before taking action. After fattening his horses and Spaniards at Chiaha for 30 days, de Soto asked for 30 women. One might wonder at the treatment that 30 women could have expected from 600 Spanish soldiers. Apparently the Chiaha were also concerned as "the cacique answered *that he would talk with his principal men* [emphasis added]; but one night, before returning an answer, all the Indians left the town" (Elvas 1557 [1993:89]). After destroying some maize fields in retaliation, de Soto withdrew his request for the 30 women, and the Indians returned to town (1557 [1993:89]). In another case, after de Soto had spent two and a half months at Chicaça, he asked for 200 porters. The cacique responded "that he would talk it over with his principal men" (1557 [1993:107]).

This is important. First, it seems clear that these services of women, at least as slaves, were not usual obligations owed to a higher leader. Second, we are told that the cacique cannot take action without talking to his *principales*, although it is possible that this was so either because the cacique was not yet "of age" in the first instance, or simply that the cacique was stalling. However, as we have seen, this was also a Natchez Sun's response to his French tormentors almost 200 years later. As we penetrate below the feudal Iberian veneer of these accounts, we almost always find "principal Indians" whose roles in the operation of these societies seem to be more than merely obeying a cacique. We can guess, but cannot prove, that there were several kinds of "principals" that are combined here. Some of them may have been cacique-level authorities, such as the later war chiefs. Others may have been subordinate town caciques, and many were probably the lineage and clan leaders of their towns (see Hudson 1976:223–226; Swanton 1928a).

---

[10] This is asserted, for what it is worth, in Garcilaso: "Este pueblo Talise no obedecía bien a su señor Coza, por trato doble de otro señor llamado Tascaluza, cuyo estado confinaba con el de Coza y le hacía vecindad no segura ni amistad verdadera, y, aunque los dos no traían guerra descubierta, el Tascaluza era hombre soberbio y belicoso, de muchas cautelas y astucias, como adelante veremos, y, como tal, tenía desasosegado este pueblo para que no obedeciese bien a su señor" [1956:243].

Prestations. Prestations were one aspect of social relations, mostly in the form of food and clothing. The de Soto documents repeatedly mention food, blankets, and skins; but they do not emphasize display items for either prestations or trade. Valued artifacts (e.g., the fan-umbrella of Tascaluca) were present, of course. Pearls, painted skins, and other "prestige" items were highly valued, but they were not the most important items in gift giving.

Tribute. De Soto heard of a marvelous land called Yupaha from a youth captured at Napetuca. Yupaha was ruled by a woman who received not only tribute, but also tribute in gold as well as clothes. We are also told that the youth was able to describe the mining, smelting, and refining of gold "just as if he had seen it done" (Elvas 1557 [1993:74]). I think that, given the report of "gold," we need to be just as careful about the "tribute." There is no reason to doubt that the reports indicate what the Spaniards *thought*, but that does not mean that this was more than a simple kind of prestation, like that described in 18th- and 19th-century Southeastern societies. In fact, the same kinds of goods continued to be used in Colonial European "gifts" to Native American chiefs (Jacobs 1950), where *tribute* is not the first word to come to mind.

At Toalli, the "lords or principal men" had "round about many large barbacoas in which they gather together the tribute paid them by their Indians which consists of maize and deerskins and native blankets resembling shawls" (Elvas 1557 [1993:75]). This account is one of the best indications that considerable storage was near the elite structures, and that this included deerskins and blankets as well as maize. Skins were an important prestation item given throughout the Southeast. We should also note that this indicates that deerskins had "value" well before the beginning of the deerskin trade from Charleston (see Chapter 8).

There are a number of explicit references to tribute in the accounts. The Spaniards were told that the Senhora of Cofitachequi was there to enforce tribute payments (Elvas 1557 [1993:86]). When the ill de Soto claimed to be the son of the sun, Quigaltam replied to this by saying if he were the son of the sun, "let him dry up the great river and he would believe him" (Elvas 1557 [1993:134]). In addition, Quigaltam said that "he was not accustomed to visit any one. On the contrary, all of whom he had knowledge visited him and obeyed him and paid him tribute, either by force or of their own volition" (1557 [1993:134]). Quizquiz was said to pay tribute to Pacaha (Biedma 1544 [1993:238]).

Perhaps the most compelling indication of expected payments to paramounts is to be found when the cacique Zamumo asked whether he should now pay tribute to the governor or to his former paramount at Ocute (Oviedo 1547–1549 [1959:II:164]). Although I have emphasized that the term *tribute* is loaded with unacceptable overtones, the Spanish understanding here was clearly *tributo*, in a feudal sense, and the question suggests, if this was reliably translated, that there was some regularization of prestations by subordinates, although this does not necessarily indicate *tribute*, in the strict sense of the term. After the exaggerated response given by this cacique to his gift of a silvered feather (see the next section), de Soto suspected that this question of tribute was "shrewd" and told Zamumo to continue to give the tribute to Ocute until the governor should order otherwise (Oviedo 1547–1549 [1959:II:164–165]).

Gifts. The relations did not always describe the various kinds of gifts and prestations as *tribute*. In many cases, more neutral terminology such as *gifts* was employed. The gifts given to the Spaniards were predominantly food and clothing, so it seems likely that whatever obligations encouraged *donas* to the chief, these were also usually in the form of food, skins, and blankets. *Donas*, "gifts," is surely a better term than *tributo*, and it is the term actually used most of the time by the Spaniards for the goods they themselves received. We may ask whether the context of goods received by paramounts was much different. As in the archaeological cases, we may distinguish between gifts of useful items such as food and clothing and gifts of so-called prestige goods.

Prestige goods. Let us examine some of the relatively rare occurrences of prestige goods as gifts in the de Soto accounts. One of the first was the gift by the Senhora of Cofitachequi to de Soto of pearls from her own neck (Elvas 1557 [1993:82]). This, however, followed gifts of food and clothing. The necklace, given as it was off the neck, does not seem to have been intended as a gift, but perhaps de Soto's stares prompted the transfer? After the "governor" crossed over to the town, he was given food, not prestige items. Given the predominance of nonprestige or display items, we need to be cautious in interpreting this particular "gift."

As for the 14 *arrobas* (~160 kg) of pearls, these were reportedly (Elvas 1557 [1993:83]) taken from the graves, presumably in mortuary temples, so they cannot be considered normal prestations. Apparently, the Señora was not concerned with this despoliation of the dead in the mortuary temple, as she is quoted as saying, "Esteem that highly? You'all[11] should go to Talimeco, my town (*pueblo*), and you'll find so much of these that your horses won't be able to carry them" (Oviedo 1547–1549 [1959:II:168]). The issue of the pearls is perplexing, since it is hard to see why the Señora was so blasé about the grave goods of the elite, presumably her own kin. As we saw in the Elvas account, she may have suggested looting the abandoned towns around. In Ranjel, she was actually suggesting going to her own mortuary temple at "Chieftown" (i.e., Talimeco = *Talwa immiko*) to get more pearls. Although each of the three main accounts has a slightly different story of how the Spaniards acquired the pearls, none of them suggest that such items were normal gifts. The pearls were much sought after by the Iberians as one of the few "riches" that the Spaniards had managed to find in Florida, but they had lost most of those that they had gotten in Cofitachequi in the battle at Tascaluca. No mention of getting more pearls was made until Nilco. Although the governor was presented with a marten-skin blanket and a string of pearls in the cacique's name at Nilco (Elvas 1557 [1993:131]), the circumstances of this second gift of pearls are hardly more clear than at Cofitachequi. The marten skin that accompanied them is as much a skin as a prestige item (see below).

Shell beads are mentioned in another instance: When Casqui aided him, de Soto "placed him in the town and gave him all that we found in it, which is much wealth for them, including some beads that are of snail shells from the sea and some small hides of cats and buckskin, and some corn that there was in the town, with which he

---

[11] The Señora was *Southern*, after all.

sent him away happy to his land" (de Biedma 1544 [1993:240]). This is "wealth," however, not "tribute." No one denies that these items were valuable, after all.

Gifts of "prestige" items were not necessarily appreciated. After the gift of a silvered feather, Zamumo (Camumo) went into a statement of joy so exaggerated that one wonders if the generally humorless de Soto was not a little suspicious: "Oh you of the sky, and this feather you give me, I shall eat with it, go to war with it, sleep with my wife with it" (Oviedo 1547–1549 [1959:II:164]). De Soto's somewhat restrained response was, yes, he could do all that (Oviedo 1547–1549 [1959:II:164]). In another instance, de Soto's gift to Tascaluca may not have been appreciated either: de Soto gave him a horse, and some half boots, and a scarlet cloak "to keep him content" (Oviedo 1547–9 [1959:II:173]). However, Ranjel (or Oviedo) commented sarcastically on how much contentment such gifts would have given the cacique under the circumstances (1547–1549 [1959:II:173–174]).

In general, the mentions of valued or display goods in these early contacts does not suggest that they were normal items for gifts or "tribute," despite their probable importance as markers of status or wealth.

Food and clothing. The major items given and received were those of everyday life, or at least items that symbolized more utilitarian purposes. At Chiaha, "homage" was paid in bearing grain to the Spanish party (Elvas 1557 [1993:87]; Ranjel also mentions nut oil, Oviedo 1547–1549 [1959:II:169]). Some 20 barbacoas of maize were awaiting de Soto at Chiaha. The term *barbacoa* here refers to raised granaries, but the same term also means any kind of raised grill or platform (hence our own *barbeque*). The implications for such quantities are discussed in more detail later.

At Xualla, they encountered a cacique of such a good disposition that he gave them porters, maize, little dogs, whatever he had. At Guasili (Guaxule), they were given, no cacique mentioned, many little dogs, and much maize (Oviedo 1547–1549 [1959:II:169]). At Chicaça, after some initial fighting, the cacique brought gifts of little dogs and deer skins (de Biedma 1544 [1993:236]). Even in areas where caciques were either absent or simply not found, gifts of food were given to the Spanish party (as at Chalaque, and Guaquili; Oviedo 1547–1549 [1959:II:168]). The dogs are probably food.

In other instances, food (fish and persimmon loaves) was given by a cacique who came in a large canoe with awnings, plumes of feathers, shields, and banners (Elvas 1557 [1993:112–113]), but not the display items. At Achese, the Spaniards were given maize tortillas and small onions (Oviedo 1547–1549 [1959:II:164]). The cacique of Tali had the towns along the road bring out maize, porridge, and cooked beans (1547–1549 [1959:II:171]). The seignior of Casqui town (*pueblo del señor de Casqui*) sent gifts of fish, skins, and blankets (Elvas 1557 [1993:11]; Oviedo 1547–1549 [1959:II:178]). Later, Casqui often sent "gifts of fish in abundance, and blankets, and skins" (Elvas 1557 [1993:118]). Gifts of "fish, skins, and blankets" were also brought by the cacique Pacaha (1557 [1993:119]). Casqui sought forgiveness for going away without permission and made de Soto "a gift of many blankets, skins, and fish" (1557 [1993:120]). While resting at Pacaha for 40 days, the two caciques competed in seeing who could provide the Spaniards with more "fish, blankets, and skins" (1557 [1993:121]). Particularly in the west, fish replaced maize for the prestations made to de Soto, probably at least partly because it was still early in the agricultural season in some of these cases, and new crops may not have ripened. However, some areas seem to have had maize left over from previous seasons, as well, so there may be some regional differences in the goods considered appropriate either as prestations or as gifts for the freeloading Iberians. The monotony of the offerings to the Spaniards is notable—fish, blankets, and skins.

When de Soto rewarded Casqui for his help in a raid on another town, not only shell beads were given, but also some "small hides of cats and buckskin, and some corn that there was in the town, with which he sent him away happy to his land" (de Biedma 1544 [1993:240]). At Autiamque, "considerable" maize, beans, nuts, and dried fruit in storage were found (Elvas 1557 [1993:128]). Gifts of "blankets and skins" came from the cacique. A lame cacique of a town called Tietiquaquo, who was subject to Autiamque came frequently to the Spaniards and "brought him gifts of what he had" (1557 [1993:129]). Fifteen men from Aguacay met the Spaniards on the road with gifts of skins, fish, and roasted venison (1557 [1993:141]). Again, the foods offered may reflect either less maize cultivation at Aguacay or simply the fact that it was early summer and new crops may not have come in as yet.

Throughout, skins were common prestations or gifts: We hear of "six or seven skins and blankets" (Elvas 1557 [1993:112]). As the Spaniards moved west, skins became a dominant gift item. The messengers from the cacique of Achese presented hides, "which were the first gifts as a sign of peace" (Oviedo 1547–1549 [1959:II:163]. Here Ranjel is telling us explicitly what we had already seen, that skins were symbolic, if useful, markers of peaceful intentions. At Quiguate, de Soto received gifts of "many blankets and skins" along the way from the cacique (Elvas 1557 [1993:121]). After burning half of Quiguate to deny shelter to attackers, de Soto was presented with a false cacique, with blankets and skins for de Soto. Finally, after much harassment by the Spaniards, the Indians came to bring gifts of clothing and fish (1557 [1993:121–122]). When a cacique of Cayas was captured, gifts of blankets and deerskins were brought at his command to the Spaniards, including two cowhides (bison; 1557 [1993:123]). The cacique of Chaguete had come to Autiamque to offer de Soto "gifts of skins, blankets, and salt" (1557 [1993:140]). After some misunderstandings, perhaps partially reflecting serious difficulties with translations, the cacique gave rich gifts of blankets and skins, and accompanied the Spaniards to his residence. At Nilco, the governor was presented, in the cacique's name, with a marten-skin blanket as well as a string of pearls (1557 [1993:131]). Marten blankets were also given at Mavila, and a marten cloak was pulled off a principal Indian at Tascaluca.

As for the skins being "tribute," we may note that, a party sent far on to the west found only "many skins" left on the roadside "as a sign of peace; for this is the custom of that land" (Elvas 1557 [1993:124]). Even out on the very edge of the Plains, skins were still being offered as gifts of peace—in social circumstances make it unlikely that these gifts are even prestations in fulfillment of obligations to "seigniors," much less "tribute."

In some areas, some indications of subordination given to the Spaniards were immaterial. They were met either at Lacane or Nondacao by weeping, "that being their custom in token of obedience" (Elvas 1557 [1993:145]). A gift of a great quantity of fish was also made, however.

Size of Chiefdoms, Towns, and Interaction. I have emphasized that my concern here is not with the location of the route taken by the de Soto party. All the same, we have to consider how reasonable some estimates have been for the distance made each day, especially if we are to use these distances to estimate the sizes and spacing of individual chiefdoms. Distance made per day has even been estimated to have been as much as 20 to 30 leagues (from the distance from Cofitachequi to Xualla), but this is impossible, even at the lower estimate of league distance of 4.19 km per league (the *legua legal*) used by the de Soto Commission. Hudson et al. (1989) have calculated distances based on the *legua comun* of 5.567 km (but cf. Little and Curren 1990:189). In general, the league varied according to circumstances and nationality. The *OED* examples of usage include a 1594 quotation indicating that the French league was 2 English miles (3.2 km) and the Spanish was 3 (4.8 km). Even at the lowest measure of the length of a Spanish league, 20 leagues per day would have meant over 80 km! If only 8 days were required to make 250 leagues, the party and pigs would have been moving at 126 km/day! It probably just seemed that way. This may be compared with the *fastest* speed made by veteran Confederate and Union infantry converging on Gettysburg—45 km in 11 hours of forced marching.

Using the longer league, Hudson and his associates (1985) estimated normal progress at some 20 to 24 *km* per day. Given their chained porters and all their pigs, 24 km per day would have been difficult, but it is not impossible. This is about the same progress as made by Alexander's armies in Classical times (D. Engels 1978:153–156). Sherman's tough Western army, marching in some of the same localities in the late winter of 1865, also managed about 24 km per day, even while they were foraging and building bridges and roads.

Size of polity. The size of territories recognizing a cacique is, then, probably best indicated by the distances traveled in terms of days. The largest chiefdoms may have been as large as 12 to 17 days' travel in length (e.g., Elvas 1557 [1993:85–86]). This could suggest a maximum length of as much as 300 to 400 km for the largest polity, although we should note that the "width" of a chiefdom may have been restricted in narrow stream valleys. Such sizes are, we should note, consistent with the "territories" of the largest later historical groups such as the Choctaw and the Creek Confederacy. In neither the de Soto nor later cases should we understand that such size implies close integration of the whole territory.

In many cases, the sizes of politically controlled areas are a little more modest. From Toasi, for example, they marched for only 5 days, passing through towns subject to the "seignior" of Talise (= Tulsa? Elvas 1557 [1993:95]; Swanton 1922:243). Chisi (Achese) was 6 days across (de Biedma 1544 [1993:229]). We also note Pacaha was only 3 days farther on from his enemy, Casqui (Oviedo 1547–1549 [1959:II:178]). About 5 or 6 days across seems to have been something like the "normal" distance across the territory of a chief, even though some paramount chiefs controlled much larger areas.

Even when longer distances are indicated, the degree of control was often slight. The best example of this was in the early days of the expedition, where there may have been less powerful chiefs. At Ucita and Mocoço, the Spanish captive Ortiz, after he had lost favor with cacique Ucita, was warned by Ucita's daughter (who saved him in the first place in a possible original of the story of Pocahontas and Smith) that Ucita planned to sacrifice Ortiz to the Devil. She told him to flee to Mocoço, since "she had heard him say" that he would welcome Ortiz. Ortiz fled that night, and reached a river in Mocoço's territory by morning. We are told that the language of Mocoço's community was different than that of Ucita (Elvas 1557 [1993:61]). What does this mean? We see evidence of conflict among subordinates of a paramount in the burning of Ucita's town by Mocoço, but we have also learned that the daughter of Ucita was able to tell Ortiz what she *had heard Mocoço say*. We also learn that the boundary between one territory and the next was only a night's journey away. Ortiz told de Soto that he had seen no gold or silver, but that he had never gone *more than 10 leagues* from where he was, and that the "Paracoxi" (at the town of *Hurripacuxi* in de Biedma) lived some 30 leagues away and was paid tribute by both Ucita and Mocoço (1557 [1993:62]). Even presuming that the paramount's authority extended as far in the other direction, this would imply only a weak level of control over an area of less than 300 km. Practical authority of a single cacique seems to have been limited here to no more than 20 or 30 km. However, in the de Biedma account, Juan Ortiz is quoted as saying that in his 12 years in Florida, he had not "heard of things only 20 leagues away" (de Biedma 1544 [1993:225]). Moving on past the town of the Paracoxi, captives were taken, "but the one who knew the most, did not know two leagues farther on from that town" (1544 [1993:226]).

On travel to Cofitachequi, the native guide(s) and porters apparently lost their way, although it is hard to know how much of this was deceit and how much real ignorance of the most direct route. Ranjel confirms that the guide was lost, but feigned madness, so Tatofa (Patofa) gave them a guide to get across the depopulated, 9- or 10-day way to Cofitachequi (Oviedo 1547–1549 [1959:II:165]). They still got lost, however, traveling without roads—note that most of the time in Florida, the Spanish were following trails, probably not much different from those outlined in Myer's classic study (1928).

Moving with the captive cacica of Cofitachequi, Elvas records, "We traversed her lands for a hundred leagues, in which, as we saw, she was very well obeyed" (1557 [1993:85–86]). However, Perico, the youth guide, had told them that this woman was not the *Senhora*, but her niece,[12] come to Cofitachequi to enforce tribute payments, but he was not believed in this (1557 [1993:86]). One suspects that "respect" could have been shown to any elite person from Cofitachequi, without there actually being subordination. Frankly, despite the understanding of the Spaniards, there are many indications that the respect given *them* was not necessarily an indication that native leaders really considered themselves subordinate to de Soto.

Seven days out from Cofitachequi, was Chalaque, and 5 days further still, Xualla. Elvas remarks on total distances at this point, indicating that from Ocute to Cofitachequi it was 130 leagues, but that 80 of these were without inhabitants (Elvas 1557 [1993:86]). As Anderson notes, the Savannah River region he has studied was probably largely uninhabited at the time of the *entrada* (1994b:71). De Soto planned

---

[12] Or perhaps the *senhora* was the niece of the Lady of Cutifachiqui, since the Portuguese is ambiguous (see John H. Hann's note on this).

to carry cacica Cofitachequi to Guaxule—5 days on from Xualla— "for her lands reached that far" (Elvas 1557 [1993:86]). Cofitachequi was said to be 250 leagues from Xualla across mountainous country (1557 [1993:86]). As noted, this would imply that the expedition made over 20 leagues per day in difficult terrain, so the distance is excessive. In any case, the "Senhora" of Cofitachequi *may* have controlled an area some 17 days' travel in length. However, this total length of travel need not reflect exercise of power so much as recognition of someone of importance.

There are indications of empty zones between communities. As the expedition moved on from Cofitachequi, they passed for many leagues across land that was very poor in maize (Elvas 1557 [1993:86]). Before reaching Chiaha, de Soto sent on an Indian messenger to tell the cacique there to have grain ready for him. He passed 5 days through uninhabited country and then was met 2 leagues outside Chiaha (1557 [1993:87–88]). As noted previously, there are indications that some towns were border zones, as in the case of Talise, where the cacique of Coça was given permission "to return to his lands" (1557 [1993:95]).

In another case west of the Mississippi, after an attack was fought off, a prisoner told them that they had been attacked by the caciques Naguatex, Maye, and Hacanac, "lord of vast lands and many vassals" under the leadership of Naguatex (Elvas 1557 [1993:143]). The mutilated prisoner was sent to Naguatex, telling him to stand and fight if he wished to deny the Spaniards their way. They reached Naguatex, "which was very extensive." We may guess, however, it was not very populous, given its scattered nature (for further discussion of this group, see Schambach in Young and Hoffman 1963).

Still farther west, in Tulla, described as the best populated land in that region, de Soto's forces were attacked: "When fifteen or twenty Indians had gathered together, they came to attack the Christians" (Elvas 1557 [1993:125]). This does not suggest that very large groups were available in any given locality!

Town size. A number of different terms were used in the original language accounts that have been translated rather loosely. *Pueblo* is probably the most common and is reasonably translated as "town." However, settlements so described were often very modest. In one case, Aguacalecuen (= Elvas's Caliquen) was a *poblazón razonable*, a "fair-sized village" (Ranjel). Other terms found include *ranchuelos* and *ranchos* (e.g., de Biedma 1544 [1993:240]).

The expedition first landed in modern Florida at the town of Ucita, where this town was the seat of the cacique Ucita. They discovered a large house (*buhío de los grandes*) like those seen in the Indies, along with smaller structures (Oviedo 1548 [1959:II:154; 1993:253]). The town consisted only of "seven or eight houses" and a chief's house on a high hill built "by hand" (Elvas 1557 [1993:57]). These were presumably large houses, and most of them were dismantled to build small houses for "a mess of every three or four"(1557 [1993:58]). It is not clear whether the houses were large enough to provide sufficient building material, or whether other canes, and so forth, were collected by the Spaniards to build the small houses.

After passing the town of *Paracoxi*, who was paid tribute by "everyone," the Spanish went to a town (*pueblo*) "that the Indians made out to us to be very large, so much so that they told us its people, shouting, made flying birds fall." However, in de Biedma's eyes, "it was a small town" (de Biedma 1544 [1993:226]).

Despite the desire of his men to stay at Cofitachequi, de Soto felt that it was too small to support the Spanish party (Elvas 1557 [1993:84]). Elvas indicated that there were also a number of abandoned "large towns" around Cofitachequi, which were apparently all occupied before a "plague" of 2 years previously (1557 [1993:83]). One suspects that it was difficult for the others to distinguish settlements so close to one another, and they are ignored in the other accounts. One may also reflect on the meaning of "large" in this context since there were "many" of these within a radius of no more than 7 km of Cofitachequi. Nonetheless, these towns may have been important enough to have mortuary establishments of their own—since by some accounts, 14 arrobas (~160 kg) of pearls were reportedly taken from their graves (1557 [1993:83]). The degree of dispersal of many towns was often considerable. Cayas is described as having dispersed, but dense, settlement (de Biedma 1544 [1993:241]).

The battle of Mavila may be taken as an indication of large concentrations of population, but De Biedma makes the circumstances of the battle of Mavila a little clearer than the other accounts. It seemed to the Spaniards that only 300 or 400 people were in the town but, in fact, some 5000 were hiding in the houses in ambush (de Biedma 1544 [1993:233]). The Spanish party in the town fought their way out, and the Spanish "encircled the entire town" (with 200 horses, 600 men), then 60–80 men dismounted and formed four parties that assaulted the town from four sides (1544 [1993:235]). All of their baggage was taken into town by their escaping porters, and the people of Mavila beat drums and raised banners against the Spanish. However, the scale of 5000 people being assaulted by four parties of roughly 20 men apiece is a little hard to understand. There can be no doubt that there were many defenders, many of whom were burned in the houses, but it is hard to imagine the technical advantages of Spanish arms being so successful against odds of 9:1 overall or 67:1 for the assault parties! The fact that Mavila could be "encircled" by a force of 200 horsemen might say something about the size of the town, but we should rather understand that the horsemen *circled about* the town, not *surrounded* it (compare Ranjel).

When Spaniards surprised the people of Quizquiz, they captured more than 300 women (de Biedma 1544 [1993:238]). The population of Quizquiz must have been considerably more than 600 persons if this number is correct.

Quiguate was the largest town encountered in Florida (de Biedma 1544 [1993:241]; Elvas 1557 [1993:121]). The Spaniards lodged in the abandoned town, filling only half of it (Elvas 1557 [1993:121]). If we assume the housing unit to be the "mess" of three or four men mentioned at the beginning of the *entrada*, this would imply that the total size of the village was over 300 houses, with reductions in scale down to as few as 40 houses if twenty-five soldiers could have been lodged in each structure.

These examples could be multiplied, but the main point should be clear. The towns and villages encountered by the earliest Spanish explorers were substantially like those seen in later historical records. I shall argue in later chapters that these ranges for both the size of towns and the size of houses are similar to those for 17th- and 18th-century towns.

Storage and Food. The kinds of gifts have been indicated in the previous discussion, but we are also interested in the amounts and the degree of central control as another measure of the power in the hands of the caciques. As noted, the above-ground storage facilities known as barbacoas represent considerable (and fairly public) amounts of stored food and clothing. We shall look first at the size of storage facilities as recorded in the accounts and then move on to an examination of the implications of the Spanish consumption of supplies in particular places. Most of the storage that the Spaniards were aware of was in the raised storehouses called barbacoas, as already mentioned. The barbacoas at Toalli, were supposed to be in the vicinity of elite houses (Elvas 1557 [1993:75]). Barbacoas in the abandoned towns around Cofitachequi were still filled with clothing (1557 [1993:83]).

By April of 1540, de Soto had lost a few men and horses, but the swine being driven along had increased from 13 sows to "300" pigs. There were also many hundreds of porters, even given some exaggeration and deaths. The swine and nearly 200 horses were surely foraging for themselves some of the time, but at Chiaha, for example, and in later Spanish accounts there are many indications that the horses were also being fed maize. The Spaniards took along enough maize for 4 days when they left Patofa (Elvas 1557 [1993:80]). At "soldier" levels of caloric intake (see D. Engels 1978:18, Appendix 1), this would mean, for modest consumption, a minimum of 1.7 metric tons up to about 3 metric tons of grain, if adjusted for loss of calories in preparation and cooking.

We do not know what else the porters were carrying besides food, skins, and some loot. More than 700 porters—as supposed to have been given by the cacique of Patofa—would have had to carry only 2–4 kg of food per bearer for the 600-odd Spaniards. Even if they were not fed as well as the Spaniards, the bearers would also have to carry some food for themselves, meaning a total load of 5–9 kg of corn each. If a daily ration of grain supplement for horses is figured in (using D. Engels's figures, 1978), the grain load per porter would rise to 10–14 kg per porter, if the horses were being ridden. Elvas notes that the horses had come from Cofitachequi "with but little maize," so we know that at least some maize was carried for them (1557 [1993:88]). Although increasing the labor force has diminishing returns because of the need to carry still more food for the additional bearers, the large numbers of porters given in the account begin to look more reasonable for such quantities.

At a little village (*poblezuelo pequeño*) on the way to Cofitachequi, the Spaniards were able to steal some 50 *fanegas* of maize (probably 2–3 metric tons; de Biedma 1544 [1993:230]), so even small places could have substantial amounts of grain in storage. A *fanega* is often defined as roughly 45 kg (100 pounds), but the measure is one that varies in different regions. Although a *fanega* can range as high as 2.6 bushels (roughly 66 kg; e.g., Lewis 1951), both the context and the amounts make a 1.6 bushel (40 kg) *fanega* seem more likely in this case. At Himahi (Aymay), when they were in need, the Spaniards found a *barbacoa* of maize, and "more than two and a half cahices"(*mas que dos cahices y medio*) of parched maize (Oviedo 1547–1549 [1959:II:165]). Worth and Hudson (in Clayton et al. 1993:275) say that a *cahiz* is 12 *fanegas*, which would make this something between 1 and 3 metric tons of parched corn. That is a lot of corn to parch, and the account specifically says that this *pinol* is *hecho*, and is *tostado*, so this was not just dried maize. A *cahiz* was normally about 18 bushels, but even that would imply nearly a metric ton of parched corn—Bourne's (1904) translation of 30 "bushels" seems more in line with what one would expect. I wonder if Oviedo did not miscopy *cahiz* for *cuartillo*, making the total only 42 kg.

At Chicaça, although it was winter (December 17), the maize was mostly still in the fields. The Spanish were able to collect enough to make it through the winter (Elvas 1557 [1993:105–106]). Including the horses, but not any bearers, in the numbers to be fed would mean that considerably more than 80 tons of maize were collected, or the production of more than 60 ha of maize fields! If the horses were able to forage, the amount of grain harvested could have been less than half as much. However, stored grain was quickly used up by the large Spanish party.

Labor. Actual and effective control of other people's labor is a condition that arises sometime between tribes and states. Claims for Mississippian chiefs' control of labor are often based in assumptions of centralized control of public labor. This assumption is largely based on the massive public works of Mississippian times, but the early data from the de Soto accounts are still important in assessing these claims for involvement of chiefs in labor allocation and control.

Native use of labor. There are indications of labor service to various chiefs. The very act of the *principales* carrying a chief represents some small indication of their labor being subject to calls by the chief, although one is reminded of the many Eastern "tribal" societies that had the custom of the headman and honored guests being carried (e.g., Cartier 1535 [1932:61]). It is also clear that the captive Juan Ortiz labored at least for the cacique Ucita in guarding the temple to prevent wolves from carrying off the corpses from within (Elvas 1557 [1993:60]). Ortiz gained favor with the cacique in this duty by saving the corpse of a son. In fact, this does not seem to have been very burdensome service. There is also mention of de Soto taking the Cofitachequi cacica and her "slave women" as hostages (1557 [1993:85]). When Tascaluca (Tascaluza) was asked to give the Spanish bearers, he said that "he was not accustomed to serving anyone, rather that all served him before" (de Biedma 1544 [1993:232]). But we cannot be sure that this "service" was primarily in the form of labor control. I can see little in these accounts that suggests that there was any "enslavement" different from that documented in many Eastern societies and in the Plains from still later records. In the de Soto accounts, in fact, most references to slavery are in the context of Spanish use of labor, not native control of labor, even of captives.

Labor demands by the Spaniards. As we have seen obliquely in the discussion of the *principales*, the almost universally negative response of each group to Spanish claims for labor created the most difficulties for the Spaniards. It is true that the harshness of the Spanish use of porters and women was responsible for some of this reaction, but that cannot simply be assumed to explain all the response. Harsh, the treatment was: We are told that most of the porters taken early on had died by March 1540, because of their "being naked and in chains" during the hard winter (Elvas 1557 [1993:74]). There are some suggestions that porters (*tamemes*) were given more freely early on during the *entrada* than later. At Ocute, the Spaniards were supposedly "given"

400 porters when they left (1557 [1993:77]). Several of the caciques encountered are reported as having expressed (through an increasingly long chain of interpreters) their lifetime happiness at being able to serve the great Lord, de Soto (1557 [1993:76, 77–78]). The cacique of Patofa (1557 [1993:80]) also "gave" the expedition some 700 porters. Nonetheless, I think the bulk of the evidence strongly suggests that the request for impressed labor itself was most often the critical difficulty in native–Spanish interactions. We should also be somewhat doubtful about round numbers such as these.

Near Ullibahali, where the Spaniards were met by "principal Indians" (*not* a cacique, Elvas 1557 [1993:94]), "necessary" porters were "given." (1557 [1993:94]). Farther on at Toasi, more porters were "given" by the "Indians" (1557 [1993:94]). At Ocute, the anger of the governor made the cacique "tremble with fear," and only then was de Soto given supplies and porters (Oviedo 1547–1549 [1959:II:165]).

Many caciques and their principal men strongly resisted the Spanish labor demands. At Mavila, Ranjel claims that 3000 of the Mavilians and porters were killed in their resistance to the Spanish call for more porters. Spanish losses of 22 men, 148 wounded, 7 horses, and 29 "others," presumably slaves taken earlier, were reported (Oviedo 1547–1549 [1959:II:175]). However large the actual Indian losses were, we may take their willingness to die, rather than be captured or recaptured, as evidence of how extraordinary the Spanish claims for labor and women were to these people and how unusual such slavery was to them.

One of the common responses to Spanish demands for food and labor was for local populations to disappear into the bush. When Talise was reached, the town had been abandoned, although de Soto was able to order the cacique to appear, and took 40 porters. However, another cacique, Tatofa and another "principal" came and also provided porters (Oviedo 1547–1549 [1959:II:165]). This documents a strong Eastern Native American tendency to "vote with one's feet" when encountering oppressive or overwhelming circumstances.

Even though the Spaniards had cooperated with the Chicaça in a military action, when the time came for de Soto to ask for porters, this "agitated the Indians among themselves to such a degree that the Spanish understood it" (Oviedo 1547–1549 [1959:II:176–177]). Despite the warning and deciding to sleep in their armor, the Indians "true to their word, entered the camp in many squadrons, beating drums as if it were in Italy[13] and setting fire, taking 59 horses" (1547–1549 [1959:II:177]). "And if the Indians had known how to follow up this victory, it would have been the last day of life for all the Christians of this army, and would have put an end to the demand for *tamemes* [porters]" (1547–1549 [1959:II:175]). At this point, Oviedo inserted a comment based on an interview with a "well-informed hidalgo" who had been with de Soto. He asked why the governor and his army needed so many porters, why they took so many women "and those who were not old or the most ugly," and why they detained the caciques and *principales* (1547–1549 [1959:II:172]). The *hidalgo* responded that they needed the porters as slaves or servants to carry the goods stolen or given to them; that some died and others wore out, so they had the need to renew them and take more.

---

[13] Spanish troops had fought in the Italian wars, participating with Imperial troops in the sack of Rome in 1527.

The women they took were to serve them and for their filthy uses and lust. They detained the caciques and principales so their subjects would not hinder their thefts (1547–1549 [1959:II:172]).

Supply of even half the numbers of porters reported from Patofa (700) and the 400 from Ocute (Elvas 1557[1993:77]) would have represented a substantial population drain on the towns supplying the porters, especially since large numbers of them never returned.

Women. The Spanish demand for women, as noted by Oviedo (1547–1549 [1959:II:172]), was another distasteful aspect of this expedition. The response of the Mavila and other peoples (Elvas 1557 [1993:104]) indicates that caciques were not used to the kind of treatment they were receiving from the Spanish. Demands for women, especially, were met by resistance, although the idea of giving bearers was little more popular. In addition to porters given at Ullibahali, 30 Indian women "as slaves" were "given." Also at Toasi, still another 30 women were given (1557 [1993:94]). At Italisi (Talise), on the other hand, although the people had fled, the cacique "gave" 26 or 27 women and deerskins and "whatever they had" (Biedma 1544 [1993:232]). There are other cases such as Chiaha, where the townspeople fled to avoid meeting the Spanish demands for more women (Elvas 1557 [1993:89]).

The Spanish surprised the people of Quizquiz, where the Spanish captured more than 300 women because "the Indian men were gone to do their labors at their cornfields" (Biedma 1544 [1993:238]). This is an intriguing comment, since normally we would expect that it would be the women who would be working the fields.

Taken as a whole, the evidence on demands for both porters and women indicate that the Spanish demands for these persons, and especially their treatment of the captives, were highly repugnant to their hosts. At the end of the Elvas account, we note that few of these captives were ever able to return home. However, one native of Coça lived to return in 1559 to his home with the de Luna expedition discussed below.

Names and Ethnicity. There are only a few points about names that are of importance to the topics here. The first is that many names that are similar to those of historical groups seem to be rather generic. The second point is that there are *some* data on ethnic identities in the de Soto accounts (as explored for the Choctaw by Galloway 1995).

The identities of many towns are uncertain. For example, *Chalaque* (Elvas 1557 [1993:86]) certainly sounds like *Cherokee*, but both names are probably *ciloki, tchiloki,* "person of a different speech" in Muskogee (Swanton 1939:60; 1946:110), which could have meant any number of non-Muskhogean speakers in the mid-16th century. *Xualla* has been compared to *Qualla,* but *Cheraw,* a Siouan-speaking group, seems just as likely on the basis of name similarity (Hann in Clayton et al. 1993:198; Hudson 1990:83–88; Swanton 1939: 60; 1946:109). Many of the descriptions give little detail that allows identification of ethnicity, except that we may note that there was often considerable linguistic diversity in localities the Spaniards understood to be within a particular paramount chiefdom. I note again that "respect" could have been shown to an elite person without actual subordination.

In other cases, when de Soto looked for Tascaluca, he passed Tallimuchase ("New Town") which had no people in it (Elvas 1557 [1993:94]). The second day, he reached Ytaua ("Somebody's Town"), which might—or might not—be the Etowah site. The trouble is that such names are not specific or unique in their meaning, and the resemblance to Etiwaw or Etowah may be a trap rather than a clue to location. It is a problem that *Coosa* is duplicated many times in later records: for example, the Cusabo of South Carolina have a group by that name, including their own Etiwaw in 1716, while there are the Alabama–Georgia presumable descendants of Elvas's Coça and Ytaua (see Swanton 1946). Although I have elsewhere commented on the lack of claims to legitimacy by using old "imperial" titles, it may be a reflection of earlier glories of Coosa that the name was used in different locations later on. I rather suspect, however, that the situation is rather more one of fission and dispersal.

Near Coça was Ullibahali ("to share out the war" = *allies?*; Elvas 1557 [1993:94]). Other names include the "leaderless" Caluça (probably *Oka lusa*, "black water" in Chickasaw or Choctaw) (1557 [1993:120]; Oviedo 1547–1549 [1959:II:176]). Who these ferocious but leaderless people were is not at all clear; perhaps the Okelousa (Swanton 1911:302). In any case, they have nothing to do with the Calusa of Florida. When the fact is considered that these names were filtered through an extremely long chain of translations, I think it is clear that there is need for caution in making identifications based on apparent similarities to historical names, even if so many of them were not potentially common descriptive names.

Ethnic identification can be difficult. For example, while *Casqui* and *Pacaha* sound much like *Kaskinampo* and *Quapaw*, it is unlikely that the names are the same. Pacaha, especially, seems to have been Tunican—but almost certainly not Quapaw—in ethnic affiliation (e.g., Swanton 1946:53–54; see discussions in Young and Hoffman 1993, most particularly Rankin 1993:213–217). It is also quite likely that most larger chiefdoms were multiethnic. There is little reason to see "confederacies" in the Southeast as reflecting only historical conditions (cf. Galloway 1994).

Overall Comments on the de Soto Accounts. In this long but still abbreviated discussion, the salient features of the de Soto accounts need to be reiterated. There is relatively little direct indication of the power of chiefs, as opposed to one or another *claim* of power. Rank differences were clear, and there were certainly important differences in prestige and dignity. Authority, however, was another matter. Just as in the case of the Natchez Suns, the councils and other official persons of the chiefdoms had considerable influence on decisions made and actions taken.

The same kind of indefiniteness exists about the kinds of support given to chiefs in the earliest historical Southeast. I think here, as in many cases later, the evidence simply does not support any considerable degree of alienation of goods from their producers, even though it is clear that "gifts" or prestations are ordinary parts of social relations between persons of different rank. The great preponderance of these transfers of goods involve food and clothing, not items denoting prestige, *per se*.

As Galloway has noted (1995), claims of very great size for these historical chiefdoms need to be assessed carefully, but some chiefs may have had a loose kind of dominance over communities and other chiefs over considerable distances. However, even paramount chiefs often controlled relatively modest territories, especially when the real autonomy of technically subordinate chiefs is considered.

Stored food in these villages was clearly mobilized by chiefs in providing food and clothing to de Soto. At the same time, it is by no means the case that we can assume the *barbacoas* or other storage facilities from which these goods were taken were the chiefs' own. I see nothing in these accounts that indicates that all, or even most, stored goods were in the chiefs' *barbacoas*, as opposed to those of the individual households. Indeed, I think that the texts of the accounts suggest that the chiefs are drawing upon the whole stores of the community.

Of all the acts of the de Soto party, the ones that caused the greatest resistance were those involving human services. Neither bearers nor women were usually given freely. In most cases, the Spaniards were put off with references to what seem to have been chiefly councils. In many cases, direct military action or flight were chosen to avoid the claims. I think it is very clear from these responses that demands for labor services on the Spanish level were not only unusual to the Southeasterners, but also abhorrent.

Tristán de Luna y Arellano

From these various origins, a serious effort to establish a permanent colony for Spain in La Florida was undertaken by Tristán de Luna in 1559–1561 (Hudson et al. 1989a, 1989b; Priestley 1936; contemporary documents in Priestley 1928; Dávila Padilla 1596). Approximately 1500 settlers were involved in an expedition to establish a permanent Spanish presence in Florida in order to protect the Spanish claim and to assist those who might suffer shipwreck on the coast of Florida. The person named the new Governor of Florida was Tristán de Luna y Arellano, a veteran of the Coronado expedition. Christian Tlaxcalans from Mexico were included in the party as free settlers. The expedition landed at Ochuse, west of Apalachee, almost certainly Pensacola Bay (Hudson et al. 1989a). Between three and six of the de Luna expedition members had been with de Soto (Priestley 1936:49–50).

At Ochuse, only a few indigenous houses for "fishermen" were found on landing, and the plan for a fortified "town" of 80 or 100 persons was staked out (Priestley 1936:105). The missionaries with the expedition allowed the military to seize maize from the natives, but Fray Pedro de Feria refused to allow them to take permanent captives as translators (Velasco to Luna, October 25, 1559 in Priestley 1928:I:64–67, 1936:107–108). However, a hurricane struck the harbor less than a week after the landing, and most of the supplies shipped with the expedition were lost (1936:109). As a result, de Luna sent an expedition inland to attempt to find food at a town called Nanipacana, probably on the Alabama River, above Mobile Bay (Priestley 1936:111–112; cf. Hudson et al. 1989a:34–39). Nanipacana contained 80 houses, but many of the houses were in ruins (Priestley 1936:112). The move of the expedition to Nanipacana was delayed for various reasons, and by the time they got to the town, the residents had carried off their stores of food. A party was sent further up the

Alabama River, finding fields for the first 35 leagues, but all the people had gone into hiding at the approach of the Spaniards (Priestley 1936:121–122). At last, in desperate straits for food, it was decided to seek out the riches of Coosa,) and a party of 150 was sent out under the leadership of Mateo del Sauz. Beginning April 14, 1560, they carried few provisions, because they expected to be able to find Indian stores along the way (1936:122–123). This was not the case, so the 57 days to get to Coosa province proved very difficult. However, the later, more energetic return to Nanipacana by Cristóbol made the same journey in 10–12 days (1936:129), so clearly the slow pace of the movement was conditioned by other factors. A messenger from de Luna having reached them in the hands of an Indian courier, they managed at last to find some maize at a place called Caxiti (Casiste? Kashita?)—probably in Coosa "province," but elsewhere identified as in the province of "Taxcaluça" (the 1561 testimony of the soldiers in Priestley 1928:II:291)—and sent 80 *fanegas* of maize downstream on some expropriated canoes under the command of Juan de Porras. Finally, the expedition reached the first town of Coosa, a town called Onachiqui, 100 leagues from Nanipacana (Priestley 1936:124, but identified later in 1928:II:291 as Talis). The Spaniards camped outside the towns to avoid confrontations in their weakened condition (1936:127). I cannot find any unambiguous statement in the accounts that Coosa was in the exact same location as in the 1540s, in any case, and I do not think that it can simply be assumed.

The 1596 account of Dávila Padilla (1596:248ff., transl. by Mrs. Bandelier in Swanton 1922:231) stresses the disappointment of the expedition at the appearance of Coosa:

> It looked so much worse to the Spaniards for having been depicted so grandly, and they had thought it to be so much better. Its inhabitants had been said to be innumerable, the site itself as being wider and more level than Mexico, the springs had been said to be many and of very clear water, food plentiful and gold and silver in abundance, which, without judging rashly, was that which the Spaniards desired most. Truly the land was fertile, but it lacked cultivation. There was much forest but little fruit, because as it was not cultivated the land was all unimproved and full of thistles and weeds. Those they had brought along as guides, being people who had been there before, declared that they must have been bewitched when this country seemed to them so rich and populated as they had stated.

Unfortunately, these reminiscences of Fray Domingo de Anunciación, recorded 30 years after the fact by Dávila Padilla, have no corroboration from documents written at the time of the de Luna expedition (Priestley 1936:129–130). The extant contemporary documents say how unsuitable Coosa was for permanent settlement, but they do not suggest the shock indicated by Dávila (as noted by Priestley in his comments, 1928:xlii). As we saw in the de Soto accounts, town size was not necessarily very large, given some of the comments discussed earlier in the de Soto accounts on relative town size. Expectations had clearly been raised so that these starving European wanderers were disappointed, but letters written at the time are merely sober and do not support the excuses made long after this failed expedition. Indeed as Sauz noted in a letter sent to de Luna in July:

> Do not marvel that the country does not please the friars, for they are inclined to have their own way and not to do anything else; they are the ones who are the most discontented. I do

not think that this is because of lack of natives, but because the soil in this country is poor, and they do not share in the assistance which may come from New Spain.   July 6, 1560, in Priestley 1928:I:220–221[14]

Those who wish to see a considerable gap between de Soto's Coosa and de Luna's Coosa have, perhaps, accepted Dávila's comments too readily (e.g., Hudson et al. 1989a, 1989b). The simpler explanation is, as Priestley noted in his comments (1928:I:xli–xliii), that Coosa may have been the worse for wear 20 years after de Soto, but that it still had the same basic outlines of settlement as earlier, consisting of a dispersed group of smaller settlements that were inclusively called Coosa. As Anunciación himself and the others said in their letter of August 1, 1560:

> They all live together in little towns, for so far we have seen none which contains as many as one hundred and fifty houses, and very few which number above forty or fifty. They have winter and summer houses. The winter houses are all covered with earth, and they sow whatever they like over them. All the towns have a good-sized plaza outside the town, in which there is a pole like the *rollo*[15] of Spain; they are very tall, and they have them for their sports. There are some towns inclosed by a pair of walls as high as a man's stature, and although there must be something between them yet it is of no value [for defense]. There are temples in some of the towns, but they are as rudely constructed and as little frequented as is uncouth the religion which they practice in them. Priestley 1928: I:238–241.

Overall, this is not so different from earlier descriptions if the difference between the cant of conquest and the excuses of disappointed colonists are allowed for. The lack of corroboration of the Dávila Padilla account is notable, especially since such a wonderful description is given by him of warfare against the Napochies (Dávila Padilla 1596, translated in Swanton 1922:231). This is, unfortunately, another in which where one of the clearest statements supporting a point of view is hearsay evidence and unreliable, at best.

Less than 4 or 5 months were spent by the party under Sauz in Coosa (in Priestley 1928:II:305, 1936:132). During this time, according to the account of Dávila Padilla, the Spaniards had helped Coosa by attacking their "rebellious" former "tributaries," the Napochies (Dávila Padilla 1596:251ff.; Anunciación et al. 1560 in Priestley 1928:I:230,y 1936:130). In the contemporary records the following is all that is said:

> We are really deeply indebted to these Indians as far as we have seen up to the present; for if twenty or thirty or ten Indians are needed to build a camp or a house they give them, showing good will in the matter. It seems that certain [other] Indians have entered their lands, demanded them and usurped them, and in so doing have caused them injuries and vexations. They have occupied the roads of these natives and cut off their communications with their own related groups, preventing trade and communication between them; moreover, they have attacked them on the roads and given them many other troubles. [These Indians] asked us, as they were our friends, had given us of whatever they had, and had placed themselves under the protection of the king, Don Felipe our lord, that we would

---

[14] "Pero no se marauille V.S. no satisfazer A los frailes la t͠rra pues son Amigos de su propia boluntad y no cunplir con mas porq̃ ellos son los q̃ mas descontentos Estan no creo yo por falta de naturales syno por ser el suelo de la t͠rra Ruin y no partiçipar de los socorros q̃ de la nueba españa pueden" (Priestley 1928:I:220).

[15] A stone column in the plaza formerly used as a pillory and indicating local authority.

show them favor and aid so that those other Indians should not prevent their communication, trade, and intercourse thus with their own natural lord. For precisely these reasons had they come to serve us and trade with us, so that we might preserve to them the use of the roads and passes. In this connection they wanted to know whether we were going to deal with them in friendship and truth. So for this reason and for the others we decided to join together to give your Lordship a report of everything. It has appeared to us right to give them favor and help, in which we are influenced by many causes which move us thereto, which your Lordship will realize better.[16] Letter of Anunciación and others to Velasco, August 1, 1560 in Priestley 1928:I:231–233

The Napochies have not been identified but may have been groups that later joined with the Chickasaw. These are the same kinds of local rivalries and local assertions of autonomy and independence that we have already seen in the de Soto accounts.

After all, we may leave the starving and disgruntled colonists to the historians at this point, since the history of the abandonment of this venture is wrapped up in lawsuits and recriminations, and, in fact, we owe the survival of many of the contemporary documents to these circumstances (see Priestley 1928, 1936).

One last item of interest is that Velasco had by 1560 found an Englishman later married and a resident in France, who had been a cabin boy on an English vessel trading along the Atlantic Coast at latitude 37° to 33° in 1546. His brief statement is included in the de Luna papers (Priestley 1928:II:177–179).

Jean Ribault

In 1562, the first French Huguenot settlement was attempted (Ribault in Hakluyt 1582:79–98; also see Shipp 1881: 495–509). On the first contact, they were met by a chief who first sent a red leather "girdle" and then met the French seated upon bay branches scattered on the ground. Crossing the river of May (probably the St. John's), they then met with still another "king." Moving along the river, the French were given painted deerskins, food, and pearls—the same general kinds of greeting gifts that we have already seen in the earlier accounts. Copper gorgets were seen, but also gold and silver, presumably from Spanish wrecks. As the French moved along, they encountered some minor reluctance to allow them to enter villages, but they continued anyway.

---

[16] En ella Ansi q̃ Para la determinaçion Dello se terna cuidado de buscar y enquirir si ay cosa q̃ Conbenga al seruiº de dios y de Su magᵗ buscar sea de manera q̃ se cunpla lo q̃ .V.S. manda estos yndios berdaderamente les somos A cargo en lo q̃ hemos bisto asta agora porq̃ si son menester Veinte yndios o treinta o diez P̃a hazer algun Rancho o casa los dan y muestran en esto buᵃ boluntad/pareçe ser çiertos yndios hauerles Entrado En sus t̃ra y en pedirselas y husurparselas y sobre Esto hazerles molestias y bexaçiones y ocuparles los caminos y quitarles la comunicaçion de sus propios naturales y estorbarles el contratarse y comunicarse y sobre esto saltarles En los caminos y otras muchas molestias pidieronnos q̃ pues ellos heran nr̃o s Amigos y nosdauan de lo q̃ tenian y se hauian puesto debaxo del anparo del Rey don felipe nr̃o señor les diesemos fauor y hayuda para que aquellos yndios no les ynpidiesen la comunicaçion y trato y el con\232\bersarse ansi con su propio señor natural como por estas causas dexauan ni mas ni menos de uenirnos a seruir y ha contratarnos q̃ les Asegurasemos los caminos y pasos y que En esto querian conoçer sy tratabamos con ellos amistad y berdad asi q̃ Para esto y para lo demas nos Juntasemos a dar a .V. señoria Relaçion de todo a nos pareçido es Justo darles fauor y hayuda y en esta determinaçion estamos Resumidos por muchas causas que a ello nos mueben y V. señoria Entendera mejor (Priestley 1928:I:230–232).

At this point, the narrative of Laudonnière (1586; Shipp 1881:499ff.) continues the account of this early voyage, telling of the naming various rivers after those of France. Finally at Port Royal Sound, some local people fled at the French approach, but they finally were able to meet with local chiefs under an arbor and collected a couple of locals to go back to France, apparently with permission. At this point some information about Chigoula (≈ Chicora of the Ayllón expedition) was obtained, but as Swanton (1922:53) notes, it is difficult to make much of this in terms of ethnographic detail. Ribault left a small group of Frenchmen at a small fort (Charlefort on the Le Moyne map of 1591). A series of caciques were contacted and befriended by these Frenchmen, all within a relatively few leagues of Charles Fort; however, even some 30 Frenchmen found it difficult to obtain sufficient subsistence from the neighboring groups and were passed along to a more distant cacique. The description there indicates not only gifts of food but also of cloth (Shipp 1881:506). However, fire and dissension among the settlers led them to abandon their settlement on a pinnace they built, finally being rescued by an English vessel (1881:507–509).

René de Laudonnière

Laudonnière had been with Ribault, and returned to the South Atlantic Coast in 1564 (Laudonnière 1586, in Shipp 1881:510–543). In this case, the settlement was made in the St. John's area, not to the north. Initially landing some 10 leagues to the north of the St. John's, there was an amicable meeting with a local *paracoussy*, chief. Meetings with the local chiefs at the St. John's River were also friendly. The French were given painted skins by some, and "silver bullets" by one chief's wife and a bow and arrows by the chief himself (1881:512). The French built a small fort in the land of Satourioua (≈ Saturiwa), according to the French, a powerful local chief. Another local chief contacted was Olata Ouae Utina at Thimogoa (probably the Uriutina of Ranjel, the Timucua).

As in other cases, one of the immediate benefits sought by friendly chiefs was military assistance against their enemies. The chief Satourioua tried to enlist Laudonnière's assistance against Timucuans "eight or ten leagues away" (in Shipp 1881:516). The attack was made by Satourioua without French assistance with many of the enemy killed and scalps taken. At this point, Satourioua cooled toward the French, since they had not helped in the attack, and refused to give up some of the prisoners to Laudonnière. Laudonnière responded with a show of force at the house of Satourioua, obtaining some of the prisoners whom he sent back to Olata Ouae Utina with gifts and some ambassadors (1881:517). These in turn, were enlisted by Utina in an attack on Patanou (≈ Potano). After traveling all night, the Patanou were not surprised by the attack, but were driven off by their first encounter with firearms, so that many women and children were taken prisoner by Utina. After all this, Laudonnière became the object of a mutinous behavior. Some of his men also ran off to become freebooters, which stirred up the Spaniards with disastrous consequences when Menéndez later killed most of the French colonists. Before that happened, however, the French had become increasingly entangled in local warfare, aiding Utina in further attacks on Patanou. A couple of Spaniards were found living among groups some 40 leagues away, who were sent to Laudonnière on his offer to give gifts for them.

These men were survivors of shipwreck some 15 years before in the land of Calos (≈ Calusa). Gifts given to the French continued to be such items as food, deerskins, and pearls (1881:525). Some leaves of cassine (for black drink) were also given. It was also recorded that permanent settlements in this region were abandoned for the hunt during the months of January through March (1881:527). The French during and after this time became very short of food. Laudonnière tried to ensure supplies of food by taking Utina prisoner but without much luck and with the result of attacks by the Indians. During these difficulties, they were discovered by John Hawkins, an English explorer (see Hawkins 1565 [1932:122] for the English account). As Hawkins noted, "Notwithstanding the great want that the Frenchmen had, the ground doth yeeld victuals sufficient, if they would have taken paines to get the same; but they being souldiers desired to live by the sweat of other mens browes" (1565 [1932:124]). All the same, despite Laudonnière's suspicions of English motives, Hawkins was very generous. Things generally went poorly until Menéndez showed up and destroyed French settlement on this coast once and for all.

Pedro Menéndez de Avilés

In response to Laudonnière, Pedro Menéndez de Avilés set out to wipe out the French and, what was worse from his view, Protestant settlements on the coast of Florida. St. Augustine was founded in the course of these activities. The Spaniards landed troops and found help from two nearby chiefs who, at least by then, had become implacable enemies of the French (Menéndez 1565 [1964:81–82]). As in so many cases, the unwillingness or inability of the Europeans to feed themselves had soured what were initially reasonably amicable relations. The French were overwhelmed and the Lutherans slaughtered. Later encountering other French soldiers and shipwrecked Lutherans, Menéndez accepted their unconditional surrender and put them to death as well. So began the history of the Spanish settlement at St. Augustine, which Menéndez had established as his base.

Of more interest here are the developing relationships between this permanent Spanish settlement and the local Native Americans. After encountering the cacique Carlos (the Calusa), Menéndez defeated them, but established an alliance by marrying Carlos's sister. The house of Carlos was described as so large that 2000 men could gather in it without being crowded, and with large windows in the house from which Pedro Menéndez de Avilés could see his men (1565 [1964: 144–146]). "The cacique was in a large room, alone on a [raised] seat with a great show of authority, and with an Indian woman also seated, a little apart from him, on an elevation half an estado from the ground; and there were about 500 principal Indian men and 500 Indian women: the men were near him, and the women near her, below them" (1565 [1964: 146]). Interestingly, the woman with the cacique was his sister, not his wife (1565 [1964: 147]).

The Spaniards tried to make peace among various caciques, and they found that the news of the French defeat had spread widely "for in that land, news of the things that happen travels fast from cacique to cacique" (1565 [1964:172]). Their efforts to place missionaries ran into resistance:

> Macoya would not accept them [Christians to teach doctrine] but took the present. He sent to tell the Adelantado that he was his friend and held him to be his elder brother, which is all the obedience the caciques of Florida can give; but that if he came to his country he would hold him to be his enemy. Menéndez de Avilés 1565 [1964:207]

The subordinance of one cacique to another is phrased in terms of brothers, not strong relations of domination. In several cases, too, the forces assembled by caciques seem to be around 1000 men or less. Finally, it is from Menéndez's base that Juan Pardo was sent to explore inland (1565 [1964:211 and elsewhere]).

Hernando d'Escalante Fontaneda

The Fontaneda [a.k.a. Fontanedo] account further confirms the other descriptions of the Calusa region (excerpt in Shipp 1881:584ff; see Swanton 1922:28ff.). There were a series of autonomous or semiautonomous chiefdoms, and Cacique Carlos was paramount chief over a series of at least 28 "major" named villages and some 22 less important communities (Fontaneda in Shipp 1567 [1881:586]). Fontaneda, who lived as a captive in the Calusa locality for 15 years, spoke four of the local languages but not the language of the Ais and the Feaga, with whom he had not lived (Fontaneda in Shipp [1881:587]). The importance of fishing was noted. Recent accounts have illustrated how hierarchical structures can emerge and exist in the absence of agricultural production (for a more complete discussion of the Calusa, see Widmer 1988).

Juan Pardo

Menéndez sent Juan Pardo on two expeditions into the interior between A.D. 1566–1568, and these have become particularly important in recent efforts to locate the communities visited by both Pardo and de Soto (Hudson 1990:x–xi). Hudson has drawn together these documents with discussions in a model for ethnohistorical publication (1990, transcriptions, and translations by P. Hoffman). In this case, it makes more sense to refer the reader to that book than to replow the same ground. I am not in complete agreement in detail with Hudson's interpretation and not particularly concerned with locations of sites, but his discussion of the implications of the accounts in terms of power and levels of control does not need to be repeated (1990:61–124). We can simply summarize the indications that the leaders encountered by the Spaniards were at what we now call chiefly levels. The documents, in Hudson's words, do not "contain enough information to determine the relationships between a paramount chief and his tributaries, subjects, and allies" (1990:65). As Hudson also notes, the "magistrates" (those "principal men") or *ynahaes*, "probably mediated more than they commanded" (1990:65). I should also note, given my interpretation of tribute or prestations, that Bandera used the term *tributo* in the context of a group of subordinate chiefs (*oratas* and *ynahaes*), asking where they should send their *tributo* of food and deerskins (e.g., Bandera 1569:folio 17 in Hudson 1990:230). Of course, I would suspect that the Spanish understanding of these gifts may have been different than that of the chiefs involved. Certainly, as in earlier times, the key items for prestations were food and deerskins. There is no question that such gifts were made and expected, but we also need to be cautious in interpreting their meaning. We should also keep in mind that the paying of obeisance (*ubidiencia*) is described in European feudal terms (e.g., Bandera in Hudson 1990:231) that may or may not correspond to what was meant by the caciques in question—who had, of course, already had some nasty experience in what was expected by the European intruders.

Hudson suggests that Cofitachequi was *nouveau arriviste* among the chiefdoms of the region (1990:67, 70; see also DePratter 1994), and the persistence of the use of mounds is also documented (Hudson 1990:70). Without getting into the details on the location of Coosa in 1540 and in 1566,[17] we may note that the suggestion that the Napochies were "tributaries" of Coosa belongs to Dávila Padilla, not to contemporary documents (cf. 1990:102). There is, however, not the slightest doubt that military action against opposing chiefdoms was a feature of the times. As we have already seen, European military aid was often sought for such purposes, and various local subordinate chiefdoms cooperated against common enemies. The Pardo accounts also document that the Europeans were interfering in local politics, elevating their supporters in political power according to feudal models (e.g., 1990:140).

Finally, Hudson's chapter entitled "The Failure of Greater Florida" summarizes the conceptions and misconceptions of the early European explorers (1990). The lack of hierarchy in chiefly societies, and their general instability, made them poor objects of "indirect rule." The deep anger felt by Southeasterners about their treatment by Europeans, even more than 60 years after the event, is also documented in later accounts (cited in 1990:173). Such long persistence about the treatment given out by de Soto is itself a clue that power relationships in the aboriginal Southeast were neither so hierarchical nor so strong as believed by the European invaders. Against the idea of tribute in food, we have to record the resistance of local societies to continuing demands for food and other goods (1990:176). We also note again, that interference with local women was greatly resented and the cause of many difficulties, again suggesting that women were not commonly part of "tribute" or other obligations owed to chiefly superiors (1990:176).

Other Accounts

The pace of European intrusion continued. In 1567, there was a French response to the massacre of the French by Menéndez (Dominique de Gourgue in Shipp 1881:562–583), in which the local people this time cooperated with the French against the Spaniards. Gourgue managed to keep some Spaniards alive to be hung so on the same trees that had earlier been used to hang the French Protestants ([1881:579]). Clearly, cooperation against enemies in raids was not limited to Native

---

[17] I would, however, call the reader's attention to the Cherokee uses of Muskogean place names and indicate that I suspect the Cherokee movement into areas formerly occupied by Muskogean speakers was underway by the mid-16th century, based on my interpretation of what happened in shell gorget manufacture in the region. Such problems considerably complicate the interpretation of locations, especially given that an old place can keep the name of a town, still called by that name somewhere else.

Americans seeking aid against "tributaries." English and French raids on Spanish settlements and forts made the restriction of settlement to well-defended places such as St. Augustine necessary (Hudson 1990:177–181).

Lowery's discussion of the Spanish settlements covers the years between 1560 and 1574 (Lowery 1959 [reprint]). The later Spanish military expeditions are examined in Worth's treatment of the period between 1597 and 1628 (1994). It seems clear that by the end of the 16th century, Spanish expectations had become an important factor in the behavior of peoples in close contact with them, even when the relations were sometimes hostile (e.g., 1994:106). After the turn of the century, it was Spanish policy for a time to send missionaries into the interior without military guards (1994:111, also cf. 106).

After an effort in 1627 was aborted because of warfare and shortages of food, a small force of Spaniards and Indians under the leadership of Pedro de Torres returned to Cofitachiqui (Cofitachequi) in 1628, for the first time since the expedition of Jaun Pardo. They found a male paramount chief (cacique *mayor*) at Cofitachiqui. The other local caciques obeyed him and recognized "vassalage" (Worth 1994:114). The recovery of freshwater pearls was described, but as a by-product of eating the clams (1994:114–115).

Spanish attention around this time came to be focused on the threat to St. Augustine and southern Florida from new English settlements to the north, and we find little more about the interior after this point (Worth 1994:116).

17th- and 18th-Century Accounts of Native Politics

After the beginning of the 17th century, European intrusions increased dramatically. There are many sources, but these no longer describe what one could precisely call pristine circumstances, whatever that may be. We can, however, recognize now that the demographic collapse in much of the East was probably not so dramatic or sudden as formerly thought (e.g., Muller 1993b; Snow 1995).

For those desiring a chronicle, Barcia's paraphrases continue to cover events up to 1722 (Barcia 1723). Here we may note that "pacification" was a feature of these times, with British settlement on the north and French settlement in the Mississippi Valley. Political power in the Apalachee area and in Spanish Florida was described in letters and records of missionary activity there, as detailed by Hann (1988: especially Chapter 4).

Authority of the chiefs in Apalachee was not great, as noted in a letter of 1617:

> The governor...has decided...not to send any religious to Apalachee because it is so far away and because it is necessary to locate a settlement or blockhouse with soldiers in that land for support and so that there would be foodstuffs for the religious, especially because it is impossible to carry those provisions overland from...St. Augustine or to assist them or to support them with what they need. And for this [reason] the religious, who went to see the land have returned, in addition to the fact that some of the Indians obey their chiefs poorly, and the chiefs would like to gain control of their Indians with the aid and support of Your majesty. Florida Friars in Chapter, Letter to the King, January 17, 1617, in Hann 1988:12

Indeed, in the 17th-century Spanish missionary letters, the most common term used for chief *by the Apalachee* was the Arawakan cacique, not one of a series of local terms recorded (Hann 1988:99). This reflects Spanish usage, but it may also indicate that the positions of relative power here may owe as much to Spanish support as to local history. This was certainly the case later on, as one Spanish authority in 1677–1678 was given the right to "install in office or remove caciques" (Hann 1988:115). Some 11 Apalachee mission centers were largely autonomous. Hann states, "The meager evidence that exists suggests that the villages functioned as oligarchical democracies in which all members of the leadership were on something of an equal footing or, at least, no great gap separated the chief from the other more important leaders" (1988:100). In general, Apalachee political structure seems to have been close to that recorded for other Muskhogean speakers (e.g., in Swanton 1928a), perhaps with somewhat less formal distinctions among elite ranks. However, the nature of the mission relationships was such that any earlier titles such as war chiefs or the like were probably lost in Spanish ranks and titles (see Hann 1988:111). By the 1680s, the Apalachee were fairly integrated into an imperial political economy that had little to do with aboriginal politics. Compulsory labor and travel restrictions were enforced that could only be escaped by leaving areas controlled by the Spaniards. Despite the disadvantages of becoming a refugee, 1300 Apalachee apparently chose to follow an English raider away from their homes in 1704 to settle in South Carolina (1988:117, 294ff.).

To the north, on the Atlantic Coast, later accounts indicate that the nature of political power, even in the Chesapeake area, well away from "Mississippian" related historical groups, was similar to that elsewhere in the East:

> When they intend any warres, the Werowances [chiefs] usually have the advice of their Priests and Conjurors, and their allies, and ancient friends, but chiefly the Priests determine their resolution. Every Werowance, or some lustie fellow, they appoint Captaine over every nation. They seldom make warre for lands or goods, but for women and children, and principally for revenge. John Smith 1624:32–33

Captain Smith's account indicates not only the reliance of chiefly authority on others, but also the nature of conflict in these societies, at least as seen by a 17th-century Englishman. These power relationships are placed into a broader context by Hantman in a study relating Powhatan's tolerance of the Jamestown settlement to copper supplied as a symbolic material (1990). One may also note that if the Monacan society was hostile to Powhatan's growing confederacy, he may have also been willing to "tolerate" the English as potential military allies against them, as the behavior described by Hantman could also be interpreted (1990:686).

Even in French accounts, d'Iberville notes of the chiefs of the Ouma: "These chiefs have no more power over their people than do the chiefs of other nations on the confines of Canada. I have noticed solely among them a little more politeness." (1700 [1981:79]). Thus, we cannot simply dismiss all differences in chiefly actions and associations in the accounts as due to observer national origin.

While we may be skeptical of the "power" of chiefs, we have to remember that custom sometimes made chiefly status the focus of life and death actions, as in the following account of d'Iberville's visit to the Taensa:

> The night of the 16th–17th lightning struck the Taensas' temple, set it on fire, and burned it up. To appease the Spirit, who they say is angry, these Indians threw five little infants-in-arms into the temple fire. They would have thrown several others into it had it not been for three Frenchmen, who rushed up and prevented them from doing so. An old man, about sixty-five years old, who played the role of a chief priest, took his stand close to the fire, shouting in a loud voice, "Women, bring your children and offer them to the Spirit to appease him" Five of these women did so, bringing him their infants, whom he seized and hurled into the middle of the flames. The act of those women was considered by the Indians as one of the noblest that could be performed; accordingly, the Indian women followed that old man, who led them ceremoniously to the hut of the Indian who was to be made chief of the nation, for the chief had died a short time before. At the death of their chief, they observed the custom of killing fifteen or twenty men or women to accompany him, they say, into the other world and serve him. According to what they say, many are enraptured to be of that number. I have strong doubts about that. That old man whom I mentioned was saying that the Spirit had become angry because, at the death of last chief, no one had been killed to accompany him and that the chief himself was angry and had the temple burned. The old man accused the French of being the ones that had caused this calamity. d'Iberville 1700 [1981:129]

French accounts do indicate that great deference was given to the chiefs (e.g., du Ru 1700 [1935:27,35]), but such respect did not mean absolute command, nor the refusal of the chiefs to engage in manual labor (1700 [1935:49–50]). If French and Spanish accounts may have had an "autocratic" bias, it is interesting to compare later English accounts of chiefs, or other leaders.

Alsop's account (1666: [1967:367]) sums up one kind of English perception, or rather perplexion, of the native systems of government they encountered:

> Their Government is wrapt up in so various and intricate a Laborynth, the speculat'st Artist in the whole World, with his artificial and natural Opticks, cannot see into the rule or sway of these Indians to distinquish what name of Government to call them by; though Purchas in his Peregrination between London and Essex, (which he calls the Whole World) will undertake (forsooth) to make a Monarchy of them, but if he had said Anarchy, his word would have pass'd with a better belief. All that ever I could observe in them as to this matter is, that he is most cruelly Valorous, is accounted the most Noble: Here is very seldom ay creeping from a Country Farm, into Courtly Gallantry, by a sum of money; nor feeing the Heralds to put Dagers and Pistols into their Armes, to make the ignorant believe that they are lineally descended from the house of the Wars and Conquests; he that fights best carries it here.

Of special interest are Bartram's and Adair's detailed 18th-century accounts of chiefdoms among Muskhogeans to the north and east of the Natchez. We have seen that these justly famous accounts do not represent circumstances that were novel to their times, but describe kinds of leadership that are well documented back to the earliest records. Here is one of the paradoxes of the historical accounts. The Natchez were only a small group by Southeastern standards, yet they were supposed to have divine, autocratic sun kings, at least according to the French. Kroeber singles out the Natchez as a "climax" expression of their culture area (1939:62ff.). On the other hand, the Creeks, Choctaws, and Chickasaws—who lived in polities that were historically as much as 10 times larger than the Natchez—are described as less organized, somehow even parliamentary, as seen in contemporary British accounts. What a coincidence—the autocratically organized French contacted autocratic Native Americans while the parliamentary British found Native Americans with systems like their own! Even with an English, "parliamentary" bias, these latter accounts of the Muskhogeans are useful as a counterbalance to the biases in other directions in descriptions of the Natchez. Where as the French accounts *implicitly* indicate the importance of the councils, the British accounts are explicit:

> This natural constitution is simply subordinate; and the supreme, sovereign or executive power resides in a council of elderly chiefs, warriors, and others, respectable for wisdom, valour and virtue. W. Bartram 1791[1928:388]

The chief is explicitly defined by Bartram (1791[1928:388]) in terms of relationships with the councils.

> At the head of this venerable senate, presides their mico or king, which signifies a magistrate or chief ruler: the governors of Carolina, Georgia, &c. are called micos; and the king of England is called Ant-apala-mico-clucco, that is, the great king, over or beyond the great water.
>
> The king, although he is acknowledged to be the first and greatest man in the town or tribe, and honoured with every due and rational mark of love and esteem, and when presiding in council with a humility and homage as reverent as that paid to the most despotic monarch in Europe or the East, and when absent, his seat is not filled by any other person, yet he is not dreaded; and when out of council, he associates with the people as a common man, converses with them, and they with him, in perfect ease and familiarity.

This is different from the Natchez in that we do have good reasons to believe that the treatment of the Natchez chief by the nonelite was more deferential than among other groups (as in du Ru 1700), but we may ask whether destabilization by warfare had weakened the traditional chief, especially at the expense of war leaders.

> The mico or king, though elective, yet his advancement to that supreme dignity must be understood in a very different light from the elective monarchs of the old world, where the progress to magistracy is generally effected by schism and the influence of friends gained by bribery, and often by more violent efforts; and after the throne is obtained, by measures little better than usurpation, he must be protected and supported there, by the same base means that carried him thither. W. Bartram 1791[1928:388–389]

The nature of economic relationships between the chiefs and the people were described in detail:

> and every man carries off the fruits of his own labor, from the part first allotted to him, which he deposits in his own granary; which is individually his own. But previous to their carrying off their crops from the field, there is a large crib or granary, erected in the plantation, which is called the king's crib; and to this each of the family carries and deposits a certain quantity, according to his ability or inclination, or none at all if he so chooses: this in appearance seems a tribute or revenue to the mico; but in fact is designed for another purpose, i.e. that of a public treasury, supplied by a few and voluntary contributions, and to which every citizen has the right of free and equal access, when his own private stores are consumed; to serve as a surplus to fly to for succour; to assist neighboring towns, whose crops may have failed; accommodate strangers, or travelers; afford provisions or supplies, when they go forth on hostile expeditions; and for all other exigencies of the state: and this treasure is at the disposal of the king or mico; which is surely a royal attribute, to have an exclusive right and ability in a community to distribute comfort and blessings to the necessitous. W. Bartram 1791[1928:401]

Adair also described the chief working with others in ordinary, domestic activities and—in passing—commented on what he felt to be inflation in the earlier accounts of the Virginia political system:

> At the dawn of it [the appointed day for planting], one by order goes aloft and whoops to them with shrill calls. "that the new year is far advanced,—that he who expects to eat, must work,—and that he who will not work, must expect to pay the fine according to old custom, or leave the town, as they will not sweat themselves for an healthy idle waster" At such times, may be seen many war-chieftains working in common with the people, though as great emperors, as those the Spaniards bestowed on the old simple Mexicans and Peruvians, and equal in power, (i.e. persuasive force) with the imperial and puissant Powhatan of Virginia, whom our generous writers raised to that prodigious pitch of power and grandeur to rival the Spanish accounts. Adair 1775:405–406

These accounts give some flavor of the contradictions between the French and British accounts. The Natchez Sun is autocratic, the Muskhogean Mico a revered first among equals. The largest native societies in Eastern North America had supposedly "simple" organization, whereas tiny little groups of a few thousand somehow were supposed to have maintained complex, centralized political structures. Does not this somehow seem a little backward? Of course, neither the Mico nor the Great Sun can be taken to have been exactly as they were described. Sometimes the French accounts *were* taken at face value by British contemporaries. For example, Hutchins commented that "this country [the Natchez] was once famous for its inhabitants, who from their great numbers, and the state of society they lived in, were considered as the most civilized Indians on the continent of America" (Hutchins 1784:50). However, we note that Adair was scornful of the earlier British descriptions of Powhatan, which he felt were inflated for political reasons "to rival the Spanish accounts." We simply *must* consider the possibility that the level of political organization in the historical Southeast was much the same across the entire area. Large and small groups alike in the Southeast were in the general range of size for chiefly kinds of societies (say, 8^4–8^5 persons). At the bottom end, societies that became too small merged with other groups in order to maintain their social and political organization (e.g., Brain 1982; Muller 1994; M. T. Smith 1987).

In general, closer attention to detail in the historical accounts warrants the need for considerable caution in interpreting the historical data purely in terms of degeneration with a few survivals of grander times. To mention just a few other problems in addition to those already illustrated, these interpretations pay no heed to the possibility that European influence may explain such elevation of the chief as actually occurred—there is a real possibility that postcontact polities were undergoing secondary state formation under European pressures (e.g., see Gearing 1962; Hunt 1940; F. Jennings 1975).

Other Observations

Before ending this chapter, one last set of observations related to status differences in the East needs to be discussed. An account of chiefdom status (Smith and Hally 1992) has concluded that (1) the 16th-century Spaniards were treated as paramount chiefs by the persons they encountered, and (2) we can therefore conclude how paramount chiefs were treated by examining the greetings made to the Spaniards. There is some truth to both of these points, yet it is not at all clear how much of the treatment of Spaniards was the "business as usual" of paramountcy and how much was novel and introduced by the particular and peculiar demands of the Spanish invaders.

Greeting strangers. There is a surprising consistency over Eastern North America and through time in the behavior associated with greeting of strangers. Some of these records have been interpreted as indicating aspects of chiefly behavior during the initial contact period (Smith and Hally 1992), but there are some problems in interpreting these behaviors as purely chiefly or as indicating strong social differentiation. First of all, many of the features that seem, at first glance, to be indications of strong social differentiation—such as eminent persons being borne upon the shoulders of others, are seen, for example, in Cartier's visit to the tribally organized Hochelaga in the Montreal locality in 1535 ([1922:61]; also Cartier 1580:45–60). Similarly, the fairly unorganized groups in the West show up with some of the same forms of greeting that have been documented in the de Soto and later 16th-century explorations (e.g., in the various La Salle accounts). What are the bare essentials of Eastern greeting behavior, then?

Beverley, in speaking of early 18th-century Virginia groups, pretty well sums up the script that was followed in greeting persons perceived to be of some higher rank (but not necessarily *paramount* rank):

> They have a remarkable way of entertaining all strangers of condition, which is performed after the following manner: First, the king or queen, with a guard and a great retinue, march out of the town, a quarter or half a mile, and carry their mats for their accommodation. When they meet the strangers, they invite them to sit down upon those mats. Then they pass the ceremony of the pipe, and having spent about half an hour in grave discourse, they get up, all together, and march into the town. Here the first compliment is to wash the courteous traveler's feet; then he is treated at a plentiful entertainment, served up by a great number of attendants; after which he is diverted with antique Indian dances, performed both by men and women, and accompanied with great variety of wild music. At this rate he is regaled till bedtime, when a brace of young, beautiful virgins are chosen to wait upon him that night for his particular refreshment. These damsels are to undress this happy gentleman, and as soon as he is in bed, they gently lay themselves down by him, one on one side of him, and the other on the other. They deem it a breach of hospitality, not to submit to everything he desires of them. This kind ceremony is used only to men of great distinction—and the young women are so far from suffering in their reputation for this civility, that they are envied for it by all the other girls, as having had the greatest honor done them in the world.

With all visitors, Beverley (1722 [1855:143–144]) notes the test of peace or war using the calumet:

> They have a peculiar way of receiving strangers, and distinguishing whether they come as friends or enemies, though they do not understand each other's language: and that is by a singular method of smoking tobacco, in which these things are always observed:
>
> 1. They take a pipe much larger and bigger than the common tobacco pipe, expressly made for that purpose, with which all towns are plentifully provided; they call them the pipes of peace.
> 2. This pipe they always fill with tobacco, before the face of strangers, and light it.
> 3. The chief man of the Indians, to whom the strangers come, takes two or three whiffs, and then hands it to the chief of the strangers.
> 4. If the stranger refuses to smoke in it, 'tis a sign of war.
> 5. If it be peace, the chief of the strangers takes a whiff of two in the pipe.

The pipe then passes alternatively down the line in order of status until all have smoked and then the party march into town after a little friendly discourse.

What is remarkable is the long-term and widespread persistence of something like these behaviors over many different kinds of social formations in the East (N.B., not just the Southeast). The calumet itself was probably a late addition to greeting behavior (I. Brown 1989). However, Galloway (1995:108) has suggested that hostility toward the earlier European explorers explained the lack of reference to the item and institution, but the mention of mats, which also were symbols of peaceful intentions, is pervasive in the accounts. The patterns involved the following features:

1. Being met some short distance outside the town by the local leadership.

They came with many attendants, hailed from far off for safety. Verrazzano 1524 [1881]

In the de Soto accounts there were also several instances of important persons coming outside their town. This was the case, for example, at Cofitachequi (Oviedo 1547–1549 [1959:II:167]) and Coça (de Biedma 1544 [1993:232]).

The King's brother came—"The maner of his comming was in this sort: hee left his boates altogether as the first man did a little from the shippes by the shore, and came along to the place over against the ships, followed with fortie men." Barlowe 1584 [1932:231]

We passed on a hill a village of Chachouma, and about 3 arpents [4 kilometers] from there we entered that of the Chicacha. They came before us and the savages took the packs of our Frenchmen and conducted us to the chief's cabin. Tonty 1702 [1982:168–169]

the chiefs of the Puans came out three leagues from their village to meet the French with their peace calumets, Guigna 1728 [1861:168]

2. The local leaders and the visitors may be carried to and from the community by bearers.

That done, the Lord and King of the countrey was brought upon 9 or 10 mens shoulders Cartier 1535 [1932:61; 1580:52]

when a chief approached, borne on the back of another Indian, and covered with a painted deer-skin. A great many people attended him, some walking in advance, playing on flutes of reed.

We traveled without seeing any natives who would venture to await our coming until the seventeenth day of June, when a chief approached, borne on the back of another Indian, and covered with a painted deer-skin. Nuxez Cabeça de Vaca 1542 [1871:31]

In the de Soto accounts, the caciques were sometimes borne on litters by principals or others as at both Cofitachequi and Coça (Oviedo 1547–1549 [1959:II:167]; de Biedma 1544 [1993:232]).

[Frenchmen came to a village on St. John's day, and a calumet was brought out] "They rubbed us when we came up and then rubbed themselves, a mark of esteem among the Indians. They took us on their shoulders and carried us to a chief's cabin. There was a hill of potter's clay to get up and the one that carried sank under his burden. I was afraid that he would let me fall and so I got down in spite of him and went up the hill, but as soon as I got to the top I had absolutely to get on his back and be carried to the cabin." St. Cosme 1699 [1861:71]

We arrived, before the chief, at his cabin; his weakness would not permit him to accompany us. He had to be carried part of the way. [First, note that the carrying may well be because of status, not illness; second, ditto for lying down.] du Ru 1700 [1935:35]

3. Attendants accompany the leader. In the de Soto accounts, the *principales*, as we saw, were nearly ubiquitous in those cases where there were rank organizations (e.g., Oviedo 1547–1549 [1959:II:173]). At Tascaluca, for example, various *principales* were closer or farther from the cacique according to rank (Elvas 1557 [1993:96]). The earlier sections discussed many of these instances in the "greeting" context.

> the cacique was in a large room and there were about 500 principal Indian men and 500 Indian women: the men were near him, and the women near her, below them. Menéndez de Avilés 1565 [1964:146]

> [The king's brother's wife had 40–50 attendants] Barlowe 1584 [1932:233]

> The chief who came some time after was dressed in a fine white cloth or blanket. He was proceded by two men, carrying fans of white feathers. A third carried a copper plate, and a round one of the same metal, both highly polished. He maintained a very grave demeanor during this visit, which was, however, full of confidence and marks of friendship. Le Clercq 1690 [1903:175]

> The chiefs have their valets and officers who follow them and serve them everywhere. They distribute their favors and presents at will. Le Clercq 1690 [1903:186–187]

> [A woman chief] had the first place in all the councils, and when she walked she was always preceded by four young men who sang and danced the calumet to her. Gravier 1701 [1861:144]

4. The parties are seated on mats (which symbolize peace). As we saw in earlier sections, the de Soto party found Tascaluca outside his house on mats and cushions in plaza (Oviedo 1547–1549 [1959:II:173]).

> The Alabamas call their country the white land, or the land of peace, and they rest on their mats, which means that they attack no one. This is an allegorical way of announcing to all the earth's nations that the war hatchet is buried and that trade can be carried on safely in Alabama territory. Bossu 1768 [1962:144]

> and they laide him down upon the foresaid mats neere to the Captaine, Cartier 1535 [1932:61, 1580:52]

> When he came to the place his servants spread a long matte upon the ground, on which he sate downe, and at the other ende of the matte foure others of his companie did the like, the rest of his men stood round about him, somewhat a farre off: when we came to the shore to him with our weapons, hee never mooved from his place, nor any of the other foure, nor never mistrusted any harme to be offred from us, but sitting still he beckoned us to come and sit by him, which we performed Barlowe 1584 [1932:231]

> The Indian Kings sate on a Form, and we sate on another over against them; Budd 1685:29

> [La Salle was too fatigued to go to town, so the chief sent a] "master of ceremonies" with 6 men, prepared a place with a "delicately worked cane-mat". Le Clercq 1690 [1903:175]

> They sat on dressed cane mat, corn seasoned with dried peaches. Gravier 1701 [1861:12]

> They made us sit on some mats near the cabin. The chief was seated there & an Englishman that I had trouble recognizing for one. Tonty 1702 [1982:168–169]

5. A special shelter may be used. The *balcões* or *balcónes* mentioned in several of the de Soto accounts appear to have been structures used for welcoming guests (Elvas 1557 [1993:75]; Oviedo 1547–1549 [1959:II:173]), although they were located near plazas, not built outside the town. The *balcões* surely must have been like "square ground cabins," such as those illustrated by Swanton (1946: Plate 59:1, Plates

99–104), or similar structures added onto a house, not balconies in the modern sense.[18]

> His house was hung round with tapestry of feathers of diverse colors, the height of a pike; moreover, the place where the king took his rest was covered with white coverlets embroidered with devices of very witty and fine workmanship, and fringed round about with a fringe dyed in the color of scarlet. Ribault 1562 [1881:505–506]

> They found the Paracoussy (chief) under an arbor with 80 others. Laudonnière 1564:511

> Meanwhile they had prepared a place under the war-chief's scaffold; [*sous l'eschaffault du chef des guerriers*] which was neat, carpeted with rush mats, and the sachems [in French, *les anciens*] were seated around them first, then the braves [*guerriers*], then the people in crowds. Marquette 1678 [1903:50, 255]

6. Sometimes, subordinate leaders are called in. The de Soto accounts abound with examples of neighboring or subordinate caciques who show up at various towns after de Soto's arrival. For example, at Cofaqui, they were met by the principal men; and cacique Patofa and another "principal" came as well (Oviedo 1547–1549 [1959:II:165]). In other cases,

> after he was come home to his house he sent messengers to eighteen or twenty villages of other kings, his vassals, and summoned them to be present at the feast and dances which he proposed to celebrate because of his victory. Laudonnière 1586:[1881:527]

7. Much discourse takes place, and sometimes the calumet ceremony is performed. Although there is no indication of the calumet ceremony as such, the pattern of long discourse and orations at first meeting is reasonably clear in the de Soto accounts from contexts surrounding events at Tascaluca and other towns:

> and being set hee made all signes of joy and welcome, striking on his head and his breast, and afterwards on ours, to shew wee were all one, smiling and making shewe the best he could of all love, and familiaritie. After hee had made a long speech unto us, wee presented him with divers things, which hee received very joyfully, and thankefully. None of his companie durst speak one word all the time: only the foure which were at the other ende, spake one in the others eare very softly. Barlowe 1584 [1932:231]

St. Cosme (1699:71) tells of "singing" the calumet, sitting on bear skins, pottery drums, and gourd rattles.

> Our Chacta notable [considerable] made his speech Tonty 1702 [1982:168–169]

> [The 80-year-old chief of Cadodaquious] "le plus éloquent haragueur de ces nations." La Harpe 1719 [1886:261]

8. Gifts are given or exchanged, in the north, sometimes wampum, but often food and clothing. In the de Soto descriptions, the gifts were very rarely items of so-called prestige goods. Rather, as discussed in detail in the section on prestations, gifts were mostly food and clothing.

---

[18] In any case, *balcão* should not be taken to require multiple stories (cf. Hann's note, Clayton et al. 1993:95), since it may simply mean a platform or scaffold projecting from the wall of a structure (It. *balco* or *palco* + *-one*).

After which conference the said Agona tooke a piece of tanned leather of a yellow skin edged with Esnoguy (which is the thing they esteeme most precious, as wee esteeme gold) which was on his head in stead of a crowne, and he put the same on the head of our Captaine, and tooke from his wrists two bracelets of Esnoguy, and put them upon the Captaines armes, colling him about the necke, and shewing him great signes of joy: Cartier 1541 [1932:95]

The chief sent a red leather belt as a gift, also painted skins, pearls, turquoises, and so on (Ribault 1562:496–7):

[given a skin] "richly painted" by the chief Laudonnière 1564 [1881:512]

[reciprocation] "wee presented him with divers things, which hee received very joyfully, and thankefully…"

[King's brother given gifts and also gave gifts to the others sitting on the mat, but the king's brother presently arose and took it all for himself] Barlowe 1584 [1932:231]

They had prepared four Belts of Wampum, (so their current money is called, being Black and White Beads made of a Fish shell) to give us as Seals of the Covenant they made with us; Budd 1685:29

and some bear meat as a refreshment, Guigna 1728 [1861:16]

9. Entertainment and dancing usually follows. The de Soto accounts indicate dancing at greeting ceremonies. For example, the cacique *grande* of Uzachile sent messengers playing flutes for ceremony (Oviedo 1547–1549 [1959:II:160], see also 173). Menéndez de Avilés (1565 [1964:146]) recorded that 500 Indian girls sang and others danced.

And the next day we were received by that small nation (très peu nombreux) amid several discharges of a few guns and amid great demonstrations of joy. Guigna 1728 [1861:168]

10. Sexual partners may be provided for high-status individuals. As already noted (at the beginning of this section), Beverley (1722 [1855:145–146]) indicated that young women were provided as sexual partners, but *voluntary* provision of sexual partners is not clearly attested in most sources, especially the earlier ones. The 16th-century Spanish demands for women are not definitely part of native practice (as also noted by Smith and Hally 1992:104, and as we saw in the discussion of labor demands by the Spaniards). Indeed, women usually kept away from the European intruders. Along the northern coastal areas, early 17th-century accounts indicate that men were "jealous" of their women, which may indicate response to earlier exploitation by European fishing vessels (Pring 1603 [1932:348]; Rosier 1605 [1932:368]). Cavelier notes that a group had left for fear the "soldiers would tamper with the women" (1687 [1861:41]). In other cases, women took flight upon sighting the French (Le Clercq 1690 [1903:173]). Although sexual demands are not uncommon in asymmetrical relationships worldwide, we have little certainty what normal practice was in this regard in the early historical East.

Other aspects. In some areas, there were other parts to the script such as weeping among the Caddo (Elvas 1557 [1993:126]; also see Early 1993a:71 and other references in Young and Hoffman 1993). However, my general point here is that the chiefly interactions described in the de Soto accounts, and later, all share a common framework that is far more widespread than are hierarchical societies in the Southeast.

In these accounts, we see many of the same elements of greeting provided to the Spaniards in the 16th-century accounts. Certainly, the Spaniards were treated as persons of note, but these behaviors were not limited only to "paramount chiefs" or even "chiefs," but were applied to any 'notable' persons. Similar patterns occur among quite nonhierarchically organized groups. Although Lankford (1984, 1988) and Smith and Hally (1992) are probably correct in linking elaborate greetings to high status, it is less clear that the character of the European–Native American interactions in relation to forcible extraction of resources is something that can be pushed back into normal conditions of subordination in the East. It is precisely in the use of force to extract goods and services that we run afoul of the essentially feudal character of European practice, and our inability to distinguish the elements in the European accounts that echo their own still-feudal relationships to king and nobility rather than normal Southeastern practice.[19] We must look closely at the behavior recounted in the various narratives, but we must also remember how negative the response of the indigenous societies was to Spanish demands, as well as to later demands by other European groups. Contrary to the impression of normalcy given in Smith and Hally's summary of the Spanish invasion, I believe accounts of towns abandoned and even burned in advance of the Spaniards, the usually hostile reaction to Spanish demands for women, and the reluctance to pay "tribute" suggest that the Spaniards were introducing European, even feudal, elements into these relationships that were neither familiar nor normal demands from the native South-easterners' points of view. In general, we must look more closely at issues of what actual behaviors were associated with chiefs in the Southeast rather than what was understood or said by the observers.

3. CONCLUSIONS

Well, enough is enough. The historical accounts provide a rich and varied set of examples of Native American life and politics from the 16th to the 19th centuries. Far from being such an impoverished record that we can draw no conclusions from it, we have a rich set of empirical observations that we can work with. A great deal needs to be done in developing a more coherent model for historical social formations in the East, but our purpose here was to provide a small correction to the too prevalent view that Native Easterners were "degenerate" and that their societies are somehow less relevant for the understanding of the prehistoric period than are more recently stud-ied societies in Oceania, for example. Some recent efforts have used Eastern historical sources to reach similar, if somewhat differently theoretically based conclusions (e.g., Anderson 1994b; McKivergan 1995). Since the bulk of this chapter was prepared, I have obtained Galloway's discussion of Choctaw "genesis" (1995). This treatment rec-ognizes the importance of the Choctaw in the colonial period, but I feel that perhaps

---

[19] See also comparative discussion in Jennings 1975:Appendix, especially 333-335, where Jennings talks about the character of "chartered conquest" and the parallels to the conquest of Ireland, in relation to English expansion.

the Spanish disappointment over not finding state systems in the region leads Gallo-way too far away from appreciating the chiefly structures that characterized both the prehistoric and historical periods (e.g., 1995:111ff.). I particularly am reluctant to see a wide gap between paramount chiefdoms and confederations.

It should be noted that the view of historical chiefdoms here does not corre-spond to the genesis of "Leviathan," the emergence of statelike power, hypothesized by Pauketat (1994) for the Cahokian polity of Mississippian times. For now, I will just say that the argument he makes is logically consistent *if* one assumes that power in any Mississippian society was sufficient to represent real control of production, and so on. I have to register my lack of conviction that the material evidence from the American Bottom supports interpretations of "hegemony," for example. Later chapters will deal with political control in Mississippian societies at greater length.

This is *not*, of course, an application of direct historical approaches in which historical materials are used to "interpret" prehistoric materials, historically tracing back markers of material connections through time. Indeed, the history of this chap-ter goes the other way, since it was empirical data on Lower Ohio Valley settlement that first led me to conclusions about the scale and economic structure of Mississip-pian society. That, in turn, led me to an examination of historical societies. With that came the realization, expressed at length here, that the complexity of the historical groups had been as much underrated, as had been the opposite case in terms of the prehistoric societies. Unlike the old idea of continuity proposed in the 1900s, the similarities this time can be a conclusion, not a presumption, as we shall see.

Chapter 3

Natural and Cultural Basis of Mississippian

> These were simple hunting folk of
> the forest; there had been a long
> regression from Hopewell grandeur
> Silverburg 1968:292

1. INTRODUCTION

Mississippian did not spring full blown out of Hopewell or arise out of the foam of the rivers. The development of Mississippian depended upon a series of natural and cultural conditions that formed the milieu of its emergence. No one, certainly not in the beginning, set out to become Mississippian. Instead, if they were like most people at most times, they were trying their level best to stay what they already were, only maybe a little fatter and happier. This chapter outlines the natural and cultural conditions of that failing struggle.

Before anything more, let us define *Late Woodland*. In some ways this is a trivial task, and in other ways, very difficult. *Late Woodland* is no more than a name given to Eastern archaeological complexes, especially ones that date between Middle Woodland and the beginnings of Mississippian. Historically, *Late Woodland* was a unit of the old "Midwestern Taxonomic System" and still retains much of the baggage of the trait-list approach. Its "type artifacts" were and are cord-marked, grit-tempered, mostly conoidal pottery vessels, and certain smaller projectile points. However, these "diagnostic" artifacts do not adequately define complexes throughout the East, and most especially do not define taxonomically clear *Southeastern* complexes. For that reason, I once tried to substitute the term *Sedentary* for *Woodland* in pan-Eastern periods (Muller 1978a). That term did not catch on despite a few distant echoes, so I shall loosely use *Late Woodland Period* here to refer to this time period, regardless of ceramic or other attributes. A *period* definition dates Late Woodland between ca. A.D. 500 and A.D. 900, although

117

materials called *Late Woodland* in terms of stages, existed no less than 100 years before and after these dates in some locations. Table 3.1 shows an approximate breakdown by arbitrary temporal segments, but the decisions about where to cut the period boundary between, say, Late Archaic and Early Woodland can only be arbitrary and for the sake of convenience in discussion. They are not necessarily meant to be representative of significant changes in any particular social systems.

Another term that has to be dealt with is *Emergent Mississippian*. Frankly, I wish we could have avoided this one altogether, as we somehow managed to do for over 100 years. As a matter of nomenclature, I think it a mistake to use teleological names that imply what something will become. In this case, it is hard for me to see that *Early Mississippian* was inadequate for those complexes that might, with some justice, be called *Emergent*. As for the others, former Late Woodland complexes in various areas are relabeled *Emergent*, because not to do this is to accept, *de facto*, claims of developmental priority for areas where so-called *Emergent* complexes have already been defined. Is there any doubt that many of these societies were developing into Mississippian? No, but is there any reason to see them as emerging rather than evolving? Was colonial Massachusetts "emergent Federalist"? Well, enough grumping. Today, for better or worse, *Emergent Mississippian* is used to refer to a stage made up of formerly Late Woodland period complexes that were becoming more hierarchical in political structure and were developing new subsistence strategies. That is to say, Emergent Mississippian complexes show some combination of elements of Mississippian—ceramic styles, mound construction, and production techniques—without necessarily having all the features that characterize full-blown Mississippian as we know it in the 11th to 13th centuries.

As a developmental "stage," *Late Woodland* itself was used to describe, in archaeology's Culture-Historical Period, what were commonly seen as degenerate cultures between the two culture-historical "climaxes" of Hopewell and Mississippian (but see Hall 1980). We shall see that this was arguably a misrepresentation of the events of Late Woodland times. Not the least of the problems was a failure to recognize how early sedentism and many other features were already present in the more southern societies after the fifth century.

The developmental parallels of a supposedly degenerate Late Woodland stage to contemporary Dark-Age European societies are rarely explicitly discussed, but nevertheless implicitly influenced interpretation of Late Woodland. Of course, comparisons are made insofar as climatological correlations are concerned (e.g., Bryson and Murray

Table 3.1. Temporal Periods in the East

Names	Other names	Representative cultures	Dates
Historic	Contact	Choctaw, Creek	A.D. 1520–
Mississippian	Late Prehistoric	Cahokia, Etowah	A.D. 900–1520
Late Woodland	Late Sedentary	Lewis, Baytown	A.D. 500–900
Middle Woodland	Hopewellian	Hopewell, Marksville	300 B.C.–A.D. 500
Early Woodland	Early Sedentary	Adena, Tchefuncte	1000–300 B.C.
Late Archaic		Poverty Point, Indian Knoll	4000–1000 B.C.
Middle Archaic			6000–4000 B.C.

1977), for example. Paradoxically, it seems hard to remember that Late Woodland complexes were the milieu in which Mississippian-period social formations developed. There is little doubt that northern temperate zone peoples were undergoing stresses in the fifth and sixth centuries. The roughly synchronous "decline" of historically documented cultures from Asia to Europe at this time is well known, but the causes of the great displacements is not so well understood. Perhaps synchronicity is just coincidence, but climate changes probably played some role, even if different peoples responded in their own ways to these changes. Each area—even each locality—had its own reasons, its own particular causes, its own course of development to be sure, but to shun comparison leads to unnecessary particularism.

Of course, Eurocentric views of the Dark Ages overlook that this was a period of persistence of the Eastern Roman Empire and of the rise of Islamic civilization. Although we may be impressed by apparent synchronicity of widespread cultural developments (such as those characterized by Kroeber 1944), we must not forget two important lessons from the Old World chronicles: (1) One area's "decline" often coincides with "florescence" elsewhere, and (2) the foundations for any cultural "climax" are necessarily to be found its preceding, "nonclimactic" period. We need to remember this as we look at developments in different parts of the Southeast. The very idea of "climax" is part of the problem, rather than a useful description of a historical event. The egalitarian attitudes that are held in nonranked societies also lead to a scarcity of the fancy artifacts that may be used to symbolize social differentiation. As a result, these kinds of social formations are less attractive to the connoisseur and are unlikely to be characterized as climaxes, even if they were in fact societies with better social and physical conditions for the mass of people.

Late Woodland has been considered almost quintessentially "tribal," just as Mississippian has been labeled as "chiefly." Our present common language concepts of both *tribe* and *chiefdom* are partly based on Eastern historical social groups, so the terms are more appropriate here than many other places. As we have seen, *tribes, chiefdoms,* and so on, are words that create problems. As noted in Chapter 1, they should be used only as approximate labels of convenience, and not as implying that some particular cluster of attributes must be present (see Fried 1975, 1978; Friedman 1975; Friedman and Rowlands 1978; Sahlins 1968; Sturtevant 1983). I and many others still use terms such as *tribe* for lack of anything better, while recognizing that it would be nice to have better terms to describe social formations that are neither simple bands nor class-based states. In using such terminology, we have to avoid begging the question. I also want to avoid compounding the problem by using still finer typologies distinguishing *Big Men* and *Great Men*, and so forth.

Some historical "Woodland" social formations were relatively large and permanently settled groups like the Iroquois. Others were highly dispersed and mobile. Although these groups may have many features in common with prehistoric Late Woodland groups, great caution is necessary in making comparisons because our evidence for the archaeological Late Woodland period suggests similar variability in prehistoric times. Upland Late Woodland sites suggest that even band-sized social groups were the rule for many archaeological Late Woodland societies until late in the period. Comparisons of archaeological Woodland and the historical groups must be done with caution. In particular, it is as important not to *interpret* either Mississippian or Late Woodland as simply being prehistoric versions of their historical counterparts.

In this book then, *tribe* is shorthand for a population in which social controls were largely informal, and leadership was achieved through personal effort or conditions. I am not using the term as an evolutionary stage through which all societies must pass on their way to civilization. Tribes certainly may arise as the result of conflict with established, more organized peoples, but conflict and intrusion are not just the result of European intrusion. Tribes often have flexible structures that can become, at least seasonally, too large for the informal leadership of hunting and gathering bands to be effective. *"Big Man"* was another name given to comparable levels of organization, because tribal leaders are often conceived to be like those of Melanesian societies in which this Pidgin word for leader implies achieved status, reinforced by good works and sponsorship of public events. In such societies, important people may decide issues of communitywide significance, but typically only in conjunction with "democratic" discussion. Social classes are absent, although there may be differences in rank, usually achieved only by good works.

Tribal social structure is commonly organized by extended kinship groups of some kind, often segmentary lineages. Strong principles of *noblesse oblige*, the obligation to be generous, are present, if without much *noblesse*. The highest status individuals may actually hold less material wealth than is possessed by others, because they have given their wealth away in exchange for respect. The distinction between *meum* and *tuum* is developed in household goods, but real property is usually held by the community or by kin-groups. Production and labor investment is largely controlled at the household and the kin group level. Public works associated with corporate entities such as male societies are common. Constructions such as men's houses or *kivas* can involve substantial labor investments, in many case equaling the labor given per household of public works in larger and arguably more complex societies.

This chapter does not attempt a political economy of Late Woodland. That is a task that requires its own studies (there is a good start on it in Nassaney and Cobb 1991b). What we need here is an overview of the social formations in which Mississippian evolved. These are the salient facts: At A.D. 500, most of the Southeast had a political landscape that was egalitarian and "tribal," in the sense discussed earlier. By A.D. 1100, social formations with chiefly rank and the germ, at least, of social differentiation were present in almost all the major floodplains in the Southeast. What caused such widespread and pervasive changes? How did they come about? This subject cannot be done justice here; but I have presented some preliminary discussions elsewhere (Muller 1986b, 1987a; Muller and Stephens 1991). What follows is more of a narrative than a formal argument. A cultural or evolutionary history of Mississippian *origins* is helpful for a political economy but not a prerequisite for it.

Social transformations such as these are built mostly using economic and political elements that already exist, but promoting them to new functions. The elements of each Late Woodland social formation surely provided the overwhelming bulk of the specific customs and behaviors that underwent qualitative and quantitative changes during the transformation. We cannot deny that contacts and diffusion occurred. But we have to ask: Why such relationships "cause" social transformations at one period, but not at another? Clearly other conditions have to be present before "contact" can make an impact on societies. If outside "influences" are postulated as causal factors, the burden of proof rests with diffusionists who must identify new, introduced elements that were missing from pre-Mississippian societies and identify their sources.

We know that raw materials such as copper and shell were being exchanged across the Southeast well back into Archaic times. We also know that mound construction goes back well into Archaic times. Horticulture may also have begun as early as the Archaic. Sites such ask Poverty Point, the Hopewell earthworks in Ohio, and—even more to the point—the platform and substructure mounds in the Southeast during the period between Middle Woodland and Mississippian, all show that public works in the service of society occurred relatively frequently and early in the Southeast, as discussed later. In any case, features such as substructure mound construction are too widespread around the world to require us to hypothesize diffusion, without physical evidence of exotic contacts such as Mesoamerican copper bells or jade. To be sure, maize is most definitely a Mesoamerican crop, but little systematic effort has been made to show comparatively that Eastern maize production was technologically and ceremonially derived directly from Mesoamerica. Maize seems to have been present in the East for no less than 700 years before it became an important food plant (see Fritz 1992; Fritz and Kidder 1992). Clearly, hierarchical social systems and mound construction were not necessarily dependent upon a maize production basis, a point I shall return to later.

With or without evidence of external contacts, researchers concerned with the origins of Mississippian need to explore how Mississippian can be modeled in terms of promoted tribal institutions. It is most probable that the tribal "captains" of Late Woodland developed into Mississippian "chiefs." Other social and economic forms were "promoted" into the Mississippian systems of organization and production. Whereas some new "ideas" may have been introduced from other areas, I see no clear argument why ideas alone would impel persons to surrender a lifeway that seems to have been both successful and attractive. In historical times, a surprising number of Europeans chose tribal lifeways when given the opportunity. In addition, the unwillingness of most historical North American tribal groups or individuals to adopt European lifeways—except under duress—is manifest in the historical records. We have to ask whether something happened to the conditions of everyday life that gave Late Woodland peoples little choice but to develop new political solutions. As a matter of tactics, if we fail to show material causes for the Late Woodland–Mississippian transformation, then there is still time enough to consider ideological and status-related causes. In any case, this book is not primarily concerned with origins.

2. BACKGROUND TO LATE WOODLAND AND MISSISSIPPIAN

The sixth to the ninth centuries in the North American East have been characterized ironically as the "good, gray period."[1] In culture-histories, this period has

---

[1] By Stephen Williams (1991, orally) in pointing out the need to look at Weeden Island and other complexes that fill in this Late Woodland "decline."

been seen as an "interregnum" between the Hopewellian and Mississippian "climaxes." Not least of the reasons for lack of interest in the Late Woodland period is that its artifacts, especially its ceramics, lack the "fanciness" that inspire an analyst's artistic soul.[2] There is a kind of blandness to many Late Woodland regional complexes that has repelled attention. Indeed, one famous archaeological prank involved a series of communications to a prominent ceramic analyst from a collector sending in some supposedly elaborate and fantastic ceramics, followed at long last by a massive shipment of plain, Baytown-period sherds. One of the key issues of Late Woodland studies is why Late Woodland pottery had such apparent stylistic uniformity (e.g., Braun 1977; Braun and Plog 1982).

What is the background for Late Woodland development? In the East, and in the Southeast in particular, more or less sedentary patterns of life developed in some places during the Late Archaic (by ca. 2000 B.C.). From that time on, a series of native North American plants were brought under cultivation in the East. These included species of *Chenopodium, Iva, Phalaris*, and others (see discussion in various papers in B. Smith 1992). None of these plants proved to be particularly promising domesticates in the long run,[3] but they did provide important dietary supplements—at least seasonally, if not in absolute caloric terms—from the second millennium B.C. on. As early as the first millennium B.C., some societies had become large enough, or at least complex enough, to get involved in large-scale public works. These early Southeastern "moundbuilders" built large earthworks at places like Poverty Point, Louisiana, and Moundsville, West Virginia. By 100 B.C., we have the first so-called "climax" in the area, named Hopewell in the Ohio Valley and north, and Marksville in the Mississippi Valley. In southern Ohio, truly large-scale earthworks were built across kilometers of bottomland. At one time, it was thought that such developments could not have been possible without agriculture, but it now seems that the role of cultivated plants of any kind in Hopewell was relatively minor. Mesoamerican crops, once thought to have been the stimulus for the development of Hopewell, were, at best, no more than minor components of Hopewellian diet, and they seem to have been altogether absent until quite late in Hopewellian times (e.g., Fritz and Kidder 1992).

A major revolution in Hopewellian studies came with the realization that *organizational* advances, rather than *production technology* improvements, may have stimulated these vast cooperative constructions (e.g., R. Ford 1974). We do not need to attribute the many regional "Hopewellian" developments to a single cause to see the common thread of economic change being rooted in "social technology." Direct production improvements as new crops or new tools seem to have played little role in these striking developments. In any case, Hopewellian cultures in the Ohio Valley and Illinois Valley change—let us avoid "decline"—into the supposedly unorganized Late Woodland folk during the fifth and sixth centuries. In the Southeast, the culture-historical changes are harder to track. Late Hopewellian-like complexes persist after A.D.

---

[2] And, to confirm my tendency to materialist interpretation, also assist in achieving publication and funding.

[3] In the sense that they were never really capable of the kind of "intensification" that could characterize later use of maize and bean.

300 in the Lower Mississippi Valley. Along the Gulf Coast, the Weeden Island complexes present a picture of continuity of mound-building on a large scale during these supposedly dark ages of Eastern archaeology. It is too strong, I think, to describe Weeden Island as "proto-Mississippian" (cf. Milanich et al. 1984), but it is easy to understand why such a term would be proposed, given the continuity between Hopewellian and Mississippian times that this complex presents. Weeden Island peoples were almost certainly not ancestral to later Mississippian peoples to the north, but they demonstrate how societies can be transformed as a result of local conditions into the kinds of societies represented by Mississippian in other areas (see also Kohler 1991). The point is that elaborate political structures are related to production capabilities in many ways, and that production and politics are intertwined in the service of the basic needs of local communities.

Even if there were evidence for extensive exchange between Mesoamerica and the Southeast in these times, the journalistic questions of where, when, who, why, and how would still remain. What needs to be done is to study Late Woodland and related cultures in the East in terms of their environment, both natural and social, and what follows is an outline of that effort.

3. THE SOUTHEASTERN LANDSCAPE AND CLIMATE

Central and Southeastern peoples during the Late Woodland and early Mississippian periods lived in environments similar to those seen at the beginning of the Historic period. The Southeastern landscape was old. Unlike the Northeast, it had escaped glacial erosion in Pleistocene times, and major geological changes were so deep in the past that even the most mountainous regions were gentle by comparison to other areas. The low areas of the broad Coastal Plain landform run for more than 3200 km from northeast to southwest. Most of Coastal Plain surface is Holocene alluvium and colluvium, poor in tool-making materials, but rich in potential for vegetation growth. Around the edges and in the uplands there are outcrops of Mesozoic and Paleozoic rocks that provided good-quality cherts for stone tools. Outside of the Appalachians and a few other uplands, the land is rolling, with rarely more than 100 m of relief. Mountainous uplands divide the Coastal Plain into a gigantic U tilted to the northeast. Humans using the landscape continually had to resolve the contrast between the upland environments and those of the floodplains of the many streams dissecting the area. The Mississippi–Ohio Drainage is on the west and north; and, on the east, the Atlantic Plain. The lowlands are dissected by mostly tributary streams in the west and by a multitude of smaller streams running into the Atlantic in the east. The western streams funnel direct human movement down to the Gulf Coast area. East of the Appalachian uplands, the streams move from mountain to shore, making north–south movement difficult, except by sea along the coast. Historic accounts of these routes from Elvas (1557) to Sherman (1891) document difficulties in movement. Thus, the landscape itself shaped the directions of movement, making some paths easy and others hard. Much human settlement by A.D. 700 was concentrated in the floodplains. This was especially so in the Interior Low Plateaus of central Tennessee and Kentucky, the Ridge and Valley landforms of eastern Tennessee, and the Interior Highlands of Missouri and Arkansas.

By Late Woodland times, the plant and animal components of the Southeastern environment had established, if not an equilibrium, at least an aspect that they would retain until the massive disruptions of the 19th century (Delcourt and Delcourt 1981; cf. Benninghoff 1968). Most of the East was covered by a vast forest that stretched westward from the coast until it gradually dwindled into prairie in the west in the face of drought and fire. Oak and hickory predominated, but here and there other components such as pine were important. The floodplains, on the other hand, were rich, swampy forests with oak, cypress, and tupelo.

Although there were some important climatic fluctuations through time, most of the Southeast has typically received over 1200 mm (48 inches) of rainfall a year, fairly evenly divided up among the seasons, but with the driest period in fall and the wettest in the summer. Although drought was always a problem, the risks involved in this area were nothing like those faced by peoples in the Plains or the Southwest. As people over time moved into the river bottoms, flooding became a more common threat to wild and domestic resources than was drought.

Temperatures are warm in summer (27°C daily mean) and yet fairly cool in winter (4° to 10°C daily mean). Figure 3.1 indicates the number of "heating degree days" in a series of cities ranging from north to south. A heating degree day is the number of degrees F below 65°F [18°C] on average for each day in the month. This particular measure is of interest, because it is a measure of energy cost for colder weather. Those cities in the regions where Late Woodland–like complexes became Mississippian are in bold lines in the chart. Mississippian, and the particular Late Woodland societies that developed into it, were not tolerant of cold winters. On the

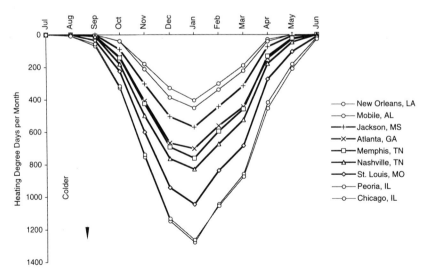

Figure 3.1. Heating degree days (from north to south). (Source: *Statistical Abstract of the United States 1975*, Table 332).

other hand, the near-tropical climates of the coastal areas such as New Orleans and Mobile were not particularly favorable to Mississippian development either.

The growing season was and is long, very long in the extreme south (Figure 3.2). This had major implications for wild-food availability in Late Woodland times. After more intensive horticulture developed, the long seasons allowed staggering of plantings—if not actual double cropping—to minimize risk from frost and flooding and to maximize yields.

All of these conditions favored rich, even rank, vegetation growth and that also favored diversity of animals. Wild resources of every kind were plentiful, and use of these formed the basis for first the establishment and, in turn, the end of Late Woodland period lifeways.

There are indications of minor climatic shifts throughout the Recent epoch, but Southeastern peoples were not threatened by these in the same way as those living in more marginal environments. The simple point is that most of the Southeast was a rich environment by almost any measure, and that the river floodplains occupied by many sedentary peoples after A.D. 500 were even richer.

It seems likely that population continued to increase after Middle Woodland times. This runs counter to the older view of Late Woodland decline, but even in the north, population may well have increased after the "fall" of Hopewell.[4] The difficulty, of course, is comparing the number of Middle and Late Woodland period people. In the northern areas of the Southeast, especially, Late Woodland populations became much more mobile. Attempting to estimate population on the basis of *number* of sites would be inappropriate, but even efforts to estimate *size* of settlements run into the difficulties of separating seasonal and permanent settlement.

4. RESOURCES AND PLACES

What resources supported populations in Late Woodland times? When did economic conditions change to those of Mississippian times? The first thing is to recognize that local circumstances varied. At the same time, it is not foolish to ask the general questions, since similar developments did occur in so many different areas, even at roughly the same time. One thing is now fairly clear: Late Woodland period societies did not depend *primarily* on horticulture, even though they had partially domesticated a series of local plants. The argument has been made that production capabilities for Weeden Island localities do indicate increased dependence on domes- ticated plants (Kohler 1991:105), and I have no problem with seeing this as playing a role there in making elite roles redundant (see Muller 1978a:306–307). There are

---

[4] In Chapter 4, I discuss some population models. In these cases, depending upon the kind of test used, the rate of increase of Hopewell ranged from a low-negative to a low-positive number. However, as in most of these cases, populations living in sedentary conditions often show declines, perhaps reflecting just the uncertainties of the data, but perhaps indicating the health disadvantages of concentration. Of course, we do not have much in the way of cemeteries for peoples who were highly mobile and perhaps increasing more rapidly than those living in more permanent settlements. If this is true, it runs counter to the traditional processual argument that sedentism leads to population increase.

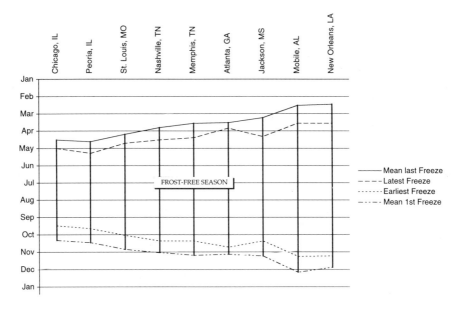

Figure 3.2. First and last frosts in the east. (Source: *Statistical Abstract of the United States 1975*, Table 321.)

arguments about the degree of dependency of Weeden Island peoples on specific domesticated plants (Newsom, personal communication 1996). However, when the area is taken as a whole, we shall see that increased use of domesticated plants is no better a marker for *decline* of central hierarchies than it is for *increased* hierarchical structures. What counts is not the *source* of food, but the quantity of it; and how much its production and consumption depends on mediation by elite brokers.

Abundant evidence indicates cultivation of native plants in the Central United States from Archaic times on (see Smith 1992). The earliest known domesticated or partially domesticated plants included a squash or gourd plant (*Cucurbita pepo*), goosefoot (*Chenopodium berlandieri*), and sunflower (*Helianthus annuus*), all before 1000 B.C. (B. Smith 1992:205). It has become clear that at least some varieties of *Cucurbita* are likely indigenous wild plants in North America (Decker 1988; also see Scarry and Newsom 1992:395–396). Other possible domesticates include knotweed (*Polygonum erectum*), maygrass (*Phalaris caroliniana*), and little barley (*Hordeum pusillum*), although these were more clearly cultivated later on. Marshelder (*Iva annua*), amaranth (*Amaranthus* sp.), and ragweed (*Ambrosia* spp.) also occur in archaeological contexts after Archaic times. The Middle Woodland period (300 B.C. to A.D. 500) saw further use of these domesticates, and in both the Midwest and the Southeast, it has been argued that production systems become more oriented toward horticultural production by the end of Middle Woodland times (e.g., Kohler 1991:105; B. Smith 1992:205). However, as Fritz and Kidder (1992; see Table 3.2) have pointed out, many areas with clear cases of "hierarchical development"—as shown in mound construction, and so on—do not seem to have much evidence for the use of any domesticates.

Table 3.2. Subsistence Data from the Lower Mississippi Valley

Complex, Site	~Date	Taxa	Status
Historic			
Natchez, Fatherland	A.D. 1540	*Zea mays* (Maize)	Cultivated
Mississippian			
Lake George	A.D. 1200	*Zea mays* (Maize)	Cultivated
Plaquemine	A.D. 1200	*Zea mays* (Maize)	Low frequency
"Late Woodland"			
Late Coles Creek, Osceola	A.D. 1000	*Zea mays* (Maize)	Cultivated
		Cucurbita pepo (Gourd, squash)	Cultivated?
		Nicotiana rustica (Tobacco)	Cultivated
Early Coles Creek, Morgan Md.	A.D. 700	no *Zea mays*	Not cultivated
Baytown, Toltec	A.D. 700	*Zea mays* (Maize)	Low frequency
		Phalaris caroliniana (Maygrass)	Not clearly cultivated
		Hordeum pusillum (LIttle barley)	Cultivated?
		Chenopodium berlandieri (Goosefoot)	Cultivated
		Polygonum erectum (Erect knotweed)	Cultivated?
		Cucurbita pepo (Gourd, squash)	Cultivated?
		Quercus sp. (Acorns)	Not cultivated
		Carya spp (Pecans & hickories).	Not cultivated
Baytown, Powell Canal	A.D. 700	*Chenopodium* spp (Goosefoot).	Not cultivated
		Polygonum sp. (Knotweed/ smartweed)	Not cultivated
		Carya spp. (Pecans & hickories)	Not cultivated
Troyville, Reno Brake	A.D. 400	*Quercus* sp. (Acorns)	Not cultivated
		Carya spp. (Pecans & hickories)	Not cultivated
Middle Woodland			
Issaquena, Reno Brake	100 B.C.	*Quercus* sp. (Acorns)	Not cultivated
		Carya spp. (Pecans & hickories)	Not cultivated
Early Woodland			
Tchefuncte, Morton Shell Md.	1000 B.C.	*Cucurbita pepo* (Gourd, squash)	Not clearly cultivated
		Lagenaria siceraria (Bottle gourd)	Not clearly cultivated
		Polygonum sp. (Smartweed)	Not cultivated
Late Archaic			
Poverty Point, J. W. Copes	1800 B.C.	*Cucurbita pepo* (Gourd, squash)	Not clearly cultivated
		Polygonum erectum (Erect knotweed)	Not cultivated
		Hordeum pusillum (Little barley)	Not cultivated

(Data from Fritz and Kidder 1992)

There is another potential problem for proposals of heavy use of native domesticates in pre-Mississippian times. It was naturally assumed that maize, as an exotic import, was one of the few C4 (photosynthetic carbon assimilation [PCA] cycle) photosynthetic plants in eastern North America. Certainly, many temperate plants have only C3 metabolisms (mostly photosynthetic carbon reduction, PCR), but a listing indicates that the PCA cycle, although discovered first in tropical grasses, is also "particularly prominent in species of the Gramineae, Chenopodiaceae, and Cyperaceae" (Taiz and Zeiger 1992:234, see also Schoeninger and Schurr 1994a). The data presented by Buikstra (e.g., 1992; see Figure 4.14 in the next chapter) and her associates indicate low C4 values until after A.D. 700 and later. These low C4 pathway indications in pre-Mississippian skeletal remains may rule out the dietary importance not only of maize, but also of some of the other known native domesticates such as chenopodium. It will be necessary to establish carbon metabolism of individual species to settle this problem. The issue of maize and other plant consumption will be addressed at more length in the next chapter.

Although it is possible that some local domesticates played a more important role in diet in some areas of the Southeast (as argued by B. Smith 1992), the bulk of Late Woodland diet was still probably derived from wild-food resources, as seen here in the Lower Mississippi Valley. A mixed, but predominantly wild economy, to be sure, would have had risks in terms of both reliability and availability. Domesticated plants (and animals) are "intensifiable"; that is, additional labor inputs generate, up to a point, additional output. It is true that greater effort in collecting may also generate greater yields, but these limits are reached sooner because of the dispersal and unreliability of wild foods, especially if alternative sites for collecting are controlled by another social group. Wild-food yields are notoriously apt to fluctuate in yield from year to year. There is a sense in which the domesticates could have played a more important role than their frequency in sites may suggest. A resource that is a "famine" food or, in a more general sense, one that is consumed at critical points in the dietary history of a person, may be critical to survival at the time of its consumption while remaining at a very low percentage of total annual diet. Such "resources of advantage" (Muller and Stephens 1991:300) cannot have their importance measured only in kilocalories.

The most important of all Mississippian crops, maize, does not seem to have been important anywhere in the central United States at the *beginning* of Late Woodland times (see Fritz 1992; Fritz and Kidder 1992; B. Smith 1992), but Late Woodland peoples in a few localities did begin the transition to something we might call intensive maize cultivation perhaps as early as the late eighth century. Interestingly, many of the earlier intensive[5] uses of maize in the Mississippi Valley seem to be to the north, while more southern societies seem to have depended less on cultivated plants, a pattern that may be consistent with the idea that the richer southern environments may not have required as much labor investment in subsistence (as suggested in Muller 1983:306, 1986b). The plant carbon metabolism profiles discussed earlier and in Chapter 4 also indicate that consumption of maize or other C4-pathway plants was infrequent until close to A.D. 900, and usually later. In any event, complexes such as Baytown (e.g., House 1990; Rolingson 1990) and Coles Creek (Fritz and Kidder 1992) developed complex mound centers in Late Woodland times without seeming to have much dependence on cultivated plants.

---

[5] As always, words such as *intensive* have to be understood in comparison to what came before, not what would follow later.

I would propose that Late Woodland societies differed from Middle Woodland societies in being more, rather than less, dependent upon a wide spectrum of plants and animals from a highly diverse range of environments. If Middle Woodland societies can be said to have concentrated in floodplain environments, Late Woodland peoples often scattered across the entire landscape. Much of this dispersal probably reflects a pattern of seasonal use of different environments. As with some historical peoples, mobility was combined with what can be described as a pattern of divided risk avoidance (for discussion of kinds of risk and security, see Halstead and Shea 1989; Jochim 1981). If, in any given season, a particular resource was scarce, then alternatives were available by virtue of mobility and low competition. As a result, some parts of the year were spent in upland rockshelters, gathering wild plants and hunting. At other times, people might concentrate on the rich resources of the floodplains, including cultivation of the plants discussed earlier. The key to this particular kind of "Late Woodland" pattern was diversity and alternative resources. Few environments or resources were without alternatives. It is possible that the introduction of the bow and arrow may have been a technological breakthrough in allowing hunters to acquire enough food to survive in the uplands (Blitz 1988, 1993:99; Ford 1974:402–403; Hall 1980:436–438; Muller 1978a:307, 1986b:141) without being tied to floodplain resources as "resources of advantage" (Muller and Stephens 1991). Shott has argued that the smaller points are not necessarily arrow points and that there may also be survivals of dart and atlatl technology in the transition to bow technology. He also argues against the greater efficiency seen in the use of bow and arrow (Shott 1993:435–438). Although he is quite right on the difficulty of objectively measuring any supposed advantage of the bow and arrow, he acknowledges—but does not come to grips with—the historical fact that the bow and arrow was not only adopted relatively quickly (even if it may have come in earlier and taken longer than assumed), but also that by historical times it had almost entirely displaced the atlatl and dart, except in those cases where thick-skinned targets needed to be attacked (such as sea mammals in the North or quilted armor in Mesoamerica). My own suspicions on this matter are that the bow and arrow allowed easier exploitation of game than was possible with spear or atlatl-and-dart technology, a point that I do not see as necessarily inconsistent with Shott's data. Of course, as Shott argues, the hypothesis of bow-and-arrow efficiency requires testing, not uncritical acceptance. However, we have to look at the differential persistence of different weapons as an indication of their effectiveness, not just measure that effectiveness in recent ethnographic contexts that are from environments vastly different from the temperate forests of the East.

Another possible technological improvement was the manufacture of better quality pottery, allowing intense boiling of wild and domestic seeds (see Braun 1983a). Cooking in this way made nutrients from small, hard seeds available, as well as assisting in exploiting otherwise inedible objects such as overmature tubers of greenbriars (*Smilax* spp., Newsom, personal communication 1996). New hunting techniques combined with improvements in the ability to extract nutrients from many classes of food might have given Late Woodland households the ability to break free of social and economic entanglements, and interdependence that bound them to the floodplains. Relative economic autonomy of a household unit made it much more unlikely that members of that household would be willing to share very far outside the immediate kin group. The "selfish peasant" has long been a topic of study as well as a problem for those who wish to impel more production by the peasants (e.g., Chaianov 1923, 1925 [1966]; Wolf 1966).

Carrying capacity is another biological concept that is fraught with difficulties. In human populations it essentially means the maximum level of population that can be supported at a given level of technology. Thus, carrying capacity of the same region for horticulturists and for hunters is quite different. One value of the concept is that it forces our attention to the minimum levels of certain resources that can support a particular population. What I have just suggested is that Middle Woodland peoples had reached something close to the number of persons that could be supported, given their technology, and social organization, and technology. If new technologies, such as the bow or better pottery, or even "better" varieties of crops, were adopted in such a society, it would have been adopted for good Middle Woodland reasons. The initial goal would certainly have been to make life better in the flood-plain-centered settlements of the time. However, new technologies have unforeseen consequences, especially for social organization, being tied as that is to the basic subsistence needs of a society. Suppose that late Middle Woodland or early Late Woodland bow hunting made taking of deer more effective away from hunted-out floodplains. At the same time, the ability to raise, store, and make palatable small, high-food-value seeds would have provided new resources. Small seeds could be stored, transported, and eaten well away from their place of origin. A new independence of production and consumption could allow each family to provide both sufficient and reliable food resources without much dependence on other families—that is, that *distribution* mechanisms may have become less important to the production units. To the extent that population did not immediately catch up with the improved conditions, the ability to hunt and eat more of the environment created conditions of "superabundance." Population would have increased, but, also, each family would have been less dependent on the floodplains where they and their forebears had been anchored for nearly a millennium. Indeed, in such circumstances the temptation (as measured in relative transportation costs) to move closer to upland resources would be very strong. The ironical circumstance is that the so-called Late Woodland "decline" from Hopewellian times probably was both a time of increase in population and of an absolute improvement in the well-being of individuals and their families. What failed was not the individual lives of Middle Woodland peoples, but rather the central organization responsible for large-scale public activities. Given some similarities of Middle Woodland public organizations to later Mississippian ones, we will need to ask both why the central organizations developed and why they did not persist in many localities.

5. POPULATION

The role of population growth in setting up conditions for change in Late Woodland society is hotly debated. It is certainly clear that many of us were too quick to account for all changes in terms of rather simplistic models of population stress.

Some have argued forcefully that since population stresses in general do not cause specific events, then population pressures are "nonexplanations" (as in G. Cowgill 1975a, 1975b). This argument seems to me to have some weaknesses. For one thing, the fact that drought, population increase, or whatever, do not always determine, of themselves, a specific *direction* of change, does not mean that they may not be proximate causes of changes in social and cultural systems. The argument does not address whether, for example, those "Mesolithic" societies that have domesticates suitable for intensification may not generally respond to "population pressure" by extension of domestication. Archaeologically identified "causes" have never been so universal or powerful as to operate in the absence of conditions and context. It is more than merely "interesting" that so many societies in so many diverse environments nearly synchronously began to associate their economies with seed-producing plants. It is correct to argue against the general assumption that population increase is a "natural tendency" requiring no explanation; but population increase is not just a theoretical concept in specific cases, but also a falsifiable proposition. It is not clear that we must ignore this part of the social and economic landscape, simply because it does not *universally* explain social change. The need to explain population pressure in precise, testable terms does not rule out its playing a role in other economic changes.

It does not seem enough to me to acknowledge that "undoubtedly, there are many instances of societies which have, for one reason or another, suffered serious stress due to resource shortages" (Cowgill 1975a:128). This view forgets what life is like when not cushioned in the bosom of rich industrial states. We have abundant physical evidence of dietary shortfalls for society after society. When severe enough, these circumstances were more than just an inconvenience. It is necessary to explore how and why these shortages occur, but rejecting an inherent population increase says little about the overall importance of population-related stresses.

Even persons otherwise not inclined to see population pressure as an "engine" of social evolution have been prepared to see it as important under certain circumstances.[6] It is obvious to most that the "material conditions of everyday life" have to meet conditions of reproduction of a society *in the first place*, or it becomes extinct. The particular mode of production highly conditions the nature of the response, but it is hard to see that the conditions of transition to *horticultural* production were much affected by what was thought by "the people with the most power" (as put by Cowgill 1975a:129). It is anachronistic to argue that such persons were already in existence, and even for complex societies with developed power relations, so much concern with elite attitudes puts a strange emphasis on elite "Will" as a determinant. Economic crises—much less famines—clearly trigger social responses, often of revolutionary dimensions, regardless of what elites think. Cowgill says that he does not want to take an idealist view as opposed to a materialist one, but his concern with what elites "like," "notions," and "attitudes" (1975a:129) seems to do just that. What,

[6] For example, "Diese Produktion tritt erst mit *der Vermehrung der Bevölkerung*. Sie setzt selbst wieder einen *Verkehr* der Individuen untereinander voraus. Die Form dieses Verkehr is wieder durch die Produktion bedingt" (Marx and Engels 1846 [1959:21]). Also see Marx 1853 [Marx and Engels 1979:67–68], 1857–1859 [Marx and Engels 1979:108]; Engels 1882 [Marx and Engels 1979:345–346]).

after all, *are* the determinants of the "attitudes" of people, elite or commoner? Population models deserve constructive criticism, but long-term selection in populations operates to increase the frequency of those behaviors that pay off (as discussed by Dunnell 1980). Population size and density are among the conditions in which selection occurs.

The power of population-pressure arguments to offend also extends to some "selectionists." Rindos has argued that population-pressure models fail because, among other reasons, such models "must assume that all resources are being consumed at as high a rate as is possible" (1984:193). This assertion is false, if Rindos means that a population-driven model *must* assume such use levels at all times. To be sure, population models commonly imply as complete usage as is possible given the mode of production *at the times of greatest stress*. However, few models hold that such conditions are normal, even when so-called "carrying capacity" is reached. An ecological, not just "evolutionary," perspective on the demography of any population (not just human) involves a complex set of alternative means of obtaining necessary resources under conditions of shortfall in some resources.

Rindos has, in effect, constructed his model in such a way as to eliminate the role of population pressure, but this conclusion follows only *if* one accepts his various simplifying assumptions (see also Rosenberg's critique from other grounds, 1990). It is somewhat ironical that the formulae employed in this effort are basically logistic equations like those that have more generally been used to model the feedback effects of population density on growth. Rindos suggests that density dependence can result from nonpopulation factors, and this illustration has considerable value. He does *not* prove thereby that "population pressure" is never important (compare Keeley 1988; and Winterhalder et al. 1988:323 on intensification effects). Whether or not population density is a important independent variable to employ in models of cultural change is an issue that deserves continuing debate; but the issue is not resolved by the fit of a few estimated data points to logistic curves. Of course, as in any case, any model's utility in explanation rests on its generality and validity, as well as its "fit."

I feel that Cowgill and Rindos understandably react to overemphasis on population density as causation, and their critiques are valuable reminders that such prime movers require their own justification and argument. However, where do such critiques leave us? For one thing, we must understand that population "pressure" can be defined only in relation to natural, social, and cultural contexts. In the intellectual history of this issue, a kind of dialectic has played in which an overemphasis on population pressure countered earlier overemphasis on the benefits of surpluses allowing supposed leisure-time benefits such as building civilization. We need to recognize at this time that population size may play an important role, *especially in nonclass societies*, in creating critical contradictions between new production systems and old social patterns. In analyzing situations, we have to balance these elements, neither prejudicially accepting nor rejecting specific causes.

"Pressure" in relation to human carrying capacity is dependent on both material and social technology. An *a priori* prediction of the levels at which "stress" results from too high population density is difficult to determine, at best. However, it is easier practically to see where and when dietary and other stresses occur. Empirically, then, population density effects can be identified from population growth curves, even though we cannot always predict the level of so-called carrying capacity. As Rindos and Cowgill have shown, population-pressure explanations alone can easily become circular arguments. All the same, no one should argue that starvation does not impact the societies in which it occurs. In the end, population density is one component in the interplay between production and social organization. These are all critical in explaining, not merely chronicling, the development of a social formation.

What does this mean for Late Woodland and Mississippian? It is embarrassing to admit that models of Late Woodland change have depended heavily on population-pressure explanations, without having very good empirical evidence for population densities at particular places and times. We have many models, but these are difficult questions to resolve empirically. Let us, then, try to tease out the individual strands of this problem. As I have noted, the number of sites in upland areas in the northern sections of the Mississippi Valley and in the Ohio Valley dating to between A.D. 500 and 700 simply explodes. At the same time, there is probably less permanent occupation in bottomlands, at least in these more northern regions, although this is harder to document. There is no indication here, it is important to remember, that bottomlands were abandoned—it is simply that more or less sedentary life in those rich environments no longer dominated social life in most places. To the south, with complexes such as Weeden Island and Issaquena-Coles Creek, what could be called Middle and Late Woodland are not nearly so different from each other, but these are also the places where such interesting social facts as mound construction also persist. In this case, the exceptions prove the rule. One can see that the process sometimes called "Mississippianization" took place over a wide area, even if *Mississippian* in the strict sense does seem to emerge on the northern frontier.

Continuity from late Middle Woodland to "Emergent Mississippian" in specific traditions such as ceramic manufacture seems well established for many regions such as the lower Ohio Valley, the Confluence area, and the lower Mississippi Valley (e.g., Kreisa and Stout 1990; Morse and Morse 1991; Muller 1986b). Continuity shows up in artifacts, but it is clear that settlement and organization undergo some dramatic, even revolutionary changes between A.D. 500 and 1000. These changes are definitely not a simple unidirectional development, however. Although complete context is valuable for any time period, the nature of Late Woodland period settlement is particularly sensitive to the kind of survey coverage in an area.

In many areas—and these tend to be some of the cases with the most extensive overall surveys—settlement is more dispersed and located away from the floodplain after A.D. 400. In the Illinois Valley, this has been well documented (Asch et al. 1979), and it also holds for the lower Ohio and adjacent areas (e.g., Hargrave et al. 1991; Muller 1986b). In other areas, it is clear that there is considerable bottomland continuity between Middle Woodland and Mississippian times, with a continuation of settlement in larger lowland settlements (e.g., Dunnell and Feathers 1991; Kohler 1991). Rudolph's paper on North Georgia is an especially good example of the difficulty in assessing the facts of the aggregation versus dispersal models of settlement (T. Rudolph 1991). In northern Georgia there was an increase in dispersal, but in that case, along the floodplains rather than into the uplands! In other areas, too, little is known about the Late Woodland period, and it is difficult to assess the importance of different environmental zones (e.g., Schroedl and Boyd 1991). Clearly, in many areas aggregation continues into Late Woodland times. Overall, however, there does appear to be a net increase in dispersal after A.D. 500, and an increase in aggregation toward the end of the Late Woodland period in many areas, especially in those regions where Mississippian appears to develop earliest.

In short, we are seeing a process of increased dispersal, but the reasons for dispersal vary and are not the issue here. Dispersal, however, means that bottomland-oriented surveys and traditional surveys that concentrate on larger sites will show the Late Woodland period as a decline in occupation—which is true for those areas so far as bottomland large sites are concerned. Such dispersal does not necessarily imply a decrease in the total number of people, however. Notably, in areas where upland dispersal did not take place, the changes from Middle Woodland times to Late Woodland times have also come to be seen as a period of increase rather than decrease.

6. ARCHAEOLOGICAL EVIDENCE FOR SOCIAL ORGANIZATION

Archaeological markers of social organization are difficult to define, but size of residential groups is one of the most important. Highly mobile band-level societies are represented by small, transient campsites, whereas "tribal" sites may sometimes be large enough to have accommodated several thousands of relatively sedentary persons. One marker that distinguishes tribal social formations from bands is the presence of small-scale to medium-sized public works. Although such "monuments" were usually present in these societies, they may not have been in forms that survive archaeologically. Tribal public works are typically small enough to have been constructed by relatively small groups working over periods of days, not months or years, and may thus be distinguished from chiefdom-level public works. Exceptions are known in both directions, so mere scale of construction is not an infallible marker for social levels (remembering again the need to avoid overtypologizing these phenomena). Size of social unit is a fairly good marker of social complexity at the bottom end (e.g., A. Johnson and Earle 1987:314; G. Johnson 1982). Bands typically are dispersed and do not maintain large groups for more than a few months. Generally groups of more than 100 or so people occur only in temporary conditions of super-abundance (in what is known as "scramble competition," Muller 1987b:248 for more discussion of this issue). One historical example of such temporarily larger gatherings is known for native Texas bands during the prickly pear harvest (e.g., Nuñez Cabeça de Vaca 1542). Tribal groups also may have seasonal rounds, but the situation is sometimes the reverse of bands: Larger groups break up into smaller ones on a short-term basis for specific activities. In practice, the distinction is blurred in that band organization of human society is so fundamental that it persists even as higher levels of hierarchy develop. Even in class-based, state-level societies, residential and work groups maintain the small-group dynamics of this fundamental human form of social organization. We have to remember that human social organization is scale dependent (e.g., G. Johnson 1977, 1982), responding with new social forms as population size increases and face-to-face communication becomes more difficult.

Differences of scale in social size may seem to form a continuum from small to large, and from complete mobility to complete sedentism, and that is true in some senses. However, organizational structure is not a continuum, since a series of thresholds have to be crossed as scale increases. Johnson has suggested that these discrete levels of structure are linked to information processing limitations (e.g., G. Johnson 1978). For example, once population reaches certain fairly narrowly defined breaking points, simple informal structures no longer suffice to resolve conflicts. At some point, an institutionalized system for resolution of conflict becomes essential, regardless of its precise form. The new institutions are almost always based on preexisting structures that are transformed, even transmogrified. Although the forms of organization can differ widely, the presence of some such structures does not. The archaeological traces of these "leaps" from one level to another are found most often in such markers as differential house sizes, cooperative construction, and display and mortuary differentiation.

7. ORGANIZATION OF LATE WOODLAND SOCIETY

In the more northern regions, the dispersal of population from relatively permanent floodplain settlement into small, wandering Late Woodland bands would have torn apart many Middle Woodland institutions. These bands, however, were embedded in "tribal" connections on a larger scale; and communal needs of various kinds persisted. Perhaps the most crucial of these was the need to find spouses from other kin groups. The dispersal of Late Woodland peoples into not-quite-hunting and-gathering bands was a partial return to a "natural" human pattern, but spouses and some resources were needed that could not be acquired in the normal annual round of a family or band. From Late Archaic times on, long-distance exchange brought exotic decorative elements across thousands of kilometers. Copper from the Great Lakes and Georgia, obsidian from the West, and conch shells from the coasts were exchanged from person to person over vast distances. The demand for fancy items was a part of the emerging distinctions in status in Middle Woodland societies. As the central Middle Woodland organizations faded away, demand for these goods became less. Exotic raw materials still moved across the East, but at a trickle compared to earlier, long-distance exchange. A decline in rank- and status-related artifacts is a direct reflection of the decline in differences of rank and status in Late Woodland. If social differentiation is the mark of "progress," then certainly there had been a social decline by A.D. 500.

Unlike the widely dispersed bands of Archaic times, however, it can be expected that some Middle Woodland traditions would have persisted insofar as they helped to provide models for local leadership and organization. Although people resided together in much smaller groups for most of the year, it can be expected that some seasons and some events provided the background for temporary "tribal-sized" gatherings. The "stone forts" of southern Illinois may have been such meeting places in later Late Woodland times (see Muller 1986b). Even true, band-level societies often have large-scale "rendezvous" during times of superabundant resources. In the temporary "tribes" of these larger gatherings, the social business of finding a spouse and establishing exchange relationships for rare materials could be carried out. The temporary leadership of these larger groups also could have preserved some of the titles and even functions of Middle Woodland leadership. We can expect that some social practices of Middle Woodland times persisted, especially in the more sedentary and larger societies farther south. As we shall see, these could provide a nucleus around which new political and economic roles could coalesce.

Social organization on the family level was probably not much different in Late Woodland times than it was in Middle Woodland, or for that matter, Late Archaic times. We have little direct evidence of how families were organized, but the elements of historical groups correspond to worldwide patterns for the various levels of political–economic organization (see Murdock 1949).

8. CONTRADICTIONS OF LATE WOODLAND SOCIETY

In this chapter, we briefly have seen how changes in the way Late Woodland people obtained their daily sustenance may have triggered social changes that they could never have foreseen when making what seemed to be simple choices. What follows is only a sketch, a set of suggestions, about how this may have happened, but such conditions should have testable consequences.

Producers

In dispersing to seek autonomy, some Late Woodland peoples eventually found themselves competing for some localized resources. To the extent that the changed lifeways were successful, it may well have been the case that population increased as calories were converted into reproduction. Unfortunately, we have little evidence to support or reject the idea of Late Woodland population increases or declines. However, if population were increasing under these circumstances it would contain the contradiction that the very success of the Late Woodland way of life would begin to restrict the ability of any given social unit to range widely. Late Woodland lifeways in many parts of the Southeast seem to have been dependent upon mobility and low population density. If population increased to levels where geographic options were cut off in hard times, the mobile Late Woodland strategy would have to be replaced with some other alternatives. Of course, in some areas, such as southern Georgia and northern Florida, mobility does not seem to have been so critical, and in these localities we see the same kinds of settlement and population concentrations that characterized Middle Woodland and would also be characteristic of later Mississippian societies.

In the northern Southeast and much of the rest of the area, the quintessential Late Woodland social group was a small, mobile band made up of a few households. Such units face problems as a reproductive unit. We may assume that there were prohibitions on marriage or reproduction with close kin. Like band-level societies everywhere, this means that small group size creates a difficulty in identifying and acquiring appropriate spouses. Complete independence could not be attained by Late Woodland peoples, since they needed to establish regional contacts to ensure reproduction. One solution is some form of scheduled gathering in of bands. The timing of such gatherings or rendezvous may come at times of high harvest potential, when larger groups will not strain local resources at the place of meeting. However, there are social stresses as well as natural ones when larger groups assemble. In such circumstances, short-term positions of authority, especially in relation to police functions, may emerge. Such roles in society have their own momentum in providing continuity in social-structure as well as providing the germs of organizations that are capable of promotion to other kinds of functions in changing circumstances.

Territories "controlled" by individual bands were mostly similar to one another. However, the bottomlands, once the headmen had disappeared or become marginal, were still the most attractive localities because of their resource richness. One may suppose that the last settlers in those territories were precisely those whose earlier roles in that environment were the most favored, that is, those who had the least reason to leave. As these people, perhaps even retaining family traditions of leadership, continued to live in the bottoms, the rich resources there could have supported their continuing to play more important roles in sponsorship of community (as opposed to band) ceremonies and activities. If, for whatever reason, the upland ranging of other bands became more restricted, these bottomland bands/lineages would have been well positioned to reassert themselves in positions of status and relative power. In that sense, the autonomous nature of Late Woodland social groups was subverted by their success, as reflected in biological reproduction.

The fundamental contradiction between production and reproduction also creates a contradiction between reproduction of a simple, dispersed community and circumstances in which some persons have differential success in social as well as biological reproduction because of their location in the landscape.

Production

The object of labor in Late Woodland societies was the foodstuffs harvested from wild sources and the cultivation of garden plots of mostly locally domesticated crops. Maize was probably present throughout much of the area, even at the beginning of the Late Woodland period, but the carbon-pathway evidence suggests that it was seldom a major contributor to the calories consumed until Late Woodland societies had already transformed themselves into something else. The same carbon-pathway evidence from human skeletons may also rule out the importance of some of the other known domesticates such as amaranths and chenopodia, if they also prove to have C4 pathways (see Taiz and Zeiger 1992, as discussed earlier).

For the most part, Late Woodland subsistence shows heavy dependence on wild foods, even though domesticates are present. It would be fairer to say that Late Woodland horticulture was *extensive*, rather than *intensive*, as is so often stated. It is notable that when and where obviously *intensive* cultivation of maize began, there were concomitant declines in the frequency of many other plant and animal foods, as scheduling conflicts became irreconcilable. Again, the care of the plants that were chosen for use, because they could be increased by planting, took time away from other activities. The plants did provide what seemed to be a more reliable source of calories. Of course, production has good years and bad years, but the worst case often has more effect on change than "normal" conditions.

Basically, Late Woodland peoples had to choose among some alternative strategies, sometimes probably even in the same year. They could attempt to remain "Late Woodland" by exploiting backwoods areas away from the relative congestion of the floodplains. This choice forced them to exploit poorer environments more subject to depletion, however. This in turn, may have had consequences in terms of finding new ways to supplement and exploit the relatively scanty upland resources.

Late Woodland people could also have chosen to try to intensify production where they were. If even the rich resources of the floodplain became strained by overexploitation—or even if population became too great to adjust to normal perturbations, then old or new crops might become attractive as resources that would allow increased labor to be turned into increased production, in ways that might not be available to circumscribed collectors.

They could also have chosen to become part of the floodplain scene, but this might have meant sucking up to those plutocrats of the Late Woodland world, the lineages who controlled the relatively concentrated but very rich resources of the wetlands. This choice would have involved some loss of the autonomy so vehemently favored by free dispersed peoples of the Late Woodland sort. Where this happened, we see Late Woodland communities that seem more like either Middle Woodland or even Mississippian peoples than like the dispersed bands more commonly seen as Late Woodland (e.g., see Sahlins 1968:86ff.).

Other strategies could have involved committing neither to autonomy nor dependence, but establishing local and regional networks with other, related communities. However, this solution probably would delay the development of subordination rather than avoiding it, as some families in the network of exchange and cooperation would have the tendency to become "more equal" than the others (see Cobb and Nassaney 1995, for discussion).

It seems likely that all of these strategies and more were tried in practice by various Late Woodland–period societies throughout the Southeast. In some areas, we see archaeological evidence of Late Woodland–period mound construction without evidence that these were supported by "surplus" production of maize or other crops. On the contrary, we may look upon the mounds as concrete representations of social relationships that did not evolve to build mounds but developed to meet much more important and critical human needs. In other places, we see little evidence of cooperation among the later Late Woodland people, but we see indications of intensification of crop cultivation. Far from providing the "surplus" as a basis for development of complexity, at the beginning we may rather see cultivation of crops and public cooperation as alternatives aimed at resolution of the same set of overall difficulties.

The means of labor utilized at the beginning of the Late Woodland period were—among other things—better pottery, domestication of plants, and improved weaponry in the form of bows and arrows. It has also been proposed that the bow and arrow may have had the effect of simultaneously improving the harvesting capabilities of individual households, while also making aggression between households more deadly. This would not have made much difference if there were lots of territory for each band, but it would have intensified the problems of interference competition as groups grew numerous enough to impinge on each other while foraging.

At the end of Late Woodland, the hoe became important in many areas, vessel forms in pottery developed into the globular vessels familiar to Mississippian specialists, and intensive cultivation of some plants was established in some regions. Once cultivation of this sort has become established, it becomes more difficult to engage in wide-ranging foraging, especially if potential rivals may raid stores during such times. In effect, the gardener became more and more tied to her land and harvest. The need to defend the cultivators and crops could transform hunters into warriors.

Elites

Even Late Woodland people periodically faced the possibility of restricted local ranges and bad years. If population and the number of bands were increasing, we would predict that there would have been more difficulties as time went by. In this kind of situation, I have speculated that headmen, especially some of those living in the richest environments, may have found themselves more often as donors than as receivers of goods. Such headmen could be expected to have heirs that might also have the same advantages. So dependency and reciprocal relationships might grow stronger with the passing of years and increases in population.

Ironically, it may have been that Late Woodland kin leaders were originally not exploiters but suppliers of resources. First *oblige*, then *noblesse*? Certainly leaders of nondifferentiated peoples often are poorer than their followers because of their generosity, which gains them still more followers. But as Sahlins tells us the Eskimo say, "Gifts make slaves just as whips make dogs" (1968:88). Sahlin's "calculated generosity" allows a donor headman to gain control over other people's production (1968:88–89). Such control may be effective but not alienating. Nonetheless, these dominant–subordinate individual social relations contain the contradictions that can create domination and subordination of the groups involved. There were no classes in Late Woodland society, and there is little reason even to see them in Mississippian, but the contrast between private lives and public works was surely blurred by emergent differentiation.

9. TRANSITIONS

From some perspectives, the transitions between Late Woodland Period societies and their more or less Mississippian descendants could be seen as gradual. There are many continuities in technology, for example. Any given kind of Mississippian production could probably be found in some developmental form in Late Woodland societies in one place or another in the Southeast. Shell-tempered pottery may have first been made here; the oldest platform-substructure mounds built earlier over there. Maize was grown in some regions long before it became important in Mississippian times. In this sense, there was little in Mississippian material life that was new, yet somehow the combination of these older technological and even social systems achieved a kind of revolutionary breakthrough at the end of Late Woodland times.

There was no sudden *areawide* end to Late Woodland; but in each region, particular societies fundamentally altered their social character, often virtually overnight. Often these changes did entail new production systems, but these were part of the phenomenon of Mississippian emergence rather than a *cause*. Likewise, the emergence of chiefs was a critical factor in defining the new lifeways, but the power of chiefs did not *cause* the power of chiefs. As we saw in the previous chapter, Historic Period populations far larger than anything we can imagine at the beginning of Mississippian times were led more than governed by their chiefs and councils. In the absence of classes, different social groups may still have had opposing interests, but it is hard to see how thuggery on the part of emerging chiefs would have been tolerated and supported in the kind of world that we can see in the later days of Late Woodland.

The following chapters take up these issues of how Mississippian worked and what it implied in considerably more detail. In all that discussion, however, we need still to remember that it was Late Woodland institutions that formed the basic building blocks out of which Mississippian was constructed.

Chapter 4

Material Conditions of Everyday Life
Biology

A day came a man consult this philosopher for to
know at o'clock it was owe to eat. If thou are rich,
told him eat when you shall wish; if you are poor,
when you may do so.
English as She Is Spoke by Pedro Carolino,
(1883[1969:104])

If it will persist, a society has to reproduce at a high enough level to maintain its population. Extinction is the evolutionary alternative if an adequate basis for biological reproduction is not provided. Although cultural perceptions affect the level of subsistence considered "basic," there are objective, biological limits below which reproduction becomes impossible and even death occurs. An excess of food may also cause problems, although obesity-related diseases were rarer in preindustrial societies than today.

Both individual and group-subsistence needs have to be considered. We can approximate the biology of Mississippian populations from archaeological data and compare these with data on Mississippian-related groups surviving into historical times. Later chapters on production will also deal with many aspects of the nutritional basis for Mississippian lifeways.

An important aspect of biological reproduction is mortality. Even populations with high birth rates have no increase if their death rate is too high. For example, many urban centers in the 18th century had such high mortality that towns were population sinks, maintaining or increasing their size only by draining off population from the rural areas around the center. Some effort will be made to suggest the character of Mississippian reproductive success. In addition, a comparison of historical and prehistoric population characteristics suggests the differences are often less than assumed.

1. MISSISSIPPIAN BIOLOGY

Physical Characteristics and Needs

In terms of "racial" classifications based largely on skulls, the prehistoric Mississippian peoples looked like modern Muskhogean-speaking peoples of the Southeast (Neumann 1952:21–23) but not much like the Plains peoples that have come to define the motion-picture "Indian." Their physical remains inform us that Mississippian populations were similar in appearance to those of the historical Southeast.

Average Mississippian adult male stature at the Moundville site, for example, was approximately 168 cm; female adult stature, nearly 160 cm, based on various, modern bone-to-height tables (in this case, by Trotter and Gleser 1958, using data in Powell 1988). At the Lake George site, figures were comparable, with adult males at approximately 172 cm and adult females at 165 cm (D. G. Ergnatz in Williams and Brain 1983:Appendix A). Figure 4.1 illustrates the range at Moundville and some other Mississippian populations. Mississippian populations in the Southeast were about the same size, even though not all of the statures in Figure 4.1 are calculated by the same methods. Other examples could be added, but this illustrates a fair consistency of stature across the area.

In prehistoric and historical Mississippian societies, variation in diet was a fact of life; and there were major fluctuations among different seasons in the availability of a balanced and adequate diet. In addition, long-term fluctuations in natural systems would have resulted in larger-scale oscillations in diet adequacy, as is well documented in Mississippian skeletal remains (e.g., Powell 1988, and many other sources cited in that work). Skeletal pathology complicates interpretation of causes, but the point is that the physical evidence shows that Mississippian people faced stress at some times, as well as doing quite well at others.

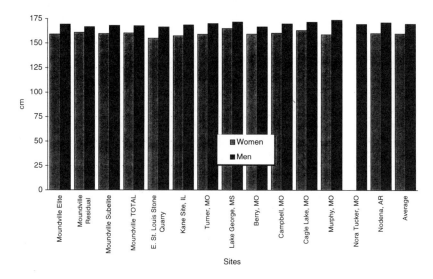

Figure 4.1. Estimated stature of various Mississippian populations.

2. PRODUCTION CYCLES AND NEEDS

The kinds of food grown, harvested, and hunted are described in Chapter 6, but we anticipate those topics here to look at the resources that supported Mississippian reproduction. Mississippian, like the Late Woodland societies outlined in the previous chapter, did not depend only on domesticated plants. Wild-food resources formed a substantial portion of the diet. As in the Late Woodland societies, this mixed economy had implications in terms of both reliability and availability of food. Domesticated plants (and animals) have the great virtue of being "intensifiable"; that is, additional labor generates additional output. There are diminishing returns beyond some point, but there can still be a fairly direct relationship between, say, the amount of land tilled and the annual yield of a crop. Greater effort in collecting may also generate greater yields, but the limit of diminishing returns is reached sooner because of the dispersion and unreliability of wild foods. Limitations on labor availability can also limit the range and intensity of productivity. Suffice it to say here that the balance of time, dependence, and productivity in the Mississippian economy first provided greater security. However, a critical contradiction in Mississippian economies is that they also introduced new risks. For example, intensifiability and diversity allowed an individual Mississippian horticulturist to avoid many problems that faced Late Woodland peoples, but crops in the floodplains meant that flooding became a risk rather than an opportunity. As with any diversified economies, shortfalls in any one of the several productive systems could bring some hardship but be compensated for by alternative production. Failures of productivity in more than one of the systems in the same year could bring disaster, however, given the increasing dependence upon a relatively few production systems.

Bruce Smith's study of the Gypsy Joint site (1978c) is one of the earliest of many illustrations that small Mississippian farmsteads had considerable similarities across the Southeast. Studies show a similar economic basis from the confluence of the Mississippi and the Missouri Rivers across the internal river systems of the Gulf Coastal Plain and many adjacent uplands. In the Black Bottom surveys and excavations, we were able to show how most Mississippian settlement was actually located in these farmsteads–homesteads, not in the major center at Kincaid (see Muller 1978b, 1986b for discussion and references to supporting work). Since that time, the massive highway salvage project in the American Bottom has shown essentially the same relationships between centers and farmsteads that were found in the Black Bottom (see Milner 1986, 1990, 1991 for a summary and references to specific volumes in the many volumes of reports). As areas surrounding centers such as Moundville have been surveyed in finer detail, similar farmstead settlements have become obvious, if not always defined in detail (e.g., Welch 1991:31). These farmsteads, as discussed in the next chapter, provide the economic basis of Mississippian life (e.g., Blitz 1993; Muller 1986b).

Diet

Many studies have shown the *potential* adequacy of the Mississippian diet. For example, Blakeman's study of the botanical remains from hamlets and farmsteads in the

Black Bottom (1974) indicated that—given sufficient quantity and some consumption of greens—the nutritional quality of the Mississippian plant diet, by itself, was surprisingly good. The addition of a fairly standard range of wild animals to the food supply (B. Smith 1974) provided a high-quality diet when sufficient quantity could be acquired. It is worth noting that many of the animals taken were also cornfield predators (Martin et al. 1951; Muller 1986b; see also Buikstra 1992:89). Penny (1983) experimentally found that historical Native American cooking techniques affected the nutritional value of foods consumed by Mississippian peoples both positively and negatively, since cooking destroys some nutrients while others would not have been available at all without cooking. Accordingly, allowances should be made for preparation alterations in our estimates for food requirements, but our rough measures are usually close enough to estimate the effect of, say, variation in acreage on food supply.

Subsistence requirements vary among individuals because of differences in size, weight, and activity. Figure 4.2 shows an estimate of caloric needs per day by different age groups (Wing and Brown 1979). In modern American populations, activity remains fairly constant between age 20 and 45, dropping off about 200 kcal/day after that (National Academy of Science [NAS] 1974:30).

For the Mississippian life tables developed later in this chapter, a population (see Muller 1986b) might be distributed in something like the manner shown in Figure 4.3, using the age-at-death data for the Turner site in Missouri. With the population so distributed and the daily requirement per age group as indicated in Figure 4.2, the average, daily, per capita caloric requirement would be some 2082 kcal.

Another way of approaching the values would be to look at the data on individual size. Average Mississippian body mass may be estimated from the stature figures (given previously) at no more than the "suggested" median mass of 64 to 69 kg of modern American males and generally like the 55 kg of modern American women (1974:29). For these masses, 1750 kcal and 1500 kcal per day, respectively, are the basal-metabolic-rate needs for active adults, to which activities would add further caloric needs. For example, a 50 kg woman engaged in agricultural and home labor (light to moderate) would have a requirement of some 2860 kcal per day (NAS

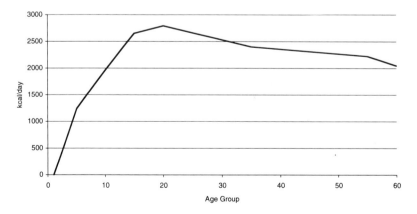

Figure 4.2. Dietary needs by age.

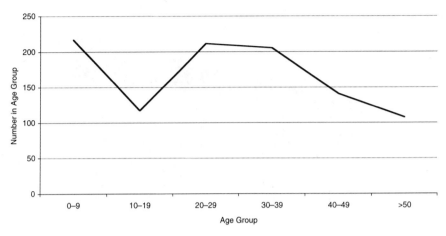

Figure 4.3. A sample Mississippian population distribution (*n* =1000).

1974:29). Recommended daily intake is 2700 to 3000 kcal/day for men and 2000 to 2100 kcal per day for women. Maintenance during pregnancy would require about 300 kcal more per day, and 500 kcal more would be needed during lactation, on the average (NAS 1974:129). Growing children have high requirements, nearly as high as for adult males for boys, or pregnant women for girls. Estimates for caloric needs developed from these figures, then, would be slightly higher than those given above, but generally comparable. In either case, the estimates are close to ethnographic data on consumption (Figure 4.4), ranging from 1706 kcal/day to as high as 2700 kcal. Given the composition of the family residential unit, the general estimate of around 2100 kcal/person/day will be used in some cases in later chapters on production and consumption.

Sources of Calories

A series of good to excellent books have recently dealt with horticultural develop-ment in the East (e.g., Green 1994b; Keegan 1987a; C. M. Scarry 1993; B. Smith 1992; Woods 1992); and other, more broad-ranging books have included papers relevant to the archaeological and biological dimensions of diet in Mississippian times (e.g., Johan-nessen and Hastorf 1994; Sobolik 1994; Verano and Ubelaker 1992). Clearly a short section cannot cover every issue from so much recent work. These are examples that struck me as particularly important, but there are considerable complications and complexities in these areas of research that are not dealt with here.

Overall, the diet of Mississippian peoples was potentially of fairly high quality. Historical data do not give us much detail on how this compares to, say, the Muskogee diet, but we do have a reconstruction of the relative amounts of different kinds of foods in historical New England (Figure 4.5, Bennett 1955). Although one can note that some items such as vegetable oils may be lower than they should be, the overall picture of heavy dependence on grain was probably even more true for the Southeastern peoples.

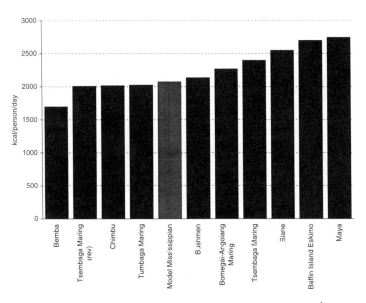

Figure 4.4. Ethnographic consumption data for comparison.[1]

The components of the Mesoamerican food dyad of maize and beans have distinctive histories in the East. The history of the these plants in the East is complex and will be discussed a little more in Chapter 6, but these plants were not introduced into the East as a part of a squash, maize, and beans complex, as was once thought. Such a combination of plants only came into place after A.D. 1200 and was probably facilitated by the networks created by Mississippian peoples, rather than being a cause of their development. The squashes and gourds (*Cucurbita* sp.) were present for thousands of years in the East and were probably local domesticates. Maize or corn (*Zea mays*) may have been present as early as A.D. 200, but, as discussed below, it was not a major source of calories until after A.D. 800–1000 (B. Smith 1992:275–276). The last of the plants to be cultivated widely was the bean (*Phaseolus vulgaris*), coming into widespread use only after A.D. 1200.

We can obtain some information from skeletal remains about the sources of the calories consumed in the prehistoric Southeast. Since animals obtain their carbon either directly or indirectly from plants, the isotopic ratios in their remains can tell us which kinds of plants they consumed, since plants use different means to obtain their carbon from the carbon dioxide in the atmosphere. As a result, the isotopes of carbon in the plant (and its remains) are slightly different. The carbon isotopic ratios in plant tissue can be identified as belonging either to the "Hatch-Slack" (PCA cycle[2]) photo-

---

[1] The sources for the ethnographic cases are as follows: Bemba (Richards 1961); Chimbu (Clarke 1971); Bushmen (Lee 1968); Bomegai-Angoiang Maring (Clarke 1971); Tsembaga Maring (Rappaport 1971, 1984); Siane (Clarke 1971); Baffin Island Eskimo (Kemp 1971); Maya (maize only) (Cowgill 1961).

[2] There are similar isotopic ratios from other metabolisms in the deserts and elsewhere (see Schoeninger and Schurr 1994a:56).

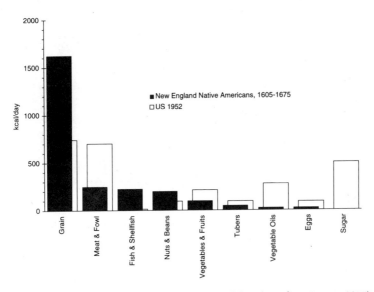

Figure 4.5. Reconstructed New England aboriginal diet. (Data from Bennett 1955)

synthetic pathway characteristic of tropical grasses such as maize or the temperate Calvin (C3, mostly PCR) pathway. As mentioned in Chapter 3, the argument for increasing use of maize in Mississippian times rests partly on C3 and C4 carbon pathway evidence. As seen there, the assumption that maize was virtually the only C4 plant in eastern North America is not correct. Most temperate plants have C3 metabolisms, but some nonmaize, consumable plants also have C4 pathways as do some animals (see Taiz and Zeiger 1992:234; also Schoeninger and Schurr 1994a:55). Whether particular species are C4 has to be determined individually. In any case, the C4 pathway data provide a maximum estimate of how much maize was consumed, realizing that there are other possible plant sources.

In Figures 4.6 and 4.7, the less negative the value of $\delta^{13}C$, the higher the consumption of C4 photosynthetic pathway plants, probably mostly maize. Note the dramatic increase in the early second millennium reflecting a relatively rapid transition to larger scale maize consumption. Maize had become an important direct (and indirect) component of Eastern diet by A.D. 1150, but it was not normally a major component of the diet before that time (e.g., Fritz and Kidder 1992; B. Smith 1992:103). Buikstra discusses the different $\delta^{13}C$ values by different periods, and the pattern is fairly stable before the transition to maize. There is, however, a broader range in the values for the postmaize transition (Figure 4.7; see Buikstra 1992), and the degree of dependence on maize varied widely by region and time.

Maize was *important* to the late prehistoric inhabitants of the East, but not *all important*. However, as will be discussed in Chapter 6, maize became one of the critical "resources of advantage" (Muller and Stephens 1983) for Mississippian peoples. Even when such a resource was not used very much, overall, it may still have

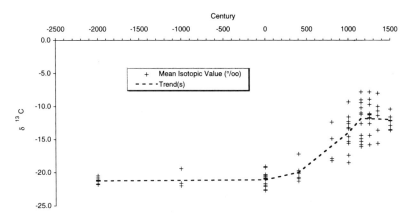

Figure 4.6. Carbon pathway δ^{13}C values by centuries for eastern North America. (The line is separate trend series from 2000 B.C. to A.D. 1, 400–800, 1000–1250, and 1350–1700.)

been of absolutely critical importance *at the times when it was needed*. The conditions that make a resource critical can be diverse. For example, a native domesticate such as maygrass (*Phalaris caroliniana*), a relative of canary grass) could never have been a major contributor to an agricultural system, yet its ripening in the spring, rather than in the fall, meant that it could relieve stores exhausted by winter consumption. Thus, it could seasonally have been critically important before new stocks of more desirable foods were available. It is not surprising, therefore, to find it persisting even after "better" cultigens such as maize came to dominate.

Maize's critical role emerges from a series of features of that plant and its cultivation. These features will be discussed at greater length in discussion of production in Chapter 6, but several important advantages can be stated briefly.

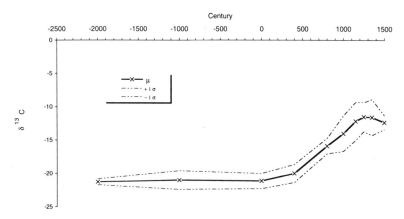

Figure 4.7. Carbon pathway δ^{13}C mean values by centuries for eastern North America. (The dashed lines are ± 1 σ; data mostly from Buikstra 1992.)

1. The advanced varieties of maize are extremely high yield, especially compared to other available domesticates in the East.
2. Maize is intensifiable; within limits, more labor yields more crop.
3. Maize is storable for longer times than are oily seeds (such as nuts) that become rancid.

These, and other, elements make maize very attractive. As Braudel points out (1981:161), maize has astonishingly low production "costs" compared to other major domesticates, and that is surely why it became important so quickly worldwide in tropical zones after the "discovery" of the New World. When things went well, maize provided Mississippian peoples with a good source of calories and even a fairly good diet, especially when consumed as hominy—a treatment that helps to correct some of the amino acid imbalances of a purely maize-based diet. Such a plant is important, since its use undoubtedly gave a substantial reproductive advantage to communities that adopted it at the beginning of Mississippian times.

Assuming maize to have been the major crop would give us some maximum figures for land use necessary to support the populations proposed here. JoAnne Penny (1983:Table 2 and Appendix A) has experimented with weights and caloric values for various Black Bottom Mississippian plant remains and found that 100 grams of raw, dry maize is equivalent to 530 grams of cooked corn meal (*sagamite*). The caloric value of this amount of maize is reduced by about 24 percent from 356 kcal to 270 kcal by cooking (1983:Table 2), and estimates of field area necessary for population support should use the latter figure.

The common bean seems to have been introduced into the East much later than maize, as noted. Like maize, the bean may have been present for a time before becoming acclimatized to Eastern conditions, but it was likely an insignificant diet component until after A.D. 1250 (e.g., B. Smith 1992:293; Yarnell 1976). Whatever the mechanisms, the time of widespread adoption of this plant is normally seen as a period of decline in Mississippian culture and population. Some of this apparent decline is probably an illusion created in a time of increasing dispersion of populations, but other factors such as climatic changes do seem to have resulted in a net decline in population. The bean may even have been a factor in this "decline" of Mississippian central authority by enhancing the productive and reproductive autonomy of individual households and communities (compare the "Schmoo effect," Hall 1980; also Muller 1986b:254–255). The value of the bean is multifold. It is high in calories, and it is superior to nonleguminous plants in providing proteins that are nearly as accessible as those from animal foods. A combined diet of maize and beans provides much better amino acid balance than either does separately. Both of these factors may have been important in the transition from "middle" Mississippian to "late" Mississippian economy at the A.D. 1250 horizon.

The other plant foods in the diet were essentially those of pre-Mississippian times (see B. Smith 1992), although their frequency of use depended on local conditions. Many of the locally domesticated and semidomesticated plants continued to supplement the higher producing Mesoamerican plants, sometimes providing alternative sources for critical nutrients such as vitamins and amino acids that are low in maize-only diets, although the method of preparation can correct for the relative

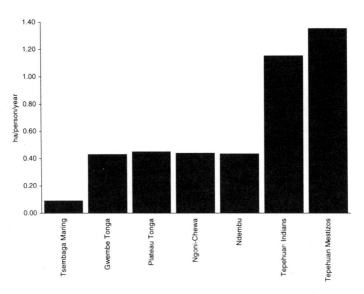

Figure 4.8. Cultivated area per person in different areas.[3]

deficit of maize considerably (e.g., Penny 1983). As in tropical Africa, local domesticates may have continued to have been sown as famine foods or for some special
purpose. Of the wild foods, the nuts consumed in quantity by Mississippians were
good sources for proteins, potentially lessening dependence on game.

Taken altogether, the domesticated, semidomesticated, and wild plant foods
available to Mississippian peoples would have provided an adequate diet, even if no
hunting had taken place. We know, however, that considerable quantities of game
were taken, much of it probably while defending gardens against animal predation
(Muller 1986b:222–226). Hunting has, of course, social values that go beyond mere
dietary needs, but there is little doubt that animal flesh providing proteins, fats, and
other nutrients was favored. One might even argue that success in providing animal
foods could have reproductive consequences in that animal proteins are generally
superior for growth to plant proteins, and certainly superior to maize alone as a basis
for fertility and childhood growth. The game animals available and exploited were
deer and a host of other, but less important, animals. We know that these animals
were hunted, but it is more difficult to estimate the quantities and contributions they
made to the overall diet.

Schoeninger and Peebles (1981) tested a sample of 132 burials for strontium
levels out of over 2000 at Moundville and found indications of more meat in the diet
of individuals designated as "elite." As we saw earlier, of course, there was little

---

[3] Data for Tsembaga Maring with low pig frequency (Rappaport 1984); Gwembe Tonga nonmaize-based
gardening (Scudder 1962); Ndembu for a mixed economy with some maize (Turner 1957); Tepehuan
Indians and Mestizos for maize-based with some nonagricultural pursuits (Pennington 1969).

difference in stature of Moundville elite and nonelite. More recently, Welch has summarized Susan Scott's work (Welch 1991:88–103) that suggests differential provisioning of persons at a "subsidiary center" with better cuts of deer. However, at the same time, it was noted that "all sites of the Moundville chiefdom had direct access to the same overall set of faunal resources and exploited them in a fundamentally similar way" (1991:103). As in other cases, there can be no doubt that there were social differences among different segments of Mississippian societies, but there should be more skepticism that these data support the interpretation that the differences were of great magnitude. The case for "nobility" and "commoners" is a long way from proved by such evidence, especially to the extent that such terms imply a classlike structure. I think it unfortunate to impose these names on Mississippian social formations in the absence of more evidence of their appropriateness. On the contrary, the social differences that we see in the historical Eastern polities would be more than sufficient to explain such archaeological biological evidence were we to hypothesize that prehistoric systems were like the historical ones. Again, the case for similarity in social status between archaeological and historical societies is not yet proved, but neither has sufficient attention been given to rejecting this possibility. In too many cases, the possibility of similarity between historical and prehistoric societies has not even been considered.

Biological Requirements for Production

From these estimates of biological needs, it is possible to estimate the amount of land necessary to support each person. First, we may ask, what is the amount of support land necessary for a horticultural people in documented ethnographic cases? Table 4.1 indicates the range for a widely varying set of production systems, but still averaging about 0.5 ha/person/year.

Figure 4.8 indicates the amount of cultivated land required for each person in a series of different economies. The average ha/person/year value is around 0.46 ha for a broader series than shown—not surprisingly, close to the old English acre. The relationship between numbers of members of a production unit (here equivalent to the household) and the area cultivated is direct in simple economies. Among the Tonga, for example, the relationship between area cultivated and the size of the

Table 4.1. Various Production Systems and Production Areas

People	ha/person/year	Source
Tsembaga Maring	0.09	Rappaport 1984:292
Yakö	0.09	Forde 1964
Bomegai-Anoiang	0.09	Clarke 1971
Gwembe Tonga	0.43	Scudder 1962
Plateau Tonga	0.45	Allan 1965:57
Ngoni-Chewa	0.44	Allan 1965:58
Ndembu	0.43	Turner 1957
Tepehuan Indians	1.15	Pennington 1969
Tepehuan Mestizos	1.35	Pennington 1969

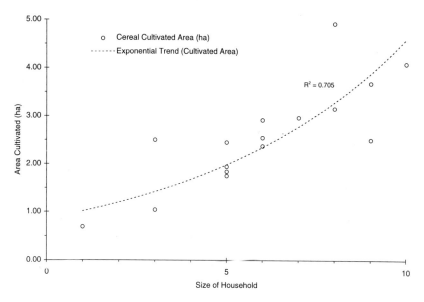

Figure 4.9. Relationship of land cultivated and household size among the Tonga (Mazulu Village, 1956–1957; data from Scudder 1962).[4]

household is shown in Figure 4.9, showing a common pattern of close relationships between these variables.

From a model life table for a representative population of 1000, as discussed above (Figure 4.3), the caloric values and the percentage of dependence upon maize yield the range of values for number of ha/person in Table 4.2.

These indicate a range from 0.07 ha/person to 0.29 ha/person of maize fields, depending on the yields and degree of dependence on this one crop. Historical figures for maize cultivation in the Great Plains indicate that the average there was also close to the range discussed earlier (Will and Hyde 1917, however with both government rationing and hunting activity.

Here we are concerned with individual and family needs, and we should note that the most probable values for Mississippian societies probably fall on this table between the 40 percent and 60 percent dependence, and at about 1200 kg/ha yields. These and similar values will be developed further in Chapter 5 in a discussion of overall population density, and still further in Chapter 6 on production. Figure 4.10 presents these ranges of values for families of 5 persons, a common estimated size for a Mississippian household.

If the nearly universal 0.4-ha/person support area figure is taken, the amount of land necessary for a family of 5 would be closer to 2.0 ha.

---

[4] Not including households with persons with external employment.

Table 4.2. ha of Maize Cultivation Necessary per Person (kcal for Cooked Maize)

% Maize dependence	ha @ 1000 kg/ha	ha @ 1200 kg/ha	ha @ 1500 kg/ha	ha @ 1700 kg/ha
100%	0.29	0.25	0.20	0.17
80%	0.24	0.20	0.16	0.14
60%	0.18	0.15	0.12	0.10
40%	0.12	0.10	0.08	0.07

Diet, Risk, and Uncertainty

Powell (1988:197) and Milner (1982); among others, have emphasized overall improvement brought by the developing Mississippian economy. Others (e.g., Cassidy 1972; Hill-Clark 1981; Hoyme and Bass 1962; Lallo 1973; Lallo and Rose 1979; Larsen 1982; and Rose 1973, 1977) have seen increasing stresses in the Mississippian societies as opposed to the preceding Late Woodland societies. These views are not so inconsistent as they seem at first glance. Risk *had* increased, but the *average* level of subsistence in good years was no doubt better than in earlier times. It is terribly important not to confuse two different kinds of risk and threat, however. One is the stress or risk suffered by the individual as an individual organism. These are the stresses measured by some of the physical evidence examined by these bioanthropologists. These individual problems, however, are not necessarily relevant to the issue of reproductive success at either the individual or social level. Short life

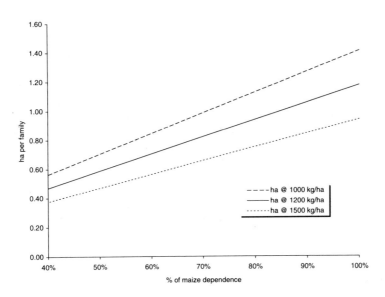

Figure 4.10. Maize garden area necessary for a family of five at different yields and levels of maize dependence.

combined with high reproductive rates is a kind of evolutionary strategy[5] followed by many successful species. It often proves to be selectively advantageous to purge the population of those elements that contribute little to reproductive success. Biological and cultural evolutionary success by no means has to be related to improvement in the *individual* standard of living within a population. Both selectional and dialectical processes are largely blind to the individual outside of those activities and events that *are* critical to the survival of the society. It is also important to distinguish between long-term and short-term processes, since activities giving short-term advantages can potentially have long-term implications that are both unforeseen and even unforeseeable.

There is uncertainty about the quantities of particular foods in the Mississippian diet, but there is evidence from bones and teeth that give us some data on the adequacy of overall diet (and the incidence of disease) during the maturation of individuals. For example, the increase of caries in Mississippian as compared to earlier populations illustrates the (dental) health consequences of an increasing dependence on horticulture, as shown by correspondence to horticultural populations elsewhere in the world (Barmes 1977; M. Smith 1986, 1987).

Another of these lines of evidence is to be found in dental pathology. Incidents of stress during the time of development of teeth can be reflected in interruption of enamel formation resulting in a condition known as *enamel hypoplasia* (Powell summarizes the nature of this pathology and gives a series of references, 1988:68–69). Easily identified in a portion of the anatomy that is normally well-preserved, enamel hypoplasia gives clues about events in a person's life that interfered with normal body functions. It does not, of course, indicate exactly what caused the stresses, but incidence of the pathology is especially useful as a measure of events at the critical period of weaning, one of the most difficult times in a person's development.

The charts in Figure 4.11 show the incidence of enamel hypoplasia at Etowah, the major Georgian "Mississippian" center, and the King site, which dates to historical times from the same general region. Each chart shows the percentage of the population that had a this kind of damage to the tooth enamel resulting from stress during the formation of the tooth. This provides a kind of window on early childhood among the two groups shown in each chart—those individuals who survived childhood, and those who died as subadolescents, in these cases (Blakely 1988a:28–29). Difficulties in enamel development can come from a number of causes and only measure a kind of generalized "stress," since these problems can occur from malnutrition or from diseases that interfere with the ability of the body to make use of nutrients in food.

The data suggest that the protohistoric King population had slightly less incidence of stresses as children than did the peak Mississippian(-like) population at

---

[5] Give me a break. I know how dangerous it is to personify and confuse evolutionary processes with concepts and terminology that suggest conscious choice. However, even "selectionist" paradigm scholars themselves employ such careless terms precisely because the alternatives make discourse cumbersome and difficult. Give me the benefit of the doubt and understand that I am not addressing the issue here of consciousness or the role of cognition in evolutionary process.

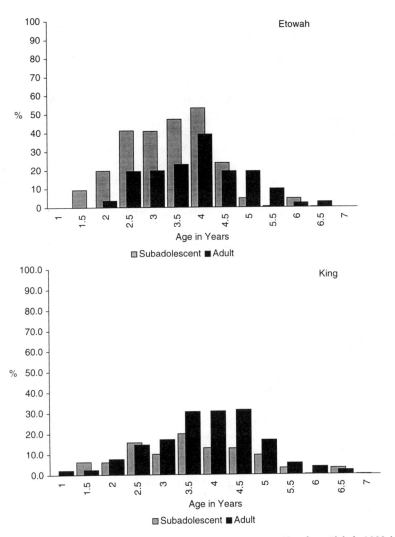

Figure 4.11. Enamel hypoplasia by age in Georgia at two sites (data from Blakely 1988a).

Etowah. The differences are especially marked in those who died as children, and Blakely interprets these differences to support a heavier dependence on hunting in the King population than was the case at Etowah (Blakely 1988a:27–28). Among those who survived to adulthood, the populations show similar levels of stress, but childhood mortality was much higher at Etowah than at the King site (1988a:27). Although this is surprising from the point of view of stereotypical views of Mississippian "decline" in post-1250 times, it is consistent with the models such as those hinted at earlier which suggest that the apparent decline in Mississippian societies throughout the Southeast may partly have been due to the introduction of crops and production methods allowing greater household production autonomy through improvements in household food production.

Similar data are available from other sites. At Moundville, a large skeletal population has been studied (Powell 1988). A number of skeletons have also been examined for hypoplasia in the American Bottom (Milner 1982). Both at Moundville and in the American Bottom, similar conditions appear to have prevailed. Some kinds of stress affected a substantial number of children in both societies, but it is important to note that less than half of all those surviving to adulthood showed any sign of these at a given time. Less than 60 percent of the people at Moundville had such problems at any of these developmental ages (Powell 1988:113). It is true that 90 percent had such problems in some samples from the American Bottom, but "severe" stress was not present (Milner 1982:193). At Moundville, "neither visual inspection nor statistical analysis suggests that the elite status segment differed significantly from the other two segments, or that the latter differed from one another in this respect" (Powell 1982:114). The physical evidence from enamel hypoplasia, like that from other lines of evidence not discussed here, is that health conditions for reproduction in these societies are neither strikingly good or bad. The data on these ill-defined "stresses" are exactly what we might expect from the life table data discussed earlier—Mississippian societies are struggling along but are not either enormously successful or disastrously failing in biological terms. The social, competitive success of Mississippian lifeways was a matter of aggregation to form groups that could outcompete others rather than a matter of pure reproductive success.

3. OTHER INFLUENCES ON POPULATIONS

Reproductive Implications of Kinship

The nature of prehistoric social organization is uncertain. Although most of the historical peoples of the Southeast had matrilineal descent systems, there were some patrilineal groups, notably the Dhegiha Siouan speakers of the Missouri–Mississippi Valleys. In either case, the resulting lineage structure had segmentary features that are well discussed by a number of authors, (especially Anderson 1994b and Pauketat 1984, if sometimes by the latter in terms that owe much to class-based social formations). The implications of a lineage-based system of rank include the presence of numerous rivals for political statuses, as well as social traditions of "power" associated with particular individuals. As clans and lineages were spread across the landscape, any faltering by the chief could quickly result in rival claims to ranked positions. In the Southeast, every "brother-cousin" can make his claims, and "sister-cousins" may also be potential rivals in some circumstances. In some senses then, the very biological genesis of power contains the contradictory legitimization of rival claims by direct and collateral kin.

Were there elite and nonelite lineages? To be sure, the historical records show that some Southeastern lineages were ranked above others. At the same time, there is less to the distinction between elite and nonelite than meets the eye at first glance. As we saw in Chapter 2, the differences were not very great in historical societies. We saw that the respect paid to a chief was extended to some close kin, but by no means did all members of particular clans or even lineages clearly receive such deference. Swanton's exposition of Creek kinship (1928a) cannot simply be pushed back into prehistoric times, but neither can its lessons on the flexibility of real kinship systems and "power" be ignored (a point made at length in social anthropological studies such as Leach 1954). It is important to recognize that there were circumstances under which the clan from which *micos* (chiefs) were chosen could be changed (e.g., Swanton 1928a: 280–281). Both the mico and the "warchief," or *tastanagi*, were chosen in terms of moiety divisions. Chiefs could be deposed as well as chosen.

In prehistoric times, claims of ranked differences at major sites such as Moundville have been made on the basis of grave associations (e.g., Peebles 1983). Peebles also noted that evidence suggested some differential access to meat, as a measure of a desired good (1983; Schoeninger and Peebles 1981). In the next section, we shall reexamine some of the evidence about status and biological indicators. In later chapters, we shall look at some other indicators of rank.

Status and Biology

What are the indications of status differences in Mississippian populations? Powell has examined the relationships between health and ranked status at Moundville in Georgia. She also summarized evidence from other Late Prehistoric complexes (1988), so it is not necessary to repeat this task, so admirably accomplished in her work. We may simply understand that little in the way of significant difference was found between mound and nonmound burials at Moundville, Etowah, Chucalissa, or the Dallas and Hixon sites. It is worth cautioning, however, that the status-related differences in adult male body size mentioned by Powell were *not* statistically significant at Moundville, and that status-related differences thought to exist elsewhere have to be accepted with caution.

One trait showing significant differences was fractures in "elite" males at Chucalissa. At that site, elite males significantly exceeded other segments in numbers of fractures, and this might be taken as an indication of a potential contribution to status by achievement in warfare (e.g. Brown 1976; Gibson 1974; Knight 1986, 1990; Lahren and Berryman 1984; Robinson 1976). Given my views on Mississippian rank and status, I welcome such evidence, but I must again urge caution in interpretation. We must remember that the non-Moundville sites in these comparisons are, on the average, quite late, generally dating after A.D. 1250—after the Southern Cult horizon that marked significant changes in the number and scale of public works across the Southeast, among other things. The skeletons studied also came from archaeological sites that are multicomponent sites or sites at which the "phase" provenience has long duration. Especially in the case of the Dallas so-called "phase", the time period from A.D. 1300 to 1550 includes a period of considerable changes in the eastern Tennessee Valley. My own studies of shell gorgets (Muller 1976, 1979, 1989) suggest that there may have been important social shifts in east Tennessee between A.D. 1200 and 1400. The possibility exists that the village burials at Dallas and Hixon sites belong to a different chronological period, and even perhaps to a different ethnic group, than some of the "elite" burials. At Etowah, we know that the "nonelite" village burials are definitely from a different time (post A.D. 1440) than the Wilbanks phase (A.D.

1250–1400) burials from Mound C.[6] In these cases, we cannot exclude the possibility that "significant" differences are referring to factors other than status. Notwithstanding these repeated *caveats*, I suspect that solidly contemporary "elite" and "nonelite" populations would probably show no more differentiation than is documented for these samples, that though the data may be flawed, the conclusions are probably pretty close to right. Certainly the differences in the more controlled sample from Moundville suggests this sort of scale is essentially correct. As Powell states, "The biological factors of age and sex exerted the strongest influence in determination of these patterns, both directly and indirectly. Ranked status seems to have played a minor role in the determination of health at Moundville, as reflected in the dental and skeletal features examined in this study" (1988:182). If this is true for Moundville—the second largest Mississippian site in mound construction—what must other, smaller Late Prehistoric social systems be like?

Disease

In an earlier work (Muller 1986b:265ff.), I drew parallels between late Medieval Europe and contemporary Southeastern groups in relation to diseases and social environments. In the Old World, we have historical records of epidemics that drastically reduced human populations. We have no comparable historical records for Eastern North America, and the only settlements that seem to show traumatic effects (literally and figuratively) on populations are at the contacts with the European invaders (e.g., Blakely 1988b). At first glance, the relatively dispersed character of much Southeastern settlement might suggest low rates of contagion of infectious disease. Although possibly true in some senses, these Late Prehistoric peoples were *relatively* packed locally by comparison to truly dispersed hunter–gatherer populations. Furthermore, by "classic" Mississippian times (ca. A.D. 1200), Late Prehistoric societies had been living on the same floodplain ridges for as much as 400 years. Any farmer can tell you that a failure to rotate a crop can lead to the buildup of diseases in a field. So it is, too, with human populations. Epidemic diseases can establish themselves and spread even in *relatively* dispersed settlement systems; witness the rapid spread of the plague in Scandinavia in the 14th century.[7]

Smallpox, measles, and many other Old World epidemic diseases were not present in the New World until the European contacts of the 16th century. Had the fanciful and fantastic contacts (see Williams 1991) between Africa, Asia, or Europe

---

[6] However, the reader should note that Jeffrey Brain, in a work of which I received a copy only after the completion of this chapter (Brain and Phillips 1996), argues for substantially later dating for most of the "Southern Cult" gorgets of many different styles. Suffice it to say here that I do not think this makes sense for many reasons, including requiring the persistence of northern Mississippian sites such as Cahokia and Kincaid much later than seems to be the case.

[7] Plague, *Yersinia* (*Pasteurella*) *pestis*, is endemic to rodent/flea populations in the New World today, but we have no evidence of the pre-Columbian spread of the Black Death into the New World from Iceland—where it is known to have spread in the 14th century—although such a connection might have been possible through Greenland Inuit populations and Viking contacts with them. However, the failure of other Old World diseases to spread through this route makes this possibility seem unlikely.

and the Americas taken place at levels to have allowed the transmission of elements of "civilization," the transmission of these diseases would surely have also occurred. At first contact with particular populations in the Old World, smallpox and measles produced death rates from 25 to 30 percent over a period of years (e.g., Gottfried 1983:5–6). The genetic makeup of Old World populations reflects strong selective pressure from these diseases, but resistance to them was lacking in the Americas, allowing certainty that these diseases were not introduced before the documented contacts. In turn, this conclusion leads to the further implication that there was no *substantial* or *sustained* contact between the Old and New Worlds before Columbus. After the initial "discovery," even the transitory contacts that took place were sufficient to introduce these diseases, which in some cases appear to have spread ahead of the actual course of exploration (e.g., Nuñez Cabeça de Vaca, 1542 [1871:74], Gentleman of Elvas 1557 [Buckingham Smith 1866:63]). Certainly there were Viking contacts in the north, but these did not constitute the types of contacts that shape civilizations, nor do they seem to have introduced European diseases into the north.

This is not to say that neither epidemics nor infectious diseases existed in pre-Columbian North America. There is evidence for a series of serious health problems in the East. Of course, most infectious diseases leave little or no traces in skeletal morphology. Even for those that do affect bone tissue, it can often be extremely difficult to distinguish among the effects of different diseases. Tuberculosis is likely to have been present, and it is significant, because it can be highly infectious and because of its ability to maintain itself as a "hidden" disease in apparently healthy individuals that may become active if stress or poor nutrition weaken the body's immune system (Buikstra 1981; Powell 1988:152–159).

Infections of the *Treponema* spirochete also seem to have been present, but it is impossible to be sure whether one particular form or another was present from skeletal evidence (e.g., Bassett in Jefferies and Butler 1982:1066ff.; Powell 1988:159ff.). Powell, working at Moundville from an epidemiological model first constructed for Illinois Woodland populations by Cook (1976), concluded that like earlier Eastern populations, nonvenereal yawslike treponemal infections were present rather than syphilis (1988:173). Such infections would probably not have depressed fertility or increased mortality, but they could have made life miserable. Another disease affecting the skeletal system was a form of osteomyelitis, probably resulting from *Staphylococcus* infections (1988:149–152). Like tuberculosis, such infections can become chronic, flaring up at times of biological stress.

Studies of Archaic health in southern Illinois (Bassett in Jefferies and Butler 1982:1055), suggest fewer problems in health at times of weaning in those populations than in later Mississippian times, when it seems likely that corn was the major solid food after weaning. Mississippian juveniles continue to show fairly high mortality, but adult mortality is generally less severe than in earlier times. Studies of the pathologies on the skeletons have shown much higher rates of bone fracture for Archaic populations than was characteristic for the later Woodland and Mississippian peoples (Steinbock 1976, Buikstra 1981).[8] In these ways the data from widely scat-

---

[8] Buikstra suggested that the differences may partially be due to differential burial patterns.

tered regions suggest that Mississippian period peoples were better off, at least in some respects.

Conflict, War, and Biology

To begin, let us not confuse war and conflict. The latter may simply be a biological phenomenon resulting from natural competition. War, on the other hand, is a *culturally* defined state of conflict between *societies*, not individuals. It can be argued that war in the strict sense does not exist prior to the emergence of classes and the state, but that is not our concern here. For now, it is enough to distinguish individual aggressive acts from those involving larger groups. The best evidence for conflict in the Southeastern archaeological record is from two kinds of sources: fortification of sites and—our concern here—trauma shown on bones. The existence of fortifications indicates the need to protect social groups but does not tell us the nature of the threat. Was it to prevent raiding, or was it a defended line placed under siege by opposing armies? It is often even more difficult to determine whether damage to human bone is the result of careless peaceful activities or the marks of combat. Even if wounds are clearly the result of human aggression, are those acts the result of person-to-person differences or warfare?

The impact of conflict is also difficult to gauge. In Kroeber's analysis of Eastern population density, he indicated that low population in the East was a result of conflict,

> Of social factors, the most direct may be considered to have been warlike habits. Reference is not to systematic, decisive war leading to occasional great destructions but also to conquest, settlement, and periods of consolidation and prosperity. Of all this the Eastern tribes knew nothing. They waged war not for any ulterior or permanent fruits, but for victory; and its conduct and shaping were motivated, when not by revenge, principally by individual desire for personal status within one's society. It was warfare that was insane, unending, continuously attritional, from our point of view; and yet it was so integrated into the whole fabric of Eastern culture, so dominantly emphasized within it, that escape from it was well-nigh impossible. Continuance in the system became self-preservatory. The group that tried to shift its values from war to peace was almost certainly doomed to early extinction. This warfare with its attendant unsettlement, confusion, destruction, and famines, was probably the most potent reason why population remained low in the East. Kroeber 1939:148

Well, we are not obliged to accept quite so grim a view of even the historical groups. It would be unreasonable to assume that the levels of conflict characteristic of historical times—with European invasions and conquests—were characteristic of prehistoric times as well. Kroeber surprisingly gives no role to either European disease or "insane, unending, continuously attritional" European military actions in his characterization of social conflict in historical times. As Frances Jennings has shown (1975), the patterns of historical warfare (even in the strictest sense) were part of the diplomatic and political practices of developing native polities in opposition to and alliance with the invading European military forces. It is true, as we have seen already, that post–A.D. 1250 evidence shows increased conflicts, such as shown among the elite persons from Chucalissa. In the Illinois Valley, there are indications of conflict among possibly different ethnic groups in late prehistoric times, even if the interpretations there are strained by having such terms as "retainer sacrifice" and "primitive state" imposed upon them (cf. Conrad 1989, 1991). In all the cases, however, the occurrence of injuries is not so great as we should expect were the situation like that hypothesized by Kroeber.

Studies such as those of Knight (1986, 1990), Larson (1971, 1972), and Sears (1961) have made interesting contributions to discussions of religious and social backgrounds of rank and conflict in the Southeast. Success in conflict was attainable, however, by persons of relatively "common" origins historically, and, although this may have been increased by the instabilities of the Historic period, we can hardly deny that instabilities existed long before the European invasions (see Anderson 1994b).

Overview

Powell indicates a set of conditions at Moundville that are probably representative of Mississippian populations, at least at the major centers: "Skeletal pathology was widespread in the population. The abundant evidence of bone inflammation, in almost all cases minor in extent, reflected a vigorous immune response to infectious diseases endemic in the population" (Powell 1988:178). She further summarizes "five levels of population experience with physiological stress" (1988:180–181) at Moundville:

1. Population-wide experience with nonspecific stress and infectious diseases that affected most members of each generation.
2. Age-graded differential experience, typified by the absence in subadults of trauma, antemortem tooth loss, and vertebral lesions from mechanical stress.
3. Sex-linked differences in the prevalence of trauma and dental caries.
4. Status-associated differences (to a minor degree) in adult male body size and skeletal evidence of iron-deficiency anemia.
5. Individual differences in growth, development, and resistance to pathological stress.

The relatively few studies of Mississippian health from other sites give much the same picture, as already noted. In line with the earlier discussion of mortality and reproduction, we see here a population that is not living in a paradise, but a biological environment that is similar to that of other "Neolithic" peoples elsewhere in the world. Under these conditions, the centers that attract "rural" populations can be unhealthy, if for no other reason that formerly dispersed people often had not had time to develop the increased hygienic measures needed by aggregated populations.

4. POPULATION PROFILES

Background to Population Studies

The state of health and reproduction of Mississippian populations has been a subject of a low-keyed but earnest debate (see Powell 1992a). One cannot honestly say that the evidence is overwhelming that health improved or declined during the transition to (and duration of) Mississippian. *Mirable dictu*, the health of particular people seems to have depended on local factors! We may expect general patterns, but, of course, the health of any population depends on many factors (e.g., food, disease, crowding, isolation), so we should not expect uniform health conditions.

The contradictions of archaeological evidence mentioned in Chapter 1 come into play here. The contradiction between archaeologists' ability to see things largely in the long term while the evidence itself is mostly from short-term activities is intrinsic to our field. This problem pervades the interpretation of human remains. A cemetery may have been in use for a long time, but short-term events such as famines or epidemics can shape its representativeness of the population, and each burial, *qua* burial, represents a brief burst of activity conditioned by circumstances that may have been just as episodic.

For this reason, among others, some have concluded that the use of skeletal populations from uncontrolled contexts is either dangerously misleading or downright impossible. Such criticisms and cautions are valuable but cannot be allowed to paralyze research. In actual practice, archaeological interpretation over time is rescued by a kind of "average," by the persistence of behavioral forms. Even within the 50- to 100-year spans that we typically control, it is possible to see patterns so long as we are not blinded by looking too closely at individual cases. We can use the evidence as a part of a research strategy that lifts itself out of its impasse by its "bootstraps,"[9] that is to say, by a kind of meta-analysis of the results overall. Our research must be theory based, with methods derived from the problem. Whole methods should not be rejected solely because current observations are of poorer quality than we would wish in an ideal world. One task of analysis, after all, is to provide targets for new data-based efforts at refutation. There are no "perfect" data, and we are doomed to inaction if we wait for them.

Although the formal data are currently inadequate for a formal "bootstrap" sampling procedure, I have discussed formal mathematical models for the growth of Mississippian populations that show consistent trends similar to those seen in historical Southeastern populations (Muller 1993b, also later in this chapter). A general discussion of the issues of Mississippian population dynamics follows.

Mississippian Population Profiles

Population profiles drawn from burials are available for a number of Mississippian sites. A grab-bag selection of these are presented in Table 4.3 as an example of the kinds of data we have. The usual, but crucial, cautions for archaeological data apply here: These data reflect the conditions of the behaviors that determined who was buried, as well as how and where. Notwithstanding these biases, the samples may be taken as representative for the sake of argument.

Given the incompleteness of skeletal populations, the variation in age-of-death percentages is not of any great significance, but all show high infant mortality. Infant mortality is often underrepresented because of burial practices and preservation prob-

---

[9]For examples of formal "bootstrap" procedures in statistical examination, see Efron and Tibshirani (1986), or Corruccini (1992).

Table 4.3. Skeletal Age Profiles for Selected Mississippian Sites[a]

Age	E. St. Louis Stone Quarry, IL	Dickson Mounds, IL	Turner, MO	King, GA	Moundville, AL	Age	Schild, IL
0–9	29.9%	35.0%	18.0%[b]	25.4%	17.7%	0	20.1%
10–19	8.0%	9.0%	21.1%	9.5%	7.1%	1–11	21.7%
20–29	12.6%	15.0%	15.7%	19.6%	23.2%	12–19	6.3%
30–39	12.1%	16.0%	17.3%	10.6%	31.6%	20–34	21.7%
40–49	19.4%	0.14	14.3%	21.2%	14.5%	35–49	15.0%
>50	18.0%	11.0%	13.7%	13.8%	5.9%	>50	15.4%

[a]Data grouped from those presented in Black 1979; Blakely 1971, 1988a; Goldstein 1980; Milner 1983a; Powell 1988.
[b]Including interpolation for Turner from Dickson Mounds data for 0–9.

lems. Moundville stands out in its high mortality in the 30–39 year age range, but the other patterns are generally similar.

From such skeletal mortality profiles, it is possible to build life tables, although it is important to be aware that each step away from the skeletal data gets a little less certain.

For example, a life table for the Turner site has been described (Blakely 1979:88) as similar to Weiss's model table MT:20.0–60.0 (1973:130), and other tables also seem generally to be within the ranges for that series of model tables (MT:20-j). Of course, Weiss's model tables are for stationary populations, an assumption that is a moot point for real Mississippian populations. The construction of any life tables also assumes a population equilibrium that may not have been present (see also Moore, Swedlund, and Armelagos 1975:63 and elsewhere).

The various life tables (Table 4.4) from data from various sources are standardized for comparison to decade-long periods from 0 to 50+ years. The tables are presented to examine variability in Mississippian populations over space and time. The standard terms (see Weiss 1973) used in the tables are as follows:

$D(x)$	Crude death rate, actual skeletal population count
$d(x)$	Number that died in interval of the "radix"—that is, *model* population size
$l(x) = l(y - x) - d(x - y)$	Number of survivors to age x of radix $l(0)$
$q(x) = d(x)/l(x)$	Probability of dying in age class
$L(x) = ((l(x) + l(x + 1))/2$	Number of years lived by survivors between x and $x + 1$
$T(x) = \Sigma L(x) - L(x)$	Yrs. to be lived by pop. now aged x before all are dead (person-years)
$E(x) = T(x)/l(x)$	Life expectancy at age x

As in the skeletal age-of-death percentages above, most of the tables share a common pattern of high infant mortality. Life expectancy at birth, $E(0)$, calculates as ca. 16 to 28 years, with life expectancy at age 20, $E(20)$, falling between 14 to 24 years. These figures are generally similar to those for pre-Mississippian groups for which data are available, as shown in the tables included for Illinois Hopewell and Illinois Archaic. The conditions for the Archaic population at Indian Knoll in Kentucky stand out as

Table 4.4. Life Tables for Mississippian and Other Groups in the East

x	[D(x)]	d(x)	l(x)	q(x)	L(x)	T(x)	E(x)
Dickson, IL [from data in Blakely 1971 (also see Black 1979:87)]							
0	35.3%	169	35	100	0.35	824	2425	24.2
10	9.6%	46	10	65	0.15	599	1601	24.7
20	15.4%	74	15	55	0.28	474	1002	18.2
30	15.9%	76	16	40	0.40	317	528	13.3
40	14.6%	70	15	24	0.61	165	211	8.9
50	9.2%	44	9	9	1.00	46	46	5.0
Schild, IL (from data in Goldstein 1980)							
0	20.1%	42	20	100	0.201	90	1607	16.1
1	21.7%	45	22	80	0.271	69	1517	19.0
12	6.3%	13	6	58	0.108	661	1448	24.9
20	21.7%	45	22	52	0.417	329	787	15.1
35	15.0%	31	15	30	0.494	343	458	15.1
50	15.4%	32	15	15	1.000	115	115	7.5
Moss, IL (from data in Goldstein 1980)							
0	0.0%	0	0	100	0.000	100	2294	22.9
1	4.9%	2	5	100	0.049	98	2194	21.9
12	12.2%	5	12	95	0.128	979	2096	22.0
20	14.6%	6	15	83	0.176	605	1117	13.5
35	68.3%	28	68	68	1.000	512	512	7.5
50	0.0%	0	0	0	0.000	0	0	0.0
Stone Quarry, IL (from data in Milner 1983a:85)							
0	29.9%	38	30	100	0.299	850	2915	29.2
10	8.0%	10	8	70	0.114	661	2065	29.5
20	12.6%	16	13	62	0.202	558	1404	22.6
30	12.1%	15	12	50	0.245	434	846	17.1
40	19.4%	25	19	37	0.518	277	412	11.0
50	18.0%	23	18	18	1.000	135	135	7.5
Turner, MO (from data in Black 1979:89: Table 31)							
0	21.7%[a]	14	22	100	0.217	892	2787	27.9
10	11.7%	8	12	78	0.150	724	1895	24.2
20	21.2%	14	21	67	0.318	560	1170	17.6
30	20.5%	13	21	45	0.452	351	610	13.4
40	14.1%	9	14	25	0.567	178	259	10.4
50	10.8%	7	11	11	1.000	81	81	7.5
Moundville, AL (from data in Powell 1988:Table 11)							
0	17.7%	18	18	100	0.177	911	2842	28.4
10	7.1%	7	7	82	0.086	787	1930	23.5
20	23.2%	23	23	75	0.309	636	1143	15.2
30	31.6%	32	32	52	0.608	362	508	9.8
40	14.5%	15	15	20	0.713	131	146	7.2
50	5.9%	6	6	6	1.000	15	15	2.5

Table 4.4. (*Continued*)

x	[D(x)]	d(x)	l(x)	q(x)	L(x)	T(x)	E(x)
Florence St., IL (from data in Emerson, Milner, and Jackson 1983:266)							
0	19%	9	19	50	0.375	122	1023	20.5
3	10%	5	10	31	0.333	234	901	28.8
12	0%	0	0	21	0.000	167	667	32.0
20	6%	3	6	21	0.300	266	500	24.0
35	6%	3	6	15	0.429	172	234	16.1
50	8%	4	8	8	1.000	63	63	7.5
King, GA (from data in Blakely 1988a:30)							
0	25.4%	48	25	100	0.254	873	2873	28.7
10	9.5%	18	10	75	0.128	698	2000	26.8
20	19.6%	37	20	65	0.301	553	1302	20.0
30	10.6%	20	11	46	0.233	402	749	16.5
40	21.2%	40	21	35	0.606	243	347	9.9
50	13.8%	26	14	14	1.000	103	103	7.5
Archaic, IL (from data in Blakely 1971)							
0	48.0%		48	100	0.480	760	2138	21.4
10	11.0%		11	52	0.212	465	1378	26.5
20	7.0%		7	41	0.171	375	913	22.3
30	11.0%		11	34	0.324	285	538	15.8
40	12.0%		12	23	0.522	170	253	11.0
50	11.0%		11	11	1.000	83	83	7.5
Indian Knoll, KY (from data in Blakely 1971)							
0	37%		37	100	0.370	815	1803	18.0
10	11%		11	63	0.175	575	988	15.7
20	41%		41	52	0.788	315	413	7.9
30	8%		8	11	0.727	70	98	8.9
40	2%		2	3	0.667	20	28	9.2
50	1%		1	1	1.000	8	8	7.5
Hopewell, IL (from data in Blakely 1971)							
0	27.89%	82	28	100	0.279	861	2960	29.6
10	8.16%	24	8	72	0.113	680	2099	29.1
20	13.27%	39	13	64	0.207	573	1419	22.2
30	13.95%	41	14	51	0.275	437	846	16.7
40	18.71%	55	19	37	0.509	274	409	11.1
50	18.03%	53	18	18	1.000	135	135	7.5

[a]Without interpolated infants from Dickson Mounds, IL data.

indicating poorer conditions in some pre-Mississippian groups. Indian Knoll is unusual for the truly awful health of its population (see discussion in Muller 1986b:77).

Even with their problems, these kinds of life tables provide a rough measure by which different populations can be compared. Figure 4.12 illustrates the actual percentage of deceased in each age class, showing the average for the "hard-core" Mississippian societies and the standard deviation, as well as the maximum and minimum values for each age class. There are other Mississippian populations for whom such tables could be constructed, but these are sufficient to illustrate the patterns.

Of course, an underlying assumption for construction of life tables is that the population was stable. The necessity for this assumption is that the birth cohorts represented by the individuals in a cemetery have to be of equivalent size, or there must be a correction for cohort size by the rate of intrinsic increase (see Moore et al. 1975:63). The problem is, in broader terms, one of compound interest. In principle, then, the constructed life table is a poor basis on which to estimate different birth- and increase rates. Even so, we may try a speculative simulation of possible demographic rates to see how well they model the kinds of skeletal-age profiles discussed above. One equation used to construct a model age distribution, $\hat{C}(x)$, is as follows:

$$\hat{C}(x) = b\hat{l}(x)e^{-r\bar{x}},$$

where the chance of survivorship from birth to age x is $\hat{l}(x) = l(x)/l(0)$, $l(x)$ is the number of survivors to age x out of the radix, b is the birthrate per person per year, r is the rate of increase per year, and $\bar{x}$ is the midpoint of the interval (Weiss 1973:6).

The life table calculations on chance of survivorship, $\hat{l}(x)$, are not going to be grossly affected unless the difference between one cohort and the next is very large (see Moore et al. 1975:61ff.), especially if we assume for the argument that each cemetery was in use for a relatively short time. We do know that Mississippian settlement was often of relatively short, continuous duration at specific sites. Other data, such as those from settlements, for example, suggest that changes in population density were relatively slow (i.e., that the rates of change were small, if not zero). To be sure, the estimation of possible values of b and r for non-stable populations from

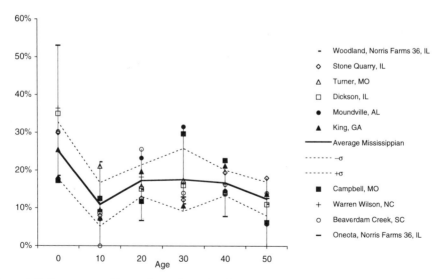

Figure 4.12. Percentages of deceased in each age class for Mississippian and roughly contemporary populations.

Table 4.5. "Best-Fit" Simulation of Birthrates (b) and Rates
of Increase (r) for Selected Populations

	b	r
Late Prehistoric		
Moss, IL	0.028	−0.084
Etowah (9Br2), GA	0.061	−0.041
Moundville, AL	0.149	−0.035
Turner, MO	0.192	−0.024
Schild, IL	0.238	−0.020
Little Egypt, GA	0.166	−0.020
Lake George, MS	0.427	−0.018
King, GA	0.243	−0.008
Dickson, IL	0.346	−0.004
Florence St., IL	0.186	−0.004
Stone Quarry, IL	0.309	0.007
Earlier		
Archaic, IL	0.513	0.013
Hopewell, IL	0.280	0.000
Indian Knoll, KY	0.331	−0.023

these equations and actual proportions in skeletal populations is only a simulation of possible rates. The precision of "best fit" values of b and r and the life table values themselves cannot be taken to be so precise as the 3-place numbers in the tables might suggest. Nonetheless, simulation of rates allows assessment of *possible* values these variables might have had in Mississippian societies. In the table that follows (Table 4.5), I have calculated the values for the birth- and death rates from the life tables using an iterative method[10] for the alteration of both the birth-rate per person per year b and the rate of increase r until the minimum summed absolute difference[11] between the modeled value of $\hat{C}(X)$ as predicted and the actual observed age distribution is reached (Weiss 1973:6, 65, 71). When analyzed, the following birth and rates of increase are "best fit" (i.e., least absolute difference) solutions:

In simulating the values of these two variables, there may be a number of possible solutions that are closer to each other in results than the precision of the real data can allow us to distinguish. Even so, it is interesting that the "best-fit" models for rate of increase, r, often show negative values for Mississippian. In Milner's model

[10] The method is part of "Solver" in Microsoft Excel™. The program substitutes different values for each variable and calculates results using observation of the rates of change until a set of conditions are met for other values. In this case, the minimum differences between the model table and the calculated life table for the site were calculated with the condition that the model survivorship value, $\hat{C}(0)$, be not less than the value of C(0)—that is, that the infant population is taken as being, at the least, no smaller than the percentage in the life value for the site.

[11] Alternatively, solving for the least sum of the squares of the differences produces slightly different answers for b and r, since the effect of the *larger* differences between the model curve and the actual curve are thus exaggerated. However, the general dimension and sign of the rates are not substantially altered overall.

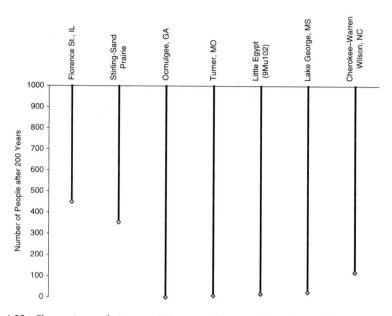

Figure 4.13. Changes in population over 200 years, with an initial population of 1000 at model rates.

of southern American Bottom population change through time (Milner 1986), he suggested that small farmstead settlement in a 15-km study area had increased about 4 percent over the Lohmann phase (A.D. 1000–1050). Thereafter the Stirling phase (beginning ca. A.D. 1050–1100), then the Moorehead (starting at A.D. 1150–1200), and finally the Sand Prairie phase (beginning around A.D. 1275 and ending before A.D. 1400[12]) population fell by about 87 percent. These population changes indicate an annual rate of increase for the Lohmann phase of 0.0008. For the Stirling to Sand Prairie phases, the long-term annual rate of increase would be –0.005, that is to say essentially the same as that calculated from the life tables for, say, the Florence Street site from Table 4.3. The similarity is encouraging, but it is unjustified to treat the model rates of increase in the table as being more than rough indications of the possible directions of population change in Mississippian times. Such rates, if they indicate the general conditions for Mississippian peoples, suggest that the Mississippians were, biologically speaking, neither prospering nor disastrously declining. Interestingly, the implications of such rates would be that many populations may have been shrinking at rates low enough for the effects to have been indistinguishable to any one generational cohort, that is, each year the group would be just a little smaller, without anyone in the society necessarily being aware of the changes.

Figure 4.13 shows the implications of these rates of increase from a starting population of 1000 and indicating the change after 200 years. The Milner study area

---

[12] These dates are those revised according to Hall's examination of radiocarbon dates (1991).

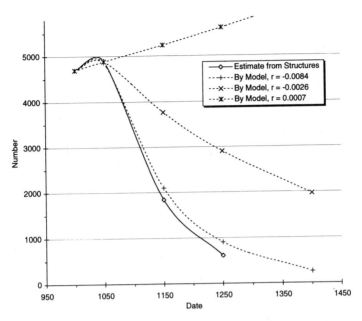

Figure 4.14. Comparison of populations from structures, with model predictions for the southern American bottom.

in the southern American Bottom (1986) is also included. The drop over the 200-year period would have taken most of these societies to near zero. The East St. Louis Stone Quarry is one Mississippian group in these simulations that would have had an increase over 200 years at the "best fit" rates—from 1000 to over 3700. However, the Sand Prairie phase, to which the East St. Louis Stone Quarry cemetery site belongs, is late (ca. A.D. 1250 to 1300–1400), and other evidence does not support *overall* population increases of this magnitude at that time (e.g., Milner 1983a:121–122; 1986). Of course, each cemetery population is a reflection of short-term, local conditions, so we should not overinterpret these results, and these figures serve as an additional reminder to be cautious in taking the models too seriously. Generally, negative rates of increase are, of course, by no means unusual for "primitive" farming populations and might provide one component in a model for the apparent decline of Mississippian between the 10th and 13th centuries.

Indeed, Milner's estimates of local populations for the southern American Bottom show declines of just the magnitude and character that are predicted from the mathematical models here of population dynamics based on local skeletal populations (e.g., 1986).

Figure 4.14 compares Milner's estimates (recalculated for slightly adjusted house size) with the model values predicted for the same area (using the Malthusian growth formula $N_t = N_0 e^{rt}$; Milner's starting population of 4692 with a rate of increase, r, during Lohmann phase times of 0.0007, followed thereafter by different rates of increase; see above, Muller 1993, in press). The lowest of the model rates (r =

–0.0084) is the minimum estimated rate from a series of Mississippian burial populations. The middle rate(r = –0.0026) is the average of the nonpositive rates from the
same study, and the positive rate (r = 0.0007) is that calculated by one method for the
Stone Quarry site (see Muller, in press).

The rates of increase used to model the skeletal population distributions are
also comparable to the mean rates found for many historical populations in the East,
although those data are highly variable because of "appearances" and "disappear-
ances" in the *records* due to of war, alliances, and avoidance of Europeans. It may be
noted that late sites in the Southeast, such as those modeled by Humpf (1992), show
distributions similar to the earlier sites mentioned, so the difficulties in interpreting
data for some of these possible contact locations dissolve into the more general
problem of explaining the Late Prehistoric population dynamics in general. Although
there are rather strident differences over the identification of these sites (Little Egypt
and King) with specific historical towns (cf. Henige 1994; Hudson et al. 1994), the
sites do represent late period populations. High negative rates for some of the historical data reflect early depopulation effects of disease after the European invasion,
although these are only rough estimates. Some historical groups had dramatic, essentially exponential growth following their being "pacified." Some of this historical
growth reflected incorporation of smaller societies, and this may be proposed in the
Mississippian cases, as well.

We can see that the modeled Mississippian rates are not strikingly different
from some of those in Table 4.6 for historical times. The similarity does not mean that
the simulation model rates are correct, merely that they are warrantable from the
marriage and kinship structures of the historical Southeast. There is, of course, no
proof that later Mississippian times were characterized by epidemics and other problems such as those faced by the historical Southeasterners.

I noted some time ago (Muller 1978b:288, 1986b:254) that the Mississippian
populations at locations such as the Black Bottom on the Ohio River were relatively
small—indeed, were similar to the figures for historical Eastern groups (see the
following discussion of town size). Low population density, of itself, has implications
in terms of the ability of a population to maintain itself. Ballonoff (e.g., 1974, 1975)
developed a structural, mathematical model for marriage structure. Although we have
neither extensive nor sound enough information to fit Mississippian data into Ballonoff's models, it is worth noting that small systems in his models require more rigid
marriage regulation rules than do large systems (1974:24). Another inference from
his discussion is that the interplay of marriage rules and small population can result
in circumstances under which population size may not be maintained. With small
generational declines (ca. 20 years), people would not be aware of depopulation until
they had reached a point at which they would begin to have difficulties in finding an
appropriately defined spouse. We can speculate that the kinds of rates modeled here
might have led to a slow loss of population, particularly once a "center" had drawn
most dispersed, outlying peoples under its control. Although Mississippian centers
were probably not the kind of population "sinks" that 17th- and 18th-century Old
World cities were, it is quite possible that the growth in Mississippian centers from
the 10th to 11th centuries may have occurred more from incorporation of outliers
than from internal population growth. Once the outliers had been incorporated into

Table 4.6. Historical Rates of Growth per Year (r)

Group	Period	Mean *r*
Coosa	1540–1832	–0.254
Creek Confederacy	1700–1800	–0.085
Biloxi	1650–1908	–0.021
Creek Confederacy	1700–1911	–0.015
Cherokee	1800–1930	0.000
Creek Confederacy	1800–1910	0.017
Chickasaw	1800–1950	0.024
Chickasaw	1650–1800	0.034
Cherokee	1650–1930	0.047
Cherokee	1650–1760	0.094

the more centralized bottomland settlements, the inexorable workings of population dynamics may have led to what archaeologists have called "abandonment," even without any of the problems with climate, production, and competition that we know to have existed.

5. PREHISTORIC AND HISTORICAL POPULATION DYNAMICS

Studies of prehistoric Mississippian and historical Native American population and population dynamics indicate the possibility that Mississippian and historical Southeastern populations were more alike in structure than is commonly supposed. This section will address the problems of Mississippian and Historic population dynamics, compare the two systems, and draw some conclusions about differences. As I argued in Chapter 2, historical groups such as the Creek—for one example—have been underutilized in examination of Southeastern political forms. There are good reasons to see the Creek as more complex than the Natchez, while possessing none of the features of the latter's supposed "state." At the same time, the grand empires sometimes attributed to prehistoric Mississippian societies are exaggerations in the other direction (cf. Dincauze and Hasenstab 1989). The great gulf between historical and prehistoric has largely been created by underestimating most Southeastern historical groups and overestimating the complexity of most prehistoric complexes.

Population Organization

Historical Groups

The population dynamics of historical populations in the Southeast form a valuable comparison for Mississippian period, because historical data on population growth and decline have been often debated with quite different kinds of conclusions having been reached. I have discussed these issues in somewhat more detail in another paper (Muller in press), but it is necessary here to set the historical situation in proper perspective, in order to understand both the historical and prehistoric situations, as shown in the Northeast by Snow (1995).

One cannot deny the terrible impact of Old World diseases upon the populations of the New World (to be discussed), but at the same time, there are reasons to doubt that these diseases were uniformly and universally catastrophic. Today, I believe it is fair to say that the evidence suggests the kind of epidemic disease history found in the records was also characteristic of earlier times—that is, that local populations suffered catastrophes, but that the whole East did not experience these problems *at the same time or with the same impact* (e.g., Milner 1980; Ramenofsky 1987; cf. Thorton 1987). It is not an apology for European invasions to understand the fitfulness and uneven impact of epidemic disease.

Population Dynamics of Historical Groups. Although we should always remember that Southeastern groups were constituted of real, historical persons, we also need to examine the broader features of their social formations. There were several different population patterns among Historic Native American populations. It would be misleading and inaccurate to consider these as "types," but there were responses ranging from successful to spectacularly unsuccessful. For political and ideological reasons, more attention was given the latter, than the former by 19th- and early 20th-century historians, such as Francis Parkman, interested in describing the "westward progress of civilization" (see Jennings 1963, 1975). Unfortunately, too many people still depend on Eurocentric histories rather than going back to primary sources.[13] Even when primary sources are cited, it is too often from excerpts in Swanton's various books and papers rather than from the original statements in context. Swanton did a wonderful job, considering his time and the questions then being investigated. His work, even today, serves as an admirable *index* to the historical accounts of Native Americans, but it does not replace them. Finally, even persons who are leading scholars in the interpretation of the historical documents have accepted exaggerated archaeological accounts of prehistoric polities while discounting the organizational complexity of groups such as the Choctaw (e.g., Galloway 1982b:146–147, 1995).

Let us examine the kinds of population histories we have for the East, particularly the Southeast. First, there are societies that are cited as examples of persistence of formerly grand, prehistoric political systems: in a few words, the Natchez and some of their neighbors. Let us look at the Natchez again, asking this time what their population structure was like.

The Natchez

We proceeded to his [the chief's] hut, which is erected on a 10-foot mound of dirt carried there, 25 feet wide and 45 long. Close by it are eight huts. Facing the chief's is the temple. These form a ring somewhat oval-shaped and enclose a public square about 250 yards wide and 300 long. Close by flows a little creek, from which they get their water. I found there a letter from M. de Montigny, a missionary at the Taensas, who left three days ago with a

---

[13] Many of the original documents are still difficult to obtain, but translations and passable transcriptions of the originals are often good enough, *if* they are used cautiously.

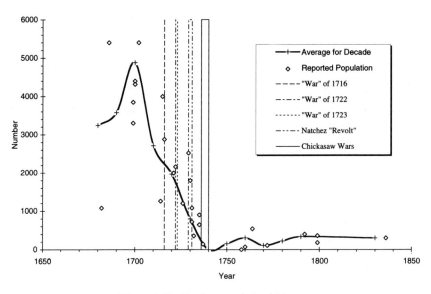

Figure 4.15. Natchez population history.

Canadian to return to the Taensas. He states that he has visited most of the huts of this nation, which he estimates at 400, within an area of 8 leagues along the bank of a small creek that waters this country.[14] d'Iberville 1700 [1981:125]

Who were the Natchez? Were they really the degenerate survivor of a once mighty empire? Do they present the historian or archaeologist with "survivals" of "primitive states"? Chapter 2 argued that the actual actions described in accounts of the Natchez "Revolt" showed that the Natchez chiefs made few, if any, *decisions* without consulting their councils. There are, to be sure, descriptions of great deference to the chief and plenty of European assertions of their "autocracy." As noted, it is also no accident that the French describe Sun Kings and the British describe (of other groups) what seem to have parliamentary systems. Surely, the Natchez chiefs at both the town and society levels were people with great spiritual and ritual importance. Other persons paid homage to them in prescribed ways, but the power of the Natchez Sun was a hollow shell. Close examination of the historical accounts does not support autocratic rule, merely autocratic manners. What was the great empire over which the Natchez Great Sun ruled? How many "subjects" did this leader have?

The Natchez were actually a quite small society of some 400 houses, as Montigny claimed, according to d'Iberville (1700, quoted above, see Figure 4.15). In the

---

[14] "Nous nous somme rendus à sa cabane, qui est élevée à une hauteur de dix pieds de haut, de terre rapportée, et large de vingt-cinq et longue de quarante-cinq. Auprès de là sont huit cabanes. Devant celle du chef est le temple, cela forme un rond un peu en ovale, et renferme une place d'environ deux cent cinquante pas de large et trois cents de long...Il marque avoir visité la plus partie des cabanes de cette nation, qu'il estime au nombre de quatre cent, dans l'espace de huit lieues de pays, sur le bord d'un ruisseau qui arrose ce pays" (in Margry 1878:4:411).

records, the Great Sun commanded at most the 1500 warriors mentioned by Tonty in 1686 (Tonty 1686 in Margry 1878:3:556) However, Tonty, later writing from memory in 1691[15] about the early contact in 1682, said only that there were "more than 300 warriors"(Tonty 1693). Most of the records over a century and a half suggest that there were rarely more than an average of 400 warriors. The largest recorded figure for Natchez population is only about 5400 people (based on the 1500 warriors, but given independently by de Bourgmont for 1702 (Bourgmont 1714). As the figure illustrates, Natchez population appears to have been declining even before their disastrous defeat by the French in 1731. Even without overt European efforts to eradicate groups, many smaller polities in the Southeast show population declines similar to those in Figure 4.15 (Muller 1993b; in press).

The Natchez cannot be identified with any certainty before the French accounts, and most efforts to do so have assumed their identity was whatever was the largest and most powerful recorded group. A brief diversion to the post-Revolt Natchez history is illuminating. In Figure 4.15, Natchez population counts continue after the supposed time of their destruction. We are told that there are no longer any Natchez, so who were these people? Many of this "destroyed people" were scattered, not dead, and were then a separate village of the Chickasaw (see the native Chickasaw map in Waselkov 1989a). Because of continuing pressure by the French and Choctaw, some Natchez, as a group, went over to the Creek to form a town there, while others may have continued to live in a Chickasaw town (*Nauchee*, or variants) until fairly late (e.g., *Nanne Hamgeh* old town mentioned by Adair 1775:195). A town of "Natchez" existed among the Creek from before the 1740s (Adair 1775:257; Hawkins 1799 [1848:14, 42]; Milfort 1802 [1956:186]; Romans 1775). A number of individual Natchez also lived in other Creek towns (same sources). Swanton reports that the last speaker of Natchez among the Creeks died before 1907, but that some speakers were still alive among the Cherokee as late as the 1920s (Swanton 1911:254, 1952:190). This history of diaspora and incorporation into surviving, larger groups is not unusual but is typical of the history of many smaller Eastern Native American "tribes".

I confess astonishment at the emphasis given to small groups such as the Natchez because of their supposed "degenerate" survivals of "complex" organization, while large societies that persisted for centuries are forgotten or dismissed as irrelevant. Small societies such as the Natchez tended to melt away over time, but larger Southeastern entities persisted and sometimes even expanded in the face of warfare, forced migration, and disease. Although the data make it difficult to explain every individual twitch in the population curves, they show that the dwindling of small groups and the maintenance of larger ones are two parts of the same overall process. Many small groups did not really become extinct, but rather merged themselves into larger polities. They often maintained an autonomous, if subordinate, existence (for more discussion of this issue, see Muller 1993b, 1994, in press).

Large social formations. Many Native American societies managed to maintain populations in the range of 10,000 to 15,000 (see Table 5.7 in the next chapter for a

---

[15] Listed in translation however as 1693 (see Galloway 1982a:21ff).

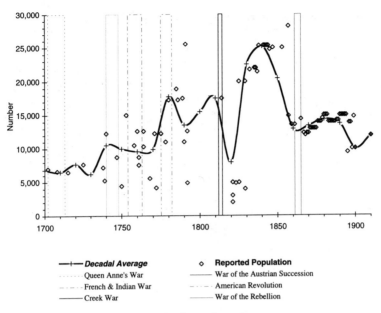

Figure 4.16. Creek population history.

list of some of these). The most successful of these groups are still well known, including the historical Cherokee, Choctaw, and Creek.

The Creek Confederacy is an excellent example of the issue at hand (Figure 4.16). A first glance at their population history, like so many others in the East, suggests poor data because of many rapid fluctuations in size. To be sure, there *are* incomplete counts, and so forth, and some of the apparent fluctuations are merely sampling error; however, more detailed attention to circumstances reveal that these census figures are better than one has any right to expect, but *they are not only counts of biological populations!* Census data on Eastern groups, large and small alike, are the same as modern data in reflecting who was discoverable at a time and place, rather than giving "true" counts of total members of a population. In addition, the early "censuses" were almost exclusively concerned with military intelligence. Although epidemics and wars ravaged these societies to a monstrous degree, we must remember that dispersals and aggregations were as much integral parts of this impact as deaths and births. Close examination of the Thornton et al. study of Cherokee population history also illustrates this point (1990).

Table 4.7 shows the population and calculated rate of increase, r, for $N_t = N_0 e^{rt}$ for each decade for the Creek Confederacy.[16] The overall average rate of increase from 1702 to 1825 was r = 0.0085; for 1715 to 1845, was r = 0.0105; and from 1775 to 1845, r = 0.0100. Peak population was reached in the 1840s. These are remarkable

---

[16] This is the finite rate, often denoted as λ, not the intrinsic rate of increase (see Pielou 1977:9 and elsewhere).

Table 4.7. Rates of Increase in Each Decade for the Creek Confederacy

Decade beginning	Average population	Rate of increase
1710	6522	−0.005
1720	7700	0.017
1730	6235	−0.021
1740	10,500	0.052
1750	9974	−0.005
1760	9575	−0.004
1770	9912	0.003
1780	17,740	0.058
1790	13,504	−0.027
1800	15,502	0.014
1810	17,500	0.012
1820	7985	−0.078
1830	22,493	0.104
1840	25,184	0.011
1850	20,413	−0.022
1860	12,907	−0.046
1870	13,379	0.004
1880	14,340	0.007
1890	13,696	−0.005
1900	10,000	−0.031
1910	11,911	0.017

under the circumstances, but the Creek did much more poorly after the Civil War. After the 1860s, Creek total reported population dropped into the 10,000–13,000 range. Although the later censuses are seemingly more precise, they reflect many political factors that are too complex to go into here. The fluctuation in finite rate of increase from one decade to the next is quite striking.

The fluctuations in Creek population are part of an overall trend of increase in size (Figure 4.17). A quick glance at Creek political history provides sufficient cause for some of the variations in counted population. The correlation between the Malthusian or exponential growth model predictions and the actual decadal averages has a $R^2 = 0.411$, and the simple exponential trend correlation with the decadal averages has an $R^2 = 0.413$.

How did the Creek Confederacy grow? At the time of the American Revolution, Romans (1775:90–91) had this to say about the Creek:

> A mixture of the remains of the Cawittas, Talepoosas, Coosas, Apalachias, Conshacs or Coosades, Oakmulgis, Oconis, Okchoys, Alibamons, Natchez, Weetumkus, Pakanas, Taēnsas, Chacsihoomas, Abékas and some other tribes whose names I do not recollect, will be the next subject of our attention. They call themselves Muscokees and are at present known to us by the general name of Creeks, and divided into upper and lower Creeks; also those they call allies and are a colony from the others living far south in East Florida.

Such a process of amalgamation was universal among larger aboriginal societies across the East and is not the least of the problems in trying to identify historical societies with their prehistoric forebears. There is no reason whatsoever to suppose that this process was solely the result of the disruptions of the Historic period. First,

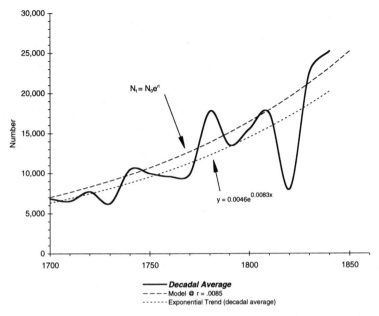

Figure 4.17. Average Creek population per decade compared to the results of an exponential trend and the Malthusian formula for population growth at $r = 0.0085$.

disruption and reformation of these societies is an institutional problem arising directly out of the internal and external contradictions of Eastern political organization (as noted in different terms by Anderson 1990, 1991, 1994a, 1994b). Second, even the earliest Eastern historical accounts give cases that can be reasonably interpreted as reflecting considerable movement of individuals, much less larger groups, among various societies (as seen in the de Soto accounts from the presence in communities of persons who were not native speakers of the majority languages).

The clouds of points in Figure 4.18 illustrate both the mass of data and the wide variation shown. The two regressions actually explain little of the variation shown, but there is a slight tendency for large groups to expand and small ones to decline even further. The critical point is that there were political and economic strategies in Southeastern social formations that allowed large groups to survive and to govern themselves without supposed "classes," "kings," or other statelike political institutions. We do not need to fantasize about what social institutions for **large** Southeastern social formations would have been like. We can, rather, look at the historical records for groups such as the Choctaw and Creek and see how they solved problems of governance of large population within the framework of the Southeastern chiefly polity form. We may even choose to compare these to even less hierarchically organized social formations such as the Illinois, Iroquois, and Huron to understand that groups as large as any reasonable estimates for prehistoric societies in the Southeast do not *require* state social formations. The behavior observed in many smaller groups, including the Natchez and Bayougoula, seems to be cut from the same cloth as for the Creek or Choctaw, notwithstanding the glories attributed to them by some French bureaucrats working for their own Sun King.

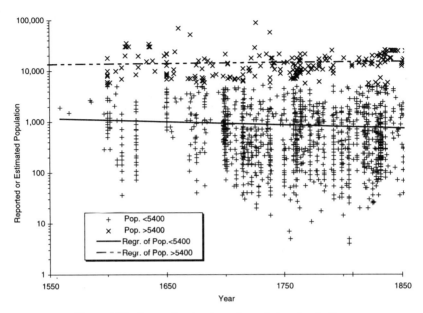

Figure 4.18. Reported and estimated populations for the East.

In these examples, we may see patterns that were probably not new, even though the stresses generating these events were certainly more severe than those that had occurred before the European invasion. The maintenance of large groups by incorporation and the tendency for declining populations to seek refuge in larger ones are arguably processes that were present well back into the Mississippian period.

Prehistoric Mississippian

As seen, simple mathematical models of population structure suggest that the "decline" of Mississippian centers in the 14th century *can* be interpreted as a consequence of the nature of Mississippian biological and social reproduction rather than a dramatic catastrophe. This does not mean that they *must* be seen so, but we should at least consider the possibility that Mississippian lifeways were locally successful more in the short term than the long term.

The Southeastern Late Prehistoric peoples are an important case of economic and social transformation. Even after A.D. 700, all of those who were later to become "Mississippian" (in the broadest sense) were no more than gardeners of crops that were largely supplemental to the chase and gathering. By A.D. 900, maize consumption in many places had become a central feature of daily life on which almost all other activities were focused. These changes took less than 200 years in most of the central Coastal Plain, perhaps much less, constituting nothing less than a "revolution." By A.D. 1200, Mississippian and related lifeways had "covered the South like the morning dew." Of course, political–economic behavior varied enormously from one region to another, but great similarities had evolved partly as a result of comparable problems faced in comparable environments. To say so does not mean that there was no impact from social, economic, and even military interactions, but these will be dealt with at greater length later in this book.

A rapid transition from more or less communal societies to hierarchical social formations inevitably created a multitude of social, economic, and even biological contradictions as egalitarian institutions became transformed by the intrusion of rank. This shift in social relations was intertwined with changes in economic structures, although not in a simple cause-and-effect fashion—some elites seemed to develop before the intensification of maize production and others, after. If the development of chiefly institutions in nonhorticultural societies rules out a simple explanation of conversion of horticultural surplus into leadership, the alternative cases suggest that it is equally wrong to see hierarchical development as causing horticultural intensification. It seems doubtful that police or military institutions were sufficiently developed to have allowed the changes to have been *compelled* by powerful, exploiting elites, but the existence of managerial elites could often have created conditions that allowed exploitation to develop.

Population Dynamics: A Bang or a Whimper? On the one hand, the expansion of Mississippian in the 10th century has sometimes been seen primarily as a result of population expansion resulting from new production methods and crops. On the other hand, there is a possibility that much of the growth of early Mississippian was the result of aggregation of "Late Woodland" peoples, formerly scattered across the landscape but now becoming concentrated in the fertile floodplains (e.g., Muller 1978a, 1986b, 1994).

However they grew, there were troubles in these developing concentrations of population. After initial spurts of growth, the best-fitting modeled growth rates (to produce the observed age-of-death distributions) for established Mississippian populations are those that have small *negative* rates of increase—that is, that show minuscule declines from one generation to the next. Mississippian communities in the floodplain would have been nothing as bad as the population sinks of early cities, but the situation would have meant that growth was, perhaps, more often a result of attraction of new persons from outside than growth within the community.

Was there a "collapse" of Mississippian in pre-Columbian times? Perhaps not, since such low levels of decline would have been virtually impossible to see on a day-to-day scale, except that sooner or later persons would have increasing difficulty in finding suitable marriage partners, and more fields in the bottomlands would have lain fallow. If one function of the leadership was to "control"—or perhaps administer—production, such circumstances would have meant real problems in providing labor for private as well as public activities. In the next chapter, the implications of labor shortages and the structure of towns and settlement will be considered.

In addition to the possibility of population decline as a result of biological dynamics, there is also the possibility that some of the "decline" in the post–13th-century period may have been a result of dispersal rather than overall deaths. This business of dispersion is the other side of aggregation. We should not see population history as being any more uniform in the prehistoric record than in the historic.

There is little doubt that some areas were, if not "abandoned," substantially depopulated, especially late in Mississippian times. At the same time, there is some indication of increases in upland Mississippian in some areas—but whether this is a *result* of the "collapse" of floodplain centers or the *cause* of the disappearance of the lowland settlements is a more difficult question. Depopulation of bottomland areas, too-persistent claims for support by bottomland chiefs, and such new productive elements as the introduction of the common bean (Muller 1978a, 1983) may have presented new options for more autonomous life away from the problems of traditional Mississippian locations. Local perturbations in production, warfare, and diseases may have led to cycles of movement from one location to others over the course of decades and centuries.

6. CONCLUSIONS

In this chapter, we have examined the biological bases for Mississippian society. We briefly examined the physical characteristics of Mississippian peoples and estimated caloric requirements that would have been necessary to support families and individuals.

Other biological evidence relates to evidence for differences among various segments of Mississippian populations in their access to the basic requirements of life. Little evidence supports the idea of dramatic differences of the sort that we might expect were any Mississippian societies to be considered "states," in the classic sense of the term.

We saw how studies of Mississippian populations, when examined as a group, reveal a possibility that Mississippian lifeways may not have always been self-maintaining. It is possible that Mississippian societies may have been dependent for maintenance of populations on mechanisms of incorporation and aggregation of "rural" population. To the extent that public labor was a component of Mississippian political economy, labor shortages may have been a persistent problem, and individual and group incorporations of "foreign" towns in the Historic period may simply be a continuation of practices that were earlier responses to the demographic character of Mississippian social formations.

Interpretation and the Corrective Effect of Models

Discussion of Mississippian "decline" and its causes may sometimes be overinterpretation, since simple, dynamic models can account for many observed changes in archaeologically known populations. On the one hand, pre-Columbian population declines have been attributed to social "collapse," often as a result of climatic changes. Studies of Historic population dynamics, on the other hand, have usually focused on epidemic disease and warfare as the prime movers. As we have seen, however, both periods can often be characterized by low negative values for rates of increase. If such reproductive conditions were characteristic of Mississippian populations, many of the supposed "problems" of explaining Mississippian population histories are eliminated, and the fluctuations may be seen as normal results of both reproductive and political instability.

On the one hand, Prehistoric populations and complexity have systematically been overestimated by being described in class–society terminology. Historic populations, on the other hand, have been underestimated by the use of "tribal" models, and their organization has too often been seen as "degenerate." These stereotypes need to be swept aside in a fresh look at both Mississippian peoples and their historical descendants.

Chapter 5

Culture and Reproduction

Sustine modicum, ruricolae melius hoc norunt.
(Wait a bit, let's ask the country folk.)
Senior clerk in the Exchequer on being asked a
tricky question, A.D. 1177

1. INTRODUCTION

The material conditions of everyday life include more than just food and drink. Human reproduction is more than a strictly biological affair, and the social and cultural characteristics of Mississippian reproduction have to be addressed, even if they are obscured by the mists of antiquity. What can be said about control of reproduction in these societies? What likely kinds of social units were there? How a society reproduces itself depends on the reproduction of the culture nearly as much as on biological reproduction. Unfortunately, the forms and character of cultural reproduction are difficult to address from archaeological evidence.

In the terminology of political economy, the term *reproduction* has a number of meanings beyond the biology of a population. It can refer to the elements of the production of labor value (material production) in that, first, the cost of production must be compensated (simple reproduction) and beyond that, a surplus value may be produced (extended reproduction for the accumulation of capital). In Meillassoux's words, "Economic reproduction takes place by producing subsistence goods—the means of producing human energy—and distributing this energy in the productive cycle, i.e., between the past, present, and future producers" (1981:51). In this chapter, however, the emphasis first has to be placed on the task of defining the nature of Mississippian producers in demographic terms, even if we were to believe, as does Meillassoux, that the "reproduction of the producers and the reproducers appears as a demographic phenomenon, but in fact it is entirely subordinate to the economy" (1981:75). Economic reproduction will also be addressed in the later chapters on production.

183

We also need to know what Mississippian populations were like in the particular and the aggregate. How large were Mississippian families, and corporate, coresident sodalities? How large or small were Mississippian communities and what was the scale of Mississippian polities? Both archaeological and historical data can inform our views of this widespread way of life.

A contrast has been drawn between what I would call an "exaggerationalist" view of Mississippian and a so-called "minimalist" view (*sensu* Stoltman 1991a:351–352). Although the size of Mississippian centers is no longer quite so prone to being exaggerated, many of the conflicts in interpretation of Mississippian complexes still stem from differences of opinion about the scale of Mississippian societies. Accordingly, it is necessary to develop arguments on the sizes of Mississippian populations. We shall begin at the lowest level, the household. This has also been the most neglected of Mississippian topics in many ways, so it is a good place to start to build a model of Mississippian settlement.

2. "A HEAP OF LIVING"— HOUSEHOLDS, FARMSTEADS, AND HOMESTEADS

A number of terms for a Mississippian domestic unit have come to be used as synonyms, but a case can be made for distinguishing among these. The simplest level, the one detected more or less easily in archaeology, is the *structure*. This term simply means the physical remains of a facility as identified and analyzed by the archaeologist. The "normal" structure in Mississippian times was a squarish to rectangular building constructed with vertical posts set into the ground and often seeming to bear the roof directly. The walls were often plastered, especially in more substantial structures, and the roof was thatch. This basic form of construction occurs widely, including some peasant architecture in Europe (hence the name "wattle and daub"). The vertical wall posts were often, even usually, set into a wall trench in Mississippian times, rather than being in individually excavated postholes. The width of the wall trenches happens to be essentially the width of a stone hoe, and the greater ease of digging a small trench with a hoe surely explains the widespread use of this technique wherever wall posts were tightly spaced. Of course, some areas that are considered to be only marginally Mississippian, if Mississippian at all, have entirely different house forms, ranging from bark- or mat-covered oval wigwams, to larger round grass-covered structures. In the de Soto accounts, what we think of as the normal Mississippian house form was not encountered until well inland at Toalli (or Capachiqui). The wattle-and-daub house form continued into historical times and was observed by many European travelers (e.g., Hawkins 1799 [1848:23, 33]; Lederer 1672:15; Membré 1682a [1903:175]). However, log cabins eventually replaced this form in the 19th century.

A *structure*, however, is not the same as a *house*. A *house* is a structure with a particular function—residence. Moreover, a *house* in Mississippian times may sometimes have been more than one structure. There were some Mississippian communities that were densely and compactly settled, but even those were made up of relatively small units that we may call "households." These small residential units were the modular building blocks of Mississippian societies. Bartram described these kinds of households as they were among the Creek in the late 18th century:

> The habitations of the Muccolgulges or Upper Crick Towns consist of Little Squares, or four oblong square houses, encompassing a square area, exactly on the plan of the <u>Publick Square</u>, — every Family however have not four of these houses—some 3,—some 2, —and some but one, according to their circumstances, of largeness of their family, &c. (1789[1995:180])

Note that we should better see that the houses are not on the plan of the "public squares" so much as the other way around. The public square replicated the household on a grander and promoted scale. Indeed, so did the location of mounds around plazas. Bartram also noted functional differences among the structures in a household square (1789[1995:180]). Some were used as reception halls, warehouses and so forth. "Public houses" were like private ones but larger and somewhat more elaborate, as recorded from the de Soto accounts onward.

The term *household* would best be limited, however, to cases in which independent arguments can be made that contiguous structures are occupied by a single family or kin group. Of course, it is reasonable to hypothesize that contiguous, contemporary structures were households. Another term, used by Polhemus, is *minimal settlement unit* (MSU) to describe pairs of lighter and more substantial structures in the Dallas phase in eastern Tennessee (1990:126–127). Although this term has the benefit of not judging the social character of the structures, its length and other assumptions seem to leave *homestead* and *farmstead* as easier alternatives.

Polhemus's discussion also has interesting characterizations of interior layout categorized in terms of public areas, but I think it would be premature to accept such a scheme for Mississippian structures in general. Certainly such variables as available light, air circulation, and many others would affect how different parts of the interior of structures were used.

The terms *household* and *farmstead* are often used interchangeably; however, the former term more closely refers to familial coresidence, whereas the latter refers to an economic function of a settlement. In order to further clarify discussion, I would suggest distinguishing between *farmstead* and *homestead*, by using the latter term to refer to a household-level place of production and reproduction, but one that is not necessarily isolated on arable land. *Farmstead*, then, can be restricted to isolated homesteads that seem to have served as horticultural production locations. This is useful since homesteads in Mississippian sites often occur in larger clusters but still retain much of the independent production character of the isolated farmstead. A farmstead, on the other hand, is the minimal level of Mississippian community.

At this point, it would be well to reiterate points that I have made elsewhere (Muller 1993a). First, the character of the homestead is virtually the same wherever in a society it occurs. That is to say that an isolated farmstead generally has essentially the same household inventory as a homestead in a larger site. Second, the larger communities are essentially repeated homesteads with some additional site functions added as size increased. Finally, although there are differences in functions of sites, these are not easily subsumed into a hierarchy of "primary," "secondary," and "tertiary centers." Most particularly, it is dangerous to assume such a hierarchy and to force sites into these types (see Muller 1993a in relation to my own earlier use of such terms). Finally, both archaeological and historical evidence attest that many activities associated with the unit took place in its vicinity, but not necessarily inside the structure (e.g., La Source 1699 [1861:80]). Special- purpose structures such as granaries might also be associated with the homestead, so the form as a whole should not be identified solely with the rectangular structures.

The Mississippian Structure and Homestead

The simple wattle-and-daub structure was usually square to subrectangular in shape. However, as one moves out of the northern Gulf Coastal Plain environments of much of Mississippian settlement, there are variations in structure form. Even so, the areas of Mississippian structures are remarkably consistent across a broad area and a number of quite different house forms. The data summarized in Table 5.1 are a grab sample of data drawn from maps and reports and are presented roughly from northwest to southeast. Where possible, the actual wall trench-to-wall trench dimensions of structures were used as given in reports. Other measurements were digitized from site maps.[1]

The largest samples are those from the American Bottom and Cahokia series. Many other areas have less complete data, since sampling excavation (as opposed to "digging the whole thing") does not always uncover entire structures. Although the data in the table are sometimes separated by phase, individual structures that were superimposed were counted as individual structures. In many cases, later structures are larger than the earlier structures in the same location. Some of these structures are not the simple square to rectangular, wattle and daub houses characteristic of "core" Mississippian, but the areas are still within the same range found in many Late Prehistoric complexes. The data are somewhat biased, since excavations were often conducted in what was perceived as the "richest" area of the site. For example, Kincaid structures turn out to be surprisingly large in this sample, but these data are from central site structures excavated in the 1930s and do not include smaller structures detected in aerial photographs that appear to be roughly the same size as other homesteads in the locality.

Across this diverse sample, the Mississippian structures have floor area *medians* ranging from a low of ca. 12 m^2 to over 52 m^2, and a few individual structures are huge. Although it does not show up clearly in this table, normal Mississippian residential structures by the mid-13th century were generally 20 to 35 m^2 in area. Earlier structures were smaller. These figures correspond reasonably well to expectations that a single structure would have served as a residence for no more than 5 or 6 persons,

---

[1] These data are selected from a large number of individual reports and local and regional summaries. The list is too large to include here, but I will be happy to provide the references on request. It will be noted that mean areas are not the product of mean lengths and widths. This reflects inclusion of partial dimensions and diameters for circular structures. Collection of data for this volume has made me more cautious about scales on published maps. Maps have inaccurate scales more often than one would suppose. In any case, the digitized dimensions of structures can be taken as accurate to within a meter or less, depending on the source material. Starting from a scanned image, *NIH Image* was used to digitize measurements.

Table 5.1. Mississippian Period Structure Size

Site/locality	μ length (m)	μ width (m)	Median area	μ area	σ	Min.	Max.
Morton, IL (11-F-9)	4.9	5.1	24.4	24.8	3.4	21.5	28.4
American Bottom, all, IL	5.0	3.6	14.8	16.4	10.9	1.8	78.3
American Bottom, Lohmann	4.8	3.4	13.3	15.1	13.6	1.8	78.3
American Bottom, Stirling	5.0	3.4	14.9	14.9	7.0	2.4	31.5
American Bottom, Moorehead	5.0	4.3	23.3	21.6	12.4	3.8	46.8
American Bottom, Sand Prairie	5.7	4.7	21.3	23.9	10.6	13.8	37.7
Cahokia, Tract 15, Lohmann	4.8	2.8	12.5	14.4	7.2	5.7	29.8
Cahokia, Tract 15, Moorehead	7.1	4.7	34.1	34.1	13.7	16.0	53.5
Snodgrass, MO	3.9	3.7	12.6	15.5	9.0	1.8	40.3
Turner, MO	4.6	4.4	19.1	21.0	9.1	7.4	44.1
Gypsy Joint, MO	4.6	4.5	21.2	21.2	6.1	16.9	25.5
Upland Southern Illinois	5.8	4.6	26.6	26.6	2.6	24.8	28.5
Kincaid, IL - Mounds	6.4	5.2	33.2	50.4	48.7	11.2	163.5
Kincaid, IL - Plaza, Village	7.7	6.1	52.4	54.5	31.8	18.2	95.1
Black Bottom, IL - small sites	4.6	4.7	18.5	18.5	6.7	8.7	27.5
Jonathan Creek Site, KY (15-Ml-4)	5.8	5.5	32.4	32.2	16.4	5.8	83.0
Angel, IN	7.4	6.5	42.0	53.3	36.2	11.7	153.6
Annis, KY (15-Bt-2)	6.9	5.8	37.9	41.4	19.2	22.1	92.6
Morris, KY (15-Hk-49)	6.4	4.8	29.3	31.2	20.4	15.5	86.5
Chucalissa, TN (40-Sy-1)	5.8	5.8	49.1	36.5	30.1	15.2	57.8
Hiwassee Island, TN (mostly mound)	10.4	8.1	92.5	95.1	48.8	1.4	212.8
Mouse Creek, TN (combined)				52.4		25.8	110.6
Dallas, TN (combined)				46.6		28.0	84.6
Lubbub Creek, AL - House Clusters	5.5	5.3	27.5	31.0	16.4	12.3	60.0
Lubbub Creek, AL - Sub Mound	6.7	6.0	38.4	42.1	20.1	20.0	75.6
Lubbub Creek Non Mound	—	—	42.0	41.5	15.6	12.0	78.0
Lubbub Creek Mound	—	—	31.0	51.8	41.8	10.0	107.0
Moundville, AL	—	—	20.5	24.7	16.6	7.0	96.0
Rucker's Bottom, GA (9-Eb-91)	5.6	5.7	30.6	31.4	19.6	4.7	165.6
Upper Saratown, NC	7.9		49.1	50.1	14.3	30.9	65.3
Warren Wilson Site, NC	6.5	5.6	39.6	36.1	7.8	20.8	45.4

that is, two adults and some children. This is less than Naroll's estimation method (1962) produces, but the inappropriateness of this estimation for noncommunal dwellings has long been recognized. This estimate is slightly more than Casselbury's estimation (1974) but not strikingly so. We may expect that few Mississippian families had more than 3 surviving children resident in the household at any given time, that, in fact, the growth of structures in rebuildings was a reflection of a growth from 2 or 3 persons to this normal size of the family (but compare a Chaianovian model of family size and production in Chapter 6). Thus, some 5 or 6 m^2 per person would be a reasonable basis for population estimation in later Mississippian complexes. Still more useful, however, given the great standard deviation in both historical and prehistoric house size, is to estimate from 5 to 12 persons per "household," taking size of structures and clustering of structures into account. By Hassan's theoretical model, this would be 22–57 m², close to the normal range for regular, nonmound structures at Mississippian sites (1981:73).

Emergent Mississippian structures in the American Bottom are another story. The small structures in early contexts in the American Bottom were so small that one wonders how they could have been usable as shelters. For that reason they are not included in Table 5.1. Mississippian structures there are difficult to push into a Mississippian pattern. They frankly look more like the Wiessner figures for roofed area among hunter–gatherers (1974). Much of the "living" space must have been the open areas of the site—remember that those Late Woodland days were not so far in the past. One must suspect that settlements in the American Bottom in Emergent Mississippian times (and even in Early Mississippian) were different in character from those of later Mississippian.

Larger structures may have held more persons and thus reflect family size, but it is likely in many of these larger buildings reflected social activities including persons outside the immediate family. Since prestige in chiefly societies involved both hospitality and skill at haranguing others, these larger structures probably served as meeting places, as well as residences. As the social distinctions of the lineage and clan were magnified and elevated into societywide functions, the space needed for elders to "hang out" would have increased.

Figure 5.1 shows number of persons per house as recorded for a series of Southeastern peoples, mostly from the Gulf Coast (see also Table 5.2), and for a series of northern and western peoples such as the Wichita and the Illinois. Unfortunately,

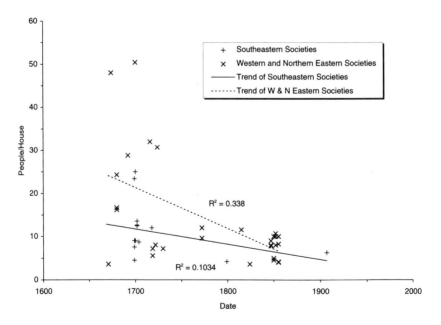

Figure 5.1. Number of persons per household in Historic societies.

Table 5.2. Historic Southeastern Persons per House

Name	Date	People/house	Men/house
Southeastern			
Tuskegee	1799	4.20	1.17
Quinipissa, Mugulasha	1699	4.50	1.00
Bayogoula	1699	7.57	2.10
Taěnsa	1700	9.00	2.50
Houma	1699	9.00	2.50
Houma	1718	12.00	3.33
Chickasaw	1702	12.41	3.45
Choctaw	1702	12.60	3.50
Choctaw	1704	8.72	—
Natchez	1702	13.50	—
Pascagoula	1699	23.40	6.50
Acolapissa	1700	25.00	15.00
Other			
Illinois	1680	16.20	4.50
Illinois	1698	11.00	3.08
Peoria	1673	11.00	2.00
Kaskaskia	1674	48.00	13.33

independent records of numbers of houses and numbers of people are relatively rare in the historical records. It is clear from other records that many societies on the "fringe" of Mississippian areas had larger communal households, so the historical data do not help much in resolving the question of whether "typical" Mississippian houses would have held only nuclear families (as among the Bayogoula, see du Ru 1700 [1935:19–20]). However, it should be noted that the Chickasaw and Choctaw, arguably "true" Mississippian descendants, both had about 12 persons per household at the beginning of the 18th century with some 3 to 4 men per house (e.g., d'Iberville 1702 [1981:174]). Although d'Iberville specifically excluded "young men 16 to 18 years old" from his Chickasaw count, counts of men in many cases may include young men who are otherwise not "adult." There are also likely effects of continuing warfare stimulated by the invading Europeans. Only the Tuskegee and the Mugulasha–Quinipissa correspond to our model Mississippian house size.

In collecting the data for Table 5.1, I was surprised at the relatively few structure clusters that could be easily interpreted as representing the "Bartram" model of multiple structures in a single homestead. Many farmsteads had just a single structure at a time, and increases in the family seem to have been more often reflected in larger scale rebuildings than in construction of new buildings to complete a compound. This probably reflects the common need to rebuild after just the length of time taken for the family to outgrow the smaller structure. If we take the average life expectancy at age 15–20 to correspond to those of the life tables in Chapter 4, and we suppose, for the argument, that establishment of a household took place about that time of life, the expected life of the members of a new family resident in a new structure would have been about 18 to 20 years. By judicious use of a skyhook, it can be suggested that the duration of a Mississippian residential structure would come out to about a minimum of 6 years (at three rebuildings by the same family) to a middle figure of about 10 years (for two rebuildings). This is the same as the figure used by Milner as a rough estimate of occupation without major rebuilding (1986:231; but see also B. Smith 1995:239–242 for a summary of discussion of this issue; also see Pauketat 1986, 1989). In the historical records there are few observations of duration, but Le Page du Pratz suggested that the 5–9 m² Natchez houses lasted for "twenty years without any repair" (1758 [1972:341]).

There *are* good examples of probable multiple-structure dwellings even in small farmsteads. In larger sites, there are more examples of apparent clusters, but it is easier to postulate such clusters than it is to *prove* their use by a single family unit. Historically, lighter structures were often used as summer cabins, and heavier structures for winter (e.g., Adair 1775:404 and elsewhere; Romans 1775:67). It has often proved difficult to document such winter and summer lodges in archaeological contexts. In some parts of the East, there are relatively good examples of distinctive summer and winter structures (e.g., see Sullivan 1987, 1995).

3. KINSHIP AND SETTLEMENT

Although we cannot know exactly what kinds of kinship patterns and land allocation shaped Mississippian households, they were probably much like those seen in general in horticultural societies, and like historical Southeastern societies in particular. For the most part, the summaries of social structure provided for the Southeast by Hudson (1976:184–257) or Swanton (1928a) can be taken as being similar to prehistoric societies in the area. Comparative historical data make it likely that descent was unilineal. Given the consistency in the historical records for the area, it is likely that the kinship systems of groups such as the Creek were like the prehistoric systems from which they were descended. Like many horticultural people, matrilineal descent was surely a common feature, although patrilineal descent systems such as those of the Omaha Dhegiha Siouan groups may have existed as well.

Unilineal descent segments or *lineages* had many social and even political functions, probably including control of marriage and land use. In the historical matrilineal groups, a male often moved to live with his wife (uxorilocal postmarital residence), while she would typically live near her mother (matrilocal postmarital residence). To the extent that there were sexual divisions of labor and ritual functions, such a pattern would have implications for gender-specific traditions. One might, for example, expect that production systems that were linked to the stay-at-home gender might show less variability in archaeological sites than those of the gender that was displaced at the time of marriage. Of course, as critics of such social archaeology have pointed out, these interpretations have to be investigated carefully, since so many possibilities for learning experiences, and so on, can be present. Unilineal systems with postmarital residence relocations even reinforce unilineality, since the stay-at-homes can have greater influence on their kin than the move-outs. Even so, the role of matrilineal male kin in historical Southeastern societies was substantial, since matrilineality by no means equals matriarchy in political terms. Positions of authority were transmitted matrilineally, from a male to his sister's son.

Lineages are groups of kin that are based on putative traceable unilineal relationships—descent from a "known" ancestor. However, as time depth increases, lineages tend to fission as a common ancestor becomes more distant and less relevant in relation to more recently branching collateral groups. For a time after fission, the segments may be ranked by their distance to the putative common ancestor, especially if that person was of importance. Over longer periods, lineage segments lose track of exact relationships but remain in a more abstract relationship to other lineages, often within unilineal kin groups called *clans* by anthropologists. Clans share a tradition of common descent, usually from a natural or mythological ancestor. Clan membership had important functions in the historical Southeast. Support in other communities could be expected from one's kin. This would mean assistance when traveling or even provisioning in times of need. Much of what is loosely called "trade" in these societies could arguably have been distribution of goods in lineages and clans, at least before the coming of the European traders. In the Southeast, males of a lineage would often have been dispersed across the region, so male-held emblems of membership in matrilineages, for example, may also have been dispersed. Given what we know to have been true historically, we can propose an outline, then, of Mississippian social and spatial organization.

Settlement in households reproduced the unilineal kin group in space. The households would have reproduced the distribution of kin on arable land *and vice versa*, given persistence of kin units in places and in relation to other kin units. Just as the public square was a grander household, so to some extent, government reproduced the ranking of local lineages and clans. Representation in the community and chiefdom was through kinsmen on town and "tribal" councils. Police functions were largely based on the threat of reprisal by members of the victim's clan. Indeed, one of the indications of the transformation of the Creek chiefdom into a Muskogee state in the 18th century was the formal exemption of council agents from clan reprisal for acts taken at the direction of the council and miko (see Hawkins 1799:64ff.; Milfort 1802).

One of the most important functions of clan membership was to define appropriate marriage partners, and clan exogamy was enforced historically. Given a likely kin basis for the proximity of households, a male would typically not find a suitable mate near his natal household. In this sense, the household could not be isolated, even if its economic production was adequate to biologically reproduce the unit. If the prehistoric groups were declining in population through time, as the models in the previous chapter suggested, principles of exogamy could create real problems for persons in identifying appropriate spouses. Under conditions of slow decline in population and more dispersal of children, particular floodplain ridges would see the kinds of abandonment and resettlement that are clearly present in the archaeological record. Those fluctuations occur as a largely random process, but one that meant that social reproduction was complicated. Land and other usufruct allocations through clans and lineages could also become problematical as some groups disappeared in a locality. Kin groups holding important offices or positions might no longer be present in the community. In short, slow declines in population over time could produce crises in local production, government, and social organization in general by the random process of some groups disappearing. Given the ranked nature of clans, the system could cease to reproduce itself well before the population had in fact reached levels that were non-self-sustaining in purely biological terms.

Like lineage segments, clans themselves often had relative rankings in terms of seniority and prestige within the councils at town or regional levels. Archaeological evidence suggests the highest ranking residents occupied the best lands, at least to the extent that the largest sites with mounds are in localities with good soils that tend to be those least likely to flood. But before it is concluded that the best lands were expropriated by the elite, we should note that it seems just as much the case that the best lands *produced* the elites! Rich lands make rich people who have the "surplus" to make others dependent upon them in hard times, fostering longer term dependencies and differences in status.

The historical records suggest that most "houses" among peoples we might reasonably conclude to have been the descendants of Mississippians were not communal residences, but were basically nuclear to small family units. As Bartram noted, a household could have more than a single structure. There were sometimes functional differences between structures such as winter and summer dwellings or storage. Each structure was placed by a set pattern of use by the family, for family production, but within the organization of land use based on kinship principles.

The structure of the household resonated throughout Mississippian life in general, forming not only the building block of Mississippian communities, but also the structure of Mississippian social life itself.

4. SITES AND COMMUNITIES

Both biological and social reproduction were inextricably grounded in the residential family unit. Clusters of such households in the same locality were the locations of groups of families, almost certainly unilineal kin. Such residential and kinship units were small in absolute terms, and the evidence suggests that the populations in these homesteads were not quite reproducing themselves biologically. Slow shrinkage of population is a definite possibility.

Social factors such as proximity to kin were surely important in locating a homestead, as they are in most societies. Mississippian local communities were scaled up from the household, not organized down from the mound center. Each social unit was a self-replicating unit in a system that was largely organized around the needs of small residential modules. Each homestead had similar requirements for survival and reproduction, so the pattern repeats itself over the broader canvas of Mississippian life. As noted in Chapter 1, Douglas Davy (1982) did a simulation of settlement in the Black Bottom that also shows how simple principles of household reproduction easily account for the overall settlement distributions observed archaeologically. A household was founded, its members reproduced. Some persons moved according to rules of postmarital residence, such as neolocality for married couples together with matriproximity of residence for females, for example. Crowding of the constrained, linear ridges in floodplains also forced establishment of new households and use of nearby empty zones. As a household aged, its land use fell off and areas either became fallow or were taken over by a new household, depending upon the need for new settlement locations at the time that production by the older household ceased. Given relatively low populations, there might not always have been new families needing land at the time of "retirement" of older productive units. In such cases, land would go fallow. Growth of plant species such as hawthorn may suggest fallow fields in some areas, although such species also occur on field margins. If a new family came into being on a filled-up ridge, then settlement would spill over to adjacent ridges or even to new fields more distant from the natal household. Some settlement even occurred on more distant lands that might be safe from flood risks, but where soils were less fertile.

The bulk of production took place within the household unit. It is unlikely that these household units *planned* to produce surpluses as such, yet the nature of localized household production is such that each household tends to follow a strategy of overproduction as a hedge against possible failure (see Chapter 6). Out of the chaos of independent, household organization would emerge—in good or normal years—production in excess of household needs. Some carryover from one year to another was possible, but storage and preservation conditions in the wet, often flooded lowlands meant that holding substantial local surpluses also meant attrition of the stored resource. As a result, the alternative of using local surpluses to aid others in the region was not so much altruistic as practical. The productive system that made each household largely autonomous also created risks that made occasional cooperative action imperative.

Land and Settlement

It is unlikely that settlements and their fields filled up the available land at any single time, except for perhaps the peak periods of occupation. Nonetheless, the amount of occupation debris found in a locality such as the Black Bottom or American Bottom, where there has been intensive, fine-grained survey, is commonly directly proportional to the amount of land above normal flooding (see Milner 1986b; Muller 1986:190–191). In addition, large and small sites alike share similar ratios of settlement area to land available for cultivation. The relationship between area of habitation and the "support area" is often very close. Support areas and their relation to population are discussed in more detail in the section on population density later in this chapter; but, as example, there is a product–moment correlation between site area (as related to structures) and support area of 0.86, with R^2 at 0.74 for the Black Bottom (see Table 5.8). The data used for these calculations in each case are based on on measurement of total contiguous areas above normal annual flooding that surround habitation areas. For this reason, they are not directly comparable to support area figures calculated differently, for example, by drawing catchment circles.

These figures reflect a certain number of individual households occupying ridges along the swales. The consistency of the relationship is another indication of the "building-block" character of these households in the formation of larger settlement units.

Towns

The household is the center of Mississippian production and reproduction, but it is not the only significant building block of Mississippian social organization. In the discussion that follows, I outline an argument for each political entity being centered on at least one "town." To do so, I shall begin with a discussion of some historical cases and then move on to compare these with a few better-known Mississippian localities. In the historical records there is great variation in what is called a *town*, ranging from a few houses to large collections of individual settlements, sometimes aggregated, and sometimes dispersed over many hectares. This creates some difficulties of comparison to archaeologically defined sites, where data are spatial, not social. Nonetheless, I shall suggesting that even when total population declined, both prehistoric and historical groups tended to maintain town size by incorporation of new persons, families, and even "tribes." A "polity" would normally have at least one "town," but the town was sometimes highly spatially dispersed. Multiple towns within a polity may indicate multiple chiefs under a paramount, but often did not do so in Historic towns. The kind of town that maintained its size through time, however, is more likely to have its own political identity and its own chief, even if these are subordinate to some other town and chief.

Creek Towns and Patterns

One political entity can serve as an example of how historical Southeastern towns were organized. Some of the best data on population are available for the Creek Confederacy, and it presents a good case study for larger Eastern polities in general. It will be recalled that the Confederacy did not have a single ethnic identity, but—on the contrary—incorporated widely different groups. Both refugee Shawnee and Natchez settled in their own towns under the political and military umbrella of the Creek chiefdom. The tendency toward dispersion for horticultural efficiency (and other reasons) in the center and aggregation on the frontiers was not absent, but it was not so pronounced as one might expect. Of course, the historical records are from a time of almost unremitting warfare, so many settlements could be expected to show some features of aggregation for defense. Certainly there are indications that recorded population dropped in times of stress, and these declines have typically been interpreted as representing loss of population in warfare. Although this may be literally true, rapid recovery in peaceful times (Figure 5.2) also suggests that we are sometimes looking at abandonment and reoccupation of the sort that characterized major French or Belgian cities in 1940–1941, rather than losses through deaths (cf. Thornton 1990). Despite fluctuations, the general tendency of Creek Confederate population was upward, even in the face of the most appalling circumstances. Some of this ability to maintain, even increase, the size of the Creek polity was not attributable to either biological reproduction or even the disappearance and reappearance of individuals in the records. Rather, in the historical accounts, refugees from other groups were often being incorporated.

Table 5.3 indicates the basic statistics on Creek town size, first for all post–1540 data, and then for specific "censuses" from 1715 to 1832. Figure 5.3 graphically presents the shifts in size of towns in this sample, showing the mean value. The vertical lines and limits in Figure 5.3 are not ranges, but represent ± 1 standard deviation from the mean. The data are those where we have information on both the number of persons and the numbers of "villages."

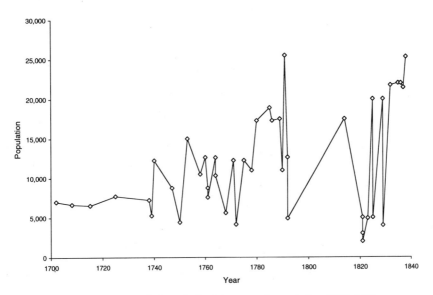

Figure 5.2. Recorded Creek Confederacy total population, 1700–1840.

The largest individual Creek towns were usually Okfuskee and Kasihta, ranging from ca. 500 to nearly 1400 people, and almost all towns were divided into a series of smaller villages. Hawkins, in 1799, noted that Okfuskee's abandonment for more dispersed settlement was underway (in a time of relative peace, in that case).

If these data are taken by frequency distribution (Table 5.4), a fair degree of consistency is apparent. However, the reader should note that the "towns" included here are those identified in the records as consisting of a single community. Some larger numbers given in the same years for what might better be called "subpolities" are not included. For example, counts for Kasihta in 1792 and 1799 specifically indicate three "villages" and are therefore excluded, as are Tukabahchee estimates just after the end date in the table. Town size remained remarkably constant despite fluctuation in the number of towns over the same time. There is no doubt that the frontier settlements had a greater need for concentration, often within the protection of palisades. At the same time, the data on the Creek and other historical Mississippian peoples suggest that the importance of

Table 5.3. Creek Town Sizes

Time	Post-1540	1715	1738	1750–1770	1750	1760	1761	1772	1792	1799	1832
Mean	257	166	224	234	109	291	170	208	294	478	269
St. dev.	306	49	175	171	85	223	98	110	311	330	144
Median	180	175	189	72	180	243	144	162	198	488	243

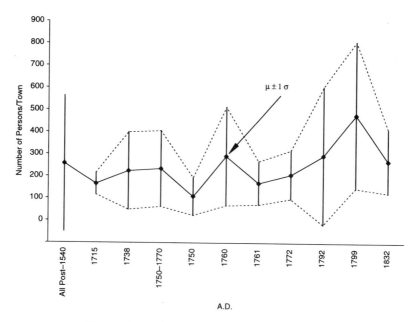

Figure 5.3. Variability in Creek Confederacy town size.

a town in political and economic terms had as much to do with its size and even, to a lesser degree, degree of aggregation. Furthermore, as these cases show, town size remained surprisingly stable despite large fluctuations in total population.

As towns became less important and less politically central, they had a tendency to scatter. They also scattered as more peaceful conditions were ensured by the *Pax Americana*, and as agents such as Hawkins encouraged dispersion into individual productive units using European agricultural methods.

In all, then, the data for historical Creek towns indicate common and rapid fluctuations in size. In addition, each larger community known as a "town" was usually made up of a series of smaller communities that were in close proximity to one another. Households and kinship were the basis of this kind of pattern. All the same, even in the midst of this variability, there is a consistency of town size within its elastic limits. Main towns tend to remain much the same size over the long term, despite overall population problems.

Historical Towns in General

In the last chapter, Mississippian societies were suggested to have had population structures that reflected low negative rates of growth. In this section, we shall examine issues of settlement and town size and the relationships of these to overall population. To begin, some historical data on population dynamics will be briefly examined, and this will then be related to the structural features of the Mississippian example I know best—that of the Lower Ohio Valley. I shall, however, relate this to

Table 5.4. Creek Population Frequency Distribution: Number of Towns in Each Size Class

To (<)	1715	1738	1750	1760	1761	1772	1792	1799	1832	1750–1775	All
50	0	3	5	1	0	0	1	0	1	1	12
100	0	2	10	3	3	2	5	0	3	8	29
150	2	3	5	3	14	3	6	2	7	20	47
200	3	2	1	7	2	3	1	0	6	12	26
250	1	2	2	1	3	0	2	1	6	4	21
300		1	1	4	0	1	3	0	6	6	19
350		0	0	0	0	1	0	0	5	1	7
400		4	1	4	2	3	3	1	3	9	21
450		1	0	0	0	0	0		3	0	4
500		0	2	1		0	1	0	1	3	5
550		0	3			0	2	0	0	3	5
600		0	0			0	0	3	2	0	3
650		0	0			0	0	3	0	1	4
700		0	0			0	0	0	1	0	1
750		1	0			0	0	0		0	1
800			0			0	0	0		0	0
850			0			0	0	0		0	0
900			0			0	0	0		0	0
950			0			0	0	0		0	1
1000			0			0	0	0		0	0
1050			0			0	0	0		0	0
1100			1			0	1	1		1	3
1150							0			0	0
1200							0			0	0
1250							0			0	0
1300							0			0	0
1350							1			0	0

Mississippian societies elsewhere and discuss whether the Lower Ohio has special features or is representative of Mississippian settlement structure.

Reported size of Eastern historical settlements, *for which both population figures and number of villages are given* (N = 328), varied widely. The smallest was as few as 10 persons in a settlement, and the highest was some 5500 persons in a single village. The latter figure, however, is a calculation for the number of houses at Coosa in the de Soto accounts, and is not based on firm data—especially as Quiguate is said elsewhere to have been the largest town they found, and it probably had no more than 250 houses (cf. Elvas 1557[1866:119]). The only other two 16th century town sizes, also for Coosa, are considerably lower, at 1925 persons in 8 villages in A.D. 1559, and 1500 in 150 villages for 1567. Only the second of these reports makes much sense. The first probably is an estimate of a whole "town" polity as opposed to individually named settlements comparable to those of the later historical record. The latter is probably a reckoning of many individual hamlets and farmsteads rather than units comparable to 17th-century data. Most individual towns in the historical record were not large.

Average sizes are more consistent. All recorded villages in the sample (from the A.D. 1600–1850 period) average 271 persons per village with a standard deviation of 391. Including the large, early figure for Coosa and other 16th-century data raises the average to 289 (see Figure 5.4a). Stability in town size is accompanied by a decrease in the number of towns per polity (see figure 5.4b).

Only 36 cases, of the more than 300 in the village-and-population data set, have total populations listed as more than 2000. Only 10 cases of average town size for a polity are greater than 1000, and only 31 listed groups have averages of more than 500 persons per village. There is a slight negative correlation between date and village size, but little of the variance is accounted for. The recorded historical data on village size indicate average size of settlement per century goes down from 486 persons per village in the 17th century to 251 in the 18th century, and then increases to 274 persons in the 19th century. However, the number of cases is small for the 17th-century data, and the lack of significant relationships between date and size show that there is no significance to the changes seen in average size for the arbitrary groupings into century-long periods. A Mann–Whitney U test of the differences from one century to another[2] indicates no statistical significance to the differences in village size by century. This conclusion is somewhat surprising, since we know that total Native American population declined markedly until the latter part of the 19th century. What the data suggest, then, is that even though total population was dropping through historical times, individuals were continuing to congregate into towns of about the same size as before. These data suggest that it will be difficult to argue that overall decreases in population are paralleled by reductions in the average town size (or, by implication, even in the complexity of political organization). If this is so for the Historic Period, one may ask whether it may not also be true of earlier times.

The historical literature is full of evidence of population aggregation, if we care to look for it. Many of the towns, even as early as the de Soto accounts, contain persons from other, sometimes former towns, and even of different ethnic groups. I suggest that this indicates a general tendency to try to maintain social life within its former parameters in the face of total population decline. There are fewer, not smaller, villages through time. Indeed, overall, there are fewer, not always smaller polities, as well. I suggest that the mechanisms that we see operating in the maintenance of social formations in the historical Southeast are of long-standing character, and that they evolved in the context of the shifting, constantly dynamic framework of unstable, so-called "chiefdoms," not just in the context of historical depopulation.

In addition, one would expect a good correlation between size of village and the number of men, not least because the total population is often a direct transformation of the recorded number of warriors. Surprisingly, the number of villages and the number of men are not at all correlated ($r = 0.05$) and the population per village and the number of men in total reported political units is also not correlated even when the small village cases are excluded ($r = 0.0057$). *A priori*, we might expect a negative

---

[2] The counts are usually by different observers and may be taken as independent measures. The assertion being tested is whether the same kind of settlement structure is present in each century.

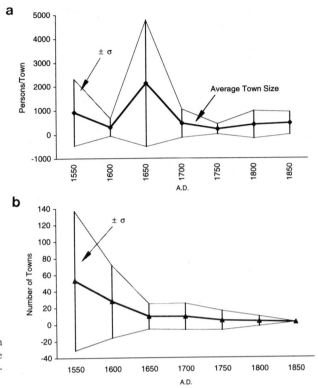

Figure 5.4. (a) Persons per town in the historic period. (b) Average number of reported towns in a polity.

correlation since it would seem that aggregation could be one response to the loss of warriors in battle—surviving warriors might be expected to show a tendency to congregate for defense in fewer villages to provide better defense. It would also seem likely that the more numerous and dispersed the villages, the fewer the number of men in each might be.

Mississippian Towns

In the Lower Ohio, the two largest Mississippian sites are Kincaid and Angel, each located in an extensive bottomland. Both have comparable amounts of mound construction—one of the sites being slightly larger in total mound construction and the other containing the largest single mound in the region. The similarities of the sites are such that one could reasonably suppose them to have been like the "white" and "red" towns of historical Southeastern peoples. At the least, they were closely related by historical connections.

In addition to the major sites, there are several smaller mound sites such as Rowlandtown, Tolu, and Orr-Herrl (locations are shown in Figure 5.6). Such sites have usually been characterized (as did Black in 1967) as satellite communities of secondary rank. There is, however, increasing sentiment among regional archaeologists (e.g., R. Berle Clay, R. Barry Lewis, and J. Muller) that mound construction at such sites may just as likely represent periods during which local authorities were relatively independent of the elites at the supposed "main" centers. In addition, palisaded, concentrated towns occurred at Southwind (C. Munson 1984), and up into the Tennessee and Cumberland Valleys in the larger sites of Tinsley Hill and Jonathan Creek. Southwind, Tinsley Hill, and Jonathan Creek sites each had some "frontier" features, such as concentration of population and fortification (see Clay's interpretations, 1976 and later).

In addition to a range of more or less dispersed settlements away from the "central" sites, there were also sites of other kinds. The best known of these are the special-purpose sites for extraction of resources—chert and salt. Transient producers, not residential specialists, usually exploited these sites. Contrary to the expectations of "specialization" hypotheses about the rise of chiefdoms (e.g., Service 1975), there is no evidence for "craft specialization" at residential locations in specific resource zones. On the contrary, even isolated upland sites conform closely to expectations for bottomland farmsteads. The main difference between upland and floodplain settlements is not in their production systems, but in the longevity of settlement in a particular location.

Figure 5.5 compares data on settlement of the Kincaid system and that of historical Creek towns. The Lower Ohio figures are slight revisions of those developed in my *Archaeology of the Lower Ohio River Valley* (1986b). The Creek data are from actual census data in the years indicated. Such comparisons are only rough, but they do indicate that overall settlement structure of the prehistoric Lower Ohio Valley is within the range of settlement size and organization seen in the historical Creek Confederacy.

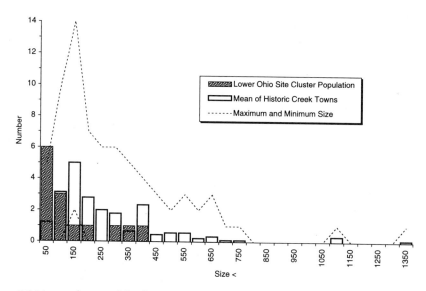

Figure 5.5. Mean and range of Creek town-size classes compared to estimated population of Lower Ohio Mississippian site clusters.

In Figure 5.5, the Lower Ohio Valley site clusters around Kincaid have been converted to a scaled population, as discussed in the section on population density (also presented in Table 5.8; also see Muller 1986b). It is not surprising that more small units show up in the archaeological sample than in the historical estimates. The relative distribution of sites by size is more important than exact figures. The data suggest that historical Creek towns cannot be taken as significantly different from the patterns observed in the archaeological data. I expect that archaeological data from historical sites, as they come available and are defined on the basis of contiguous scatter of debris, will show spatial clusters that are even more similar to the prehistoric patterns than are the population data.

The relationship between projected and known numbers of structures and "site area" at archaeological sites is also close (as discussed in more detail below, and shown in Table 5.7). As a result, although estimates may be off true Kincaid locality "town" (in this case, site clusters) sizes by some constant value, the comparison serves to illustrate relative town-size ranks.

Comments on Size and Complexity

So far I have compared population structure between Mississippian times and data from historical Eastern societies. The *lack* of disjunction between one historical period and another—and the similarities to prehistoric Mississippian settlement—suggest that Eastern populations tended to maintain town size, even if the number of polities and the number of towns decreased. These comparisons also suggest that the supposed disconformities between social practice in historical and prehistoric times are exaggerated.

I want to make it clear that I am not arguing that declines in mound construction and population are of no significance, merely that these cannot be taken as *a priori* evidence for collapse of political structures. The Medieval European case is a clear example of how the combination of climate ("Little Ice Age"), invasion (Islamic), epidemic disease (plague), and warfare (internal and external) does not automatically translate into immediate destruction of fundamental organizational principles.

No one should argue that Eastern North American societies did not change, but we *can* reasonably argue that the social conditions of Mississippian at its peak are more directly reflected in the social conditions of Mississippian peoples in the Historic Period than many have allowed. As noted, two contradictory impulses seem to have been at work here. The first impulse is a natural desire to show the complexity of prehistoric Eastern populations in response to the popular misconceptions that they were simple hunters and warriors. The second problem is that historical societies have often been underestimated as degenerate, not least by those historians seeking to justify a manifest destiny. Unfortunately, such exaggerated views of pre-European social formations have often been compared to the historical misrepresentations, resulting in a huge gap. I suggest that the levels of complexity in both periods are roughly comparable. However, one consequence of the European Invasion may have been formation of incipient secondary states under the pressure of warfare. Instead of causing a decline in aboriginal political organization, the invasion of North America, as in so many other places, may actually have stimulated the formation of states for self defense.

Prehistoric Polity Size

To look at the size of Mississippian communities, we need to look at the basis of settlement and community structure in more detail. The discussion of the Lower Ohio Valley case that follows is a further development of estimates presented in more detail in my book on that region (1986b). It is based on a very nearly 100 percent survey of an entire bottomland and substantial survey of the whole valley from the Wabash to the Mississippi.

Mississippian settlement in this locality, like most others, typically occurred on ridges in the bottomlands along major streams. Fertile soils and relative freedom from annual flooding were key factors in site location, but access to a broad range of wild-natural resources was as important as the potential of the land for maize cultivation. In fact, as we see from data on Terminal Late Woodland (a.k.a. Emergent Mississippian) settlement, concentration on these environmental zones predates the maize-intensive horticultural systems of fully developed Mississippian. There are also some Mississippian settlements in upland zones, but these are rarer and often seem to be somewhat later as well.

The question arises of the degree of aggregation of Mississippian population (as expressed in settlements) in the floodplains. One way of assessing aggregation and dispersal is through the use of Voronoi tessellation (also known as Thiessen polygons, see Haggett 1965; Hodder and Orton 1976: Chapter 4). These figures are simply lines drawn between sites in such a way that each point within the boundary is closer to the enclosed site than to any other site.[3] The first tessellation (Figure 5.6) is for the entire Lower Ohio Valley from Angel to the Mississippi–Ohio confluence area. The zones defined around the so-called primary sites (Kincaid and Angel) and the supposed "secondary" sites do not show the hexagonal patterning but are often linearly divided along the curving river systems. The divisions, especially when geographic features are considered, are fairly uniform, however.

The second Voronoi tessellation (Figure 5.7) is for the Black Bottom locality only, but includes all Mississippian sites in the floodplain and on the first terrace area. This figure also illustrates the linear nature of local Mississippian settlement, similar to the Valley as a whole. In this case, the primary resource on which the curved band of Mississippian settlement concentrates is that associated with certain soil types. As in the valley, the distribution of sites is fairly evenly spaced along the higher ridges that would have been fertile horticultural land.

Both of these figures graphically support the long-standing observation that Mississippian population concentrated on a few resources and that settlement was fairly evenly distributed on lands having agricultural and bottomland resources. The Lower Ohio Valley is better known than many Mississippian settlement systems in terms of nearly complete survey at a scale that reveals small, farmstead-level settle-

---

[3] The Voronoi tesselations are generated by the Systat 5.2 program for the Macintosh.

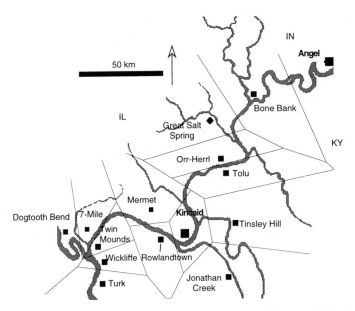

Figure 5.6. Voronoi tessellation of major Mississippian mound sites (and the Great Salt Spring) in the lower Ohio River Valley.

ments; but similar patterns can be found in other localities as recent work in the American Bottom and also in the Moundville localities illustrates (Bareis and Porter 1984; Peebles 1987b).

One statistic for measuring settlement aggregation is the "Nearest Neighbor" statistic originally developed for botanical distribution studies (Clark and Evans 1954; Pielou 1977:154–155). Even though the Nearest Neighbor statistic has its

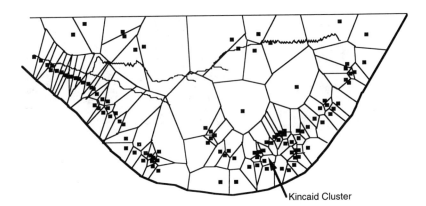

Figure 5.7. Voronoi tessellation of Mississippian settlement in the Black Bottom of the Ohio River. (The arrow points to the Kincaid Mounds site cluster location. The Black Bottom is approximately 8 km north–south and 16 km east–west.)

problems in interpretation (cf. Pielou 1977:156; Pinder, Shimada, and Gregory 1979), it provides a rough measure for the intensity of patterning. Of course, how one views any set of locations in terms of aggregation depends upon the background "universe" to which it is compared. In Figure 5.8 the Mississippian settlement of the Black Bottom is fairly aggregated when all the bottomland is examined for settlement—settlement is restricted to high, fertile ridgetops. The distribution of Mississippian settlement is nearly random, however, if settlement is examined only in its distribution on those ridges alone. The site clusters in Figure 5.8 and Table 5.5 are defined by the dissection of the floodplain and represent settlement on contiguous areas of high-fertility soils that are above normal annual flooding. The names are arbitrary, reflecting natural features, such as lakes, separating zones of occupation. Whether such site clusters correspond to Mississippian communities is difficult to judge, but such close proximity ensured that, whatever the *original* reasons for settling together on these ridges, the settlers would have soon become some kind of community.

For the unadjusted statistic, the pattern of settlement in the Black Bottom proper (Figure 5.8) appears to vary from aggregated to random to uniform as the distance from the major site, Kincaid, increases. Aggregation is most pronounced in the center of this linear band of settlement. It has often been suggested that there appears to be some suppression of smaller Mississippian settlement in the vicinity of the large sites, and that may be one factor in the pattern shown. In addition, the further away from Kincaid in the bottomland, generally, the more narrow the ridges become, producing a linear, but uniform, distribution. The pattern is reminiscent of the transitions noted for cellular automata (order → complexity → chaos, see Waldrop 1992:234) A nearby, probably auxiliary, Mississippian settlement zone, the so-called "Upper Bottom" has a pattern that is essentially random overall, as reflected

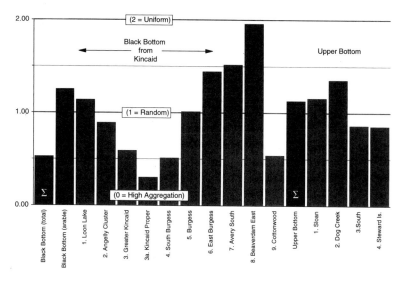

Figure 5.8. Nearest Neighbor statistical values (calculated according to Clark and Evans 1954) for Black Bottom and Upper Bottom site clusters, Lower Ohio Valley.

in Nearest Neighbor statistical values near 1.0. Indeed, these statistics for the Lower Ohio Valley conform to what we know about population density from other data. Mississippian settlement was constrained to certain soils and elevations in the flood-plains but does not usually fill those zones to the extent of forcing uniform (hexagonal) settlement spacing.

Table 5.5 indicates the R values for the Nearest Neighbor statistic as graphically presented in Figure 5.8, as well as providing additional data on the settlement patterns in two of the three major Mississippian site zones in the Lower Ohio. Note that the site areas in this table are the total areas with habitation debris, not areas of the site cluster (or within palisades at Kincaid). The data may be even more consistent than the table indicates since the most variant values are generally in zones where survey coverage is slightly less complete or more problematical because of factors such as alluviation. Even so, the consistency of the data is striking, within the parameters of the variation in aggregation already discussed. The R_{cor} column is the figures as adjusted for edge effect according to the Pinder et al. correction for square areas (1979). This correction shows that clustering is much more pronounced in terms of overall area.

Even given problems in interpretation of this statistic, the measures of aggregation and dispersion in Mississippian settlement, high aggregation is a feature of the richest zones in the bottomland, and the measures that might suggest random or

Table 5.5. Nearest Neighbor Statistic, R, and Site–Land Ratios for the Black Bottom, Ohio Valley

	N	Site area	Area	Area/ site area	Area/site	R=	R_{cor}=
Black Bottom (total)	151	40.8	4900	120.2	32.5	0.53	0.00
Black Bottom (arable)	151	40.8	881	21.6	5.8	1.25	0.02
1. Loon Lake	24	8.8	161	18.3	6.7	1.14	0.02
2. Angelly	11	4.1	58	14.0	5.3	0.89	0.02
3. Greater Kincaid	34	9.7	179	18.5	5.3	0.59	0.01
3a. Kincaid Proper	20	6.2	77	12.5	3.9	0.31	0.01
4. South Burgess	6	2.1	46	21.5	7.7	0.51	0.01
5. Burgess	18	3.4	57	16.7	3.2	1.01	0.02
6. East Burgess	8	1.8	33	18.1	4.1	1.45	0.03
7. Avery South	15	3.7	27	7.3	1.8	1.52	0.04
8. Beaverdam East	4	0.3	10	30.3	2.5	1.96	0.05
9. Cottonwood	3	0.9	21	23.3	7.0	0.54	0.01
Upper Bottom	33	9.2	190	20.6	5.8	1.13	0.02
1. Sloan	14	6.2	60	9.7	4.3	1.16	0.02
2. Dog Creek	12	1.4	83	58.9	6.9	1.35	0.02
3. South	3	1.2	25	21.7	8.3	0.87	0.01
4. Steward Is.	5	0.5	22	45.8	4.4	0.86	0.01
mean=	12.6	3.6	61.4	22.6	5.1	1.0	0.0
SD=	9.0	3.1	51.0	14.1	2.0	0.5	0.0

All areas are in ha.

uniform settlement are away from the richest areas. The implications for Mississippian reproduction are fairly clear. The distribution of Mississippian families may have been slightly concentrated on the main political centers, but the distributions suggest the main factor in location was the availability of fertile soils above normal flooding.

5. POPULATION DENSITY

I shall first briefly discuss some aspects of historical Southeastern demography to see what kinds of impact historical depopulation had on such variables as town size and the size of these social entities. I shall ask if there is justification for the often-expressed opinion that early historical population losses so disturbed historical groups that their settlement and social structures were fundamentally disrupted (cf. M. T. Smith 1987). I also shall compare historical Southeastern data on settlement to several cases of prehistoric Mississippian settlement to see if there are similar patterns to those of the historical data.

Historic Populations

A doubly false dichotomy is created when it is supposed that prehistoric Mississippian societies were large and that their historical descendants lived in scattered and unorganized refugee camps. Were historical polities really small, scattered remnants? The simple fact is that there are many cases of historical political entities of over 20,000 persons (e.g., Table 5.6). Not all of these figures are of equal reliability, but they are solid enough to show that the largest historical groups were as large as the largest reasonable estimates for prehistoric Mississippian polities. When the "cant of conquest" is removed from our consideration of these polities, we find that they functioned on high levels. They pursued effective, if not ultimately successful, political and military strategies against the invading Europeans (e.g., Jennings 1975). Among other things, these population figures demonstrate that the political and economic structures described in the 18th century **were** adequate for chiefly societies of substantial size. However "degenerate" these political structures were supposed to be, they were nonetheless capable of providing governance for societies of 20 or 30 thousand people.

In Table 5.6, if number of men is given, the original sources normally indicated *only* the number of "warriors." These numbers have been converted into total population using a multiplier of 3.6, which is based on an average of the historical sources in which both total population and number of warriors are given independently by the same observer. The census data are from times of considerable conflict, and the ratio of males to total population is only a little different than the same ratio in postwar Germany (e.g., Lexikon-Institut Bertelsmann 1975:117, 246), reflecting the effects of World War II on German gender ratios.

In short, the rumors of the death of large-scale chiefdoms in the historical East are much exaggerated. Confederacies such as the Choctaw and the Cherokee were as large as any prehistoric groups, with populations well in excess of 20,000.

Table 5.6. Aboriginal Groups Reported as Larger Than 20,000 People

Name	Date	Pop.	Men	Villages	Sources/notes
Cherokee	1500	30,000			Thornton 1990:15–18; cf. Mooney, 1928 (Ubelaker 1976:260)
Huron (Wyandot)	1615	30,000		18	Champlain, in Hodge 1907:587
Huron (Wyandot)	1616	35,000			Brebeuf; Hewitt in Hodge 1907:587
Huron (Wyandot)	1616	30,000			Sagard; Hewitt in Hodge 1907:587
Apalachee	1618	30,000			Lowery MSS, in Swarton 1946
Apalachee	1635	34,000			Lowery MSS, in Swarton 1946
Florida (many)	1635	30,000		44	Swanton 1922:439; mostly Timucuan & Guale
Timucua Group	1635	30,000		44	Letter, 44 Missions
Timucua, Guale	1635	30,000		44	Swanton 1922:439; mostly Timucuan & Guale
Cherokee	1650	22,000			Mooney 1928 (Ubelaker 1976:260, cf. Thornton 1990:15–18)
Tuscarora	1650	? 21,600	6000	24	"Early Times", Cusick in Hodge 1910:842
Miami	1657	24,000	8000		Renault, *Jes. Rel.* 44:246
Illinois	1660	70,000	20,000	60	Jesuit Rel. for 1660 in Hodge 1907:597
Choctaw	1700	21,600	6000	50	"Chaquitas"; d'Iberville 1700, Margry1880 iv:427
Choctaw	1725	28,800	8000		1725–1726, Bienville (see fn Adair 1775[1930]:302)
Choctaw	1726	90,000	25,000		Le Page du Pratz 1758[1972:295]; doubt over estimate
Cherokee	1735	21,600	6000	64	Adair 1775:227 according to old "Traders"
Choctaw	1738	57,600	16,000		High estimate, Swanton 1946:123, 1952:184
Cherokee	1746	21,600	6000		Documents in Anderson & Lewis 1983 in Thornton 1990:31
Choctaw	1764	21,500			Hutchins 1784
Creek Confederacy	1791	25,500	5500		Swan, M'Gillivray in Schoolcraft 1851-1857(5):263–264
Creek Confederacy	1832	21,733			1832-1833 Census, all; Sen Doc 512:334-394; in 1922:438
Cherokee	1835	22,542			Georgia, NC, Tenn., Alabama, beyond Miss.(est)
Creek Confederacy	1835	22,000			US Indian Office (USIO) Census; Swanton 1922:443
Creek Confederacy	1836	22,000			USIO Census; Swanton 1922:443
Creeks & Seminoles	1836	26,000			Gallatin 1836:101 "War Dept."
Creek Confederacy	1837	21,437			USIO Census; Swanton 1922:443
Creek Confederacy	1838	25,293			USIO Census; Swanton 1922:443
Creek Confederacy	1841	25,338			USIO Census; Swanton 1922:443
Creek Confederacy	1842	25,338			USIO Census; Swanton 1922:443
Creek Confederacy	1843	25,338			USIO Census; Swanton 1922:443
Creek Confederacy	1844	25,338			USIO Census; Swanton 1922:443
Creek Confederacy	1845	24,754			USIO Census; Swanton 1922:443
Creek Confederacy	1847	25,000			USIO Census; Swanton 1922:443
Creek Confederacy	1853	25,000			USIO Census; Swanton 1922:444
Choctaw	1856	22,707			US Department of Indian Affairs (USDIA)
Creek Confederacy	1857	28,214			Schoolcraft, Swanton 1922:444
Cherokee, West	1859	21,000			Thornton 1990:87
Cherokee	1860	21,000			Mooney 1928
Cherokee, West	1882	20,336			Thornton 1990:105

(continued)

Table 5.6. (*Continued*)

Name	Date	Pop.	Men	Villages	Sources/notes
Cherokee	1884	23,000			Ann. Rep. Indian Affairs; Thornton 1990:106
Cherokee, West	1890	25,978			Citizens of the Nation; Thornton 1990:108
Cherokee	1902	28,016			Incl. tribal repudiated, Mooney in Hodge 1907:247
Cherokee	1907	25,000			Mooney 1928 all
Cherokee	1910	31,489			US Census
Choctaw	1916	20,601			USDIA, 1916-1919, OK, MI, LA and elsewhere
Cherokee	1923	38,947			Indian Office Census, in OK+NC
Cherokee	1930	45,238			US Census

Population Density

Questions about population density are central to much of our understanding of Mississippian society. On the one hand, we have estimates that are like what Adair scornfully called "the reputed establishment of extensive and puissant Indian American empires" (Adair 1775:459–60 [1930:426–427]). These are figures for sites such as Cahokia that suggest populations of tens of thousands, and even more. As James B. Griffin once noted, if population figures for Cahokia had been as high as some of these estimates, the accumulation of human wastes alone would have gone a long way toward the construction of Monks Mound, suggesting to another colleague of mine that this would truly have been the original "effluent" society. The question of mound construction will be dealt with in subsequent chapters, but it is enough to note here that both the scale of construction and the numbers of persons necessary to carry out such construction programs have also been exaggerated, as have been the nature and quantity of prehistoric production and exchange. Still, the crux of the matter comes down to how many people there were at these Mississippian sites.

The following Lower Ohio Valley Mississippian population estimates are firmly grounded in empirical evidence for numbers and size of sites, combined with extensive knowledge of the local geography. Those who wish to see those "puissant" Native American empires have difficulties with such low population estimates, and I have heard dismissal of Kincaid as unusual in its low population—quite a comedown for a site once called a "prehistoric Illinois Metropolis."[4] Kincaid has even been described as merely a "small" Mississippian site, not like the really big centers. Although Kincaid was certainly small by comparison to Cahokia in both mound construction and total population, it is not a small site by the standards of any other Mississippian centers. The total palisaded area is no less than 50 ha, and probably includes more like 70 ha. This is as large or larger than the palisaded areas of Cahokia or Moundville (see the scale maps in Morgan 1980). The largest mound at Kincaid ranks about 12th among all Mississippian mound construction, and the site as a whole is roughly fifth

[4] Surely by comparison to the nearby modern Metropolis, Illinois, with a population of some 7000.

among all Eastern sites in total mound construction (see Chapter 6 for more detailed discussion). Kincaid or Angel cannot simply be dismissed as small and untypical. Concentration on the large-scale features of Mississippian mound centers has naturally created a rather grand view of Mississippian, but the basic module of settlement remained the household–farmstead, not the pyramids of the rich and famous. So, let us look at settlement and population, and how they are related.

The population figures that can be projected for areas where we have detailed information are much more in line with historical figures than the exaggerated views of thousands of persons, which have sometimes been postulated.[5] At the same time, Mississippian populations were often dispersed so that the traditional central sites may have been less than 30 or 40 percent of total populations. Many, perhaps even most, Mississippian persons lived in small farmsteads of no more than 3–4 structures, not in "centers." Such homesteads may cluster together into slightly larger settlements or "hamlets" of 6–15 households. Many of the historical records of community organization show us these smaller "towns." Even within these somewhat larger communities, however, evidence indicates that the nature of the composition of the household and the economic activities taking place in the homestead are the same as in more isolated farming locations. Each structure seems to be essentially the same as every other structure in terms of archaeological contents, especially when there is evidence of residential use.

I have already commented on the close relationship between area of site and "support area" (i.e. good horticultural land above annual flooding). Figure 5.9 expresses this graphically in another way, relating numbers of sites to support areas.

In the Black Bottom and in the American Bottom, the relationships between structures and *site* areas are also very consistent, as shown in Table 5.7. The site areas and numbers of structures are given for selected sites where well-defined site limits based on controlled surface collections are available or otherwise precise limits are defined (e.g., Blakely 1988b; Fortier 1985; Milner 1983b, 1984b, 1984c; Muller 1986a). The similarity of these estimates for these two different Mississippian localities is striking. The "maximum" and "minimum" figures for structures are only marginally related to temporal differences, and the actual site area per contemporary house is lower than shown here. For other sites in the American Bottom with more broadly defined site areas (and multiple components), the amount of site area per Mississippian structure is much higher, For example, the Stirling phase components at the Sponemann (Jackson, Fortier, and Williams 1992) and BBB Motor sites (Emerson and Jackson 1984), have around half a hectare per structure, although the earlier Edelhardt component at the latter site is similar to the figures that follow. Such differences reflect different ways of defining site limits, but there may also be some

---

[5] I have explained the assumptions underlying the site estimates in more detail in Muller 1986b. However, these are maximum figures for the mid-13th century period when nearly all sites seem to have been occupied. For reasons explained in my *Archaeology of the Lower Ohio River Valley*, there are likely to have been few habitation sites not detected in our long-term survey of the Black Bottom, and excavations and controlled surface collections have confirmed our site-size estimates. Site areas with appreciable alluviation are generally too low for regular habitation, and the river channel has been relatively stable at this point for many thousands of years.

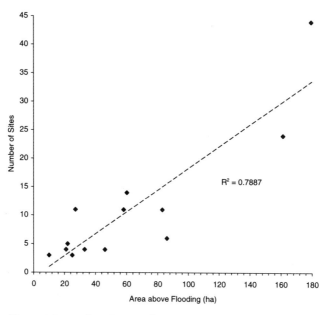

Figure 5.9. Number of sites and support area in the Black Bottom only.

development of even more dispersed settlement in the later American Bottom phases. The site–area comparisons provide another piece of evidence that suggests that despite its regional diversity, Mississippian has some elements of widespread similarity in organization, as well.

These data also show a weak trend toward reduction of area per structure as site area increases [the regression formula is ha/structure = .195 − .028 × site area(ha)]. While expected and significant, the relationship is weak (R^2 = 0.225).

Table 5.7. Site Areas and Numbers of Structures

Site	Site area (ha)	Min. no. of structures	Max. no. of structures	Ha/structure (range)	
IASMx109, Black Bottom, IL	0.30	2	2	0.20	0.20
BBPp105, Black Bottom, IL	0.30	1	2	0.30	0.20
BBMx213, Black Bottom, IL	0.4	1	5	0.40	0.08
Robinson's Lake, American Bottom, IL	0.77	10	10	0.08	0.08
IASMx66(1), Black Bottom, IL	0.84	4	6	0.21	0.14
Robt. Schneider, American Bottom, IL	0.91	5	5	0.18	0.18
Turner, American Bottom, IL	1.16	6	6	0.19	0.19
IASMx66(all), Black Bottom, IL	1.35	8	8	0.17	0.17
King, GA	2.05	25	25	0.08	0.08
Kincaid 1A,B, Black Bottom, IL	2.25	15	15	0.15	0.15
Julien, American Bottom, IL	2.95	22	22	0.13	0.13

These Mississippian sites do not appear to have usually been so compact or crowded that compression effects were important. The range of area per structure is presented in Figure 5.10.

At slightly over 30 m² per structure (not including extramural living areas), some 2–2.4 percent of total site area was structure floor. More broadly defined site areas (such as those usually entered in state site records) have only about 0.1–0.8 percent of the larger area in actual structure floor. Figure 5.10 shows the ranges of numbers of structures. Figure 5.11 shows the relationship of the number of structures to the total site area. Recall that number of structures is based on controlled surface collections and excavations and projections from known areas of occupation. The data are most directly related for the Black Bottom, where alluviation since occupation has made only "living" areas visible archaeologically. The estimation of site area differs somewhat for the American Bottom sites (Robinson's Lake, Robt. Schneider, Turner, and Julien) but in all cases are determined from controlled-surface-collection data (Fortier 1985; Milner 1983b, 1984b, 1984c). The slope is similar, and the greater number at Cahokia may reflect the generally smaller size of structures in that locality. The area of the King site in Georgia is calculated by palisade enclosure, so it is surprising that it falls as close to the others as it does.

The regression relationships indicated here would not hold for areas where site area cannot be so tightly defined, and especially not in unalluviated areas. I would expect that more careful measurement of site areas according to explicit criteria would allow similar calculations for other localities.

The patterns for the American Bottom sites, the Black Bottom sites, and others are consistent enough to justify their use for estimation of numbers of structures at other sites, at least as a maximum measure. Of course in reality, many structures were not contemporary, and taphonomic uncertainties can mean the loss of structure data. I emphasize again that the estimates refer *only* to narrowly defined occupied site areas, *not* to the areas in records that combine many discrete surface scatters together.[6] In the American Bottom data given earlier, the site area given usually includes *all* 10-m² units that have occupational debris present. For the Black Bottom site definitions, the base grid unit was typically 3 or 6 m², and site location surveys always broke down site areas into the minimal *contiguous* areas of site surface scatter.

Given a pattern of homestead units located in relation to land, it is possible, in turn, to project *maximum* population figures. Of course, actual population would have been lower, because of the assumption of contemporaneity of nonoverlapping structures. In the Black Bottom, I had earlier estimated population of the different site clusters on the basis of the local data only (Muller 1986b:Table 6.5), and my older estimates are slightly revised *downward* as a result of including the non-Black Bottom sites in the tables above. Table 5.8 indicates the estimates for the Black Bottom around the Kincaid site and for an upstream bottomland known as the "Upper Bottom."

---

[6] For example, of the sites from the American Bottom in Table 5.7 for which we have data, the Robinson's Lake site was originally listed as being 18.8 ha total, with 9.6 ha in the right-of-way, but the surface collection defined an area of 0.77 ha. The Turner site was 11.1, 9.1, and 1.16 ha, respectively. Julien was 25.8 ha in total area, of which 5.7 ha was in the right-of-way, and the defined site area was 2.95 ha.

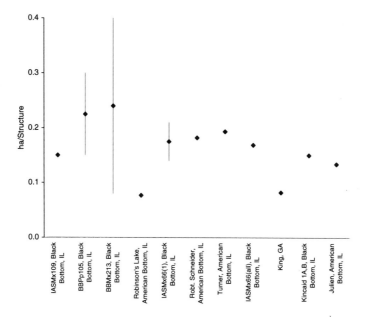

Figure 5.10. Range of hectares per structure at various sites.

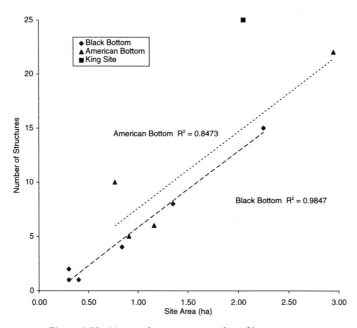

Figure 5.11. Measured site area to number of known structures.

In this table, the estimate of 5 persons per structure is used, as it has been in many other cases (e.g., Black 1967:547). A second column of estimated population is based on the 12 persons per structure found in some historical Chickasaw and Choctaw settlements (see above). This, however, seems unreasonably high for the roughly 30 m² buildings under discussion here. Some structures had nonresidential functions, of course, and a few at Kincaid itself were more than large enough to have accommodated such a number. The assumption of contemporaneity is generally false, although it is often the case that the maximum number of nonoverlapping structures may be close to the actual maximum during the peak use of a location. I am comfortable with the estimates for the Kincaid locality clusters given here for the 5 persons per structure. As we have already seen, they are quite comparable to historical town and village sizes. The figure for Angel, however, is something more of a problem. Black estimated that there were "about one-half million square feet of area which show signs of having been lived upon with varying degree of intensity"—that is, some 4.6 ha. He further estimated that there were "perhaps as much as 2,400 square feet per family dwelling unit"—about 0.022 ha per household. This figure is only one-tenth of

Table 5.8. Lower Ohio Valley Mississippian Population Estimates from Site Areas (in ha) and Structures[a]

Zone	Support area	Number of sites	Observed site area	Est. number of structures	Estimated pop.@ 5	Estimated pop. @12
Black Bottom						
BB I	161	24	8.8	55	274	659
BB II	58	11	4.1	26	129	310
Kincaid (BB III)	179	44	10.8	68	339	813
BB IV	46	4	1.9	12	59	143
BB V	86	6	1.0	7	33	78
BB VI	33	4	1.5	9	45	109
BB VII	27	11	2.8	18	88	212
BB VIII	10	3	0.3	2	10	24
BB IX	21	4	0.9	6	28	68
BB Other	—[b]	16	3.8	24	120	287
Black Bottom I–IX	621	111	32.2	201	1006	2414
BB Total	—	127	36.0	225	1126	2702
Upper Bottom						
UB I	60	14	6.2	39	193	463
UB II	83	11	1.4	9	44	106
UB III	25	3	1.2	7	37	89
UB IV[c]	22	5	0.5	0		
UB total	190	33	9.2	55	274	657
BB & UB total	811	160	45.3	280	1399	3359
Angel Site total[d]	—	—	4.6	29	145	348

[a]Based on the assumptions of 5 persons per structure and 6.3 structures per occupied ha; all structures assumed to be contemporaneous residences.
[b]Sites where no support area can be defined.
[c]Probably refuse areas.
[d]Angel occupied area is from Black 1967.

the estimates of site area to structure given above, so Black's estimate of the number of households (not the same as *structures*) is slightly more than 200, for a total population of over 1000 persons (1967:547). As Black himself noted, this seems large, but not impossible as a maximum. The estimate of 145 persons from the table above is likely to be too low for Angel, so we must either revise Black's estimates of occupied area upward, or note that some sites had greater density of occupation. I suspect that the true answer is even more complex, however. There are likely to be many similarities, but surely some differences, reflecting local conditions. At Kincaid, the majority of population of the "town," in the historical sense at least, lived outside the palisades of the main site. By Black's figures, a larger percentage of the intramural site at Kincaid would have had actual habitation (some 15–22 percent at Kincaid, 9–12 percent at Angel). We lack comparable localitywide surveys on a fine-grained basis for the Angel bottomlands, but I would be surprised if the site is so different from Kincaid as Black's estimates would suggest (see my earlier discussion, 1986b:207). The Angel site area is somewhat over two-thirds of the area of the Kincaid site (1986b:207). At the same time, the scale of mound construction at the two sites is quite close (1986b:202). Nonetheless, it has been suggested that upwards of 80 percent of all Angel phase persons lived in the Angel site proper (C. Munson, personal communication). If this were so, it would suggest a very different pattern indeed from that at the otherwise similar Kincaid site and its locality. Table 5.9 indicates the amount of contiguous support area there would have been at the two population estimates given in the earlier table.

Table 5.10 indicates the population estimates and support areas for the same site clusters given in Table 5.8 but recalculated at Black's higher density figures. These estimates are much higher and more like the traditional views of Mississippian "metropolises," even though some might think even Black's estimates to be too low. Are the extensions of Black's estimates to other sites reasonable? I think not. First, the resulting estimate of numbers of structures is quite simply wrong for the density of structures in the smaller Black Bottom sites. Second, the historical data correlate much more closely to the lower population estimates based on the Black Bottom data than do the larger settlements based on the Angel estimates, as Black himself was well aware (1967:547). Finally, even though Black's estimate is possible for the Angel site proper, the extension of the same figures to the other settlement clusters produces very high, even impossible, densities of persons for the potential horticultural zones. An individual human being cannot live on the production of 0.06 ha for a year at the likely levels of production—a mere 0.15 **acres** simply does not provide enough resources. These estimates are probably no less than 10 times higher than could reasonably be supported by the Mississippian mixed horticultural, collecting economy, even allowing for horticulture on adjacent soils (see Chapters 4 and 6 on production for more discussion of Mississippian subsistence, land area, and biological needs).

As I indicated in an earlier discussion of this issue (Muller 1986b:213–215), somewhat larger populations *can* be proposed if higher production figures are accepted for Mississippian horticulture, but even for these estimates, the smallest amount of land to support a person on maize would have to be at least 0.102 ha per person per year (Davy 1982:219; discussion of production in Chapter 6). Applying this high-production figure to the support areas defined would yield a total population for the Kincaid site proper of about 1755 persons, total maximum Black Bottom population of 6088, and Kincaid locality bottomland total of nearly 8000 persons (Muller 1986b:214). Although no comparable definition of site support area is available for the Angel site, the area within the site proper (less the "occupied" area) would have supported 300 to 400 persons at 0.102 ha/person/year (Table 5.11).

These figures represent a considerable range, but they are warrantable in range by comparison to historical group sizes, although the smaller estimates are closer to the normal town sizes recorded (as discussed earlier). At first glance, the smaller estimates for the intramural population of the central sites may seem too small to those accustomed to exaggerated *ad hoc* estimates. However, the historical data indicate how small some of the largest historical towns were when only their immediate local settlement was counted. As we have seen, the actual total population of an historical "town" in the broader sense is not far off the 200–300 persons of these estimates. Confusion among Europeans about just what a town was, is surely the cause of the widely varying number of "towns" for the same historical people given in accounts only a few years apart. The same sort of uncertainty about the town limits

Table 5.9. Lower Ohio Support Areas per Person at 5 Person per Structure and 12 persons per Structure

Zone	Support area	Observed site area	Est. num. of structures	5 persons per struc.		12 persons per struc.	
				Estimated pop.	Support area per person	Estimated pop.	Support area per person
Black Bottom							
BB I	161	8.8	55	274	0.59	659	0.24
BB II	58	4.1	26	129	0.45	310	0.19
Kincaid (BB III)	179	10.8	68	339	0.53	813	0.22
BB IV	46	1.9	12	59	0.77	143	0.32
BB V	86	1.0	7	33	2.65	78	1.10
BB VI	33	1.5	9	45	0.73	109	0.30
BB VII	27	2.8	18	88	0.31	212	0.13
BB VIII	10	0.3	2	10	1.00	24	0.42
BB IX	21	0.9	6	28	0.75	68	0.31
BB Other	—	3.8	24	120		287	
BB I-IX	621	32.2	201	1006	0.62	2414	0.26
BB total	—	36.0	225	1126		2702	
Upper Bottom							
UB I	60	6.2	39	193	0.31	463	0.13
UB II	83	1.4	9	44	1.88	106	0.78
UB III	25	1.2	7	37	0.68	89	0.28
UB IV	22	0.5	0				
UB total	190	9.2	55	274	0.69	657	0.29
BB & UB total	811	45.3	280	1399	0.58	3359	0.24
Angel Site total	—	4.6	29	145	—	348	—

Table 5.10. **Recalculation of Lower Ohio Population Estimates at Black's Proposed Density**

Zone	Support area	Observed site area	Est. number of structures (Black)	Estimated pop. (@ Black's est.)	Support area per Person (Black)
Black Bottom					
BB I	161	8.8	394	1,969	0.08
BB II	58	4.1	185	926	0.06
Kincaid (BB III)	179	10.8	486	2,431	0.07
BB IV	46	1.9	85	426	0.11
BB V	86	1.0	47	233	0.37
BB VI	33	1.5	65	325	0.10
BB VII	27	2.8	127	635	0.04
BB VIII	10	0.3	14	72	0.14
BB IX	21	0.9	40	202	0.10
BB Other	—	3.8	172	859	
I–IX	621	32.2	1444	7219	0.09
BB total	—	36.0	1615	8077	
Upper Bottom					
UB I	60	6.2	277	1,384	0.04
UB II	83	1.4	63	316	0.26
UB III	25	1.2	53	265	0.09
UB IV	22	0.5	22		
UB total	190	9.2	414	2072	0.09
BB & UB total	811	45.3	2030	10,150	0.08
Angel Site total	—	4.6	208	1042	—

would seem likely for prehistoric Mississippian societies in those locations where lack of external threats allowed dispersion across the horticultural production zones. I again quote Adair's (1775: 281 [19300:302], emphasis added) comment on historical Choctaw settlement:

> The barrier towns, which are next to the Muskohge and Chikkasah countries, are compactly settled for social defense, according to the general method of other savage nations; but the rest, both in the center, and toward the Mississipi, are only scattered plantations, as best suits a separate easy way of living. *A stranger might be in the middle of one of their populous towns, without seeing half a dozen of their houses, in the direct course of his path.*

As I noted some years ago for the Black Bottom (1986b:215), ethnographically documented agricultural labor needs would have required slightly less than 1500 persons to cultivate *all* of the support area lands in a single year. Taken together, I feel that the lower ranges are more likely to have been correct, but that larger communities and polities did emerge on occasion, just as in the historical record. Even at the largest estimates possible from support areas, the largest polities would have been smaller than earlier efforts to see prehistoric Mississippian populations in the "tens of thousands" (e.g., Fowler 1989:206) for single *sites*. "Tens of thousands," however, is not unreasonable for the largest whole polities. For example, the entire Black Bottom

Table 5.11. Lower Ohio Population Estimates Based on Support Areas and Production Yields

Site cluster	Support area (ha)	Population est. based on		
		.102 ha/yr.	.405 ha/yr.	Site area
Black Bottom				
BB I	161	1578	398	294
BB II	58	569	143	138
Kincaid (BB III)	179	1755	442	363
BB IV	46	451	114	64
BB V	86	843	212	35
BB VI	33	324	81	49
BB VII	27	265	67	95
BB VIII	10	98	25	11
BB IX	21	206	52	30
BB I–IX	621	6088	1533	1079
Upper Bottom				
UB I	Å60	588	148	207
UB II	83	814	205	47
UB III	25	245	62	40
UB IV	22	216	54	0
UB I–IV	190	1863	469	294
Kincaid Locality Bottomland <BB and UB>	811	7951	2002	1373
Angel Intramural Area (less occupation)	42	415	105	181

is some 28 km² in area. If its population was as large as 1200 persons, the bottomland (not including surrounding uplands or terraces) would have had a population density of about 43 persons per km². This number is close to the estimate arrived at by Milner for a study zone in the Southern American Bottom (Milner 1986, discussed earlier in Chapter 4).

Milner's estimates were developed from known structural remains, phase-by-phase, using a formula involving duration of each phase and structure. Milner made two estimates, one based on residential occupancy at 6.12 persons per structure, and a second based on the different average sizes of structures in each phase. For comparison with the figures developed above, Milner's tables are recalculated here (Table 5.12) using the same 5-person-per-structure figure used above for the Black Bottom and Angel.

These estimates (for these sets of assumptions) are actually somewhat lower for total area density than the earlier estimates for the Black Bottom. The big differences in the hectare per structure figures surely reflect differences between the definitions of "support area" in the Black Bottom and "habitable area" in the American Bottom. However, the estimates per total area turn out to be quite similar. What we are seeing here, I feel, is that most Mississippian settlement was actually much alike, with scattered households and fairly low density. Figure 5.12 is a spindle diagram of the populations calculated per phase in Milner's study area.

Table 5.12. Southern American Bottom Population Density[a]
(Structure Longevity of 10 Years)

Phase	"Habitable" area		Total area (persons/km²)
	Ha/structure	Persons/ha	
Lohmann	5.10	0.98	36.5
Stirling	4.89	1.02	38.1
Moorehead	13.04	0.38	14.3

[a]Recalculated for 5 persons/structure from Milner 1986: Table 5.

An older, huge population estimate of 25,500 people for Cahokia was based on density data from Powell Tract and Tract 15A (Gregg 1975). Unfortunately, this estimate is grounded in some numerical miscalculations[7] that doubled the actual area of the quadrilateral-delimited site to some 13.2 km² instead of the actual 6.6 km². This error has become embedded in American Bottom literature from Fowler (1975) to Milner (1991:34). The miscalculation also carries over into the estimate for the land below 127 m above sea level within the quadrilateral boundaries, as well, so that the low ground area is closer to 306 ha than the some 600 ha (1500 acres) given (Gregg 1975:132). Corrected density measurements *by Gregg's calculations* for the "central town" of Cahokia are given in Table 5.13.

Gregg used a value of 1.86 persons per structure, which is—as he noted— a conservative figure (Gregg 1975:132), but one which might be consistent with small structure size in some Cahokia phases. Using this figure (*and* assuming that the site density on all the higher ground in the Cahokia site was comparable to that at the Powell Tract and Tract 15A), the estimate, *by this method*, of the Greater Cahokia site population would be nearly 13,000 persons (not 25,500; Gregg 1975:134). The often-cited editor's note on the same page using Casselbury's estimation method (in this case, 3.1 persons per structure) should be corrected to 21,700. If the estimate of 5 persons per structure that I have used elsewhere is substituted, the estimate for the site would be just over 35,000 persons, however! Gregg made an effort to make his figures conservative by not counting overlapping structures, and so on. Of course, later work in the American Bottom, such as Milner's study, has replaced this earlier and necessarily cruder estimate. Even so, the estimates based on these (mis)calculations have come to have a life of their own, and they still appear in the marvelous Cahokia Interpretive Center exhibits. By comparison to the estimates for the site areas discussed (Table 5.9), the two tracts at Cahokia show much higher density than is the case in most American Bottom or Black Bottom site zones. Only the Robinson's Lake site in the American Bottom and the King Site in Georgia have area–structure ratios similar to Tract 15A, and none is so dense as the settlement for the Powell

---

[7]Gregg multiplied the diagonals of a quadrilateral to obtain the area instead of using the formula Area = ½ a b sin(θ). The angle θ of the two diagonals in this case is 88°, so sin(θ) is close to 1.0, and the error resulting from multiplying the diagonals is only slightly more than double the actual area.

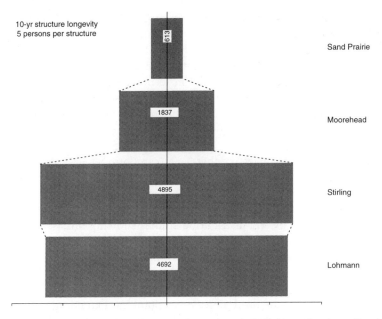

10-yr structure longevity
5 persons per structure

613

Sand Prairie

1837

Moorehead

4895

Stirling

4692

Lohmann

Figure 5.12. Population size estimates for Milner's Southern American Bottom zone by phase. (Recalculated for 5 person per structure from Milner's data for 10-year structure longevity.)

Tract. I would suspect that more fine-grained sorting out by phases would reduce this apparent density, but such an extreme figure cannot be used as a general measurement for the entire Cahokia site, much less the entire American Bottom.

Another problem with many population estimates for the American Bottom is that they seem to assume that all soil groups above some elevation are equally likely to have had Mississippian use. In most areas, this is most definitely *not* the case—factors such as vegetation and distance to river or marsh mean that most of the bottomlands were not exploited for residential purposes, at least. Although all bottomland soils were fertile, not all were equally attractive or accessible to Mississippian farmers and settlers. We must note that the FAI-270 right-of-way goes down a linear segment of its bottomland that is at a consistent distance from the river and follows other

Table 5.13. Correction of Gregg's Estimates of Population Density for the Cahokia Site[a]

Phase	"Habitable" area		
	Structure/ha	Ha/structure	Persons/ha
Powell Tract	26.45	0.04	49.19
Tract 15A	14.83	0.07	27.58
Average	20.64	0.05	38.38

[a]Area miscalculation corrected.

features of interest to modern engineers. The FAI-270 transect is not a random or necessarily representative sample of the entire bottomland, although it is much better than projecting Tract 15A to the entire bottomland. For this reason, if no other, generalizations from the American Bottom, like those from the Black Bottom or elsewhere, can be applied only with caution to other cases. A more detailed look at the soils and vegetation conditions of the American Bottom using modern GIS techniques is underway, and this may considerably reduce the estimates of land that was likely to have been lived upon by Mississippian gardeners (Milner, personal communication, 1993).

I see no problem in suggesting that American Bottom Mississippian populations may have been larger than those in other areas. The American Bottom is an enormous bottomland, and it is not inconceivable that it was more densely filled up than was the case elsewhere I would feel more comfortable with this proposition, however, were it to be backed up by site distribution studies showing Mississippian settlement on all such flood-free zones in that bottomland.

As the Voronoi tessellation of the Black Bottom (Figure 5.6) shows, much of the bottomland settlement was linear along the ridges having the very most fertile soils (see Muller 1986b). The American Bottom is in some senses the reverse of the Black Bottom situation—the Black Bottom is a point bar extending out into the river, whereas the American Bottom is a series of "cut-off" meanders with oxbow lakes. Both areas share common ridge and swale characteristics, and large parts of both localities would have been inundated annually (see Milner 1993). The difference in scale is enormous. The Black Bottom is some 28 km^2 in area, whereas the American Bottom is more than 628 km^2. About 22 percent of the Black Bottom is "support area," as defined here. We will never be able to survey the heavily urbanized American Bottom area in the complete fashion done in the Black Bottom, but new computer-based geographic studies are under way and should yield more precise data on Mississippian settlement in relation to terrain and soils. In the meantime, if the percentage of the landscape that was suitable for bottomland Mississippian settlement was roughly the same in the two areas, we would have some 13,000 ha of "support area" in the American Bottom. At approximately the same density as the Black Bottom populations, this would yield a total American Bottom (*not* Cahokia) population of ca. 27,000 persons. The greater Cahokia site (including the mound areas outside of the palisade) would—by this rough estimate—have had some 1300 persons. These estimates are within the range of the largest historically documented, ethnographic societies for the Southeast. While the estimate for the entire bottomland still seems high, it is not impossible for peak occupation of the American Bottom. The estimate for the Kincaid site itself at this level is certainly reasonable by comparison to other Mississippian sites, "exaggerationalist" estimates aside.

Even the smallest populations estimated here for these sites would have provided sufficient labor for activities such as mound construction (see Muller 1986b:200–204; and below). The central, palisaded towns probably were, like so many walled settlements elsewhere, refuges for much larger populations that were normally dispersed over the surrounding countryside in peaceful times. Thus, the problem of sufficient personnel to "man" the bastions raised by Black (1967) is not particularly critical to the issue of normal, intramural residential density.

Finally, a few observations on the geographic size of polities are appropriate. Although both historical polity (as shown in Chapter 2) and prehistoric extent are very difficult to estimate, we note again that the largest territories found in the early 16th century seem to have been about 300–400 km in maximum extent. If the Lower Ohio Valley centers of Kincaid and Angel were ever the twin major towns of a single polity, then the full extent of such a unit could have been about 250 km long. If Cahokia controlled the conjunction of the Illinois and Mississippi to that of the Kaskaskia, its extent could have been over 200 km. A 400-km-long territory could have existed between Peoria and Cairo, Illinois, although it is difficult to see what markers for this "control" there are in archaeological data. Although some gorget themes do occur throughout this possible territory, it is important to note that they are too late in time to mark a Cahokia-centered polity, regardless of whose dating scheme for the gorgets is used. If each mound center is taken as representing a more or less autonomous polity at some time, then the "normal" polity extent in the Lower Ohio would have been about 28 km, with a range from 6 km (separated by the river) to 48 km. In the confluence area of the Mississippi and Ohio Rivers, the normal distance between one small mound center and another is smaller, usually a dozen or so kms. Hally has analyzed Georgia Mississippian chiefdoms and found essentially the same geographic extent (Hally 1993). Polity organization would probably have fluctuated through time between multiple small polities, each surrounding a single small town-center, to much larger but more fragile polities containing several major town-centers within a paramount chiefdom.

6. CONCLUSIONS AND COMMENTS

Households

The beginning of a Mississippian community was, at the least, the establishment of a household. At first, the households probably consisted of only one structure and its surrounding living areas and even gardens. In time, as posts rotted and the family grew, the structures would be rebuilt in larger sizes. At an isolated farmstead, this often seems to have taken about three rebuildings before the location was abandoned or a new house site chosen.

Sometimes, instead of just rebuilding a larger house, additional structures were added. Sometimes these served additional, nonresidential purposes. When such structures were built, they usually were placed at right angles to each other with a common courtyard—a pattern that holds for almost all Mississippian construction, from houses to platform mounds.

Each of these homesteads had certain basic functions that appear even at the permanent houses of the most specialized settlements, such as those engaged in hoe production. Later chapters examine these production aspects as the household took on other functions in becoming "elevated" in Mississippian life, but it seldom lost its primary production capabilities.

Communities

Homesteads were located on land that was probably allocated by kinship organizations. Settlements on contiguous, usually linear, ridges must have soon taken
on community functions, sometimes concentrated at a somewhat larger collection of
structures, centrally located. Mississippian site areas and numbers of structures are
fairly closely related to immediate arable land area. At least in the Black Bottom, there
is little evidence of use of even slightly less fertile ridgetops adjacent to known areas
of settlement.

Town Size, Dispersion, and Aggregation

Historic descriptions of native Eastern populations explicitly or implicitly drew
attention to the phenomena of aggregation and dispersion as dynamics of those
populations. From the de Soto accounts on, some settlements are described as highly
concentrated in central locations, whereas comments are made about the lack of
concentration of other groups.

Concentration of population has often been linked to richness of soils, and
dispersion to either poverty of production capabilities or to external threat. Abandonment of a normal, diffuse, settlement pattern is the common response to various
kinds of stress, especially military threat. The interplay between aggregated settlement and dispersed settlement is complex. To some extent, power conditions the
response. The essence of power here is the ability of the polity to defend itself
adequately in the aggregated state, and also the ability of a central authority to
exercise its authority. Dispersed settlement is inconsistent with conditions of conflict,
especially given that the pattern of warfare in the East was that of raids on outlying
settlements and isolated individuals. At the same time, dispersion is consistent with
any emergency so great that it places the burden for survival solely on the individual
household production unit. Destruction of central food stores by Europeans warring
on Native American groups forced dispersion, even in the face of continuing threats.
Depending on the balance of power, large towns can either be a better defense or
simply an easier target.

Of course, dichotomous modes of settlement on this dimension are worldwide
and have long been recognized. As noted in Chapter 2, educated (i.e., literate) 17th-
and 18th-century travel commentators would have known the distinctions made in
Classical sources between Gaulish and Germanic settlement. Caesar emphasized the
roles of buffer zones (Caesar 51 B.C., *Gallic Wars* [4]:3; [6]:23, 30 and elsewhere) and
the part that land plays in internal social distinctions (6:21). Tacitus echoed and
amplified these distinctions in *Germania* in A.D. 98:

> It is well known that the nations of Germany have no cities, and that they do not even
> tolerate closely contiguous dwellings. They live scattered and apart, just as a spring, a
> meadow, or a wood has attracted them. Their villages they do not arrange in our fashion
> with the buildings connected and joined together, but every person surrounds his dwelling
> with an open space. Tacitus 98:[16] (1942:716–717)

There are plenty of indications of similarity in site dispersion and aggregation
between the historical and the Mississippian examples. In recent discussions of

Choctaw settlement by Galloway, she draws attention to dispersion as though it were necessarily an indication of lack of centralization of political power (e.g., 1995:111 and elsewhere). Geographic and political centralization should not be confused, and both aggregation and dispersion may be contingent results within the same overall organization of settlement. Which is present at any given time depends on both external and internal conditions but has much less to do with centralization of political authority than does the overall size of the polity. Thus, Galloway's argument about paramountcies sometimes makes too-dramatic distinctions between supposedly different social formations (e.g., 1995:112–113), while she presents us with a discussion of processes (summarized in her Chapter 9) that may prove to have wide applicability not only to Choctaw ethnogenesis, but also to Mississippian complexes in general.

Population Density

The existence of extremely large historical polities is a much-forgotten fact of Eastern history. The implications of overlooking the size of these groups is part of the artificial gap between historical and prehistoric. The other is the exaggeration of the size of the prehistoric sites. There is no need to apologize for the political and social complexity of the Southeast and Mississippian. We do not have to exaggerate the nature of the social systems of the American Bottom to appreciate that they were arguably the most complex political developments of all of North America north of Mexico. At the highest peak of their power, the chiefs of Cahokia *may* have played important roles in ordering the lives of as many as 20 or 30 thousand people. But so, after all, did the councils and chiefs of the Choctaw in the early 18th century.

The Farmstead and Society

In speaking of the distinctive characteristics of the French peasantry after the Revolution, Marx hit upon the social implications of the kind of social situation that we have also seen—to be sure, on a somewhat different scale—in the Mississippian countryside.

> The small-holding peasants form a vast mass, the members of which live in similar conditions but without entering into manifold relations with one another. Their mode of production isolates them from one another instead of bringing them into mutual intercourse. The isolation is increased by France's bad means of communication and by the poverty of the peasants,. Their field of production, the small holding, admits of no division of labour in its cultivation, no application of science and, therefore, no diversity of development, no variety of talent, no wealth of social relationships. Each individual peasant family is almost self-sufficient; it itself directly produces the major part of its consumption and thus acquires its means of life more through exchange with nature than in intercourse with society. A small holding, a peasant and his family; alongside them another small holding, another peasant and another family. A few score of these make up a village, and a few score of villages make up a Department. In this way, the great mass of the French nation is formed by simple addition of a homologous magnitudes, much as potatoes in a sack form a sack of potatoes. Marx 1852 [1975:170–171]

There are some important similarities between the French peasants and the Mississippians. The Mississippian farmstead inhabitants stood in the same kind of relative isolation as did the French peasants. Of course, such isolation is social, not geographical. It stems not only from the dispersal of horticultural activities across the floodplain, but also from the relative economic autonomy of the household (and by extension, the lineage). The Mississippian producer normally found herself able to provide adequate subsistence to her family. Beyond the nuclear family, she was able to call on her mother or sisters and her matrilineal male kin, and perhaps even her affines, for assistance. It was probably only after household and lineage stores were exhausted that the broader society as a whole was called upon for assistance.

Remember that the Mississippian cultivated floodplains are the most risky lands available, if also the most productive. The record summer floods of 1993 stand as a recent reminder of the dangers to producers who have put all of the eggs into the floodplain basket. As we shall go on to discuss in later chapters, the implications of small parcel–based production, organization by lineages, and the lack of diversity on the productive level was profound in shaping the directions, character, and scale of Mississippian political economy. The small, nearly autonomous producers of "Emergent Mississippian" times, dispersed across high-risk lands, would have had little diversity of relationships with others. Like their predecessors of a few years earlier, they would have been able to produce most of their needs, even surpluses in normal to good years. Yet, at the same time, their commitment to their floodplain fields would prove, sooner or later, to be a commitment that could endure only with wider, broader, and more regional integration to share risks across larger areas and even different environments. Yet, how can the autonomous, homogenous, and relatively simple social systems of the family and lineage provide the basis for such regional integration? The contradiction between production means and reproductive needs is one, but not the only, root of the institutions of Mississippian chieftainship.

Chapter 6

Mississippian Production I
Base

> The earth must be laboured before it gives its
> increase.
>
> Joseph Addison, *Spectator*, 1712

Mississippian was supported by horticulture and collecting. In each activity, there were sufficient resources to support comparatively large populations. With both combined, Mississippian peoples had a little insurance against problems in either. In order to understand how these production systems worked together, and with other production strategies, we need to look at the components of Mississippian modes of production. Meillassoux has proposed, although not precisely in the same way, such studies for noncapitalist systems in general (1972).

Mississippian modes of production were no more a unitary taxonomic unit than was Mississippian itself. For all that, there are a number of elements in Eastern Late Prehistoric societies that were shared. We shall examine some of these components of the production system, in turn. First, there are the basic components in the system—the material items produced and consumed, and the direct production technology involved in this process. Then we shall look at the production system, with treatment of the social organization of production, insofar as we can suggest its character. This will involve a number of issues, including the question of the role of elites in the production system—to what extent were they managing, appropriating, or supported by surplus-labor?

1. OBJECT OF LABOR

Economic production involves territory and the goods produced or harvested from it. Although the use of territory is critical, archaeologists have difficulties in approaching that topic directly. Accordingly, we shall have to come at the topic from the other side—the goods that were produced and consumed. Food items are the most important of these, so the first task is to look at the material basis of life itself, beginning with food plants and then moving to other dietary resources. In each case, the resources have to be identified, and then the problems of their production considered. There was a broad range of domesticated and wild-food resources, but it will suffice here to examine the major components without trying to catalogue or discuss every single contributor to the Mississippian diet.

A few words on evidence and the underlying scheme of this treatment seems called for. Although evidential problems are endemic to archaeology, the problems of *taphonomy* become especially critical in analyzing food remains. There is such apparent concreteness, and percentages are sometimes calculated out to three decimal places for archaeological samples representing a few grams of burnt matter. Taphonomy—"the science of burial" (and, by extension, of survival under archaeological conditions)—has wrestled with the questions of what kinds of materials survive and in what degree. We know that hickory nutshells, for example, are more durable than acorn shells, so archaeologically recovered plant assemblages reflect such differential preservation. Other factors affecting the survival of particular materials include the kinds of cooking methods employed. When nuts were roasted or their shells used as fuel, charring of shells would aid in preservation after burial in a *midden* (a "refuse pile"). Boiled greens and soft tissues, on the other hand, may only be preserved under exceptional circumstances. The methods of archaeological recovery also affect what kinds of evidence are available. Coarse-meshed screening of archaeological deposits mean that smaller items are discarded, so that fine-mesh screens and techniques such as fluid flotation are necessary. Because various recovery methods are employed in different excavations, reports may present falsely divergent pictures of what was, in aboriginal times, essentially the same economy. All the same, these are the data we have, and we should not take the path of refusing to do what we can with them.

Mississippian Sustenance

Full-blown Mississippian economies depended mostly on cultivation, especially of maize. Yet as discussed in Chapter 3, the timing of Mississippian emergence indicates that corn, more properly maize (*Zea mays*) cultivation *per se* cannot be taken as the only, or even primary, trigger for the emergence of Mississippian organization. Some communities even seem to have taken up maize cultivation more as the *result* of the emergence of elites rather than the other way around. A second important Mesoamerican crop, the common bean (*Phaseolus vulgaris*), as noted, does not appear in the East until close to the end of the first "climax" of Mississippian, so it cannot be involved at all in the emergence of Mississippian cultivation. Eastern North American peoples had raised various, probably local, squashes and gourds (Cucurbitaceae) since Archaic times. At the least, the spread-out character of these introductions and the hundreds, even thousands, of years between the various importations indicate the absence of any strong, direct contact between the East and Mesoamerica. By A.D. 1000, maize cultivation was critical, and we shall return to the Mesoamerican crops after first examining wild plants and native domesticates that were important even before the acclimatization and widespread use of maize. These native plants were important for Mississippian peoples. Some were domesticated in the region, whereas others were exploited as wild resources throughout the Mississippian period.

The overall pattern was that of a mixed economy, dependent upon a broad range of activities, but always depending, in the last analysis, on the twin legs of horticulture and collecting:

> In March and April they live much vpon their Weeres, and feed on Fish, Turkeys, and Squirrells and then as also sometymes in May they plant their Feilds and sett their Corne, and live after those Monethes most of Acrons, Wallnuts, Chesnutts, Chechinquamyns and Fish, but to mend their dyett, some disperse themselues in smale Companies, and live vpon such beasts as they can kill, with their bowes and arrowes. Strachey 1612 [1953:80]

The Mississippian Hunting "Pattern"

An early study of Mississippian exploitation of animal resources was undertaken some 20 years ago by a graduate student at the University of Michigan (B. Smith 1975). It is remarkable how this work has held up. Smith's general points have been somewhat revised, of course, as new data have become available, but the basic outline of what Mississippians hunted remains close to the picture painted by Smith.

Mississippian hunting patterns are interesting examples of how simple choices in human behavior can affect other behavior as well. In Late Woodland times, the hunting pattern was fairly open and opportunistic. It seems likely that the animals hunted were fairly representative of the desirable species available in the surrounding environment (e.g., B. Smith 1975:120 in relation to low occurrence of wapiti).

By Mississippian times, the animals taken were from a smaller range of species. In addition, many animals occur at lower frequency in the list of animal remains when they do appear. In part, this reflects a shift to a horticultural basis for the economy. As field activities dominated some portions of the year, opportunities for foraging and hunting activities were correspondingly reduced. In addition, as we shall see, the fields themselves were a magnet for many species—precisely the species that are so well represented in the Mississippian faunal record.

It is interesting, however, that some sites do not fit the typical residential site pattern. For example, the Great Salt Spring salt-making site showed associated broad-ranging hunting that resulted in an assemblage more similar to that of Late Woodland or Fort Ancient than to the normal day-to-day hunting represented at Mississippian residential sites (see Breitberg 1986, 1988, 1990a, 1990b, 1992; also in Muller et al. 1992). At this site, some persons engaged in a Late Woodland-like pattern of hunting, while others were making salt. The bone evidence from the Great Salt Spring also suggests that extraction of bone fats from pounded and boiled bones was another use for the large reduction vessels (usually called "salt pans") that dominate the ceramic assemblage there. The evidence does not suggest a great strategic shift in "hunting pattern" but merely that both the Late Woodland and Mississippian peoples took what they needed, where they could get it, and when they were able. If sufficient game were available around the fields, then that was the game taken. If one were away from home after harvest and could range out while other members of the household were making salt, then a broader range of species would be taken in areas where there were few permanent residents to deplete large game.

I am also suggesting that Mississippian hunting reflected the relatively high populations in the horticultural production areas, so that slowly reproducing species would become rarer, and "weedy" animals capable of pioneering the human disturbed floodplains would come to predominate. In metaphorical terms, the "oaks" of the animal world are being replaced in these cultivated and settled bottomlands by the animal equivalents of goosefoot, cane, willow, and cottonwood.

Species and Frequency. One of the difficulties in understanding Mississippian animal use is that the bottomlands occupied by Mississippian peoples have extremely poor conditions for bone and shell preservation. In many areas, for example, virtually all shell in shell-tempered pottery has been leached out, leaving impressions in holes in the baked clay. Bone is sometimes preserved well in large features or in heavy midden, but its absence elsewhere can be interpreted as largely due to having been dissolved. However, even under such localized, better preservation, there are often fewer animal remains than one who has worked in areas such as the Plains might expect. It is difficult to assess how much animal diet there really was in peak Mississippian times.

Figure 6.1 indicates how much mammals dominate the usual faunal assemblages. However, as careful controlled studies have shown, this dominance also reflects the larger sizes of the mammals represented, most of which are deer (see Table 6.1). The columns in the table are shown in the figure with the first site (Snodgrass) on the inside, and so on, out. The particular species chosen are simply those that are identified in many different sites, and so could be compared in terms of percentages. However, these comparisons are certain to reflect recovery and preservation factors,

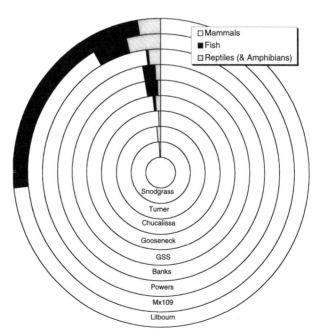

Figure 6.1. Proportions of classes in selected Mississippian faunal assemblages.

Table 6.1. Faunal Assemblages at Some Mississippian Sites (% MNI)

Taxa	Snodgrass (%)	Turner (%)	Chucalissa midden (%)	Gooseneck (%)	Great Salt Spring (%)	Banks (%)	Powers Fort Str.1 (%)	Mx109 (%)	Lilbourn total (%)
Mammals	98.8	97.5	97.3	95.3	94.2	92.3	91.8	89.1	65.9
Fish	0.0	0.0	—	0.6	2.1	1.8	0.2	3.9	22.0
Birds	0.4	1.1	2.0	3.2	2.4	5.1	6.6	2.8	10.1
Reptiles (& Amphibians)	0.8	1.4	0.7	1.0	0.6	0.8	1.5	4.2	2.1
Odocoileus virginianus	85.2	72.9	74.2	78.6	52.1	79.7	64.8	63.6	51.8
Cervus canadensis	2.6	0.0	2.9	0.0	18.8	0.0	0.0	0.0	0.0
Castor canadensis	0.4	1.7	0.7	1.7	3.0	0.7	3.0	10.5	1.6
Ursus americanus	0.0	5.9	3.4	0.0	13.7	2.3	0.0	0.0	0.0
Procyon lotor	4.7	5.1	2.4	0.7	2.9	4.0	3.6	4.2	2.9
Meleagris gallopavo	0.3	0.7	1.5	2.8	2.2	1.6	5.1	4.5	1.4
Didelphis virginiana	0.3	0.7	0.7	0.7	1.1	1.5	2.6	3.1	0.7
Sciurus niger	0.0	0.1	0.6	0.1	0.4	0.1	2.9	0.0	0.5
Aplodinotus grunniens	0.0	0.0		0.0	0.9	0.2	0.0	1.8	4.7
Sylvilagus floridanus	0.2	0.2	0.4	0.2	0.2	0.3	0.9	0.0	0.5
Amia calva	0.0	0.0		0.2	0.7	0.1	0.0	0.4	1.7
Sylvilagus aquaticus	0.0	0.1	0.2	0.0	0.1	0.6	0.4	0.0	1.1
Marmota monax	0.0	0.1	0.0	0.0	0.5	0.0	0.0	0.7	0.0
Ictalurus spp.	0.0	0.0		0.0	0.3	0.2	0.0	0.4	3.3
Lepisosteus sp.	0.0	0.0		0.0	0.2	0.1	0.0	0.2	1.1
Sciurus carolinensis	0.0	0.0	0.0	0.1	0.2	0.1	0.0	0.0	0.3

and so to underestimate small animal remains. Figure 6.2 shows the same classes as represented from more recent excavations, with more efforts at recovery of small bone. These are the data from the Cahokia ICT-II work reported by Kelly (1991). The differences from the first chart probably do not indicate differences in Mississippian food habits, merely differences in recovery.

Mammals were extremely important relative to other animals, and even with improved recovery methods, the mean Cahokia ICT-II fauna MNI (= minimum number of individuals) was still 49.9 percent mammal, and 39.0 percent *of total* MNI was white-tailed deer, even including all the smaller species!

These are percentages based on minimum number of individuals and so do not reflect the relative amount of food from each species, which would be even more tilted toward mammalian species and deer in estimates of how much meat was consumed. Smith estimated meat yield for his MNI, and his ranks based on that are compared in Table 6.2 to the mean percentages from the sites categorized in Table 6.1.

Reidhead worked out an elaborate linear programming model for Fort Ancient and Late Woodland in Southeastern Indiana (1981). This is an extremely useful study, although the actual patterns discussed are not much like Mississippian in general. What is directly useful here is that Reidhead explicitly laid out a set of assumptions

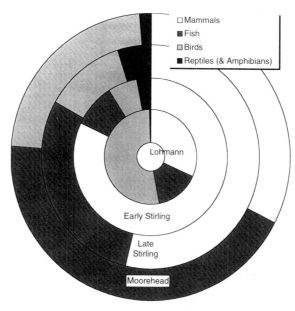

Figure 6.2. Cahokia ICT-II faunal assemblage by class (data from Kelly 1991).

and data on "costs" of acquiring various animal and plant resources. An effort on this scale and scope can certainly be revised, but Reidhead's estimates are well warranted and seem useful, even if future research might scale one or another resource up or down. Table 6.3 gives a summary of some of the key animal resources, with annual averages from Reidhead's seasonal estimates. These are averaged from Fort Ancient data by seasons (1981:45–47) to give a relative scale for ease of access. More accurate estimates could be worked out for other areas following Reidhead's methods, but I think these are probably close to what we would find for many Mississippian localities. Another useful source on the subsistence of the Southeast, especially those closer to the regions, is Larson (1980).

Comparison of the various tables poses some interesting research issues for future work. Chief among these are the reasons for divergence of actual remains to what might be expected if effort per mass were the determining factor. As we shall see, however, many animals do correspond to the least-cost expectations.

Large Animals. White-tailed deer (Odocoileus virginianus). In many ways, white-tailed deer are an incredibly rich resource. They, like willow trees, reproduce quickly under "scrub" conditions. When forage is plentiful, white-tailed deer may restrict their movement to less than 3 square km. They also tend to follow the same paths as they move around this area. Even when fleeing, they will try to work their way back to their original location (Rue 1968:448–450). These behaviors make hunting them a little easier than more wide-ranging species. Bucks do move around more during rutting season in late fall. Deer can live from 8 to 11 years in the wild. Each doe normally has two fawns each year, and a substantial percentage of modern herds may

Table 6.2. Primary Animal Groups Exploited in Mississippian Times

Smith's rank (meat yield)	Species	Mean MNI % in Table 6.1
1	White-tailed deer (*Odocoileus virginianus*)	68.9
2	Raccoon (*Procyon lotor*)	3.0
3	Fish (Class Pisces)	1.7
4	Migratory Water fowl (various spp.)	3.7
5	Wild turkey (*Meleagris gallopavo*)	2.9
6	Beaver (*Castor canadensis*)	3.3
7	Opossum (*Didelphis virginiana*)	1.6
8	Swamp rabbit (*Sylvilagus aquaticus*)	0.2
	and Cottontail rabbit (*Syvilagus floridanus*)	0.3
9	Alligator snapping turtle (*Macroclemys temminicki*) and snapping turtle (*Chelydra serpentina*)	1.5 (all reptiles)
10	Domestic dog (*Canis familiaris*)	—
11	Fox squirrel (*Sciurus niger*)	0.7
	and grey squirrels (*Sciurus carolinensis*)	0.1
12	Black bear (*Ursus americanus*)	3.2
13	Wapiti (*Cervus canadensis*)	—

Ranks based on B. Smith 1975:10.

be newborn fawns (Rue 1968:460). Births typically occur in early spring. Younger, inexperienced animals are also easier to hunt.

Fall and winter "yarding" into larger groups seems to be less common in southern areas where forage is more abundant (B. Smith 1975:19). However, canebrakes—the primary river bottom environment exploited by many Mississippian peoples—were a favored refuge in hard winters (Rue 1968:447).

Table 6.3. Estimates of Cost in Person-Hours of Various Wild Animal Foods (from Ft. Ancient Data in Reidhead 1981:45–47)

Animal resource	Reidhead's density per sq. km	Annual average	
		Cost/100 kg (fresh)	Cost/100 kg fresh (dried and stored)
Fish (kg/km²)[a]	24,216	25	53
Mussels (kg/ km²)[a]	151,474	40	—
Deer	15.44	85	124
Wapiti (elk)	1.16	133	172
Turkey	7.72	164	202
Beaver	9.65	170	209
Waterfowl (seasonal)	360.26	192	227
Opossum	9.21	235	256
Bear	0.26	279	318
Raccoon	11.58	309	348
Squirrel	123.55	683	721

[a]Fish and mussels are masses/km² *for surface area of water*, (the rest are for numbers/ km²).

The combination of large size, restricted ranges, and high reproductive rates makes deer an attractive game animal, especially to Late Prehistoric peoples who were strongly tied to their fields and homes. Deer normally weigh about 63 kg, of which about 33 kg is usable meat. The largest white-tailed deer recorded was nearly 193 kg (Rue 1968:441)! In their classic study of wildlife and plants, Martin et al. (1951:268–269) indicate that the diet of the deer is based on twigs of shrubs and trees, but the overall diet is extremely broad-based, including acorns, fruits, and crops—especially maize (also see Rue 1968:448). On occasion, from 25 to 50 percent of the diet may be maize. Acorns are also a major source of food in fall and winter.

Since the deer is a forest "fringe" animal, it thrives when humans create open areas (such as fields) within forested areas. This means that the normal practice of Mississippian horticulture would have favored and attracted deer. Thirteenth-century declines in Mississippian "centers" as foci of settlement may have been matched by an increasing dependence on hunting, but this remains speculative until we have better data on late Mississippian faunal assemblages. As Rue (1968:465) pointed out, the Historic period was one of a boom in deer populations until intense hunting pressure (and expansion of settlement) in the mid-1800s began to extirpate deer in many localities. The low point of deer populations was in the 1890s. As discussed later in the chapter on distribution, there were enormous numbers of deerskins traded in the mid-18th century. Between 1699 and 1715, England imported, on the average, nearly 54,000 deerskins annually just from Charles Town, peaking at over 160,000 in a single year (Crane 1964:111). Historic pressures on deer were massive, although there were considerable annual fluctuations. The ability of deer populations to survive such hunting is remarkable and helps us to understand why this species was far and away the most common large prey animal for Mississippians.

Figure 6.3 shows the rates of increase calculated from deer percentages by age in Waselkov's study of deer hunting in the East (1978). Life tables for prey deer (not necessarily, indeed probably, not representative of deer away from hunted areas) were calculated, and rates were estimated by the same methods used for human populations in Chapter 4. The chart shows a dramatic decrease in the rate of increase of hunted deer populations by this measure in Mississippian times. A third-order polynomial regression shows "Date" accounting for about 68 percent of variability in rate for the combined Late Woodland, Mississippian, and historical Oneota deer populations as represented in archaeological sites. If Fort Ancient peoples are included, the explained variability is reduced by about half, since there is great variability in the Fort Ancient data. In his study, Waselkov suggested, on the basis of modality of age of killed deer, that Mississippian peoples had a different hunting strategy of using deer drives as opposed to stalking of deer (1978). However, stalking and driving are not the only alternatives, and I suggest that the unimodal tendency for Mississippian is an indication of "vermin" hunting in fields (see Beverley 1722 [1855:255]) as well as more organized hunting. Simply taking the deer that were eating the corn would have produced as good a cross-section of the deer population as drives.

Reidhead's estimates of cost per 100 kg of deer flesh (see Table 6.3) are the lowest by far of any large animal, and his estimates are based on an assumption of

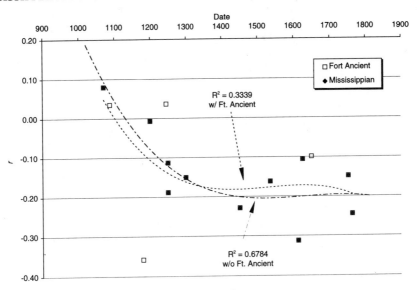

Figure 6.3. Modeled rates of increase for deer from percentages of killed animals in Eastern archaeological sites of various periods.[1]

organized hunting rather than incidental collecting. This low cost, combined with good flavor, and cornfield predation seem enough to explain the heavy use of this animal in Mississippian times.

Wapiti (Cervus canadensis). Wapiti, commonly known in North America as elk, occurs in Mississippian faunal assemblages, but at lower levels than was the case in pre-Mississippian times. Its occurrence at special-purpose sites such as the Great Salt Spring illustrates that Mississippian peoples had no prejudice against using wapiti. As a grass-eating herd animal, elk were simply not all that common in the territorially restricted range of most Mississippian farming settlements. I suspect this is one situation in which the areas hunted by Mississippian peoples differed from the northern elk density estimates used by Reidhead (1981; see Table 6.3) which show person-hour cost for elk being lower than for many animals that were taken by Mississippian hunters. Elk, at any rate, are not likely to be found in cornfields.

Bear (Ursus americanus). The black bear, unlike some of its Western cousins, has done better under European settlement and hunting pressure than would be

---

[1] As with the human populations, there are many assumptions that have to be made to do such modeling, but the purpose is not so much to discover a "true" rate of increase as it is to see what the implications of such rates might be and what they might imply if they were true. As in the human case, the percentages for the first cohort were not included, because we know how poorly these fragile bones preserve in archaeological sites.

thought of such an animal (Rue 1968:21, 24). This may suggest that the species might have similarly responded to Mississippian hunting. Bear meat and oil is widely reported in the historical accounts, although bear bone is uncommon in Mississippian archaeological remains.

> They also make a great use of Bears fat as oil; the flesh the traders have learned them to make into bacon, exactly resembling that of a hog; but all these dishes suit but ill the palate of a European, and when they have any deer or buffalo flesh at home, it is so dried as to have no taste in it. Romans 1775:67–68

Bears are omnivorous and compete directly with humans for many foods, including roots, acorns, and berries. Acorns are often the main "fattening" food eaten before winter hibernation and up to 50 percent of the diet at such times can be acorns (Martin et al. 1951:220; Rue 1968:26). Bears commonly catch wounded or weak deer and often raid human camps for food. The occasional taking of bears, as with so many other objects of Mississippian predation, could have easily come about through the competition of humans and bears for the same resources. It is also possible that the high amount of winter fat stored in wintertime by dormant bears may have made them attractive prey at that time (as they were in the North; see Quimby 1962:226–227). Reidhead's estimate of time investment (Table 6.3) placed bears at a high cost, and this may be another factor in explaining why bears are not common in Mississippian sites.

Bison (Bison bison). The bison, so important in these regions in historical times (it was hunted in central Kentucky by Daniel Boone in the 1740s), was entirely absent until the late 17th and early 18th centuries. Notably, high hunting levels depleted the bison in these areas rapidly in the 18th century; and it may be that the expansion of the bison into this range was a result of depopulation of the area after the 16th century. A bison that wandered across the frozen Mississippi River in Mississippian times probably had a short life expectancy.

Small Animals

> They have another sort of hunting, which is very diverting, and that they call vermin hunting; it is performed a foot, with small dogs in the night, by the light of the moon or stars. Thus in summer time they find abundance of raccoons, opossums and foxes in the corn fields, and about their plantations: but at other times they must go into the woods for them. Beverley 1722 [1855:255])

This kind of hunting is probably what many of the supposedly lazy men were doing when not observed by European visitors. There are a considerable number of these "vermin" animals, including some already discussed earlier.

Raccoons are cornfield predators and fields can be severely damaged by their nocturnal raids (Martin et al. 1951; Rue 1968). Raccoons also eat acorns and would be found together with other mast-feeders such as deer during the fall. Although raccoons are not true hibernators, they tend to den up when temperatures are lower than –2° C (Rue 1968:92), where they could be relatively easily found in dead trees in winter hunting (see Reidhead 1981:149). By Reidhead's estimates, raccoons would be expensive animals to hunt, with a higher cost per 100 kg than bear or *wapiti* (Table

6.3). The near ubiquity of the raccoon is another case in which its role as a pest in fields would virtually force Mississippian peoples into taking this animal in order to protect their crop.

Both the gray (*Sciurus carolinensis*) and the fox squirrel (*S. niger*) were taken by Mississippian peoples. Historically, there are not many references to squirrels of either kind, but squirrels are mentioned as an important part of the diet from March to April by John Smith (1612:22). However, as with the other main game animals of Mississippian times, these are also cornfield predators (Martin et al. 1951). Simple traps were probably used, although Smith explicitly mentions bow hunting of squirrels (1612:22). Squirrels were surely among the animals taken in historical times by boys guarding the maize fields during the day.

O'Brien indicates that pet squirrels were traded historically (1991:150), but the Swanton reference she gives is quoting sources on trade with Havana in the early 19th century, not referring to exchange among Native Americans (in Swanton 1922:344, 1946:738; from Williams 1837:242), Strachey (1612 [1953:79]) explicitly denies that squirrels or other small animals were kept and grown in the historical mid-Atlantic, and there is no reason to believe that there were domesticated squirrels in the Southeast prehistorically. There is an interesting account of Apalachee use of squirrel, turkey, or raccoon in making a smelly, boiled-down "stew" as a countermeasure against ritual actions against them in the ball game (1676, in Hann 1988:342). In Reidhead's estimates of cost (1981), squirrels rated as a high cost per 100 kg, requiring by his estimate nearly 683 person hours to obtain that much squirrel, but he also recognized that other evidence suggested this was conservative. However, trapping or hunting in maize fields would require considerably less effort than that calculated in Reidhead's tables. This is another case in which maize-field hunting seems strongly indicated.

Birds. Poor preservation of bones in Mississippian sites in the bottomland means that the light bones of many bird species are underrepresented, and this problem was compounded by earlier recovery techniques that failed to recover many small bones.

The turkey is one of the major game animals taken by Mississippian peoples. although the turkey does eat maize, showing up to 10 percent dependence at times; it is also a "low-cost" species by Reidhead's estimations (1981:151–155).

Songbirds are especially important eaters of corn (Martin et al. 1951). Historic records indicate that planting was timed to coincide with wild-fruit ripening to help keep the songbirds away from the newly planted maize (Adair 1775:405). We do not, however, have indications that songbirds were taken in any quantity.

Many Mississippian peoples lived close to what are today major flyways for migratory waterfowl, and these species were taken seasonally. The Cahokia faunal data referred to earlier, using modern recovery techniques, show that mallard, teal, and other waterfowl were fairly common at some sites (Kelly 1991). Interestingly, so were swans, and even cranes were represented. Surprisingly, some waterbirds, marsh-shorebirds, and upland game birds also consume maize, although not in large quantities (Martin et al. 1951). Of course, modern game reserves and commercial hunting locations leave maize fields to attract Canada geese in southern Illinois today. So even some seemingly unlikely animals could partially have been taken by Mississippians in their outfields.

Fish and other riverine resources. Despite the fragility and poor preservation of fish remains, it is likely that fish were important in the Mississippian diet. Yields of fish from floodplain sloughs could have potentially been large (Limp and Reidhead 1979). The sloughs were restocked annually by flooding. This was the other side of the risk to crops from flooding—that flooding brought a fresh harvest of alternative foods directly into the floodplain. This is reflected in Reidhead's estimates for the costs of collecting fresh fish as being only 25 person-hours per 100 kg of fresh fish (Reidhead 1981:45, 132ff.).

New recovery and analysis techniques are now showing us that fish were seasonally important in many regions (e.g., Schoeninger and Schurr 1994b). It will be remembered that as the time since the last harvest increased, de Soto was more and more given fish, not maize, as aid or prestations. A sort of trade-off between maize and fish as seasonal alternatives may have been the rule in Mississippian times, although recovery of fish remains in earlier archaeological work was poor. Just in case anyone wonders, I am not proposing that the fish were taken in Mississippian maize fields too, despite early and late flooding of ridgetop fields. Of course, those adjacent sloughs full of fish trapped after floods were surely prime locations, even as they are today for fishermen along the major streams.

The evidence—in the form of shell temper in Mississippian pottery—suggests mussels were heavily used in Mississippian communities. It is by no means clear that the mussels in the shells were consumed as food. At the Great Salt Spring in Illinois, the species represented included some that are today considered unpalatable (J. Bloom in Muller 1992). Shell was crucial to the manufacture of pottery, and it would seem likely that the quantities taken were enough to suggest "clamming" rather than merely gathering up dead shells on the shore. If the shells were needed for pottery making, it would seem likely, as well, that the more palatable species were being consumed, if only as a by-product of shell collecting. As in so many cases, one production activity is linked with others. The estimated number of person-hours needed to collect 100 kg of fresh mussel flesh is only 40, including transportation and processing time (Reidhead 1981:46, 139ff.). Mussel collection is practically limited to times of low water.

Other animals. As we saw in the tables, a small percentage of animal remains consisted of small creatures such as turtles or even toads. Some of these are surely just incidental to Mississippian food habits, although a few would have provided small amounts of meat. Some of these animals may simply have been brought into settlements or been taken there by animals or children. All in all, their frequency is so small as to play no major role. A few are so unpalatable that their actual consumption, if it were clearly established, would hint at emergency situations such as famine.

Patterns. I think that what I am suggesting here is pretty clear by now: Just as Mississippian exploitation of resources such as lithics tended to be opportunistic, so their hunting patterns tended to focus on prey "of opportunity" that were either drawn to the maize fields or were encountered—or more accessible—during other activities such as salt making or gathering wild foods. Of course, I am not saying that Mississippians never hunted, as such, simply that the surviving record suggests that most of the animal resources could have been by-products of activities that were not "hunting" *per se.*

Aside from Wood's hunting station in Missouri (1968), there is less evidence of Mississippian hunting stations than one would expect if hunting had been a major activity. There certainly are traces of Mississippian use of rockshelters, but the Mississippian use of such sites between A.D. 900 and 1400 is minor by comparison to their use by Late Woodland peoples between A.D. 600 and 900. As noted, the Great Salt Spring salt-production site, however, does show game patterns that are substantially different from those found at Mississippian domestic sites, and Mississippian men probably pursued organized hunting in the vicinity while women made salt, if the pattern of historical times was followed. Of course, salt sources are just as attractive to many game animals as are maize fields, so even here the pattern may be more incidental than primary.

Plants

Recent studies of Mississippian plant resources have covered the ground well. To cite just a few that will lead the reader into this extensive literature, the reader should see Ford (1985), Green (1994b) B. Smith (1992), and Woods (1992). What follows are brief highlights of the known use of wild and domesticated plants in Mississippian life.

Wild Plants. Wild plant foods remained important in Mississippian times. Substantial portions of the diet came from collected or even, one might say, semidomesticated plants. Most important of these were the many different species of nut resources available in the region. The difficulty is not whether nuts were important, we know that; but *how* important they really were, given striking differences in preservation. Even so, Table 6.4 presents a broad range of species that are preserved in the archaeological record from the Lower Ohio Valley. Similar data are available from other areas (e.g., Lopinot 1994; Welch and Scarry 1995) but are more different in detail than in the major outline.

Famine foods, of course, are those used as backups by horticultural peoples whose crops have failed:

> In failure of their crops, they make bread of the different kinds of Fagus, of the Diospyros, of a species of Convulvus with a tuberous root found in the low cane grounds, of the root of a species of Smilax, of live oak acorns, and of the many young shoots of the Canna; in summer many wild plants chiefly of the Drupi and Bacciferous kind supply them. Romans 1775:84–85

One reason such crops are used primarily as famine foods is that their cost of production in person-hours is relatively high, at least in relation to caloric return. For example, tubers yield only about 110–156 kcal/person-hour in Reidhead's estimates (1981).

Table 6.4. **Plant Remains in Lower Ohio Valley Mississippian**

Genus/OTHER	Species	Family	Common name	Environment
Acalypha	sp.	Spurge	(Three-seeded Mercury)	Woods, waste ground
Acalypha	*ostryaefolia*	Spurge		Woods, roadside
Acer	spp.	Maple	[Maple]	Wet woods
Amaranthus	sp.	Amaranth	(Pigweed)	Waste ground
Ambrosia	*artemisiifolia*	Composite	Common ragweed	Waste ground
Ambrosia	sp.	Composite	(Ragweed)	Waste ground
Arundinaria	*gigantea*	Grass	Giant cane	Swampy ground
Carya	*illinoensis*	Walnut	Pecan	River bottom woods
Carya	spp.	Walnut	[True hickory]	
Carya	sp.	Walnut	(Hickory, pecan)	
Chenopodium	*berlandieri*	Goosefoot		Waste ground
Chenopodium	*album*	Goosefoot	Lamb's quarters	Waste ground
Chenopodium	sp.	Goosefoot	(Goosefoot)	Waste ground
Crataegus	sp.	Rose	(Hawthorn or red haw)	[Fallow fields, wood margin]
Desmodium	sp.	Pea	(Beggar's tick)	Woods
Diodia	*teres?*	Madder	Rough buttonweed	Dry or sandy ground
Diospyros	*virginiana*	Ebony	Persimmon	Fallow field
Fagus	sp.	Beech	[Beech]	Moist woods
Fraxinus	spp.	Olive	[Ash]	
Galium	sp.	Madder	(Goosegrass, cleavers)	
Gleditsia	sp.	Pea	(Honey locust)	
Gleditsia (cf.)	*triacanthos*	Pea	Honey locust	Bottom, swampy woods
GRAMINEAE	[Family]	Grass		
Gymnocladus?		Pea	[Kentucky coffee tree]	Woods, bluff base
Iva	*ciliata*	Composite	Marsh-elder	Moist waste ground
Juglans	*nigra*	Walnut	Black walnut	Woods
Juniperus	*virginiana*	Cypress	Red cedar	Dry sandstone blufftops
LEGUMINOSAE	[Family]	Pea		
Liquidambar	*styraciflua*	Witch-hazel	Sweet gum	Woods
Liriodendron	*tulipifera*	Magnolia	Tulip tree	Wet woods
Magnolia	*acuminata*	Magnolia	Cucumber tree	Wet woods
Morus	*rubra*	Mulberry	Red mulberry	Wood margin
Phalaris	*caroliniana*	Canary Grass	Maygrass	Fields
Phaseolus	*vulgaris*	Pea	Common bean	Fields
Phytolacca	*americana*	Pokeweed	Pokeweed	All habitats
Polygonum	*lapathifolium*	Buckwheat		Moist ground
Polygonum	*pennsylvanicum*	Buckwheat	Smartweed	Moist ground
Polygonum	sp.	Buckwheat	(Smartweed)	
Portulaca	*oleracea*	Purslane	Garden purselane	Fields, cultivated areas
Potamogeton	sp.?	Pondweed	Pondweed	All habitats
Prunus	*americana*	Rose	American plum	Moist woods, waste ground
Prunus	*serotina*	Rose	Wild black cherry	Woods, waste ground
Prunus	sp.	Rose	(Plum)	
Pyrus ?	sp.	Rose	(Pear)	Road margins, escapee
Quercus	sp.	Beech	(Red oaks)	Dry woods
Quercus	sp.	Beech	(White oaks)	Dry woods, moist woods
Quercus	sp.	Beech	[Oak]	
Rhus	sp.	Sumac	(Sumac, poison ivy)	Woods, waste ground
SALICACEAE	[Family]	Willow	[Willow]	

Table 6.4. (*Continued*)

Genus/OTHER	Species	Family	Common name	Environment
Strophostyles	*helvola*	Pea	Wild bean	Wood margin
Strophostyles	sp.	Pea	(Wild bean)	Wood margin
Sysyrinchium	sp.	Iris	(Blue-eyed grass, "pigroot")	Prairies, wide range
ULMACEAE	[Family]	Elm		
Viburnum	sp. ?	Honeysuckle	(Arrow-wood, black haw)	
VITACEAE	[Family]	Grape	(Grape, Virginia creeper)	Woods
Zea	*mays*	Grass	Maize, corn	Fields

Data from Blakeman 1974, Lopinot 1991, and other sources

Nuts. Nuts provided easily stored resources for the period between one horticultural harvest and another. Nuts were extremely important food products. They are typically high in both fats and proteins, nutrient components lacking in a maize-based diet. Many vegetarian diets use nuts to substitute for animal proteins. Even if hunting had been far more important than it seems—from the surviving evidence—to have been, the fact is that stored nut oils were generally a more reliable wintertime source of fats than were most thin, winter game animals. Collection of nuts could wait until after harvest of domesticated plants, so long as competition from squirrels or other animals was not too great. Hawkins described women collecting nuts at the end of November, for example (1796, in Grant 1980:5). The "return on investment" of nuts, the number of kcal produced per unit of labor, varies according to species. Because of hard shells and high processing costs, some nuts are not as productive as one might expect. Hickory nutmeats reduced to oil would actually be somewhat easier to acquire than nutmeats for direct consumption, since one could pound up the nuts and boil out the oils (see Reidhead 1981), giving about 500 to 600 kcal per person-hour.

Various methods were used to extract oils from nuts (e.g., Adair 1775; Beverley 1705; Bourgmont 1714; Lederer 1672). It seems likely that both animal fats and nut oils were also boiled down in reduction vessels at the Great Salt Spring, as well as brine. In historical times, hickory and other nuts were so processed into an oil or a kind of aboriginal nondairy creamer:

> The walnuts, Chesnuts, Acornes, and Chechinquamens are dryed to keepe. When they need them they breake them betweene two stones, yet some part of the walnut shels will cleaue to the fruit. Then doe they dry them againe vpon a mat ouer a hurdle. After they put it into a morter of wood, and beat it very small: that done they mix it with water, that the shels may sinke to the bottome. This water will be coloured as milke, which they cal Pawcohiscora, and keepe it for their vse. John Smith 1612:12 [1969:346–347]

> ... they likewise use hickory nuts in plenty, and make a milkey liquor of them, which they call milk of nuts; the process is at bottom the same as what we use to make milk of almonds; this milk they are very fond of, and eat it with sweet potatoes in it. Romans 1775:67–68

> They parch their Nuts and Acorns over the fire, to take away their rank Oyliness; which afterwards pressed, yeeld a milky liquor, and the Acorns an Amber-colour'd Oyl. In these, mingled together, they dip their Cakes at great Entertainments, and serve them up to their guests as an extraordinary dainty. Lederer 1672:15

These are only a few of many comments on this practice, which seems to have been nearly universal (e.g., see Adair 1775; Beverley 1722; Bourgmont 1714).

Acorns (*Quercus* spp.) are not rare in archaeological contexts, but they are bound to show up less often than hard-shelled nuts such as hickories. In some of the historical records, they are simply mentioned as a food source, but in others they are mentioned specifically as a famine food. The problem with acorns, of course, is their high tannin content. Some white oaks are supposed to be sweet enough to eat without processing, however (e.g., Peterson 1977:204); and individual trees vary in "sweetness." In California, a long leaching process was carried out, but we do not know what techniques, other than choosing sweet trees and separating oils, were used in processing acorns in the East.

The trade-off between the historically most often mentioned nuts— acorns and hickories—is that the hickories are hard shelled, requiring high labor and energy to exploit, whereas acorns are easier to shell but have labor and energy costs associated with tannin reduction. In an experiment of my own, I tried to boil some shelled whole, large, red oak acorns and found that repeated boiling in fresh water only made them unpalatable, as opposed to inedible. Of course, since tannin is water soluble, the common process of extracting oil from crushed and floated nutmeats would have leached out much of the tannin incidentally.

One thin-shelled species of hickory, pecan (*Carya illinoensis*), is easy to shell. As a result, pecan trees were still left standing in otherwise cleared fields in localities such as the Black Bottom well into the 1970s. The frequency of pecans in the vicinity of archaeological sites suggests that this may have been common prehistoric practice as well. It has even been suggested that the relationship between Mississippian peoples and hickories may come close to being a kind of "sylvaculture" (Munson 1985).

Walnut (*Juglans nigra*) is not common in the woods of much of the Southeast, but it occurs in low frequency in many areas. It is similarly represented in Mississippian contexts: present, but not common. Other nuts are represented in low frequency. The major species are those growing in the wet forests of the floodplain and in the immediately adjacent areas of the uplands.

Other wild plants. Amaranths, marsh elder, knotweed, and chenopods are relatively common in Mississippian sites, and various persons have made a strong case for domestication of these plants, discussed in the next section (Asch and Asch 1985; Cowan 1985; B. Smith 1992; and many others). Even wild variants, however, would have produced at a fairly high level, to judge from experimental collections of modern wild varieties (see Asch and Asch 1978; Reidhead 1981:196; B. Smith 1992:198). The percentages of various small seed plants vary from site to site, however. In the Black Bottom farmsteads, on the one hand, the percentages of *Amaranthus* and *Chenopodium* were minor, but *Polygonum* was at about 18 percent of nonmaize remains (Blakeman 1974; Muller 1986b:219). In the American Bottom, on the other hand, the amaranths and chenopods are close to ubiquitous at many sites (Lopinot 1994). At

Moundville, some, but not all, samples have frequent occurrence of many of these seed producers (Welch and Scarry 1995).

Hawthorn (*Crataegus* spp.) is a field margin or fallow field tree. It may be that its presence is an indication of leaving some fields fallow. "Old fields," as they were called, are well documented historically around newer settlements, and these would have been prime sources for both hawthorn and berries (*Rubus* spp.) such as blackberries. Persimmon (*Diospyros virginiana*) was widely used in Mississippian times. Ripeness would commonly come in October, but availability of this fruit could continue into winter. Grapes (*Vitis* spp.) are another plant commonly found on field or meadow margins. These field-margin and fallow-field species should serve as a reminder that old fields are not entirely out of production, even though no cultivated crops are grown on them.

Many of the plants exploited could have been used as greens or as teas, as well. Persimmon leaves, for example, make a tea that is high in vitamin C (Peterson 1977). Amaranth and chenopods are still widely used as pot greens, and many more species could have been used without leaving much archaeological evidence. A wide range of plants was used either as famine foods or as supplements (e.g., Romans 1775:84–85).

Native Domesticates. The importance of native domesticates has always been difficult to assess. Frankly, most of these plants seem to have contributed little to the overall caloric intake of the average Mississippian household, although they may have been much more important earlier. At the same time, as I emphasized earlier, the importance of a crop cannot be assessed solely in terms of percentage of annual caloric intake. Both dietary needs and seasonal importance of a crop may make it a crucial resource during some short period of time, without its overall contribution being substantial.

Seed crops. Various starchy seed crops were important. Goosefoot (*Chenopodium berlandieri*) is now fairly well established as a domesticated species in the later prehistory of the East (see work in B. Smith 1992). Amaranth (*Amaranthus* spp.) is a possible early domesticate, but a definite domesticated variety may only have come into the western part of the area quite late (1992:294). Small seeds, even after having been modified through domestication, are still hard to harvest, but the yields in terms of kcal/person-hour are high. Smith (1992: Chapters 7 and 8) provides experimental harvest yields for *Chenopodium* and discusses parameters of its potential use in Mississippian and other Late Prehistoric cultures. Starting from Smith's yield and labor estimates, *Chenopodium* values are nearly 6000 kcal/hr! Combined small seed yields of *Chenopodium* and *Amaranthus* calculated from Reidhead's data are lower, at ca. 2225 kcal/hr, but this is still high. Chenopods and amaranths are more common at some sites than others. Erect knotweed (*Polygonum erectum*) is yet another possible domesticate, although it seems to have been more common in Illinois than elsewhere (Asch and Asch 1985:183; cf. Cowan 1985). All of these species, like maize, are harvested in the fall, so there was some potential conflict in scheduling. It seems likely that the continuation of use of these native domesticates was contingent upon a number of local factors. Probably first among these was the ability of the people to depend upon maize, that is, I would expect the frequency of all of these starchy seeds to be a reflection of the risk associated with maize cultivation in that locality.

Marsh elder (*Iva annua*) is oily seeded, like sunflower (*Helianthus annuus*) and squash (discussed later), and these also appear to have a long history of cultivation in the East (e.g., Asch and Asch 1985; B. Smith 1992; Yarnell 1994), although poor preservation of these seeds may mean they are underrepresented in the archaeological record. Smith's figures for experimental *Iva* harvests average out over 4000 kcal/person-hour (1992: Chapter 8).

Maygrass (*Phalaris caroliniana*, a relative of canary grass) was not recognized in the early analyses from the Black Bottom (Blakeman 1974; Muller 1986b), but it is present at most other locations and typifies an early harvest plant that could have been seasonally significant. Although its potential for enhancement as a cultivated crop seems to have been low, its spring ripening made it potentially of more importance at some times of year than its numbers might indicate. Even a modest crop, when other resources are low or exhausted, could be welcome. Little barley (*Hordeum pusillum*) is another plant harvested in the spring, shortly after maygrass (Asch and Asch 1985:190–195).

Lopinot's ubiquity indices have been recalculated by phases in Figure 6.4, in which maygrass and little barley are both spring starchy seeds, and chenopodium and knotweed are fall harvest plants. Presentation here by phase obscures some variability within phases, as discussed by Lopinot (1994:137–138); but it also minimizes local effects in those cases where there are multiple-site data. These indices indicate fluctuations in use through time, with the low point of both kinds of harvests being at the height of population and, presumably, maize use in Lohmann to Stirling phases.

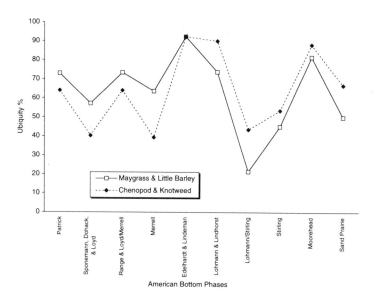

Figure 6.4. Ubiquity indices of small seed crops in the American Bottom. (Recalculated for phases from Lopinot 1994: Table 1.)

Cucurbits. The Archaic Period gourd remains were almost certainly domesticated from local wild forms (see Decker 1988;Heiser 1979), but it is unclear whether any cucurbits from Mesoamerica were later added to these (such as *Cucurbita argyrosperma,* which may have occurred in the 1400s in Arkansas;Yarnell 1994). Some Cucurbitaceae are native to the East, and it is difficult to be certain from archaeological or other evidence which domesticated squash and gourd species, if any, are Mesoamerican in origin (see discussions in Green 1994b; C.M. Scarry 1993; B. Smith 1992:40; Smith, Cowan, and Hoffman 1992). Whatever their origins, the squashes of Eastern North America were important food plants by Mississippian times. It can be difficult to distinguish varieties of this extremely variable genus, *Cucurbita,* but it is unlikely that any known *Cucurbita* species or varieties were introduced at the same time as maize. Yields for squash are high, estimated by Reidhead for the Upper Ohio Valley at over 6000 kg/ha in squash fields and over 3000 kg/ha when interplanted with maize (the latter still producing at normal rates, Reidhead 1981:205–206)! Reidhead's estimate for monocultural field production cost for fresh squash was 13.3 person-hours/100 kg, and that stored squash required a total of 26.4 person-hours/100 kg. Although these direct labor costs[2] of squash production seem to compare favorably to some 207 hours for each 100 kg of maize, maize cultivation is, in fact, much more productive when nutritional value is taken into account. One hour of labor, by these estimates, would produce only about 800 kcal of squash, but more than 1/700 kcal of maize, and perhaps as high as 3500 kcal.

As productive as squash is, it presents storage problems as well as problems of palatability and nutrition (e.g., see Richards 1961:47, 53, 84ff.). Stored squash converts about one-third of its starches to sugars, and loses one-third of its carbohydrates in storage after 3 months—and more than half, after 6 months (Philips cited in Whitaker and Davis 1962:202–203). Carotene content apparently remains high. While some varieties hold up well when dehydrated (mostly *C. maxima*), varieties such as Arikara, Cheyenne, Dakota, Fort Berthold, and Omaha scored only good to poor in dried preservation (Whitaker 1962:204–205). The term *squash* is, in fact, derived from Narraganset *asquutasquash*—"eaten green or raw." For whatever reasons, it is notable that the cucurbits, widespread and productive as they are, have not had the worldwide agricultural "success" of maize, and these problems and the low caloric value per kg of fresh plant are surely part of the explanation. Although we know squash was dried for wintertime use, these watery tissues require a considerable investment of time to preserve in this way, further increasing final costs of production.

Mesoamerican domesticates. As noted in Chapter 4, the components of what was once called the "Mesoamerican" trinity of squash, maize, and beans now are seen to have had separate histories in the East. Cucurbits are considered likely

---

[2] I have used the term *labor cost* rather than *labor value* here, because true labor value is a much more complicated value to estimate, including among other things reproductive costs, and so on. These labor costs are only direct production investments as recalculated, mostly based upon Reidhead's estimates (1981), with some corrections and amendments.

local cultigens, and the bean was not introduced until late in Mississippian times (see Yarnell 1994).

Maize. Maize had probably been introduced into the East as early as the third century of the current era (B. Smith 1992:274), and the long delay before it became a major component of diet may be partly due to acclimatization to temperate climates. Smith summarizes some of the other possible explanations for the lag between the first appearance of maize and its becoming a major dietary component (1992:275–276). These include the idea that maize was ceremonially controlled by Middle Woodland elites and became accessible to the society as a whole only after the decline of these elites. This explanation, of course, does not explain maize's scarcity or absence in Late Woodland times when such elites had disappeared. Maize may also have been consumed green as a delicacy, leading to poor preservation. However, the carbon-pathway data show such usage was limited. Even if maize was initially a only a food supplement, it may still have been more important than its percentages of seeds or total consumption would seem to indicate.

As noted in Chapter 4, maize was important in the East, but in most cases, it probably accounted for little more than half the calories consumed. In many cases, wild foods of one form or another still predominated. Maize was another critical "resource of advantage" (Muller and Stephens 1983). As a food plant, maize shares with many other crops the feature of being intensifiable—that is, more planting in the ordinary way will yield a correspondingly greater harvest. We have already seen evidence—in its phenomenally rapid spread after it was introduced into the Old World—of its substantial advantages. It is incredibly productive compared to many other crops. The advantages of maize are especially pronounced in comparison to other potential food crops in the East, especially local domesticates such as chenopodium or maygrass. Maize has the advantage of great productivity in relation to the amount of seed that must be reserved. As an early Maryland account pointed out in 1635:

> That which the Natives use in the Countrey, makes very good bread, and also a meate which they call Omene, it's like our Furmety, and is very savory and wholesome; it will Mault and make good Beere; Also the Natives have a sort of Pulse, which we call Pease and Beanes, that are very good. This Corne yields a great increase, so doth the Pease and Beanes: One man may in a season, well plant so much as will yeeld a hundred bushells of this Corne, 20 bushells of Beanes and Pease, and yet attend a crop of Tobacco: which according to the goodnesse of the ground may be more or lesse, but is ordinarily accompted betweene 800 and 1000 pound weight. Anonymous (Calvert?) 1635:22

Romans (1775:67–68) indicated how maize was used:

> Their common food is the zea or the Indian corn, of which they make meal, and boil it; they also parch it, and then pound it; thus taking it on their journey, they mix it with cold water, and will travel a great way without any other food. They also have a way of drying and pounding their corn before it comes to maturity; this they call Boota Copassa (i.e.) cold flour; this, in small quantities, thrown into cold water, boils and swells as much as common meal boiled over a fire; it is hearty food, and being sweet, they are fond of it; but as the process for making it is troublesome, their laziness seldom allows them to have it.

Historic production of maize before the development of modern hybrids was indicated at 1177 kg/ha for the Mandan in 1878, 1281 kg/ha for the Maya, 1702 kg/ha for the United States in the 1870s, and 1514 kg/ha for US production in the 1880s. Various estimates suggest a premodern production level of around 1200 kg/ha (roughly 20 bushels an acre). Reidhead (1981) used a higher figure of 1570 kg/ha (25 bushels an acre), and such production is not unlikely for floodplains that can yield as high as 7700 kg/ha (roughly 125 bushels an acre) under modern cultivation. Braudel (1981:161) cites Colonial central Mexican dry yields of ca. 600 to 700 kg/ha, which would roughly double the time and labor estimates. However, he also cites much higher yields elsewhere.

Another advantage of maize is that it holds up well in storage. The amount of grain that was in storage can be estimated from one of the earliest historical accounts. According to Elvas, when the De Soto expedition was approaching Chiaha, a message was sent by the cacique of that place, indicating that 20 barbacoas of maize were waiting (1557 [Smith 1866:66, 77; see Chapter 2), presumably enough for the 2 month supply requested by De Soto for his 600 men and an undetermined number of porters, although most porters were apparently being supplied on this section of the journey on a town-to-town basis (1557 [1866:66]). If one assumes (1) that the figures refer to food for the Spanish only, and (2) that the 20 barbacoas did contain enough grain for a 60-day stay, then—if some 2500 kcal/day were required by each of the Spanish warriors—the barbacoas would have contained between 25,000 to 33,000 kg of maize, or about 1.3 to 1.6 tons per barbacoa. That some 30 tons of grain could be diverted to such guests is surprising at first glance and seems to indicate great power of, and "tribute" payments to, the cacique of Chiaha. However, in the first place, we do not know whether these barbacoas were entirely those of the cacique or not. As in so many cases, even if they were, the picture alters somewhat when broken down into finer detail. At the historical levels of production mentioned in the preceeding paragraph above, the grain set aside for the Spanish would have represented no more than 27 ha, and perhaps as little as 20 ha, of fields. Such an extent of fields would have required between 3000 to 4000 person-days of labor, which is to say the production for a year of 18–27 field-workers (by Lewis's 1951 measure of field labor of 143 person-days/ha in Mexico, and assuming a 5-month field season and average yields). Such a commitment of resources was high, but hardly requiring so-called "tribute" from large territories. Such a commitment of resources would not have been trivial for a society of some 5000 people, but it would hardly require tributary donations from large territories. For comparison, ridgetop areas with Mississippian occupation around the Kincaid site totaled some 621 ha (Muller 1986b:214), and there may have been some periods when nearly all that land was in use. The stored food at Chiaha would have been no more than 4 percent of the total annual *local* support base for a polity the size of Kincaid at its peak. We also need to recall, however, that by late winter and early spring, fish were substituted for maize in prestations to de Soto, and this may indicate that maize supplies in storage were running short.

Maize fields had "productivity" that went well beyond the nutrition from maize kernels. Data from Martin et al. (1951)—detailing a long-term collection effort examining the stomach contents of wild game—show that the heaviest dependence on maize by wild animals for the Southeast was by songbirds, but many larger animals had considerable reliance on maize, when and where it was available (1951:31, 40). The game animals most attracted to maize fields are those that are most common in

Mississippian sites (see also Muller 1986b:223). Surprisingly, or not, maize turns out to be the second most important single plant food nationwide for wild animals, as measured by stomach contents, second only to some 65 species of pondweed (*Potamogeton* spp.)— much beloved by Northern waterfowl. In the Southeast, maize comes in second to oak (acorn) in percentage of diet and first in numbers of wild species eating the crop. Aside from the attractiveness of maize itself to the major Mississippian prey species, the farming practice of clearing fields in areas surrounded by standing forest would also have had the effect in increasing browse.

Beans. As noted in earlier discussion, the common bean, *Phaseolus vulgaris*, does not become important until after A.D. 1250, although it may have taken some time to acclimatize to Eastern conditions (e.g., B. Smith 1992:293, Yarnell 1976). The bean may have enhanced productive and reproductive autonomy of individual households and communities (e.g., Muller 1986b:254–255). The bean also has the virtue of being capable of being interplanted with maize without much loss of yield in either plant (e.g., Reidhead 1981:206). The stalks of the maize serve as poles for the beans, thus reducing labor in production. The value of the bean is threefold: First, it is high in calories; second, it is superior to nonleguminous plants in providing proteins that are nearly as accessible as those from animal foods; and third, it helps to maintain soil fertility if it is manured into the soil. These factors may have been important in the transition from "middle" Mississippian to "late" Mississippian economy at the A.D. 1250 horizon. However important the bean may have been in North America, it has not had the same impact on world agricultural systems that maize has had. In Africa, for example, the bean has made little headway against other legumes such as cowpeas and the peanut (see Allan 1965:38, et seq.).

Interplanting of all of these food plants was practiced, and volunteer plants were often encouraged, as Pring (1603[1932:349]) indicated far north in New England:

> and not farre off we beheld their Gardens and one among the rest of an Acre of ground, and the same was sowne Tobacco, pompions, cocumbers and such like; and some of the people had Maiz or Indian Wheate among them. In the fields wer found wilde Pease, Strawberries very faire and bigge, Gooseberries, Raspices, Hurts, and other wild fruits.

Raw Materials

The manufactures of the Mississippians were relatively simple. A quick catalogue of produced items covers most of the assemblages recovered archaeologically. There was the construction or manufacture of such items as houses, canoes, wooden tools, baskets, and clothing requiring plant resources. Other containers and clothes were made from animal products. Pottery and ceramics were made from clay. Some objects were made of stone, and others of bone or other animal materials. There were also some minerals used for pigments, and for a few other purposes.

Plant Resources

We have already seen how plants were used for sustenance, but we need to consider that many of the by-products of harvesting such foods would also produce some quantities of nonedible resources as well.

The evidence for Mississippian use of wood in most areas suggests that whatever trees were handy were the ones used most frequently, always recognizing that some woods might be left for last or not used at all, despite their propinquity, because of poor durability for a given purpose. We also need to remember that the woods preserved best in the archaeological record are those that preserve best! For example, pine stakes for laying out archaeological sites rot quickly in floodplain settings, whereas white oak stakes survive for several years. Even so, there are higher frequencies of what modern builders would consider poor materials than one would expect if durability were a major focus of prehistoric builders and manufacturers.

The bottomlands of the major rivers would have provided thatch, reeds, and other plant materials necessary for known Mississippian manufactures in considerable quantities within short distances of every homestead. Most kinds of wood found in the oak–hickory forests of the Southeast and Midwest were available within relatively short distances of every person's home. This is not to deny that there were preferences for some woods over others. On the whole, however, Mississippian use of wood was as opportunistic as its use of other resources. Whatever was close was usually good enough, even if its properties might have been less desirable than some other species.

One major resource that is often mentioned in Mississippian discussions is that of firewood. It is certainly true that historical people from large northern Plains villages had to go considerable distances for firewood. However, in the historical records for the East, there is little mention of difficulties in obtaining firewood, except for Northern peoples such as the Illinois—who were often, like the Plains peoples, in floodplains surrounded by grasslands (e.g., Liette 1702:110). The Eastern United States is not like the Great Plains. Historic source after source explicitly comments on the great woods surrounding historical towns and settlements. Firewood was so short of being a problem for these Eastern peoples that they burnt their cleared timber in the fields rather than saving it for firewood (e.g., Catesby 1731). In addition, woods were purposely burnt "in a circle of five or six miles compass" for hunting (Beverley 1722 [1855:124]). Such hunting practices do not develop or persist in areas where wood availability is a serious problem. Beverley even claims, "The wood grows at every man's door so fast, that after it has been cut down, it will in seven years time grow up again from seed, to substantial firewood" (1722 [1855:98]). Although bottomlands may have sometimes had enough settlement to exhaust immediately available firewood, almost everywhere there were large upland forests within a few kilometers that could be exploited with acceptable costs.

Another factor in lack of evidence for wood exhaustion is that populations were small, as discussed in earlier chapters. Indeed, the persistence of settlement in many bottomland environments over long periods of time is in itself a modest argument against the exaggerations of population that persist.

Salt production at the Great Salt Spring involved substantial consumption of firewood for each kg of salt produced (Muller 1992). Over some 500 years, vast deposits of ash and debris from salt production piled up. Examination of the wood used, however, shows that much of it was wood that had fallen and lain on the forest floor (Lopinot, in Muller 1992). European salt production used up firewood rapidly.

In short, even in such special production circumstances, the evidence does not support a general idea of fuel exhaustion.

Animal Resources

The early historical evidence supports an area-wide use of skins as one of the primary goods used in prestations to leaders and guests of high status. Given the wide geographic distribution of this behavior in the earliest historical records, I think it likely that it was a well-established areal pattern of considerable time depth. There are few archaeological traces of this, however. Perhaps one day we shall be able to show that animal exchange goods present in one region came from another. For example, jackrabbit fur in Georgia might indicate some kinds of reciprocity in animal products for the Georgian-made shell gorgets that have been found at Spiro (Muller 1966a; Phillips and Brown 1978).

Surviving animal raw materials are largely in the form of bone and shell items. There are few indications of widespread exchange of bone items in the Mississippian period, but sea shells, especially the lightning whelk, *Busycon perversum* (or *contrarium*), were important, if not common. Unlike most other Mississippian raw materials, these are most definitely not available locally or even regionally for most of the Mississippian peoples of the East. The distribution of objects made from exotic shell will be discussed in more detail in Chapter 8, but for now it should be enough to note that the kinds of shell for making display goods such as shell gorgets were from the East coast.

Over the several centuries of Mississippian exchange, considerable quantities of shell were exchanged, finding their way from the Gulf well inland, even beyond the northern fringes of the Mississippian world. However, we have to understand that this widespread distribution had historical roots going well back into Archaic times. Although the number of exotic shells brought into Mississippian sites was greater than that found at Archaic or even Hopewellian sites, I suspect that the quantity of exchange of shell is largely proportional to the overall population in the East, rather than representing qualitatively different mechanisms of exchange at different times. Manufacture of items from shell, especially marine shell, is well attested in the American Bottom. As I will argue in the next chapter, I do not believe that this manufacture constitutes true production for trade or full-time specialization. I have been glad to see more recent discussions of this topic have toned down claims for true specialization (compare Yerkes 1989 or 1991 with Yerkes 1983; cf. Muller 1984a, 1986b). Although shell items were not produced for trade (i.e., were not *commodities*, in the strict sense), they were certainly exchanged. However, it is important that we not confuse such behaviors as ritual exchange of display items with commercial trade—a completely different sort of economic event.

Freshwater shellfish were widely exploited; but they are resources, like many others, that were available near most Mississippian sites and settlements. The same is true of the freshwater pearls that are less common in the archaeological record than one might expect from their prominence in the de Soto accounts. A few pearls were even given to the Spanish in their passage, although they took more, as we saw in Chapter 2. The importance of pearls as indigenous prestations is not at all clear—given the desperate desire of the Spanish for something of value to justify their activities.

The historical evidence indicates much use of skins, feathers, and so on, but these are seldom preserved in the archaeological record in a form that allows us to say much about their acquisition or even their use. Some of the rare cases of preservation are from contexts adjacent to copper in "elite" graves, the salts of which have preserved fragile materials. However, we can hardly judge these as typical only of elites, since similar opportunities for preservation are not commonly present in small-site circumstances.

Mineral and Lithic Resources

Salt. Salt is a relatively localized resource (Figure 6.5, but showing only some of the major sources), typically occurring at those places where faults have brought groundwater down to buried salt deposits. Of course, the nearest seacoasts were potential salt sources as well. The next chapter will deal with this resource and the idea of specialization associated with it in detail. For now it is enough to note that salt is not so important physiologically as past discussion has sometimes indicated (e.g. Bunge 1873,1874; cf. Dauphinee 1960, especially p. 400). However, there is no denying the psychological and habituating nature of salt appetite, and availability of salt (or its rarity) has often played a role in social development. Today, of course, salt is widely recognized as one of the basic fast-food groups, along with fat and sugar. People love these flavors, and they will consume far more of them than is needed, when they can. Social value is even symbolized in salty terms such "not worth his salt," "below the salt," and the like.

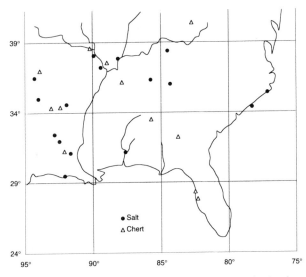

Figure 6.5. Some of the major chert and salt sources in the Southeast.

Even though salt is not available everywhere, there are salt sources within relatively easy range of most Mississippian centers. As we shall see in the next chapter, salt production appears to have been a domestic activity, not the result of the specialized production systems for exchange that were formerly proposed (Muller 1992, next chapter).

Chert. Chert (Figure 6.5) is also a raw material—an object of labor—as well as being a tool of labor in processed form. This is another of the resources seen by some as indicating centrally controlled or, perhaps, specialist production. Work is still underway on the data collected from one of the largest and most important sources of chert—the Mill Creek quarries in southern Illinois, but the preliminary results are inconsistent with the idea of external dominance and full-time specialization there (see Cobb 1988, 1993a, b, c) and at the similar Dover quarries. Most Mississippian tools were locally made from local cherts, even when those were not of particularly good quality. The key word in Mississippian chert use is "expedient," that is, proper to the ends desired at as low a labor investment as possible. For some purposes, raw materials with special properties were required; but more often than not, whatever was available was used, even if it would be only marginally serviceable. The use of river gravels was common, even when small and of poor quality. The number of fine, curated tools made of any kind of chert is quite small in comparison to rough, sharp flakes that were used briefly and discarded.

One task requiring, or substantially benefiting from, special raw materials was the manufacture of stone hoes. These tools required several distinctive characteristics in the chert from which they were made. Perhaps foremost was the quality of toughness and resistance to breakage. I well remember that a prominent French prehistorian once came to a professional meeting in Illinois and gave a demonstration of flint knapping. However, without realizing what they had done, the organizers had provided him with Mill Creek chert that had not been heat treated. The difficulty of flaking this intractable material was soon revealed in his repeated *sotto voce* cries of "*Merde!*" Resistance to breakage, of course, is a crucial virtue in a tool that will be struck into the bricklike clays of the floodplains.

A second property of the cherts needed for hoes is that, given the difficulty of chipping them, it is far easier to do so if they are found in tabular form. At the Mill Creek sources, raw nodules may approximate the final form of the tool, requiring little more than trimming of the cortex to make a hoe. Small wonder, then, that the cherts from such sources were widely sought. However, to anticipate later discussion, their distributions falsify claims of central control (see Chapter 8, Muller 1995b; cf. Brown et al. 1990).

Other Mineral Resources. Other minerals were used to a lesser degree. Among these was fluorite (or fluorspar) that was used to make ornaments. The main Mississippian source for fluorite seems to have been in the Lower Ohio Valley. The mineral does occur widely in limestone in the Midwest; however, but most of the distinctive purple crystals are probably from the southern Illinois and Kentucky sources. There is no evidence of anything but the most simple kind of acquisition and distribution. As one would expect, the Mississippian sites closest to the source area have the highest frequency of artifacts made from fluorite.

Shalelike coal was also used for ornaments such as lip plugs and the like. On a few occasions in the Black Bottom locality, crushed coal was also used as temper in making pottery (it was reduced to coke in the firing process). One small pit feature south of the main plaza at Kincaid had ash fill with high levels of sulphur that is almost certainly coal ash (Weigand 1976). Fragments of coal and cinders from burnt coal are common markers for Mississippian sites in the Black Bottom locality (Muller 1986b).

Copper was a mineral, or rather metal, that was of great attractiveness to Easterners at initial contacts until the value was debased by overtrading by the Europeans (see John Smith 1624). The archaeological evidence supports the same kind of use of copper for goods that can be accurately described as "display" items, often called "prestige goods" (Goodman 1984). As with various shell artifacts, the evidence supports widespread *exchange* of repoussé copper plates, but, nothing suggests true commerce in them. The archaeological evidence is silent upon the question whether such goods were parts of prestations (as in so-called "tribute"). Although most pre-Mississippian copper seems to have come from the Lake Superior region, the Mississippian copper seems, insofar as tests have been done, to have come from Appalachian area (the mountains, not the people, see Goad 1978; Goodman 1984).

Earth. The earth itself was an object of labor, and not just as fields. Mounds were built basket load by basket load, of silty clay loams. The soil was dug up near the mounds, and many mound sites have marshy borrow-pit areas visible nearby. The stability of piles of earth as substructure platforms reflected both the nature of their soil and the accumulated wisdom of the prehistoric builders. It would not have taken long for mound builders to learn practically what the maximum angle of repose was for particular soils. As recent collapses at Monks Mound at Cahokia have shown, the amount of moisture and other features can adversely affect how well the mound holds together. One should point out that this is one case of an element that is substructural being superstructural as well. We shall return to mound construction as a form of production under the discussion of elites and their roles. Mounds are the clearest locus for elite control, or at least management, of labor.

I would be remiss if I did not also mention the use of clays to make ceramics. In most Mississippian regions, reasonable quality clays for the manufacture of pottery were available locally. Most production of pottery seems to have been both domestic and local. Mississippian pottery does include a magnificent array of very fancy and well-made vessels (e.g., Holmes 1903). Some vessels were distributed widely outside their probable places of origin, but the vast bulk of Mississippian pottery was, in fact, rather plain and quite local. Virtually everywhere archaeological types such as "Bell Plain" and "Mississippi Plain," simple jars or bowls, and lack of much real decoration characterize ceramic assemblages (see Chapter 7). The point is the ordinariness of *most* Mississippian use of clay, notwithstanding the presence of some marvelous examples of the potter's art.

Comments on Objects of Labor

Most evidence from Mississippian "manufacture" shows opportunistic and ex-pedient use of raw materials. The inventory of materials used was limited and most raw materials were easily obtainable by each household without much effect on the success of other families. A few raw materials were more limited in distribution, such as shell from the Coast or chert for stone for hoes from Mill Creek or Dover. Some systems of indirect acquisition through exchange existed for these goods. Even in these cases, however, there seems to be little evidence that acquisition of such raw materials was undertaken by a few specialists, rather than by the domestic producers themselves. Even some of the exotic items appear to have entered exchange net-works rather more as a by-product of other activities than having been the special object of labor of specialist producers. Most goods and resources needed for a Mississippian way of life were available within a relatively short distance of every person's home, usually within a day's journey out and back, and rarely more than a few days away.

Human activities in seeking out raw materials were certainly motivated by personal goals such as acquiring prestige. Undertaking of a historical materialist approach to Mississippian does not mean that the realm of motivation and immediate cause can be ignored. These attitudes are not immaterial, literally, since they are related to how societies develop in their evolutionary and dialectical contexts. Their relevance to studies of raw materials acquisition and the "objects of labor" is that persons make choices about which material is more suitable or less so. The germ of trade arises in the barter of one less desirable object for one more desired. In this exchange process, it is possible for each partner to feel that they have had the best of the deal, and in the sense of evening out the distribution of useful goods across the society, they may both be right.

Having said this to be so, I am somewhat nonplussed by efforts to deny social and material causes for the desires of individuals. Material causes are mediated through the wills of humans, but the test of dialectical and evolutionary processes is that—given the long term—behaviors with socially useful and biologically positive consequences will prevail. The evolution of cooperation takes place within the frame-work of desire but has material causes and relations that are features of how things work, not how people think (e.g., Axelrod 1984; Holland 1975). In the short term, economic choices at the level of acquisition reflect individual goals and ideas. In the long term, on the other hand, selection operates to resolve the contradictions be-tween individual choice and social needs.

2. TOOLS OF LABOR

Manufacture and Use of Tools

The material tools used in Mississippian production were relatively simple. These are the standard production kit of Neolithic peoples everywhere: stone tools, pottery vessels of various kinds, and a broad range of tools made of other natural materials. However, we should also understand that tools can include more than just hoes or knives. One, perhaps *the*, distinguishing characteristic of our species is that it can transform both social and natural phenomena into tools just as material in their effects as a hoe.

The manufacture of most tools was relatively simple. The raw materials were generally available directly to each producer. There was little opportunity for one person or group to monopolize either the sources or, most particularly, the "means of production" of these artifacts. It is extremely unlikely that any of the critical resources needed by a Mississippian family could have been effectively denied to them, except by a common decision of their family and neighbors. There also is little, if any, indication in the early historical literature, and certainly little archaeological evidence, that production of certain goods was under the patronage of elites. The idea of attached specialists is a useful concept, and it may well apply to other circumstances, but I cannot see that the evidence for Mississippian societies supports such kinds of production. The essence of controlled production (*alienation*) is that the nonproducer "controller" has to have some means of restricting the unauthorized production *or* distribution of goods. In Mississippian production, most economically important, and even most exotic, raw materials were available to everyone, requiring only the effort of getting them, or the connections with neighboring peoples needed to obtain goods from more distant sources. I see little in the primary historical records—before the establishment of European "factors" (traders)—of the ability of any *individuals* to prevent others from seeking access to raw materials or finished goods. There are some indications by the late 17th century of groups attempting to control materials or sources in opposition to other societies, but these are not relevant to alienation of persons within the same society. I will discuss the evidence for exchange and distribution of goods in Chapter 8 (see also Muller 1995b).

On the contrary, the manufacture and use of the tools were within the capabilities of every normal person. This does not mean that there were no artisans of greater skill at one task or another. However, few Mississippian tools required more than modest learning to make or use, and most persons would have acquired these skills while growing up. Esoteric knowledge was in the realm of ideas, not technology and production.

Even ideas can be considered tools, especially in areas of technological knowledge such as the practical physics or chemistry needed for various activities. However, in the realm of ideas as tools, there surely could have been little purely technical knowledge that could have been monopolized by elites. The old spouse's tales about the priest telling the farmers when to plant is a fantasy. Any farmer would soon have had clear enough markers of when and where to plant without divine or other spiritual guidance. Such knowledge would have developed long before the "priests" were there, and it is hard to see how it could have been suppressed. On the other hand, priests or shamans may well peddle a different kind of knowledge (e.g., how to avoid mythical and spiritual risks to crops) in such a way as to lead believers into perceived risks without spiritual guidance. So long as the costs paid for such advice are modest, garden magic and its ilk will be subscribed to. Surely the farmers would have needed spiritual guidance to keep spirits and such like dangers away.

Horticultural Implements

Cultivation of maize and other crops was the basis of horticultural production. Stone hoes (Figure 6.6) were often employed in the central riverine localities. Charles Cobb's continuing studies of this chert-production system at the famous Union County, Illinois, sources are providing new data on the social context and technical characteristics of stone hoe and other chert production. An unplowed residential site near the quarries promises to provide valuable evidence on the domestic contexts of chert production as analysis proceeds (Cobb 1993, personal communication 1996).

Mississippian chert hoes are often elongated ovals in shape, with highly distinctive use polish (e.g., Figure 6.6). It is probable that persons living at the major "hoe chert" sources found ready exchange for any production beyond their immediate needs. In that sense, they probably could be called "part-time specialists." Such overproduction and exchange is, however, a universal phenomenon that occurs in all human societies. Such activities are surely one genesis of trade and commodity, but they lack the distinctive social features and social implications of these. The houses these people lived in near the quarries, the food they ate, the production of the food that they ate—all were much like those of any Mississippian residential site. No great store of exotics from trade, no indications of greater wealth, nor any other of the markers of merchants or specialists are found. Even the uniformity of the end product seems less a result of specialist production than of the requirement that the end product meet regular needs. Given the centuries of Mississippian occupation of their bottomlands, the number of stone hoes, broken stone hoes, or even flakes from the special hoe cherts is much smaller than one might expect if they had been absolute

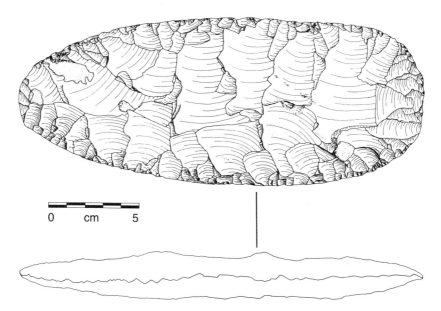

Figure 6.6. "Typical" stone hoe (from Southern Illinois, drawn by Brian DelCastello).

necessities for farming and digging. I think we may take it that they were good tools that made the job of cultivating crops and digging wall trenches, and so on, much easier, but that other kinds of digging implements were adequate in the absence of stone hoes.

The next chapter will briefly address the character of hoe production, and Chapter 8 includes discussion of the forms of distribution of stone hoes. If nothing else, the substantial number of stone hoes indicates that Mississippian exchange cannot be characterized as being solely concerned with exotic, finely made goods. The diversity of Mississippian exchange is important in considering models emphasizing valuables exchange at this social level (see Brumfiel and Earle 1987).

Use of the hoe is not discussed much in historical records, aside from illustrations such as those of de Bry (in Hariot 1590), in which the hoes, like their users, were translated into European forms. A somewhat similar system of horticulture in Mexico, but in different soils and conditions, required about 143 person-days/ha of field (Lewis 1951). It is not, I think, unreasonable to use this as a working estimate of required labor investment for Mississippian field cultivation (see Muller 1986b).

Fields and Their Use

A garden or field is an ambiguous "thing." Is it a tool for extracting resources from nature, or is it an object of labor? Of course, it is both and more. For convenience's sake, fields will be discussed here, but they could as easily be put into the previous section. The establishment of a field is a distinctive mode of behavior, although smaller scale "clearing" of areas probably characterized preparation of a locality for settlement. In fact, many Mississippian fields were really just extensions of the homestead and were immediately adjacent to the structures and areas where people lived. The same pattern continued over the East in Historic times:

> Their houses are in the midst of their fields or gardens, which are small plots of ground. Some 20 acres, some 40, some 100, some 200, some more, some less. In some places from 2 to 50 of those houses together, or but a little separated by grouves of trees. Neare their habitations is little small wood or old trees on the ground by reason of their burning of them for fire. John Smith 1624:31

The division between "in fields" and "out fields" is often made, but it would have been difficult to tell where one ended and the other began, either historically or archaeologically. Of course, the presence of fields around structures meant probable benefits from household debris as a kind of natural manure.

Mississippian archaeologists have often argued for long duration of settlement and cultivation of floodplain areas (e.g., Muller 1986b); but a recent reexamination of Mississippian farming practice has argued for the "necessity" of incorporating a "shifting" horticultural regime into models of Mississippian horticulture (Baden 1995). Baden has done us a major service by introducing solid agricultural science into this discussion. However, I think there are a few problems with the specifics. There are definitely indications in upland areas of Mississippian patterns of abandonment and reoccupation that would be consistent with a model of shifting cultivation and fallowing. For example, Hargrave, and Butler, and their associates found such indications at the Bridges site (1983). Baden's point that soil nitrogen is not renewed by alluviation is important. All the same, Baden's model is based more on upland agricultural studies than on alluvial floodplain—studied not least because upland lands are the ones historically troubled with soil exhaustion. At the least, I believe the time before soil exhaustion for major Mississippian settlements must be longer than Baden allows.

Baden's ethnographic cases supporting the idea of shifting cultivation are mostly Northern, not Southeastern. However, one Southeastern source he quotes is William Bartram (1791 [1928:315]), who does refer to "frequently" breaking up of towns. Such instances are not quite so simple as it seems at first glance. First, Bartram asked his question why such events occurred of a trader at Apalachicola during a stroll to a nearby abandoned town, which was only a "mile and a half" from the new settlement. "Old" Apalachucla (= Apalachicola) was surrounded by "expansive old fields," but the move is said to have been occasioned by flooding and "vengeful spirits"—as a result of blood having been shed in a "white" town (1791 [1928:314]). No mention is made of soil exhaustion as a cause of *this* particular abandonment. Moreover, the new town of Apalachicola, occupied by the bulk of the occupants of the old town, was only 2.5 km away and was occupied for over 20 years, very close to the old site. This relocation only moved the settlement about a 20-minute walk from the old area. The general answer given by the trader at Apalachicola about field exhaustion was really as much concerned with shortages of game animals, and it is hard to see how a 2.5-km move could have helped either problem much. In addition, the conclusion appears to have been that of the trader, perhaps drawn by him more from European views and practices, rather than representing aboriginal viewpoints.

Another reason for doubting that exhaustion was so rapid and recovery so long for bottomland fields is that we have indications of historical use since the early 19th century of many of these fields under even more intensive European practice. These fields seem to be more fertile than the upland soils of Baden's model, although he quite correctly points out that family tales of agricultural practices have more than a little in common with tales about fishing success (Baden, personal communication). Even so, I think that the historical evidence cannot be easily brushed aside. There is good archaeological evidence, for example, of the use of the Armiesburg soils around Kincaid from ca. A.D. 900 to later than 1300. For Kincaid, Baden suggests that complete abandonment would have to occur at roughly 134 years after first use of the area. From archaeological evidence for duration of settlement, I think, wherever the adjustments must be made, the abandonment time should not be less than 200 and probably closer to 300–400 years. The low negative rates of increase modeled for Mississippian populations in Chapter 4, of course, may be directly linked to field yields. We do have some evidence (in the form of hawthorn and a few other plants) that fields may have stood fallow, but it is equally possible that those species were present only as field margin, rather than "old field," plants, as already discussed. If Baden is right in his estimates of time to abandonment, then we shall have to find evidence of either importation of food from outside or periodic abandonment at many major Mississippian sites.

In fact, I like the idea that "cycling" of Mississippian communities was partly tied to soil fertility. It provides a much more down-to-earth cause of this phenomenon than an appeal to structural contradictions alone. If, of course, we accept Baden's model for the sake of argument—even with extended periods before exhaustion and with shorter fallow periods—the implication is to deflate even further ideas of massive settlement in Mississippian floodplain areas, unless we are willing to propose elaborate models of "surplus" extraction from distant areas. As will be discussed later, mound construction and other activities at the major sites suggest that they, at least, were occupied fairly continuously over something like 200 to 300 years.

The use of fields is tied to the number of persons being supported, typically at the almost universal figure of one acre (.404 ha) per person per year, as we saw in Chapter 4. This old English measure is astonishingly resistant to differences in environment and plants being cultivated, as shown by data from many different kinds of horticultural systems around the world, probably because it is a measure of how much effort a producer will expend with expectation of a return.

3. AGENCY

The question of agency in Mississippian is complex. It involves issues of what and why as well as who. Those who believe in complex production systems in Mississippian have correspondingly assigned various tasks to hypothetical specialists, a topic discussed at greater length in the next chapter. Here, I shall try to avoid the problems of task and labor differentiation and deal first with the issues of personnel available for production activities.

Individuals and Households

The first level of all economic systems is the individual, the "economic man" of classical economics. Here primary economic choices are made, and these choices have become the basis of much recent economic theory. There is a danger in giving individual choice too much importance, however, in that the combination of choices *en masse* does not necessarily, nor even usually, replicate the structure of individual choices. As efforts to model economic theory in terms of complexity theory have shown, there are emergent features to economic systems that result from seemingly simple individual choices interacting to create results that are neither foreseen by the actors, nor by the economic theorist who only looks at the conscious wants of individuals (e.g., see Anderson et al. 1988; Kauffmann 1992; popular discussion in Waldrop 1992). The individual's choice is certainly important. Human beings are actors who make conscious and other choices about what activities they will undertake, when they will schedule those activities, and how long they will continue them. At the same time, not even the "economic man" is free of constraints. Western economists, as noted back in Chapter 1, often deal theoretically only with wealthy industrial societies and assume a minimum "safety net" underlying the choices made. Real people in most societies, however, cannot make individual choices in such splendid isolation of physical survival. There are harder choices than that between Maxim's and McDonalds'.

An individual Mississippian cultivator faced real and concrete risks when she had to decide how much to plant and when to do so. She could not expect that reckless and totally selfish choices on her part would be "insured" by others in the short run, much less the long term. As we saw in Chapter 4, individual Mississippian consumers commonly underwent periods of stress in their everyday lives while growing up. There were years when there was too little to eat, when crops were flooded, when frosts came too early. As I have already argued, these are powerful inducements to several courses of individual choice that have implications for society as a whole. One framework of individual choice was that the planter worked with her household, first of all, and then with her kin—who in all probability were major players in allocation of usufruct rights to resources, especially land. A second frame of decision making was whether an individual person, family, or small community would try to make it on its own. I think few would argue that most Late Woodland peoples went for large-scale cooperation. Each of the more northern Late Woodland producer units, whether that is considered as a person or a small community, would have been in the position of Robinson Crusoe or the Swiss Family Robinson. Autonomy of this sort is possible when populations are small or when resources are plentiful—in either case, relative to technological means of extracting resources.

At some point, however, a natural contradiction comes into play. Small numbers and plentiful resources are biologically contradictory. But as numbers increase, competition for resources also increases. Strategies that were regional and extensive—in the sense of requiring large ranges and having alternatives available for any given resource—are forced into local and intensive modes. Of course, these are the classic contradictions underlying the development, adoption, and intensification of domestication. But these are also the conditions that can favor the establishment of reciprocal social relations with others—in effect, restoring a regional extent of alternative resources, but in this case through people, not land.

In all of this, the place of the individual producer becomes embedded in a matrix of social ties, of social security achieved through sharing among consanguinous kin, and even with affines. Alliances by marriage certainly reduce conflict and help to minimize competition by creating both friends and hostages in other communities. These same relationships, however, have economic consequences as channels for the movement of goods among and between communities. In the original context, these relationships are generally reciprocal, so long as failures are local and not regional, one producer as likely to be a donor as a recipient of emergency aid. Or would be, that is to say, were resources and risks distributed evenly across the landscape. In fact, communal sharing of risk and resources has its own contradictions as well. Some persons and households were likely to have been sited so that their risks were lower and their productivity greater than others.

The typical mechanisms of sharing in small-scale societies are reasonably well known and show patterns that have been recognized for a long time (from Mauss 1923–1924 [in 1950] to Sahlins 1972 and beyond). For one example, in a carefully documented study of the Gwembe Tonga (Scudder 1962, especially Appendix B), each family of roughly six people had about three unmarried persons to cook for. Sharing in this case, extended to these persons whose homes would show up as separate and separated structures in an archaeological context. Of course, in times of scarcity, larger kin groups, even affines, may be called upon for help. As the spheres of sharing extend beyond consanguineous kin and affines, communal standards of sharing come into play.

The contradiction in these relationships, especially those on the communal level, is that asymmetry can arise out of differences in local conditions. Egalitarian sharing, the commune, bears within its breast the specter of differentiation. To the extent persons in favored locations may be the subject of obligations from those who more often come up short, efforts to balance these obligations are usually expressed in either goods or services. This is not a new argument, of course, and it has a certain flexibility that makes it fit everything with appropriate *post hoc* tweaking, yet even just so stories can sometimes be just so. This is a premonetary version of the problem of primitive accumulation. How do surpluses arise, and how do they come to be distributed and used asymmetrically in societies that start off mostly egalitarian in structure? Sahlins has summarized a series of cases showing production above minimal levels (1972:102–122, and elsewhere).

The balance of risk and productivity in the Mississippian economy was such as to require planning at the individual level to prevent failure. Shortfalls in any one of the productive systems could bring real hardship as population increased, and alternative strategies such as hunting or collecting became less viable. Shortfalls in more than one of the major productive systems in the same year could bring disaster. In these circumstances, prudent management of the household economy will necessarily aim at producing more than the absolute minimum required for survival in the next year. The simple fact is that horticulturists know from repeated experience that the environments that they farm are subject to repeated and even periodical risks such as flooding. Under these circumstances, the household has to produce more than the bare minimum necessary under the best possible production conditions. In short, common prudence and memory of recent shortages will mean that a producer will plant enough to ensure a little extra, just in case.

Household Structure and Production

The structure of the Mississippian household can be conjectured from archaeological, comparative, and ethnohistorical data. In Chapter 5, we saw that the typical Mississippian household was probably within the range of the Southeastern household of some 4 to 9 persons. Given the small size of many structures, the traditional estimate of around 5 persons, as discussed earlier, is probably not far off.

The following table (Table 6.5) is an idealized model of Mississippian household structure in relation to the ratio between consumers and workers (C/W). The table is based on Chaianov's model of family development from Vologda budget values as simplified by him (Chaianov 1923:15; 1925[1966:58]). The assumptions upon which my modifications are based are those listed here:

1. Childbearing is limited to four children
2. A new surviving child is born each fourth year
3. A child leaves home at 18, but half (possibly female) remain nearby

Table 6.5. Idealized Mississippian Consumer/Worker Ratio over Time

Age of couple	Year of family	Married couple	Children 1	2	3	4	Consumers	Workers	C/W ratio
18	1	**1.8**					1.8	1.8	1.00
19	2	**1.8**	0.1				1.9	1.8	1.06
20	3	**1.8**	0.3				2.1	1.8	1.17
21	4	**1.8**	0.3				2.1	1.8	1.17
22	5	**1.8**	0.3				2.1	1.8	1.17
23	6	**1.8**	0.3	0.1			2.2	1.8	1.22
24	7	**1.8**	0.3	0.3			2.4	1.8	1.33
25	8	**1.8**	0.3	0.3			2.4	1.8	1.33
26	9	**1.8**	0.5	0.3			2.6	1.8	1.44
27	10	**1.8**	0.5	0.3	0.1		2.7	1.8	1.50
28	11	**1.8**	0.5	0.3	0.3		2.9	1.8	1.61
29	12	**1.8**	0.5	0.3	0.3		2.9	1.8	1.61
30	13	**1.8**	0.5	0.5	0.3		3.1	1.8	1.72
31	14	**1.8**	0.5	0.5	0.3	0.1	3.2	1.8	1.78
32	15	**1.8**	**0.7**	0.5	0.3	0.3	3.6	2.5	1.44
33	16	**1.8**	**0.7**	0.5	0.3	0.3	3.6	2.5	1.44
34	17	**1.8**	**0.7**	0.5	0.5	0.3	3.8	2.5	1.52
35	18	**1.8**	**0.7**	0.5	0.5	0.3	3.8	2.5	1.52
36	19	**1.8**	**0.7**	**0.7**	0.5	0.3	4	3.2	1.25
37	20	**1.8**		**0.7**	0.5	0.3	3.3	2.6	1.27
38	21	**1.8**		**0.7**	0.5	0.5	3.5	2.6	1.35
39	22	**1.8**		**0.7**	0.5	0.5	3.5	2.6	1.35
40	23	**1.8**		**0.7**	**0.7**	0.5	3.7	3.3	1.12
41	24	**1.8**			**0.7**	0.5	3	2.7	1.11
42	25	**1.8**			**0.7**	0.5	3	2.7	1.11
43	26	**1.8**			**0.7**	0.5	3	2.7	1.11
44	27	**1.8**			**0.7**	**0.7**	3.2	3.4	0.94
45	28	**1.8**				**0.7**	2.5	2.8	0.89
46	29	**1.5**				**0.7**	2.2	2.5	0.88
47	30	**1.5**				**0.7**	2.2	2.5	0.88
48	31	**1.5**				**0.7**	2.2	2.5	0.88
49	32	**1.5**					1.5	1.9	0.79
50	33	**1.5**					1.5	1.9	0.79
51	34	**1.5**					1.5	1.9	0.79
52	35	**1.5**					1.5	1.9	0.79
53	36	**1.5**					1.5	1.9	0.79
54	37	**1.5**					1.5	1.9	0.79
55	38	**1.5**					1.5	1.9	0.79

Boldface are counted as producers.

4. After leaving, each child contributes on average 0.1 to labor, 0.0 to consumption (for both male and female)
5. Adult productivity and requirements fall off after age 45

Table 6.5 illustrates probable changes in the production capabilities and relative production capabilities of the family over a 38-year history (i.e., from the couple's marriage or becoming independent of the parental household) at 18 years of age until the couple reaches a modeled lifespan of 55, after which, in any case, the household would likely cease to be an independent productive unit. Figure 6.7 presents the curves for a 5-year, moving average to smooth out the unrealities in assuming sudden jumps in productivity at specific ages.

Given the level of success of Mississippian reproduction, the model presented represents a "best-case" scenario for reproductive and productive success. It illustrates the important point that the productive history of this basic economic unit—the family—is not constant through time, but changes as a reflection of the composition of the coresidents at a given point in their history. Chaianov's model drew attention to the alteration in consumer–worker ratio after—in our case— the midpoint of the family development. In the Russian peasant cases studied by Chaianov, the duration and potential size of the individual household is larger, but probable lineage linkages and the proximity of Mississippian households to each other probably produced circumstances not unlike the Russian case, after all.

In the Russian case, however, productivity and consumption requirements of women are set lower than for males, reflecting both socially defined roles and sexual dimorphism. Gallatin speculated (1836:153) that dependence on women's labor for cultivation limited the range and intensity of agricultural productivity in Native American societies.

> In order that the cultivation of the soil may promote that increase of mankind, which is limited only by the quantity of land fit for cultivation, it is necessary that the annual agricultural labor should produce a quantity of food, at least equal to the annual consumption of the whole existing nation. The labor of women alone is not sufficient to produce that result. A portion of their time is necessarily employed in the other domestic occupations which must always fall to their share; and the residue is unequal to the task of raising food adequate to the whole consumption of the nation. But it fell short everywhere of that which was required; and the result was, that, after producing an increase of population proportion-

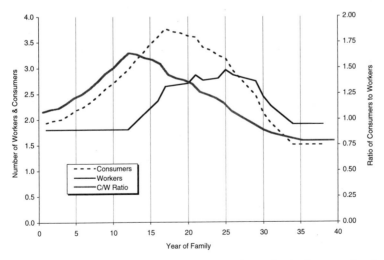

Figure 6.7. Consumers, workers, and consumer/worker ratios during the development of an hypothetical Mississippian family (smoothed, 5-year, moving average).

ate to the additional supply, that increase was again ultimately limited by the quantity of
game which the territory afforded.

He felt women's responsibilities for cultivation among Eastern Native Americans
meant that field labor was therefore insufficient "to promote any but a very limited
increase of population" (1836:108) because of other household responsibilities. On
the other hand, a strong community organization may mean that the actual time
spent in direct child care by women in larger settlements might be minimal, with
older children and elderly persons taking on much of this load (see Chapter 1 and the
labor figures given by Grossman 1984). In this case, we may generalize Gallatin's
conjecture for sexual division of labor to note simply that it is the relative lack of time
spent by *any* producers that limits the "increase" of such societies. In the absence of
coercion, "Neolithic" producers, like their peasant cousins, do not commonly spend
much more time than is required by household midterm needs—hence the
Chaianovian limitations on production emphasized by Sahlins (1972).

Communal Life

At the beginning, the family, defined both by kin and physical proximity, is the
focus of the individual producer in all spheres of production. As pointed out in
Chapter 1, this is true to a remarkable degree even in complex economies, but it is an
even more conspicuous aspect of small societies. In hunter–gatherer economies, as in
Late Woodland times, the family band may in fact move to localized resources in
order to exploit them, and when the whole family does not move, goods collected at
remote locations will usually be processed and partly distributed by the collectors to
their kin. When production takes place at remote locations, of course, there is a
certain potential for "skimming" of the returns, but the biological proximity of the
group makes sharing have survival value in biological as well as social terms. As a
community, as opposed to a family, emerges out of the combination of sedentism and
localized production, there is less "sociobiological" justification for sharing, yet the
old 19th-century observation that such societies tend to be "communal" remains true.
Why? Why not nature "tooth and claw," with every biological segment struggling for
scarcer and scarcer land and food resources? Well, there is some truth to the observation that biological distance in communities is still close when compared with more
remote groups, but the essence of the situation is that communal economies are a
successful way to resolve the contradictions that isolation presents. As Axelrod
(1984) and others have shown, there is a logic to cooperation that favors cooperation
over selfishness in the long term, at least in agent-to-agent settings.

In the course of concentrating in bottomland settlements, Mississippian people
made other changes in the way they approached storage, and these also had implications for social relations. At least in upland sites, the general, earlier system for storage
seems to have been in storage pits. Storage pits are essentially private storage facilities,
and how many and how much one has remains obscure to others. In wet bottomlands,
pit storage was not practicable, and the general Mississippian pattern appears to have
been aboveground storage in houses or in *barbacoas*, like those observed in early
historical records (see Chapter 2). Although the contents of such a structure are not

completely public, it is pretty clear from the historical records that these facilities were easily identified and the Spanish were able to "forage liberally" upon them. In a closely settled community, and even in dispersed farmsteads, storage in the house or in special storage houses becomes much more public, with a corresponding reduction in the ability of a potential donor to claim shortages when asked for aid. The principle of *noblesse oblige,* mentioned earlier, is an extension of public demands upon private stores. To be a donor, however, brings those social asymmetries to the fore and tends to translate private surplus into public prestige—and even into an ability to mobilize clients in activities that further enhance the prestige of the patron.

As noted earlier, individual decisions about how much to plant would often produce short-term surpluses. These were private, but could be used socially. Surplus is a taxing problem. Childe (e.g., 1954) and others before him (e.g., Morgan 1877) treated the creation of surplus as the event that made possible the development of civilization (cf. Pearson 1957). The problems of why there might be a surplus and what its existence or not might imply has been the subject of extended discussion, especially in relation to buffering of risks (e.g., see Halstead 1989; other papers in Halstead and O'Shea 1989). Surpluses are certainly culturally defined, and mobilization of resources may effectively "create" a surplus where one is otherwise not present. The apparent contradiction between risk buffering and the Chaianovian version of the principle of least effort (see Sahlins 1972:87) is more apparent than real. People need not *seek* to produce a surplus as such, but they surely will recognize the risks inherent in recent (i.e., short-term) fluctuations of conditions, and they will produce for what they perceive as the worst case. It is wrong, therefore, to argue that domestic producers do not produce relative surpluses (cf. Halstead 1989:69). The longer the interval since hard times, of course, the more likely that production will decline to be closer to the mean set of conditions. Of course, one evolutionary advantage of large-scale, complex systems is that they may maintain longer term "memory" of bad conditions, and may allow geographical diversity to mitigate local disasters. Data supporting this kind of production cushion may be found implicitly in many of Sahlins's examples (1972), and more explicitly in Allan's discussion (1965). Allan defines a "normal surplus" for Tonga production that is quite substantial, and his data on production indicate, even minimum production in an average year, was well in excess of minimum subsistence requirements (Allan 1965:38–40). An archaeological argument based on this viewpoint is presented by Halstead (1989).

So, in many years, perhaps even the majority of years, a surplus resulting from safety margin production will not be needed. What, then is to be done with it? Practically, the principle that surplus depresses production holds even in such simple economic systems, so the good of all in the long term means that some means of taking surplus production out of circulation is developed—usually through means that may enhance the prestige of the surplus producer. One such means is public feasting that "burns" surplus production in great, short-term episodes of "redistribution." In such public feasting, the immediate control of the surpluses may be taken by village heads, who typically "own" the rights to sponsor the events. Here is certainly one likely avenue for the promotion of village heads to chiefs who are able to call on donations. These donations could eventually develop from voluntary gifts into the coercive tribute of full-fledged states. An intriguing discussion of the problems of surplus, public goods, and labor may be found in Hawkes's paper and the accompanying comments (1993) on why hunter–gatherers work.

Labor

In the Mississippian case, we have good reason to conclude that the bulk of labor was done in the household, by the household, and for the household. However, certain kinds of labor that may not have been household labor, *per se*, produced conspicuous results, such as mounds and special goods such as hoes, salt, and fancy goods. It remains an issue for argument about how much labor in Mississippian times took place outside the domestic setting or was even controlled by elites. Since the next chapter will deal with Mississippian specialization, it is only necessary here to outline the issue of personnel involved in labor, noting cases of potential differentiation. As noted earlier, the argument on specialization is partly drawn between those who see *specialization* as a continuum of labor commitment and those who see qualitative differences. In the following section, I shall first discuss historical data on labor organization and character. I want to emphasize that this is not a claim that Mississippian organization was identical to that of the historical period. However, while the historical data should not be used to *interpret* prehistoric use of labor, it certainly can be used to suggest and even warrant hypotheses about how labor may have been organized. These, of course, require testing with archaeological data.

Division of Labor

Direct observations of divisions of labor are difficult in archaeological settings but not impossible. Evidence of household distinctions in labor has often been found (e.g., Pauketat and Woods 1986). Certainly, production in the early historical East was marked by sexual division of labor (e.g., Martire d'Anghiera 1533 [1555:25]; Joutel 1687 [1962:112]). John Smith's account (1612:22) makes the usual value judgments on different kinds of work:

> The men bestowe their times in fishing, hunting, wars & such manlike exercises, scorning to be seene in any woman like exercise, which is the cause that the women be verie painefull, and the men often idle. The women and children do the rest of the worke. They make baskets, pots, morters, pound their corne, make their bread, prepare their victuals, plant their corne, gather their corne, beare al kind of burdens and such like.

In 1700, du Ru was trying to build a chapel for Christian worship, and he commented on the sexual division of labor among the coresident Bayogoula and Mugulasha [Mougoulacha] with the same kinds of judgments. It was difficult to convert the women, but "I believe the men here are unusually difficult to reform, being naturally indolent and more idle. It is the women who do nearly all the work" (1700 [1935:29]). However, some accounts do suggest more male participation in agricultural activities, as at the Tunica mission:

> The men do here what peasants do in France; they cultivate and dig the earth, plant and harvest the crops, cut the wood and bring it to the cabin, dress the deer and buffalo skins

when they have any. They dress them the best of all Indians that I have seen. The women do only indoor work, make the earthen pots and their clothes Gravier 1701 [1861:134–135, 1906:132–133]ff. rt.

It is not clear whether this reflects differences in Tunica work custom or the influence of missionaries. Certainly by the time of the American Revolution, groups such as the Choctaw and some Creek communities had fairly intensive male participation in field production (e.g., Romans 1775:86; Hawkins 1799 [1848:34,35]).

It is nonetheless the case that males in many historical Eastern societies typically engaged in the *heaviest* horticultural labor deemed beyond the capabilities of the women alone. In that sense, there is some reason to see a female-dominated horticulture as less intensive than full-scale agricultural systems.[3] Historically, the rise of central control of agricultural production in most societies shifted production from a female horticulturist to a male peasant farmer. However, it must also be remembered that the labor devoted to cultivation is not usually at high levels in non-class societies (e.g., Grossman 1984; Richards 1961).

Women's work *was* difficult and hard, but it should be remembered that many male economic activities, such as hunting, took place out of view of these observers. Liette said that the men rested and gambled under ramadas in front of the cabins while women were working, (but then he observed that the men were engaged in night fishing (1702[1962:131]), certainly less obvious than daytime field work. Indeed, many productive subsistence activities went unobserved by European soldiers and priests. Male labor was often seen as "recreation" rather than labor.

Given the wide geographical distribution of these patterns of gender differences in the East, the Plains, and elsewhere in North America, there seems little reason to reject the idea that a similar pattern of labor organization was true of Mississippian as well. I think that there are enough data to warrant such an hypothesis, but there are also enough exceptions to make efforts to test the gender associations of particular industries important.

Other than gender distinctions, there seems to have been little labor differentiation in the historical Southeast. Although leadership roles themselves might be conceived as "specialist," even the households of the elite differ more in degree than in kind in their accoutrements and economic behavior. Specialization, in the economic sense, implies dependent social relations that are difficult to see in historical or prehistoric Eastern peoples (see Chapter 7).

Effort

What intensity of effort was necessary to survive in the East? One common theme in the historical record is that labor among Eastern aboriginal groups was scarcely an end of itself. LeMoyne d'Iberville, like many others, commented on labor

---

[3] Bruce Smith (1992:207) speaks of the term *horticulture* as having "vague connotations of small vegetable gardens," and takes exception to it, even as applied to Hopewellian cultivators. However, the term *agriculture* has quite explicit implications of large-scale, specialized production that seem especially inappropriate for *any* prehistoric cultivation system in the East.

and effort in the Lower Mississippi Valley: "These Indians are the most beggarly I have yet seen, having no conveniences in their huts and engaging in no work" (d'Iberville 1699–1702 [1981:3]).

The European invaders found enthusiasm for production of surpluses to be lacking. Father du Ru (1700[1935:47]) had a common European view of the work ethics of the Native American population in his chapel building project at the Bayougoula:

> We have finally begun, and the way the Savages went at it I thought that we should complete the building to-day, but they did not keep it up. These people soon lose their fire and usually they spend more time in discussing what they are going to do, and in contemplating what they are going to do, and in contemplating what they have done than they do in actual work on the undertaking. By and large we three Frenchmen here have done more than all the village together, but it is something to have made a start.

After a while, enthusiasm for du Ru's project waned, and "it took a little display of temper" on du Ru's part to make the work go on, and again "it was necessary for the elders to set the example" in order "to prevent the young people from playing" (1700 [1935:51]).

Du Ru's (1700[1935:53]) comments, even though loaded with unsympathetic value judgments, emphasize that heavy labor was not necessary to produce subsistence sufficiency:

> I am again struck by the dominant preference of these tribes for indolence. They do without things that we regard as absolutely necessary, merely because it would require a little effort to get them. If they have more corn than they actually need for food, this is less due to the quantity they sow than to the fertility of their soil which, alone, is responsible. The Mississippi is full of fish and there are very good ones here, but very few of the Savages take the trouble to fish. By the looks of their cabins one would say that they lack the ability to do good work, but it is only the desire to do it that is wanting. I discovered that, when I had them make my garden. The soil here is marvelous for it, but it would require labor so they have only tiny gardens where they raise tobacco. Two or three leagues from the village there is excellent hunting, but this is too far from them. They prefer to let the buffalo and deer there alone. Turkeys, also, set and lay eggs at all seasons. But all the women do is to boil Indian corn; they seem to find that almost too much for them. It is true that these people always have a pot on and eat at all hours. However, some women spin wool and bark but this work does not amount to much.

The view of aboriginal plenty in both horticultural and natural production was nearly universal:

> This, and a great deal more, was the natural Production of that country, which the Native Indians enjoy'd, without the Curse of Industry, their Diversion alone, and not their Labour, supplying their Necessities. The Women and Children indeed, were so far provident, as to lay up some of the Nuts and Fruits of the Earth, in their Season for their further Occasions: but none of the Toils of Husbandry were exercised by this Happy People, except the bare planting a little Corn, and Melons, which took up only a few Days in the Summer, the rest being wholly spent in the Pursuit of their Pleasures. And indeed all that the English have done, since their going thither, has been only to make some of these Native Pleasures more scarce, by an inordinate and unseasonable Use of them; hardly making Improvements equivalent to that Damage. Beverley 1705 [1947:156], also 1722[1855:126]

> They commonly have pretty good crops, which is owing to the richness of soil, for they often let the weeds outgrow the corn, before they begin to be in earnest with their work,

owing to their laziness and unskillfulness in planting: and this method is general through all those nations that work separately in their own fields, which in a great measure checks the growth of their crops. Besides, they are so desirous of having multum in parvo, without much sweating, that they plant the corn-hills so close, as to thereby choak up the field.
Adair 1775:407–408 [1930:438–439]

On the other hand, some peoples (such as the Tohome and Mobile) were described as very hardworking or, rather, industrious: "Ils sont fort laborieux, travaillent beaucoup à la terre" (d'Iberville 1702 [1880:514, 1981:169]). In another case, Romans (1775:83) contrasted the Choctaw to other groups:

Their way of life in general may be called industrious, they will do what no uncompelled savage will do, that is work in the field to raise grain; and one may among them hire not only a guide or a man to build a house, or make a fence, but even to hoe his grounds; nay they will for payment be your menial servants to the meanest offices; no other unsubdued savage will do any more of all these than be your guide; they are very ingenious in making tools, utensils and furniture; i have seen a narrow tooth comb made by one of these savages with a knife only out of a root of the Diospyros that was well finished as i ever saw one with all the necessary tools; this shews their patience.

But Romans also noted that a sense of property had become established among the Choctaw by his time (1775:81).

In short, depending on circumstances, incentives, and need, historical Eastern groups worked hard in their fields or not—just like any other people. However, the advantages of good climate, rich soils, a great diversity of wild foods, and productive domesticated plants made a high degree of social control of food production unnecessary. The challenge of Mississippian archaeology in the Southeast is to come to grips with the issue of whether large-scale public labor expenditure in things like mound construction required more complex production systems than those that seem to have been nearly universal in historical times.

Subsistence Production

In general, ordinary production activities in the historical East were based on the substantial production advantages of maize over other crops. As Locke noted (1674[1912:209]), the initial labor investment was great, but the yield was vastly greater than those characteristic of Old World plants:

The Indian corne requires most labour in planting and tillage as 5 to 1 compard with wheat, and is of a courser tast, but nourishes labourers better, and bring a far greater increase commonly 50 for one.

Although propaganda to encourage new European settlers often made such yield claims suspect, the fact is that maize really was highly productive by comparison to the crops Europeans were used to. Beverley commented on the large yields of maize: "So that oftentimes the increase of this grain amounts to above a thousand for one" (1705 [1947:143], 1722[1855:114]). Nor were fields large by European standards: "Their fields are not big, considering the number of people they have" (d'Iberville 1699–1702 [1981:64]).

Planting and harvest had elements of community labor. For example, even after considerable effort by American authorities to encourage individual farming, the Koasati town among the Creek had public field labor in 1799:

> These Indians [Koasati] are not Creeks, although they conform to their ceremonies; the men all work with the women and make great plenty of corn; all labor is done by the joint labor of all, called public work, except gathering in the crop. During the seasen for labor, none are exempted from their share of it, or suffered to go out hunting. Hawkins 1799 [1848:35]

In earlier times, goods and land were sometimes set aside for the temple and the keepers of the temple, as among the Tensas:

> At the last quarter of the moon all the cabins make an offering of a dish of the best food they have, which is placed at the door of the temple. The old men take care to carry it away and to make a good feast of it with their families. Every spring they make a clearing, which they name the field of the spirit, when all the men work to the sound of the tambour. In the autumn the Indian corn is harvested with much ceremony and stored in magazines until the moon of June in the following year, when all the village assemble, and invite their neighbors to eat it. They do not leave the ground until they have eaten it all, making great rejoicings the whole time. This is all I learnt of this nation. The three villages below have the same customs. Tonty 1693 [1903:141]

Some 80 years later, Adair (1775:405–406[1930:436–437]) described what seems similar organization of field labor among the Choctaw, Chickasaw, and their neighbors. Members of the elite worked alongside the general public:

> Among several nations of Indians, each town usually works together. Previous thereto, an old beloved man warns the inhabitants to be ready to plant on a prefixed day. At the dawn of it, one by order goes aloft and whoops to them with shrill calls. that the new year is far advanced, that he who expects to eat, must work, and that he who will not work, must expect to pay the fine according to old custom, or leave the town, as they will not sweat themselves for an healthy idle waster. At such times, may be seen many war-chieftains working in common with the people, though as great emperors, as those the Spaniards bestowed on the old simple Mexicans and Peruvians, and equal in power, (i.e. persuasive force) with the imperial and puissant Powhatan of Virginia, whom our generous writers raised to that prodigious pitch of power and grandeur to rival the Spanish accounts. About an hour after sunrise, they enter the field agreed on by lot, and fall to work with great cheerfulness; sometimes one of their orators cheers them with jests and humorous old tales, and sings one of their most agreeable wild tunes, beating also with a stick in his right hand, on the top of an earthen pot covered with a wet and well-stretched deer-skin: thus they proceed from field to field, till their seed is sown.

Overall, production in historical groups was based on household labor, when it was not cooperative. Cooperative labor seems to have been most common to support the "priests," and other elite, and for common stores. Agriculture was the task of all households and members of all households, including those of the elites, engaged in these activities—apparently in more than just symbolic fashion.

As the records indicate, historical production at the household level was normally sufficient to ensure a sufficiency of subsistence produce, especially when horticultural production was combined with wild products from hunting and gathering. Beverley commented on the negative impact of European overuse of these resources (1705; and there was also a well-established historical trade in deerskins). By later historical times, the availability of wild products appears to have been less than usually assumed for Mississippian times. Perhaps this depletion of resources explains Romans's discussion (1775:86) of male activities and hunting among the Choctaw:

> They help their wives in the labour of the fields and many other works; near one half of the men have never killed a deer or turkey during their lives. Game is so scarce, that during my circuit through the nation we never saw any, and we had but two or three opportunities of eating venison in as many months;

On the other hand, the absence of hunting resources may simply reflect the large population reported for the Choctaw through the entire historical period. Ample documentary evidence supports an important social as well as economic role for hunting activities, so "vermin" hunting was not the whole story in historical times.

Other Production

Common goods were also manufactured largely within the household unit (e.g, Stephens 1982), and according to Adair (1775:422), mostly by women:

> The women are the chief, if not the only manufacturers; the men judge that if they performed that office, it would exceedingly depreciate them. The weight of the oar lies on the women, as is the case with the German Americans.

As already noted, elites sometimes, perhaps even usually, participated in production activities. Although the anonymous source believed to be Calvert was speaking of Maryland, his description rings true for the area:

> They have also Cockorooses that are their Captains in time of war, to whom they are very obedient; But the Werowance himselfe plants Corne, makes his owne Bow and Arrowes, his Canoo, his Mantle, Shooes, and whatever else belongs unto him, as any other common Indian; and commonly the Commanders are the best and most ingenious and active in all those things which are in esteeme amongst them. The women serve their husbands, make their bread, dreste their meate, such as they kill in hunting, or get by fishing; and if they have more wives than one, as some of them have (but that is not generall) then the best beloved wife performes all the offices of the house, and they take great content therein. The women also (beside the houshold businesse) use to make Matts, which serve to cover their houses, and for beds; also they make baskets, some of Rushes, others of Silke-grasse, which are very handsom. Anonymous [Calvert?] 1635:27

So we see that historically most elite personages participated in "common" kinds of activities, although, to be sure, this labor might sometimes be more symbolic than not.

Forced Labor

The issue of forced labor and slavery in preclass societies has a long history of discussion without much light having been shed on the matter. At one time, the origin of classes was seen as being the result of conversion of conquered peoples into a slave "class." However, although forced labor by captives is widely attested, the actual institution of *slavery*, in any useful sense of the term, is harder to recognize, even historically. Insofar as slavery represents a conversion of people into property, slavery in societies in which *property*, as such, plays so minor a role, is a moot question. What actually happened is simple—a captive was taken in warfare and brought back to the home society of the captor. What then took place is the crux of the matter. In the historical record, we commonly find evidence for several different kinds of treatment of captives. One response, especially on the northern frontier of what had earlier been Mississippian, was to torture and kill the captive in a public ceremony of some kind. The bravery of a captive warrior was a matter of honor for both sides. A second treatment of captives was to incorporate them into the captor society. Such was the fate of Daniel Boone with the Shawnee in northern Kentucky. Formal adoption was often undertaken, or the captive might move from a condition of captive gradually to one of a full-time participant in community affairs. Finally, there was a residue of persons in the historical records who seem to have been just "slaves"—persons retained for their forced labor.

In the de Soto and early accounts there are some indications of the Spanish buying slaves, but it is impossible to conclude that the aboriginal perception of these persons being "exchanged" was the same as the European. I do not think that the Garcilaso references are reliable enough to be used as evidence for slavery, although there are indications there of captives being maimed to prevent their escape (1605 [1956:340–341, 1951:487–488]).[4] By the late 17th century, there is no doubt that some persons were slaves in the classic sense, but this was a direct reflection of an extensive European slave trade, as is clear from contemporary documents describing, for example, Illinois capture of slaves for sale to others (Dablon 1678 [1878:247]):

> ... du sud et de 'oüest, où ils vent faire des esclaves, desquels ils se servent pour trafiquer, les vendant cherement a d'autres nations, pour d'autres marchandises.

Similar practices are also attested for the Arkansas and for the mid-Atlantic (LeClercq 1690; Woodward 1674), but always in the context of a developed trading system with, and directed toward, the Europeans.

In short, there is not much evidence of class distinction for so-called "slaves" until the commercialization and commoditization of all exchange goods in the context of transatlantic metropolitan economies.

4. ELITES AND PRODUCTION

Again, our best historical sources, from those closely attuned to the realities of Native American political economy, are very clear on how these historical elites worked within the relations of production. Adair (1775:426–427, 459–460) deals with the topic at some length:

> This leads me to speak of the Indian method of government.— In general, it consists in a fœderal union of the whole society for mutual safety. As the law of nature appoints no frail mortal to be a king, or ruler, over his brethern; and humanity forbids the taking away at pleasure, the life or property of any who obey the good laws of their country, they consider that the transgressor ought to have his evil deeds retaliated upon himself in an equal

---

[4] It is terribly tempting to use Garcilaso here, not least because this same section emphasizes the nonterritorial basis of Eastern warfare. Unfortunately, one cannot just pick and choose what one likes, ignoring what one does not.

manner. The Indians, therefore, have no such titles or persons, as emperors, or kings; nor an appelative for such, in any of their dialects. Their highest title, either in military or civil life, signifies only a Chieftain: they have no words to express despotic power, arbitrary kings, oppressed, or obedient subjects; neither can they form any other ideas of the former, than of "bad war chieftains of a numerous family, who inslaved the rest." The power of their chiefs is an empty sound. They can only persuade or dissuade the people, either by the force of good-nature and clear reasoning, or colouring things, so as to suit their prevailing passions. It is reputed merit alone, that gives them any titles of distinction above the meanest of the people. If we connect this with their opinion of a theocracy, it does not promise well to the reputed establishment of extensive and puissant Indian American empires.

Adair was responding to what he saw as exaggerations in the earlier sources, and his "parliamentary" Native Americans should be taken no more or less seriously than the "sun kings" of the French accounts. However, there is this difference between the French and this British colonial description: The societies described by Adair were at least four times larger than the Natchez! On the eve of the American Revolution, Native American societies such as the Creek and Choctaw had arguably transformed themselves into secondary states capable of challenging some aspects of the local power of the intrusive colonial societies. What is lacking from the accounts are efforts of individual chiefs to exert personal control of resources of any kind, even with the examples set by the Europeans in front of them! As in the Natchez revolt, where there is evidence of "pressure" being exerted, it is by the society as a whole, or at the very least by those "principal men," not by chiefs alone. We need to recall that few Mississippian societies were anywhere near the size of the Choctaw polity.

Mounds

Mounds are the most obvious expression of Mississippian elite dominance, but not certainly domination. Not all observers have seen them as emblems of dominance:

It has been for sometime a subject of enquiry, when, and for what purpose, these mounds were raised; here it explains itself as to the purpose; unquestionably they were intended as a place of safety to the people, in the time of these floods; and this is the tradition among the old people....The name is *o-cun-li-ge*, mounds of earth, or literally, *earth placed*. But why erect these mounds in high places, incontestably out of the reach of floods? From a superstitious veneration for ancient customs. Hawkins 1799 [1848:38–39]

Even though Hawkins's explanation may have something to it, what do mounds really represent? It is not wrong to accept the usual assumption that physical elevation of some members of the community reflected their social elevation as well. Both living and dead members of such a family were elevated, and this is a fairly good indication that the status symbolized by mounds was ascribed rather than achieved.

Scale

Mound sites are large and small. Figures 6.8 and 6.9 show different mounds as they were depicted in Thomas's survey in 1894. Table 6.6 shows the largest individual mounds from Late Prehistoric times, but these data are usually not so precise as those that I have published for the Kincaid and Angel sites (Muller 1986b), since they are based on mound dimensions from site reports, maps, and many other sources, some

Figure 6.8. Etowah Mound A, Georgia, in the late 19th century (from Thomas 1894: Plate XV, fac. p. 294).

of which are sketchy. They are, however, based on the best dimensional data I have available in each case and calculated by the same formulae to ensure as much comparability as is possible.[5] This table shows the immense size of Monks Mound by comparison to the other larger mounds. Also note that 4 other Cahokia mounds are in the top 20. Some mounds are not included in these rankings, either because of their probable dates or my doubts about the accuracy of their dimensions. The pattern of some sites having fewer, but larger mounds may suggest some differences in the way "power" was distributed, or at least how it was transformed into the making of mounds in different Mississippian societies. In both Tables 6.6 and 6.7, older data for Moundville volumes have produced much higher figures, so that the mound known as Moundville B would be about 85,000 m³, and the site total would be over 250,000 m³ in the second table (Welch, personal communication 1996). I do not know how these volumes were calculated, but even if they are accepted, the point remains that Cahokia is at an entirely different scale.

Table 6.7 presents the 20 largest *sites* from the Late Prehistoric East, insofar as I can measure total size. These data are totals for sites from the same measurements in the earlier table. Not all mounds at all sites survive, at least in a manner that allows reasonable estimates of their dimensions. We know that some sites (marked with asterisks in the table) were larger than their presently measurable volumes, although this is true to a lesser degree of other sites listed. For is reason, the relative rank of sites is not to be taken too seriously— aside from Cahokia at over *1 million* m³, the important observation is that all other Late Prehistoric sites are each less than 155,000 m³ total of mound construction. Monks Mound alone at Cahokia is many times larger than the total volume of mound construction at any other *site!* The list of mound construction volumes for the some 65 sites for which total volume exceeds 3000 m³ is not marked by clear breaks, but simply grades off from large to small.

---

[5] In cases where I have only base dimensions, I have calculated an average angle of repose in order to estimate the dimensions of the tops of the mounds.

Figure 6.9. A small mound in Desha County, Arkansas (from Thomas 1894: Figure 147, p. 240).

As I pointed out in 1986 (1986b:201ff.), fewer persons are needed to account for even the largest of these construction projects than one would suppose at first glance. Erasmus's (1965) experiments with Mexican workers using digging sticks indicated that a worker could produce as much as 2.6 m^3 of fill in a warm-weather working day of 5 hours. A modern contractor's estimation tables for shovel work in heavy soils (e.g., Page 1959) give 1.2 m^3 in the 5 hours. Even given differences in

Table 6.6. Largest Late Prehistoric Mounds

Rank	Site	State	Volume
1	Cahokia 38 (Monks)	IL	731,000
2	Etowah Mound A	GA	114,000
3	Angel A	IN	72,000
4	Ocmulgee	GA	65,000
5	Winterville 1	MS	63,000
6	Cahokia 48	IL	60,000
7	Lake George A	MS	56,000
8	Moundville 1	AL	53,000
9	Carson D	MS	48,000
10	Mott 1	LA	45,000
11	Cahokia 60	IL	42,000
12	Kincaid Mx8	IL	41,000
13	Cahokia 42	IL	41,000
14	Pack Mound A	TN	40,000
15	Mayersville A	MS	39,000
16	Mound Bottom A	TN	35,000
17	Cahokia 31	IL	35,000
18	Moundville 2	AL	33,000
19	Lake Jackson 2	FL	31,000
20	Obion (main)	TN	29,000

Table 6.7. Largest Eastern Late Prehistoric Sites in Total Mound Construction

Rank	Site	State	Volume
1	Cahokia	IL	1,007,190
2	Moundville	AL	153,377
3	Etowah	GA	140,702
4	Winterville	MS	109,908
5	Kincaid	IL	93,061
6	Mound Bottom *and* Pack	TN	90,688
7	Angel	IN	87,706
8	Lake George[a]	MS	74,049
9	Ocmulgee	GA	64,517
10	Kolomoki	GA	57,726
11	Mott[a]	LA	56,421
12	Mayersville[a]	MS	52,589
13	Toltec[a]	AR	50,105
14	Mound Bottom	TN	49,582
15	Anna	MS	48,499
16	Arcola	MS	43,361
17	Pack	TN	41,246
18	Lake Jackson	FL	40,478
19	Fitzhugh[a]	LA	33,206
20	Troyville[a]	LA	29,560

[a]Partial totals for these sites.

tools and enthusiasm, the costs of construction, including lifting and spreading (see Muller 1986b) were probably close to 1 person-day per 1.25 m³. These are the figures used in the estimates of time below.

As Figure 6.10 shows, a community of 5000 persons could have erected all of the mounds at Cahokia in about 250 years, with an annual community labor "cost" of only 4 days per household of five people! Kincaid, with only a population of 1250 persons and the same degree of public labor, could have built all of their mounds in about 100 years. For Moundville at 1250 people, it would have required about 160 years, and about 40 years with 5000 total population. There has been a tendency to look at massive public works and to overestimate the actual costs. Labor donations in societies with little vertical differentiation have labor donations to community projects as high as 40–45 days, and moderately complex historical societies have had more than 150 days of community labor for a household per year (Erasmus 1965:280–281).

As once I pointed out (1986b), partly on the basis of nonmound construction estimates from Lafferty (1977), mound-building labor at Kincaid much exceeds the totals of other known public-labor commitments. This is clearly the case at other Mississippian sites as well. Of course, there were periods of more intensive labor. At Kincaid, the maximum single-mound-stage addition was about 6000 m³ (Muller 1986b:203) A single stage was presumably completed in one work period, so the maximum mound-building effort at Kincaid would have involved about 4800 person-

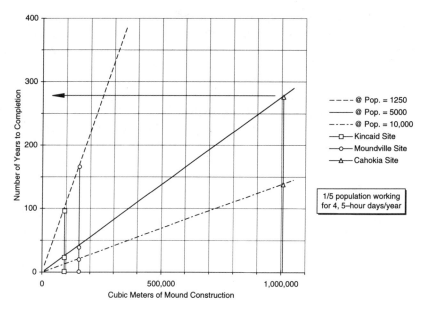

Figure 6.10. Labor costs of mound construction.

days of labor in 1 year. With an estimated 240 families (i.e., 1200 persons), in the Black Bottom, this would imply only 20 workdays per household. Again, even this maximum effort for a small total population would not present any kind of problem in terms of labor shortages or unavoidable scheduling difficulties.

Hierarchy

Another question is what practical social purpose a mound had. Surely social elevation was symbolized by vertical elevation; but who managed to build mounds and what do they represent?

That mounds were important symbols of "power" cannot be denied. For example, the "construction" of litter burials out of goods and bones from earlier burials at Spiro probably represents, as James Brown suggests, "an attempt to concentrate the powers of the ancestors within the bowels of the mound that was erected on top of them" (personal communication 1996). It could also represent efforts to create "new" ancestors for "usurpers" whose own lineages were not so grand or, at least, not local. In either or both cases, the dead support and justify the power of the living. The historical records, with the peculiar possible exception of the *reported* (in Elvas and Ranjel, but not in de Biedma) indifference of the Lady of Cofitachequi to Spanish search for pearls among the dead, generally indicate great concern about the deceased ancestors of the serving chief.

As mentioned in passing, in Chapter 5, the elevation of a mound, as a symbol of the elevation of the individual sponsoring the work, is surely as often an indication of the independent power of that sponsor as of his or her subordination to external political authorities. Since there was such importance to mortuary remains as validation of power, probably even to targeting the rival's ancestors in his or her "temple" for destruction, it would be surprising to me if the ruling chief would encourage or even allow the construction of mounds at locations under his or her authority. As discussed by Anderson at length (1994a,[6] 1994b), because of the clear threat of rival claims by the "subordinate" chiefs or even relatives, there would seem little reason for the paramount or central chief to have assisted the local personage in making the assertion to authority that a mound usually, and nearly universally, represents.

Decline in Mound Construction

It is easy to overestimate the scale of mound building and to underestimate what can be accomplished by relatively small numbers of well-organized workers. Populations large enough to build mounds were certainly present in historical as well as prehistoric times. Thus, we come to what may be the best argument for a scale difference between prehistoric and historical Mississippian—the fact that mound construction or other kinds of large-scale public investment appears to be rare in most historical groups. In M. Smith's argument (1987:89ff.), the "loss" of secondary mound center construction is equated with loss of political control. However, the contrary may be true. These "secondary centers" may more often reflect degrees of local autonomy rather than subordination. In such a case, the loss of secondary power centers would be a consequence, not of loss of political control, but rather of survivors banding together because of declines in total population. As Smith puts it: "Depopulation and decentralization of sixteenth century chiefdoms led to increasing recombinations of refugee groups" (1987:142). I am suggesting that the same effect can occur without the "decentralization" of which Smith speaks. I have already suggested the possibility that such aggregation was present well before the 16th century. The "recombinations" are these peoples' best attempts to maintain as large a society as possible. In Late Mississippian contexts, what mound construction there was would have been concentrated in fewer sites. In addition, other activities such as warfare may have used up surpluses that would have been converted into mounds in earlier times. Warfare almost certainly had this effect in the Historic period.

The initial decline in mound construction occurred before the early European–Native American contact period. Although dating of mounds is often uncertain, there was probably more small-mound construction in late times than usually recognized. The construction of *large* mounds did decline after A.D. 1300, and even earlier to the north. Figure 6.11 shows the necessarily rough estimates for dates of completion of various mounds throughout the Southeast, and even this schematic repre-

---

[6] Anderson's paper on factionalism has very useful points to make that are probably mostly correct, but its strong dependence on Garcilaso de la Vega and, to a much smaller degree, on Dávila Padilla (1596) is unfortunate, since these are both indirect sources that are likely to be least reliable precisely in the discussion of such matters as relations of power.

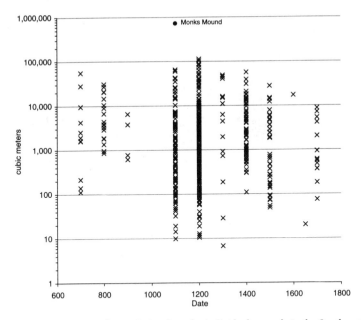

Figure 6.11. Estimated completion dates for individual mounds in the Southeast.

sentation indicates a decline. However, *decline* is by no means the same as *cessation*. In the data on mounds, there appears to have been a late Mississippian change in scale. Some areas were effectively abandoned, whether this resulted from slow reductions in population incrementally or by actual emigration. However, a view of Mississippian overall decline is too narrowly focused in parochial regional interests. The southern complexes continued to flourish later than their northern Mississippian counterparts.

However impressive Mississippian mounds are, they represented a small part of the political economy of specific peoples, especially in light of how small their labor costs could have been. Mound construction is an economic and symbolic act of community, perhaps in support of the elite roles. Trigger has spelled out how this material expenditure—as an example of conspicuous consumption—may be a transformation of social relations into a concrete representation (1990). I would have said *labor* was the measure, rather than *energy* the *currency*; but Trigger's discussion is a valuable reminder of the interrelation among things, social relations, and persons. Such labor investments may be nonetheless symbolic for also having had practical value, I might add.

Although the onset of massive public works is a excellent archaeological marker of the emergence of a new social order, the cessation of such cooperative labors is not nearly so significant a marker of social change. For example, we know that the post-Giza Egyptian polity continued to be highly organized, even more organized, after Dynasty IV, but the only period of really large-scale pyramid construction is in Dynasties III and IV (Figure 6.12).

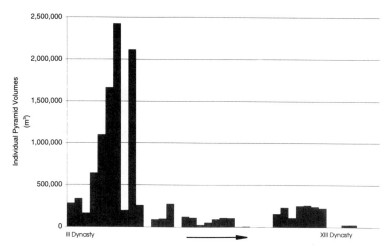

Figure 6.12. Egyptian pyramid construction though time (from pyramid dimensions in Edwards 1961, and other sources).

Some have come close to suggesting that large-scale emblems of power are meaningless for archaeological interpretation, because they do not occur in every case, or because there were "powerful" societies without such obvious markers. There are, however, few cases in which it has been seriously argued that massive public works were *necessary* components of some complex of power. It is easy to imagine political complexity without pyramids, but it is hard to imagine pyramids without some degree of complexity. The presence of these material symbols is significant, not their absence. They are usually sufficient grounds for proposing diversified organization and coordination, but not necessary evidence to do so.

In general, mound construction is the kind of simple, public labor project that is common worldwide at the first blush of political power. It is often associated with societies in which the tensions between public good and private goods are poorly defined. Mounds are conspicuous consumption but not wasted effort. They represent public commitment to cooperative labor as much as the power of the chiefly sponsors. They enhance the prestige of both the chief and the ordinary people of a town. The power of the chief and the community were inextricably interwoven—the names of historical caciques and their towns were usually linked.

One more thing also needs to be considered—Mississippian mounds were platforms for houses, and their layout and organization magnified those of the ordinary household. They were the household writ large—magnified into a public display of grandeur, but still a house. Even the "temples" were houses of the dead, who were warehoused to validate the power of the living. The mounds symbolized the elevated households of the powerful persons who mobilized the endeavor—and, not incidentally, the community that actually performed the labor. Such a pattern of magnification and transformation of the domestic into the political is characteristic of many societies (compare Fustel de Coulanges 1864, on ancient Rome; Vogt 1965, on Maya).

The elite, therefore, also lived in households—elevated as they were, literally as well as symbolically, above the rest of the population. The nature of the household remained much the same in both elite and non-elite contexts, however, in terms of the archaeologically accessible evidence of the material conditions of everyday life. I would suggest that an important difference between the Cahokia site and other Mississippian centers, aside from its great size, of course, is that its postulated 3-tier social system literally elevated its midrange elite (e.g., the *principales*) as well as the top-rank elite upon mounds. Otherwise, the layout and organization of households at Cahokia are much like that of smaller sites.

Production and Patrons

We have little historical evidence of the sponsorship of any form of production by the elites, except for those kinds of "production" associated with or resulting from the sponsorship of festivals. I feel it is reasonable to argue that mound construction was one such class of production in prehistoric times. There are historical accounts, such as those of du Ru and others in the Lower Mississippi Valley, that some fields were set aside for elite purposes. These, in fact, were generally associated with festivals, since the crops grown in them would be used for that purpose. These fields were worked by the public, who were mobilized for that purpose on a set day.

Artistic endeavors—so-called "prestige goods"—may have been sponsored, but there is little evidence that I can find in either the historical or archaeological record of such a practice for Mississippian societies. What we know archaeologically is that some persons seem to have done more of some of these production activities than others, but what we do not find is any clear evidence that their households or even themselves were in anyway exempted from other activities on that account. Most of these activities seem to have been done by too many people to be good candidates for either sponsored and/or specialist production. In short, the suggestion of "attached" specialists in Mississippian society so far has no more evidence behind it than the older idea of so-called "craft specialization." As noted in Chapter 8, the somewhat higher concentration of display goods in the hands of the elite may be expected from causes that have no connection to their sponsorship, or not, of specialist production. Neither condition is absolutely impossible, especially at Cahokia, but I cannot see that either has yet been proved to be necessary from the evidence we now have. The next chapter deals with this issue at greater length, so let us go on to see what Mississippian elites do seem to have done in terms of production sponsorship.

Production Mode and Leadership Character

The likelihood that the Mississippian household can be considered a kind of module from which to build more complex communities has implications for Mississippian social structure. A household as a primary social unit has a kind of limited horizon, and its importance in Mississippian societies is part of the reason why these did not develop into statelike social formations.

Marx in the *18th Brumaire* (1852[1975:17–171]) discussed the relationship between isolated, nearly self-sufficient production units and political development in pre-Second Empire France, taking up where we left off in a quotation at the end of the last chapter:

> In this way, the great mass of the French nation is formed by the simple addition of homologous magnitudes, much as potatoes in a sack form a sack of potatoes. In so far as millions of families live under economic conditions of existence that separate their mode of life, their interests and their culture from those of other classes, and put them into hostile opposition to the latter, they form a class. In so far as there is merely a local interconnection among these small-holding peasants, and the identity of their interests begets no community, no national bond and no political organisation among them, they do not form a class. They are consequently incapable of enforcing their class interests in their own name, whether through a parliament or through a convention. They cannot represent themselves, they must be represented. Their representative must at the same time appear as their master, as an authority over them, as an unlimited governmental power that protects them against the other classes and sends them rain and sunshine from above. The political influence of the small-holding peasants, therefore, finds its final expression in the executive power subordinating society to itself.

I think that, with due recognition to economic and social differences, much the same situation held for largely autonomous Mississippian households. Of course, 18th- and 19th-century French peasantry were not Mississippian horticulturists. The French peasant was a specialist producer of sorts or, at the least, the last gasp of the domestic economy in a nation-state economy. The French peasantry, if not exactly a class, stood in opposition to existing classes. The French peasantry were embedded in a state-level system of long standing, so their conditions are certainly different from those of the Mississippian producer-families. Nonetheless, the same features that prevented the French peasant from achieving a form of class consciousness also hindered the independent development of anything like classes in Mississippian society. Production is linked to the political and economic superstructure. Since the households in the same locality are subject to the same local conditions as other households, local alliances with other kin groups provide only a modest buffer against broader scale problems. It is in these circumstances that the local horticultural producers, like their French counterparts, find their independence to be a burden, find their economic autonomy to be risky. Under these circumstances, they need some form of regional support system; the bureaucracy that administers that regional system becomes, in fact, their "master, as an authority over them, as an unlimited governmental power that protects them ... and sends them rain and sunshine from above"(Marx 1852[1965:171]). On a much smaller scale, the kinds of pressures that Marx suggested produced Napoleon III from a simple peasant mass, in a *non-class* society may produce a "chief" whose power rests precisely in the "provision of rain and sunshine from above"(1852[1965:171]), or—failing that—in the provision of relief for those whose crops and fields have failed them. The scale of Mississippian society did not allow the great power that was exercised by the French emperor, but the dignity and even authority that *was* held by Mississippian chiefs far exceeded anything seen in the Southeast before.

5. LOCATION

Local and Dispersed Production

Years ago (1986a), I made a distinction between *producer specialization* and *site specialization*. I had thought this a fairly obvious point that was sometimes overlooked simply because of loose usage and confusion of criteria for localized production as opposed to true craft specialization, referring to actual differentiation of labor in the classic economic sense. I suppose the distinction has proved useful, since it has often been cited in the literature on production. However, I have somewhat regretted that I used the term *specialization* at all in the sense of a location of production, since this is really only a limited activity zone, in any real sense. The simplest limited activity sites are those that are both close to a particular resource and do not possess other features that make them attractive for a more diversified range of activities. So it is that a low ridge adjacent to a slough may have come to be used predominantly in dry seasons for fishing. A cherty blufftop area may have been used only or primarily for obtaining and processing blanks for tool manufacture. Other kinds of sites were less "limited," to the extent that they were attractive for a broader range of acquisitive and manufacturing behaviors. The "typical" Mississippian site, to the extent that there is such a thing, was a location used for many purposes. In the end, it comes down to what we have seen again and again in this society, that a household or groups of households had the full range of human living literally "taking place." There need not have been a gradual range in Mississippian production in space and time between large and small sites. Some sites surely had functions and activities that did not take place everywhere, but the differences between household activities at large sites and small sites were generally less than commonly proposed or appreciated.

Scale of Production

From time to time, claims for large-scale Mississippian production have also been made, often in combination with discussions of localization of production. There is no doubt that some Mississippian production locations are marked by extensive middens or widespread production debris. Of course, this is commonly true at relatively localized sources; but their extent, like that of large Paleo-Indian sites in the Northeast, more often reflects centuries of reuse rather than truly large-scale production. At the same time, there can be little doubt that the scale of production of raw materials such as chert or salt was certainly greater at the peak of Mississippian that it was before or after. Before we can accept claims of massive Mississippian production systems, we need better chronologies of occupation and of production activities, together with some demonstration that contemporary activities exceeded the scale observed historically in the Southeast. The best cases so far, for organized production are the palisade lines and single-mound stages, and neither of these represents what could be described as subsistence or materials production.

6. TIME

Amount of Labor Investment

I have already discussed some kinds of labor "costs" in discussing mound construction and crops, so I am merely going to comment here on the costs of production, such as the making of goods. What we need are more models like those for mound construction that examine probable labor and energy *costs* and *investments*, even though neither of these terms is particularly felicitous. Not the least of the usefulness of such estimations lies in providing concrete targets for improvement.

Despite the problems of pinning down fine-grained chronologies for Mississippian production, we do have many cases of short-term and some middle-term kinds of production activities. Of course, the most common activities are those involving home and hearth—food preparation and the preparation of raw materials for use in production are the key activities in the household units. Some kinds of production, such as making pecked stone items and engraved shell or other shell objects, were almost certainly activities undertaken over many weeks and even months. My own experimentation with making a small shell gorget suggests that even taking out a blank disk from a whelk shell must have involved many tedious hours of cutting with stone tools. Over 2 hours of cutting with a graver on chert blades produced a barely visible groove in the surface of the shell. Even with a high-speed rotary hobbyist tool with carbide-steel bits (after wearing out several conventional tool bits) and Carborundum™ cutting wheels, I spent some 4 to 5 hours in cutting out a small blank.

Production of shell items in Melanesia was normally time-consuming, and the production of shell artifacts was embedded in a domestic setting, while their exchange was either with uxorial kin and husband or in the context of the broader Kula exchange system itself (Malinowski 1922: Chapter 15; also Weiner 1976). I would suggest that even at its greatest "florescence," the manufacture of display goods and other items in Mississippian society shared many aspects with Melanesian shell production (and other Melanesian skilled production; e.g., Gerbrands 1967). The key is that such activities do not, as a rule, displace primary subsistence activities but are undertaken alongside them, or as an auxiliary activity in off times or seasons.

Schedule of Production

We cannot say much, nor do we need to, about the scheduling of production in Mississippian societies, except that subsistence activities were bound to have precedence in most decisions about timing of production activities. Some kinds of production appear to have been curtailed by early Mississippian times as a result of the shift to horticultural production. Some hunting and collection activities that conflicted with higher priority activities relating to crops were abandoned altogether or reduced in intensity. Of course, gender differences in production activities may have reduced some scheduling conflicts. Other activities were deferred until planting or harvest were complete and fields could be left alone safely for a time. Altogether, Mississippian producers faced the same kinds of problems faced by domestic producers everywhere—everything is done in the home, mostly by the same people, so there is always difficulty in the busiest times in finding the necessary labor. In such a situation, hard choices have to be made about which activities will yield the greatest return. Maximization of *desired* return for a minimum of effort is not, after all, only a capitalist or class–society choice. Optimization of some kind is an evolutionary alternative, not just a personal choice, affecting the survival of individuals and societies. The world is not linear in its organization, but human efforts to exploit resources *are* largely linear and sequential, so a kind of script can be given for the sequence of choices faced in practice by producers. Although we do not know the details well, we know that certain activities followed one another in a repeating, annual round of all kinds of production.

Winter was the slowest time for subsistence production. If the preceding year had been good, stored food in the form of grain, nuts, and other dried and preserved foods would last through the winter and early spring. Such a time would surely have been used for auxiliary production of implements, clothing, gear, and display objects for the year to come, just as European farmers used such times for "harness mending." Of course, if stored food proved inadequate, then a terrible struggle would have begun to eke out enough food until new food resources were available. Hunting was one of the few ways to obtain much wintertime additional resources, and some denning or hibernating animals might be taken then, even conserved for such times.

Spring, of course, was a time of renewal of resources, but early spring could easily be the hardest time of all if stored resources had run out. A number of famine-food plants and animals might be taken at this time that would have been ignored otherwise. However, with enough stored food in reserve, this would have been a time of working the fields, preparing the first planting, and harvesting early wild and domesticated products. The primary scheduling conflicts at this time would be those between collecting enough to meet current needs against the preparatory labor needed for the main harvests later on in the year. If stored foods were still available, they might well have been consumed in a feast together with new, spring crops (e.g., Le Page du Pratz 1758, on the feast of the Month of the Deer [March]). In historical times, "tribute" owed the chief was brought in for the feasts, although this seems more like "potluck" than tribute to me. Spring is one possible time for public works associated with consumption of some of the previous year's surplus, together with the new crops of various kinds. The first "stomp" dance of the historical Creek was probably such a ceremonial occasion (Swanton 1928b:550–551). Symbolic acts of renewal combined with practical acts of relief of shortages in such times.

Summer provided a rich harvest of wild resources, while labor was required for maintenance of fields for later harvest. Aside from protecting the growing plants from animal and plant invaders—an activity that doubtless had its own production by-products—many historical peoples found this an ideal time to abandon their fields temporarily and go out on long hunts. We have little evidence of this in Mississippian times, but there are indications of extensive hunting at great distances in more northern historical societies.

The late summer to early fall, depending on the local harvest time, was also a time of festivals celebrating the new maize crop. This is another likely possibility for public works, using up the last of the old crop and heralding the advent of the new. Historically, the harvest-festival maize may have sometimes been grown in special fields reserved for that purpose and tended by males (Le Page du Pratz 1758).

The best of all seasons had to have been fall. After all the problems of shortages of stored foods and other scarcities of needed resources in many other times of the year, at last there was plenty of everything. However, this very plenty is a kind of "convoy" strategy that evolved among prey species—"scheduling" their times of maximum risk with as many alternatives as possible, ensuring that there would be so many targets that predators could not possibly take them all. Fall is a time of plenty, but also a time of making many decisions about what game and plants to take, and which to ignore, although this is more true in the northern Mississippian localities than in the more southern ones. Even in southern Mississippian, however, the planting of early *and* late maize crops in different fields would still mean some overlapping of activities. The Mississippian choice in most localities developed into one that placed the primary emphasis on harvesting crops, keeping open the possibility of shifting to wild resources when there were disastrous failures in horticultural production. Otherwise, some persons might be detached to collect or hunt at harvest, especially since animals would have also been attracted to the ripe foods in the fields. Most people, however, would have first completed the labor of harvest, and only then shifted to collection of the most desirable wild foods, even though many plants and other resources might have already been past peak harvest by this time. For example, production of salt in the Lower Ohio was undertaken mostly in fall, mostly after maize harvest in that locality (Muller 1992).

The end of the fall season also involved much preparation of the domestic and wild products for storage. Both storage preparation and cooking affect the nutritional value of the foods, and preparation and processing often require significant amounts of labor. More detailed studies of Mississippian production systems need to pay more attention to these labor and energy costs, along the lines already done for Fort Ancient complexes (Reidhead 1981).

7. COMMENTS AND CONCLUSIONS

Mode of Production

The nature of production among Mississippian peoples was domestic, expedient, and practical. The vast majority of needed resources for construction and manufacture were available locally and available directly to each household without outside control or restriction. The exceptions were few and their importance in terms of survival questionable. There was no *monopoly* in Mississippian society of any resource that was critical to survival. There were certainly differences in access to the raw materials of life but no evidence that anyone could deny anyone else such critical goods by virtue of their status or rank. The differences seen in recent studies of access to some goods (Jackson and Scott 1995) do not seem to suggest that the necessities of life were denied to some and given to others.

Object of Labor

The natural resources of a region were the main objects of labor, whether field or raw material. Mississippians use of their environment had some impact upon it in terms of vegetation and game availability. Indeed, lighter Mississippian use of uplands may have allowed some restoration of pre–Late Woodland conditions in the uplands, although we cannot honestly suppose the impact in either pre-Mississippian or Mississippian times to have been great. It is possible that the use of fire in hunting may have had more effect than clearing upland fields. In the floodplain localities, there were, however, substantial changes from earlier times. Concentrations of populations in the relatively circumscribed floodplains meant that at least the best soils were pretty much all cleared at one time or another. The extent of Mississippian settlement in the Black Bottom corresponds closely to the areas cleared for cultivation in the same locality by 19th- and early 20th-century American farmers.

Copper, marine shell, and probably furs and feathers were all exchanged widely, but these imported materials pale in comparison to stone hoes in both mass and survival importance, so far as we can tell from archaeological evidence. Chapter 8 examines the patterns of their distribution to see what the nature of exchange was for these goods. Their local use, however, shows little sign of the often-proposed concentrations around the elites at central sites *in those cases where we have an adequate sample of nonelite contexts.* It is certainly the case in the Black Bottom that so-called "prestige goods" are not especially limited to central sites or to persons that can reasonably be entitled "elite," and there is increasing evidence that this was also the case in the American Bottom and elsewhere. Indeed, I will venture to predict that once we have a good look generally at small sites, as well as the large ones, this will turn out to be the common situation in Mississippian societies, not the rarity some now feel it to be.

Tools of Labor

Most Mississippian tools were expedient rather than carefully made and curated artifacts. The most important imported raw material and finished tool in terms of being directly related to survival was the stone hoe. Yet, as I suggested earlier, the numbers of these objects and their by-products in absolute terms are relatively less than one might expect if they were absolutely necessary for Mississippian horticultural production, when the extent and great area of Mississippian settlement is taken into account. After all, 3 or 4 hundred years of stone hoe use and sharpening by every single producer would mean many more hoe chips and much more Mill Creek or Dover flakes (from recycling broken hoes into flake cores) than are actually found at Mississippian sites.

The fields themselves were a kind of tool in organizing land for production (as noted long ago by Marx 1867 [1906:199; 1965:52ff.]), and issues of soil fertility have been raised that will require a closer look in the future at possible indications of periodic abandonment and resettlement.[7]

---

[7] I must, however, say that if the fields were used for shorter periods, as suggested in Baden's model, and by fewer people, then the mystery of the missing hoes would also be explained, even if every producer used these implements. This would imply, however, that Mississippian societies were even smaller than I have suggested.

Agency

Mounds as an indicator of public activity suggest organized labor, but the scale of that labor has often been exaggerated or simply misunderstood. The labor investment in mounds is properly thought to be symbolic, but like all symbolic behavior, it derives from real causes. Of course, mounds were refuges from floods; but, more importantly, they were material reflections of duties owed, of social obligations resulting from asymmetrical economic relationships. Here was not true alienation of labor, given that the scale of labor owed was relatively small. But it was a social obligation owed in labor to one who did not own the workers, but who had claims upon them that were beyond those relatively symmetrical relationships that exist within families and among *most* clan members. Other kinds of labor were either domestic or communal. Little solid evidence exists for any real *control* of labor by elites, although they can surely be seen as *mobilizing* labor.

The Household Unit of Production Labor

In nearly every aspect of Mississippian production, the household was the unit that seems to have had the responsibility of both reproduction and production. Mississippian settlements were made up of clusters of these entities, and the production activities seen archaeologically or historically are similar from the smallest to the greatest.

Elites

I do not want to downplay the importance of elites in Mississippian society, however much that may seem to be the case. Chiefs, their families, and other officers were surely the most important individuals in Mississippian society. However, no good purpose is served by an exaggeration of their importance, either. Events such as major festivals, surely including major commitments of public labor, were sponsored by various levels of elite members of society, but the absolute differences in access to goods of any kind were less than an archaeology based on large, central sites has suggested. I think more work in the immediate hinterlands of any large site will, as it has in the Black Bottom and the American Bottom, show us societies with relatively little "hard" social differentiation.

Location

Most Mississippian production, like most Mississippian residence, was localized in small homesteads. Although claims have been made for nondomestic localization of particular "industries," I do not consider that these are yet firmly established for any Mississippian production system, including Cahokia (see Chapter 7). I suspect that it will prove impossible to do so. This is not to deny that a low level of localization of special kinds (NOT *specialization*) of production is common. Differences of skill and talent will exist, but even highly localized and large-scale (for Mississippian) production sites that have been investigated at the Union County chert quarries or the Great Salt Spring have not shown specialist production. I do not see the evidence for either ceramic or shell-object manufacture as suggesting true specialization, either, although these show the kinds of differences that could be the germ of specialization.

Time

Finally, the timing of Mississippian production is marked by the same constraints that affect horticultural producers anywhere. The development of horticultural systems initially frees societies from some risks, but it ties populations to places and times to an even greater degree than is characteristic of hunters or collectors. It is simply that the choices at any given time are so much more constrained and the alternatives fewer.

Chapter 7

Mississippian Production II
Differentiation

Και κεραμευς κεραμει κοτεει
(The potter is hostile to the potter.)
Hesiod

1. DIFFERENTIATION OF PRODUCTION

Specialist production has played an important part in theories of the development of social stratification in an extensive literature on that topic in economics and political economy. For the most part, specialization has been proposed as developing in one or another contexts—in production of staple commodities (e.g., Engels 1891, Service 1962, 1975) or in production of finely made goods (as per Earle 1987). This chapter will discuss some of the theories about specialization and its roles in terms of the case for developing hierarchy in Mississippian societies. I want to stress that the concept of *specialization* is most useful when it is returned to its meaning in economic theory and not redefined in some form that is unique to archaeology. It is also important that any proposal for specialist production be defined in a logical, *testable* way that addresses the core issues. Some degree of specialization has been widely proposed in association with developing hierarchies in the East (e.g., Pauketat 1987b, 1994; Prentice 1983, cf. Prentice 1985; Yerkes 1983, 1986). As I noted in the last chapter, time and more evidence have brought greater caution, and most recent claims for labor differentiation in Mississippian are qualified or phrased in terms such as "part-time" or "household" specialization (e.g., see Pauketat 1987b, 1994; Prentice 1985). The term *craft production* has been introduced recently in order to avoid dealing with the issue of specialization, but there is still a problem. *Craft*, itself, seems to confuse the recent informal usage of *craft* as *hobby*, as in "craft show," with its traditional use in economics and history to refer to a skilled trade, business, or profession by which persons earn their living.

289

In this chapter, I shall provide a little background for discussions of specialization and then outline some tests for conditions of specialization in Mississippian archaeology, with more extensive discussion of some specific cases.

Background

Specialization has been an important component of theories about the evolution of hierarchical distinctions ever since scholars postulated the "Great Divisions of Labor" (from Marx 1852 and Engels 1891, up to Tosi 1984) as critical events in the development of "civilization." The problem of identifying either domestic or specialist production has been considered important enough to generate a substantial number of studies (e.g., J. Arnold 1984; P. Arnold 1991, Brumfiel 1987; among many, many more). Specialization is by no means the only postulated organizational feature of hierarchical development, but the elites themselves may become "specialists" in a nontrivial sense. *Efficiency* "in the division of labor" is often ranked as an important variable in understanding stratification (e.g., Lenski 1966; Turner 1984). Production for external exchange and the increasing importance of balanced reciprocity are also seen as part of the process of social differentiation (e.g., Durkheim 1893; Luhmann 1982:198ff.).

"Resource concentration" has also played an important role in other theories of the origins of hierarchical systems (Carneiro 1970), although such approaches do not necessarily involve specialization, as such. Some theoretical discussions do place specialization at the very core of the development of hierarchical systems (e.g., Jacobs 1967; Service 1962,1975). Service focused on specialization in production of staple goods as a precursor to hierarchical development that provided differential production bases for "redistribution" (Service 1975). In such terms, the uneven distribution of critical natural resources is supposed to have led to specialized production at restricted localities, thus encouraging the development of local hierarchies.

However, as Earle has shown in the Hawaiian case, redistribution of the sort proposed by Service does not appear to exist there (1977, 1978). Rather, local production was similar from one location to another but, according to Earle, was used to provide "staple" finance supporting "nonproducers" (1987). In Earle's analysis, what he calls "craft specialists" in this highly developed chiefdom were used to convert "staple finance" into "wealth finance" used to exert control over larger areas. Variants of this "prestige goods" model have become popular in Mississippian studies (e.g., Welch 1986, 1991). In this sense, a distinction between specialist production of elite goods as opposed to the domestic production of staples is important. As Earle and others have suggested (1987; Muller 1987a), staple-production specialization does not seem to have been common, if it *ever* occurred, in developing hierarchical societies. An alternative focus of specialization may have been display (a.k.a. "prestige,") goods production by workers dependent on elites (Earle 1981, 1987). Unfortunately, this issue is still largely unresolved, since rigorous tests have only been applied to a few proposed cases of staple or "wealth" production. Mississippian archaeologists, as we have seen in the previous chapters, now have enough data on production to assess the nature of proposed specialist production in more detail than has been the case earlier.

Among other problems, there has also been a confusion, especially in archaeology, of different levels of phenomena such as "site specialization" (or even "tool specialization") with "producer specialization" (Muller 1984a; also see Goody 1982:3–7 for a similar distinction). The mere presence of a tool kit defined for some particular task, for example, is not sufficient evidence of a particular *social status* for the person using the tools. Localization of production can be caused by many factors as well. Nonspecialist production can be localized at concentrations of natural resources, so spatial concentration is by no means a sufficient indicator of the specialist character of production. In archaeological literature, unfortunately, terms referring to supposed specialization of various kinds have been very loosely applied, often in ways that are at odds with usage in other fields. Costin has provided a valuable catalogue of the current terms as redefined in archaeology (1991) but has not undertaken the task of assessing whether these definitions are useful or merely idiosyncratic to our field.

Craft specialization, especially, is one of those social phenomena that follows a version of Yoffee's Rule (originally put forth in the context of "states", 1993:69) that may be generalized and paraphrased as: "If you can argue whether it is or isn't, then it isn't." Only divorcing of specialization from its social and economic context makes it seem merely different in degree from !Kung manufactures that Clark and Parry called "specialization" in a very broad sense (1990). On the contrary, true specialization is not something that can long persist as merely a few workers in a larger mass of domestic producers, since the very presence of specialists creates a whole set of social interdependencies that fundamentally transform production as more and more workers find themselves becoming producers, sellers, and purchasers in noncommunal settings. I repeat: specialization is a social, as much as an economic, transformation of the relations of production—as everyone seems to acknowledge and then forget. There are certainly different kinds of "real" specialization, such as the distinction of "attached specialists" made by Earle (1981). Nonetheless, specialization, in the strict sense, implies that production is the manufacture of *commodities* for exchange, that specialist producers no longer can directly provide sustenance to refresh and reproduce their own labor power, and that relationships of exchange replace those of kin, among many other alterations of relationships to people and things. Commoditization of product, in turn, makes it much, much easier for "nonproducers" to extract surplus value from the producer. These are, I suggest, revolutionary, not incidental, changes in the organization of a society.

Craft specialization is a key factor in the distinction between *Gemeinschaft* and *Gesellschaft*. Whole new sets of social distinctions and relationships come into play when survival of the producers depends upon their craft rather than their domestic context (see Meillassoux 1981, for examples of the interaction of domestic with nondomestic economies). This is not merely a terminological quibble over how much time is spent at a craft before it is "specialized," but a fundamental theoretical problem concerning one basis of hierarchical development. Nor is the issue simply one of different philosophical schools. The research on this topic contributes to the debate over this important transition in social life. No primary examples of these developments have survived for examination, so the problem is fundamentally an archaeological one.

Finally, not the least of the problems in dealing with specialization is a tendency to treat the specialist (or not) character of production as a "type" of organization that can be identified by some trait list of criteria. Although we do need to look at the conditions or criteria that mark different production systems, it is critical that these be considered in the context of a political economy, as parts of modes of production, rather than isolated types of behavior (as also noted forcefully by Cobb 1993d). As one of the best-known, nonstate systems, clarifying the issues of Mississippian specialist production has broad significance in the study of political economy in nonstate, nonclass, but hierarchically organized societies.

To treat craft specialization, *a priori*, as a gradualistic development begs the whole question of its role—whether as cause, effect, *or* insignificance—in the major social, political, and economic transformation of society that occurs sometime and somewhere between "tribes" and "states." The simple observation that once there were only small, nonhierarchically organized societies and today there are almost only large-scale, class societies may be sneered at as "neoevolutionary." Nonetheless, it seems to me that this is one of the more important questions that we deal with as archaeologists, and we need to deal with it better than we have done so far.

Dimensions of Specialization

In the more general literature on political economy, efforts have been made to define the dimensions of specialization. For example, Blau(1977:187) has categorized the range of task variability as it is concerned with variation among persons and across time periods (Table 7.1).

One kind of specialization is tasks that vary from one specialist producer to another, but are routinized for each producer through time (3, Table 7.1). A second form of specialization (4, Table 7.1) is characterized by variability both among persons and through time. Blau characterizes this form of division of labor as "specialized expertness" along the lines of medical specialists as opposed to general practitioners (1977:188). It is difficult to identify this kind of activity in production systems, since a broad range of different "expert" activities would have been involved in each specialist's activities.

The key to specialization is not only variation among persons and tasks, but also the relationship of the tasks to the full, annual cycle of production. Of course, seasonal and other environmental variation necessarily causes some simple temporal and spatial variation in production. For this reason, it is critical to determine the time span over which "repetition" is defined. In the Mississippian cases to be discussed below, the evidence shows a production situation that is essentially repetitive over time and persons. A typical Mississippian producer would have performed much the

Table 7.1. Tasks and Specialization

		Task variability among persons	
		Repetitive	Variable
Task variability among time periods {	Repetitive	1. All same routine	3. Routinized division of labor
	Variable	2. All same "craft"	4. Specialized division of labor

same activities each year and at the same time as other producers. Although it is possible that elites were exempt from some productive activities, little evidence suggests that even the elite activity cycle would have been distinguished except by preferential access to the same resources utilized by all households. Skilled persons may have produced wealth items during inactive periods in the horticultural cycle, but the distribution of such producers argues against their being considered specialists, as opposed to merely persons with special skills (often misleadingly called "part-time specialists"). Variability in persons and time exists under such conditions, but since the activity in question is supplemental and not in conflict with primary productive activities, it should not be taken as proof of "division of labor." Blau (1977:188) points out that the organization of routinized division of labor may require expert management and organization. A somewhat similar concept of work organized almost entirely by repetition of a small repertoire of actions for each worker is called *Arbeitszerlegung* by Bücher (1898). Such kinds of specialization seem to be a *sine qua non* for machine production, but assembly-line production is not a serious concern in societies at the Mississippian level.

Other, more or less formal models of social differentiation are found in works such as those of Turner (1984) and Lenski (1966). Turner treats specialization ("differentiation of productive positions") as a special case of homogeneous subpopulation development (1984:147–152). In Turner's model, specialists ought to be engaged in "modal behaviors that distinguish them from others." In general, this argument is that specialists ought to be distinctive from other segments of their society in more than just their productive technology. As applied to Mississippian production, this would imply that true specialists might be expected to mark their occupational status with patterns markedly different than those of agricultural producers, even in their domestic circumstances. These differences need not be at castelike levels to be distinguishable in the archaeological record.

It may be asked what kinds of goods might be expected to show the earliest development of specialization. Clearly, Service's model suggests that the earliest specialist production should be in those areas of primary production most closely associated with subsistence. Salt and hoe production qualify under these models as likely primary foci of specialization. Earle suggested that specialization may first appear in the context of wealth conversion (e.g., 1987). In that model, display or fancy goods production would be the likely early focus of specialization.

In the economic and sociological literature on social stratification and specialization, sources generally agree on the broad profile of specialist production. Its features include differentiation of specialist producers from other producers in both productive and domestic circumstances, homogeneity of production, and an emphasis on exchange. The literature also supports a close association of specialist production, as defined here, and the full development of hierarchies. The relative timing and course of development of specialist production in relation to hierarchical organization and other social forms in prestate systems is a question at the root of social theory. Mississippian production is an especially apt test case for this investigation because of its pristine context. This is a hierarchical system that does not show much differentiation, but claims for specialization have been made for production of display goods, salt, and chert.

Proposals of specialization in archaeological contexts include complexes in the Near East (e.g., Tosi 1984), the Aegean (e.g., Renfrew 1972), among many other areas—but often for societies that meet Yoffee's Rule for being states. Unfortunately, many of the criteria suggested as markers for craft specialization are *not* necessary "test implications" for that economic status. In many cases, the criteria seem better for identifying specific craft specialists in societies *for which specialization is a given* than they are for identification of whether or not specialization itself exists. This situation is another reason why nonstate systems such as Mississippian are important to study.

Evans (1978) summarized a series of expectations for craft specialization. Even though Evans used the term *craft specialization* in a very broad sense of merely a skill not otherwise present in a society (even suggesting that craft specialization was present in the Paleolithic), his suggestions for identifying it are more narrowly defined. He suggested (1978:115) that specialization should (1) be limited to a small percentage of the society, (2) replace basic subsistence activities to some degree, and (3) therefore, be dependent upon other producers (through exchange). Other criteria included the presence of workshops, tool kits, storage for craft products, limited resource exploitation, and so on. For reasons I have mentioned and discussed elsewhere (Muller 1984a, 1986a, 1987a), I believe that the term *craft specialization* should be restricted to producers whose livelihoods depend upon their craft. Even so, Evans's basic criteria were, and are, an extremely useful starting point for placing the discussion of specialization on a firmer basis. At the same time, *as Evans explicitly pointed out* (1978:115), many of his criteria for recognizing specialist production are clearly neither fully necessary nor sufficient to establish specialization without attention to their "societal or communal context." Unfortunately, some discussion of specialization has tended to apply criteria such as the presence of "specialized" tool kits as though they were invariant markers of specialist production, regardless of context. It is also unlikely that true specialization would meet the first of Evans's criteria of being limited to a few members of a society, since the onset of specialization, as discussed elsewhere, forces more and more members of a society into specialization, because of the second and third of these criteria (see Jacobs 1967). For example, in full-scale class societies, even primary food producers become specialists—"peasants."

Rice (1981, 1989) has drawn attention to some other markers of specialization. Among the most important of these is the presence of standardization of both the products *and* the means of production. Of course, some kinds of standardized production can occur in nonspecialist production (see Hodder 1983:86–88). For example, no one, to my knowledge, has ever proposed that the highly standardized form and size of Mississippian structures is an indication that they were built by "craft specialists."[1] Clearly, conformity to needs can produce a kind of standardization that has nothing to do with any form of specialization.

---

[1] Although Pauketat (1994:172–173) does propose that Early Cahokia houses were built by nondomestic "work crews," to explain the rapid transition to wall-trench construction. It is hard to see why this is necessary, since there was an equally rapid adoption of this technique, even in isolated farmsteads, all over the Mississippian world.

Another key feature of specialist production is production for exchange. Blau (1977:195) raises this to the level of a theorem: "The division of labor depends upon opportunities for communication." Through scale and skill, specialist production is usually more efficient than nonspecialist production; and the quantities of goods produced, almost by definition, exceed the needs of local consumers. Whether there is "surplus" in more than a temporary sense is not germane here, but production for exchange clearly requires temporary surpluses of goods beyond the producer's own needs in that class of goods. Exchange exists without specialization, but specialization nearly always implies exchange; and evidence for exchange is important in assessing claims for specialist production. Indeed, the presence of true trade and markets may be taken as a strongly supporting a conclusion of specialist production in cases where they are present. Markets, in the strict sense, are not a *sine qua non* for specialization, but markets of some kind are probably the most common means of distributing the production of specialists.

In addition, there has come to be an argument, sometimes stated fairly explicitly (as in Renfrew 1982:265), that subsistence surpluses are necessary to support specialist producers. Although this is true if we consider individual producers and households, we have to remember Sahlins' point that societies, not just individuals are provisioned (1972: 187n; also see Halstead 1989:69). A detailed consideration of whether specialization "costs" or "pays" is not critical to our concerns in identifying whether specialization existed in Mississippian societies, but it is certainly possible that early or "emergent" specialization may have brought in new outside resources. It is not impossible that a little extra production for exchange of some goods such as salt or chert may have become like "profit centers" in the quaint terminology of late-20th-century capitalism. In a very real sense, one impetus to developing specialist producers would be that their provisioning and more besides could be carried by the external consumers of their commodities, rather than by the society in which they reside. This also raises the issue of whether the role of elites in sponsoring specialists is a usual condition for specialization.

Patronage of a simple sort is characteristic of societies that are weakly differentiated (e.g., Gerbrands on Melanesian woodcarving, 1967), but there is a fine line between sponsoring an event and commissioning an object. The role of ironworkers as unattached, wandering specialists in some regions of West Africa is well known, and the degree of attachment to elites is highly variable (see Meillassoux 1981:37–38, who makes a distinction between a *specialty* and *specialization*).

In other circumstances, there is what has sometimes been called "specialization" of production on a village level. For example, the production of some goods for the Kula took place in circumstances in which certain items were only made in certain places (Malinowski 1922). This, of course, is not specialist production, but rather ritually (or economically) *restricted* production in relation to an exchange system. The goods produced are valuables for exchange but not commodities.

Costin has surveyed specialization and presented a general discussion of the identification of specialization (1991). She is, however, dealing more with "organization of production" than "specialization" (as the title of her Figure 1.4 tacitly acknowledges). As a discussion of "the organization of production," her summary is quite useful. She has taken an explicitly gradualist view of specialization (1991:4) that is, I believe, fundamentally wrong. Her treatment is thus somewhat marred as a discussion of *specialization* by its insistence on massing together all kinds of production as occurring along an putative *continuum* of specialization. Even so, many useful elements are to be found in Costin's "typology of specialized production." She appropriately adopts (1991:7) some aspects of a discussion developed by Peacock for Roman ceramic production (1982), but Peacock's concern is another of those distinguishing among different kinds of specialization in a society that was indisputably "differentiated." It is a different research problem to distinguish between specialization or its absence in societies that are not known to have been differentiated.

Costin discusses organization of production in terms of four "parameters": **context** (by which she refers to the degree of elite sponsorship), **concentration** (spatial extent), **scale** (on a gradation from kin to factory), and **intensity** (part-time to full-time production activities). From these dimensions she constructs eight types. Table 7.2 indicates the relation among Costin's parameters and her types. The table has been modified from Costin's original presentation in the order of the rows and columns, arranged here by her criteria of intensity and scale.

Resorting this table in this way helps to illuminate some of the difficulties if the word *specialization* is used. *Corvée*, for example, refers to an element of compulsion in mobilization of labor power in many societies but does not have much to do with specialization of any kind. One way or another, societies attempt to make tasks that need to be done seem desirable, so the issue of labor mobilization may have less to do with the exercise of force than one might initially expect. In addition, features such as *nucleation* and *dispersal* constitute dimensions that are more contextual than criterial. Costin's discussion is a step in the right direction, but we have to tease apart these issues more fully to find those that are most relevant to "specialization."

2. WHAT NEEDS TO BE DONE?

As nearly everyone agrees, production has to be assessed in terms of its social context (e.g., Cobb 1993d; Costin 1991; Costin and Hagstrum 1995; Evans 1978;

Table 7.2. Costin's Parameters and Production Types

Type	Intensity (% time)		Scale (composition)		Context (elite sponsorship)		Concentration (spatial)	
	Part-time	Full-time	Labor	Kin-based	Attached	Independent	Nucleated	Dispersed
Dispersed workshop		X	X			X		X
Nucleated workshop		X	X			X	X	
Retainer workshop		X	X		X		X	
Individual workshop		X		(X)	X		(X)	
Dispersed corvée	X		(X)	(X)	X			X
Nucleated corvée	X		X		X		X	
Individual	(X)	(X)		X		X		X
Community	(X)	(X)		X		X	X	

Adapted from Costin 1991: Table 1.1.

Muller 1986a). How are we to do this? I set out some of the dimensions that needed to be examined at the Great Salt Spring in a National Science Foundation proposal in 1988 (BNS-8907424; also see Muller et al. 1992). This categorization covered some of the things we needed to do to test for producer specialization, but only as a beginning, not as a complete analysis of production activities. The following list is generalized from those in terms of attempting to set an archaeological context:

1. Extent of activity
2. Intensity of activity
3. Continuity of activity (including duration and seasonality)
4. Differentiation of activity (including limited activity areas)
5. Production and consumption character (especially in domestic contexts)
6. Indications of external goods and exchange

Each of these dimensions, and more, is important to the assessment of the social context of proposed specialist production. The nature of these variables can often be assessed with data from Mississippian sites—ranging from large mound centers, on one end of the scale, to small farmsteads, on the other. A comparison of proposed "specialists" in each case has to be made with domestic producers elsewhere in the Mississippian society.

Extent of Activity

One of the central, and often overlooked, aspects of any production system is its spatial scale. Any kind of "concentration" can only be judged in terms of a context, and production localization has to be assessed on spatial scales of community, locality, and region. *Extent* is a relative term that has to be placed in both social and geographic contexts. Localization of production, as already discussed, can occur for many reasons. Sometimes the reasons are obvious: Catlinite production in Minnesota must necessarily have been carried out where the raw material was available. Of course, localization of nonspecialized *and* specialized production can occur for many reasons. For example, gender division of labor can produce localization under circumstances in which the sexes congregate or cooperate in their work. Thus, a men's house may have a high degree of localization of male production activities, without the slightest degree of nongender differentiation of production. Of course, these kinds of activities provide the raw material from which such institutions as craft guilds can be built as a society differentiates. Nonetheless, the impression of continuity is false, since the *social* and *economic* contexts of a men's house and a guild are by no means the same—just as a flipper is no longer a paw despite its having evolved from one.

In fact, the spatial distribution of production is not the best place to look for solid evidence of production specialization except under very special circumstances such as *barrio* production systems. To be sure, a conclusion of true specialization might be strengthened by the presence of coresidential neighborhoods in which *only* certain production activities took place. These patterns, however, are unlikely in early specialist systems, precisely because the spatial clustering of producers is usually a response, or at least a correlate, of large-scale production. Nonetheless, although spatial patterns are rarely "criterial attributes" that can be used to identify production "types," they are important background from which to judge other criteria such as scale of production.

Intensity of Activity

On the whole, intensity of activity is often a better place to examine the character of production than is spatial concentration, since truly large-scale production is unlikely in nondifferentiated production systems. The catch, of course, is that there must be *contemporaneous* large-scale production, not just masses of archaeological evidence. As we shall see, massive cultural deposits at limited-activity production sites such as chert quarries and salt springs in Mississippian times do not prove that activities *at any one time* were intensive. Another problem in using intensity as a measure is that of actually deciding how *much* it takes to be *intensive*. These measures are necessarily relative and must take the scale and size of the society and the producer scale into account.

Again, intensive production of woven goods in a men's structure, for example, is not significantly "specialist" in any very useful sense if the men involved are not undertaking this activity for exchange *and* are not using time that would ordinarily be used for socially necessary labor. The essence of specialization is the transformation of auxiliary production skills into socially necessary labor—labor that is meeting the basic needs of the biological and social reproduction of the producers. The intensity of production has to be measured against such standards, and placed into its social context, before it is a meaningful indicator of specialization. Archaeological detection of this transformation is not easy. Nonetheless, an increase of production to a scale far beyond what can be used by the producers and their immediate neighbors will often be associated with specialist production. Production on a local, rather than regional, scale will rarely be associated with true specialist production. In fully differentiated societies, the "auxiliary" labor beyond that needed for reproduction may be conceived as "surplus labor." If this labor is compelled in one form or another, it creates value beyond that which is socially necessary. The alienation of this labor—in effect, its confiscation by persons who somehow control production—is seen as the source of "profit" in laborvalue theory.

Continuity of Activity

Another issue, closely related to intensity, is that of continuity through time of intensive production. A seasonal use of a resource, such as a certain stand of prickly pear in early historical Texas, may have been quite intensive while it lasted but was restricted to only a brief period each year. Indeed, given that basic family needs have been met for the year, it is possible that person(s) may have devoted essentially full time to some activity for some particular period of time. Again, this is the sort of thing that might be called a temporally restricted "part-time specialization." However, the time spent in such activities is in addition to primary economic activities; it is supplemental, although by no means economically insignificant. Before we can argue that an activity was specialized we must assess continuity in terms of professional activity within the normal cycle of production.

Differentiation of Activity

As discussed earlier, spatial differentiation in the sense of extent is fairly easy to detect archaeologically. As I pointed some time ago (1984a), this kind of spatial differentiation *may* occur with profoundly domestic production systems as well as with specialist production. So-called "site specialization" is of little significance unless it can be related to *social* differentiation of production.

Social production differentiation is less easy to detect archaeologically but—as discussed in the following sections—may show up in combinations of distinctive characteristics of both domestic and production locations. Again, limited activity areas are "work places," but not necessarily "workplaces," in the sense of a locus of a profession. Nor is specialized production necessarily only found separated from the home. In advanced capitalist settings, for example, both cottage industries and piecework are kinds of specialist production within societies in which middle men and entrepreneurs control the access of the producer to markets. Such a production system might look like domestic production but it is really dispersal of production in an entirely different social and economic matrix. A true "cottage industry" (formerly *Hausindustrie*, but more commonly *Verlagssystem* or Putting Out System, Bücher 1898) involves a middleman of some kind and constitutes, in effect, a form of piece wages. It has been very commonly associated with capitalist production of fabric and clothing. It is unfortunate that "cottage industry" has been misapplied to a concept of domestic locus of supposedly specialist production in the American Bottom (see following discussion, and Prentice 1983; cf. Prentice 1985 and Pauketat 1987b).

Another reason for the connection between specialist production and increasing scale of a society is that craft division of labor is one effective solution to increasing the scale of production to meet overall societal needs. Indeed, here is where the kind of feedback loop envisioned by Jacobs (1967) comes into play. When specialization of production separates individuals from subsistence production and even from production of their own raw materials, the scale of production of those support supplies has to increase on the part of those responsible for subsistence or raw materials production. The more specialists, the more likelihood that others will have to become specialists in order to supply the specialists. Under such circumstances, domestic or individual production levels may be insufficient because of shortages of labor, inefficiencies caused by individual production, and so on. Thus, specialization can often require collective production, particularly specialization in a number of fields, in order to increase the scale from the individual level to the social level. These involve *social*, rather than just *kin*, relationships. This is why Evans's criteria of restriction of specialization to a few persons may be only a transitory stage on the path to true specialization.

Production and Consumption Character

The location of production provides many useful clues to the nature of production, especially when this is separated from normal domestic contexts. These are locations at which the criteria discussed earlier in relation to extent, intensity, and so on, can be assessed. However, the workplace may offer little or no evidence of the social and economic context of the producer who worked there. Meals consumed in a workplace, for example, may have been brought in from cooking locations, without suggesting that these were specialist producers receiving food in payment for their production. Any limited-activity site will, of course, have a consumption-oriented profile for *other* activities. How different the case is, however, if we can show that producers of goods, both at limited-activity sites and in their domestic setting, were *not* engaged in normal-subsistence production activities! If their domestic setting is entirely consumption-oriented, we surely must suspect that they were, in fact, specialists. On the other hand, if we find that the household of a maker of an item is still an ordinary household, showing the same kinds of production and consumption characteristic of all other domestic producers, we may rightly consider the argument for specialist production to be unproved.

Detection of production technology in the various activities undertaken at a location is relatively straightforward. Fortunately, these data also provide a good basis for assessing specialization. The organization of production in domestic sites and locations is also accessible through comparison of households among themselves and in relation to those from other Mississippian sites. The presence of local elites should be visible in differential access to either fancy goods or even basic products. The means of perpetuation of the system is less important in a test for specialization, but stratigraphic data provide evidence for persistence of the patterns.

Indications of External Goods and Exchange

The last of the rough guides outlined here is whether locations of residence and production show indications of exchange. Without a *quid pro quo*, there cannot be any "pros," no specialization. Goods exchanged for the goods produced are a necessary condition for the demonstration of specialist production, although this may be harder to detect in "attached" specialization. Specialist production involves the production of a local surplus of some goods and their exchange for other goods. The trick is being able to prove this in archaeological research. For example, exchange goods may not be sufficiently localized in terms of sources to allow an archaeological judgment of their "exotic" character. Many kinds of "payment commodities" might simply not preserve in most sites.

Although I would not use the term *specialization* to describe production in the Kula Ring, there are certainly many exotic items moving across the participating societies. So the mere presence of exotic or valuable goods alone does not signal the condition of "trade," as opposed to more generalized kinds of exchange. Exchange goods are a necessary, but not sufficient, condition of specialization.

The character of the goods themselves sometimes suggests their production character. Wheel-made pottery is not impossible to produce in nonspecialist conditions, but the investments required in both equipment and training make true wheel-thrown pottery a likely marker for specialist production, *in the appropriate contexts*. As we shall briefly see later, other forms of production requiring less commitment to large-scale production or investment of time in learning are correspondingly less useful as proof of specialization.

3. PRODUCTION OF GOODS FOR EVERYDAY LIFE

Differentiation of labor throughout the Southeast seems to have been low, fitting well within models of domestic production (Muller 1984a, 1986a, 1986b, 1987a). Despite some localization of production, goods do not seem to have been alienated from the producers. Even so, although claims for specialization have been made historically for both "ordinary" and "elite" associated social contexts. We shall start here with evidence for those goods that were used in everyday life. First, I shall briefly review our work aimed specifically at this issue in the Lower Ohio Valley.

The Lower Ohio

The early goals (ca. 1967) of the Lower Ohio Valley Project at SIUC were to investigate the organization of Mississippian from a settlement-subsistence perspective. Specifically, we were testing ideas about the origins of hierarchical societies that were then being proposed (e.g., Fried 1967; Service 1962). We were also interested in claims for militaristic expansion of a Kincaid "state" made by Sears (1968) although without accepting the premise of that suggestion. As other important writings about the development of complex societies were published (e.g., Carneiro 1970, Service 1975), Lower Ohio Valley Mississippian provided a useful source of data on the importance and sequence of developments in production systems and settlement (Muller 1978b, 1984a; Rackerby and Muller 1971).

After the late 1960s, the emphasis shifted from settlement subsistence to political economy, but the program has been true to its original goals of investigating several general questions: (1) How complex was Lower Ohio River Valley Mississippian?, (2) What degree of social differentiation had developed?, (3) How was this related to systems of production?, and (4) How can this regional development be related to general theories of hierarchical organization and development?

The nature of production in Lower Ohio Valley Mississippian society, in the context of a "minimal" chiefdom, provides data relevant to proposals about the importance of production organization in evolving hierarchies. The Kincaid–Angel phase(s) is exceptionally well known as a result of long-term research programs in the Lower Ohio Valley region (see summary in Muller 1978b, 1986b, but also see my autocritique, 1993a; also Green and Munson 1978). As a result, production systems can be studied in their cultural context, and these data can be used to assess hypotheses about the level of organization necessary to account for the archaeological remains.

Evidence from this research program in the Ohio Valley has shown some striking features of these Mississippian production systems, falsifying hypotheses that developing, "chiefdom-level" societies had specialistlike production (e.g., Service 1962, 1975). In the Lower Ohio, production of basic foodstuffs and other goods shows consistent characteristics across the entire settlement system. Large and small sites alike share a common profile of production tools, "status" or probable "valued" goods, and indications of day-to-day activities (see Figure 7.1 and discussion following).

Large sites such as Kincaid resolve themselves into clusters of homesteads that on closer examination are essentially indistinguishable from farmsteads located further away from the mound center (see Muller 1976, 1978b, 1984a, 1986b, 1993a for bibliography and citations of relevant theses and dissertations including Blakeman 1974; Butler 1977; Davy 1982; Lafferty 1977; Martin 1991; Riordan 1975; and Santeford 1982). Survey and testing programs upstream (e.g., Ahler et al. 1980; Butler et al. 1979) have shown a similar pattern of settlement and organization throughout the valley between the Wabash and the Tennessee confluences. Even small upland valley Mississippian sites show the same general archaeological profile (e.g., Canouts et al. 1984). None of these sites shows evidence of being the locus of any "specialist" production of locally concentrated resources. To the contrary, every indication suggests that production in Mississippian society in the Lower Ohio Valley was profoundly "domestic." Differential concentration of resources in upland areas, for example, did not lead to specialization on hunting. Other work in the region supports the general conclusion of the domesticity of Mississippian production in the Lower Ohio Valley (e.g., Black 1967; Clay 1976; Cole et al. 1951; Green and Munson 1978).

As we saw in Chapter 5, a "typical" Lower Ohio Valley Mississippian site is a little larger than 0.25 ha in area and consists of the remains of only a few structures. Some larger hamlets and centers have larger areas with up to 1.0–1.25 ha of contiguous settlement. Clusters of homesteads and larger groupings in large centers at Kincaid and Angel range up to 8–10 ha in total extent. In the cases of Angel and Kincaid, the areas of palisaded zones are from 35–70 ha, but only about 8 percent of the enclosed area was actually occupied.

In Figure 7.1, it should be remembered that ratios for a series of categories of artifacts vary according to the activities that took place at various sites, their duration of settlement, and many other factors. Nevertheless, the same pattern holds generally for a diversity of sites in different locations. In the figure, IAS Mx 66 is a hamlet-sized settlement that had stone-box graves associated. BB Pp 105 is a small site just outside the palisade line at Kincaid. BB Mx 164 is a site located on a ravine on the terrace above the Black Bottom (see Muller 1986b). Site 25D2–35 is a transient, at least, residential location near a poor-quality chert source (Muller 1985). Sites 25D3–22, –23, and –24 are refuse areas near a hamlet located in a small bottomland near Kincaid known as the Upper Bottom (probably all included in the older site number IAS Pp 25 [≈ UC Pp^{y}28]). Site 25D3–24 also had Middle Woodland and Late Woodland components. The samples from these are very small, however, being based on deep trenching (see Ahler et al. 1980).

Homesteads were normally dispersed, but they surely maintained ritual and economic links to each other in each neighborhood and also to larger centers such as Kincaid. Most of the homesteads were located in the same basic environment. There is little hint in the settlement patterns of dispersal across diverse ecological zones proposed in former models of specialization after the fashion of Service. In fact, even most Mississippian sites that are outside the main valleys are most often located near whatever kinds of wetlands are locally present. The most striking exceptions to this generalization are the blufftop settlements associated with salt and chert production, as discussed later in sections on those production systems. One site in southern Illinois, Millstone Bluff, is also a blufftop site, but is not obviously associated with any distinctive kind of economic activity. Investigation of this site began in the 1996 SIUC Field School in Archaeology. Other kinds of settlements away from the main valleys correspond pretty closely to bottomland settlements in character (e.g.,

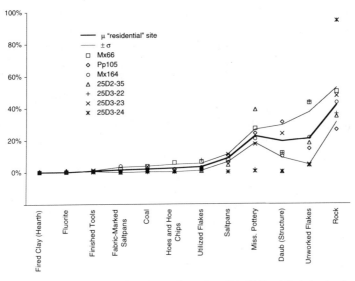

Figure 7.1. Variation in some major artifact classes for Lower Ohio Valley Mississippian "residential" and other sites.

Canouts et al. 1984), but there is some reason to believe that soil exhaustion and a kind of shifting cultivation pattern may have been necessary away from the main valleys, at the least (see Hargrave, Oetelaar, Lopinot, Butler and Billings 1983). There is a tight correlation between the number of structures at a site and the area of potentially arable land (see Figure 5.11). Prehistoric settlements and households appear to be similar to each other and on the same scale as those throughout the Historic period (as shown in Figure 5.5, also see Muller 1993b, in press).

Figure 5.6 showed the linear character of Lower Ohio Valley Mississippian settlement, and Figure 5.7 illustrated the same point on the local level in the Black Bottom itself. The majority of sites in any given community, as we saw in that discussion, were roughly the same size, built up in the same way as the others, and showed only minimal differences from the "best" to the "worst" houses in any community.

The degree of alienation of surplus products or labor from the individual households appears to have been low, based, among other things, on both the biological evidence (Chapter 4) and the scale of labor investment for probable elite-sponsored work such as mound construction (Chapter 6; Muller 1986b:200–204). This society was pretty clearly ranked, but little evidence exists for *stratification* in Fried's sense. In this nonstratified society, some possible stimuli for specialist production may be found in both unevenness in distribution of some natural resources and, more importantly, in terms of some diversion of household production into surplus goods for exchange. However, neither of these proves the existence of specialization.

Households and communities that were adjacent to concentrated resource areas were fortunate and were surely able to translate their surplus production into exchange. However, there is no proof that any of the "surplus" was other than that described as "normal surplus" (Allan 1965). There is really no evidence in all the data that we have of substitution of production of surplus goods for any other economic activity. Mississippian surplus seems to have been primarily that resulting from extra yield in good years as a result of planning for the worst case. There may have been some "spare-time" production of some goods for exchange, but this does not seem to have replaced ordinary subsistence activities. So far, there is no evidence that the goods were alienated from the local production units. Most producers were working even with exotic raw materials in a way that suggests that they were engaged in supplemental production rather than as true craft or full-time specialists (Muller 1984a, 1986a; Meillassoux 1981:37).

Lithic resources show a production pattern that is similar to that found for other so-called "subsistence-oriented" goods. Fluorite is somewhat concentrated in distribution, but it outcrops here and there along the bluffs of the Ohio River between the Saline River and the Black Bottom. It seems unlikely that Kincaid directly dominated either the famous Union County or Dover chert sources, each located some distance away. Morrow has suggested that Archaic use of the Union County cherts may have been a by-product of hunting or other periodic activities outside the locality, rather than an indication of exchange (1982:1317, following a point made by Binford 1979:260–261). Given the great distances over which Historic groups in the area ranged, it would not be unreasonable to see Mississippian groups ranging over considerable distances to obtain valued raw materials.

Some moderate quality chert sources are available within the region (Ahler et al. 1980; Butler et al. 1979; Muller 1985), but much chert was brought into the localities for use in making stone hoes and other finished tools. No chert resources of any kind exist in the Black Bottom proper, but some poor-quality cherts were available in terrace gravel, and slightly better cherts were found across the river in Kentucky (Nance 1984). Some moderate-to-poor-quality, rarely used cherts occurred at Cave-in-Rock between Kincaid and Angel. What may be limited-activity Mississippian sites there could reflect some transient use of the resource (Muller 1985). Although these sites have not been tested, associated domestic debris from surface collections shows a pattern different from the "modular" Mississippian farmstead/homestead. The most striking differences are that the habitation areas (Muller 1985) at these chert sources show (1) light occupation with little associated midden, and (2) a striking absence of edge "microflakage" (sometimes called *utilization*) on lithic debris at both the processing stations and in the habitation areas. Microflakage is commonly associated with both opportunistic use of flakes and with breakage resulting from trampling in areas of high traffic flow. In this case, its absence suggests that habitation near the chert and fluorite sources may not have been intensive. However, microflakage had not occurred, despite the fact these samples were from modern park areas with moderate foot traffic. Either intermittent or even seasonal exploitation of the local lithic resources seems indicated both by the habitation remains and by the scanty evidence for core processing. Thus, chert exploitation seems likely to be nonspecialist in these contexts, although the sites are clearly limited activity sites (e.g., see 25D2–35 in Figure 7.1). Chert working at other, more usual, primarily residential Mississippian sites in the Lower Ohio Valley also shows no clear indications of "specialist" production (such as restriction to specific sites or site areas, standardization of form or size, etc.). This also appears to be the case generally in the American Bottom (Holley 1995; Pauketat 1987b; cf. Pauketat 1994) and at Moundville (see Welch 1991:167). These will be briefly discussed later in this chapter. Although craft-specialist production of artifacts such as stone hoes has often been suggested, none of the known lithic production sites in the Lower Ohio Valley proper are consistent with that model. For these reasons, chert production was not especially useful in our search for developing specialization in this particular region. However, Cobb's work has explored the dimensions of chert production at the famous Union County, Illinois, quarries (1988, 1993a,b,c), and this will also be discussed in a later section of this chapter, together with a discussion of the Dover chert quarries.

Evidence in the Black Bottom and the Lower Ohio Valley indicates that ceramics production, like almost all activities, was domestic. The use and distribution of ceramics are much more uniform than previously thought. Riordan's dissertation (1975) is the most detailed examination of the ceramics from the smaller sites tested in our work in the Black Bottom. His work shows surprisingly similar ceramic profiles among a range of different sized, and putatively different function, sites.

Most of the pottery in Mississippian sites in the Lower Ohio Valley is plain coarse-shell tempered vessels (Figure 7.2). Coarsely crushed shell-temper characterized 98 percent of the sherds from Kincaid (Cole et al. 1951:309). A small percentage is fine-crushed shell-temper, found in what are commonly thought of as fancier forms such as plates. Decorative techniques were rarely used, a truth not easily deduced from the overwhelming temptation to illustrate the very rare, but "nicer" vessels from any given site. It is interesting that about *half* of *all* plate sherds recovered were illustrated in the Kincaid report (1951), with over 240 Mississippian ceramics illustrations. I would guess that this overrepresentation of fancy goods is similar to that in other Mississippian site reports. Digging mostly at big sites has often badly skewed our view of what constitutes Mississippian "prestige" goods.

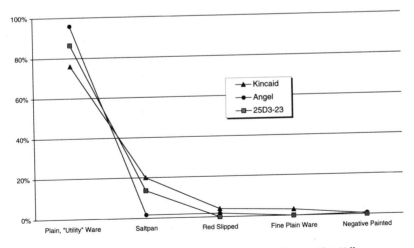

Figure 7.2. Major ware and ceramic categories in the Lower Ohio Valley.

As Figure 7.3 shows, the supposedly "elite" plate vessel forms are actually relatively more common in the farmsteads and hamlets than in the excavated portions of central mound sites. Plates make up 0.6 percent of the sherds at small sites and 0.2 percent at Kincaid. Orr counted some 32 plate sherds out of nearly 15,000 sherds! (in Cole et al. 1951:309).[2] Another "elite" form, the bottle, is about equally common in large and small sites. It is true, of course, that the rare goods are much better chronological indicators than plain, coarse-ware pottery, but the percentages of such vessels at small sites in the Black Bottom do not support the conclusion of important social differences between the dwellers of the central site and those scattered about its "hinterlands."

Given the differences in sample size and in collection techniques, however, it is not surprising that there should be differences in the percentages of rare types. Martin (1991) compared the assemblages from UC Mx^v 1C, at the main Kincaid center; IAS Mx 66, a hamlet cluster; and BB Mx 164, a short duration farmstead, in terms of ceramic variables using evenness and richness measures. Although sample size proved to be a problem, he concluded, as had others before him, that there was considerable consistency in the activities reflected in ceramics at these sites. In short, much of the proposed distance of elite settlements from even isolated farmsteads tends to melt away under close scrutiny. The ceramic evidence suggests little differences among Black Bottom families in their ability to acquire and use various kinds of fancy and plain pottery.

The same is true of other classes of materials. Although we have only tiny fragments of copper from smaller sites, these also are similar to the finds at larger sites with much larger samples in terms of the percentage of the assemblage. Such materials at the small sites are indicators of the presence and working of raw materials. Coal and fluorite, for example were worked at all sizes of sites. Although soil conditions have destroyed most shell and bone at floodplain sites, the distribution of various other finely made goods across the East as a whole simply does not bear out the conclusion that they were limited to the centrally located "elites." On the contrary, shell gorgets, for example, occur at all kinds and scales of sites. We also should remember the elaborate objects recovered from quite modest sites in the American Bottom. Of course, many kinds of finely made objects did find their way into the burials of the wealthiest and most central persons in Mississippian societies, but we should not forget that their poorer cousins in the villages also had access to these same goods.

Mississippian societies in the Lower Ohio Valley clearly had hierarchical political structures with leaders that could be accurately described as "chiefs," but the economic and political basis of their power was not redistribution of the rationing, "specialist" form proposed by Service (Muller 1978b, 1984a, 1987a). Nearly 20 years of survey and testing in the Lower Ohio Valley have shown that production was essentially uniform in practice from one location to another and that, in normal to good years, local farmsteads would have been capable of supporting themselves and

---

[2] These percentages for Kincaid are those given in the report (Cole et al. 1951:145ff.), but close examination reveals inconsistencies in the samples used as the total count for a given comparison, no doubt reflecting the diversity of the people working on various sections at different times.

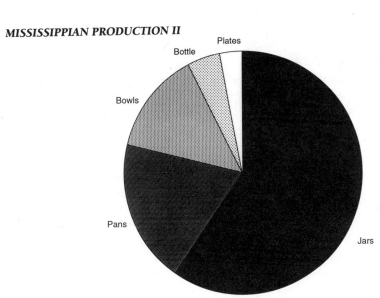

b. Black Bottom Sites Total

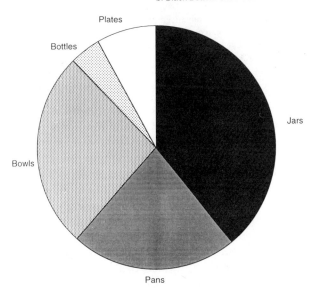

Figure 7.3. Vessel forms at Kincaid and other sites in the Black Bottom. (Cole et al. 1951; Riordan 1975).

of contributing to community stores, as well. As I have detailed elsewhere (e.g., Muller 1986a, 1987a), little evidence exists to date in the Lower Ohio Valley for wealth-conversion specialist production in either of the main sites—Kincaid or Angel. There is no evidence in the Lower Ohio Valley for concentration of specialist production in either the mound centers or in smaller sites, although there are many indications of production of goods of the sort usually considered to be "valuables" (Muller 1978b, 1986a, 1987a). Production of so-called "valuables" and other goods (see Douglas and Isherwood 1979) alike was dispersed across the community, and evidence of this production is found in sites of all size ranks. It is doubtful that many individuals in the Mississippian societies of this region could accurately be characterized as "nonproducers." In this view, Lower Ohio Valley Mississippian stands in contrast to the more highly developed chiefdoms of Polynesia, as described by Earle (1978).

In technology after technology, Lower Ohio Valley Mississippian, and I think this is true of Mississippian complexes in general, fails to provide clear examples of specialist production of either utilitarian or valued goods. Thus, a once-upon-a-time proposed craft-specialist model of Mississippian salt production at sites such as the Great Salt Spring would be a striking and important social phenomenon.

Great Salt Spring Test for Specialization[3]

The Context of Mississippian Salt Production

> Specialization was probably more advanced in the East, *although it is less often reported in the literature*. The rich and variegated material culture of a tribe like the Iroquois is proof of craft specialization. The lively trade which occurred in pre-Columbian times and continued after Europeans settled America is further evidence of specialization. In the Southeast, salt was a common article of trade, *and the persons connected with its making by evaporation in pottery saltpans were most certainly specialists*. Driver 1969:172[emphases added]

Such claims for "specialist" production of salt in Mississippian times surely include the production of salt at the Great Salt Spring. The Great Salt Spring was one of the earliest identified salt production sites (Cramer 1814, Sellers 1877), and one of the most famous. Our work at the Great Salt Spring (Muller 1984a, 1986a, 1986b; Muller and Avery 1982; Muller et al. 1992) was motivated by a desire to test the hypothesis of specialist production at this large and complex site.

As noted earlier, we came to the Great Salt Spring to investigate its proposed "specialist" production system from an extensive base of survey and excavation in the Lower Ohio Valley. Given generalized and domestic subsistence and other production, the proposed specialization of Great Salt Spring Mississippian salt producers stood out as highly anomalous. If, in fact, these salt producers could be shown to have been specialists, then the Mississippian case would not be so strong a counterexample to theories of development like Service's and would provide contrasting data for models like Earle's concept of attached specialists. If specialization were taken to be a cause, precursor, or even a component in the early formation of elites in this region, then it must have occurred in such activities as salt or chert production, since there is little evidence for it in ordinary Mississippian sites. It is, by the way, a misconception that salt or chert production is somehow more "low skill" than other kinds of Mississippian production. These tasks, especially if we were to hypothesize large-scale production, require no less knowledge of practical chemistry and physics

---

[3]This section is a summary of discussion presented in Muller et al. (1992) and other reports on the Great Salt Spring.

than the skill level required for production of conch shell, fluorite, or coal display items, for example. It is organization of the task, not its complexity, that is at issue. I repeat, it is wrong to confuse complexity of a task with the social character of its production.

Finally, a word or two must be said again about the question of salt as "one of the few trade items that could be classified as a necessity rather than a luxury" (Wentowski 1970:42). Salt is often seen as a critical but restricted-source material, necessary for the maintenance of human life, so it was natural to argue for its being a focus of production for exchange. As I indicated in the last chapter, much of the scientific basis for connecting sodium chloride consumption with horticulture rests on a hypothesis raised by Bunge (1873, 1874), that increased sodium intake was necessary because of a need to eliminate potassium as a result of decreased animal foods and increased plant food consumption. However, as Dauphinee (1960) and others have pointed out, little evidence supports this specific explanation of the strong connection between salt appetite and vegetarian diet. Rather, the connection simply seems to be that many plant foods lack sodium, and the shortage has to be made up. However, even a diet of largely plant foods normally would provide the small physiological minimum requirement (ca. 200 mg sodium/day). Heavy sweating may require as much as an extra 7 g/day of sodium chloride, however (NAS 1974:9; e.g., see Andrews 1983). Nonetheless, where plentiful, salt is almost always consumed in greater quantities than can be justified by any physiological need (e.g., Dauphinee 1960: 404). The large number of potential sources in the Southeast, combined with evidence for a mixed diet in Mississippian times, does not support the idea that sodium chloride was a "necessity," but there is no reason to doubt that it was a highly desired item of production, exchange, and consumption (as noted in the previous chapter; Avery 1983). Salt may also be used in ceramic production to prevent lime-spalling (Rye 1976, Stimmel 1978), although Avery's experiments indicate that salt was not always necessary for this purpose (1983).

Salt does have a long history of its use in dominance relationships, as in British India or in Medieval Europe (Braudel 1981). For such reasons, it has been suggested that salt trade may have played an important part in the origin of Maya civilization (see discussion in Andrews 1983:133–135). Whatever the reasons for the demand for salt, salt producers and/or the persons who controlled salt production have stood in positions of potential dominance over people who wish to obtain salt. No one has been bold enough to suggest that salt springs might have served as primary foci for social differentiation in Mississippian society, but these limited, concentrated, and potentially controllable resources are significant in testing for differentiation. If specialization were present at them, it would raise a whole set of new hypotheses about the origins of Mississippian relations of subordination. Since craft specialization is widely accepted as an important event in the development of other kinds of social differentiation, its presence or absence in low-level hierarchical societies such as Lower Ohio Valley Mississippian is also important as a test case for examining the relative priority of social developments required by general social theories.

Earlier work at the salt springs in the East (e.g., Brown 1980a,b; Keslin 1964) and at the Great Salt Spring (Blasingham 1972; Cramer 1814; Peithman 1953; Sellers 1877) generally concentrated on stratigraphic concerns and the technology of salt production without directly addressing the mode of production. That the mode of production cannot be simply assumed is shown by the case of the Maya, among whom salt production was apparently less than a craft-specialist activity, even though their sociopolitical organization was more complex than Mississippian. Andrews comments on the coordination of Maya seasonal salt production with the agricultural activities that formed the true basis of livelihood (Andrews 1983:112–113). It may be, however, that Maya exchange of salt was undertaken by trader-specialists (Andrews 1983:113), even though the producers may not have been specialists. This is an important example of why a production system has to be examined in its broader social context.

The Site

The Great Salt Spring site is located in southern Illinois on the Saline River, a tributary of the Ohio between upland, unglaciated hills to the south, and the Wabash floodplain and till plains to the north. The site is approximately 90 km east of Carbondale, Illinois. It was first reported as an archaeological site in the early 19th century (Cramer 1814), although it was known as a historical and aboriginal salt production area for more than a century before that. Archaeological excavations date from the 1870s to the present (Blasingham 1972; Muller 1984a; Muller et al. 1992; Peithman 1953; Sellers 1877). The entire Great Salt Spring "site" consists of two major areas along the Saline River: (1) a bottomland salt-production zone around the saline springs, and (2) an area atop an 30-m-high escarpment that was described as a "residential" zone by Sellers (1877). All areas of the site are forested and understory growth is largely poison ivy, especially in the low areas (see Muller 1984a and 1986b, for maps and more detail on the earlier work at the site). The lowland salt production site extends for over 500 m along the south bank of the Saline River. Evidence of prehistoric use of the escarpment-top site consists of looted stone-box graves, a few possible structure depressions, and debris—including saltpan sherds and thin "utilitarian" Mississippian pottery.

Whatever else it may have been, the Great Salt Spring site was a locus of salt production, and its role in the development of regional integration is important in testing opposing theories of the origins of complex societies.

The Fieldwork

Our work at the floodplain salt production area of the Great Salt Spring site (Muller 1984a, 1986a, 1986b, 1987a; Muller et al. 1992; Muller and Avery 1982) showed that all of that 500-m long zone was devoted to salt production and to the manufacture of tools used in salt making. Virtually no "domestic" debris is associated with this portion of the site, and the vast majority of the ceramics are thick, saltpan sherds. The tool assemblage is extremely uniform in content (as demonstrated by various statistical tests, see Muller 1984a; Muller et al. 1992). The salt-production assemblage sharply contrasts with the associations found at Mississippian farmsteads, hamlets, and centers in our previous 20 years of work.

The Great Salt Spring floodplain area is an extraordinary site. Only a small range of activities are represented there. Salt manufacture and auxiliary activities such as hunting were virtually the only activities carried out at the site during its use from around A.D. 800 into Historic times. The little domestic debris that is present is mostly reflective of temporary use of the locality, rather than any substantial permanent settlement.

The augering and excavations at the supposed residential area showed that area was also characterized by a similarly uniform archaeological assemblage (Muller et al. 1992). This assemblage may also be characterized as being largely the result of activities clearly related to salt production, either directly or indirectly.

The technology associated with the exploitation of salt included a fairly uniform tool kit. Large to medium-sized saltpans were made from clays available at the site (Holt in Muller et al. 1992). Brine from natural saline springs was evaporated in these saltpans, often over specially made distinctive clay-lined hearths (see Muller 1984a: Figure 4). "Saltpans" at nonsalt spring locations were probably used for reduction of liquids in general, or for other purposes, but their primary use for salt production at salt spring sites is not questioned. Vessel size and the size of auxiliary production components vary (see Muller and Renken 1989), although the tool kit for salt production is similar over a large area of production. There is not much evidence of such indications as standardization (see Muller 1984a, 1986a; Muller et al. 1992). The kinds of archaeological remains are those that could be expected for a seasonal pattern of salt exploitation like that described for the historical Natchez:

> The Indians come a great way off to this place to hunt in winter and make salt. Before the French trucked coppers with them, they made upon the spot pots of earth for this operation: and they returned home with salt and dry provisions. Le Page du Pratz 1758[1972:153]

It is not surprising that salt springs were centers for salt production, just as chert outcrops were for chert production, and so on. Localization of extraction is environmentally determined in these cases. Although localization is created by resource concentration, it does **not** necessarily imply producer specialization. It may encourage the development of craft specialization as the society becomes larger and more complex, but localization will occur in any system of exploitation of concentrated resources.

The evidence from the low areas of the Great Salt Spring alone, while consistent with nonspecialist production, was not decisive in falsifying hypotheses of "full-time" producer specialization, except on the grounds of Occam's razor, precisely because the upland "residential" context had not been examined. The central issue facing us as we began work on in the supposed "residential" zones was to examine the social context of salt producers and salt production at the Great Salt Spring in comparison to the social and economic context of Mississippian elsewhere in the region. This is where we return to the criteria for judging specialization that were described earlier.

Extent of Use

Survey sampling of bottomlands near the Great Salt Spring locality has shown few Mississippian farmsteads of the sort identified elsewhere in the Lower Ohio Valley (Muller and Avery 1982; Muller et al. 1992). The Great Salt Spring site is not, in fact, close to high quality soils of the sort normally chosen for Mississippian cultivation, although regional Mississippian settlement is known for areas of even poorer quality soils under special circumstances (Butler 1972, 1977; Davy 1982; Muller 1986b, 1978b; Muller and Davy 1977; Muller, Stephens, and Powell 1981). It is difficult to define a potential support area for the Great Salt Spring site that is comparable to that defined in bottomland environments; but there is little indication of intensive Mississippian use of this locality outside the Great Salt Spring.

Aboriginal use of the Great Salt Spring is documented between ca. A.D. 800 and the late 18th century, so even with low levels of small homestead settlement at any one time, the density of structures and features in some areas should have approached those of the residential zones of large sites like Kincaid or Angel. This proved not to be the case.

Although excavations of the Great Salt Spring site constitute only a small percentage of its total surface area, the site area has been augered and shovel tested at a 10-m interval with additional soil probes (Muller and Avery 1982). Because of this, it is among the best-known Mississippian salt extraction sites (see also Brown 1980a,b; Early 1993; Keslin 1964). The intensive use area of lowland salt production totals about 2.8 ha. This zone shows no residential use but has extremely deep, dense, and complex deposits resulting from salt production and the firing of ceramic saltpan vessels (Muller 1984a; Muller and Avery 1982). The escarpment-top site zone is scattered over a huge area, although site density is not uniform. Stone-box graves on a nearby ridgetop suggested the presence there of other site zones, but shovel testing revealed no use areas.

The auger-and-shovel test program, together with excavations, revealed widespread areas of salt production on the blufftop and the floodplain, but no identifiable permanent occupation like those at typical Mississippian residential sites. Site distributions on the blufftop are essentially linear, with the densest materials concentrated along the north escarpment. Discarding of refuse on the slopes may be partly responsible for this pattern. There has been, however, modern American agricultural use of the area, and some deflation of the zone has apparently occurred as a result. Even so, the bulk of utilization of the blufftop was in those areas most accessible from the springs on the floodplain below. As we discovered, however, only limited areas of even the main blufftop zone could be described as partially residential, and even that appears to have been predominantly transient use. Of course, the presence of stone-box graves in the use zone does not necessarily imply permanent residential use of a site (e.g., Funkhouser and Webb 1932; Muller 1985). There is no clear evidence for fortifications, although what may have been some small-scale fortifications may have been visible on the blufftop zone before cultivation of the area in the early 20th century (Sellers 1877). The blufftop zone had the natural defense of steep slopes, especially if salt burning had left the area sparsely timbered. However, botanical evidence from the site indicates that much of the wood burned had been lying on the forest floor, not freshly cut (Lopinot in Muller et al. 1992). No mounds are present in the immediate locality. A large, permanent settlement is not present at the site. However, a few structures were present in the blufftop zone. These were not typical Mississippian "houses," however, in their contents, although they were substantially built. It seems likely from the debris occurring in them that the excavated structures were more shelters for salt production than residences. Despite their important similarities, differences exist in the nature of the assemblages between the blufftop zone and the floodplain zone. Plain saltpans, for example, were more common in the blufftop zone, apparently largely as a result of size differences in the vessels being used (see Muller and Renken 1989; Muller et al. 1992).

In what we called the "floodplain" zone (actually the first terrace, T_1), the depth of the cultural deposit and artifact density generally increases as the distance to the salt spring(s) decreases (see Muller et al. 1992: Chapter 5). Actually, none of the floodplain proper (T_0) showed any evidence of aboriginal use in our augering to more than 2 m below present surface. Virtually all of the western T_1 zone was utilized in salt production, with a total area of utilization of approximately 0.9 ha. About 0.8 ha of area in the "central high ground" between what are believed to have formerly been two separate springs was utilized for salt production. Close to 0.98 ha was used for salt production in the areas to the east of the main spring. The auger-and-shovel test program in the blufftop zone indicates that, in all the areas tested there, 266 10 × 10 m units had cultural material present. The "utilized" area on the blufftop is estimated to be somewhat greater than 2.66 ha total. Together with the utilized areas in the floodplain zone, the total area with archaeological remains at this site appears to be about 5.42 ha out of a total "site" area of over 100 ha. The heavily utilized area is a little smaller than the "occupied" portions of mound centers in the region, but the total area over which these deposits occur is larger than the areas enclosed by palisades at Kincaid or Angel.

In terms of the various hypotheses suggested at the beginning of our project, it is now quite clear that the Great Salt Spring is not comparable to other Mississippian sites in the nature of its settlement. It is not constituted of a series of small Mississippian homesteads engaged in Mississippian domestic production, nor even persons producing salt on a yeararound basis. All indications are that the vast majority of use of the site was transient, as will be discussed. Even in the case of a substantial structure excavated in the 1990–1991 seasons, evidence indicates that the location was used more for salt production than primarily as a residence. Nor have we found any evidence that even the users of this structure were present throughout the year, making salt or anything else. Transient use, *per se*, is sufficient to force rejection of the most extreme hypotheses of salt-production specialization at this site, but it does not force rejection of more moderate hypotheses relating to possible seasonal production within a specialist framework. More importantly, the data on transient use form an important backdrop for the discussion of other aspects of salt production at this site.

Intensity of Use

Mississippian farmsteads were usually occupied through several rebuildings of their pole, wattle, and daub structures. Artifact finds at smaller sites are sparse, contributing materially to their low archaeological visibility. New studies of duration of normal Mississippian farmsteads in the American Bottom (Pauketat 1986, 1987a) suggest that ceramic associations will be useful in estimating the duration of settlement at such sites. Settlement density at centrally located sites in ridge complexes and/or mound sites appears greater than at farmstead and hamlet sites, but this is generally an artifact of longer term reuse. Thus, site density often measures central

location and the attractiveness of an area for serial use rather than scale of contemporaneous settlement. In the low-lying areas around the Great Salt Spring, salt production was carried out from roughly the 9th to the 18th century, and the complex
structure of the archaeological remains reflects continued reuse of areas for different
activities associated with salt production. In "burning" salt production (as opposed to
unaided evaporation), large amounts of wood ash are generated over time and midden buildup can be substantial (as in the low-lying area around the spring). Deep
middens are rare atop the escarpment. Even 19th-century observers recognized that
saltpan sherds indicated that some of the escarpment-top area was used for salt
production (Sellers 1877).

Intensity of use is known from a number of lines of evidence. I have made some
rough estimates of numbers of vessels and the levels of production implied by those
estimates (Muller et al. 1992:301–306). The estimates of the maximum number of
vessels in use at any given time can be quite large, and the quantity of salt produced
would seem enormous. Tons of salt were produced in Mississippian times at this site
complex, but the length of time of exploitation was more than 500 years. As we shall
see, when taken altogether, the estimated quantity of salt produced would have given
a population of 5000 consumers about what the National Academy of Sciences con-
siders to be a "safe and adequate" level of sodium consumption per day!

Extensive buildup of middens resulted from reuse of the same areas over time.
Although deep archaeological deposits are sometimes taken as evidence of high intensity of use, it is well to remember that repeated, but transient, use can also result in
deep deposits, especially if the vessels used in production broke easily and weathered
poorly between episodes of use so as to render them unfit for reuse. It is hard to
imagine full-time specialists at this site so poorly equipped in terms of day-to-day
amenities, as the remains from this site indicate. Such kinds of domestic debris are
quite compatible with the kind of "picnicking" that would accompany seasonal or
occasional use of the salt springs.

As recently as 1986, we still thought that the blufftop area might be the center
of substantial residential use (see Muller 1986b); but we now know that that part of
the site was also used primarily for salt production. Even the few relatively permanent structures that have now been found have contents that are inconsistent with
interpretation of them as ordinary Mississippian domestic units (Muller 1991; Muller
et al. 1992). It is clear, however, that the blufftop was used less intensively for salt
production than was the floodplain zone. One indirect line of evidence for fairly light
levels of overall exploitation at any one time is that the floodplain area seems to have
been "continuously" used for some 800 years. The deep midden and the large number
of hearths indicate that huge amounts of firewood were used in salt reduction. Given
the amount of firewood needed, only fairly small-scale production at any one time
could have allowed production to have been concentrated within the 500-m-ong
floodplain site area. This is especially true if limb fall was the preferred fuel. Evidence
for use of fallen timber in burning (see Lopinot in Muller et al. 1992), is surprising,
given the amount of wood ash present in the site areas. All zones seem to have seen
peak use in the 13th century, and it is possible that much of the blufftop production
dates to that century (see Muller and Renkin 1991; Muller et al. 1992). Very wide
dispersal of salt production over a large area in the 13th century suggests a pattern of

spacing out of independent producers, rather than concerted efforts by cooperating specialists (see the following discussion of dating).

The strong evidence for transiency—from the combination of a general lack of permanent shelter, the burning of fallen timber in salt production, the purity of the floral assemblages by season, the lack of domestic production, and so on—is inconsistent with normal perceptions of *full-time specialization* as it has commonly been defined. It is very consistent with the kind of use of salt sources described for historical Native Americans. Historic sources on salt production largely presented a picture of individual families or groups coming to salt sources on a transient, often seasonal, basis (see Muller et al. 1992). While at the salt sources, family members not engaged salt production took part in hunting and collecting activities. Production beyond immediate family needs may have occurred, but we have no real evidence of specialist "traders" engaged in salt or other exchange prior to European times. The bulk of exchange seems to have been incidental to other kinds of events such as rituals, marriage, aid to those in need, and so on. Such exchange is consistent with the long-term but relatively low-intensity use of the site. During the busiest times of the year, probably in the autumn, the site would have had many persons from all over the Lower Ohio Valley present and engaged in salt production. During other times, the site might have had only a few persons present.

Nonetheless, the total scale of production at the salt springs was large. Tons of salt were produced at the Great Salt Springs and in a smaller area (we think) at a nearby springs called Half Moon Lick. In a peculiar way, however, the extent of the salt-production activities are a testament to the dispersal of the activity across broad zones. This production was extensive but dispersed, just as might be expected if salt production were in, say, family or lineage hands. It is not concentrated in the way that full-scale, full-time historical American production was.

Continuity of Use (Duration and Seasonality)

Background. Early historical aboriginal salt production in the Southeast is poorly documented but seems often to have been a seasonal or transient activity (e.g., Le Page du Pratz 1758 [1972:153], see Swanton 1946 for a summary of the sources).

The question of settlement at the Great Salt Spring is important. Did a permanent settlement of Mississippian producers live there throughout the exploitation of the Great Salt Spring? If the site were a focus for the development of specialists, we would expect to see a permanent population at the site, even though one might imagine other possibilities. Over the time of exploitation of the saline springs, we would also expect to see the character of domestic activities become increasingly differentiated from a standard Emergent Mississippian pattern (i.e., Douglas or Duffy phase in this Wabash confluence locality).

Normal Mississippian sites, ranging from farmsteads to large centers, were occupied throughout the year, or at least as much of the year as a site was above water. If the character of the blufftop zone at the Great Salt Spring were similar, occupation should have been persistent and household inventories should also have been similar. Under conditions of specialist production, however, persistence of settlement should be coupled with not only a distinctive tool kit for salt production and auxiliary activities, but also by markers of exchange and distinctive status. We now know, however, that residential use of the Great Salt Spring was entirely, or nearly entirely, transient.

Different aspects of continuity have to be considered—seasonality, permanence of occupation, and duration. These issues relate to the question of how this huge site was used through time.

Seasonality. Evidence for the heaviest use of the site as being in the autumn is substantial, although the evidence also supports some use of the site through much of the year (Lopinot in Muller et al. 1992). However, individual botanical samples from the site have an extraordinary seasonal purity with little mixing of plant remains from different seasons. This pattern supports short-term visits rather than long-term residence as being favored by the exploiters of the saline springs. Such a pattern contrasts strongly with that found at other Mississippian sites where products of widely separated seasons are found together—reflecting storage at the time of production and consumption later. The pattern of food remains at the Great Salt Spring is consistent with importation of some already partially processed food (such as maize kernels) and then supplemention during the visit with local plants and animals. It is notable that corncobs are relatively rare at the site in relation to the number of kernels recovered (Lopinot in Muller et al. 1992). Although this could indicate importation of shelled maize in "payment" for salt, it is more likely that it represents shelled maize brought to the site by transient producers.

The faunal analyses (Breitburg in Muller et al. 1992) show animal species are present at the site that could have been taken most easily in the fall or in the late winter. As with the botanical data, there are indications of use of the site throughout the year as well. Use at different seasons in this case does not seem to indicate permanent residence during all seasons, of course; but simply that transient salt makers might come to the site at any times when the springs were not flooded.

An interesting, although by no means conclusive, indication of season is to be found in the form of the distinctive salt-boiling hearths. These small-to-large, clay-lined pits had fluelike extensions on one side. These "flues" most often point toward the northwest. Prevailing winds at the site are from the southwest for most of the year, but the wind blows from the northwest in January through March and in October (Wallace and Fehrenbacher 1969:4). At that time of year, the wind would have blown into the hearth, promoting more efficient combustion—consistent with the high degree of ash rather than charcoal from the site. The zoological and botanical evidence also suggest fall or late winter to early spring usage. In addition, the best chance of finding a rain-free period at the Great Salt Spring would be in September to early November. The latter part of this period would be after harvest, but temperatures would still normally be fairly comfortable, so that substantial shelters would not be necessary.

Indeed, the Great Salt Spring had only a small number of substantially built structures. However, there is evidence that more ephemeral shelters made of cane, daub, and other materials were erected here and there near the edge of the escarpment.

In general, the use of the site as seen in the floral and faunal assemblages and from other evidence is consistent with transient, nonspecialist production systems. These patterns are difficult to interpret in ways that would support craft-specialist production. As in the case of the area utilized, the data on seasonality cause rejection of the more extreme versions of specialist hypotheses. Of themselves, these data make it clear that virtually no one in this society could be seen as working at the site on a yeararound basis, engaged in full-time salt production.

Permanence of Occupation. One apparent line of evidence against the site having been primarily used transiently is the presence of substantial cemetery areas. More than 150 years of looting and vandalism have made it impossible to tell how many graves there were, but a large area has been dug up in the blufftop zones. Several comments may be made on this issue. Mississippians in general did not find it necessary to live permanently at a place in order to be buried there. This is shown to be so by the presence of large stone-box grave cemeteries on hilltops, without closely associated habitation, on the Kentucky side of the Ohio River near Paducah (see Funkhouser and Webb 1932). Similar patterns of burials being placed away from residences are known for other Mississippian complexes as well, such as the stone-box graves in the Cave-In-Rock State Park, another locality characterized by transient occupation, at least in the immediate vicinity of the graves (Muller 1985). In the American Bottom locality, graves are often separated from contemporary occupations (e.g., Milner 1984a). The bodies or bones of individuals must sometimes have been transported for some distance before burial. At the same time, some individuals *were* buried near, or even in, hamlets during Mississippian times. Still other individuals received special burial treatments in the large sites, but not all large-site burials are of "elites." The common use of wood picked up from the forest floor referred to earlier is further evidence that much use of the site was not continuous or permanent.

Duration and Dating. Radiocarbon dates from the Great Salt Spring are in accord with the typological evidence that the site was used from "Emergent" Mississippian times up to close to historical times. Good charcoal samples, as opposed to ash, were relatively rare in the floodplain areas, apparently as a result of very efficient burning of fuel in the prepared hearths. For this reason, it was somewhat more difficult to choose useful samples from the floodplain areas. However, the range of dates from the 10th–15th centuries is reasonable, representing the long persistence of salt production at the site. The blufftop dates, as well as many from the floodplain zones, are directly contemporary with the mid-13th-century peak periods of Mississippian population and settlement identified elsewhere in the lower Ohio Valley (Muller 1986b; Muller and Renken 1989). It is possible that the apparent increase of 13th-century use of the blufftop area reflects a correspondingly less intensive use of the floodplain at that time, but this view is unlikely, in my opinion. Given the overall nature of the use of the salt resource, I would suspect that the increased use of the blufftop is partly a reflection of the greater numbers of people present in the lower Ohio Valley during this period, with concomitant increases in the numbers of visitors to the site.

It would be nice to have more detailed chronological data to examine the question of absolute contemporaneity of use of the blufftop and floodplain site areas. However, the overlapping radiocarbon dates make it difficult to argue for any significant chronological factor in the use of these two areas, except that the duration and intensity of use of the blufftop area was less. On both artifactual and chronometric grounds, the most likely situation is that the various site areas were in use at the same times. The important points about the dating of salt production at this site are that (1) it begins early in Mississippian times and continues up to historical times; (2) the dates from the excavated samples are predominantly from the 13th century and are thus coeval with the best-known Mississippian assemblages from the rest of the Ohio Valley, so that (3) the differences between Mississippian exploitation of the Great Salt Spring and other sites must be attributed to something other than temporal differences.

What do the production levels seen at the Great Salt Spring imply in terms of consumption and demand? We can at least model some of the parameters. We know that wide areas of high fertility floodplain localities were settled by roughly contemporaneous communities in the 13th century (Muller 1986b:212ff.). With widespread settlement at this time, the maximum figures of ca. 1200–1500 persons for the Black Bottom and 300–500 for the Upper Bottom may also be close to *peak* population. If Angel is taken to be of similar size (and I believe it should be for reasons outlined in Muller 1986b), the total Lower Ohio Mississippian *town* population would be around 2500–3000, and bottomland population *for the entire region* would have been something less than 10,000 total. This would suggest something on the order of 500–2000 households at any one time. If every other household made an expedition to the Great Salt Spring or the Half Moon Lick in a given year, this would imply some 250–1000 salt-production visits per annum! At 3–5 vessels per visit, some 750–5000 vessels might be in use in a given year. These estimates are consistent with those sherd counts in the hundreds of thousands (see Muller et al. 1992: Chapter 10), where for 150 years of use, the average number of vessels in use would be more than 2800 vessels *per annum*. If the full 550-year range of use is taken instead, then the *average* number of vessels in use in a given year would be 776 vessels. As noted earlier, these estimates are consistent with a reasonable, annual salt consumption for such a population, given the normal salinity of the springs and allowing for five uses of each salt pan (see Muller et al. 1992 for more detail). Populations of the known sizes of Lower Ohio Mississippian settlements could easily have consumed even these estimates of salt production at the Great Salt Spring and the Half Moon Lick without producing a single gram for external exchange. If a modest level of exchange of salt is factored in, the apparent hugeness of salt production becomes easily understood.

Of course, the vessel number and other estimates are multiplied by one another, so that it would be foolish to place too much trust in them. The estimates are only important in that they demonstrate that the substantial levels of use actually seen archaeologically at the Great Salt Spring *are*, nonetheless, consistent with a model of salt production based on domestic units rather than upon occupational specialization. I will discuss efforts to use such multiplied numbers to prove specialization of labor as we come to the issues of chert production.

Differentiation of Use (Limited Activity Areas)

The Great Salt Spring "site" is actually a series of moreorless distinct sites separated by nonutilized areas, but it is not unreasonable for comparison to group such uniform remains into the main zones of the floodplain and the blufftop.

Floodplain zone. The general conclusions after the completion of our work at the Great Salt Spring are basically those outlined in earlier reports on the 1981–82 seasons (Muller 1984a; Muller and Avery 1982). All seasons of work revealed a consistent picture:

1. There is great uniformity of materials across the floodplain site zone. For example, in a Q-mode factor analysis (Muller et al. 1992), the excavation units in the floodplain site area all loaded heavily on Factor 1 (> 0.89), except for one unit (4938.5E 5001.5N) that loaded heavily on Factor 2. This latter unit is disturbed and is also the most distant from the spring(s). Almost all the variability is explained by the first factor, which could probably be identified as something like "salt production." As many as three salt springs may been present historically in the site, but only one spring today is salty. The use zone extends more than 500 m along the Saline River, involving substantial transport of brine from any springs to the reduction locations. The terrain divides the floodplain zone into three areas of higher ground, all of which were used in salt production. These areas are historically subject to annual flooding. Our testing program in the lower portions of the floodplain zone proper (T_0) demonstrated that the top 2m of deposits there do not contain cultural material. The three higher areas, on the other hand, contain massive quantities of debris.

2. The cultural debris in the floodplain zone consists very largely of saltpan sherds, burnt clay, mussel shells, discolored stone (sandstone, limestone, and quartzite of local origin), and little else. Although thin "utility" ware Mississippian pottery does occur, it is a minority of the total sherds present. Some fancier ceramics are found, but the quantities or unusual character of these on closer analysis have proved less striking than was thought earlier (Muller 1984a:505). Fired, clay-lined basins that preserve wiping and finger marks on their surfaces are nearly ubiquitous in the floodplain zone. Correlation of any given artifact class with any other class is typically very high, and factor analysis of the floodplain materials alone produces predominantly single-factor results regardless of the methods of factoring employed.

3. Normal "domestic" kinds of refuse are almost entirely lacking. No traces of permanent structures were found in the testing program in the floodplain, and the full range of Mississippian lithic tools is absent. Chert flakes and tools are extremely rare. *Even if the mass of saltpans and other salt-production tools are removed from the analysis,* the remaining assemblage is still untypical for Mississippian domestic assemblages from the Lower Ohio Valley.

4. The fired-clay basins (hearths) and high-temperature firing of surfaces in the deep deposits show widespread burning activities. This is also supported by the ashy fill and the large amount of charcoal flecks present. Much of this burning was related directly to saline-water reduction, but some was the result of firing of saltpans and other vessels.

5. Although bone is present and preservation is generally superb, almost all of the bone is splintered into very small pieces of the sort characteristic of heat damage to bone (Shipman 1981) or of smashing of bone of the sort

seen in Late Prehistoric (Late Horizon) sites in California (e.g., Jewell 1961:18). Such a pattern may be the result of boiling of bone to extract fats. Considerable numbers of whole and fragmentary mussel shells of a number of species were found throughout the refuse deposits and in small basin pits with very dark fill.

These and other data indicate how undifferentiated the floodplain zone is. The main activity at the salt spring floodplain zone was the production of salt. Most of the other activities that occurred there are easily related to salt production, the clearest examples being the quantities of materials, tools, and debris from the manufacture of salt pans. The work shows a textbook example of a limited-activity site. To call such a site "specialized" has some truth in it, but such terminology is misleading in implying "producer specialization" as well.

No habitation remains are known from the Great Salt Spring floodplain zone. Some burials have been reported from the spring area, but none were found in any of our work there. The evidence from the artifacts themselves is that the same activities took place throughout the site.

The Blufftop zone. The escarpment-top site areas proved to be less diverse, as we expected, but there are still important differences in relation to the floodplain zone. The major 19th-century account of the site (Sellers 1877) indicated probable structural remains. However, what Sellers called the main "residential" area is, instead, predominantly a salt-production area with only transient occupation. Even a substantial structure investigated in 1990 and 1991 was not like a "typical" Mississippian domicile in contents. In fact, depending on the variables included in analysis, the structure contents look more like the floodplain salt-production areas than the rest of the blufftop, reflecting concentration of salt-production activities in the structure. Cemeteries of stone-box graves were present, but they have been destroyed by generations of looters and were not investigated in our project.

There are a number of possible dimensions of residential and production differences, including

Behavioral Pattern	⇐ Range of Behavior ⇒		
Residence	Permanent	Seasonal	Transient
Production	Full-time	Seasonal	Occasional
Specialization	Full-time	"Part-time"	Domestic

Many combinations exist, even from these short lists. For example, permanent residents could have been earning their subsistence through salt production, but engaging in it only seasonally. Or, transient production may have taken place on a "as-needed" basis by domestic units, as seems to be the case here. The evidence supports transient residence with domestically organized seasonal to occasional production.

If Mississippian production at the Great Salt Spring site were organized in the same manner as other Mississippian production systems, our expectations were for any permanent residential areas to have a low degree of differentiation in use areas. Specifically, the domestic debris associated with any structures should have been similar in profile to those from usual Mississippian farmsteads and homesteads elsewhere. In the event, permanent residential areas were absent, but the pattern of low differentiation of use areas was true, although with different activities than at homesteads. Had the subsistence of the Great Salt Spring producers been dependent on exchange with external producers, we would have expected to find a pattern of domestic debris characteristic of consumption rather than production of basic subsistence items. In such a case, the material remains in the residential area would have had a profile that would be distinct from domestically producing Mississippian farmsteads. True craft specialists should also be expected to display their social status through distinctive decoration, elaboration, and artifacts. Depending upon settlement structure, these might be localized in residential areas. Although the site profile is certainly distinct from normal Mississippian households in lacking permanent residential units, these differences are not of the kind or quality expected of producer specialization. "Absentee" producer specialization is not inconceivable, but it is unlikely.

What we actually found was very different than these expectations. The pervasive transiency of the entire site was a surprise to us. We had initially anticipated that we would find at least some permanent settlement associated with this site zone. Early's suggestion (1993:230; cf. Muller 1995a) that our earlier interpretations had simply missed a domestic component buried in the mass of salt production debris is not true: many components of normal Mississippian domestic life are absent, not merely rare, at the site (to be discussed).

Salt springs are absent atop the escarpment, so salt production there required portage of the brine for a distance of more than 30 m vertically and from 600–800 m horizontally. This compares to portages of up to 250 m in the floodplain zone. Sellers had suggested that salt production on the south-facing slope was a possible indication of solar evaporation (1877:584–585). The efficiency of solar evaporation in this humid environment is uncertain. Some of the distinctive hearths found in the bottom zones are also present in the blufftop zone, and there are many more amorphous burned areas associated with salt production. Poorer preservation of these hearths is characteristic of the shallower deposits atop the hill, but the overall pattern of materials found in the blufftop zone is similar to that of the floodplain. The number of hearths relative to the density of materials is not much different from the low-lying areas, and there is therefore little reason to see solar evaporation as playing any greater role on the blufftop.

Low spatial differentiation of activities was found everywhere in the site, and the only structures seem to be as much salt-production areas, or more, as other blufftop-site areas. Although the potential causal relations are too complex to provide simple yes–no test implications, close association of salt-production facilities on the blufftop with quasi-domestic units does not support strong craft specialization (among other things, similar reduction processes are ubiquitous in Lower Ohio Mississippian sites).

A Q-mode factor analysis for the blufftop zone produced results similar to analysis for the floodplain. Most of the blufftop excavated units loaded heavily on Q-mode Factor 1 (contributing over 0.56 of the variance overall). Unlike the floodplain zone, however, there were a number of units that also had heavily loading on Factor 2 (contributing about 0.37 of the variance overall). A couple of units on the blufftop had high-positive loading on Factor 3 (less than 0.07 of variability). The interpretation of the "meaning" of these factors is less significant than the lack of variation in the site as a whole. It is clear, however, that more variation is present in the blufftop than in the floodplain.

Such extreme indications of specialist production as *barrios* within a residential area—with distinctive residential groups of specialist salt producers, traders, and so on—were completely absent at the site. Because true specialization creates the need for further labor differentiation in support personnel, the absence of such a situation is a clear indication of the lack of anything like an "industrial" level of salt production. However, no one should really have expected such levels of production in Mississippian anyway. The presence of specialist *barrios* would be significant, but their absence is not important in assessing claims for lower levels of craft specialization.

Character of Production

The evidence on artifact assemblages at the residential and hilltop production areas is important in assessing specialization at this site. In the first place, the assemblage profile gives some indication of the range of activities that took place. Full-time salt producers whose activities varied throughout the course of the annual cycle (such as gathering wood through the winter, boiling salt in some other season, and engaging in exchange activities at other times) might be seen as similar to Blau's (1977) "specialized expert," but it would still be expected that tasks within each portion of the productive cycle would have been routinized. Standardization of production technology and practice is primarily a reflection of intensity of production, but the implements of even "specialized experts" would be expected to be more "standardized" than those of nonspecialists.

The assemblages from the site show a high degree of "standardization" in terms of such things as percentages of different artifact classes. However, it would be wrong to interpret this kind of standardization as being that referred to in the literature on criteria indicating specialization. That kind of specialization refers to standardization of production tools and product (e.g., Rice 1981; and also Chapter 1).

Figure 7.4 shows the Great Salt Spring as a whole and remains from the structure area compared to the averages and standard deviations of more ordinary Mississippian sites in the Lower Ohio Valley (as given in Figure 7.1).

This figure shows that the general areas at the Great Salt Spring and the structure areas generally are alike and, in many cases, fall outside 1 standard deviation of the means for specific classes at more typical Mississippian sites in the region. Note that the largest portion of the ceramic complex at the Great Salt Spring is saltpans. Perhaps the most notable difference overall is the almost complete absence of the distinctive clay-lined hearths from non-salt-producing sites in the region.

Hearths and Evaporation. Solar evaporation has been proposed for the site (Sellers 1877), but it may be instructive to note that one excavated basin on the blufftop near the structure filled with rainfall soon after its excavation. This water-filled, burned basin retained its water without appreciable loss for a period of 2 weeks until it was backfilled. Although the basin was shaded for part of the day, the area did receive some direct sun. Humidity was quite high, even though the site was drier than other localities in the region. Under such conditions, the use of natural evaporation would not have been very efficient, especially given the need to protect exposed saltpans from rain.

On the other hand, it has to be noted that our project lost few days to rainfall during the five seasons of work at the site (from mid-June to early August). Heavy storms often blew in from the southwest or northwest, but usually failed to rain much in the areas where we were working.

Hearths are rarer in the blufftop than in the floodplain. However, so is general density of use, and some areas on the blufftop have been cultivated. Even so, they are still present in fairly large numbers and constitute the most common type of feature found in the site as a whole. The different relative density seems to be mostly a reflection of the lower density of production (and perhaps duration of production) in the blufftop zone.

The ubiquity of hearths of different kinds, the huge numbers of apparently fire-stained broken rock, and the deep, ashy middens in the floodplain all indicate that heat reduction played an important role in the production of salt at this site. There were some differences in the processes used in different site zones, but these do not seem to be very significant. The average size of the saltpans used in the blufftop

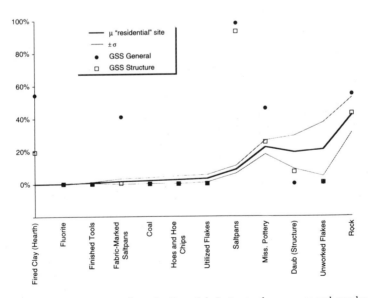

Figure 7.4. Comparison of percentages from the Great Salt Spring to the averages and standard deviations of the sites shown in Figure 7.1.

zone was less than in the floodplain zone. In addition, the distinctive hearths of the floodplain zone are rarer in the blufftop zone. It is possible that some prereduction of the brine may have taken place in the floodplain zone, with final production stages on the blufftop, but it is difficult to see how this can be settled one way or the other. It is, perhaps, just as likely that the blufftop smaller vessel size is a reflection of smaller quantities of brine being reduced there—simply as a function of the distance of the area from the salt springs.

Ceramic vessels in production. The size and numbers of saltpans at the site were substantial. Cramer described what the site was like at the beginning of the 19th century, before cultivation and intensive American salt production: "At, and in the neighborhood of these works, is to be found fragments of ancient pottery of an uncommon large size, large enough it is stated, to fit the bulge of a hogshead and thick in proportion" (1814:272). In fact, the average size of the vessels was substantial, like those of other salt-producing sites.

Vessels from other sites provide some comparative data on saltpan size. H. M. Brackenridge is cited by Holmes as saying that some vessels at Ste. Genevieve, Missouri, were "as large as a barrel" (1903:29), similar to Cramer's comment—and perhaps even derived from that popular source for early travelers. J. Jones (1880:42) found a large fabric-marked vessel in a mound at Nashville that had a diameter of 109 cm ("forty-three inches in diameter") with a depth of 7.62 cm ("three inches in height"), implying a volume of roughly 36 l (by the formulae discussed in Muller et al. 1992). By way of a comment on descriptions of shape, Jones's description of the vessel as "flat" (1880:42) seems from the context to be an argument for a basket-molded, shallow vessel rather than one that is flat bottomed in the usual sense. Holmes visit to the Kimmswick salt springs in 1901 resulted in restored vessels with diameters of 50–76 cm diameter ("20 to 30 inches," 1903:29) The Thruston collection contained a vessel some 78 cm (31 inches) in diameter, with an actual flat base (Holmes 1903:30, Plate IIIa). Holmes also quotes an *Alton* (Illinois)*Telegraph* account of materials from Cooper County, Missouri, "shaped like shallow pans, and on inch and a half in thickness and near 4 feet across the rim" (1903:31). Based on these and other accounts, I. Brown indicates the range of diameters from 50–80 cm (1980:22).

Webb and Funkhouser report a vessel from Tolu, Kentucky, with a diameter of 140 cm (1931:391, Table II). The averages for the vessel thickness in the small selection from Tolu in Table 7.3 was 0.98 cm, the maximum rim-thickness average, 2.13 cm, and the average diameter, 90.8 cm. These estimates of diameter may seem large, but Sellers (1877:580) was told of intact vessels found at the Half Moon Lick site near Equality, Illinois, as having a diameter of nearly 140 cm ("between four and five feet diameter"). About 140 cm is a fair estimate of the size of the largest saltpans.

The radiocarbon dates from the Great Salt Spring, the saltpan sherd frequencies, and vessel-diameter estimates suggest that no simple model of chronological trends in saltpan style will suffice to explain the variation in surface treatment at this site, and I would suggest caution in such interpretations elsewhere. Rather, present data at the Great Salt Spring suggest strongly that surface treatment of saltpans is a result of a combination of technical and functional considerations involved with the size and use of the reduction vessels. Larger vessels are more likely to be mold-made, and

**Table 7.3. Selected Saltpan Measurements at Tolu Site, Kentucky
(Modified from Webb and Funkhouser 1931: Table II)**

Thickness of wall (cm)	Max. thickness of rim (cm)	Form of rim	Diameter of vessel (cm)	Kind of weave	Method of application
1.00	1.70	Mold mark?	90	Single-twined weave	Oblique
1.00	2.85	Mold mark?	100	Single-twined weave	Oblique
1.10	2.70	Mold mark?	80	Single-twined weave	Oblique
1.00	1.90	Mold mark?	100	Single-twined weave	Oblique
1.10	2.85	Mold mark?	70	Single-twined weave	Oblique
0.90	2.10	Straight rim	140	Single-twined weave	Square
1.05	2.30	Mold mark?	70	Single-twined weave	Square
1.00	1.90	Straight rim	80	Modified twined weave	Oblique
0.80	1.70	Mold mark?	100	Single-twined weave	Square
1.00	1.70	Straight rim	60	Single-twined weave	Oblique
1.00	2.30	Straight rim	120	Single-twined weave	Oblique
0.75	1.60	Straight rim	80	Single-twined weave	Square

hence have some kind of surface texturing from lining the mold (see Muller and Renken 1989).

Average estimated surface areas for the jars and saltpans at the Great Salt Spring are similar, with the former at roughly 3200 cm², and the latter at more than 3100 cm². Bowl surface area would be at only slightly more than 500 cm², whereas the average circumference of rims would be at 80 cm. Overall estimates of the size and shape of thinware (as defined in the analysis sheets as ceramics less than 0.75 cm thick) suggest that much of the thinware sherds at the Great Salt Spring site are from "bowls" that probably should be considered as small saltpans. This is means that the count of salt-producing vessels as opposed to ordinary cooking or eating vessels is underestimated in the comparisons to domestic sites given here. The jars found at the site could certainly have been used for salt reduction, although they would have been less efficient than saltpans. In short, there is little about the ceramic complex at the Great Salt Spring that strongly supports the presence of many, if any, activities not related to reduction processing (certainly of salt and, perhaps, reduction of game remains and boiling of acorn mush or other foods).

Other materials. Lithics and other categories at the Great Salt Spring site are a mere shadow of what they are in bottomland Lower Ohio Valley Mississippian farmsteads and towns. Most of the lithic assemblage described as "common" in Cole et al. (1951:114ff.) is virtually or actually absent, despite the large size of the sample from the Great Salt Spring. When the lithic assemblage from the Great Salt Spring is compared to a "typical" hamlet-level site like IAS Mx 66, the difference can plainly be seen (Table 7.4, Figure 7.5).

Although there are relatively unimportant differences in the percentages of various kinds of broken rock, the main differences in the assemblages are those in the number and kind of flakes, especially "utilized" or "microflaked" flakes. Hoechips are rare at all sites, but much more rare at the Great Salt Spring. The differences overall

**Table 7.4. Comparison of Some Great Salt Spring Categories to a
Black Bottom Hamlet (by Units)**

	GSS				Mx 66			
	Total	Mean/unit	St. dev.	Maximum	Total	Mean	St. Dev.	Maximum
Sandstone	71,344	46.3	153.15	1882	5300	240.91	206.88	691
Broken rock	10,558	6.85	26.99	378	107	4.86	9.12	30
Pebbles	1735	1.13	4.47	55				
Unworked flakes	1835	1.19	3.11	31	2034	92.45	76.68	337
"Utilized" flakes	125	0.08	0.4	5	258	11.73	10.26	37
Fluorite	29	0.02	0.45	17				
Cores	24	0.02	0.15	3	23	1.05	1	3
Hoechips	21	0.01	0.12	2	162	7.36	6.34	20
Bifacial tools	23	0.02	0.13	2	88	4	10.43	50
Points	25	0.02	0.13	2				
Iron concretions	337	0.22	3.09	100				
Unworked coal	210	0.14	1.95	60	103	4.68	7.54 .	31

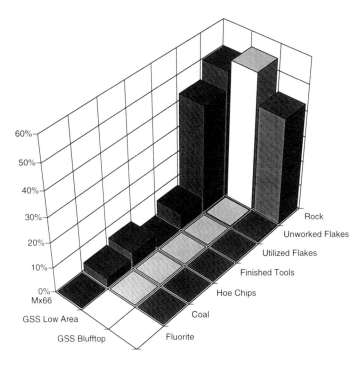

Figure 7.5. Comparison of some lithics categories at the Great Salt Spring (GSS) and the Angelly site (IAS Mx 66).

are striking, even on simple inspection. The Great Salt Spring clearly does not present the same range of production activities as that present at the many farmsteads, hamlets, and towns of the Lower Ohio River Valley.

Indications of External Goods and Exchange

If salt were produced by craft specialists, it would be produced for external exchange. Producers should have received imports in exchange for their production. Excavations showed that some of the nonsalt production items found at the Great Salt Spring were "exotic" by comparison with materials from small farmsteads in the Kincaid locality. However, many of these were items such as small molded "figurines" that were exceptionally crude and are not convincing evidence for "trade." Many of fancier items (such as negative-painted pottery) normally found in the farmsteads and homesteads are lacking entirely at the Great Salt Spring production areas.

Salt is water soluble, so it rarely produces good archaeological evidence that might be tested for source areas by chemical studies, for example. Nor do we have any likely candidates for salt containers, such as *augets*, that might allow us to identify "exports" of salt. Salt surely was a highly prized exchange item in Mississippian times, however, as it was in early historical times. Salt processing was easiest at the salt spring areas; and, even without specialization, producers at the Great Salt Spring probably exchanged surplus salt for other goods. So the mere presence of exotic items, of itself, would not prove specialization here. Rather, judgments of the character and quantity of such goods in relation to exchange would have to be made. The absence, however, of significant quantities of exotics is critically important, in that it is hard to justify a model of production *in Mississippian* that would place the control of production far away from the producers, leaving them with nothing to show for their labor.

Direct exploitation by transients from "a great way off" (Le Page du Pratz 1758[1972]:153) would also explain some exotic assemblages at the Great Salt Spring site, but exotic items in campgrounds are poor support for specialist production, even if many such items were present. Since so few exotics are even present in this sort of context, we may suppose that the salt makers tended to travel "light" on their forays to the salt-production locality. This further strengthens the idea of a regional rather than purely local exploitation of this resource.

In terms of sources of chert used at the Great Salt Spring, lithic materials show diversity of sources; but there is so little chert from the site that the pattern of use is difficult to compare with ordinary Mississippian sites. There are no good chert sources in the immediate Great Salt Spring locality except for cobbles in glacial till, so *all* cherts are exotic in one sense. None of the character of the lithic assemblage is such that it could be reasonably interpreted as indicating imports of exotic cherts for the support of resident salt producers (of the sort proposed in principle for early specialist production in the Near East by Jacobs, 1967).

In terms of ceramics, there can be little doubt that nearly all ceramics used at the Great Salt Spring were made on the spot from local clays and other abundant local raw materials such as river mussels (Holt and others in Muller et al. 1992). As already indicated, the majority of thinware vessels are not jars—as at residential sites—but bowls. Many of these simply seem to be small saltpans rather than eating dishes. The percentages of "fine" wares are lower at the Great Salt Spring than they are at the farmsteads and hamlets of the main river valley. Again, the numbers of the "fancy" ceramics is so small everywhere that the differences among various sites need to be interpreted with caution. Examined overall, however, the ceramic assemblage from the Great Salt Spring is *not* consistent with most of the expectations of a "specialist model" of salt production. The assemblage is consistent with transient use of the site, with local production of the main tools used in salt production. On-site specialist producers are absent, together with the rich "trade" assemblage of imported goods that one would expect them to receive in exchange for their salt. Although we have only anecdotal and historical information on the grave furniture from the site, the grave accompaniments seem to have been as sparse in display goods as is the rest of the site. They certainly were not extremely "rich" in materials as compared to other stone box graves in the region.

Taken altogether, then, the Great Salt Spring does not show the degree of evidence for "trade" or (more properly) "exchange" that would have been expected for the full-time or craft-specialist models that were commonly presented before our work at the site.

Conclusions

Six major conclusions of the Great Salt Spring's character may be summarized:

1. Extent of occupation and use—Salt production was ubiquitous. Most of the site had either no residential use at all or was only occupied transiently. Even a substantial facility, Structure 1, in a meter-deep pit (on the upslope side) proved not to be a "typical" Mississippian house, but seems to have been a shelter for salt production. Testing and augering revealed a few other potential structures, but there were very few structures at the site as a whole.

2. Intensity of use—Salt production was cumulatively extensive over the site, with some zones with as much as 3-m deep middens of ash and debris from burning reduction of brine. Salt manufacture did not display the standardization to be expected of specialist production. Residential use was transitory across the site, even in a substantially built structure. Most construction of shelters was light and insubstantial.

3. Continuity of use—Most botanical and faunal evidence suggests heaviest use of the site occurred in October and November, but evidence of spring and summer species indicates some year-round exploitation. Most botanical assemblages are relatively pure in seasonal terms, supporting the conclusion of mostly transient, short-term use.

4. Differentiation of use—The site as a whole is one, large, limited-activity site. Spatial differentiation is quite low, with—for example—Q-mode factor analysis of site materials yielding strong indications of a common factor underlying variability at the site. Although the blufftop and floodplain zones are different in a few ways, those differences are mostly related to variables of distance, transport, and intensity of use.

5. Production and consumption character in the domestic context—The only materials that represent a "domestic" or residential context at the site are clearly from transient use. Although the Great Salt Spring site is different in specific ways from "typical" Mississippian households, it shares a major principle of labor organization with all regional Mississippian: Production is centered around small, in this case probably domestic, units and is not organized by craft or industry.

6. Indications of external goods and exchange—On one level, many non-salt-producing materials at the site are exotic, in line with transient use. However, no areas have much in the way of wares or goods that might indicate their use in exchange relations for salt.

Thus, the work at the site has shown a number of site features, including:

1. Salt production occurred over a long period in Mississippian times, but heaviest use coincided with the previously identified 13th-century peak of regional population.

2. Different site areas represent temporally distinct episodes, but virtually all site areas were in use in the 13th century.

3. Structures are generally absent. Evidence has been found for a few temporary structures, but only two certain "permanent" facilities have been identified.

4. The predominant activity in *all* site zones, including the structures, was salt production. Contrary to our first impressions of the structure, however, the assemblage there has proved to be rather like the salt-production activities elsewhere in the site. There are some fancier ceramics with the structure, but these do not constitute an assemblage that can legitimately be described as "elite" or "trade-oriented."

The data show a pattern of production that is best explained by nonspecialist production.

Salt Production at Other Sites

Salt was, in fact, widely available throughout the Southeast, and there are a number of salt springs in different localities (see Figure 6.6; Brown 1980b: Chapter 6; or Wentowski 1970: Chapter 4). The fact that salt was available within a few days' travel from many Mississippian communities must have played a role in preventing any one salt source from having a monopoly on this prized material. Before moving on to other production systems, however, I want to briefly discuss other salt-production localities to see how we may interpret their character in light of the research at the Great Salt Spring.

The Missouri Salt Springs

Keslin undertook his study of the St. Marys, Missouri, salt springs as a part of a training program for the University of Missouri in 1957 and 1958 (1964). The sites are located along Saline Creek in Ste. Genevieve County. A number of various kinds of sites were tested or sampled, including four salt-producing areas. The kinds of materials recovered were basically similar to those of the Great Salt Spring site, with large quantities of saltpans, hearths of various kinds, and relatively low numbers of chert flakes. Figure 7.6 shows the relative proportions of "utility" Mississippian pottery and saltpans at the Ste. Genevieve sites and at the Great Salt Spring for comparison.

The actual ratios of chert flakes and bifaces or bifaces alone to both Mississippi Plain sherds and to saltpan sherds are actually even lower at the Missouri sites than they are at the Great Salt Spring, although different recovery methods and conditions make the data less than completely comparable. As at the Great Salt Spring zones, stone-box graves were found near the salt production areas (e.g., Keslin 1964:117ff.). The association of a few "trade" sherds of Cahokian type coincides with high frequency of fabric marking of the saltpans, which was primarily a reflection of larger sized vessels. This may be a hint of extra production of salt for some exchange from this locality to the St. Louis locality, some 80–90 km north. However, one should not make too much of this possible exchange relationship, as the total number of "northern" sherds is small: three sherds of Powell Plain, one sherd of Ramey Incised, three sherds of Tippets Bean Pot, and a few others at Kreilich, for example, and less at the Cole site! Some trade network! Of course, the closest salt producing sites to St. Louis and the American Bottom are actually those near Kimmswick, Missouri (see Bushnell 1907, 1908; also Adams 1941, 1949) which are less than 30 km south of the St. Louis Mound site in modern downtown St. Louis.

No indications, in admittedly small-scale testing, were found of structures at the Kreilich or Cole sites. The Fortnight site did have daub. If this was actual daub rather than clay-lined hearth fragments, the site may have had some structures. There was little utilitarian Mississippian pottery from the site, as shown in Figure 7.6. Overall,

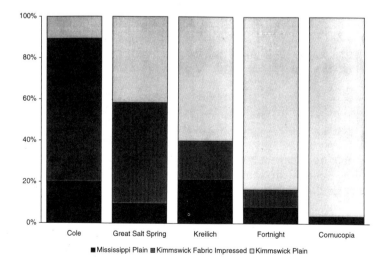

Figure 7.6. Percentages of plain "utility" pottery (Mississipp Plain) in relation to Saltpans (Kimmswick types).

Keslin concluded that exploitation of at least the Kreilich and Cole sites was probably carried out by persons resident elsewhere (1964:68–69, 94).

The Missouri salt-producing sites are much like the Great Salt Spring, with the expected local variations in detail. Unlike the Great Salt Spring, there are various kinds of Mississippian residential sites, even including mound sites, near these salt-production areas, but there are no indications that the sites were used by craft specialists producing for trade. Mind you, exchange of goods was important in these localities, and the St. Marys site (MacCurdy 1913) is one location that has shell gorgets in several styles, perhaps linking Spiro to Etowah (see Muller 1966a; Phillips and Brown 1984). There is no reason, however, to see salt production at the Missouri salines as the center of these exchange activities. Rather, it is more likely that salt was just one of many goods that were sometimes exchanged.

Avery Island

The initial work at the Avery Island, Louisiana, salt springs sites was carried out by Gagliano (1967), who was able to show that salt production had taken place in the Plaquemine period, but using ordinary bowls rather than saltpans. Subsequent work at Salt Mine Valley (Brown 1980a; Brown and Lambert-Brown 1979) confirmed this situation. Brown (1980b, 1981) suggested that a narrow, flowerpot-like mold form and baked clay supports were of a form used in salt production known in the Old World as *briquetage* (Kleinmann 1975; Nenquin 1961). Brown suggests that some other small and crude vessel forms, perhaps even including Cahokia "stumpware" may also be indications of salt molding. This may be, but note that the "mold" theory seems to be based on no more than a few miniature vessels at the salt-production area itself. The absence of more of these is explained by their being exported with the salt in them. However, so far as I am aware, such objects are equally rare at possible consumer sites where one might expect to find them discarded. The claim of molding salt is not unimportant, since in the Old World cases, the molds (*augets*) themselves were standardized to ensure salt cakes of equal size for exchange in what may have been true specialized production for trade (e.g., Kleinmann 1975:45). As Brown explicitly recognizes, however, the whole *briquetage* hypothesis is intriguing but far from proved. It is notable that the cases from other areas that are cited as possible indications of this kind of salt production are mostly fairly late, many in the 15th and 16th century, like the Avery Island salt production itself. I think the evidence is too scanty at present to accept that specialist *briquetage* production of salt was established late in the prehistory of the Lower Mississippi Valley. Demonstration of a truly standardized production and trade system will require, among other things, proof that *auget*-like vessels were in fact exchanged widely over the region and have a standard volume.

Arkansas Salt Making

One of the more detailed studies of prehistoric salt production in the Southeast is that carried out at a small Caddoan salt-making site in Arkansas by Ann Early and her associates (1993b). The Hardman site, as it is called, is only about the size of a typical Mississippian farmstead in the Black Bottom—0.25 ha. Column samples and stripping of the site produced over 28,000 sherds. However, the vast majority of them were plain saltpans (Figure 7.7). As can be seen, the assemblage has many similarities to those at other Mississippian salt-producing sites. The saltpans here were not quite like the usual forms from Mississippian contexts but shared the common features needed to assist in reduction of brine into salt, such as shallowness in relation to diameter.

Although most sherds were too small to allow determination of saltpan dimensions, illustrations in the report suggest that at least one vessel had a radius of about 34 cm. The illustrated sherds appear to be from flat-bottomed pans that seem to be quite shallow. The minimum volume would have been around 8–9 l, based on a few photographs of larger sherds. There were a number of "hearths," but some of these were quite large (ranging from 1–22 m²; Williams, in Early 1993b:47), and the larger hearth features could be pottery firing areas (see Muller 1995a). Early concludes, "The salt trade seems never to have reached the scope of a full-time enterprise" (1993b:233). She also concludes that salt making at this site probably mostly was related to local domestic consumption, and exchange items are missing from graves at the site (1993b:232). There were domestic structures on this Caddo site, with perhaps two structures having been occupied during the peak use of the site (Williams, in Early 1993b:42–46). There were, however, also a number of "ephemeral postmold arcs" (1993b:42, 44) that suggest to me that there may have been temporary structures erected during transient use of the site at other times. However, Williams suggests the possibility that these were platform storage bins (in Early 1993b:45).

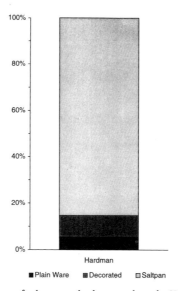

Figure 7.7. Percentages of saltpans and other vessels at the Hardman site, Arkansas.

Hoe Production

Hoes made from hard cherts were implements that were widely used in Mississippian times. Given that the total mass of exchanged goods for these artifacts may have exceeded all other items exhanged, the production of hoes is another important test case in looking at Mississippian production systems. Two major hoe source areas are those in Union County, Illinois, and those near Dover, Tennessee. Each of these, as summarized in the last chapter, was especially well suited for hoe manufacture both in terms of the shape of nodules and their hardness and resistance to breaking.

Mill Creek

The hoe production locality at Mill Creek, Illinois, is different in settlement character than that found near the Great Salt Spring. Overall, the settlement pattern is somewhat like that at the Ste. Genevieve, Missouri, salt springs in the sense that there is evidence for long-term residence and even the construction of small mound centers in these localities.

The largest center near the Union County quarries in Illinois is actually in the main valley of the Mississippi River at the Linn site (Cobb 1991; Thomas 1894:155–159). This small center had a palisade enclosure of about 11 ha and more than five small mounds with a total volume in the neighborhood of 6000 m³. The largest mound (Mound A) was about 4 m high and had a volume of about 3000 m³. Thomas referred to about 100 structure depressions visible on the site in the late 19th century, although the accompanying map only located 30 "hut rings" (1894). Either of these figures is within the ranges we saw for historical Southeastern towns. The presence of other small polities in the neighborhood may have resulted in more aggregation than is typical for the interiors of larger Mississippian complexes. The Linn site is located so that there would have been fairly easy passage up "hollows" to the Mill Creek quarries. Considerable quantities of chert flakes and many indications of processing Mill Creek chert are found on the site, which has not been professionally investigated since the late 19th century. Other small mound sites are located within 10 km of this site, and there seem to have been a number of probably autonomous communities in the broad bottomlands north of a constriction in the Valley known as Thebes Gap. Just below Thebes Gap lies the Lower Mississippi Valley proper and a large number of small polities that seem to have characterized Mississippian political structure between the Ohio Confluence and modern-day Memphis.

In the immediate vicinity of the quarries and workshops is the Hale site at Mill Creek, Illinois. This site had one square mound a little over 2 m high and another possible mound with stone-box graves (Thomas 1894:148–154). Together they would have represented less than 1000 m³ of construction. A number of stone-box graves was excavated by the Smithsonian workers. It is notable that little in the way of exotic items was buried with these people—grave goods consisted of some shells, bone or shell pins, and a few fragments of copper (1894). So far as I have been able to determine, the excavation of a few more graves in the 1970s yielded similar results. These are not the rich graves of some hoe-making guild masters. There was, however, one unusual grave that had three persons buried in it, two of whose heads had been removed and were placed beneath the head of the central figure (1894:154; see Figure 7.8). It would seem reasonable that this arrangement reflected some kind of subordination (i.e., they might have been persons killed to accompany a local chief), but it would be easy to overstep the evidence since we do not know if these peripheral individuals were contemporary or redeposited, for example. One does not know how accurate Thomas's illustration might be, but the limbs of the flanking figures are shown as partially disarticulated. Since it was common in the Southeast to keep the remains of ancestors in mortuary shrines for some time, it may be just as likely that the flanking burials are kin who predeceased the central figure. Putting the heads together, of course, could symbolize many kinds of relationships.

Another possible mound is located about 3 km to the south. The locality around the Hale site has a number of smaller sites, most with evidence of workshop activities. Many of the workshops also had residential use, but not all. The quarries themselves showed evidence not only of mining the chert, sometimes as deeply as 4.5 m down (Phillips 1899, 1900), but also of doing the initial trimming of the nodules before removing the chert to the workshop sites (from analysis of the Smithsonian collections by Cobb 1988; also Holmes 1919; Phillips 1900).

Additional workshop and quarry sites were found in surveys by SIUC graduate students and staff leading up to Cobb's dissertation (1988) and his subsequent NSF-sponsored work in the locality (1995; Cobb and Thomas 1994). In the course of the latter work, testing at a site believed to be a quarry revealed a Mississippian blufftop

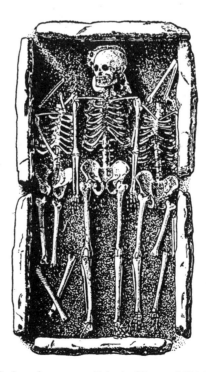

Figure 7.8. Stone-box grave at Hale site (Thomas 1894: Figure 81).

settlement. Subsequent investigations by Cobb and his associates at this site, Dillow's Ridge, have produced valuable data on the residential context of Mill Creek hoe production. Analysis of this site and several years of testing and excavation are not yet completed. However, preliminary results have revealed a site of extraordinary character—a blufftop residential site with many workshops around it. Not only hoes, but also a special bipointed knife form known as a Ramey knife were made at the site (Figure 7.9). The knives should, I think, not be confused with finely made goods (a.k.a. "prestige goods"). Similar artifacts were also made at the Dover work shops (Gramly 1992). In fact, the number of pieces of Ramey knives at Dillow's Ridge was actually higher than the number of hoe fragments in the 1993 season at the site (Cobb 1995:15). Projectile points of the ubiquitous Mississippian small triangular form were also common, along with large flake scrapers. Surprisingly, given the huge quantities of debitage available from workshop production of hoes and knives, there were also bifacial cores. Perhaps these served some kind of chopper function.

The blufftop was packed with houses that were rebuilt many times over a long period of occupation. My own interpretation of the finds at this site suggest that there is a standard Mississippian domestic production system here that has had the production of considerable quantities of stone tools added onto it; that is, I cannot see that the evidence suggests that hoe and knife production had supplanted local production for consumption, yet clearly more stone tools and blanks were being prepared than would have been needed locally, although the totals do not add up to much excess production per annum (Brian Butler, personal communication 1996). If there were justification for the term *part-time* specialization, this kind of system would be it.

The ceramic assemblage, for example, looks much like those from other Mississippian residential sites, allowing for geographic and temporal differences (see Table 7.5). Saltpans and large bowls are more common than one might expect, so it is clear that some kind of reduction process was being practiced. Perhaps animal fats were being boiled off in pans from game hunted with the arrowheads, butchered with the knives and scrapers, and bone pounded up by the chopper cores. There is no possibility that major salt production took place at this site.

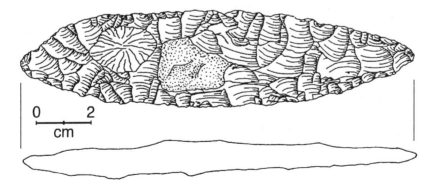

0   2
cm

Figure 7.9. Ramey knife from Dillow's Ridge (drawn by Brian DelCastello in Cobb 1995).

**Table 7.5. Percentages of Vessel Forms at
Dillow's Ridge**

Vessel forms	%
Bowls	37.8
Jars	34.4
Plates and pans	12.8
Seedjars	3.9
Everted lip	3.9
Bottles	3.9
Stumpware	2.8
Rectanguloid bowls	0.6

From Cobb and Thomas 1994

When the contents of the houses at Dillow's Ridge are examined after filtering out the production of objects from the local chert, what is left seems as much domestic as any site where we have no evidence for concentration of production in any one technology. Indeed, the vast quantities of chert debitage at these sites has to be put up against the centuries during which production of these goods took place. There is no doubt that hoe and Ramey knife production at a site such as Dillow's Ridge was far more intensive than production *of these items* at other sites. That does not mean their production was industrial, by any means. Remember that other Mississippian sites are located in alluvial floodplains, where nearly every piece of rock had to be brought into the location. If wood chips, cane fragments, or other items worked at domestic sites preserved as well as chert flakes, we would see far more "workshops" than we do!

In general, the Dillow's Ridge site indicates that Mill Creek Mississippian producers were taking advantage of the rich resources of their locality. However, there is little in the way of surviving goods or "riches" that seem to have been returned to them from other localities. Neither Dillow's Ridge nor the Hale mound site appear wealthy or favored by comparison with Kincaid or Cahokia peoples. Nor does the Linn site or any of the other local Mississippian sites show any indication that *they* were the "entrepreneurs" benefiting from the work of the Mill Creek knappers. Rather, the Linn site evidence, such as it is, simply indicates that those people, too, were collecting raw material in upland foraging activities and processing the materials in their domestic setting, albeit at much higher levels than those located at greater distances.

Finally, there is another problem with making the residents of Dillow's Ridge, at least, big suppliers of hoes to the American Bottom. The earliest radiocarbon date for the site is A.D. 1230, the most recent date A.D. 1495 (corrected intercept, data from Cobb and Butler, personal communications 1996) and the mean date for the site is A.D. 1350! All but the earliest of these are after the effective end of Cahokia as a major center. In the case of Dillow's Ridge, the possibility exists that the blufftop settlement and many of the features of the site may reflect alteration of settlement possibilities after most long-distance exchange in Mississippian had dropped off precipitously.

Perhaps these are the descendants of peoples who formerly lived at sites such as Linn and Hale. It is clear that we still need to look at earlier Mississippian sites in this locality to see what exactly was happening at the time of the regional peaks in the Mississippi and Ohio Valleys, respectively. However, I cannot see that we can conclude from present evidence that chert tool manufacture and exchange were the "cutting edge" of Mississippian social and economic differentiation.

Dover

The Dover locality is near the present Tennessee town of that name, close to both the Tennessee and Cumberland Rivers, and near the Civil War Fort Henry. The chert found there is a distinctive fossiliferous, and hard, variety that shares many of the properties of Mill Creek chert. We do not have the data needed for a full comparison of the Dover hoe production systems to Mill Creek. However, several things are reasonably clear. The distribution of Dover chert tools was more restricted than Mill Creek tools. These were not exchanged as widely as Mill Creek hoes or knives. Even at Kincaid, for example, Dover chert does not predominate, despite the fact that Kincaid is directly downstream from Dover by either the Tennessee or Cumberland. Although Mill Creek is closer to Kincaid, it is an overland, not a water journey. This suggests that (1) Dover was not as favored a raw materials source given its likelier greater ease of access, or (2) perhaps water transportation was not as highly developed as we believe. Neither of these observations is compatible with the idea of massive specialization of hoe production at Dover.

Gramly (1992) has presented a complex series of production estimates at some small sites at the Dover quarries locality. From these he concludes that full-time producers were engaged in production there. However, it is necessary to look at the details of these estimates to see whether they are sufficient to prove the case.

Gramly's estimates are built upon a series of conjectures about the site, about density of artifacts, and about duration of production. If one accepts his final estimates, then it would, indeed, seem that for a small family living at the location, an annual production of over 3200 large stone tools in a year—working "13–21.5 hours" per day—would indicate full-time specialization. But how are these figures obtained?

One central problem with Gramly's assumptions is the proposal that the debris at each of two small sites tested (Cross Creek and Turkey Pen) represented the debris of only 1 year's production. In fact, neither of these sites is likely to have represented only 1 year's production for a single producer family. Cross Creek was a workshop site with a mound of debris. Although we are not given overall site limits, a small trench produced about 2200 kg of chert, among which some 200 "implements" were discovered (1992:19). However, by extending the estimate to a broader area, for which we are given little evidence, the total site volume is taken to be some "4078.4 kg"—note the precision of the 0.4 kg for this estimate. The Turkey Pen site was estimated to have some 2400 kg of debris, although only a little over 1900 kg was actually excavated (1992:20). After producing these *estimated* volumes, Gramly then indicates, "I am inclined to believe that the pit at Turkey Pen represented one year's waste from the manufacture of flaked tools by a family of craftsmen whose house once stood nearby" (1992:20). This is the argument that is given for this assumption, which is treated thereafter as a simple truth. A "median" is calculated from these two points, so 3900 kg per year is used to estimate the duration of use of other workshop areas!

Gramly uses the phrase "hamlet/workshop" for these sites; but only one of the sites tested by him, the Revnik site, had a structure. Even that structure is by no means a typical Mississippian building. In fact, as Gramly describes it, it is "an open rectangular pattern of medium-sized postholes" (1992:15). By "open" here is meant that it only had three walls! The area enclosed with posts is about 6 × 4.5 m, but less than 4 × 4.5 m are claimed as "house" by Gramly (1992:15). The reason for this conservatism is that the northern portion of the structure area is packed with lithic production debris, so that if the entire structure were taken together, it would be rather easy to interpret it as an open lean-to shelter for transient lithic workers. In fact, there is little reason to see this structure as a "house" in the normal Mississippian sense. There *is* evidence for a domestic presence at the site, in that production and consumption debris are present. From the information we have, it is not possible to tell whether this might be more of a campsite than a year-round presence. Indeed, contrary to hypotheses of specialized production, the domestic debris does indicate that a broad range of domestic *production* activities were undertaken at the site in addition to manufacturing Dover tools.

Each link of the chain forged by Gramly has some weaknesses. The Revnik site is described by Perino in his foreword: "41 tons of debitage were recovered and among this debris were found nearly 9000 objects of human manufacture" (in Gramly 1992:ix). It is easy to see how Perino came to this conclusion, but the truth is that we are not told in the report what the quantities were in the some 92 m² actually excavated! The figures given by Perino are, rather, *estimates*, apparently calculated by multiplying the number of total squares by the unspecified densities that resulted in a density contour map. However, when one examines this map, it becomes obvious that the estimates are inaccurate. It seems likely that somehow each square in the higher density zones was counted more than once, since calculation of the areas and densities on Gramly's map—even at his probably exaggerated estimates of density—would only be about 24,000 kg, not the 37,423 kg (i.e., 41 short tons) he claims for the site.

From his table (Table 7.6), Gramly added up the numbers of tools in Categories 1–4, then divided them by the sum *of the first 4 categories* to get a percentage to estimate numbers in his formula: Flat adzes 0.42N + knives 0.20N + hoes 0.13N + k. b. adzes 0.25N = N (1992:87). It makes sense to apportion Category 5 (fragmentary bifaces) according to this formula, but I do not understand why this would be appropriate for Categories 6–10. By the counts and masses in his Table 1, the percentages used to estimate numbers of artifacts can only be used for (at best) about 74 percent of the debitage, The other categories—hammerstones, utilized flakes, scrapers, cores, and gravers—total 26 percent of the mass and about 48 percent of the counts that seem to be erroneously distributed among *estimated* numbers of finished tools for export. Even accepting Gramly's assumptions for the sake of this argument, there would only have been some 18,000 kg of supposed *tool production* debris at the Revnik site after adjusting for overcount and misapportionment, not the 37,000 kg calculated by Gramly.

Table 7.6. Gramly's Estimates of Total Numbers of Flaked Stone Implements at the Revnik Site

Category		Number	Mass (kg)
1	Flat adzes	609	128.07
2	Knives/swords	294	14.9
3	Hoes	189	51.42
4	Keeled, bellied adzes	357	32.06
5	Fragmentary bifaces, not further identifiable	3108	403.82
6	Hammerstones	147	43.51
7	Utilized flakes	210	19
8	Unifacial scrapers	819	59.16
9	Beaks or spurred gravers	3024	98.78
10	Blocky cores	42	6.8
Total		8799	857.52

Data from Gramly 1992:14

The first two columns of numbers in Table 7.7 are the numbers resulting when the corrections to totals and distribution among categories are made. However, there is another way to estimate the number of artifacts per volume of debris. At the Cross Creek site that really forms the basis for the estimated "annual" production figure, there were in fact "nearly 200 implements" in the "approximately 2273 kg of debitage" (1992:19). If this *were* part of a single annual production achievement, then we would expect a similar ratio in other debris—that is, one discarded "implement" for every 11.4 kg of debris. If this ratio is used to estimate how much of the 18,000 kg of tool debris could be apportioned among the four main categories, it yields the total and annual production estimates for the Revnik site, as always, following, for the sake of argument, Gramly's assumptions about time (11.5 years of production) and apportionment of tools.[4]

At the latter estimates, suddenly the production per year—*even accepting an 11.5 year time span for all production at the site*—becomes rather modest, with a total annual production of only about one artifact every other day, rather than the 21.5-hour days estimated by Gramly. At Gramly's production estimates, as corrected, a full-time production unit of five people, consuming an average of 2000 kcal/day/person, would have needed to have received a minimum of 0.7 kg of dried maize per artifact in order merely to provision themselves. At the much lower figures, it would have required a "price" of nearly 8 kg per artifact just to get enough to eat! Of course, in the end, such multiplication of estimates by estimates are not very compelling either way. It is, however, clear from these that it is hard to make a very strong case for full-time specialization at the Revnik site or at other sites in the Dover locality, even following Gramly's assumptions about production. The Dover production systems show much evidence that production was not solely limited to exploitation by

[4] Of course, the apportionment to classes and numbers is based on the numbers of discards and broken specimens, but this seems to be how Gramly made his larger estimates as well.

Table 7.7. Tool Production Estimates for the Revnik Site

Tools	Gramly's estimates (corrected)		Estimates by ratio of tools to debris	
	Totals	Per year	Totals	Per year
Flat adzes	7481	650	665	58
Knives	3562	310	317	28
Hoes	2315	201	206	18
Keeled, bellied adzes	4453	387	396	34

Based on data in Gramly 1992

full-time residents, much less full-time specialists. The kinds of debris, the absence of true, weatherproof houses, and even the chronology from the sites are consistent so far with an argument of primarily transient use. There is, as I mentioned before, some evidence from some of these sites at Dover that there may have been residential areas nearby, as was the case at Dillow's Ridge and at the Missouri salines. What has not been done yet is to show that the nature of the domestic life of any of these residents is consistent with their being full-time specialist producers, rather than ordinary Mississippian people who happened to be near a wonderful resource.

Finally, as at Dillow's Ridge, there is the embarrassment that the dated production episodes are all rather late. The more or less reasonable dates from Gramly's excavations range from A.D. 1320–1480 with the mean about A.D. 1385. These dates are essentially at the end of Mississippian times in the regions to the north. There were still southern Mississippian societies, but total Mississippian population in the Southeast was probably smaller than it would have been a century or two earlier. So far as I can tell, the hoes seem to have been exchanged most widely well before the Revnik site was used. Residential use of Dillow's Ridge, and possible residentially based exploitation of the Dover area, are both late enough to rule out these particular sites as being relevant to lithic tool importation for the "High" Mississippian of Cahokia, or even Kincaid. As I have argued, the "decline" of Mississippian after the mid-13th century is by no means universal, but it seems odd for *specialist* production of hoes and other stone tools to be present in times of declining populations and more widely dispersed polities. Perhaps, like the Great Salt Spring, earlier exploitation was predominantly transient, and residential concentrations at both Dillow's Ridge and Dover took place after the decline of nearby competing centers.

4. PRODUCTION OF DISPLAY GOODS

We actually know less than one would think about the production of display goods in Mississippian societies, given the amount of importance attached to it by some. Of course, as for the more mundane production systems, assessment of the production of what I would prefer to call "finely made" or "display" goods, for lack of better terms, is difficult without placing these into their social context. As I have already suggested, the restriction of "prestige" goods to the elite and to elite sites is largely, though not entirely, an artifact of where we have dug. Close attention to production of rare goods in small sites in both the American Bottom and the Black Bottom has shown that such goods are rare everywhere but occur about as frequently at small sites as at larger ones. Of course, in the latter cases, the larger totals of all artifact classes make even rare classes of goods appear in archaeological samples in greater numbers, though not in higher percentages. In the discussion that follows, I will briefly discuss production of such items at a series of locations.

The Black Bottom

Display goods production, as opposed to the use of display goods, seems to have been widespread and not restricted to limited groups. As already noted, fluorite, coal, marine shell, and copper represent supposed "valued" goods used in making Mississippian fancy items. The processing of such "wealth" items has sometimes been proposed to have been done by specialists. Yet all of these materials are known from small sites well away from Kincaid (except for marine shell because of poor preservation conditions). Coal and fluorite, at least, were processed at these small sites. No evidence supports an argument that this processing was done by specialists in any useful sense of that term. Rather, nearly every household seems to have participated in the production of the coal and fluorite ornaments made in the Kincaid locality. The evidence might suggest sexual division of labor, but hardly more than that.

In shell gorgets, for example, the present evidence indicates that these objects were made and used at both large and small Mississippian sites, generally; and this is also true in the Lower Ohio and surrounding regions specifically. The next chapter will discuss their distributions in terms of exchange connections within and between various regions, but that discussion will also reveal that these objects have wide distributions that are not completely restricted to major sites, notwithstanding the much greater degree of archaeological digging that has taken place there.

Other Mississippian Regions

Claims for one level or another of specialist production have been made for other Mississippian complexes in the Southeast (e.g., Hardin 1981; Prentice 1983, 1985; Yerkes 1983, 1986). The absence of craft specialization in the Kincaid–Angel phase(s) does not show that specialization never existed in any Mississippian system, but I remain skeptical of claims of craft specialization in which the production systems have not been evaluated within the context of the broader culture (see Muller 1986a, 1987a). Differences in craftsmanship exist in all levels of economic production. but the key element of true craft specialization is the roles of specialist producers within the production organization of their societies. Identification of craft specialization cannot rest solely on the presence of one or two criteria without attention to the social contexts of production. I would especially resist claims of craft specialization for industries in which the simpler hypothesis of domestic production has not been tested and rejected (Muller 1986a). The use of an explicitly defined proposal for each production system is critical to testing, but often usage and argument have tended to be rather loose.

A complete critique of claims of specialization for all Mississippian societies would be its own book and should involve much detailed reanalysis of the evidence presented. Nonetheless, I would like to comment on the problems and bright spots in the study of production of display goods in Mississippian social formations.

American Bottom

Discussion of American Bottom "specialized" production was stimulated in 1983, when Yerkes proposed that microdrills at Cahokia were "specialized" tools, at least in the sense of having been used for a limited range of activities. As he quite properly pointed out then, they were not necessarily used by "full-time" specialists, nor did "specialized" tools necessarily support what he called *craft specialization*. Moreover, he rejected the then commonly assumed idea of "guild" production areas, as derived from the then-popular state-level model for Cahokia (e.g., Porter 1969). At the same time, starting from the generalized definition of craft specialization in Evans, Yerkes did conclude that microdrills were "specialized tools" used for shell-bead production and that "additional archaeological evidence can be used to satisfy most of the criteria for craft specialization outlined by Evans," while noting that more work is necessary before the "nature of Mississippian craft specialization can be fully apprehended" (1983:514). Yerkes stated that "demonstrating that craft specialization existed at Cahokia does not prove that the site was the urban capital of a true state" (1993:514). Of course, the terminology here follows that of Evans, so that *this kind* of specialization is certainly *not* an indication of *any* form of social structure or formation. In response to my critique of some aspects of this proposal (Muller 1984a), Yerkes made his gradualist assumptions about specialization explicit (1986:403). Although I personally believe it is important to treat specialization as a social fact, not as a list of traits, that issue cannot be settled here. The debate on the degree and kind of organization of shell and other production in the American Bottom continues.

A closely related set of issues has developed around claims of a "cottage industry" organization of production at Cahokia (Prentice 1983). I think what was meant was "domestic economy" as blurred by a rather foggy view of specialization from the heights of Monks Mound. In a later article, Prentice moderated his terminology considerably by claiming only "part-time" specialization but still attempted to salvage an idiosyncratic (to anthropology, at the most) usage of the term *cottage industry* to describe a system of production for "trade" in Mississippian homes (1985). I have already signaled the difficulties I have with such terminology, and the response to Prentice's article by Pauketat (1987b) has, at the least, placed Prentice's conclusions about the nature of domestic production into a broader context. As Pauketat concluded, Prentice's "analysis is insufficient to warrant the identification of part-time specialist households" (1987b:82).

Claims for some degree of specialization continue to be asserted for shell production (e.g., Yerkes 1983, 1989). More recently, Yerkes (1991) has accepted a "primitive state" model (*à la* Conrad 1989:93–98). Here one of the key issues is brought out explicitly, for Conrad—despite the latitude of his definitions of these concepts—found no mention in his "ethnographic survey" of secondary sources of "professionalism in the arts and crafts among the Natchez" (1989:97). Yet, as Conrad goes on, "Prehistoric Middle Mississippian sites across the greater Southeast, however, among them Cahokia, have yielded such quantities of finely made articles, often of a politico-religious nature that it *is assumed* that specialized artisans under state control did exist" (1989:97, emphasis added). On the next page, Conrad(1989:98, emphasis added) reiterates this point:

> Even without ethnographic analogy, *occupational specialization would be assumed at Cahokia* from the existence of very large quantities of exotic materials, fine craft objects, tremendous and well-planned earthworks and fortifications, large numbers of people living and working together in a naturally constricted area, and the localization of certain work areas.

This fairly well illustrates the problem with this argument about specialization at Cahokia. The conclusion is already drawn that Cahokia was some kind of state. Therefore, it is merely a matter of *identifying* specialization, rather than having to *prove* its existence. There is more than a little circularity to this viewpoint, since the criteria used to *identify* the state character of the site are often based on the presence of the very criteria at Cahokia that are *deduced* from the conclusion that it was a state. If one can *assume* specialization, it certainly simplifies the task, to be sure; but there are more than a few of us who want some hard evidence before we reach such conclusions.

Research has shown that the proposed shell-working tools occur widely in the American Bottom (e.g., Milner 1983a, 1984b, 1990, personal communication; Milner et al., in Bareis and Porter 1984:162, 163; Vander Leest 1980; cf. Ensor 1991 for the Tombigbee region and its critique by Blitz 1993:158–162). Although there is some concentration in elite contexts, as discussed later, the overall pattern seems more consistent with widespread domestic production than craft specialization. The presence of microdrills, even where localized as claimed by Yerkes (1991), seems weak evidence for true "specialization" of production in the American Bottom (see also Yerkes 1986; Muller 1984a, 1986a; Pauketat 1987b; especially Holley 1995). I am afraid that Yerkes's citation of supposed craft specialization of shell-goods production by hunter–gatherers in the Channel Islands of California (cf. Arnold 1984) is less compelling to me as "specialist production" for either case than it is to him. The argument is essentially one of scale, but large quantities of any finished goods do not necessarily indicate specialist production. Evidence for the social context of the supposed specialized producers still has to be produced. In the relatively large scale engraved shell production for Spiro, there are indications that many different artisans were involved (Phillips and Brown 1975–1983: 6:xvii). From their conclusions, Griffin (1984:3, emphasis added) has suggested:

> If this is true, it would suggest that a large percentage of the male(?) population was capable both of the technology and ideology necessary during one or two generations. It would seem to eliminate the domination of the production by only one or a few "privileged" sacerdotal individuals. *It should eliminate the proposal that there was specialization of labor in a "cottage" industry.*

The lack of evidence for the actual use of the tools for shell production at the microlith production areas is explained away as being the result of discard of used tools at the place of renewal of the tool. The problem is more likely to have been one of preservation. Even so, the mere localization of a kind of production and its supposed concentration in a geographically limited area are by no means proof of specialized production. The case that Yerkes makes (1991) is mostly based on claims about the Kunnemann Tract in "downtown" Cahokia, so it is worthwhile to compare his interpretation of this area with those of one person who has conducted fieldwork there (Holley 1995). When Holley assessed standardization of these lithic assemblages, he concluded that the statistics "do not indicate that exacting standards were used in the production of either blades or drills" and that a preliminary investigation of the shell beads also "suggests that these beads are far from standardized in reference to diameter" (1995:52). Holley concluded, " The perspective gained from a consideration of the microlithic technology at the Kunnemann Tract is that the production regime was not rigid and exacting" (1995:52). Holley does note in a postscript that standardization in these contexts is difficult to place in context at an appropriate level (1995:62). This is certainly so, but the fact still remains that standardization of *these materials* cannot be claimed as a argument in favor of specialized production at the Kunnemann Tract. In terms of assessing the localized context of this production, Holley concluded that the western area of production was "to state the obvious, not the site of a 'factory' for the manufacture and use of microdrills" (1995:58). Holley suggests the possibility of status distinctions in access to raw materials and shell production, but his conclusion is that "I identify this production as *accretional* as opposed to specialized, in that it represents an accumulation of tasks on the domestic schedule of households" (1995:59).

It may be the case at Cahokia that there was some localization of shell-artifact production, as noted by Pauketat (1993:139). Rare household auxiliary activities could, for example, be expected to be more visible in areas of denser occupation. However, the areas where such production took place are still extensive in time and space. Production activities were widely dispersed across the social landscape. As Pauketat noted, "It is anticipated that, besides the Kunnemann Tract, similar densities of shell-working tools or shell refuse exist in the Powell Tract and to a more limited extent in the Dunham and Ramey Tracts and the Groves Borrow Pit Area." Pauketat did state that "it may be concluded tentatively that Kunnemann Tract shell workers probably did not perform domestic tasks with expedient tools to the same degree that other American Bottom Mississippians did. This would certainly qualify the Kunnemann Tract artisans as 'specialists' no matter whose definition is used" (1993:139). Even allowing for Pauketat's "probably" and "tentatively," I think his "certainly" and "no matter whose definition is used" are a little premature.

It is certainly *possible* that some attached specialists were involved in necklace production in this location at the Cahokia site, but neither the evidence presented in Pauketat's analysis, nor in subsequent discussion of the topic (1994), has yet really done more than to warrant the hypothesis of "qualitative and quantitative distinctions between central and rural craft production" (1993:139). Even a *quantitative* difference at the Kunnemann Mound itself does not eliminate the truth that many kinds of what he called "craft" production are not limited to one or another locations in the American Bottom, but occur in a wide diversity of locations in sites of many kinds. Even if there were some kind of so-called "specialization" at some locations, it is clear that it would have coexisted with nonspecialist production at others. This would be structurally and logically unusual, to say the least. I wish to point out that, contrary to what Pauketat suggests (1993:139), I never argued that "every Cahokia household dabbled in shell-working (cf. Muller 1987a:17)." Quite to the contrary, my discussion of Cahokia on that page followed that of shell gorget manufacture in which I explicitly pointed that it would be unjustified to conclude that all men made shell gorgets. What I did say was—as I still believe to be the case—that

> there can be no doubt that some persons were more skilled than others at certain tasks, nor can there be any doubt that manufacture of shell beads took place somewhere; but I cannot see that the level of production localization, the quantity of the material processed, nor the restriction in production locations were sufficient at Cahokia to justify a conclusion of "craft specialist" shell workers who earned their living at this task. Muller 1987a:17

This does not constitute a claim that every household was identical.

I also note, as I did in 1987, that the large scale of wampum production in the historical East, in the context of a well-documented historical system of trade with Europeans, took place without any indication of craft specialist production of those items. Only European producers seem to have made a craft of this production, not Native Americans. I point to this example merely to remind people that even large-scale production of goods does not always imply specialization of production, as many historically documented production systems worldwide show.

Frankly, whether production systems are *craft*, or not, is the issue, and to use that term begs the question. If finely made goods production were an auxiliary activity, it may well be that some households would engage in it, more or less, to the degree that they were relieved from ordinary domestic production. That is to say that one possibility is not so much elite-sponsored producers (i.e., attached specialists) as simply elite producers, perhaps just like those of the Kunnemann Mound. I think the possibility that shell-bead production may have been a common household production activity of elites *themselves* has not been sufficiently considered here. What *is* certain is that we need to have more data on the domestic contexts of these production systems for the entire social formation than we have so far. There are bound to be social differences in production, distribution, and consumption that are related to social rank. These differences must be distinguished from differences that are due to occupational differentiation. What the evidence does suggest is that *if* there were either distinct elite-sponsored production or an elite production system at Cahokia, it does not seem to have lasted throughout most of the Mississippian occupation of the American Bottom (e.g., see Pauketat 1992 on exotic goods distributions).

Before moving on to some modest views of Cahokia's production systems, I should mention some more exuberant views of production at Cahokia. Conrad's typological assignment of the site to his understanding of Service's "primitive state" has already been mentioned (1989). For O'Brien, Cahokia is an example of "early state" economics (1991). Dincauze and Hasenstab propose that Cahokia was the "core" for an Iroquois "periphery" (1989). Peregrine also takes a broad, extended and "power-based" world-systems view, beginning from a "prestige-good" economy that he sees as embedded in a set of core-periphery relationships (1991, 1995). I do not think that the use of terms such as *state* has yet been justified for Cahokia, and I cannot see how world-systems models have any real fit to social formations that were so strongly *local* and *regional* in scope. King and Freer have also proposed a world-systems perspective for Mississippian (1995). I think the problem with these world-systems discussions is not what is said about Mississippian so much as it is the insistence on forcing it into a framework suggesting something quite different from what is actually being described (see, especially, Peregrine 1995:256–261). As King and Freer acknowledge, "Most would agree that earlier systems, especially those dominated by classless societies, may not possess the same logic as the modern world-system," but they go on to say, "However, these differences should not preclude the use of world-systems theory to understand the dynamics of precapitalist societies" (1995:268). I am afraid that I don't find this assertion convincing. World-systems theory has real problems even in dealing with noncapitalist class systems (as noted by King and Freer 1995:276; also see Stein 1995). It seems to me that by its generalization to noncapitalist, *nonclass* systems, it becomes little more than a metaphor asserting that exchange and power were important.

There are, however, American Bottom researchers who view Mississippian neither from the periphery (as per Stoltman 1991b), nor from the summit of Monks Mound, but rather from the solid comparative basis provided by the large-scale highway-construction transects across that bottomland (see Bareis and Porter 1984 for a preliminary summary). Their voices should be heard in addition to those of "exaggerationalist" persuasions. Milner has written at length about the tendency to exaggerate differentiation in the American Bottom (1982, 1986, 1990, 1991, 1993). After noting some of the examples mentioned earlier, Milner observed, "Regardless of the merits of particular arguments for task specialization at mound centers, available evidence is insufficient for discriminating among different levels in the incidental to full-time work continuum," especially noting the lack of more than "minor variation in activities at the level of the farmstead" (1990:14). Mehrer, in considering the countryside around Cahokia, found evidence for households that were "specialized in hosting community activities" (1995:166). He continues:

> These nodal points appear to be the homes of locally prominent families who were part-time ceremonial specialists, but who also produced their own food. There is no evidence for full-time specialization in the countryside beyond the generally accepted notion that rural families functioned primarily to provide for their own subsistence and to produce a surplus for exchange or tribute. In the same sense, there is no evidence to suggest that these households existed merely to support the temple-towns with their surplus production.
> Mehrer 1995:166

Despite mischaracterization of my supposed "minimalist" views on Cahokia (e.g., Stoltman 1991a:352), I certainly am among those impressed by the magnificence of Monks Mound and the site surrounding it. The implications of its incredible scale in comparison to other Mississippian activities suggest that the period of its construction could have been a period of increasing social differentiation. However, if we want to investigate the role of specialization in the development of hierarchical political economies, we must not merely conclude that Cahokia's scale allows us to "assume" the character of either production or political structures.

Moundville

The Moundville site in Alabama may have been more complex socially than many Mississippian sites, except, of course, for Cahokia. Thus claims for a prestige-goods economy there with specialist production of some goods, most notably fine-ware ceramics, are especially important (see Steponaitis 1991; Welch 1991). In this section, the issue of ceramic production will be discussed first, and then discussion of other production systems at Moundville. If there is any hope for identifying developing specialization in Mississippian social formations, Moundville and Cahokia are, after all, the best bets.

Ordinary Mississippi or Bell Plain vessels used in Mississippian sites were predominantly of local and domestic production (cf. Gramly 1992:89). The domestic context of their use, the diversity of form and size, and their distributions all indicate predominantly local manufacture and use. There are, of course, those "migrating potsherds"—so-called "trade sherds"—that have been elevated into spheres of influence and the like. A realistic assessment of the percentages and contexts of exotic ceramics indicate what a minor role such vessels played in large and small sites alike.

There are some well-made, complex ceramics in the Mississippian world, however. Some kinds of vessels such as effigies and elaborate fine wares indicate an increased labor commitment to their production, and some may have had considerable symbolic and ceremonial importance. From Cahokia down to the smallest Mississippian farmstead, the patterns of these objects suggest that they were created by persons, mostly women, with much greater than ordinary skill, but there is no context that I know of that provides clear evidence for the idea that the majority of even fine wares were *specialist* produced.

Probably the best possible case for "specialist" ceramics would be something like wheel-made pottery. The only thing remotely similar to that level of production organization found in Moundville (or other Mississippian) contexts is some ceramics from Moundville that appear to have been made in molds (Hardin 1981; van der Leeuw 1981). There was also a suggestion that a "few potters" made, as Welch concluded, a "disproportionately large number of fine-ware vessels," arguing that only "some form of craft specialization accounts for the observed data" (1991:144–145). I suggest that the situation is not quite so clear as that. However, Welch has noted that the "conclusions about Moundville" drawn here "are pretty much exactly what I conclude about Moundville." In saying "some form of specialization" Welch was not using the terms as defined here, but rather sought to indicate "that not every household made all the things they used in daily life" (personal communication 1996).

There is no doubt that Welch's data prove the special skills of some ceramic artists at Moundville. They, like some of the textile producers discussed later, were engaged in highly complex production activities. However, the complexity that most often marks true specialization is complexity such that the task is beyond the capability of an unsupported single producer, not the complexity that indicates the producer's high level of skill. What we have in the Moundville engraved pottery is more like the latter than the former. The complexity of the Moundville techniques reflect the careful manufacture of a few items of greater than ordinary artistry—not mass production of the sort characteristic of ceramic specialists in Mesoamerica or the Near East. The skill of the real specialist is more the skill of speed and high output than the skill of the artist, and we should not confuse the two. In West Irian, Gerbrands found a village of just under 700 inhabitants had about 20 *wow-ipits* or wood-carvers. These wood-carvers were artists whose skill was greatly admired and who did the majority of wood carving of display goods. Yet these apparent specialists are in fact primary producers like all other men, save only that they are commissioned (N.B., not *attached*) to carve display items, not because no one else could do these activities, but because the *wow-ipits* are so much better at them (Gerbrands 1967:36). Those days spent in wood carving are subsidized by the commissioner of the work by the latter taking over those duties for that time. In this case, the prestige accrues not only or even primarily to the commissioner, but to the *wow-ipits*. As Gerbrands indicates, that is the primary "payment" rather than compensation in the economic sense (1967:36–37).

Welch especially notes that the mold technique probably would not qualify as a technique "not accessible to everyone" (1991:182). This too, is like the skill differences among those 20 recognized wood carvers out of 700 villagers in West Irian. We are speaking of talent, not of skills that could not have been duplicated, if more crudely, by ordinary producers (e.g., Gerbrands 1967:169–170). Indeed, one should also remember that the engraving part of the decoration of these fancy vessels at Moundville is probably close to the final stage of production and could have been done by anyone, at any time, after the manufacture of the vessel itself. While it is convenient to speak of a "single potter" (Welch 1991:142), this is an "analytical individual" (Redman 1977) rather than necessarily indicating a single, living person, although these vessels really are very similar.

Even assuming, for the sake of the argument, that the types and varieties in Table 7.8 are independent of the stylistic attributes that were used to identify the individual artists, I think the case from this table for a high concentration of production of Moundville Engraved in the hands of a "few potters" is weak. First, the total number of vessels here is only 269 vessels out of slightly under 1000 whole vessels at the site. Moundville Engraved is, of course, an analytical creation of archaeologists, but it is the kind of decorated ware representing a tiny percentage of all ceramics at Mississippian sites. Second, the number of potters represented, even in this analysis, *is very close to the total number of vessels*. There are 238 analytical individuals for 269

Table 7.8. Moundville Engraved Attribution to Analytical Individual Potters

Type	# of vessels	# of potters	Expected % of pots/potter[a]	Average #/potter	Largest # of pots by 1 potter	Largest % of Σ pots by 1 potter
Moundville Engraved *Hemphill*	138	130	0.77	1.06	3	2.17
Moundville Engraved *Wiggins*	47	39	2.56	1.21	9	19.15
Moundville Engraved *Taylorville*	28	19	5.26	1.47	6	21.43
Moundville Engraved *Tuscaloosa*	21	18	5.56	1.17	2	9.52
Moundville Engraved *Northport*	16	14	7.14	1.14	3	18.75
Carthage Incised *Carthage*	19	18	5.56	1.06	2	10.53
Total	269	238	0.42	1.13	9	3.35
Moundville Engraved only	250	220	0.45	1.14	9	3.60

[a]As calculated by Welch, 1991: Table 5.2.

vessels, or only about 1.13 vessels per identified potter. The maximum number of vessels attributed to a single artist is only 9, and the table gives the maximum number from each variety. It *is* "significant" in a number of senses that one skilled artist made 8 more pots than most other producers; but it is not *significance* that forces us to a conclusion of "specialization." The large number of different artists involved in this activity surely is counter to our expectations for true conditions of "craft specialization." It is certainly not the case that we have to argue that every household was engaged in the manufacture of finely made pottery in order to reject the specialization hypothesis (see Welch 1991:143–144). There is nothing about a domestic context for any production system that means every single household engaged in all activities.

We also must consider that individual style differences are not likely, in fact, to be independent of the stylistic elements used to identify ceramic varieties. We have to be skeptical about the independence of the measures of variety and individual style. When we group all Moundville Engraved together, the overall "concentration" in the hands of a "few individuals" tops out at no more than 3.6 percent of all Moundville Engraved for the largest single producer. I would also suggest that "overrepresentation," to the degree it actually occurs here, of some producers in elite burials could reflect a number of social ties other than those of specialist producers to their patrons. Perhaps one grandmother had an especially fine reputation as a potter? An aesthetic sense was not lacking prior to the development of craft specialization. Welch is quite right in being concerned about who produced what, and for whom. These are data that may prove to be very useful in a number of ways, but the reader has to be cautious in not interpreting Welch's argument to be one that implies "craft specialization."

Were these techniques being used to produce a large number of vessels for trade? Not so far as I can see from these data for either inside or outside Moundville. The analyses of Hardin and van der Leeuw do not show that mold-made vessels were mass produced, but merely that they were complex in production. Most Moundville vessels were not produced in this fashion. In this sense, *this* mold manufacture is different from our normal understanding of what mold manufacture means in real specialized ceramic production. Do these scholars suggest that all 238 recognized potters were "specialists?" Do they really mean to imply that the data on production of Moundville Engraved and a single bottle form suggest that *all* Moundville pottery was made by these same artists? Remember, too, that mold-made pottery appears to have been made at Lubbub Creek as well as at Moundville (Blitz 1993:128, citing Cyril Mann's work). Blitz's comparison of village and mound contexts in the Tombigbee data do not support the idea of restriction of availability of fine wares (1993:145).

There is really not much indication of the kind of localization of production that would result from most of the work being done by only a few producers (cf. Welch 1991:145–146). The evidence, instead, merely suggests that the hazardous (to people with thatched roofs) open kilns were located where they were unlikely to set fires. We need to remember that *all* Mississippian pottery was fired somewhere, and surely the vast bulk of this cannot be seen as the result of specialist production, even were we to accept the case for the fine wares. Caches of raw materials such as shell and clay would be significant in the right context (Welch 1991:146–147), but, again, every pottery producer needed these materials, and localization of production in relation to spatially restricted firing areas is not a very strong argument for or against specialization. Blitz's data from the Tombigbee, however, do somewhat strengthen the idea that farmsteads in Alabama Mississippian contexts may have been more temporary and less involved in production that was the case in the Ohio Valley. However, these same data do support the similarity of distribution of fine wares at large and small sites alike (1993:157–158).

Welch closes with a disclaimer that "I make no claim as to whether these potters were full-time specialists or only part-time specialists: I merely argue that there was some specialization of pottery production" (1991:149). Insofar as *part-time specialization* merely implies differential levels of production, this is surely true. By Yoffee's rule, of course, it fails, and, more importantly, it fails to show the necessity of postulating specialization at all, in the strict sense, to explain the particular patterns of production, insofar as they are revealed in these data from Moundville. As I have noted, Welch and I differ more in terminology and in the problems we are most concerned with than we do in terms of conclusions about the character of production at Moundville or other Mississippian sites.

Much lithic material at Moundville is suggested by Welch to have been found only in finished form at outlier sites, and in production contexts at Moundville itself (1991:166–167). If this really proves to be the case when more complete data on the non-Moundville sites are available, it would be significant. However, I cannot see that the current data are adequate to assess this question (note Welch 1991:198). Much the same would have been said of Kincaid, Cahokia, or any other large site at a time when we had only scattered data from outliers and little or no data from individual households. It is most definitely not the case in the Black Bottom, for example, that discoidals are found only at Kincaid, although that could have been said before we actually looked at the small sites in detail. There are indications of household production of discoidals in the Tombigbee (Blitz 1993:158). The differences in scale between a site such as Moundville and the homesteads around it mean that rare forms are more easily seen at large sites. In addition, surface collections are notoriously likely to be biased toward finished forms rather than production debris. Welch asserts, on the basis of comparison to assemblages from single-mound sites, that "all the nonlocal materials demonstrably worked within the Moundville chiefdom were worked only at Moundville. There is *no* evidence for the manufacture of items of nonlocal materials at the outlying sites" (1991:170). But given the "limited extent of excavations," which Welch acknowledges (1991:170), I think this generalization is premature. The same reservation has to be applied to similar conclusions about other exotic goods and exchange goods such as galena (e.g., 1991:176). Although Welch concludes that the Moundville community was "qualitatively different from other communities in the chiefdom" (1991:177), I would suggest that research directed specifically to this point at hamlets and farmsteads may yet show more quantitative than qualitative differences. To be sure, all we have to do is to look at the mounds themselves to see that there are important differences between a site such as Moundville and its hinterland. Nonetheless, the scale and character of differences in production systems, and especially the assessment of the scale and character of production activities, cannot be judged without being placed in a social and production profile for all levels of sites. Moundville may well have been a "prestige goods economy" (1991:178), but we need more evidence before we can accept that this, in turn, was based on the presence of any kind of "attached specialists." Of course, Welch explicitly recognizes the "lack of evidence" for the "mobilization" of craft goods part of the prestige goods model as well as the failure to detect "interdistrict exchange of subsistence goods" (1991:181). I would also add that clear evidence for "attachment" of these proposed specialists is also lacking. The need for more data on context at different sites is also stressed by Blitz (1993:128, 155). The Tombigbee, after all, is not so far from Moundville, and it does provide a context, albeit on a smaller scale, in which we have a much more representative cross-section of the society. Blitz (1993:178) sums up this situation pretty well in a statement that applies widely to Mississippian chiefdoms, given that I might avoid certain terms he uses:

> All evidence indicates that fineware ceramics, microdrills, marine-shell beads, and discoidals were produced within the household. It is unlikely that all of these prestige items, in contrast to many utilitarian artifacts of local materials, were produced in every household. Thus there was some "specialization" or variability in production of prestige items at the household level. However, part-time, low-level production of these artifacts was probably a widespread domestic activity. This household variability and the intensity of production are within the magnitude attributable to individual ability, skill, and episodic opportunities. There is no unequivocal evidence of specialized areas for craft production segregated from household contexts, nor is there evidence of restricted access to specific technology, knowledge, or raw materials. If this level of production is to be considered craft specialization, it clearly fails to meet the criteria of most accepted definitions (e.g., Evans 1978; Michaels 1987, in Ensor 1991).
>
> Household production of prestige goods at farmsteads, the presence at farmsteads of fineware ceramics, abundant marine-shell beads and ornaments, and the occasional fragments of stone disk palettes and other rare prestige goods are contrary to expectations about access derived from the Moundville models. Instead of centralization of production and restriction of access to an elite, the widespread distribution of these wealth items and the materials to make them reveals that the ability of would-be elites to monopolize durable wealth was minimal. This does not mean that ambitious individuals did not have opportunities to benefit from unequal disbursement of nonlocal materials or finished goods. Rather, these opportunities were severely limited at the modest social scale of two-tiered settlement systems and subject to regional social dynamics beyond local control.

Textiles

Finally, a few words can be said about analyses of textiles that have been found in various Mississippian contexts. As can be expected, the direct survival of textiles is extremely rare, but the impressions of huge numbers of cloths have been found in the fabric-marked saltpans referred to in the sections on salt production.

It may be debated whether particular textiles were a "staple" or a "prestige" good. As the historical examples in Chapter 2 showed, "clothing" of some kinds does seem to have been controlled directly or indirectly by chiefs. However, the historical examples often seem to involve deerskins rather than textiles. Like many other goods, textiles can be either mundane or display goods, depending upon the labor value that they represent and the symbolic role that may be assigned to them. Ordinary textiles in Mississippian times do not show much indications of specialization. In Drooker's discussion of Wickliffe textiles in the Ohio–Mississippi Confluence region, she notes that these fabrics were well made, but that their "nonstandardization" in many attributes "argues that these fabrics were not all produced by the same hands" (1992:170).

Drooker's treatment of textiles followed analyses by Kuttruff (1988). These analyses revealed how very "costly" some Late Prehistoric textiles—such as those from Spiro, Oklahoma—were in terms of labor value. As Drooker sums up the case, "This is the level of intricacy that might possibly require specialist artisans for its production." She goes on to conclude, "However, even though it seems unlikely that all women made them, their apparent rarity argues strongly against any full-time crafts-people being dedicated to their production" (1992:232). Again, this parallels what we have seen in other areas of Mississippian production.

5. SUMMARY

With a few exceptions, the idea of staple production specialization for Mississippian in particular (and nonstate societies in general) has been abandoned by most researchers. Given substantial agreement on this, I would only remind everyone that this was not the case even a few years ago. I trust that future *rejection* of staple specialization in particular cases will still be based on solid evidence rather than being as freely assumed as was its former *acceptance*. I am firmly convinced that Eastern staple production—that is, production of the goods that were essential to reproduce the society—was everywhere concentrated in the hands of domestic producers. However, having drawn this conclusion, I do not think that research into Mississippian staple and domestic production can now cease, with all interesting questions answered. Quite to the contrary, Mississippian provides an important example of the relationships between domestic and community-based production and developing elites.

When display goods are considered, we find the same kind of picture in many technologies that we see in shell production at Cahokia and elsewhere—some persons with greater skills than the average producer were making finely made goods that represented considerable investments of time. But at the same time, the evidence that we have to date is consistent with social and production contexts similar to those seen in Historic social formations in the Southeast, rather than indications of "craft specialization." We find "artists" rather than craft producers, and, like modern artists, most of these had to have "day jobs" as well as their special skills. I would like to see evidence or argument for the "attachment" of proposed specialists for any of these cases, although Pauketat (1993) does suggest that the locational restriction of production may be an indication of attachment to the Kunnemann elite. As I noted in my discussion earlier, such producers may have been high-ranking individuals themselves rather than "attached."

Like specialized staple production, display-goods specialization should neither be assumed nor rejected *a priori*. Too often specialization has been assumed to exist prior to any examination of the archaeological record. Specialization is not inconceivable for Mississippian societies, especially for those of the largest scale; but Occam's razor applies. Those who propose that particular production systems in Mississippian society were "specialist" must show that simpler, domestic production systems are inadequate to account for the observed archaeological data. If the existence of specialization is not directly tested, the "proof" of specialization too often consists merely of identifying material remains that *could* have been produced by specialists.

The data from the Mississippian cases contribute to a general picture of specialization and hierarchical development. It seems that full-time or "craft" specialization is unlikely to have been a common feature of hierarchical societies developing out of nonranked societies. In the Mississippian cases, where the issue has been tested explicitly, it seems that "specialists" were absent, with the possible exception of the developing elites themselves. Certainly there can be no suggestion that staple-goods production of any kind was the focus of developing division of labor. Even display-goods production seems unlikely to have been handled by true specialists, as opposed to skilled persons. Although there are still claims for specialist production in Mississippian societies, we have seen that these are, nowadays, mostly couched in terms of "part-time" specialization. Only a few have been bold enough to have argued for *craft specialization* in the economic sense of the term. Even if it were eventually proved that there were a few cases of true specialization in Mississippian societies, it is hard to avoid a conclusion that this was not the case normally. Thus, it seems unlikely that specialized production can be seen as a major feature, much less a cause, of the early development of ranked societies at a chiefly level. Rather specialization, as such, is much more likely to have been a *result* of the functions of the elite, rather than a cause or foundation for their power.

These relationships of supposed subordination, hypotheses of tributary relations, and other related issues require a fresh approach to Mississippian societies. Control of chronology is important, but archaeologists have been too concerned with local culture-historical sequences. It is fruitful to try out political and economic theories based on exotic ethnographic cases, but such efforts can too easily become procrustean if they are pushed beyond reasonable limits. What is important is to be more concerned with empirically based investigations to understand what Mississippian political economy really was.

Chapter 8

Distribution, Exchange, and Consumption

El dar es honor, Y el pedir dolor.
"To give is honor, and begging is grief."
Spanish proverb

1. DISTRIBUTION, EXCHANGE, CONSUMPTION, AND NETWORKING[1]

Allocation of goods in the broadest sense includes three related but different aspects in economic theory:

1. The division of wealth among the members of society as individuals and families.
2. The division of the *value* of the output of goods among the producers and other factors involved in the production process.
3. The movement of goods into the paths of exchange or commerce.

The first kind of allocation is the first concern of this chapter under the heading of distribution. The second kind of allocation of *value* in state-level societies concerns monetary payments, which take such forms as wages, rent, interest, and profit, but it is of little concern where values are generally held by communal producers within the context of kin groups or other social bodies. In the absence of money, distribution of value must, of necessity, be in payments in kind. Even so, the problem of allocation remains—the necessity and ability to control who gets what and how much. The third kind of allocation will be discussed under the heading of exchange.

---

[1] Some of the data and discussions on interaction in the Southeast have been presented in a different form in related papers (e.g., Muller 1995b).

In capitalist societies, the law of supply and demand is seen by many as governing the distribution of value. This is part of the fiction of "rational" economic choice, since even in the most free-market, bourgeois settings, value is determined by social choices that are not based on pure "economic" factors. Monopoly, regulation, and such intrusions into "free markets" shrink in importance in comparison to social choices resulting from cultural "values" of many kinds. One may argue that these social and cultural "values" are economically "rational" in terms of long-term "evolutionary pressures" on *societies*, but the choices made by *individuals* in such settings can hardly be so described (compare the debate on sacred cows in India; Diener 1980; Harris 1978, 1979).

Distribution and exchange are really the same process, except that the former is taken most often to refer to allocation of goods within a single social formation, whereas the latter usually refers to movement of goods across social boundaries. In both cases, a product leaves the control of the producer and finds its way to a consumer. Class-based societies tend to have both internal and external allocation in the hands of specialists whom we may call traders or merchants. Nonclass societies tend to have few intermediaries except those whose kinship ties or rank involve them in allocation of goods of some kind. It is not uncommon for external allocation in such societies to be handled by extension of similar social ties, as in fictive kinship, to the external consumer. In this chapter, in line with usage in other fields, the term *trade* will be used to refer to exchange that is mediated by exchange specialists, as opposed to the myriad mechanisms that can characterize the neutral term *exchange*. *Consumption*, for the archaeologist, is not easily distinguished from distribution, being the goal and end of that process. Nonetheless, consumption is an important topic that deserves more attention than it normally receives, or—I am afraid—than it receives here. I want to stress in the strongest possible terms that I can see little good, and much harm, in loosely confusing *trade* and *exchange*, *market* and *distribution*, and *trader* and *exchanger*.

Some theories hold that "trade" (in the strict sense) can only arise as a result of uneven development, with cheap raw materials being acquired by overpricing fancy finished goods (e.g., Mandel 1968:182). But *trade* by those "merchants who are foreigners who bring luxury goods for the king and the nobles" (1968:182–183) is not typical of the mechanisms by which goods moved from one nonclass society to another, something that occurred long before the emergence of specialist traders. Nor is it clear that "exchange" must, as trade is supposed to do, emerge out of resource unevenness. Of course, unevenness of resources *does* encourage exchange, but exchange does not necessarily have to be "casual and occasional" (1968:49). On the contrary, it occurs commonly and regularly in many kinds of social formations. Examples could be multiplied worldwide, but it suffices to remind the reader that Gulf Coast shell, for example, was being exchanged into the Upper Great Lakes long before the emergence of ranked societies in the area. Few of the archaeologically visible resources in these exchanges seem to have had any value as staples, but there were surely no "kings" demanding luxury goods in these early cases! Uneven development *in the sense of difference in complexity* makes little sense as the main engine of exchange among societies that were so uniform in structure and most resources as were Archaic period peoples. Notwithstanding some efforts to force Mississippian into a framework of uneven development, I find it hard to see how the supposed "peripheral" peoples were so economically behind the Mississippian "core" as to make the argument work.

The idea of regional specialization or incipient specialization as a generator of uneven development also fails to make much sense for the East at any time period. Service emphasized specialized production and redistribution, and Mandel also postulated a different sort of localized "specialization" divorced from redistribution (1968:53ff.). As in Service's case, Mandel's generalized kind of specialization seems so reasonable, *a priori*, that it might even be so, but there seem to be no real examples of such social events that hold up under close analysis. As we have seen in the discussion of production, exchange occurs in terms of uneven quantities of goods of many different kinds; but these seem to be the results of ordinary, rather than truly specialized, production. Of course, there is no doubt that localized or specialist production and subsequent exchange exist in state-level systems, capitalist and noncapitalist. Likewise, true uneven development may be characteristic of the relationships of some early states to their peripheries. The issue is whether specialization and trade emerge before or after the great transition to class-based organization. Is *trade* something that develops in class societies, or is it a cause of the development of class societies?

The simplest kind of "exchange" is hardly exchange at all; it is the distribution of goods within the reproducing and producing unit—the family, often in a broad sense. Beyond simple kin-based distribution, the main prerequisite for exchange is normally the existence of a "surplus," although high priority needs can certainly encourage efforts to acquire outside resources as well. As we have seen in the discussion of production, forward-looking production strategies will produce a "normal surplus" in many, even most, years. Although a labor cost was incurred for the normal surplus, the effective marginal labor cost here was close to zero,[2] and the use-value to a society that has a sufficiency of the good is also close to zero. Hence, these goods have little but exchange-value to their producers, since their labor of production was expended only at the level that was deemed sufficient to produce socially necessary goods.

First, one place that a normal surplus has value to the producer is in distribution of it to those for whom its use-value is higher. The exchange-value in this context may simply be for its ability to provide social security of the "You scratch my back and I'll scratch yours" variety—generalized reciprocity. As noted before, unevenness of distribution of the normal surplus—in the sense that some localities may be more favorable locations for production of surplus—may lead to some asymmetry of obligations. Even so, there has to be some social mechanism to encourage those in favored areas to continue to produce surpluses rather than scaling back their production to the minimal level required for their own reproduction. Part of the answer is, of course, that natural perturbations affect even those in favored areas, so—even though their risk may be less than others—it may still be high enough to keep them producing fairly regular local surpluses.

Second, all social formations have differences in prestige and status that give "immaterial" rewards to the donors in asymmetrical relations for their extra commit-

---

[2] Marginal cost was close to zero in the sense that only the minimum necessary labor for worst-case planning was expended. Any additional crops harvested beyond those needed for daily life cost nothing more than the labor cost any rational producer would have already expended.

ment. Such rewards confer a real and material selective advantage on social groups that can properly support social security through increased production and leveling distribution, as well as enhancing the individual advantage accruing to the surplus producer. Although this is not the *redistribution* of Service 1975, the argument and effect is similar. The goods distributed through a society in this fashion, of course, are likely to be staple goods. However, display goods produced in off-times (i.e., time not spent in socially necessary labor) may well prove useful means of establishing and supporting exchange networks that become much more economically important in times of shortages. For such links to be most effective, these display goods should mark relationships not only between adjacent chiefs, but also should be expected to be found in the hands of primary producers. It is important to note that this "net-work" pattern of production and distribution of display and staple goods can exist without the "attached specialists" that are often part of the idea of the "prestige-goods" model. Some concentration of display goods by elites is to be expected, since these are persons who through production and prestations are economically impor-tant members of their societies. Nonetheless, in this simpler model, the production and exchange of display goods is not the source of the power of the chief nor of elites in general, but is a reflection of both elite and nonelite competition for prestige in the context of generalized and nonspecialist production. I argue in this chapter for this network model, but a final proof will require much more than can be done here.

Distribution can be a "value-adding" activity insofar as a good has no use-value unless it can be obtained by the consumer–user. In this sense, exchange is not necessar-ily a parasitic activity, but rather the first glimmerings of "service"-oriented labor. Exchange has some dimensions that echo those of productive systems. If "goods" are treated as "raw material," then the activities of acquisition, processing (transporting, packaging, publicity, etc.), and "sale" may be conceived of as labor investment on the part of the exchangers (whether or not they may be the actual producer). These labor costs of transport and other activities have to be considered as part of the labor-value of a good. In class-based systems, it is clear that some costs related to merchandising are "nonproductive" (see Mandel 1968:201). Where exchange, rather than trade, is in-volved, most labor costs associated with distribution can probably be considered pro-ductive, since no subsidy for "nonproducers" is involved. Such distinctions and problems are not so much relevant to the conditions holding in most nonstate societies as they may be in understanding the rise of class or, especially, bourgeois states.

Distribution, exchange, and consumption—just like production—each have di-mensions such as agency, what goods were favored, what degree of control existed, spatial extent, value, organization, and measures of success. Except for the fact that there is little transformation of use-values of the sort characteristic of production, activities relating to distribution and exchange are typically parallel to those in pro-duction. This parallelism is especially clear in societies in which distribution is largely in the hands of the producers themselves, so that production and distribution are sequential behavior for the same individual. Of course, consumption by the producer is the simplest form of consumption as well.

One of the key issues of agency is whether control rested with any nonpro-ducers, such as traders or simply members of the elite ranks. Most theories suggesting nonproducer control of distribution and exchange in Mississippian societies have concentrated on supposed elite control of distribution as an important part of the power of the chief, but almost inadvertent claims for merchant-based alienation of product have been made by using terms such as *trader* and *market* without justifying them or attempting to argue their suitability.

The first question is how and to what degree the elites may have controlled the *internal* distribution of goods. Concepts such as redistribution, "attached specialists," and "staple finance" have played important parts in theories of the emergence of elites in general, as we have seen in discussion of the concepts of specialized production systems. Second, did the elites have special functions in the mediation of exchange regionally, as between one center and another? These questions are at the root of some theories of the rise of elites that place emphasis on their external relations as a means of gaining control of social relations of exchange, even going from control of external exchange first, to the total control of all exchange. In some sense did chiefly leaders such as those in Mississippian preempt the emergence of specialized "traders" by taking control of external exchange? If leaders were not involved in exchange themselves, were there, as in Medieval societies, emerging commercial travelers who comprised a sort of Mississippian bourgeoisie? Finally, was it possible for the elites to determine the consumption of a "commoner" family? Were the chiefs so powerful that they could successfully prevent ordinary persons from acquiring the essentials of life? I think it should be obvious what my feelings would be about efforts to force Mississippian exchange events into such terminology.

There is still much to be done in investigating distribution, exchange, and consumption in Mississippian societies, but this chapter will concentrate on two classes of goods, one "utilitarian" and the other "display," to see if either is consistent with the kinds of control sometimes postulated for Mississippian social formations. Consumption is the conversion of use-value and represents an investment in reproduction, among other things, returning to the basic issues of Chapter 4. In discussing reproduction and production, much evidence relating to distribution and consumption has already been presented.

Before proceeding, it may be helpful to say a few words about the kinds of tools that archaeologists have developed to deal with the distribution of goods. Since 1975, it has been common to employ a set of distinctions and patterns suggested then by Colin Renfrew. The types defined by Renfrew are direct access, reciprocity of several kinds, down-the-line, central place redistribution, central place market exchange, middleman trading, emissary trading, colonial enclave, and port-of-trade (Renfrew 1975). After what we have seen of Mississippian societies, only the first three of these seem relevant for Mississippian distribution of goods, although claims have been made for more complex exchange relationships such as market economies (e.g., Porter 1969). Direct access, strictly speaking, is not a method of exchange, but rather a description of the simple acquisition of raw materials—one simply goes to the place of origin and gets raw materials. These may either be taken home for processing, or some or all production may take place at the place of origin. Reciprocity simply refers to the close and largely informal distribution of goods within the reproducing unit (ranging from the family to the community) and their close kin and coresidents, but something like these social ties may be constructed with outsiders with whom exchange relations may be formed. Down-the-line exchange refers to the effective extension (from the analyst's point of view) of the simple kinds of reciprocity over large areas involving many donors and receivers. Central place redistribution seems a theoretical form that may not exist prior to class differentiation, and it now seems extremely unlikely for any prehistoric or historical Eastern society. The remaining types of exchange are true market and state-level forms involving markets and real traders.

Renfrew's discussion of exchange has stood the test of time well and hardly needs to be discussed at more length, except to note that the essence is that person-to-person exchange will show relatively smooth drop-off as the square of distance from the source. Both raw materials and the few finished goods that were taken from one place to another without interference by mediators typically show density declines proportionate to the square of the distance. Such falloff patterns reflect increasing size of the area over which goods can be distributed, since, of course, Area = πr^2 (where r = distance from the artifact's place of origin). Since the area here is social as well as geographical, the population within the area also affects the number of items found as a result of person-to-person exchange patterns—including down-the-line exchange. Mediation by secondary centers of distribution or traders can be expected to have their own gravity falloff curves from the secondary center, not just that from the original source. These relations will be used to look at the nature of exchange of various items.

2. MISSISSIPPIAN DISTRIBUTION

Because distribution is so intimately linked to domestic production, this section will concern issues already presented in one form or another in previous chapters. Distribution in Mississippian societies was carried out on two levels, at least. At the farmsteads and local clusters, most goods were distributed as they were produced, that is to say, domestically. On the level of the whole community around a site such as Kincaid or Angel, however, the patterns of sharing and exchange could have been affected by the more prestigious members of the community. These persons, the elite, were not completely separated from their fellows by differences in production activities. The households of the elite probably looked and acted much like other households, most of the time. The real differences between the elite and others were probably clearest at times of festival and display. Large-scale gatherings of the community were almost certainly sponsored and partially controlled by the elite. Although it is difficult to identify public events in the archaeological record, features such as plazas suggest areas used for public ceremonies. Public construction, as evident in the mounds and other site features, also commonly serves as a time of festival—as in 19th-century American barn raisings. So although it is nearly impossible to "see" distribution or redistribution in action, it is possible to see the effects that these events have.

The public works that are so evident in the larger sites are important evidence of social cooperation. It is clear that many people came together to work on these projects and shared not only the experience but also many material goods in the process. Even if mound building was the occasion for no more than a "potluck" festival, the sharing of goods would have been substantial. Of course, it is likely that these were the occasions for opening the public or chiefly granaries and calling in obligations of all sorts to provision the "ceremony." Not only material goods are shared at such events. Information, spouses, and services are acquired through the social networks created in these settings. So it is probably right to place strong emphasis on the mounds built by Mississippian people, because they were one focus of the key organizational characteristics that distinguish Mississippian societies from the less complex contemporaneous groups to the north and east. They represent a kind of material consequence of local and regional distributive activities. The continuity shown in much Mississippian mound construction suggests that prestige and the rights to sponsor community events were concentrated in places, at least, and probably in families who lived in those places. This tends to provide a steadier system of distribution and consumption of goods than is possible with authority that is more transitory.

On the local level, it is more difficult to see what patterns of goods' distribution there were. As we have noted, production and use of display goods seem to have taken place throughout the bottoms around a site such as Kincaid. The raw materials, at least, were accessible to nearly everyone. Exchange of finished goods produced at the domestic level might have been coordinated by the elites at central sites, but surprisingly little historical or archaeological evidence suggests such a degree of control in Southeastern societies. As we have seen, display goods are not limited to large or politically central sites. This has been taken to reflect the reward of local clients by elite patrons (as in Marx 1852 [1975]), but the evidence available to us is consistent with the proposal that local manufacturers of things like fluorite beads and figurines were able to control their exchange to a substantial degree—and to acquire other kinds of fancy goods and raw materials, even including the right to go directly to sources as an alternative to exchange.

One of the telling indications of the level of social difference in Mississippian societies is that the differences between the individual houses of Mississippian peoples and those of the "tribal" Late Woodland societies that preceded them are small and came about more through gradual change than radical transformation. So far as the domestic context of daily life was concerned, Mississippian and Late Woodland activities differ less than one might expect, given the economic transition to more intensive, maize-based horticulture. As I suggested in Chapter 3, the new production capabilities of Mississippian may have actually increased the autonomy of the household in some ways, since the primary economic choice became that of how *much* production. In such cases, the relations to emerging chiefs may not have been terribly significant, most of the time. The differences that do exist are in the development of elite homes, but even these echo the form of the ordinary domicile in most respects save that of size. The houses of the elite Mississippians differed from their "commoner" cousins more in their being used as public as well as private edifices, as discussed in Chapter 5. Moreover, the layout of public facilities echoes the layout of the humble, multistructure homestead. Houses, people, and spaces were promoted but not altered out of recognition between the lowest and the highest.

Nor does the biological evidence collected on elites and nonelite persons indicate a vast gulf in their ability to acquire the necessities of life, as shown by the data discussed in Chapter 4. There we saw that the stature of Mississippian persons was similar regardless of their rank, in circumstances where other factors, such as temporal differences, can be minimized. The data on health and diet at neither Cahokia nor Moundville—arguably the locations where we might expect the greatest social differentiation—support much difference between elites and other segments of the same societies (e.g., Milner 1982; Powell 1988). In short, the evidence for differential access to staples, to the necessities for basic reproduction, does not support claims for elite control or alienation of staple production.

The data in the two previous chapters have also suggested that evidence for both possession and manufacture of many display items is not appreciably different from large to small sites. Much, although certainly not all, of the supposed concentration of "wealth" items by elite-status persons is due to excavation emphasis on larger and "elite" contexts. As in the case of staple production, the dispersal of production and the evidence for so-called "part-time" specialization is not particularly compatible with the application of a "prestige goods" model to Mississippian, insofar as that model postulates strong elite control of production and exchange of any goods. I just cannot see that present data on Mississippian production and exchange provide evidence for "wealth" conversion. I am *not* denying that the elites played an economic role, quite to the contrary. I certainly do not feel that their "power" was a purely symbolic matter. I *do* conclude that elite control of internal distribution of goods in Mississippian societies is more assumed than tested, much less proved. To me at least, this seems a serious problem for discussion of the puissance of Lords and Ladies in Mississippian societies. Although it is not premature to create a model of power relationships before we have laid out more clearly what the dimensions of real, day-to-day power were, such models cannot be taken as already "proved." The power to command has clear economic and material implications, and those who wish to argue for real power in Mississippian societies need to address this issue more explicitly.

The key issue for future research into the structure of Mississippian social relations will be the effort to link the indisputably domestic character of most activities to the equally indisputable elevation of elites, often literally on top of large-scale public works. At the same time, the outlines of Mississippian internal distribution are relatively clear. Like the historical chiefs of the Southeast, Mississippian elites were respected leaders who led societies that retained considerable "freedom" both locally and domestically. Every person was not a chief, but to be a chieftain may well have been potentially within reach of fairly large segments of Mississippian societies. The evidence we have suggests that the real power of chiefs depended on their ability to collect and distribute prestations of food and clothing rather than on control of display items otherwise forbidden to their followers. I have already discussed *tribute*, so I merely want to reiterate here that I feel that the use of the term in the absence of proof of a true "tributary" relationship is prejudicial to judgments about those relationships and begs the questions we have about the nature of movements of goods among followers and leaders in the Southeast. I have earlier suggested that the term *prestation* is slightly preferable, since it has fewer implications of class distinctions among those involved in subordinates' economic relations to elites.

Shortages of food seem to have affected most members of any given local community, and in these circumstances the social obligations and friendships built up to the elite and to other individuals and groups became important in ensuring sharing of scarce resources. In historical documents, we have an echo of the social insurance functions of central elites in such statements as those of Bartram, quoted in Chapter 2 (1791 [1928:401]). These statements emphasized the domestic character of production and most distribution, while acknowledging a special role for the chief in providing "comfort and blessings to the necessitous."

3. MISSISSIPPIAN EXCHANGE

In culture-historical interpretations of the East, interactions with surrounding societies—such as diffusion and warfare—were seen as the unifying processes that linked these people together historically. The culture area reflected exchange and migration, whereas warfare and conflict were seen as cultural traits that limited the increase of the same people. Long-distance contacts with Mesoamerica were seen as the origin of such traits as platform mound construction and many symbolic representations. Today, it has become clear that long-distance exchange with Mesoamerica was extremely rare (or absent in any direct sense) and that the development of Mississippian owed little to direct contact between the Southeast and Mesoamerica. Nonetheless, as suggested in Chapter 2, there were long-distance movements of goods within the East that continued from Paleo-Indian times (e.g., Anderson 1995; Jefferies 1995; Johnson and Hayes 1995), even into the Historic period (see Muller 1989, 1995b, in press). Although most exchange was of raw materials, there were relatively brief horizons during which finished goods also found their way far from their places of manufacture. The most important of these horizons are the Hopewellian and the Late Prehistoric "Southern Cult" or "Southeastern Ceremonial Complex." In the discussion that follows, we shall look at the indications of external exchange for both staple and display goods to see whether their patterns of distribution are consistent with various models of control and mechanisms of exchange in the Southeast.

The historical literature that has been taken as evidence for trader specialists really does not support that interpretation on close examination (compare the actual texts in such sources as Joutel 1687; Lane 1586; Lederer 1672; Nuñez Cabeça de Vaca 1542[1871: 85–86]; and many others). In Chapter 2, the dangers of choosing and picking what one wishes from the ethnohistorical accounts were emphasized. Nonetheless, the literature has often been used rather too broadly. For example, John Kelly (1991:78) had this to say about Mississippian "trade" of "commodities":

> The distribution mechanism for commodities such as marine shell and Mississippian vessels throughout the Mississippi Valley was probably traders similar to those observed by Hernando de Soto in the Southeast five hundred years later (Varner and Varner 1951:254).

In this instance, Kelly's case for generalizing the modern commercial concept of "gateway city" to Cahokia is considerably weakened by begging the question with terms such as *commodities* and *traders*. The problem of the use of historical sources is more serious. As in the case of political generalizations, the question of the existence of traders (actually, *mercaderes*) is exactly the sort of situation for which Garcilaso's 1605 "history at a distance" is least worthy of trust. What did Garcilaso (the Varner and Varner reference cited by Kelly) tell us about this "trade"? The first native informant said that he had worked for some merchants who, Garcilaso notes in an aside, did not seek gold or silver; but a second youth (presumably Elvas's Perico) was more helpful. He told the Spanish that the merchants that he had worked for had the trade of gold and silver as their primary business! Can we accept the *trade* without the *silver* and *gold*? The danger of picking and using only confirming evidence should be clear. We need to be skeptical about the claims of either tribute or trade in gold in the Southeast. There are other problems with this "evidence" for traders—what was actually said at this point, according to Elvas, was that certain goods were being paid to the chieftainess in *tribute* (1557 [in Clayton et al. 1993:74]). In Elvas, nothing is said at this point by about either *trade* or *merchants*.

Many of the other examples commonly cited for *trade* either are from times when European trade in deerskins and beaver had begun to commoditize Eastern exchange relations, or seem to be European misunderstandings of *exchange* rather than trade, *per se*. It is also striking that the English sources speak of trade more often than do the French. This reflects, again, the different interests of the reporters rather more than an indication that *trade* was more important in early contact Virginia societies than in the Mississippi Valley.

Exchange did take place, of course; but there is a big difference between someone "trading" and someone being a trader. In the same way, there is a difference between someone being a warrior and being a professional soldier. Even in historical times, the supposed *pochteca*-like role attributed to traders has no basis:

> We can find no authentic instance of immunity granted to Indians engaged in commerce who belonged to a hostile tribe unless from considerations having no relation to their occupation. Myer 1928:740

Elites may have had some influence over the distribution and exchange of some exotic items. They surely had external alliances that gave them advantages in acquiring display goods. I would, however, appreciate a formal argument that what we see in the Southeast would require more complex exchange than that of the Melanesian Kula Ring (e.g., Malinowski 1922; Weiner 1976). The Kula Ring was largely uncontrolled, even though chiefs encouraged exchange by their ability to underwrite the construction of expensive sailing vessels. As Malinowski suggested, these shell–display-goods exchanges promoted all kinds of other exchanges. Recent analyses (Weiner 1976) have furthered a kind of dialectic of these exchanges, involving the contradictions between private and public benefit. The Melanesian examples illustrate how societies with weak hierarchical development can have long-distance movement of goods without political *control*. Although groups such as the Tsembaga Maring are characterized as "Big-Man" societies, not chiefdoms, we find indications of exchange of display goods as well as staples (Rappoport 1984).

The Tsembaga Maring move many kinds of goods, including prestige items, from one group to another. As we have seen in Chapter 2, a good case has been made for Late Woodland exchange (see Cobb and Nassaney 1995) along similar lines in times when there can be no question of elite management or control. Much the same is true of Archaic exchange.

World-systems theory as applied to Mississippian has been mentioned earlier, but it is, of course, more concerned with asymmetrical exchange than with production. As I noted, the extension of the terminology of these asymmetries to noncapitalist, nonclass societies stretches the discussion to the breaking point. In a metaphorical sense, such discussions (e.g., King and Freer 1995; Peregrine 1995) are helpful in drawing attention to power and exchange, but the terminology of capitalist and class systems encourages a view that makes Mississippian sound too much like European cultures. This problem is exacerbated by use of documents that are among the most likely to be "tainted" by a verbal reinterpretation into European forms that is just as striking as de Bry's visual transformations of native Easterners (e.g., the use of Garcilaso and Dávila Padilla in King and Freer 1995:271, 279 and elsewhere, see Chapter 2). Whatever was translated into *tributo* needs to be understood as meant by the original speakers, not what was meant by the Iberian chroniclers. The same applies to all the prestations, exchanges, and supposed commercial relations found in the historical records for the East. It would be enough of a problem if historic, especially colonial, native exchange practices were simply extended back into the past, but the problem is worsened when it is the European understanding of those relations that is assumed to be true for Mississippian as well. There is little in the archaeological record for Mississippian that supports the kind of superstructure represented by world-systems theory.

What

The kinds of goods produced in Mississippian societies have already been discussed in earlier sections, and these, of course are the same goods that were, on occasion, exchanged. Exchanged "display" goods were diverse both in the form of raw materials and in finished goods—including fluorite, coal, lithics, copper, chert tools, and, of course, marine shell. Other goods—such as feathers, skins, and perishable items that we rarely see in archaeological contexts—were surely exchanged. Both utilitarian items such as hoes, a "staple" good, and display items such as engraved shell have been found long distances away from their places of origin. *Busycon* whelk shell, for example, came from the Florida Keys, but found its way in raw-material form as far away as eastern Canada and the northern Great Plains (Muller 1966a, 1989; Phillips and Brown 1978:26–27).[3] As we shall see shortly, finished goods made

---

[3] T. E. Pulley of the Houston Museum of Natural Science identified some of the Spiro materials and noted that there were species present that could only have come from either the Huastec area in Mexico or from the Florida Keys (Phillips and Brown 1978:26–27). Given the continuity of distributional evidence linking Mississippian peoples down to the Keys and the lack of evidence for Mexican goods in the Southeast, I cannot see that the Veracruz connection is likely (see Muller 1984b).

from these shells also have wide distribution away from their places of manufacture. It is important to remember that utilitarian objects and raw materials are moved just as far as display, presumably "symbolic," items.

We know that goods were exchanged widely on local and regional levels, but it is difficult to assess how important these exchanges were to local survival. Did particular groups really depend upon their neighbors in other localities to any major degree? During hard times there may have been considerable dependency, but exchange and nonlocal distribution was certainly less critical in ordinary years. Regional ties, made material through exchange goods of both utilitarian and display forms, were in this sense a backup system against local disasters. The same regional relationships also meant cooperation in other affairs such as military defense against other regional powers or groups, of course.

On the level of exchange outside the region, a wealth of evidence exists for external sources for many kinds of goods and raw materials. The far reach of pottery from Cahokia and other sites indicates the establishment of long-distance exchange relationships. What is more difficult to determine is whether these relationships were direct or indirect ("down-the-line").

When

The earliest identifiable, widespread interactions in Archaic times were predominantly of raw materials. Marine shell and native copper linked the Gulf Coast and the Lake Superior regions. The Hopewellian Interaction Sphere horizon also involved copper, marine shell, and other goods that were often moved well over 1000 km from their origin. During the Hopewellian, both finished goods and raw materials were widely exchanged. After ca. A.D. 400, the amount of finished goods exchange dropped off, but there was still detectable exchange in many raw materials. After A.D. 700, the tempo of long-distance exchange—always as detectable by archaeology—picked up, continued until A.D. 1250, and thereafter persisted at a reduced level into historical times. The main period of widespread interaction was that of the Southern Cult or Southeastern Ceremonial Complex which took place close to the end of most intensive, areawide interaction, generally within a few decades either side of A.D. 1250.

Avenues of Exchange

Although there were important highways (often called "warpaths") across overland areas in Historic times, water transportation appears to have been at least as important. Large canoes are documented in historical times, and archaeological finds elsewhere in the Southeast have shown that prehistoric Mississippian people made similar vessels. Lafferty (1994, 1977) concluded that considerable quantities of goods could have been moved long distances at relatively low cost using such canoes. Actually proving that large amounts of cargo were being moved from one locality to another is more difficult. Many major Mississippian centers are located in places that could have controlled major river routes for such exchange (as well as being fertile floodplains for horticulture).

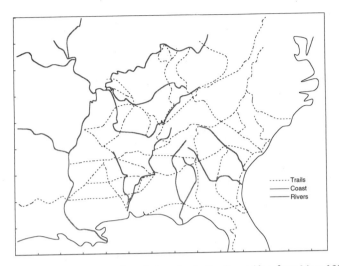

Figure 8.1. Some major trails and rivers in the Southeast (data from Myer 1928).

Trails in the Southeast were quite clear to Europeans entering the area from de Soto's time and later, and something like the same trail system probably existed well back into pre-Mississippian times. Myer's last work, unfortunately unfinished at the time of his death, was to try to trace the approximate routes of these trails (1928). Figure 8.1 shows the approximate locations of a few of the more major of these trails. PreInterstate American roads, of course, still often reflect these routes. The historical American practice of floating downstream on the rivers and returning via overland trail was also a likely prehistoric practice, and the many rivers of the Southeast were major avenues of movement of people and goods. One should note that although the terms *trail* or *path* are those historically applied to these routes, they are much more extensive than are the *roads* of the Chaco region in the Southwest—and usually are more obvious to the eye when actually sought out. There is much more to be done with this topic, and there are hopeful signs of a revival of interest in trails and their traces (e.g., Morrow and McCorvie 1993).

Goods and Distance in the Southeast

The exchange of goods in Mississippian times seems rarely to require more complex models than simple "down-the-line" movement of goods from one local group to their neighbors and beyond (see Muller 1995b and below). The following discussion briefly illustrates a few aspects of the movement of stone hoes and of fancy shell goods during the "Southern Cult" horizon and the late Mississippian period. Brief definitions of the styles have been presented recently (e.g., Muller 1989), but the content and themes of these styles is of less interest for this discussion than their distributions. As noted, the gorgets are clearly within the range called "prestige goods," whereas the stone hoes are not.

Mill Creek Hoes

More recently, Brown et al. have examined stone hoe distributions. Figure 8.2 shows the distributions of these widely exchanged items (from the same data used in Brown et al. 1990). The area shown centers on the major river systems around the confluences of the Mississippi with other streams. In the figure, the size of each circle is proportional, on a log scale, to the number of items found in a county. Most of the hoes in this data set were visually identified as being from the Mill Creek Union County, Illinois, and others were identified as either kaolin (a term for another Union County chart type) or as being from Dover, Tennessee. Of course visual identifications are always somewhat problematical, but in this case it seems likely that most of these attributions are correct. A particular "Dover" hoe might really be Fort Payne chert from the Lower Cumberland, but that would not materially affect its distinction from Mill Creek.

Following the treatment by Brown et al. (1990), I will use the relationship of falloff of distribution as the logarithm of the distance to examine the artifact distributional patterns as a device for understanding the questions that must be posed. It is very important to remember, as most do, that these falloff curves can be overinterpreted. Peaks have been too glibly taken as indications of different patterns of distribution without assessing other explanations. However, if used cautiously, falloff curves do have investigatory value, even though they may be only weak "proof" of kinds of exchange relationships.

In their analysis of stone hoe distribution, Brown et al. present their data on distribution in "falloff" curves by distance from the source. They further relate these

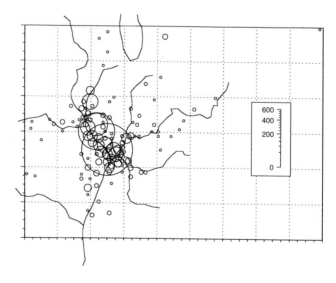

Figure 8.2. Map showing the distribution of stone hoes around the Mississippi–Ohio confluence. (The size of the circle represents the number of stone hoes according to the scale at the right. The base map scale is in km from an arbitrary 0,0 location in southern Arkansas. Data from Brown et al. 1990, courtesy of J. Brown.)

data to gravity models. The latter indicate the relations between two areas in terms of the "mass" of population in each area in a manner derived from Newtonian physics (e.g., Hodder and Orton 1976:188; Renfrew 1975). The basic idea is essentially that in directional trade, "control" of goods by a secondary center of distribution (e.g., a chief passing out these goods to his or her followers) will show up as secondary peaks, each with its own "gravity" falloff. In Figure 8.3, there is a decided peak at Cahokia and its environs. Does this imply Cahokia control of Mill Creek hoe distribution?

I have previously discussed these relationships (Muller 1995b), but when I wrote that paper, I did not have the original data that were later very kindly provided by James Brown. These data allow distinguishing among different directions from each proposed "center of distribution." The product–moment correlation between the logarithm of distance from the sources in Union County, Illinois, and number of Mill Creek hoes in *all* directions is 0.732 (the adjusted r^2 is 0.532; without the St. Clair County part of the American Bottom, the correlation of the remainder of the counties goes up to 0.794 with an adjusted r^2 of 0.628). The influence of Cahokia on the distribution of stone hoes outside the American Bottom does not seem very great, at best. All of the statistical relationships discussed in this section are significant at $\alpha = 0.01$, with $p = 0.0001$.

Figure 8.3 shows the number of Mill Creek hoes *only* in the "Northern Mississippi" region (the river, not the state) as defined by Kerber in Brown et al. (1990), plotted here by 20-km intervals against distance from Union County, Illinois, together

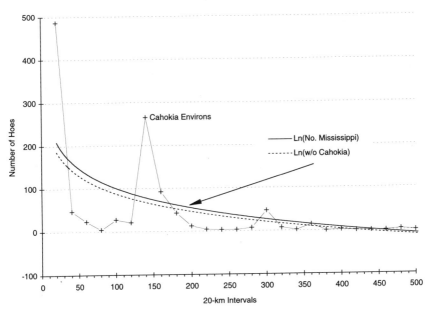

Figure 8.3. "Northern Mississippi" Mill Creek hoes in 20-km intervals from Union County, Illinois (data courtesy of J. Brown).

with a regression curve of number against the logarithm of distance. In this case, the overall correlation of numbers of Mill Creek Hoes per "Northern Mississippi" county to Ln(distance) is 0.828, adjusted r^2 = 0.678 for all (if the American Bottom is omitted, r = 0.908 and adjusted r^2 =0.821). If only the same distributions are taken at the logarithm of the distance *from Cahokia* (as St. Clair County, shown in the figure), then the correlation actually drops slightly to 0.733 (with an adjusted r^2 = 0.527). Such patterns are consistent with the importance of Cahokia as a way station and a populous locality, but not as a center of *control* of distribution. The distributions of Mill Creek hoes even a little way from Cahokia are clearly more related to their distance from Union County than they are to St. Clair County.

If there were significant "influence" of Cahokia on hoe distributions, we would expect it to show up most clearly in the northern distributions shown grouped by intervals in Figure 8.3. Taking Cahokia as the "source" of these materials weakens the correlations rather than strengthening them. Quite aside from the "attraction" of relatively large populations in the American Bottom, much more archaeological work has been done there. In short, removal of the Cahokian outlier does not appreciably alter the regression. Brown et al. concluded that Cahokia did not control distribution of hoes "to the south" (1990:268), but close examination of the realities of Figure 8.3 indicates that the "impact" of Cahokia even to the north is largely a visual artifact of using a line-plot in which the very high numbers in the American Bottom environs (a reflection of population, as noted by Brown et al.) create a large "bump." However, if one leaves out the American Bottom locations and looks at the adjoining points on the graph, those fit a gravity decay distribution *from Union County* better than they do a secondary source at Cahokia.

I should also mention that Brown et al. demonstrate some interesting possibilities in using a distributional approach to assess relative population, given that the quantity of a particular exchanged good is known (1990:269). Of course, the known quantities do reflect archaeological as well as prehistoric interactions. When relatively coarse measures are used for items that are common, the limitations of archaeological knowledge may be less significant. For goods that are rare, accidents of finds can seriously bias interpretations if they are not allowed for.

It is important to remember that Cobb's work with the Union County source areas has shown that there is evidence for small-scale, perhaps even often transient, production (Cobb 1988, 1993a, 1993b, 1993c, 1993d, 1995), with the cautions already discussed in Chapter 7. Taken altogether, the distributions of hoes of all kinds from the likely sources are strong indicators either of direct access or simply down-the-line exchange.

Shell Gorgets

It is possible to estimate a "center of distribution" for each style based on the distance as weighted by the number of gorgets found at a specific location (Figure 8.4). These "centers" are the locations from which the weighted sum of distances to each actual find spot is at a minimum. Since this measure is sensitive to outliers, the "centers" for different styles of shell gorgets cannot be taken too earnestly, but do indicate the general distributions of these styles, using my terminology for style

Figure 8.4. Computed "centers" for Late Prehistoric Gorget styles (based on minimum total sum of distance × number of items).

names (Muller 1989).[4] The styles plotted include Eddyville (anthropomorphic and spider themes from the Mississippi–Ohio confluence) and the Hightower (anthropomorphic and spider themes from the upper Tennessee). Some Moundville styles and related themes are not shown. The center of distribution of the Hixon style (a slightly later continuation of the Hightower style) is also shown, but these objects sometimes occur in association with another style (Williams Island) up to early historical times. The Eddyville style is similar to the materials identified as "Braden" style on Spiro, Oklahoma, shell cups, also not shown here.

The shell-mask theme also shown in the figure is not strictly a gorget form but is often found in association with later gorget styles, although it is clear that it is not limited only to late associations. Nashville style is the "scalloped triskele" gorget of the mid-15th century. Lick Creek and Saltville are "rattlesnake" gorget forms from the uppermost Tennessee Valley and adjacent areas of the Carolinas. These also begin about the mid-15th century and continue into the mid- to later 16th century.

The Citico "rattlesnake" gorget style is mostly associated with late 16th century to later contexts in the eastern Tennessee and adjacent localities (see Muller 1966a, 1966b, 1989). As I noted in Chapter 2, I find the proposed association (e.g., Hally et

---

[4] Since this book was completed, I have received a copy of Brain and Phillips's (monograph 1996) on shell gorgets of the Southeast. Although I have not had time to examine the work in full detail, I cannot agree with many of the stylistic distinctions made. Unfortunately, Brain and Phillips use some of my terms for new clusters of materials, so that the reader should note that I am using the terms here as originally defined by me (Muller 1966a, 1966b, 1979, 1989, and elsewhere). I also believe that Brain and Phillips's dating of many styles is far too late, having been influenced unduly by a few heirloom situations.

al. 1990:133; Hudson et al. 1985; M.T. Smith 1989:138–9) of my *Citico* style (Muller 1966a, 1966b, 1979, 1989) with a political unit in general and particularly with the Coosa chiefdom. *If*, mind you, *if* it were a good idea to treat any gorget style as symbolizing political entities, I would expect Coosa and its related peoples to have been associated with what I call the Williams Island and Hixon styles (Muller 1966a, 1989).[5]

Figure 8.5 presents the abstract distribution of shell gorget styles by location (center of each symbol) and relative number (size of the symbol) for the period a few years either side of A.D. 1250. Spiro shell cups (at 35° N, 95° W) are the largest corpus of engraved shell art from the Southeast. If shown here, they would indicate another very large triangle at that location. Other goods found at Spiro include objects that were almost certainly executed by the same artisans as goods found in sites in the Mississippi and Tennessee Valleys.

---

[5] I say this for several reasons. First, the Citico style proper is generally later than the de Soto entrada, although it seems to have its origins about that time. Second, the Citico style is structurally and morphologically closely related to the earlier Lick Creek style, which has a much more restricted distribution well to the north of anything we might imagine to be Creek (Muller 1966a, 1979). In particular, the Citico gorgets are, more often than not, associated with historical materials in what are most likely to be Cherokee contexts (e.g., Thomas 1894:337–339).

It would also be expected that stylistic unity would occur in those artifacts made by or for social groups engaged in "chiefly" activities (cf. Hally et al. 1990:133), not in domestic circumstances, such as household pottery. Thus, shell gorget styles might generally be a good possibility to examine, but the associations of Citico gorgets are not what we would expect them to be if they were "chiefly" artifacts. Even if questions of contemporaneity and dating were not at issue, Citico gorgets are more commonly associated with "village" rather than "mound" burials (as at Etowah). The Hixon and particularly Williams Island styles, however, *were* in place in the southern portion of the eastern Tennessee Valley ca. 1500, and more to the south in slightly later times. Their stylistic affiliations are to earlier "middle" Dallas and Wilbanks phase styles in this area going back to the mid-13th century. In numerous cases, the Williams Island gorgets have been associated, like their 13th-century stylistic forebears, with mound burials. The main distribution of Williams Island and Hixon gorgets after the mid-16th century is in central Alabama in historical "Creek" contexts. In addition, their distribution outside their probable areas of origin is associated with other Muskhogean-speaking groups such as the Apalachee. The distribution of Citico gorgets is supposed to coincide with the Coosa chiefdom (cf. Galloway 1995), but I feel that the Williams Island and Hixon gorgets fit better both geographically and in terms of their historical associations. The shell gorget distributions cannot, of themselves, settle the issue, but an identification of Coosa with the Williams Island and Hixon styles would be as consistent with the arguments about Coosa's location made by Little and Curren (1990) as with the northern locations proposed by Hudson and associates. Moreover, Citico gorgets have a distribution that extends well north and west of the Coosa boundaries drawn by Hudson and his associates. If Citico gorgets were the marker for Coosa, then Coosa would have extended well into western Virginia and western North Carolina (Muller 1966a, 1966b). The Virginia distribution is, I should note, north of the northern limit of Coosa as outlined by Hudson et al. (1985:733). The common form of Citico gorget is also rare in the southern part of their Coosa "province." The relationship between the transitional Citico–Lick Creek gorgets and distance from Murray County also is not significant (p = 0.93). So far as the Citico theme is concerned, it is difficult to see any of these as controlled from the putative Coosa in Murray County. The identification of this gorget form as a marker for the Coosa chiefdom is not supported by its distribution, its falloff curves from the supposed center of the chiefdom at the Little Egypt locality, nor by its historical derivation from the Lick Creek style.

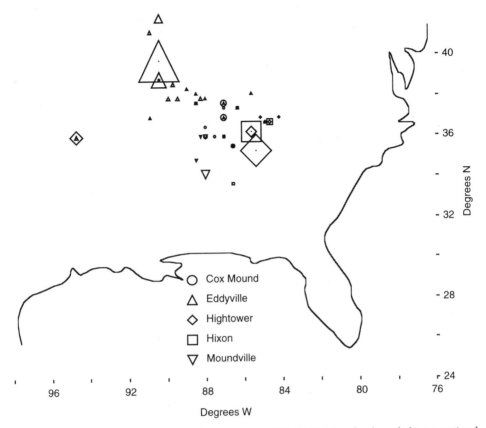

Figure 8.5. Southern cult gorget–style distributions, ca. A.D. 1200–1450. (Size of each symbol is proportional to the number of gorgets at the location. Spiro Craig-style gorgets and shell cups in the "Braden" style are not included.)

The distributions shown in Figure 8.5 are partly related to the communication provided by major river systems. The known trails across the Southeast do not correspond as closely, but these distributions reflect Mississippian settlement along rivers. Of course, we know overland routes much less certainly than we do water routes. The "centers" such as Etowah, Moundville, and so on, show larger numbers of goods, with the exception of Cahokia where only a few "Southern Cult" items in the strict sense have been found. Of course, A.D. 1250 is late for American Bottom Mississippian. For reasons I have discussed elsewhere (e.g., Muller 1989 and references in that paper to other work), I believe that these goods are a relatively good temporal marker for the mid-13th century—*so long as they are not confused with later styles or jumbled together into a broad Southeastern Ceremonial Complex that covers all fancy goods made by Mississippians and their neighbors!* There is no doubt that the dates of (re)deposition of some of these objects are later than this time period, but I do not believe that these dates can be taken as representing the period during which the artifacts were produced or distributed.[6]

Although engraved shells are common at larger sites, these are not limited to large, or elite, contexts. Their find spots, as we have seen earlier, are less of an indication of elite locations than a simple correlation with population and archaeological research. Nor, as indicated, do the burial contexts and grave-lot associations support an assertion that these are necessarily "prestige" markers for elite persons, unless we circularly conclude that presence of a shell gorget automatically confers elite status on a burial. Each of the styles is largely restricted to a single region (leaving aside the complex issue of the Braden style at Spiro and the Eddyville style in the Mississippi–Ohio confluence, see Brown 1989; Muller 1989).

Figure 8.6 shows the distribution of very late prehistoric and early historical gorgets with the so-called "rattlesnake" theme. These are most often associated with proto-Cherokee and historical Cherokee contexts (not, note well, Creek). The Saltville style, however, appears to be associated with protohistoric Piedmont Siouans. These are not Southern Cult styles, nor are they even Mississippian styles. Nonetheless, they do illustrate both the differences in the complexity of gorget origins after Southern Cult times, as well as showing important similarities in the kinds of distribution at widely separated times in the Southeast.

As the graphs show in terms of the spread of individual styles, there is far more long-distance movement of finished goods between centers in the 1250 period than later. However, "rattlesnake" gorgets were sometimes transported over very long distances. Even the early Lick Creek style is sometimes found in association with a distinctive style of gorget from the South Atlantic Coast or with the Nashville style.

The analysis of the distribution of goods during the Late Prehistoric period has been approached in a number of ways. For example, Brown (1989) has discussed the stylistic divisions of the Southern Cult from a revisionist view of the various styles defined in the late 1960s and later (e.g., Muller 1966a, 1979; Phillips and Brown 1978, 1984).

I will present a few of the patterns for the shell gorget styles and examine them in terms of distance from various "centers," somewhat arbitrarily chosen in terms of known density. I will first examine the Eddyville pattern as seen from the often-used view from the summit of Monks Mound at Cahokia. I do so, not because Cahokia is the distributional center of these styles, but as a measure of the often-claimed "hegemony" of Cahokia over the areas in which Eddyville gorgets have been found. As noted, the Eddyville style is essentially the same as Braden A, as defined at Spiro, and I feel that it is possible that the origin of many of the Spiro Braden artifacts was from eastern sources. However, the distances are great, and there is much to be explained about the relationship between the Spiro people and those in the Mississippi–Ohio Confluence. The intraregional relationship of Cahokia to other sites where Eddyville gorgets have been recovered is also obscure.

---

[6]This is another issue upon which I very strongly disagree with the late dates given to the bulk of Southeastern gorgets in Brain and Phillips (1996). Some of these dates, I believe, would place many northern gorget styles as being later than seems possible for sites such as Cahokia and Kincaid, to mention only one problem area.

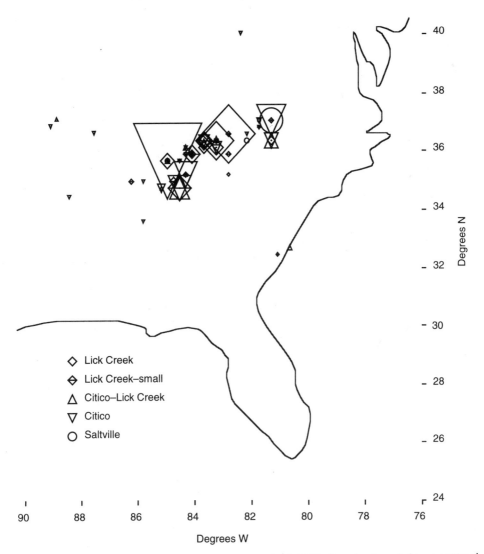

Figure 8.6. "Rattlesnake" gorget–style distributions, ca. A.D. 1450–1650. (Size of each symbol is proportional to the number of gorgets at the location.)

Figure 8.7 shows the falloff curve for Eddyville gorgets of several different kinds from the Cahokia site. The relationship is astonishingly good, given that these gorgets do not have a single source area, and certainly do not all originate at Cahokia, not least because some of the themes represented are absent or rare in the northern local variants of the style. The natural logarithm of the distance from Cahokia correlated with number of gorgets has an r value of 0.487 (with an adjusted r^2 of 0.207, significant at the α = 0.01 level with p = 0.0087). For the hypothetical center (at 38.5° N, 90° W) shown in Figure 8.4, the r^2 is 0.239.

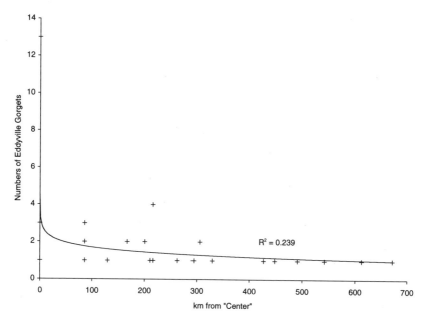

Figure 8.7. "Eddyville" gorget distributions from the hypothetical "center" of distribution. (The "center" is near Cahokia. Braden A shell cups from Spiro are not included.)

If data are grouped into 50-km intervals the correlation is 0.9, as shown in Figure 8.8 (see also my discussion in Muller 1995b:330–333)! As with the hoe distributions, the statistical correlations indicate that it would be misleading to interpret what appear to be secondary peaks as secondary centers of distribution.

In the East, the Hightower style is associated with the period of construction of Mound C at Etowah. Grave lots and other associations place the period of dispersal (not necessarily of deposition in every case) in the mid-13th century. The largest number of known Hightower gorgets is from Mound C at Etowah, Georgia, and the calculated "center" of dispersal is near that site. Figure 8.9 shows the distance distribution from Etowah. Even including the Spiro items in this style, the correlation is good with $r = 0.639$ (adjusted r^2 of 0.365, significant at the $\alpha = 0.01$ level, with p = 0.0078). As with the Eddyville style, neither the curve nor any other aspect of the distribution of these objects at the peak of the so-called "Southern Cult" force an interpretation of elite control at secondary centers. As with the hoes, the simplest explanation is simply that goods are moving from one place to another without much of any kind of mediation except that of one person exchanging goods with another.

The next group is the distributions of the rattlesnake gorget styles of Figure 8.6. These are considerably later in time than the Southern Cult items (see Muller 1989, 1995b) and should not be considered Southern Cult in the strict sense of that term. However, the patterns of distribution of these objects, while more local, shows the same pattern as the earlier styles. Figure 8.10 shows the down-the-line distribution of the 15th-century Lick Creek style, which has a relatively restricted distribution. In the figure, small Lick Creek gorgets are included, but these appear to continue to be made into Citico times. If these are omitted, the r^2 for Ln(distance) and number is 0.97!

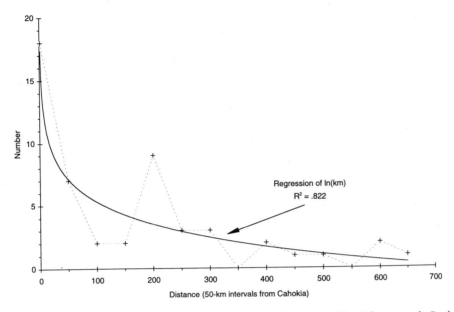

Figure 8.8. "Eddyville" gorgets in number and distance from Cahokia (grouped by 50-km intervals. Braden A shell cups from Spiro are not included.)

Figure 8.11 shows the Citico style gorgets of the late 16th and 17th century as plotted from Hamilton County, Tennessee, their weighted center of distribution. Here the distribution shows a moderately strong correlation to Ln(distance). However, both stylistic examination and the distribution pattern suggest that these objects were made throughout their core area of distribution as well as exchanged (Muller 1966a, 1979). I cannot see that the peaks of local occurrence in this instance are likely to be indications of mediation by chiefs. The Citico pattern is at least as consistent with local manufacture and exchange. A pattern of uxorilocal residence for males and their

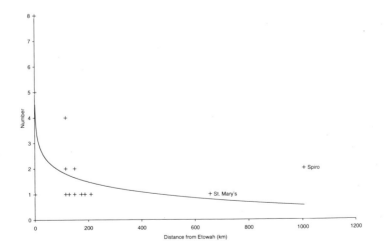

Figure 8.9. Hightower gorgets as calculated from the Etowah site.

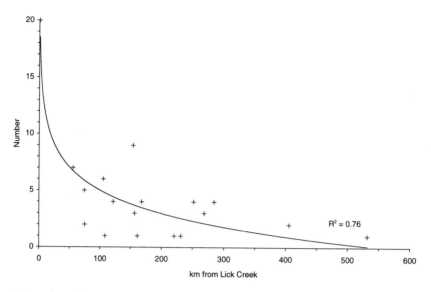

Figure 8.10. Lick Creek gorgets and the regression line of the logarithm of the distance from the Lick Creek site.

movement about the region could be as easily explained as a pattern of control of the manufacture or distribution of these objects from a single place.

As shown in the figure, the "typical" Citico gorgets have their best correlated falloff from the Chattanooga locality (Hamilton County, Tennessee). The correlation is 0.704 with an adjusted $r^2 = 0.47$ (which is significant at $\alpha = 0.01$, with $p = <.0001$). On the other hand, the spread of these gorgets in the eastern Tennessee Valley is quite wide, with the second largest center of their distribution in Smyth County, Virginia, and the third most common peak at Bartow County, Georgia. What appears to be a stylistically transitional form between the earlier Lick Creek style and the Citico style has a more narrow distribution. This Citico–Lick Creek form, as shown in Figure 8.11, has its largest find spot in the Etowah locality, but nearly the same number were found in Caldwell County, North Carolina. The examples from Etowah are *not* from Mound C context, and date to ca. A.D. 1550 or later, not to the mid-13th century. There is a correlation between distance from Bartow County, Georgia, and the numbers of this form ($r = 0.62$, adjusted $r^2 = 0.34$), but the relationship just fails to be significant at the $\alpha = 0.01$ level with $p = 0.0135$. Measures of the relationships between numbers of Citico gorgets and distances from Murray County, Georgia—the proposed location of Coosa according to Hudson et al. (1985)—show an adjusted r^2 of only 0.043 and insignificance at $p = 0.162$. Even though there is a significant relationship to the distance from the Citico site near Chattanooga, I repeat that the falloff curves do not strongly support *any* one local place of origin. As noted earlier, the stylistic evidence itself suggests that a number of persons made these gorgets in many locations throughout the eastern Tennessee Valley, but that finished goods were moved about the region freely. As I have hinted, if I were forced to place an ethnic identity on the Citico style of gorgets, I think that they are far more consistent with what we know about the locations and timing of post–de Soto Cherokee expansion than with de Soto–period Creek chiefdoms.

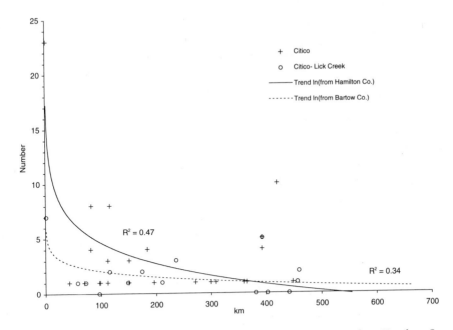

Figure 8.11. Citico gorgets and the regression of the logarithm of the distance from Hamilton County, Tennessee, and from Bartow County, Georgia, for the Citico–Lick Creek transitional form.

Other Goods

I believe the patterns are clear enough to warrant a view of exchange in the Mississippian Southeast that does not require much intervention by elite lords or by merchant traders. This exercise could be repeated for any number of different items that have been proposed as "commodities" in the Southeast. For example, ceramic exchanges are often predicated on the basis of the presence of pottery types (e.g., Steponaitis 1983, 1991). Fortunately, new research into such things as identification of the chemical composition of raw materials will become increasingly important in pinning down actual movements of goods from one locality to another (e.g., Steponaitis et al., 1996). Such studies will allow much more exact discussions of what goods and how many actually were moved from one place to another. These researches cannot but help to improve the data needed to identify the likelihood of elite or other mediation in exchange in the Southeast.

Interaction, Polities, and Persons

The identity of the peoples engaged in these episodes of exchange is, nonetheless, obscure in terms of linking prehistoric styles or phases to historical groups. Certainly realignments and reorganizations of specific polities occurred as a result of Old World diseases and invasions. We can note, however, that the historical Muskhogean-speaking groups of the Southeast were often associated closely with the styles that are most clearly descended from the styles of the Southern Cult proper. The historical confederacies of the Southeast no doubt owe much of their immediate *raison d'etre* to European invasions, but Cahokia, Moundville, and Spiro do not show patterns of exchange that appear very different from those of historical times. There are regional and temporal differences in exchange frequency, of course. For example, the highest frequency of items per burial at Moundville occurs around A.D. 1250, but the highest total of exotic goods in burials peaks with the maximum number of burials around A.D. 1400 (Steponaitis 1991:210–211). This later period, of course, is after the reduction in size or actual abandonment of the Mississippian settlements near the Mississippi–Missouri confluence and in the Ohio Valley. However the average number of exotics with each burial is low, only about 0.4 items per burial. The period with the most exotic items was at ca. A.D. 1250 (Steponaitis 1991).

As discussed in the previous two chapters, in these chiefdoms, production of almost all goods was on a domestic level, not very different in that regard from tribal-level societies. Of course, we must understand that domestic production and the *potential* for every household to produce every kind of object is not a denial that some skilled artisans produced more fancy objects than did ordinary Mississippians. By the times that chieftains were well-established in the Southeast, it is clear that differences of status and rank were expressed in clothing and accoutrements of symbolic significance. However, "prestige goods" (e.g., Earle 1978, 1987; Johnson and Earle 1987:Chapter 7) show little sign of their manufacture having been under elite control. In this chapter, we have also made a case that access to such goods was widespread. Elites seem to have had little role in controlling such access. Ultimately, of course, goods do not move so much from one location to another as they are transferred from one person to another. What is key is the nature of the social relationship involved in the dyad of supplier and receiver. Each has a social place, and the interactions are affected by the kin or other ties linking producer to consumer as well. The distribution of both hoes and shell gorgets is consistent with the idea that simple production is involved in which the production has vested the producer with control of the use-values and exchange-values of the objects. Personal styles predominate in the shell engravings, and the nature of the styles is inconsistent with the idea of workshop production by specialists. The most likely path of distribution of both hoes and gorgets was first of all within the broad domestic setting, including kin at other locations. The second path was probably in some kinds of exchange within ritual expressions of solidarity. Although possessing a "prestige" object no doubt conferred prestige, the prestige was as likely to be conferred from the object as from the honor of the donor; that is, these objects may be of social value, without being tokens of the admiration of a seignior. This is another aspect of the possible network character of these relationships as opposed to the classical version of a prestige-goods economy.

It is, however, likely that elites had, through such avenues as alliance relationships to other regional elites, somewhat greater access to such goods and possibly some indirect influence over their distribution and exchange. This is not what a "prestige goods" economy requires of them, however. As I have suggested in passing, the Kula ring should be as carefully examined as the exchange and production systems of Polynesia have been by Southeastern archaeologists. It seems likely, by reading between the lines, that elites played some role in sponsoring festivals that probably involved much exchange of all kinds—ritual, gambling, and purely staple.

There is not much evidence that I can see that the historical European practice of giving out medals to allied or dependent chiefs had precedents in pre-European social relations. Shell gorgets do not seem to have had the same purposes as European medals and metal gorgets (see Jacobs 1950).

Another possible means for the enhancement and transformation of status into rank is through risk management, but that is a topic that leads us away from our external exchange theme toward internal distribution. Certainly, the ability of chiefs to draw on alliances with other chiefs to provide succor in times of need would be a very practical reason for ordinary folk to commit themselves to chiefs. There can be little reason to doubt that Southeastern chiefs did resemble European lords in one important respect at least—*noblesse oblige*. Both prestations to and gifts from Southeastern chiefs in historical times seem more often to have been in staple goods such as food and clothing, rather than in tokens of elite power (in addition to the sources discussed in Chapter 2, see Jacobs 1950). The obligation of the chief to provide a social security net under the domestic producers seems to have been strong.

I remain extremely skeptical that power and relations of exploitation of the sort that seem to characterize some developed chiefdoms and states were important in the Southeast until quite late, although simple thuggery could have occasionally played a role in the growth of elites. Even such champions of exploitation theories as Marx and Engels, however, recognized that positive functions played some part in leadership, at least prior to the emergence of classes. This is especially true for societies in which "voting with one's feet" was still possible (and well documented in historical records, back to the 16th-century abandonment of towns at the approach of Spanish conquistadors; see Chapter 2).

To judge from historical records in the Southeast, nonelite interactions were also likely to have been important. There is no evidence, however, for any special social status of trader (Myers 1928) in this area. Rather, persons ranged out in visits to other groups as a part of their domestic and kinship-based economies. Much the same may be said of supposed "markets" in the Southeast. There were gatherings and festivals, and much exchange took place during them, but these never seem to have achieved a true market character, even at the height of European trade in actual commodities.

4. CONSUMPTION

Consumption is a kind of end product and synthesis of production and distribution. It is the process of realization of use-value, and production itself is consumption—"production supplying the external object of consumption and consumption the conceptual object of production" (Marx 1859 [1977:198]). Consumption of staple goods is a necessity for survival and reproduction of a society. There are at least as many kinds of consumption as there are modes of production or distribution, but many of these are less important in the context of a profoundly domestic economy than they are in modern industrial states. For example, although one can imagine how *capital consumption*, the using up of some goods in the course of production of other goods, might be adapted to noncapitalist economies, the purpose and usefulness of such a conversion are unclear. It seems sufficient to recognize that consumption has the same dimensions as other human activities. There is, however, the distinction between productive and nonproductive consumption mentioned earlier. However, be warned that "nonproductive consumption" in neoclassical economic theory includes consumption of goods for public services such as schools or roads! Presumably, mound construction would be nonproductive as well. It is important to understand the distinction, not because there was much "nonproductive" consumption in Mississippian societies, but because the demonstration of "nonproductive" consumption would provide a strong boost to theories emphasizing the thuggery of power.

In general, consumption completes production by destroying the product. It is a concluding act. Its close connection with production, however, does not mean that production and consumption are identical (Marx 1859 [1977:198–199]).[7] Marx could also see the growth of consumption as driving technological change (e.g., Marx 1846 [1975:662]). That is to say, an understanding of consumption and its consequences should not be ruled out of a political economy on grounds that political economy deals only with relations of power and politics.

In social formations without differentiation, consumption is largely collective, like production and distribution. With division of labor, consumption itself came to reflect classes and professions. Indeed, the test of specialized production at the Great Salt Spring, summarized in Chapter 7, was partly based on the probability that true specialists would show distinctive, consumption-oriented artifactual profiles, coupled with indications of consumption of exotic goods from their exchanges with "customers." Like production, the mode of consumption depends upon the state of development of the consumer.

The issue of surplus is also linked to that of consumption. A surplus may be produced as a result of normal production. However, not all goods in excess of immediate needs are true surplus, since there is "deferred consumption" in the form of goods kept for consumption in later times. These savings may not be available for immediate consumption without placing future survival at risk.

Mississippian Consumption

Household Consumption

Mississippian consumption, like production and distribution, seems to have involved fairly uniform and equitable distribution of goods. The data on health presented in earlier chapters suggests that problems were widely shared across the communities rather than being concentrated among the lower ranking members of the society. The data on reproduction also suggest that outlying sites were in effect subsidizing the reproduction of the larger sites, however. This may have happened not through the moving in of goods into the centers, but through actual movements of people, consuming the primary costs of biological reproduction at small sites, but, perhaps, moving into the less healthy and more crowded and risky larger sites later in life. Other data on production, distribution, and exchange already discussed also show that the levels of consumption at all sites were surprisingly consistent.

---

[7] A comment by Marx that a "Hegelian" at this stage would see consumption and production as identical because of their connection is, I think, another indication that Marx does not fit into the "realist" camp as suggested by McGuire (1992:114) and others.

The de Soto chronicles indicated that the Spanish taking of stored grain some-times created real hardship later in the same year. This shows that these stores cannot be understood always as true surplus goods, controlled by the elites and produced beyond levels necessary for reproduction. If the goods were necessary for the later survival of the group, it is also hard to see these stores as true tribute for the use of the chief and the elite, if their use was essential rather than reserved for privileged consumption. That is to say, such stored goods represented merely deferred consump-tion rather than primitive accumulation of "royal capital." It would be unwise simply to ignore the evidence that earlier times had consumption circumstances that were quite similar. Elsewhere, the conclusion was reached that diets of most subsistence cultivators, "while monotonous, distasteful, and often insecure, are not on the aver-age inadequate physiologically" (Clark and Haswell 1970:172).

Elite Consumption

I suppose that it might be conceivable that social differentiation in Mississip-pian societies grew, as it were, "out of the tip of the arrow." By such a view, Mississip-pian elites might simply have been those "bad war chieftains of a numerous family, who inslaved the rest" who constituted the only Muskhogean concept of despotism (Adair 1775:427). If Mississippian chiefs were simply local thugs running a psycho-logical and economic "protection racket," we should expect to see differences be-tween elite and general-population consumption reflecting that kind of domination. In really hard times, the elites would, in such a model, do well, but the mass of people would starve as the wiseguys of a Mississippian Don took first call on essential resources. In fact, as we have seen in earlier chapters, the persons buried in the main "elite" contexts are arguably little more than marginally better off in health and indicators of stress than were so-called "commoners". The evidence seems fairly conclusive that high rank in Mississippian societies did not confer the power to take essential food from the mouths of their "subjects". There certainly were differences in consumption by elites and others, but these differences seem to relate to markers of social status. They do not seem to have been indications of the ability of chiefs to take away the necessities of life from their followers (see Jackson and Scott 1995).

As for nonproductive consumption by elites, there is little evidence in the historical records that the chiefs were primarily nonproductive. The willingness of chiefs, even "autocratic" ones, to lead by participation in many kinds of labor activi-ties is documented as often as are indications of the deference given to them. I would not be surprised if the individual "Great Sun" of Cahokia was exempted from many kinds of normal activities, but I would be very surprised if the "Great Sun's" retinue proved to be nonproducers as a family, much less a class. I suspect that we might generally find that the wealthier members of Mississippian societies had some advan-tages in consumption, but the evidence and arguments to date have hardly warranted this hypothesis, much less tested it. I repeat, the bulk of current evidence at Missis-sippian sites in general is that elite consumption is only slightly better, if any better, than that of the ordinary Mississippian people. At the very least, this seems to be the case for staple goods. For display goods, the evidence does not unambiguously sup-port elite "control" at this point, notwithstanding claims to the contrary. Conspicuous consumption is a wide enough marker of prestige that we should not be surprised if some kinds of display goods were consumed conspicuously in competition for rank status. I would especially expect to see this at centers where there was developed rivalry with adjacent polities. Where any burial with fancy grave goods is treated as elite, we cannot be surprised that sometimes only elite persons have fancy goods!

5. CONCLUSIONS

Given the patterns of exchange as they are, *domination*, as opposed to individual *dominance* within societies, is hard to justify as an explanation for regional or even local integration in the Southeast. This seems to be true before, during, and after Mississippian times. Patterns of exchange, rather, developed in the give and take of social relations among communities and among the leaders to whom communities owed fealty. Relations with external elites provided additional prestige for local leaders who had somewhat easier access to valued goods. However, the patterns suggest that leaders could claim no monopoly to such relations and exchanges. Most long-distance exchange relations in the Southeast are reasonably well modeled by simple, down-the-line movements of goods from diverse and dispersed centers of production.

The few examples given here illustrate that the patterns of exchange and interaction in the Southeast are consistent with what we have learned in recent years about the generalized character of production and political economy in small-scale, developing, chiefdom-level societies. Just as there was little evidence for full-time, craft specialization (in the strict sense, see Muller 1984a, 1992), and production of every kind of goods and raw materials was profoundly domestic, so external relationships also seem to be explainable in terms of the external relations of domestic, not only elite, units. In short, the economies of these societies were still in many ways at what we formerly thought of as a "tribal" level, even though there were emergent groups of persons who gathered central administrative roles. These roles were probably partly obtained through risk management by allocation of stored resources gained by prestations from the normal surplus of the primary producers. In historical times, gifts (a.k.a. "tribute") given to leaders were mostly staple goods, exactly what would be expected if they were partly provisioned by others, and partly serving to provision others in turn (even including the Spanish). Other factors probably included the elites' developing influence over external relationships and their social ability to stimulate fealty on the part of their followers. The evidence on the nature of external exchange in the Southeast does not support models of elite development that emphasize such features as "power" and authoritarian control of resources. These "power" models too often emphasize features of elite protoclasses that come into being only as chiefly societies develop into class societies.

I do not want to be misunderstood as suggesting that Mississippian societies and their relatives were "tribal" or less than complex. Quite to the contrary, the ease with which historical Eastern polities transformed themselves into "incipient" states under European military pressures illustrates how well their ancestors had done in establishing areawide traditions of hierarchy and political order. A suggestion that most prehistoric Mississippian peoples were at the political level of their historical descendants *should* not be seen as "degrading" the complexity of Mississippian except by those who have accepted the "cant of conquest" that treats historical Southeastern Native Americans as "degenerate."

Chapter 9

Contradictions of Mississippian Political Economy

> When people want to understand the rise or
> disappearance of anything, they usually imagine that
> they achieve comprehension through the medium of
> a conception of the *gradual character* of that rise or
> disappearance. However, changes in being take
> place, not only by a transition of one quantity into
> another, but also by a transition of qualitative
> differences into quantitative, and, on the contrary,
> by a transition that *interrupts gradualness* and
> substitutes one phenomenon for another.
> G. Hegel, *Wissenschaft der Logik*, Bd. I,
> 1812:313–314.

1. WHAT IS WHAT?

This book is a beginning analysis of the political economy of what are loosely known
as Mississippian social formations. I do not see this as a particularistic task. I have
painted with a broad brush, since in this book I more interested in the similarities
that make these societies recognizable than I am in their differences. I have, when
concerned with other problems, explicitly called for understanding the diversity of
Mississippian complexes (e.g., Muller and Stephens 1991). I have not tried to survey
all expressions of Mississippian evenly—I have taken my data where I could find
them. This is not a culture-historical textbook. However, to those who say that these
conditions couldn't apply to *their* Mississippian, I say "*De te fabula narratur*" (This
story is about you). Although the complexes where data are available *may* all be
atypical, I think there are enough general similarities to ask for empirically grounded
arguments for differences rather than assumptions.

What is it that makes these societies Mississippian? Is there a Mississippian
political economy? Mississippian everywhere had a common basis in maize horticul-

ture. However, as societies on the edges of the Mississippian world amply illustrate, this alone was not enough to make a people Mississippian, not any more than shell-tempered pottery made them so. I have purposely not defined a separate Mississippian mode of production, not least because I am uncertain whether this mode is at all distinctive, rather than a form similar to that of most large, nonstate societies. Regardless, it is their particular mode of production, and the social relations contained in it, that makes a people Mississippian, not mounds, not pottery, or even chiefs.

In this book, I have built up from the domestic level to ranked hierarchies. This approach does not mean that we should or can ignore nondomestic Mississippian social structures. I have not claimed to have covered every important issue relating to Mississippian political economy, but I hope that I have shown some benefits of integrating economic bases with social mechanisms in investigating key questions about these hierarchical, but classless, societies. Elites were important, but so were the so-called "commoners." A balanced approach is necessary, but one built on evidence. We especially need to avoid begging the question through the use of loaded terms such as *trade* and *tribute*. If some social group is described as a *class*, how can one avoid seeing the whole society in terms of opposing class interests? Terminology should be as neutral as possible to avoid prejudgment of the conditions of a particular time and place. If it is claimed that elites are able to divert critical resources from the mass of population, let us see the physical evidence rather than presumptions based on loose metaphors and the terms employed.

One question I have asked in this book, admittedly somewhat polemically, is how much a simple model of Mississippian suffices in explaining the facts of Mississippian archaeology. I believe those who argue for complex interpretations—Mississippian states, Mississippian kings, and Mississippian markets—bear special burdens to show why models postulating level of complexity like those of Historic times are inadequate. Frankly, I resent my efforts to understand Mississippian having been characterized as *minimalist*, a term that offensively imputes to me a prejudice to make Mississippian less grand than it is. It is in this spirit that I have, perhaps a little peevishly, responded in kind by characterizing some views as "exaggerationalist." I would honestly rather debate the size and organization of these societies than call names. I started with ideas about "my" Mississippian complex that were quite as grand as anyone's, but 30 years of empirical investigations have showed us, not what we might wish it to be, but rather what kinds of models suffice. To the others, I again say, "*De te fabula narratur.*"

Although I have made criticisms where I felt them to be necessary, I hope that these will not be taken as the main focus of this book. Rather, I have tried to present an extensive bottom-up view of Mississippian. As long as this process has been, and as long this book has become, what is presented here remains necessarily incomplete and preliminary.

I am not opposed in principle to the idea that the biggest Mississippian complex might be qualitatively different than the rest, but this is not something that can be assumed simply on the basis of size. The size of Cahokia warrants investigation of its possible "statelike" organization, but it does not prove it. Even the largest population estimates for Cahokia ever given by professional archaeologists are smaller than the largest historical population estimate for the Choctaw—who have been supposed by some to be an organizationally decadent confederacy. If large size doesn't suffice to make the Choctaw complex, why should it do so for Cahokia? Of course, in each case, size is only one of many variables to be considered in assessing complexity.

In Chapter 1, I sketched an outline of political economy as a topic and summarized the theoretical context of this book. The study started from an historical materialist position that concentrates especially on the material conditions of everyday life, but that also appreciates that the ultimately determining nature of these is mediated by social and political conditions, not merely by technology. The concept of *mode of production* was outlined and the book was largely structured in the form of a mode-of-production analysis. I then presented an outline for a discussion of Mississippian political economy. I indicated that I would try to analyze material conditions, and the social and political structure that was built upon and constitutes a whole with, those everyday conditions.

Chapters 2 and 3 filled in the foreground and background of Mississippian social forms, respectively. The historical literature was surveyed for evidence about historical social relations and political authority. I concluded that there was a paradoxical over- and underestimation of Historic Native Americans in the East. On the one hand, overblown terminology had been used for some small societies, whereas the complexity of large-scale, persisting social formations was treated as being in some senses, at least, "degenerate." Anthropologists and archaeologists nearly universally abhor expansionist ideology, but they have not perhaps allowed for the degree to which such ideology permeates many historical sources. They have also not always sufficiently allowed for cultural differences among Spanish, French, and English observers. Historic Easterners were engaged in difficult struggles to save their lives, their societies, and their cultures, and many of them did remarkably well in responding to overwhelming political and economic pressures. They proved capable, at least in the larger groups, of maintaining both town and polity size. They were able to respond flexibly to appalling loss of life from disease and warfare through such processes as aggregation and reformation of smaller groups within larger ones. I suggested that some of these historical processes may have also been characteristic of pre-European times, although the causes of reformation of social groups were, perhaps, different. I again want to make it clear that I have *not* used Historic Eastern social forms to interpret Mississippian social formations, but I *have* suggested that there is evidence that supports comparable levels of integration for the two periods. Some specific mechanisms of integration may have been common to both historical Easterners and their ancestors.

Some kinds of "Eastern models" for the prehistoric East might better be investigated before we feel the need to draw on the social forms of Medieval Europe or Oceania. I certainly have not hesitated to compare Mississippian to the latter, of course, but I think I have shown enough attention to historical data on the East to justify looking more broadly. I am a little mystified at discussions of Mississippian that, in effect, divide these peoples from their descendants—hardly mentioning historical Native Americans, while being filled with comparisons to Old World societies. This would not be surprising for the 19th-century Eurocentric historians who denied Native Americans not only their lands, but also their pasts; but anthropologists should be more alert to such biases in their historical sources. Mississippian societies are not "lost civilizations." They are here still, changed to be sure, but perhaps not so much more changed than are the descendants of their European adversaries. Modern Choctaw and others carry on traditions that have their roots in the Southeastern Late Prehistoric.

I also suggested that developing Mississippian peoples used the social forms of pre-Mississippian social and economic relations as their building blocks. There is little indication that the social roles of Mississippian chiefs, for example, were modeled on anything other than the most powerful people they had known from the previous generation. Each generation built on and transformed, in fact, promoted, the social forms that preceded theirs. This is another reason why our models of Mississippian political economy need to be constructed from the bottom up, since in the first instance, the Mississippian economy is built on the basis of the domestic economy of its homesteads. These produced the food that filled, or not, the bellies of Mississippian peoples. Yet the conditions of production at the homestead level became considerably more complicated for the Mississippian homestead than for Late Woodland domestic producers. Late Woodland producers were not tied to specific locations, at least during most of their period and in the more northern localities. Mobility and the resulting production alternatives were key elements in cushioning the natural and social perturbations of production. As communities were formed that were tied to fields filled with crops requiring months to mature, the dynamics of community life were transformed. Although we do not understand the particular historical developments in every case, it is clear that kinds of leadership that had remained flexible and informal throughout Late Woodland times then became more important and less informal.

It is in this context of sedentism, increased production, and, paradoxically, sometimes greater risk, that we should be able to see the promotion of tribal heads to chiefs. As alternative production strategies were cut off, continuity between one year and the next, and one locality and the next, became more important. Leadership became extended in time and space. Local integration was replaced by regional integration, and short-term leaders became cross-generational chiefs. Yet it would be a mistake to emphasize cross-generational continuity too much in this context, because the evidence also supports a high level of insecurity for Mississippian chiefs. Claims of chiefly descent were probably always subject to challenge, especially by other members of the same kin groups, but also by others whose economic successes might enable them to establish rival claims to chiefly dignity. Archaeologically this is reflected in the "blinking" on and off of Mississippian complexes noted by Anderson (e.g., 1994a). The dispute over precedence by the caciques of Pacaha and Casqui (Chapter 2) illustrate such rival claims at first contact with the Europeans.

In analyzing Mississippian modes of production, I began with the most basic aspect of successful Mississippian societies—their ability to reproduce their populations and their social forms. Mississippian persons seem to have had a mostly adequate, if risky, basis for day-to-day living. The distribution of food across the societies showed maize was a critical factor in the evolutionary success of Mississippian in comparison to non-Mississippian social formations. Maize was not the *cause* of these developments, of course. In fact, some societies developed hierarchical systems rather like Mississippian without having had much, if any, dependence on maize. What was important was not one particular crop, but rather the conditions of limited alternatives combined with risk for domestic producers.

However, evolutionary success—differential persistence—does not have to mean improvements in the life of individuals. Group survival may be enhanced in relation to other local and regional societies almost independently of individual well-being, for example. Because of this, evidence of individual biological stress cannot be simply interpreted as implying that a particular society was failing in a social or biological sense. The morality of evolutionary success values differential survival and reproduction, not happiness. Emergent Mississippian societies could have outcompeted and eliminated potential rivals on a local and regional basis during their flourishing days of formation without necessarily being stable in the long term. Virtually all human societies that developed through aggregation into sedentary, densely settled groups have faced the same contradiction. The ethics of a mobile society in terms of sanitation, water and resource conservation, and so on may not be consistent with new, settled conditions. The success of a group in building a large population that can dominate a region can also create a new reservoir for disease and other kinds of risks. Ironically, until things are sorted out, individual health and life span may actually decline after (and even during) a time of group success. Some risks were present in Mississippian societies, and there were important contradictions within Mississippian reproductive success.

The biological differences between elites and nonelites also proved to be relatively slight. In stature, dental pathology, and other measures, elites seem to have been biologically like other members of the same societies. The elites seem to have shared the good and bad years. Indeed, given the probable "flexibility" of rank in the Southeast, similarity may reflect upward and downward mobility as well. These measures are not the only way to look at the empirical standing of the elite in relation to others, but the similarities are particularly telling as a caution against elevating elite rank in Mississippian to classlike levels.

Much of the Southeast was transformed either into Mississippian or something much like it during the few centuries after A.D. 900. An effort to look at reproduction through life tables, admittedly an imperfect measure, suggested some rather surprising things about these transformations. Mississippian social formations around the 10th century were increasing in size, extent, and population. Yet taking the population curves represented in Mississippian cemeteries as representative, one finds that these population distributions, particularly after the 11th century, could have typically been characterized by slight negative rates of increase, rather than the strong positive values that one might expect from overall Mississippian expansion. I argued some time ago that population growth was an important stimulus to Mississippian transformations (e.g., Muller 1978a, 1986b), and I am still inclined to see population increases as having been important in stimulating Mississippian social forms under certain conditions. However, many of these populations, especially after the initial period of formation of Mississippian social forms, may have been maintained by immigration and aggregation as much as by natural increase. Such a process would have had negative affects on smaller communities as they subsidized the reproduction of the larger centers at their own expense. In turn, the long-term result may have been gradual, local population declines that may have been the proximate causes of the disappearance of some Mississippian social formations by the 15th century. Of course, climate and other factors almost certainly also played some role in these "abandonments" along the northern limits of Mississippian life ways. The same kind of aggregation and absorption of other social formations that occurred in historical Eastern polities may also have characterized prehistoric developments, especially after the beginning of the 14th century.

There seem to be economic and political pressures that forced or allowed town size to remain fairly constant in the Historic period, even in the face of drastic social change. Prehistoric towns had a similar scale and tendency to persist at a certain size, or not at all. The basic unit of town life still remained the household, of course. Even the layouts of mound centers, with their plazas and mound groups, reproduce the scaled-up courtyard and buildings of a homestead. The isolation of many individual producers in farmsteads was also seen as having social implications in terms of relations to both other producers and elites. The question of population estimates was also treated to show the consequences of accepting the larger estimates for the size of Mississippian settlements. Many estimates turn out to be so large as to be difficult to justify in terms of potential productivity of the areas occupied.

I discussed production next (Chapter 6), from the simple details of the raw materials and their transformation into use-values in the context of domestic production. The overwhelming evidence supports the domestic character of labor in production. The dynamics of Mississippian production in these domestic contexts were related to the reproductive dynamics of the growth and decline of households. Division of labor was by gender, not by social class. The evidence amply demonstrates that most products were created under the control of individual production units within a domestic setting. This includes not merely the food consumed, but even such "prestige" goods as shell gorgets. The domestic production force was sufficient, almost, to meet all the needs of the local community. The key, after all, is in the word *almost.* In that tiny (as a percentage of total labor) difference lies the genesis and support of the whole superstructure that makes Mississippian distinctive. If local production had been completely sufficient, then Mississippian would, after all, not have been different from Late Woodland in such interesting ways.

However, one of the exceptions to domestic production is, of course, the most visible remains left by Mississippian peoples. Large-scale public investments in mound construction are clear, but we should not forget that the scale of this labor is but a relatively small part of the total labor expended by Mississippian producers. Even the slightly more than a million cubic meters of fill at Cahokia could have been erected in only 250 years of one *4-day* festival per year by one-fifth of a total population of 5000 people. With 10,000 persons total, the time required would have been halved. Such a labor investment is most impressive in its results, but it is hardly necessary to postulate "*corvée* labor" to explain it.

A number of proposals of "craft specialization" for Mississippian have been made over the years. Most of these have turned out not to be really proposals for professionalization (i.e., craft production, in the strict sense), but rather suggestions of something that has come to be called "part-time" specialization. Despite my long-standing criticism of this terminology, I suppose it would be acceptable if we were all to agree to make it clear what this term means. However, it is essential that we understand that this usage completely divorces the term *specialization* from any implication of complexity, either economically or politically. "Part-time specialization" is merely the ordinary division of labor by skill that occurs in all societies, and there hardly seems any important reason to dignify it with a separate term. Real craft specialization, however, has very strong implications—it indicates that a set of social interdependencies have been created that place the survival of the craft specialist into the hands of other persons. Whether such a dependency is seen as being to a member of the elite who becomes the producer's patron or simply a condition of mutual interdependencies, as in a market, this new social relationship creates fundamental contradictions in kin-based or communal societies. The patron or the customer becomes all important to the specialist, weakening or even destroying other social relationships.

Because some claims of specialization have been put forward with great vigor and assurance, I did present a detailed analysis of salt production, simply because salt—creating an almost habit-forming appetite—should have been a focus of specialized production and exchange if such were present. Other goods, both staple and display, and their production, were also discussed, including hoe production and a few kinds of display goods. These staples and the display-goods production cases are largely inconsistent with a "specialization" interpretation. The manufacture of such items is mostly dispersed across Mississippian communities. The concentration that does occur, such as that in shell-bead production at Cahokia, may represent an elite production activity, perhaps one that actually does involve "attached" specialists, but I would like to see more evidence on exactly who was doing what at these locations than we have so far. Even the strongest of the cases seem to me to be explainable without concluding full-time specialization was present.

. Finally, the distribution and consumption of all kinds of goods showed the same domestic character that permeated production in Mississippian social formations. Both utilitarian (including staple) and display goods show patterns of internal and external distribution that are consistent with down-the-line or person-to-person spread, rather than supporting the idea of powerful redistributive elites. The simple falloff curves of goods to distance have truly remarkable correlations by social science standards. There is little in these cases that is left to explain once the distance to source has been determined. Inside Mississippian societies, the goods so often characterized as "elite" turn out to be widely shared and as common in even homesteads and small sites as they are in supposed elite contexts. Of course, there *were* markers of status and rank. We may expect that some goods, both staple and display, will have more often found their way into the hands of the elite than of those who were less well connected. What we have is a society, however, that met its needs more by *networking* than by the kinds of labor mobilization proposed in models of prestige-goods economies. The ability of many persons at small, isolated farmsteads to obtain exotic raw materials and fancy display goods speaks to the lack of social distance between top and bottom in Mississippian societies. In Historic times, it was certainly possible for persons to achieve considerable status and rank if their talents were great enough. The access to display goods and the instabilities seen in prehistoric Mississippian chiefdoms suggest no less in prehistoric times.

2. WHAT IS TO BE DONE?

The issues addressed in this book are far from resolved. Although the arguments about such features as "states" or "craft production" are partly terminological, there are real differences about specifics as well as on the kinds of view that should be taken generally. In concluding, I want to draw attention again to some of the theoretical and empirical issues that characterize Mississippian studies and Mississippian itself. These are issues that *can* be investigated. Some of them have been explored in this book, but others represent areas of future research. In this section, I have ranged rather more broadly than before from what we know empirically about Mississippian to some things we *need* to know, or even might wish to know.

I have found the framework of historical materialism to be useful to me in these analyses. I cannot say whether I might have reached the same or different conclusions if I had worked from a processual or neoevolutionary perspective. I can only say that historical materialist approaches have the analytical advantage of forcing a kind of holistic approach that emphasizes the interplay among events, their consequences, and the resulting changes in form and structure. An historical materialist method strikes a middle road between the vulgarism of environmental determinism and the idealism of neo-Hegelian pure reason. You readers will have to judge whether you find it useful in your own cases. Certainly, one danger in the approach is a tendency to become doctrinaire, but I have tried to remain flexible. Whether there is a "dialectic of nature" is immaterial in many ways, since a dialectical approach can be justified as a useful method for human analysis of events, especially human events. The dialectic, at the very least, draws attention to actions and their consequences within the context of "contradiction." This is not, of course, the contradiction of formal logic, of "A" and "not-A." Rather, these are contradictions such as large populations having group survival advantages as opposed to their health disadvantages. These are not only opposing factors, but also actions and consequences that are linked inextricably within the same events. Everything cannot be reduced to some underlying set of principles or relations, but neither can all such apparently contradictory tendencies be assumed to reflect lack of underlying unity. Ultimately, any proposal of dialectical relationships has to be subjected to standards of evidence, consistency, adequacy, and utility—just like other kinds of argument. In classical historical materialism, the goal was to identify "key" or "determining" contradictions out of the myriad contradictions present in all phenomena. As noted in the first chapter, there are many problems with this, both in practice and in theory. Nonetheless, even if it had no other uses, a dialectical analysis has didactic and heuristic value in drawing attention to causes and effects as interaction. In the discussion that follows, I try to define some kinds of interactions that characterize Mississippian studies, at least.

Population Growth and Decline

At least at the beginning, population grew, from whatever causes. This growth reflected the evolutionary success of Mississippian. Larger populations can smother out smaller social groups by using up local resources, even if not by actual conflict.

However, the more people, the greater the problems, especially in social and sanitation areas.

The very acts that made life better had embedded in their consequences the potential for making things worse in new and unforseeable ways. As maize and other floodplain resources provided a sustainable and intensifiable resource, fertility may have gone up. The bottomlands and their fertile soils could also have attracted more and more people from the uplands. The attractiveness of social groups for other humans seems clear enough, but there must often have been little real choice once such clusters of settlement began to form in a region. Seasonal settlements became relatively permanent settlements and then permanent settlements. Upland resources of game and wild foods could not offer the year-to-year assurance of the rich, wild resources of the floodplain, combined with crops that allowed planning from one year to the next. More particularly, it must have been difficult for small family groups to compete with these larger settlements. Sedentism and diets that were more steady from one year and season to the next provided the first kick to increased reproduction, as well as to aggregation. Data on "Emergent" Mississippian and early Mississippian reproductive success are not so common as for later times, but there do seem to be the initial increases that one might expect would result from a new and more competitive political economic system. It is, of course, very difficult to know how much of the reproductive success of early Mississippian was due to improvement of sustenance, and how much was due to aggregation of formerly dispersed upland peoples immigrating into floodplain environments. One might expect to see indications of immigration in local ceramic traditions, but these may have be obscured for archaeological detection by the small scale of particular events and by the relative simplicity and evenness of Mississippian ceramic styles. Whether the increases in the size of Mississippian societies were due to immigration, natural increases, or both, the scale of life changed quite radically from earlier times. Institutions to ameliorate periodic shortfalls that had sufficed in Late Woodland times could not have easily handled the greater demands on them in the more crowded, larger Mississippian settlements. In this context, the old social institutions relating to sharing and public acts of mercy must necessarily have been transformed in character and scale. Yet, at the same time, we should not expect that these changes so transformed early Mississippian social structure that its Late Woodland roots were unrecognizable.

The security of fertile floodplains could become a kind of trap. People came to depend upon floodplain resources *and* the social system they had built there, but at the same time, the reproductive success of individuals was not necessarily enhanced. Indeed, the individual's well-being did not really enter into the equation, and groups could continue to grow by aggregation. Eventually this could have caught up with these societies as they used up their hinterland populations. Perhaps that is one factor in the changes in northern Mississippian during the late-13th–14th centuries.

Although I suggested earlier that historical warfare was stimulated by the presence of hostile European powers, each seeking allies against the others, it is also true that conflict was not new to the Mississippian Southeast. Although evidence such as body injuries only weakly supports this for prehistoric Southeasterners, the presence of fortifications and aggregated towns also has to be considered. Of course, conflicts may have been another factor in the slow declines in population over time.

Population seems to have peaked earlier in the north. As these centers declined, some southern centers came into their periods of maximum extent. There may have been some movement from more northern areas into the southern societies, but there is little evidence of large-scale "migrations" of people, not least, perhaps, because there weren't all that many people left in the north by those times. The Historic records, as noted, suggest that towns in the earliest periods of contact were already "multiethnic" in a way that supports the idea that portions of their populations had formerly been separate, autonomous groups. Part of the "rise" of a new chiefdom, or the persistence of an older one, seems to have been its ability to assimilate new elements.

If the Mississippian town required a certain size to function economically and socially, then some aspects of the cycling of Mississippian chiefdoms may have followed from the political economic contradictions implicit in population dynamics. Even if the negative reproductive rates modeled earlier in this book were characteristic of these societies, the rates were still close to replacement, so that a few new persons from another town could have kept town (and even polity) size at the minimum required to provide the economic and political reserves necessary to ensure relative safety in times of hardship.

Production Cycles and Natural Events

Natural perturbations affected health, as we know from skeletal remains, but how critical were these in providing an economic basis for chiefly government? The tensions created by natural perturbations in relation to nascent, regional political economies have already been discussed at some length. It does need to be remembered that the unpredictability of natural events such as floods plays a more direct role in relatively small societies than they do in large ones. The number of persons on whom one can depend for aid in hard times is simply more limited than in nation states. I have argued that the scale of Mississippian societies reflects that risk, insofar as the interplay of population size and predictability of outcomes is concerned. This is far from arguing for population determinism. What I am suggesting is that the various conditions are simultaneously favoring sedentism, increase in localization of population, and integration of political life on a regional scale. Yet the consequences of these events may be an increase in dependency and the need for still greater integration and aggregation. If the mode of production cannot respond flexibly enough or provide long-term stability, then there may be centrifugal pressures, *at the same time*, encouraging dispersal, emigration, and abandonment of localities. Whether dispersal or aggregation occurs in a particular place is dependent on the specifics of each location, but the same kinds of mechanism are at work in both cases. The relations between these different kinds of historical process in Historic times are clearly linked to internal and external problems. In relation to social problems and natural perturbations, population density is not just cause or effect, but is part of dialectical processes.

Domestic Economy and Community Economy

Another contradiction is that between the domestic and community economies. As land became an important factor in survival, kin groups may have taken over much of the allocation of fields. Unfortunately, we do not have much evidence about how this actually worked out in either Historic or prehistoric times. If kin groups allocated land, one problem may have emerged from the probability that aggregating communities included persons whose membership in the group, through marriage, capture, or simply immigration, did not entitle them to a share. The conflicting claims of residence and kin are involved. Marriage alliances could solve some problems, but what about a woman immigrant in a matrilineally based land-allocation system? Would her marriage to a male member of the matriclan entitle her to land? There is some discussion of allocation of lands to *resident* families among the Creek (e.g., Bartram 1789 [1853:37–39]), but the chief, as such, does not seem to enter into the allocation that is said to be by "the town or community." Goods produced belonged to the producer, however, not the community, although a share of the crop was placed in the "Public Granary, which is called the King's crib, because its contents are at his disposal, though not his personal property, but considered the tribute or free contribution of the citizens of the State, at the disposal of the king" (1789 [1853:40]). These stores are explicitly said to be set aside for aid to individuals or towns in want. The bulk of production, in most cases, was stored in each producer's "own crib." Whether the "community" that allocated land was in fact kin, town council, or chief is nearly impossible to determine. Even without knowing exactly what was happening, it is likely that there were tensions in regard to the use of the communal/chiefly share as opposed to that taken for domestic use by the producers. Such tensions can hardly be mentioned in the same breath as real class interests, but social-group interests do not exist solely in class societies. It would be inappropriate to apply class-conflict models to this situation, but it is not inappropriate to ask about the nature of conflicts of interests between different ranked groups. This is another reason for applauding efforts to deal with the political aspects of the "Lords" of the Southeast, however much I may regret some of the terminology employed.

Other issues arise. What about the allocation of production to distant kin or even distant towns? Would individual households in favored locations find the shelter of kin or community distribution of goods to be useful or even tolerable if they are mostly donors rather than recipients? Societies need to reward overproduction by the talented, but the traditional models of lordly gifts do not seem to work very well in the cases studied so far.

What about the relation of the household and town to elites? Was there a kind of chain of command through *principales* who were kin? Or was the relationship of the household more directly to the chief, thus weakening kin ties in opposition to relations of fealty? Hard times and good times brought different problems, and social structures that were necessary and sustaining in hard times could become tyrannous and obnoxious in good times. What kinds of internal or external threats were necessary to accept the chief's demands? Although these issues will be difficult to approach archaeologically, it is still possible to see that we must look very closely at the archaeological evidence for production, distribution, storage, and consumption on a regional scale. A good start has been made at Cahokia, where both small domestic settings and the central community have both seen extensive archaeological work (e.g., Mehrer 1995; Milner 1990, 1991; Pauketat 1993, 1994). At Kincaid, the outlying communities are reasonably well known, but more work is needed at the central site to help interpret the data from excavations carried out in the 1930s. Moundville and Etowah both need more work on the regional scale before we can compare what we know of the central site to life in smaller and more dispersed communities, although many useful models have already been presented (e.g., Peebles 1987b; Steponaitis 1991; Welch 1991). Ultimately, if we want to understand the production systems of Mississippian communities, we have to examine communities on a regional, as well as local, scale.

Elites but Not Classes

Although our historical sources say little about the wealth of most chiefs and *principales*, there were discernible differences in their homes and regalia.

Within the communal and domestic economy, there were some forms of elite wealth. The practice of making prestations of portions of production to the chief's granary surely made the subsequent donations of those goods to needy persons and towns a source of respect for the chief. As we saw in Chapter 2, however, even the French sources on the Mississippi Valley sometimes comment on the *dignitas*, dignity, of the chiefs, while recognizing their lack of *potestas*, true power or authority. Such persons are leaders, but they are not able to command. This, in itself, creates contradictions. Who can lead when no one follows? This power and lack of power was not an incidental feature of either Historic or Mississippian political life but follows directly from the practical autonomy of the domestic producers, coupled with their potential dependence on the chiefs and on each other.

Prehistoric chiefs seem to have been, and Historic chiefs certainly were, strongly embedded in relations of receiving and reallocating subsistence goods, but what about markers of wealth? As we have seen, most likely archaeological candidates for wealth markers are distributed across Mississippian societies in ways that give little support to the idea of their being controlled by sumptuary custom. Few "prestige goods" were identified in the earliest historical accounts. Pearls, for example, seem to have been primarily mortuary accompaniments for the dead members of the chief's lineage. Some display goods such as "fans" seem to have been markers of status, but these were not, so far as we know, offered to the European intruders. Copper items seem, by the early 17th century, at least, to have been "valuables" in the Middle Atlantic region, but our records place them into an economy created by the European "sale" of copper in seeking food and supplies. The commercial interests of British traders and some others dominated so completely in later times that we cannot see much that clearly reflects wealth in goods for chiefs. Some chiefs did become wealthy in trade with Europeans, however (e.g., Bartram 1789 [1853:38]).

How did elites "control," if at all? Were they able to demand a percentage of production, and on what basis? How voluntary was the donation? Was it as voluntary as stressed for the Historic period by Bartram and Adair? Although Spanish sources sometimes speak of *tributo*, what can we conclude about the nature of prestations in Southeastern societies? Was the primary support of chiefs from tribute or from "numerous" kin, or did they draw on a large body of "made men"? Evidence suggests that the households of the elite in Mississippian times were far from "nonproducing" units.

Who were the *principales*? How could we identify them in a Mississippian context? The description of Creek social organization by Swanton illustrates how complex these offices may have been (1928a). There are real difficulties in attempting to draw up an organization chart for the various titles of "honored men," war chiefs, and so on. To speak of "levels" of hierarchy in such a case distorts the character of the different titles and ranks. I see little in the historical record that indicates that the composition of councils was determined by the chief. Some offices appear to have been filled from the chiefly lineage, but the bulk of the positions seem to have been like the structures described for the Creek by Swanton (1928a). As Anderson (1994b) stressed in his analysis of the Savannah River complexes, the historical records (as well as comparative data from other chiefly societies) support the idea of similarity of roles at different levels. If every person could not be a chief, there were still far too many potential rivals for any chief to have felt very secure. Anderson is certainly correct in singling out the contradictions in leadership as an important factor in Mississippian cycling. We may, of course, also ask, as he does, how these challenges to chiefly dignity might have been related to economic and environmental difficulties in Mississippian times.

The problem of local autonomy also deserves attention. The archaeological evidence supports the similarity of town size and town structure between Mississippian and Historic societies in the Southeast. As noted, the similarity of town structure to larger scale political structures in the Southeast even led Hudson to call each "town" a chiefdom (1976:202). This is correct insofar as many, if not all, towns possessed nearly the full political apparatus that characterized the political structure of a polity as a whole. I agree with Anderson and Hudson in seeing this as characteristic of Mississippian chiefdoms, rather than an artifact of Historic period aggregation. Each town chief, each "twin chief," each "war speaker" and "war chief" represented potential rivals for the *dignitas* of chief. Probably the war chief (*Tastanagi thlako* among the Creek) was the greatest threat to both the chief and public order, as perhaps the only person who ever held *potestas*, the power to command, even if only temporarily. It is significant that Adair's informants mentioned the office of war chief as a potential source of tyrannical rule, when he was trying to find out if they had the concept of a "king."

Some historical chiefs were clearly subordinate to others, yet the actual instances of paramountcy—as opposed to claims of paramountcy—in the historical record are relatively rare. Since every "town" had a sort of "shadow chief," the difference between an ordinary chief of more than one town, and a paramount chief, whose first-rank followers were themselves rulers of several towns, could not be very clear when the towns themselves were often dispersed in groups of hamlets and farmsteads. There *were* subordinate chiefs, but both the distance between the paramount and the subordinate and the number of subordinates has been exaggerated, I think. The term *confederacy* has widely been used for the large-scale polities of the later historical period and deserves some consideration as a more neutral term for the Prehistoric period in place of the somewhat prejudicial *paramount chiefdom*.

It would be going much too far to suggest that each mound group implies a separate or autonomous polity. However, it is also going too far to interpret all smaller mound centers near larger ones as being in a subordinate rank in relation to a paramount chief. Mound construction involved the sponsorship of a public event. One might suppose that such events were fairly regularly scheduled for particular parts of the annual cycle, so that participation in one such sponsored event may have meant not participating in another. If, as I think we may also suppose, participation involved bringing in goods to share during the celebration, then there are limits to how many such events could involve the same "subjects" in a given year. If a chief were, in fact, caught in a subordinate relation to another chief, would not the first act expressing autonomy be to appropriate the mound-construction labor available to the dominant chief? Might not, then, most mounds represent symbolic expressions of autonomy, as well as representing the "votes" of the builders themselves as to where they might choose to participate in public events?

In any case, the social-geographical landscape of Mississippian societies reflects their political economies to a high degree. The oppositions between large sites and small, aggregated and dispersed, mound construction or not, and many other similar conditions are not logical contradictions, but dialectical contradictions. These are different forms that result from the operation of a Mississippian political economy as it encountered different objective conditions.

Social groups of various kinds were probably also involved in other kinds of oppositions in Mississippian societies. I believe that it is fundamentally wrong to impose the framework of class interests and opposition on nonstate societies like Mississippian. However, there are different interests on the part of different social groups even in small-scale societies. To the extent that a society is large enough to have any kind of subgroups, there will be group-related rivalries. Such rivalries are not limited to humans but occur in other social primates and even more widely. Yet human intelligence, even foresight, makes for much more complex interactions and expression of group interests than in nonhuman societies. Even in kin-based political organizations, there are different statuses such as elders and new adults. When this is complicated by internal ranking of, for example, lineages or clans, then the kinds of social tensions created can be complex without, strictly speaking, being complex in the form of states.

Kin conflicts may generally be less bitter and structurally divisive than those of nonkin-based groups, but this does not mean that all is necessarily harmonious. When kin elders become part of a council, their relationships with the chief and with their own kinsmen may come into conflict—are they more council or clan? If Mississippian chiefs ever tried to exert statelike power, one might suppose that one way to achieve such an end would have been to somehow "attach" the council and other confederacy officials—to "secularize" them into being more representative of the chiefly power to the clans, than the other way around. Such officials would be perhaps better cases for "attached specialists" in Mississippian societies than were producers of display goods—if, indeed, the elites were not themselves also producing display goods. Although the data from Cahokia or elsewhere seem insufficient to make the case now, it would be interesting to see more research specifically aimed at identifying the social and economic behavior of differently ranked individuals. Differences far short of stratified classes should be visible in production, distribution, and consumption patterns, but representative samples rather than a grab-bag of comparisons are needed.

Much the same can be said about comparisons of the Mississippian elites in general to the mass of the population. The use of terminology such as "commoners" is ill-advised, but we need to settle the issues of differences in productive capabilities and practices between the ordinary members of the polity and those who have taken prestige and rank into their hands. Even though I believe that other contradictions are more central in the development of Mississippian polities, these social contradictions must still have been important.

The issue of justice—the mediation of disputes—is one of the critical issues in understanding how "developed" Mississippian political structures were. Up to the point of secondary state formation under European pressure, the Historic pattern seems to have been that of "justice" being determined by the kin of the victim. In discussing the promotion of police functions in the nascent Creek state, both Hawkins (1799) and Milfort (1802), described how the right of revenge was taken away for actions authorized by the council (not, it will be noted, by the chief). This is simply another case in which contradictions exist between the polity and the traditional domestic institutions. However, there is hardly any area more difficult to investigate from an archaeological perspective.

Goods without Specialists

Despite my skepticism about specialized production in Mississippian, there were certainly skilled producers. In a few cases, these producers may have actually made the majority of some kinds of goods, even if the whole group of producers *could* have produced the items. Most historical evidence from the Southeast strongly supports the majority of production having been done in a domestic setting. Archaeologically, the circumstances seem to have been similar. The bulk of goods involved something more than casual and expedient manufacture, and were widely dispersed across domestic sites. Skill differences for more complex goods meant that some kinds of artifacts and goods were produced more often by talented persons who might have had some support from less-skilled persons wishing to obtain such items. Some internal exchange of these goods may have occurred in the framework of distribution of goods along clan and kin lines, but some may well have contributed to asymmetry of relations among persons of different levels of skill. Just as a more skilled farmer could perhaps acquire a kind of following though her skills and her ability to contribute more than her share, so might someone who was especially skilled at flint knapping or making shell gorgets also become involved in making objects for others. We have no real evidence on whether a skilled producer of any kinds of goods could have used those skills to amass wealth, but it seems more likely that the "payments" for production were essentially the costs of reproduction of the producer, with no "profit," as such, except for the enhancement of prestige for such a producer. However, prestige can be a kind of deferred consumption too, in that someone who has been predominantly a donor in exchange may have more just calls on goods when he or she *does* need them. The accumulation of actual goods and deferred rights to goods at some future date can be significant in creating social tensions. Even in relatively small and undifferentiated societies, myths and stories are told to teach the lesson of avoiding asymmetrical calls on the goods of others, lest one have to repay the gift at some future time. Such widespread fear of being in social debt to another indicates the importance of such contradictions of interests on the part of skilled producers and their fellow "citizens." This is another reason why the changes between communal social forms and conditions of rank are significantly *not* gradual, but changes that tend to collapse from old forms to the new—from egalitarian to ranked. The probable expectations would be that the number of persons whose social roles implicitly involve asymmetry of exchange would be relatively few. The formation of classes, on the other hand, implies that substantial portions of a society stand in asymmetrical roles in regard to the mass of producers. Commoditization of production is a key factor in allowing accumulation of values that further increase the differences between the basic producers and those who are able to alienate their production. In the slave-holding states of antiquity, not only were there differences in wealth, but humans themselves became commodities. The ratio between producers and elites in such cases probably could be expected to follow something like the formulae for ratios between predators and prey (or, perhaps better, parasites and their host species). Detailed efforts to enumerate the ratio of elites to nonelites in Mississippian societies would provide some insights into the likelihood of statelike models. Based on an impression of house floor areas and sites with mounds as compared with other sites, I would guess that only a tiny percent of any Mississippian population was socially exempt from primary subsistence activities by virtue of their rank in the society. Even at the top of that range, such a low number of nonproducers does not provide much support for ideas of class or near-class distinctions implying appropriation of goods from producers.

Of course, production of nonsubsistence goods entails a whole group of contradictions, large and small. Time has to be taken from production of goods directly used in reproduction to make goods that may or may not assist in those tasks. The social contradictions between the producers and consumers have already been discussed, but similar kinds of asymmetrical relations can come into being as production comes to involve raw materials that are not directly accessible to the producer. An especially good flint knapper knocking out the odd hoe in the American Bottom was probably in a significantly different social situation than the person of similar skill working at the Union County quarries. At over 150 km from the sources, the American Bottom producer was likely to have been dependent upon others for the raw material to make a hoe, whereas some other kinds of artifacts were made from raw materials that were more likely directly acquired. An exchange system that involves larger numbers of persons increases the potential for the development of conflicts and dependencies. Although it is unlikely that the failure to obtain "good stuff" from Mill Creek would have made a vast difference in the life of an American Bottom flint knapper, it might have made that producer less able to meet reciprocal obligations that may have been deferred earlier. However, it is important to note that the kinds of movement of raw materials that we are discussing are not carried out by traders but are down-the-line exchanges that probably involved either real or fictive kin relations closer to the sources. Although there may have been third parties involved in acquisition of raw cherts of all kinds at Kincaid, both Dover and Mill Creek cherts were perhaps a little more easily acquired directly than in the American Bottom. Although the Dover sources are about 90 km away from Kincaid, the return with a canoe-load of chert would have been downstream all the way, so transportation costs would have been low. Mill Creek was overland, but only about 70 km. Although there may have producers for exchange at both sources, the patterns of distribution of the hoes generally, it will be recalled, was down the line.

We know next to nothing about the exchange, or not, of salt, but we have good evidence of predominantly small-scale domestic production by transient producers at the Great Salt Spring. In such a case, there would have been social and economic pressures on families to share their salt production with others who had not been able to make the production trip in a given year. Salt is attractive enough that some have even characterized it in terms more characteristic of addictive drugs. As a result, salt must have been a highly desirable gift or prestation. From Asia to Mesoamerica, salt has often played an important role in relations of domination because of this, but neither our historical records nor the character of the production itself give us the slightest indication that such relationships had developed in the East. No effort seems to have been made by either traders or elites at major sites to control or "garrison" salt sources to monopolize their use and exchange. The absence of such efforts at control of sources constitutes a powerful argument for the lack of state-level power in Mississippian.

Display goods, especially, require some separate discussion, not least because they have become part of the dominant model of Mississippian economic structure under the rubric of "prestige-goods economy." Although such items have been widely interpreted as displays indicating rank, we need to remember that it is distinctiveness of display that communicates status, not necessarily the individual items displayed; that is, a simple amulet to protect one against rattlesnake bite may have a high enough "price" that it is most often found with wealthier persons, but it still does not have to be an *emblem* of rank, even though its presence allows the identification of a ranked (or wealthy) person in practice. This example, although somewhat contrived, has some historical grounding. It illustrates the danger of imposing extravagant symbolic interpretations in the absence of evidence about the actual uses of artifacts.

Even granting a direct display role to an artifact, we have to recognize that the wide distribution of these items reflects a whole chain of production–exchange relationships, of which we see only the beginning and the end. Many display items, shell gorgets, for example, show evidence of curation over long periods before they found their way into their final archaeological context. In other cases, objects seem to have been manipulated in order to provide legitimation of ranking (as at Spiro). We need to remember that these objects were not only made and used, but also were exchanged over long distances. Highly valued, their value was surely more in giving and receiving them than in possessing them. Property and wealth seem less important in many of these cases than symbolic expression of interdependence. I have suggested that these are icons of networks rather than emblems of wealth. I suggest their use is not particularly involved in wealth conversion or provisioning so much as it is in marking deferred accumulation and reproduction. These may well be items that confer as much prestige in the giving as in the getting, representing not the asymmetry of wealth and poverty, but the social symmetry of reciprocity. The use of wampum as prestations in the Midatlantic and Northeast provides some points of reference that can be interpreted in this framework rather than in that of "tribute" and "shell money" (e.g., see, John Smith 1624).

3. CONCLUSION

When we look back at the social formations of the Late Prehistoric Southeast, we find distinctive features that do not correspond to the abstract models that have been proposed for the transition from "tribe" to "state." We find no evidence for the kinds of administrative organization of production by specialization and redistribution that were proposed first in the 19th century and elaborated in the 1960s. If there is any redistribution at all, it seems to have been a kind of warehousing and relief mechanism. In this sense, there may have been an administrative component to the development of chiefs, but the evidence suggests that the differences between a chief and the remainder of the population were much less striking than in state formations. Even the quasi-redistributive role of a chief was only a backup, in effect, for the same kinds of warehousing and distribution carried out at virtually all levels of Mississippian society. In this context, I have suggested that the production, distribution, and consumption of goods in Mississippian society is domestic- and community-oriented within social networks. Mississippian central mound sites and Mississippian farmsteads do not represent a series of radically different social levels, each with its own distinctive markers. On the contrary, Mississippian is, in effect, a modular society with a structural form that ranges from the farmstead at its smallest, but could be scaled up to community, town, mound center, and even paramount chiefdom. Each of these levels promotes the form of the "level" below it. That great plaza, even at Cahokia, is like an elevated version of a cluster of homesteads around their courtyard. The mode of production was "communal," but it had promoted kin leaders into cross-generational chiefs.

The evidence suggests that Mississippian had the same kinds of difficulties in adjusting to the crowded conditions of large towns that are nearly universal worldwide at periods of rapid increases in aggregation. In addition, a number of the largest Mississippian centers were located on what was effectively a northern frontier in terms of climate. With internal and external conditions changing, there was an apparent decline of Mississippian in the 13th–14th centuries. However, there are indications of some improvements just before the European invasions. Unfortunately, at this point, it become impossible to say what might have happened had Mississippian social formations been left alone. What we can say is that a number of Mississippian-descended societies were able to survive in the face of terrible warfare and disease. Groups such as the Choctaw, Chickasaw, and Creek demonstrated their ability to survive. I have argued that their historical features are not "degenerate," but simply represent a very late Mississippian solution to problems posed by the expansions of nation states around them.

References

For historical sources, I have normally listed references under the original date of publication or writing, with the date of the publication as cited in brackets. This gives prominence to the important date—the date of origin, rather than the reprint date, and so on, although these are given for the sake of locating the materials.

Adair, James, 1775, *The History of the American Indians, Particularly Those Nations Adjoining to the Mississippi*, London: Edward and Charles Dilly. [Reprinted 1930 Society of Colonial Dames, facsimile of 1930 ed. New York: Promontory Press]

Adams, Percy G., 1980, *Travelers and Travel Liars: 1660–1800*. New York: Dover. [Reprint with corrections of 1962, Berkeley: University of California Press]

Adams, Robert M., 1941, Archaeological investigations in Jefferson County, Missouri, 1939–40. *Transactions of the Academy of Science of St. Louis* 30(5):151–221.

Adams, Robert M., 1949, Archaeological investigations in Jefferson County, Missouri. *Missouri Archaeologist* II(3&4):1–72.

Ahler, Steven, Jon Muller, and Joel Rabinowitz, 1980, *Archaeological Testing for the Smithland Pool, Illinois*. Research Paper No. 13, Center for Archaeological Investigations, Southern Illinois University at Carbondale.

Allan, William, 1965, *The African Husbandman*. Edinburgh: Oliver & Boyd.

Allen, P.M., 1982, The genesis of structure in social systems: the paradigm of self-organization. In C. Renfrew, J. Rowlands, B. Seagraves, eds., *Theory and Explanation in Archaeology*, pp. 347–374. New York: Academic Press.

Alsop, George, 1666, A character of the Province of Mary-Land. In C. C. Hall, ed., 1967, *Narratives of Early Maryland, 1633–1684*, pp. 340–387. New York: Barnes and Noble. [Reprint of 1910, Charles Scribner's Sons]

Althusser, Louis, 1970, *For Marx*. New York: Vintage Books. [Translation with added material and comment of 1965 *Pour Marx*, Paris:Librairie François Maspero]

Althusser, Louis and Étienne Balibar, 1970, *Reading Capital*. New York: Pantheon Books. [Trans., abridgment, rev. of 1968, *Lire le Capital*. Paris: Librairie François Maspero]

Ambrose, Stanley H., 1987, Chemical and isotopic techniques of diet reconstruction in eastern North America. In W. F. Keegan, ed., *Emergent Horticultural Economies of the Eastern Woodlands*, pp. 87–107. Occasional Paper No. 7, Center for Archaeological Investigations, Southern Illinois University at Carbondale.

Ames, Kenneth M., 1991, Sedentism: A temporal shift for a transitions change in hunter–gatherer mobility patterns. In S. A. Gregg, ed., *Between Bands and States*, pp. 108–134. Occasional Paper 9, Center for Archaeological Investigations, Southern Illinois University at Carbondale.

Anderson, David G., 1990, Stability and change in chiefdom-level societies: An examination of mississippian political evolution on the South Atlantic Slope. In M. Williams and G. Shapiro, eds., *Lamar Archaeology: Mississippian Chiefdom in the Deep South*, pp. 187–213. Tuscaloosa:University of Alabama Press.

Anderson, David G., 1991, Examining prehistoric settlement distribution in Eastern North America. *Archaeology of Eastern North America* 19:1–22.

Anderson, David G., 1994a, Factional competition and the political evolution of Mississippian chiefdoms in the Southeastern United States. In Elizabeth Brumfiel and J. Fox, eds., *Factional Competition and Political Development in the New World*, pp. 61–76. Cambridge, U.K.:Cambridge University Press.

Anderson, David G., 1994b, *The Savannah River Chiefdoms: Political Change in the Late Prehistoric Southeast*. Tuscaloosa:University of Alabama Press.

Anderson, David G., 1995, Paleoindian interaction networks in the Eastern Woodlands. In M. Nassaney and K. Sassaman, eds., *Native American Interactions: Multiscalar Analyses and Interpretations in the Eastern Woodlands*, pp. 3–26. Knoxville: University of Tennessee Press.

Anderson, Perry, 1976, *Considerations on Western Marxism*. London:NLB.

Anderson, Philip W., Kenneth J. Arrow, and David Pines, eds., 1988, The Economy as an Evolving Complex System: The Proceedings of the Evolutionary Paths of the Global Economy Workshop, held September 1987, in Santa Fe, NM. Evolutionary Paths of the Global Economy Workshop. *Santa Fe Institute studies in the Sciences of Complexity*, vol. 5. Reading, MA: Addison-Wesley.

Anderson, William L. and J. A. Lewis, 1983, *A Guide to Cherokee Documents in Foreign Archives*. Methuen, NJ: Scarecrow Press

Andersson, Malte, 1994, *Sexual Selection*. Princeton, NJ: Princeton University Press.

Andrews, Anthony P., 1983, *Maya Salt Production and Trade*. Tucson: University of Arizona Press

Anonymous [Calvert, Cecil?], 1635, *A Relation of Maryland; Together, with a map of the Country, the Conditions of Plantation, His Majesties Charter to the Lord Baltemore*. London: William Peasley. [Facsimile reprint, 1966, March of America Facsimile Series 22, Xerox]

Arnold, Jeanne, 1984, Economic specialization in prehistory: Methods of documenting the rise of lithic craft specialization. In S. Vehik, ed., *Lithic Resource Procurement: Proceedings from the Second Conference on Prehistoric Chert Exploitation*, pp. 37–58. Occasional Paper 4, Center for Archaeological Investigations, Southern Illinois University at Carbondale.

Arnold, Philip J. III, 1991, *Domestic Ceramic Production and Spatial Organization: A Mexican Case Study in Ethnoarchaeology*. Cambridge, UK: Cambridge University Press. New studies in archaeology.

Arzigian, Constance, 1987, The emergence of horticultural economies in southwestern Wisconsin. In W. F. Keegan, ed., *Emergent Horticultural Economies of the Eastern Woodlands*, pp. 217–242. Occasional Paper No. 7, Center for Archaeological Investigations, Southern Illinois University at Carbondale.

Asakawa, K., 1931, Feudalism: Japanese. In *Encyclopaedia of the Social Sciences*, Vol. 6, pp. 214–219. New York: Macmillan.

Asch, David, and N. Asch, 1978, The economic importance of *Iva annua* and its prehistoric importance in the Lower Illinois Valley. In R. I. Ford, ed., *The Nature and Status of Ethnobotany*, pp. 301–341. Anthropological Paper 67, Museum of Anthropology, University of Michigan, Ann Arbor.

Asch, David, and N. Asch, 1985, Prehistoric plant cultivation in west-central Illinois. In R. I. Ford, ed., *Prehistoric Food Production in North America*, pp. 149–203. Anthropological Paper 75, Museum of Anthropology, University of Michigan, Ann Arbor.

Asch, David L., K. Farnsworth, and N. Asch, 1979, Woodland subsistence and settlement in west-central Illinois. In D. Brose and N. Greber, eds., *Hopewell Archaeology: The Chillicothe Conference*, pp. 80–85 Kent. OH: Kent State University Press.

Aston, T. H. and C. H. E. Philpin, eds., 1988, *The Brenner Debate: Agrarian Class Structure and Economic Development in Pre-Industrial Europe*. Cambridge, UK: Cambridge University Press.

Avery, George, 1983, *Salt, pots, and diet: Replication studies of Late Prehistoric shell-tempered ceramics*. M.A. thesis, Department of Anthropology, Southern Illinois University at Carbondale.

Axelrod, Robert, 1984, *The Evolution of Cooperation*. New York: Basic Books.

Baden, William W., 1995, *The impact of fluctuating agricultural potential on Coosa's sociopolitical and settlement systems*. Paper presented at the 52nd Southeastern Archaeological Conference, Knoxville, TN. [Also http://cvax.ipfw.indiana.edu/~baden/coosa/ or directly from baden@cvax.ipfw.indiana.edu]

Bailey, Anne M., 1981, The renewed discussions on the concept of the Asiatic mode of production. In J. S. Kahn and J. Llobera, eds., *The Anthropology of Pre-Capitalist Societies*, pp. 89–107. London: Macmillan.

Bailey, Anne M. and Josep R. Llobera, eds., 1981, *The Asiatic Mode of Production: Science and Politics*. Boston: Routledge & Kegan Paul.

Balfet, H., 1966, Ethnographic observations in North Africa and archaeological interpretation: The pottery of the Maghreb. In F. R. Matson, ed. *Ceramics and Man*, Viking Fund Publications in *Anthropology 4*.

Ballonoff, Paul, 1974, Statistical theory of marriage structures. In P. Ballonoff, ed., *Mathematical Models of Social and Cognitive Structures*, pp. 11–27. Illinois Studies in Anthropology No. 9. Urbana: University of Illinois Press.

Ballonoff, Paul, 1975, Structural models and correspondence problems: Mathematical anthropology, *Sococial Science Information* 14 (3/4):183–199.

Barcia Carballido y Zuñiga, Andrés González de, 1723, *Ensayo cronologico para la historia general de la Florida contiente los descubrimientos, y principales sucesos, acaecidos en este Gran Reino, à lose Españoles, Franceses, Suecos, Dinamarqueses, Ingleses, y otras Naciones, entre si, y con lose Indios: cuias Constumbres, Genios, Idolatria, Govierno, Batallas, y Astucias, se refieren: y lose Viages de algunos Capitanes, y Pilotos, por el Mar del Norte, à buscar Faso à Oriente, ò vnion de aquella Tierra, con Asia. Desde el año dfe 1512. que descubrió la Florida, Juan Ponce de Leion, hasta el de 1722.* escrito por Don Gabriel de Cardenas z Cano (pseud.). Madrid: Nicholas Rodriguez Franco. [1951, *Barcia's chronological history of the continent of Florida: Containing the discoveries and principal events which came to pass in this vast kingdom, touching the Spanish, French, Swedish, Danish, English, and other nations, as between themselves and with the Indians whose customs, characteristics, idolatry, government, warfare, and stratagems are described; and the voyages of some captains and pilots through the Northern Sea in search of a passage to the Orient, or the union of that land with Asia, from the year 1512, in which Juan Ponce de Leon discovered Florida, until the year 1722.* Transl. by Anthony Kerrigan. Gainesville: University of Florida Press]

Bareis, Charles J., and James W. Porter, eds., 1984, *American Bottom Archaeology: A Summary of the FAI-270 Project Contribution to the Culture History of the Mississippi River Valley*. Illinois Department of Transportation, University of Illinois, Urbana.

Barker, Alex W. and T. R. Pauketat, eds., 1992, *Lords of the Southeast: Social Inequality and the Native Elites of Southeastern North America*. Archeological Papers of the American Anthropological Association, No. 3.Washington D.C.:American Anthropological Association.

Barlowe, Arthur, 1584, Captain Arthur Barlowe's Narrative of the first voyage to the coasts of America. In Henry S. Burrage, ed., [1932] *Early English and French Voyages, Chiefly from Hakluyt, 1534—1608*, pp. 227–241. *Original Narratives of Early American History*. New York: Charles Scribner's Sons.

Barmes, David E., 1977, Epidemiology of dental disease. *Journal of Clinical Periodontology* 4:82–92.

Barnett, William A., John Geweke, and Karl Shell, eds., 1989, *Economic complexity: Chaos, Sunspots, Bubbles, and Nonlinearity: Proceedings of the Fourth International Symposium in Economic Theory and Econometrics* (1987, Austin, TX) Cambridge, UK: Cambridge University Press.

Bartram, John, 1751, *Observations on the Inhabitants, Climate, Soil, Rivers, Productions, Animals, and Other Matters Worthy of Notice Made by Mr. John Bartram in His Travels from Pensilvania to Onandago, Oswego and the Lake Ontario, in Canada*. London: J. Whiston and B. White.

Bartram, William, 1789, Observations on the Creek and Cherokee Indians. mss. [published 1853, *Transactions of the American Ethnological Society*, 3(1), with prefatory and supplementary notes by E. G. Squier.; Chapter III in G. A. Waselkov and K. E. Holland Braund, eds., *William Bartram on the Southeastern Indians*, 1995, pp. 139–186. Lincoln: University of Nebraska Press.]

Bartram, William, 1791, *Travels through North and South Carolina, Georgia, East and West Florida*, James and Johnson, Philadelphia [1928 reprint in Mark Van Doren, ed., *Travels of William Bartram.*, New York: Macy-Masius; 1955 facsimile edition of 1928, New York:Dover].

Bawden, Garth, 1989, The Andean state as a state of mind. *Journal of Anthropological Research* 45:327–332.

Bennett, M. K., 1955, The food economy of the New England Indians, 1605–1675. *Journal of Political Economy* 63(5).

Benninghoff, William S., 1968, Biological consequences of Quaternary glaciations in the Illinois region. In R. Bergstrom, ed., *The Quaternary of Illinois*, Special Publication No. 14, pp. 70–77. Urbina:University of Illinois, College of Agriculture.

Bender, Barbara, 1985, Emergent tribal formations in the American midcontinent. *American Antiquity* 50(1):52–62.

Benson, Henry C., 1860, *Life among the Choctaw Indians, and Sketches of the South-West*. Cincinnati: L. Swormstedt and A. Poe.

Berliner, Joseph S., 1962, The feet of the natives are large: An essay on anthropology by an economist. *Current Anthropology* 3(1):47–77.

Bettinger, Robert, 1991, *Hunter–Gatherers: Archaeological and Evolutionary Theory*. New York:Plenum Press.

Beverley, Robert, 1705, *The History and Present State of Virginia in Four Parts*. London: R. Parker. [1968 reprint of 1705 edition, *The History and Present State of Virginia*. Charlottesville: Dominion Books, University Press of Virginia]

Beverley, Robert, 1722, [1855] *The History of Virginia in Four Parts*. Richmond, VA: J. W. Randolph. [Reprinted from the author's 2nd ed. of 1722].

Biedma, Luys Hernandez de, 1544, Relation of the Conquest of Florida Presented by Luys Hernandez De Biedma in the Year-1544 to the King of Spain in Council. [translated from the original document by Buckingham Smith in 1904, Edward G. Bourne, ed., *Narratives of the Career of Hernando de Soto*, pp. 3–40 (Volume II) New York: A. S. Barnes. Translation by John E. Worth 1993 in Clayton, et al. *The De Soto Chronicles: The Expedition of Hernando De Soto to North American in 1539–43*. Volume 1, pp. 225–250. Tuscaloosa: University of Alabama Press]

Binford, Lewis, 1979, Organization and formation processes: Looking at curated technologies. *Journal of Anthropological Research* 35(3):255–273.

Binford, Lewis, 1987, Data, relativism, and archaeological science. *Man* 22:391–404.

Binford, Sally R. and L. R. Binford, eds., 1968, *New Perspectives in Archaeology*. Chicago: Aldine.

Black, Glenn A., 1967, *The Angel Site*. Indianapolis: Indiana Historical Society.

Black, Thomas K. III, 1979, *The Biological and Social Analyses of a Mississippian Cemetery from Southeast Missouri: The Turner Site, 23BU21A*. Anthropological Papers No. 68, Museum of Anthropology, Ann Arbor: University of Michigan.

Blakely, Robert L., 1971, Comparison of the mortality profiles of Archaic, Middle Woodland, and Middle Mississippian skeletal populations. *American Journal of Physical Anthropology* 34:43–54.

Blakely, Robert L., 1988a, The life cycle and social organization. In R. L. Blakely, ed., *The King Site: Continuity and Contact in Sixteenth-Century Georgia*, pp. 17–34. Athens: University of Georgia Press.

Blakely, Robert L., ed., 1988b, *The King Site: Continuity and Contact in Sixteenth-Century Georgia*. Athens: University of Georgia Press.

Blakely, Robert L. and L. A. Beck, 1981, Trace elements, nutritional states and social stratification at Etowah, Georgia. In *The Research Potential of Anthropological Museum Collections*, edited by A. -M. Cantwell, J. B. Griffin, and N. A. Rothschild, eds., Annals of the New York Academy of Sciences 376:417–431.

Blakely, Robert L. and B. Detweiler-Blakely, 1989, The impact of European diseases in the 16th-century Southeast: A case study. *Midcontinental Journal of Archaeology* 14(1):62–89.

Blakeman, Crawford, 1974, *The Late Prehistoric paleo-Ethnobotany of the Black Bottom, Pope and Massac Counties, Illinois*. Ph.D. dissertation, Department of Anthropology, Southern Illinois University at Carbondale.

Blakeslee, Donald J., 1981, The origin and spread of the calumet ceremony. *American Antiquity* 46(4):759–768.

Blanton, Richard, Steven Kowalewski, Gary Feinman, and J. Appel, 1981, *Ancient Mesoamerica: A Comparison of Change in Three Regions*. New York: Cambridge University Press.

Blasingham, E., 1972, *The Prehistoric and Historic Uses of the Saline Springs, Gallatin County, Illinois*. Ms. on file, Center for Archaeological Investigations, Southern Illinois University at Carbondale.

Blau, Peter M., 1977, *Inequality and Heterogeneity: A Primitive Theory of Social Structure*. New York: Free Press.

Blitz, John H., 1988, Adoption of the bow in prehistoric North America. *North American Archaeologist* 9(2):123–145.

Blitz, John H., 1993, *Ancient Chiefdoms of the Tombigbee*. Tuscaloosa: University of Alabama Press.

Bloch, Marc, 1931, Feudalism: European. In *Encyclopaedia of the Social Sciences*, Vol. 6, pp. 203–210. New York: Macmillan.

Bloch, Marc, 1961, *Feudal Society*. Chicago: University of Chicago. [translation of *La Société Féodale*]

Bogan, A. E., 1980, *A comparison of Late Prehistoric Dallas and Overkill Cherokee subsistence strategies in the Little Tennessee River Valley*. Ph.D. dissertation, Knoxville:University of Tennessee.

Boisvert, Richard, 1977, *A Reconnaissance and Evaluation of Archaeological Sites in Hardin Co., Ky*. Kentucky Heritage Commission Report No. 5. Lexington:Kentucky Heritage Commission.

Bossu, Jean-Bernard, 1768, *Nouveaux Voyages aux Indes occidentales; Contenant une Relation des differens Peuples qui habitent les environs du grand Fleuve Saint-Louis, appellé vulgairement le Mississipi; leur Religion; leur governement; leur moeurs, leur guerres et leur commerce*. Paris:Le Jay (later edition of 1769, Amsterdam). [1962] Translation: *Travels in the Interior of North America, 1751–1762*. Norman:University of Oklahoma Press (trans. Seymour Feiler)

Bourgmont, Etienne de Véniard, sieur de, 1714, L'Exacte Description de la Louisianne. translated *as* Exact Description of Louisiana, of Its harbors, Lands and Rivers, and Names of the Indian Tribes That Occupy It, and the Commerce and Advantages to Be Derived Therefrom for the Establishment of a Colony. In [1988] *Bourgmont, Explorer of the Missouri, 1698–1725*, ed. and trans. Frank Norall, pp. 99–112 (Appendix A). Lincoln: University of Nebraska Press.

Bourne,Edward G., ed. and trans., 1904, *Narratives of the Career of Hernando de Soto*, 2 vols., New York: A. S. Barnes.

Boyd, C. Clifford and G. F. Schroedl, 1987, In search of Coosa. *American Antiquity* 52(4):840–844.

Brain, Jeffery P., 1982, La Salle at the Natchez: An archaeological and historical perspective. In P. K. Galloway, ed., *La Salle and His Legacy: Frenchmen and Indians in the Lower Mississippi Valley*, pp. 49–59. Jackson: University Press of Mississippi.

Brain, Jeffery P., 1985, Introduction: Update of De Soto Studies since the United States De Soto Expedition Commission Report. In 1985 reprint of Swanton 1939, *Final Report of the United States De Soto Commission*, pp. xi–lxxii. Washington, DC: Smithsonian Institution Press.

Brain, Jeffrey P. and Philip Phillips, 1996, *Shell Gorgets: Styles of the Late Prehistoric and Protohistoric Southeast*. Cambridge: Peabody Museum Press.

Braudel, Fernand, 1981, *The Structures of Everyday Life* [Volume I of *Civilization and Capitalism, 15th to 18th Century*]. New York: Harper & Row.

Braun, David P., 1977, *Middle Woodland—Early Late Woodland Social Change in the Prehistoric Central Midwestern U.S.* Ph.D. dissertation, Department of Anthropology, Ann Arbor:University of Michigan.

Braun, David P., 1983a, Pots as tools. In J. A. Moore and A. S. Keene, eds., *Archaeological Hammers and Theories*, pp. 107–134. New York: Academic Press.

Braun, David P., 1983b, *Social Evolution, Prehistoric Central Midwestern U.S., 200 BC–AD 600*. Draft Proposal. Mss. on file at Center for Archaeological Investigations, Southern Illinois University at Carbondale.

Braun, David P. 1987 Coevolution of sedentism, pottery technology, and horticulture in the central Midwest, 200 B.C.–A.D. 600. In W. F. Keegan, ed., *Emergent Horticultural Economies of the Eastern Woodlands*, pp. 153–181. Occasional Paper No. 7, Center for Archaeological Investigations, Southern Illinois University at Carbondale.

Braun, D. P. and S. Plog, 1982, Evolution of "tribal" social networks: Theory and prehistoric North American evidence. *American Antiquity* 47:504–525.

Breitburg, E., 1986, *Late Prehistoric Vertebrate Assemblages from North-central Kentucky*. Report on file at the Kentucky Heritage Council, Frankfort.

Breitburg, E., 1988, Chapter 9: Faunal Remains. In C. A. Turnbow and W. L. Sharp, eds., *Muir: An Early Fort Ancient site in the Inner Blue Bluegrass*, pp. 215–242. Archaeological Report 173, University of Kentucky Program for Cultural Resource Assessment, Lexington.

Breitburg, E., 1990a, *Analysis of the 1982 Great Salt Spring Site Faunal Remains*. On file at the Department of Anthropology, Southern Illinois University at Carbondale. (Muller et al. 1992, q.v.)

Breitburg, E., 1990b, Chapter 12: The faunal assemblage. In P. A. Webb, ed., the *Petitt Site: An Emergent Mississippian Occupation in the Thebes Gap Area of Southern Illinois*. CAI Research Paper No. 58, Center for Archaeological Investigations, Southern Illinois University at Carbondale.

Breitburg, E., 1992, *Faunal Remains from the Great Salt Spring Site, Gallatin County, Illinois*. Report on File at the Center for Archaeological Investigations, Southern Illinois University, Carbondale. (Muller et al. 1992 q.v.)

Brookfield, H. and Paula Brown, 1963, *Struggle for Land: Agriculture and Group Territories among the Chimbu of the New Guinea Highlands*. London: Oxford University Press.

Brown, Ian W., 1980a, Archaeological investigations on Avery Island, Louisiana, 1977–78. *Southeastern Archaeological Conference Bulletin* 22:110–118.

Brown, Ian W., 1980b, *Salt and the Eastern North American Indian: An Archaeological Study.* Lower Mississippi Survey, Bulletin No. 6. Cambridge, MA: Peabody Museum, Harvard University.

Brown, Ian W., 1981, The role of salt in Eastern North American prehistory. Louisiana Archaeological Survey and Antquities Commission, Anthropological Study No. 3. Department of Culture, Recreation, and Tourism, Baton Rouge.

Brown, Ian W., 1989, The calumet ceremony in the Southeast and its archaeological manifestations. *American Antiquity* 54(2):311–334.

Brown, Ian W. and Nancy Lambert-Brown, 1979, *Archaeological Investigations at Salt Mine Valley (33-I-5).* Lower Mississippi Survey, Petite Anse Project Research Notes No. 8. Peabody Museum. Cambridge, MA: Harvard University.

Brown, James A., 1971, The dimensions of status at Spiro. In J. A. Brown.ed., *Approaches to the Social Dimensions of Mortuary Practices,* Society for American Archaeology, Memoirs 25:92–112.

Brown, James A., 1976, A reconsideration of the Southern cult. *Midcontinental Journal of Archaeology* 1:115–135.

Brown, James A., 1989, On style divisions of the Southeastern ceremonial complex: A revisionist perspective. In P. Galloway, ed., *The Southeastern Ceremonial Complex: Artifacts and Analysis,* pp. 183–204. Lincoln: University of Nebraska Press.

Brown, James A., 1991, Afterword. In M. S. Nassaney and C. R. Cobb, eds., *Stability, Transformation, and Variation: The Late Woodland Southeast,* pp. 323–327. New York: Plenum Press.

Brown, James, R. Kerber, and H. Winters, 1990, Trade and the evolution of exchange relations at the beginning of the Mississippian Period. In B. Smith, ed., *The Mississippian Emergence,* pp. 251–280. Washington D.C.: Smithsonian Institution Press.

Brumfiel, Elizabeth, 1987, Specialization and utilitarian crafts in the Aztec state. In E. Brumfiel and T. Earle, eds., *Specialization, Exchange and Complex Societies,* pp. 102–118. Cambridge, UK: Cambridge University Press.

Brumfiel, Elizabeth and T. Earle, eds., 1987, *Specialization, Exchange and Complex Societies.* Cambridge, UK: Cambridge University Press.

Bryson, Reid A. and T. J. Murray, 1977, *Climates of Hunger: Mankind and the World's Changing Weather.* Madison:University of Wisconsin Press.

Bücher, Karl, 1898, *Die Entstehung der Volkswirtschaft.* Tübingen: Verlag der H. Laupp'schen Buchhandlung. [Various editions, English, *Industrial Evolution.* Translated 1967 from the 3d German ed. by S. Morley Wickett. New York: Burt Franklin]

Budd, Thomas, 1685, *Good Order Established in Pennsilvania & New Jersey in America.* No publisher or place. [1966 facsimile reprint, Readex Microprint]

Buikstra, Jane E.,ed. 1981, *Prehistoric Tuberculosis in the Americas.*, Scientific Papers No. 5, Northwestern University Archaeological Program, Evanston, IL.

Buikstra, Jane E., 1992, Diet and disease in late prehistory. In J. W. Verano and D. H. Ubelaker, eds., *Disease and Demography in the Americas,* pp. 87–101. Washington D.C.: Smithsonian Institution Press.

Buikstra, Jane E., W. Autry, E. Breitberg, L. Eisenberg, N. van der Merwe, 1988, Diet and health in the Nashville Basin: Human adaptation and maize agriculture in Middle Tennessee. In B. V. Kennedy and G. M. LeMoine, eds., *Diet and Subsistence: Current Archaeological Perspectives,* pp. 243–258. Calgary:Chacmool 19th Conference

Buikstra, Jane E., Jill Bullington, Douglas K. Charles, Della C. Cook, Susan R. Frankenberg, Lyle W. Konigsberg, Joseph B. Lambert, Liang Xue, 1987, Diet, demography, and the development of horticulture. In W. F. Keegan, ed., *Emergent Horticultural Economies of the Eastern Woodlands,* pp. 67–85. Occasional Paper No. 7, Center for Archaeological Investigations, Southern Illinois University at Carbondale.

Buikstra, Jane E., Jerome C. Rose, and George R. Milner, 1994, A carbon isotopic perspective on dietary variation in late prehistoric Western Illinois. In W. Green, ed., *Agricultural Origins and Development in the Midcontinent,* pp. 155–170. Report No. 19, Office of the State Archaeologist. Iowa City, IA.

Bunge, G., 1873, Ueber die Bedeutung des Kochsalzes und das Verhalten der Kalisalze in menschlichen Organismus. *Zeitschrift für Biologie* 9:104–142.

Bunge, G., 1874, Ethnologischer Nachtrag zur Abhandlung über die Bedeutung des Kochsalzes und das Verhalten der Kalisalze in menschlichen Organismus. *Zeitschrift für Biologie 10*:111–132.

Bushnell, David I., 1907, Primitive salt making in the Mississippi Valley. *Man* 13.

Bushnell, David I., 1908, Primitive salt making in the Mississippi Valley, II. *Man* 35.

Butler, Brian M., 1972, Early vegetation of the Kincaid area. Manuscript on file, Center for Archaeological Investigations, Southern Illinois University at Carbondale.

Butler, Brian M., 1977, *Mississippian settlement in the Black Bottom, Pope and Massac Counties, Illinois.* Ph.D. dissertation, Department of Anthropology, Southern Illinois University at Carbondale.

Butler, Brian M., 1991, Kincaid revisited: the Mississippian sequence in the Lower Ohio Valley. In B. Lewis and T. Emerson, eds.,*Cahokia and the Hinterlands: Middle Mississippian Cultures of the Midwest*, pp. 264–273. Urbana: University of Illinois Press, in cooperation with the Illinois Historic Preservation Agency.

Butler, Brian M., Glen P. Harrell, and Mary C. Hamilton, 1979, *An Archaeological Reconnaissance of the Illinois Portions of the Smithland Pool of the Ohio River.* Research Paper No. 5, Center for Archaeological Investigations, Southern Illinois University, at Carbondale.

Caesar, Caius Julius, 51 B.C. *Gallia.* Roma. Translation in 1957, Moses Hadas, ed., *The Gallic War and Other Writings.* New York: The Modern Library.

Campbell, T. N., 1959, Choctaw subsistence: Ethnographic notes from the Lincecum manuscript. *Florida Anthropologist 12*:9–24.

Canouts, Veletta, E. E. May, N. H. Lopinot, and J. Muller, 1984, *Cultural Frontiers in the Upper Cache Valley, Illinois.* Research Paper No. 16, Center for Archaeological Investigations, Southern Illinois University, at Carbondale.

Carneiro, Robert, 1970, A theory of the origin of the state. *Science 169*:733–738.

Carolino, Pedro, 1883, *The New Guide of the Conversation in Portuguese and English.* with an introduction by Mark Twain. Boston: James R. Osgood and Co. [reprint 1969, as *English as She Is Spoke*, New York: Dover Publications]

Cartier, Jacques, 1534, The first relation of Jaques Carthier of St. Malo. In Henry S. Burrage, ed., [1932] *Early English and French Voyages, Chiefly from Hakluyt, 1534—1608*, pp. 4–31. Original Narratives of Early American History. New York: Charles Scribner's Sons.

Cartier, Jacques, 1535, Cartier's second voyage. In Henry S. Burrage, ed., [1932] *Early English and French Voyages, Chiefly from Hakluyt, 1534—1608*, pp. 37–88, Original Narratives of Early American History. New York: Charles Scribner's Sons. [from Hakluyt 1600, trans. by Ramusio]

Cartier, Jacques, 1541, The third voyage of discovery made by Captaine Jaques Cartier. In Henry S. Burrage, ed., [1932] *Early English and French Voyages, Chiefly from Hakluyt, 1534—1608.* pp. 93–102. Original Narratives of Early American History. New York: Charles Scribner's Sons.

Cartier, Jacques, 1580, *A Shorte and Briefe Narration of the Two Navigations and Discoveries to the Northwest Partes called Newe Fraunce*, translated by John Florio. London:H. Bynneman, [1534 and 1535 voyages; facsimile reprint 1966, Xerox].

Case, Karl E. and Ray C. Fair, 1989, *Principles of Economics.* Englewood Cliffs, NJ:Prentice-Hall.

Cassidy, C.M., 1972, *Comparison of Nutrition and Health in Preagricultural and Agricultural Amerindian Skeletal Populations.* Ph.D. Dissertation, Department of Anthropology, Madison:University of Wisconsin.

Casselbury Samuel E., 1974, Further refinement of formulae for determining population from floor area. *World Archaeology 6*(1):117–122.

Catesby, Mark, 1731, *The Natural History of Carolina, Florida and the Bahama Islands: Birds, Beasts, Fishes, Serpents, Insects, and Plants:....* Vol. I. [two volumes, second 1743] Published by the Author, sold at W. Innys and R. Manby, London. [Alan Feduccia, ed., 1985, *Catesby's Birds of Colonial America.* Chapel Hill: University of North Carolina Press]

Cavelier, Jean, 1687, Relation of M. Cavelier. [1861] In John Dawson Gilmary Shea, ed., *Early Voyages Up and Down the the Mississippi Valley, by Cavelier, St. Cosme, Le Sueur, Gravier, and Guignas*, pp. 13–42. Albany, NY: Joel Munsell. [Margry 1877:2:501–509; "Journal de l'Abbé Jean Cavelier," part only; Margry 1878:3:583; "Mémoire de l'Abbé Jean Cavelier sur la nécessité de continuer l'entreprise de son frère, 1690"]

Chaianov, Aleksandr Vasilevich (Tschajanow, Alexander; Chayanov, A.V.), 1923, *Die Lehre von der bäuerlichen Wirtschaft: Versuch einer Theorie der Familienwirtschaft im Landbau*. Berlin: Verlagsbuchhandlung Paul Parey. [shorter version of below]

Chaianov, Aleksandr Vasilevich, 1925, *Organizatsiya krest'yanskogo khozyaistva. Iz rabot Nauchno-Issledovatel'skogo Instituta s.-kh. ekonomii*. Moskva Tsentral'noe tovarichestvo kooperativnogo izd. In 8°, III. [translation as A.V. Chayanov, 1966, *The Theory of Peasant Economy*, edited by D. Thorner, B. Kerblay, and R. E. F. Smith. Homewood, IL: American Economic Association.]

Childe, Vere Gordon, 1954, *What Happened in History*. Harmondsworth, UK: Penguin.

Chippindale, Christopher, 1993, Review of *Processual and Postprocessual Archaeologies: Multiple Ways of Knowing the Past*, edited by R. Preucel. *American Anthropologist* 95(1):208–209.

Claessen, Henri J. M. and Pieter van de Velde, 1985, Social evolution in general. In H. J. M. Claessen, P. van de Velde, and M. E. Smith, eds., *Development and Decline: The Evolution of Sociopolitical Organization*, pp. 1–12. South Hadley, MA: Bergin and Garvey Publishers.

Clark, Colin, and M. Haswell, 1970, *The Economics of Subsistence Agriculture*. 4th ed., New York: St. Martin's Press.

Clark, John and W. J. Parry, 1990, Craft specialization and cultural complexity. *Research in Economic Anthropology* 12:289–346.

Clark, Philip J. and Francis C. Evans, 1954, Distance to nearest neighbor as a measure of spatial relationships in populations. *Ecology* 35(4):445–453.

Clarke, William C., 1971, *Place and People: An Ecology of a New Guinea Community*. Berkeley: University of California Press.

Clay, R. Berle, 1976, Tactics, strategy, and operations: The Mississippian system responds to its environment. *Midcontinental Journal of Archaeology* 1(2):138–162.

Clay, R. Berle, 1979, A Mississippian ceramic sequence for western Kentucky. *Tennessee Anthropologist* 4(2):111–128.

Clayton, Lawrence A., V. J. Knight, Jr., and E. C. Moore, ed., 1993, *The De Soto Chronicles: The Expedition of Hernando De Soto to North American in 1539–43*. Tuscaloosa: University of Alabama Press.

Cobb, Charles R., 1984, Dissertation proposal, Department of Anthropology, Southern Illinois University at Carbondale.

Cobb, Charles R., 1988, *Mill Creek chert biface production: Mississippian political economy in Illinois*. Ph.D. dissertation, Southern Illinois University at Carbondale.

Cobb, Charles R., 1991, One hundred years of investigations at the Linn Site in Southern Illinois. *Illinois Archaeology* 3(1):56–76.

Cobb, Charles R., 1993a, *Archaeological Investigations on Shawnee National Forest Property* (NSF Grant BNS-91-20222, Letter Report No. 1, Results of Field work. mss. on file, Shawnee National Forest, Harrisburg, IL.

Cobb, Charles R., 1993b, *Archaeological Investigations on Shawnee National Forest Property* (NSF Grant BNS-91-20222, Letter Report No. 2, Laboratory Analysis Progress Report, mss. on file, Shawnee National Forest, Harrisburg, IL.

Cobb, Charles R., 1993c, *Upland Mississippian Settlement in Southern Illinois*. Paper presented at the 50th Southeastern Archaeological Conference, Raleigh, NC.

Cobb, Charles R., 1993d, Archaeological approaches to the political economy of nonstratified societies. In M. Schiffer, ed., *Archaeological Method and Theory*, vol. 5, pp. 43–100. Tucson: University of Arizona Press.

Cobb, Charles R., 1995, *1995 SIUC Field School Investigations at the Dillow's Ridge Site (11-U-635)*. Mss. on file, Center for Archaeological Investigations, Southern Illinois Unversity at Carbondale.

Cobb, Charles R. and Michael S. Nassaney, 1991, Introduction: Renewed perspectives on Late Woodland stability, transformation, and variation in the Southeastern United States. In M. S. Nassaney and C. R. Cobb, eds., *Stability, Transformation, and Variation in the Late Woodland Southeast*, pp. 1–10. New York: Plenum Press.

Cobb, Charles R., and M. S. Nassaney, 1995, Interaction and integration in the Late Woodland Southeast. In M. Nassaney and K. Sassaman, eds., *Native American Interactions: Multiscalar Analyses and Interpretations in the Eastern Woodlands*, pp. 205–226. Knoxville: University of Tennessee Press.

Cobb, Charles R. and L. A. Thomas, 1994, *Investigations at the Dillow's Ridge Site (IAS U-635), An Unplowed Mississippian Village in Union County, Illinois* [Draft of June 5, 1994]. Mss. on file, Center for Archaeological Investigations, Southern Illinois University at Carbondale.

Cohen, Ronald and Elman R. Service, 1978, *Origins of the State: The Anthropology of Political Evolution.* Philadelphia:Institute for the Study of Human Issues.

Cole, Fay-Cooper, R. Bell, J. Bennett, J. Caldwell, N. Emerson, R. MacNeish, K. Orr, and R. Willis, 1951, *Kincaid: A Prehistoric Illinois Metropolis.* Chicago:University of Chicago Press.

Conrad, Lawrence A., 1989, The Southeastern ceremonial complex on the northern middle Mississippian frontier: Late Prehistoric politico-religioius systems in the Central Illinois River Valley. In Patricia Galloway, ed., *The Southeastern Ceremonial Complex: Artifacts and Analysis,* pp. 93–113. Lincoln: University of Nebraska Press.

Conrad, Lawrence A., 1991, The Middle Mississippi cultures of the Central Illinois River Valley. In B. Lewis and T. Emerson, eds., *Cahokia and the Hinterlands: Middle Mississippian Cultures of the Midwest,* pp. 119–156. Urbana: University of Illinois Press in cooperation with the Illinois Historic Preservation Agency.

Cook, Della C., 1976, *Pathologic states and disease process in Illinois Woodland populations: An epidemiological approach.* Ph.D. dissertation, University of Chicago.

Cook, Della C. and Jane E. Buikstra, 1979, Health and differential survival in Prehistoric populations: Prenatal dental effects. *American Journal of Physical Anthropology* 51:649–664.

Corruccini, Robert S., 1992, Bootstrap approaches to estimating confidence intervals for molecular dissimularities and resultant trees. *Journal of Human Evolution* 23: 481–493.

Corsi, Marcella., 1991, *Division of Labour, Technical Change, and Economic Growth.* Aldershot, Hants, UK: Avebury.

Costin, Cathy L., 1991, Craft specialization: Issues in defining, documenting, and explaining the organization of production. In Michael Schiffer, ed., *Archaeological Method and Theory,* vol. 3, pp. 1–56. Tucson: University of Arizona Press.

Costin, Cathy L, and Melissa B. Hagstrum, 1995, Standardization, labor investment, skill, and the organization of ceramic production in Late Prehistoric highland Peru. *American Antiquity* 6(4):619–639.

Cowan, C. Wesley, 1985, Understanding the evolution of plant husbandry in Eastern North America: Lessons from botany, ethnography and archaeology. In R. I. Ford, ed., *Prehistoric Food Production in North America,* pp. 205–243. Anthropological Paper 75, Museum of Anthropology, University of Michigan, Ann Arbor.

Cowgill, George, 1975a, Population pressure as a non-explanation. In A. Swedlund, ed., *Population Studies in Archaeology an Biological Anthropology: A Symposium,* pp. 127–131. Memoirs of the Society for American Archaeology 30, *American Antiquity* 40(2).

Cowgill, George, 1975b, On causes and consequences of ancient and modern population changes. *American Anthropologist* 77(3):505–525.

Cowgill, George, 1986, Archaeological applications of mathematical and formal methods. In D. J. Meltzer, D. D. Fowler, and J. A. Sabloff, eds., *American Archaeology Past and Future,* pp. 369–393. Washington, DC: Smithsonian Institution Press.

Cowgill, Ursula M., 1961, Soil fertility and the ancient Maya. *Transactions of the Connecticut Academy of Arts and Sciences* 42:1–56.

Cramer, Zadok, 1814, *The Navigator; Containing Directions for Navigating the Ohio and Mississippi Rivers;* Pittsburgh: Cramer, Spear Eichbaum.

Crane, Verner W., 1964, *The Southern Frontier: 1670–1732,* 3rd Printing [1929 original]. Ann Arbor:Ann Arbor Paperback, University of Michigan Press.

Crummey, Donald and C. C. Stewart, 1981, *Modes of Production in Africa: the Precolonial Era.* Beverly Hills: Sage Publications.

Dablon, Father Claudius, 1678, [1903] The voyages and discoveries of Father James Marquette in the valley of the Mississippi. In J. D. G. Shea, ed., *Discovery and Exploration of the Mississippi Valley,* pp. 1–69. Albany, NY: Joseph McDonough. [2nd ed., orig. 1852] [French text of first voyage: Recit des voyages et des decouvertes du P. Jacques Marquette, pp. 235–258]

Dalton, George, ed., 1968, *Primitive, Archaic, and Modern Economies: Essays of Karl Polanyi.* Garden City, NY: Anchor Books.

Dauphinee, James A., 1960, Sodium chloride in physiology, nutrition and medicine. In D. Kaufmann, ed., *Sodium Chloride: The Production and Properties of Salt and Brine*, pp. 382–453. New York: Reinhold Publishing Corporation.

Dávila Padilla, Augustín, 1596, *Historia de la fundacion y discurso de la provincia, de Santiago de Mexico, de la orden de Predicadores por las vidas de sus varones insignes y casos notablles de Nueua España*. Madrid. [Edicion segunda, Brusselas]

Davis, T. Frederick, 1935, History of Ponce de León's voyages to Florida. *Florida Historical Quarterly* 14:1–70.

Davy, Douglas M., 1982, *Proximity and human behavior: Settlement locational pattern change in prehistoric Illinois*. Ph.D. dissertation, Department of Anthropology, Southern Illinois University at Carbondale.

Decker, Dina, 1988, Origin(s), evolution, and systematics of *Cucurbita pepo* (Curbitaceae). *Economic Botany* 42(1):4–15.

Delcourt, Paul A. and H. R. Delcourt, 1981, Vegetation maps for eastern North America: 40,000 B.P. to the present. In R. C. Romans, ed., *Geobotany II*, pp. 123–165. New York: Plenum Press.

De Montigny, Mr., 1699, Letter of Mr. de Montigny. In J. D. G. Shea, ed., [1861] *Early Voyages Up and Down the the Mississippi Valley, by Cavelier, St. Cosme, Le Sueur, Gravier, and Guignas*, pp. 75–79. Albany, NY: Joel Munsell.

DePratter, Chester B., 1994, The chiefdom of Cofitachequi. In C. Hudson and C. C. Tesser, eds., *The Forgotten Centuries: Indians and Europeans in the American South, 1521–1704*, pp. 197–226. Athens: University of Georgia Press.

DePratter, Chester B., Charles M. Hudson, and Marvin T. Smith, 1985, The Hernando de Soto Expedition: From Chiaha to Mobila. In *Alabama and the Borderlands: From Prehistory to Statehood*, pp. 108–126. R. Reid Badger and Lawrence A. Clayton, (eds.), Tuscaloosa: University of Alabama Press.

Desan, Wilfred, 1966, *The Marxism of Jean-Paul Sartre* Garden City, NY: Anchor Books.

d' Iberville, Pierre LeMoyne, 1699–1702 [1981] *Iberville's Gulf Journals*, trans. and ed. Richebourg Gaillard McWilliams. University: University of Alabama Press. [translation of Journals, A.D. 1699–1702. French text in Margry 1880– 4: 131–209; 4:393–444; 4:503–523]

Diener, Paul, 1980, Quantum adjustment, macroevolution, and the social field: Some comments on evolution and culture. *Current Anthropology* 21(4):423–431.

Dincauze, Dena F., and Robert Hasenstab, 1989, Explaining the Iroquois: Tribalization on a prehistoric periphery. In Timothy C. Champion, ed., *Centre and Periphery: Comparative Studies in Archaeology*, pp. 67–87. London: Unwin Hyman.

Dobb, Maurice, 1973, *Theories of Value and Distribution since Adam Smith: Ideology and Economic Theory*. Cambridge, UK: Cambridge University Press.

Dobyns, Henry F., 1966, Estimating aboriginal American population: An appraisal of techniques with a new hemispheric estimate. *Current Anthropology* 7:395–416.

Dobyns, Henry F., 1976, *Native American Historical Demography: A Critical Bibliography*. The Newberry Library Center for the History of the American Indian. Bloomington: Indiana University Press.

Dobyns, Henry F., 1983, *Their Number Become Thinned*. Knoxville: University of Tennessee Press.

Doolittle, William E., 1992, Before there was a cornbelt: A prospectus on research. In W. I. Woods, ed., *Late Prehistoric Agriculture: Observations from the Midwest*, pp. 217–240. Studies in Illinois Archaeology, No. 8. Illinois Historic Preservation Agency, Springfield.

Douglas, Mary, and Baron Isherwood, 1979, *The World of Goods*. New York: Basic Books.

Driver, Harold E., 1969, *Indians of North America* (2nd rev. ed.) Chicago: University of Chicago Press.

Drooker, Penelope B., 1992, *Mississippian Village Textiles at Wickliffe*. Tuscaloosa, AL: University of Alabama.

Duby, George, ed., 1988, *A History of Private Life: II. Revelations of the Medieval World*. Cambridge, MA: Belknap Press of Harvard University Press.

Dunn, Stephen P., 1982, *The Fall and Rise of the Asiatic Mode of Production*. Boston: Routledge & Kegan Paul.

Dunnell, Robert C., 1980, Evolutionary theory and archaeology. In Michael B. Schiffer, ed., *Advances in Archaeological Method and Theory*, vol. 3, pp. 35–99. New York: Academic Press.

Dunnell, Robert C. and James K. Feathers, 1991, Late Woodland manifestations of the Malden Plain, Southeast Missouri. In M. S. Nassaney and C. R. Cobb, eds., *Stability, Transformation, and Variation: The Late Woodland Southeast*, pp. 21–45. New York: Plenum Press.

Durkheim, Emile, 1893, *De la division du travail social*. [1984 *The Division of Labour in Society*, trans. W. D. Halls. New York: Free Press.

du Ru, Paul, 1700, Journal of Paul du Ru, February 1 to May 8, 1700. MS. copy in E. E. Ayer Collection, Newberry Library. [1935 *Journal of Paul du Ru*, (February 1 to May 8, 1700), trans. Ruth Lapham Butler, Caxton Club, Chicago]

Dye, David H. and C. A. Cox, eds., 1990, *Towns and Temples along the Mississippi*. Tuscaloosa: University of Alabama Press.

Earle, T. K., 1977, A reappraisal of redistribution: Complex Hawaiian chiefdoms. In T. K. Earle and J. E. Ericson, eds., *Exchange Systems in Prehistory*, pp. 213–229. New York: Academic Press.

Earle, T. K., 1978, *Economic and Social Organization of a Complex Chiefdom: The Halalea District, Kaua'i, Hawaii*. Anthropological Papers No. 63, Museum of Anthropology, Ann Arbor: University of Michigan.

Earle, T. K., 1981, Comment on P. Rice, "Evolution of Specialized Pottery Production: A Trial Model." *Current Anthropology* 22(3):230–231.

Earle, T. K., 1987, Specialization and the production and exchange of wealth: Hawaiian chiefdoms and the Inka Empire. In E. Brumfiel and T. Earle, eds., *Specialisation, Exchange and Complex Societies*, pp. 64–75, Cambridge, UK: Cambridge University Press.

Earle, T. K., 1989, The evolution of chiefdoms. *Current Anthropology* 30:84–88.

Earle, T. K., ed., 1991, *Chiefdoms: Power, Economy, and Ideology*. Cambridge, UK: School of American Research Advanced Seminars, Cambridge University Press.

Early, Ann, 1993a, Finding the middle passage: The Spanish journey from the swamplands to Caddo Country. In G.A. Young and Michael P. Hoffman, eds., *The Expedition of Hernando de Soto West of the Mississippi, 1541–1543. Proceedings of the De Soto Symposia, 1988 and 1990*, pp, 68–77. Fayetteville: University of Arkansas Press.

Early, Ann, ed., 1993b, *Caddoan Saltmakers in the Ouachita Valley*. Arkansas Archeological Survey Research Series No. 43, Fayetteville.

Edwards, I. E. S., 1961, *The Pyramids of Egypt*. London: Pelican.

Efron, B. and R. Tibshirani, 1986, Bootstrap methods for standard error, confidence intervals, and other measures of statistical accuracy. *Statistical Science* 1:54–77.

Elvas, Gentleman of (Fidalgo Deluas), 1557, *Relaçam verdadeira dos trabalhos q ho gouernador dõ Fernãndo de souto e certos fidalgos portugueses passarom no descubrimẽto da prouincia da Frolida. Agora nouamẽte feita per hú fidalgo Deluas*. Evora. [Translations in Hakluyt 1611; Buckingham Smith 1866; Clayton et al. 1993]

Emerson, T. E., 1992, The Mississippian dispersed village as a social and environmental strategy. In W. I. Woods, ed., *Late Prehistoric Agriculture: Observations from the Midwest*, pp. 198–216. Studies in Illinois Archaeology, No. 8. Illinois Historic Preservation Agency, Springfield.

Emerson, T. E., and D. Jackson, 1984, *The BBB Motor Site*. American Bottom Archaeology, FAI-270 Site Report No. 6 for the Illinois Department of Transportation by the University of Illinois Press, Urbana.

Emerson, T. E. and R. B. Lewis, eds., 1991, *Cahokia and the Hinterlands: Middle Mississippian Cultures of the Midwest*. Urbana: University of Illinois Press.

Emerson, T.E., G. Milner, and D. Jackson, 1983, *The Florence Street Site*. American Bottom Archaeology. FAI-270 Site Report for the Illinois Department of Transportation by the University of Illinois Press, Urbana.

Engels, Donald W., 1978, *Alexander the Great and the Logistics of the Macedonian Army*. Berkeley: University of California Press.

Engels, Friedrich, 1873–1886 *Dialektik der Natur*. Mss. not published in Engels's lifetime. First publication 1925 in German in the USSR. In *Marx Engels Werke*, Band 20:305–570. Berlin: Dietz Verlag. [English trans., 1940, New York: International Publishers]

Engels, Friedrich, 1878, *Herrn Eugen Dührings Umwälzung der Wissenschaft*. {Anti-Dühring}. [Many editions, *Marx/Engels Werke*, Band 20:1–303. Berlin: Dietz Verlag. [English trans., 1977 Moscow: Progress Publishers]

Engels, Friedrich, 1881–1882 Zur Urgeschichte der Deutschen. In *Marx/Engels Werke*, Band 19:425–473. Berlin: Dietz Verlag. [English trans. 1979 as "A contribution to the early history of the Germans," in Marx and Engels, *Pre-Capitalist Socio-Economic Formations* pp. 298-360. Moscow: Progress Publishers]

Engels, Friedrich, 1882, *Die Entwicklung des Sozialismus von der Utopie zur Wissenschaft.* Berlin: Vorwärts. [Rev. chap. from Engels 1878, *Anti-Dühring*]. *Marx/Engels Werke*, Band 19:189–228. Berlin: Dietz Verlag. [English trans. *Socialism: Utopian and Scientific.* Many editions, in *Selected Works*, 1975, pp. 394–428]

Engels, Friedrich, 1886, Ludwig Feuerbach und der Ausgang der klassischen deutschen Philosophie. *Die Neue Zeit* 4 & 5. *Marx/Engels Werke*, Band 21:259–307. [English trans. as "Ludwig Feuerbach and the end of classical German philosophy," Many editions, in *Selected Works*, 1975, pp. 584–622]

Engels, Friederich, 1890, Letter of September 21 [-22], 1890, to J. Bloch in Königsberg. In 1965, *Selected Works* (3rd ed.), Karl Marx and Frederick Engels. Moscow: Progress Progress Publishers, pp, 682–683.

Engels, Friedrich, 1891, *Der Ursprung der Familie, des Privateigenthums und des Staats. Im Anschluss an Lewis Henry Morgan's Forschungen.* [Vierten, ergänzten Auflage] Stuttgart. [1st publication, 1884, Hottingen-Zürich] [1962, *Marx/Engels Werke*, Band 21:25–173. Berlin: Dietz Verlag] [English translation 1975, The origin of the family, private property and the State. In *Karl Marx and Frederick Engels Selected Works*, pp. 461–583. Moscow: Progress Publishers]

Engels, Friedrich, 1894, Nachwort, "Soziales aus Russland." In Internationalles aus dem "Volksstaat." [*Marx/Engels Werke*, Band 22:421–435] In English translation as "From the Afterword to 'Soziales aus Russland,'" in Marx and Engels, 1979, *Pre-Capitalist Socio-Economic Formations*, pp. 475–481. Moscow: Progress Publishers]

Engels, Friedrich, 1895, Engels to J. Bloch in Königsberg, September 21, 1890. *Der sozialistiiche Akademiker* 19. [In *Marx/Engels Werke*, Band 37. Berlin: Dietz Verlag. [English translation, In 1979, *Pre-Capitalist Socio-Economic Formations*, selections from K. Marx and F. Engels, pp. 520–525. Moscow: Foreign Languages Publishing House]

Ensor, H. Blaine, 1991, The Lubbub Creek microlith industry. *Southeastern Archaeology* 10(1):18–39.

Erasmus, Charles J., 1965, Monument building: Some field experiments. *Southwestern Journal of Anthropology* 21:277–301.

Evans, Robert K., 1978, Early craft specialization: An example from the Balkan Chalcolithic. In C. L. Redman, M. J. Berman, E. V. Curtin, W. T. Langhorne Jr., N. M. Versaggi, and J. C. Wanser, eds., *Social Archaeology: Beyond Subsistence and Dating*, pp. 113–129. New York: Academic Press.

Ewers, John C., 1974, Symbols of chiefly authority in Spanish Lousiana. In J. F. McDermott, ed., *The Spanish in the Mississippi Valley, 1762–1804*, pp. 272–286. Urbana: University of Illinois Press.

Feinman, Gary and Jill Neitzel, 1984, Too many types: An overview of sedentary prestate societies in the Americas. In M. Schiffer, ed., *Advances in Archaeological Method and Theory*, vol. 7, pp. 39–102. New York: Academic Press.

Fenton, William N., 1953, *The Iroquois Eagle Dance: An offshoot of the calumet dance.* Bureau of American Ethnology, Bulletin 156.

Firth, Rymond, 1963, *We, the Tikopia*, (abr. ed.). Boston: Beacon Press.

Flannery, Kent V., 1968, The Olmec and Valley of Oaxaca: A model for inter-regional interaction in formative times. In E. P. Benson, ed., *Dunbarton Oaks Conference on the Olmec*, pp. 79–110. Washington, DC: Dunbarton Oaks Research Library and Collection.

Flannery, Kent V., 1972, The cultural evolution of civilizations. *Annual Review of Ecology and Systematics* 3:399–426.

Ford, Richard I., 1974, Northeastern archaeology: Past and future directions. *Annual Review of Anthropology* 3:385–413.

Ford, Richard I., ed., 1985, *Prehistoric Food Production in North America.* Anthropological Papers No. 75, Museum of Anthropology, University of Michigan, Ann Arbor.

Forde, C. Daryll, 1964, *Yakö Studies.* London: Oxford University Press.

Forrest, Stephanie, ed., 1991, *Emergent Computation: Self-Organizing, Collective, and Cooperative Phenomena in Natural and Artificial Computing Networks.* Center for Nonlinear Studies (Los Alamos National Laboratory, Special Issues of *Physica D*). Cambridge, MA: MIT Press.

Fortier, Andrew C., 1985, The Robert Schneider site. In F. Finney and A. Fortier, *The Carbon Dioxide Site and the Robert Schneider Site*, pp. 171–313. American Bottom Archaeology, FAI-270 Site Reports No. 11 for the Illinois Department of Transportation by the University of Illinois Press, Urbana.

Foster-Carter, Aidan, 1978, The modes of production controversy. *New Left Review* 107:47–78.

Fowler, Melvin L., 1969, The Cahokia site. In M. L. Fowler, ed., *Explorations into Cahokia Archaeology*, pp. 1–30. Illinois Archaeological Survey, Bulletin No. 7. Urbana: Illinois Archaelogical Survery.

Fowler, Melvin L., 1974, Cahokia: Ancient capital of the Midwest. *Addison-Wesley Module in Anthropology* 48:1–38. Menlo Park, CA: Cummings Publishing.

Fowler, Melvin L., 1975, A Pre-Columbian urban center on the Mississippi. *Scientific American* 233:92–101.

Fowler, Melvin L., 1978, Cahokia and the American Bottom: Settlement archaeology. In B. Smith, ed., *Mississippian Settlement Patterns*, pp. 445–478, New York: Academic Press.

Fowler, Melvin L., 1989, *The Cahokia Atlas: A Historical Atlas of Cahokia Archaeology*. Studies in Illinois Archaeology No. 6, Illinois Historic Preservation Agency.

Fowler, Melvin L., 1991, Mound 72 and Early Mississippian at Cahokia. In J. Stoltman, ed., *New Perspectives on Cahokia: Views from the Periphery*, pp. 1–28. Madison, WI: Prehistory Press.

Fowler, Melvin L., 1992, The Eastern horticultural complex and Mississippian agricultural fields: Studies and Hypotheses. In W. I. Woods, ed., *Late Prehistoric Agriculture: Observations from the Midwest*, pp. 1–18. Studies in Illinois Archaeology, No. 8. Illinois Historic Preservation Agency, Springfield.

Frankenstein, Susan and M. J. Rowlands, 1978, The internal structure and regional context of early Iron Ages society in Southwestern Germany. *University of London Institute of Archaeology Bulletin* 15:73–112.

Franklin, Benjamin, 1729, *A Modest Inquiry into the Nature and Necessity of a Paper Currency*. Philadelphia: B. Franklin [Reprinted in 1836 Jared Sparks, ed., in *The Works of Benjamin Franklin...*, Vol. II, pp. 253–277. Boston: Hilliard, Gray, and Company]

French, B.F., editor, 1846–1875, *Historical Collections of Louisiana...*, 3rd series, New York, A. Mason, J. Sabin, Wiley and Putnam. [1976 reprint by New York: AMS Press]

Fried, M. H., 1960, On the evolution of social stratification and the state. In S. Diamond, ed., *Culture in History*, pp. 713–731, New York: Columbia University Press.

Fried, M. H., 1967, *The Evolution of Political Society: An Essay in Political Anthropology*. New York: Random House.

Fried, M. H., 1975, *The Notion of Tribe*. Menlo Park, CA: Cummings Publishing.

Fried, M. H., 1978, Tribe to state or state to tribe in Ancient China? In D. N. Keightley, ed., *The Origins of Chinese Civilization*, pp. 467–493. Berkeley: University of California Press.

Friedman, Jonathan, 1974, Marxism, structuralism and vulgar materialism. *Man* 9:444–489.

Friedman, Jonathan, 1975, Tribes, states and transformations. In M. Bloch, ed., *Marxist Analysis and Social Anthropology*, pp. 161–202. New York: Wiley.

Friedman, Jonathan and M. J. Rowlands, 1978, Notes towards an epigenetic model of the evolution of "Civilisation". In J. Friedman and M. J. Rowlands, eds., *The Evolution of Social Systems*, pp. 201–276. Pittsburgh: University of Pittsburgh Press.

Friedman, Jonathan and M. J. Rowlands, eds., 1978, *The Evolution of Social Systems*. Pittsburgh: University of Pittsburgh Press.

Fritz, Gayle J., 1992, "Newer," "better" maize and the Mississippian emergence: A critique of prime mover explanations. In W. I. Woods, ed., *Late Prehistoric Agriculture: Observations from the Midwest*, pp. 19–43. Studies in Illinois Archaeology, No. 8. Illinois Historic Preservation Agency, Springfield.

Fritz, Gayle J., 1994, In color and in time: Prehistoric Ozark agriculture. In W. Green, ed., *Agricultural Origins and Development in the Midcontinent*, pp. 105–126. Report No. 19, University of Iowa, Office of the State Archaeologist. Iowa City.

Fritz, Gayle J. and T. R. Kidder, 1992, Recent investigations into prehistoric agriculture in the Lower Mississippi Valley. *Southeastern Archaeology* 12(1):1–14.

Funkhouser, W. D. and W. S. Webb, 1932, *Archaeological Survey of Kentucky*. Lexington: University of Kentucky, Reports in Anthropology and Archaeology No. 2.

Fustel de Coulanges, N.D., 1864, *Le cité antique*. Paris: Hachette. [Trans. 1956, *The Ancient City*. New York: Doubleday and Co.]

Gagliano, Sherwood M., 1967, Occupation sequence at Avery Island. *Coastal Studies Series, No. 22*. Baton Rouge: Louisiana State University.

Gallagher, James P., 1992, Prehistoric field systems in the Upper Midwest. In W. I. Woods, ed., *Late Prehistoric Agriculture: Observations from the Midwest*, pp. 95–135. Studies in Illinois Archaeology, No. 8. Illinois Historic Preservation Agency, Springfield.

Gallagher, James P. and Constance M. Arzigian, 1994, A new perspective on Late Prehistoric agricultural intensification in the Upper Mississippi River Valley. In W. Green, ed., *Agricultural Origins and Development in the Midcontinent*, pp. 171–188. Report No. 19, University of Iowa, Office of the State Archaeologist, Iowa City.

Gallatin, Albert, 1836, A synopsis of the Indian tribes within the United States east of the Rocky Mountains, and in the British and Russian possessions in North America. *Transactions and Collections of the American Antiquarian Society*, Vol. II, Part I, pp. 1–266.

Galloway, Patricia K., 1982a, Sources for the La Salle Expedition of 1682. In Patricia K. Galloway, ed., *La Salle and His Legacy: Frenchmen and Indians in the Lower Mississippi Valley*, pp. 11–40. Jackson: University Press of Mississippi.

Galloway, Patricia K., 1982b, Henri de Tonti du village des Chacta, 1702: The beginning of the French alliance. In Patricia K. Galloway, ed., *La Salle and His Legacy: Frenchmen and Indians in the Lower Mississippi Valley*, pp. 146–175. Jackson: University Press of Mississippi.

Galloway, Patricia, K., editor, 1982c, *La Salle and His Legacy: Frenchmen and Indians in the Lower Mississippi Valley*. Jackson: University Press of Mississippi.

Galloway, Patricia K., 1987a, The Minet relation: Journey by river. In Robert S. Weddle, ed., *La Salle, the Mississippi, and the Gulf*, pp. 17–27. College Station, Texas: Texas A&M University Press.

Galloway, Patricia K., 1987b, Annotation to the Minet Relation. In R. S. Weddle, ed., *La Salle, the Mississippi, and the Gulf*, pp. 17–126. College Station: Texas A&M University Press.

Galloway, Patricia, K., ed., 1989, *The Southeastern Ceremonial Complex: Artifacts and Analysis*. Lincoln: University of Nebraska Press.

Galloway, Patricia K., 1991, The archaeology of ethnohistorical narrative,. In D. H. Thomas, ed., *Columbian Consequences: Volume 3 The Spanish Borderlands in Pan-American Perspective*, pp. 453–469. Washington, DC: Smithsonian Institution Press.

Galloway, Patricia, K., 1994, Confederacy as a solution to chiefdom dissolution: The Choctaw case. In C. Hudson and C. C. Tesser, eds., *The Forgotten Centuries: Indians and Europeans in the American South, 1521–1704*, pp. 393–420. Athens: University of Georgia Press.

Galloway, Patricia K., 1995, *Choctaw Genesis: 1500–1700*. Lincoln: University of Nebraska Press.

Garcilaso de la Vega, el Inca, 1605, *La Florida del Ynca. Historia del Adelantado Hernando de Soto, Gouernador y capitán general del Reyno de la Florida, y otros heroicos cauallera Españoles e Yndios; escrita por el Ynca Garcilasso de la Vega, capitán de su Magestad, natural de la gran ciudad del Cozco, cabeça de los Reynos y provincias del Perú*. Lisbona: Pedro Crasbeeck, Reprinted 1956 Fondo de Cultura Económica, México. [Translations: 1881 in Shipp 1881 (from the French translation of P. Richelet); 1951, *The Florida of the Inca...*, by John G. and J. J. Varner, Austin: University of Texas Press; 1993, in L. A. Clayton, V. J. Knight, and E. C. Moore (trans. C. Shelby for the De Soto Expedition Commission in 1935)]

Gearing, Fred, 1962, *Priests and Warriors*. American Anthropological Association, Memoir 93. Washington D.C.: American Anthropological Associations.

Gerbrands, Adrian, 1967, *Wow-Ipits, Eight Asmat Woodcarvers of New Guinea*. The Hague, The Netherlands: Mouton.

Gibbon, Guy, 1984, *Anthropological Anthropology*, New York: Columbia Unversity Press.

Gibson, J. L., 1974, Aboriginal warfare in the protohistoric Southeast: An alternative perspective. *American Antiquity* 39:130–133.

Goad, Sharon I., 1978, *Exchange networks in the prehistoric Southeastern United States*. Ph.D. dissertation, Department of Anthropology, University of Georgia, Athens.

Godelier, Maurice, 1977, *Perspectives in Marxist Anthropology*. Cambridge Studies in Social Anthropology No. 18. Cambridge, UK

Goldstein, Lynne G., 1980, *Mississippian Mortuary Practices: A Case Study of Two Cemeteries in the Lower Illinois Valley*. Evanston, ILL: Northwestern University Archaeological Program.

Goodman, Claire G., 1984, *Copper Artifacts in Late Eastern Woodlands Prehistory*. edited by A.-M. Cantwell. Evanston, ILL: Center for American Archeology.

Goody, Esther N., ed., 1982, *From Craft to Industry: The Ethnography of Proto-industrial Cloth Production*. Cambridge, UK: Cambridge University Press.

Goody, Jack, 1976, *Production and Reproduction: A Comparative Study of the Domestic Domain*. Cambridge Studies in Social Anthropology No. 17. Cambridge, UK: Cambridge University Press.

Gorodzov, V.A., 1933, The typological method in archaeology. *American Anthropologist* 35:95–102.

Gottfried, Robert S., 1978, *Epidemic Disease in Fifteenth Century England: The Medical Response and the Demographic Consequences*. New Brunswick, NJ: Rutgers University Press.

Gottfried, Robert S., 1983, *The Black Death: Natural and Human Disaster in Medieval Europe*. New York: Free Press.

Gould, S. J., 1977, *Ever Since Darwin: Reflections in Natural History*. New York: W. W. Norton.

Gould, S. J. and N. Eldredge, 1977, Punctuated equilibria: The tempo and mode of evolution reconsidered. *Paleobiology* 3:115–151.

Gramly, Richard Michael, 1992, *Prehistoric Lithic Industry at Dover, Tennessee*. Buffalo, NY: Persimmon Press.

Grant, C. L., ed., 1980, *Letter, Journals and Writings of Benjamin Hawkins* (2 vol.). Savannah, GA: Beehive Press.

Gravier, James [Jacque], 1701, Journal of the voyage of Father Gravier. [1861] In J. D. G. Shea, ed., *Early Voyages Up and Down the Mississippi Valley, by Cavelier, St. Cosme, Le Sueur, Gravier, and Guignas*, pp. 115–163. Albany, NY: Joel Munsell. [Also in 1906, R. G. Thwaites, *Jesuit Relations* 65:100–179]

Green, T. J. and C. A. Munson, 1978, Mississippian settlement patterns in Southwestern Indiana. In B. Smith, ed., *Mississippian Settlement Patterns*, pp. 293–330, New York: Academic Press.

Green, William, 1994a, Perspectives on Midwestern agricultural origins and development. In W. Green, ed., *Agricultural Origins and Development in the Midcontinent*, pp. 1–6. Report No. 19, Office of the State Archaeologist, University of Iowa, Iowa City.

Green, William, ed., 1994b, *Agricultural Origins and Development in the Midcontinent*. Report No. 19, Office of the State Archaeologist, University of Iowa, Iowa City.

Gregg, Michael, 1985, A population estimate for Cahokia. In *Perspectives in Cahokia Archaeology*. Bulletin 10, pp. 126–136. Urbana: Illinois Archaeological Survey.

Gremillion, Kristen J., 1994, Evidence of plant domestication from Kentucky caves and rockshelters. In W. Green, ed., *Agricultural Origins and Development in the Midcontinent*, pp. 87–103. Report No. 19, University of Iowa, Office of the State Archaeologist. Iowa City.

Griffin, James B., 1952, Culture periods in Eastern United States archeology. In J. B. Griffin, ed., *Archeology of Eastern United States*, pp. 352–364. Chicago: University of Chicago Press.

Griffin, James B., 1978, Foreword. In B. Smith, ed., *Mississippian Settlement Patterns*, pp. xv–xxii. New York: Academic Press.

Griffin, James B., 1983, The Midlands. In J. D. Jennings, ed., *Ancient North Americans*, pp. 243–301. San Francisco: Freeman.

Griffin, James B., 1984, Art and archaeology. *Quarterly Review of Archaeology* 5(2):3–5.

Grossman, Lawrence S., 1984, *Peasants, Subsistence Ecology, and Development in the Highlands of Papua New Guinea*. New Jersey: Princeton University Press.

Guigna, Louis Ignatius, S.J., 1728, Guigna's Voyage up the Mississippi. In J. D. G. Shea, ed., [1861] *Early Voyages Up and Down the the Mississippi Valley, by Cavelier, St. Cosme, Le Sueur, Gravier, and Guignas*, pp. 167–175. Albany, NY: Joel Munsell.

Haas, Jonathan, 1981, Class conflict and the state in the New World. In G. D. Jones and R. R. Krautz, eds., *The Transition to Statehood in the New World*, pp. 80–101. Cambridge, UK: Cambridge University Press.

Haeckel, Ernst Heinrich Philipp August, 1869, *Über Arbeitsteilung in Natur- und Menschenleben. Arbeitsteilung in Natur-und Menschenleben*. Berlin: C. G. Luderitz, Sammlung gemeinverständlicher wissenschäftlicher Vortrage. 4. ser., Heft 78.

Haggett, P., 1965, *Locational Analysis in Human Geography*. London: E. Arnold.

Hall, Robert L., 1980, An interpretation of the Two-Climax Model of Illinois prehistory. In D. L. Browman, ed., *Early Native Americans: Prehistoric Demography, Economy, and Technology*, pp. 401–462. Mouton, The Hague, The Netherlands: World Anthropology.

Hall, Robert L., 1991, Cahokia identity and interaction models of Cahokia Mississippian. In B. Lewis and T. Emerson, eds., *Cahokia and the Hinterlands: Middle Mississippian Cultures of the Midwest*, pp. 3–34. Urbana: University of Illinois Press in cooperation with the Illinois Historic Preservation Agency.

Hally, David J., 1993, The territorial size of Mississippian chiefdoms. In J. B. Stoltman, ed., *Archaeology of Eastern North America: Papers in Honor of Stephen Williams*, pp. 143–168. Mississippi Department of Archives and History, Archaeological Report No. 25.

Hally, David J., 1994, The chiefdom of Coosa. In C. Hudson and C.C. Tesser, eds., *The Forgotten Centuries: Indians and Europeans in the American South, 1521–1704*, pp. 227–253. Athens: University of Georgia Press.

Hally, David J., Marvin T. Smith, and James B. Langford Jr., 1990, The archaeological reality of de Soto's Coosa. In David H. Thomas, ed., *Archaeological and Historical Perspectives on the Spanish Borderlands East: Columbian Consequences*, Vol. 2, pp. 121–138. Washington, DC: Smithsonian Institution Press.

Halstead, Paul, 1989, The economy has a normal surplus: Economic stability and social change among early farming communities of Thessaly, Greece. In Paul Halstead and J. O'Shea, eds., *Bad Year Economics: Cultural Responses to Risk and Uncertainty*, pp. 68–80. Cambridge, UK: Cambridge University Press.

Halstead Paul and J. O'Shea, eds., 1989, *Bad Year Economics: Cultural Responses to Risk and Uncertainty*. Cambridge, UK: Cambridge University Press.

Hann, John H., 1988, *Apalachee: The Land between the Rivers*. Ripley P. Bullen Monographs in Anthropology and History, No. 7. Gainesville: University Presses of Florida.

Hann, John H., 1994, The Apalachee of the Historic Era. In C. Hudson and C. C. Tesser, eds., *The Forgotten Centuries: Indians and Europeans in the American South, 1521–1704*, pp. 327–354. Athens: University of Georgia Press.

Hantman, Jeffrey L., 1990, Between Powhatan and Quirank: Reconstructing Monacan culture and history in the context of Jamestown. *American Anthropologist* 92(3):676–690.

Hardin, Margaret, 1981, The identification of individual style on Moundville engraved vessels: A preliminary note. *Southeastern Archaeological Conference Bulletin* 24:108–110.

Hardy, Charles O., 1933, Market. In Edwin Seligman, ed., *Encyclopaedia of the Social Sciences*, Vol. 10, pp. 131–133. New York: Macmillan.

Hargrave, Michael L., Charles R. Cobb, and Paul A. Webb, 1991, Late Prehistoric ceramic style zones in Southern Illinois. In M. S. Nassaney and C. R. Cobb, eds., *Stability, Transformation, and Variation: The Late Woodland Southeast*, pp. 149–176. New York: Plenum Press.

Hargrave, Michael L., G. Oetelaar, N. Lopinot, B. Butler, and D. Billings, 1983, *The Bridges Site (11-Mr-11): A Late Prehistoric Settlement in the Central Kaskaskia Valley*. Research Paper No. 38, Center for Archaeological Investigations, Southern Illinois University at Carbondale.

Hariot, Thomas, 1590, *A Briefe and True Report of the New Found Land of Virginia*, ... (with illustrations by John White, engraved by Theodor de Bry). Frankfurt am Main: Theodor de Bry.

Harn, Alan D., 1975, Cahokia and the Mississippian emergence in the Spoon River area of Illinois. *Transactions of the Illinois State Academy of Science* 68:414–434.

Harn, Alan D., 1978, Mississippian settlement patterns in the Central Illinois Valley. In B. Smith, ed., *Mississippian Settlement Patterns*, pp. 233–68. New York: Academic Press.

Harris, Marvin, 1978, India's sacred cow. *Human Nature* 1:28–36.

Harris, Marvin, 1979, *Cultural Materialism: The Struggle for a Science of Culture*. New York: Random House.

Harris, Marvin, 1994, Cultural materialism is alive and well and won't go away until something better comes along. In R. Borofsky, ed., *Assessing Cultural Anthropology*, pp. 62–75. New York: McGraw-Hill.

Hasebroek, Johannes, 1928, *Staat und Handel in Alten Griechenland: Untersuchen zur antiken Wirtschaftgeschichte*. Hildesheim: Georg Olms Verlagsbuchhandlung. [1966 reproduction reprint Tübingen: Verlags J. C. B. Mohr (Paul Siebeck)].

Hasebroek, Johannes, 1965, *Trade and Politics in Ancient Greece*. New York: Biblo and Tannen [reprint of 1933 English ed.]

Hassan, Fekri A., 1981, *Demographic Archaeology*. New York: Academic Press.

Hatch, James W., 1976, *Status in death: Principles of ranking in Dallas culture mortuary remains*. Ph.D. dissertation, Department of Anthropology, Pennsylvania State University, University Park.

Hatch, James W. and R. A. Geidel, 1983, Tracing status and diet in prehistoric Tennessee. *Archaeology* 36:56–59.

Hatch, James W. and P. S. Willey, 1974, Stature and Status in Dallas Society. *Tennessee Archaeologist* 30:107–131.

Hatch, James W., P. S. Willey, and E. E. Hunt Jr., 1983, Indicators of status-related stress in Dallas society: Transverse lines and cortical thickness in long bones. *Midcontinental Journal of Archaeology* 30:49–71.

Hawkes, Kristen, 1993, Why hunter–gatherers work: An ancient version of the problem of public goods. *Current Anthropology* 34(4):341–361 (with comments).

Hawkins, Benjamin, 1796, (see Grant, 1980).

Hawkins, Benjamin, 1799, *A Sketch of the Creek Country in the Years 1798 and 1799*. Ms. in possession of Georgia Historical Society, published 1848 in *Georgia Historical Collections* III, Part I, pp. 13–83. Another copy of mss. in Peter Force Papers, Manuscript Division, Library of Congress. [1938 reprint of 1848 with additions in *The Creek Country*, as by "Hawkins, et al.," pp. 19–80. Americus, GA: Americus Book Company; also reprint by Kraus Reprints Co., 1971 facsimile reprint of the 1848 publication].

Hawkins, John, 1565, The voyage made by M. John Hawkins Esquire, 1565. In Henry S. Burrage, ed., [1932] *Early English and French Voyages, Chiefly from Hakluyt, 1534—1608*, pp. 114–132, Original Narratives of Early American History. New York: Charles Scribner's Sons.

Hayden, Brian, 1975, The carrying capacity dilemma: An alternative approach. In Alan Swedlund, ed., *Population Studies in Archaeology: A Symposium*, pp. 11–21. Society for American Archaeology, Memoir 30.

Hays, Denys, 1966, *Europe in the Fourteenth and Fifteenth Centuries*. New York: Holt, Rinehart and Winston.

Hegel, Georg W. F., 1812, *Wissenschaft der Logik* . Nürnberg: Johann Leonhard Schrag.

Heider, Karl G., 1969, Visiting trade institutions. *American Anthropologist* 71:462–471.

Heiser, C.B. Jr., 1979, *The Gourd Book*. Norman: University of Oklahoma Press.

Henige, David, 1993, Proxy data, historical method, and the de Soto expedition. In Gloria A. Young and Michael P. Hoffman, eds., *The Expedition of Hernado de Soto West of the Mississippi, 1541–1543. Proceedings of the De Soto Symposia, 1988 and 1990*, pp. 155–172. Fayetteville: University of Arkansas Press.

Henige, David, 1994, Life after death: The posthumous aggrandizement of Coosa. *Georgia Historical Quarterly* 78(4):687–715.

Herskovits, Melville J., 1952, *Economic Anthropology: The Economic Life of Primitive Peoples*. New York: W.W. Norton & Co.

Hietala, H., ed., 1984, *Intersite Spatial Analysis in Archaeology*. Cambridge, UK: Cambridge University Press.

Hill, M. Cassandra, 1986, *A study in adaptation: The dynamic interplay of culture, biology, and environment for a Late Woodland population in Alabama*. Paper presented at the 43rd Southeastern Archaeological Conference, Nashville, TN.

Hill-Clark, M.C., 1981, The Mississippian decline in Alabama: A biological analysis. *American Journal of Physical Anthropology* 54:233.

Hilton, Rodney, ed., 1976, *The Transition from Feudalism to Capitalism*. London: Verso.

Hindess, Barry and Paul Q. Hirst, 1975, *Pre-Capitalist Modes of Production*. Boston: Routledge & Kegan Paul.

Hindess, Barry and Paul Q. Hirst, 1977, *Mode of Production and Social Formation: An Auto-Critique of Pre-Capitalist Modes of Production*. London: Macmillan.

Hobsbawm, Eric J., 1965, Introduction. In *Pre-Capitalist Economic Formations*, by Karl Marx, pp. 9–65. New York: International Publishers.

Hobsbawm, Eric J., 1984, Marx and history. *New Left Review 143*:39–50.

Hodder, Ian, ed., 1982, *Symbolic and Structural Archaeology*. Cambridge, UK: Cambridge University Press.

Hodder, Ian, 1983, *The Present Past: An Introduction to Anthropology for Archaeologists*. New York: Pica Press.

Hodder, Ian, 1991, Postprocessual archaeology and the current debate. In R. Preucel, ed., *Processual and Postprocessual Archaeologies: Multiple Ways of Knowing the Past*, pp. 30–41. Occasional Paper No. 10, Center for Archaeological Investigations, Southern Illinois University at Carbondale.

Hodder, Ian and C. Orton, 1976, *Spatial Analysis in Archaeology*. Cambridge, UK: Cambridge University Press.

Hodge, Frederick W., 1907, *Handbook of American Indians North of Mexico, Part 1.* Bureau of American Ethnology, Bulletin 30, Smithsonian Institution, Washington, DC.

Hodge, Frederick W., 1910, *Handbook of American Indians North of Mexico, Part 2.* Bureau of American Ethnology, Bulletin 30, Smithsonian Institution, Washington, DC.

Hoffman, Paul E., 1994a, Lucas Vázquez de Ayllón's discovery and colony. In C. Hudson and C. C. Tesser, eds., *The Forgotten Centuries: Indians and Europeans in the American South, 1521–1704,* pp. 36–49. Athens: University of Georgia Press.

Hoffman, Paul E., 1994b, Narváez and Cabeza de Vaca in Florida. In C. Hudson and C. C. Tesser, eds., *The Forgotten Centuries: Indians and Europeans in the American South, 1521–1704,* pp. 50–73. Athens: University of Georgia Press.

Holland, John H., 1975, *Adaptation in Natural and Artificial Systems.* Ann Arbor: University of Michigan.

Holley, George, 1991, *Cahokia as a state?* Paper presented at the Society for American Archaeology Annual Meeting, New Orleans, LA.

Holley, George, 1995, Microliths and the Kunnemann tract: An assessment of craft production at the Cahokia site. *Illinois Archaeology* 7:1–68.

Holmes, William H., 1903, *Aboriginal Pottery of the Eastern United States.* Bureau of American Ethnology, 20th Annual Report, Smithsonian Insitution, Washington, DC.

Holmes, William H., 1919, *Handbook of Aboriginal American Antiquities. Part I: Lithic Industries.* Bureau of American Ethnology Bulletin 60. Washington, DC: Smithsonian Institution.

Honerkamp, and R. B. Council, 1995, *Wither Coosa in Chattanooga?* Paper presented at the 52nd Annual Meeting of the Southeastern Archaeological Conference, Knoxville, TN.

Hood, Victor P., 1977, *The Davis–Noe site (40RE137): A study of functional variability in Early Mississippian subsistence settlement patterning.* A.A. thesis, Department of Anthropology, University of Tennessee, Knoxville.

House, John, 1990, Powell Canal: Baytown period adaptation on Mayou Macon, southeast Arkansas. In B. Smith, ed., *The Mississippian Emergence,* pp. 9–26. Washington, DC: Smithsonian Institution Press.

Howard, James. H., 1968, *The Southeastern Ceremonial Complex and Its Interpretation.* Missouri Archaeological Society Memoir No. 6. Columbia: Missouri Archaelogical Society.

Howard, James. H., 1981, *Shawnee! The Ceremonialism of a Native American Tribe and Its Cultural Background.* Athens: Ohio University Press.

Hoyme, L. E. and W. M. Bass, 1962, Human skeletal remains from the Tollifero and Clarksville sites, John H. Kerr Reservoir Basin, Virginia. *Bureau of American Ethnology Bulletin* 153:329–400.

Hudson, Charles, 1976, *The Southeastern Indians.* Knoxville: University of Tennessee Press.

Hudson, Charles, 1988, A Spanish–Coosa alliance in sixteenth-century north Georgia *Georgia Historical Quarterly* 72(4):559–626.

Hudson, Charles, 1990, *The Juan Pardo Expeditions: Exploration of the Carolinas and Tennessee, 1566–1568.* Washington, DC: Smithsonian Institution Press.

Hudson, Charles, 1994, The Hernando de Soto expedition, 1539–1543. In C. Hudson and C. C. Tesser, eds., *The Forgotten Centuries: Indians and Europeans in the American South, 1521–1704,* pp. 74–103. Athens: University of Georgia Press.

Hudson, Charles, C. B. DePratter, and M. T. Smith, 1989, Hernando de Soto's expedition through the southern United States. In J. T. Milanich and S. Milbrath, eds., *First Encounters: Spanish Explorations in the Caribbean and the United States, 1492–1570,* pp. 77–98. Gainesville: University of Florida Press.

Hudson, Charles, C. B. DePratter, and M. T. Smith, 1993, Appendix I: Reply to Henige. In Gloria A. Young and Michael P. Hoffman, eds., *The Expedition of Hernado de Soto West of the Mississippi, 1541–1543. Proceedings of the De Soto Symposia, 1988 and 1990,* pp. 255–269. Fayetteville: University of Arkansas Press.

Hudson, Charles, M. T. Smith, and C. B. DePratter, 1984, The Hernando DeSoto expedition: From Apalachee to Chiaha. *Southeastern Archaeology* 3(1):65–77.

Hudson, Charles, M. T. Smith, C. B. DePratter, and E. Kelley, 1989a, The Tristán de Luna expedition, 1559–1561. *Southeastern Archaeology* 8(1):31–45.

Hudson, Charles, M. T. Smith, C. B. DePratter, and E. Kelley, 1989b, The Tristán de Luna expedition, 1559–1561. In J. T. Milanich and S. Milbrath, eds., *First Encounters: Spanish Explorations in the Caribbean and the United States, 1492–1570,* pp. 119–134. Gainesville: University of Florida Press.

Hudson, Charles, M. T. Smith, D. Hally, R. Polhemus, and C. B. DePratter, 1985, Coosa: A chiefdom in the sixteenth century Southeastern United States. *American Antiquity* 50(4):723–737.

Hudson, Charles, M. T. Smith, D. Hally, R. Polhemus, and C. B. DePratter, 1987, Reply to Boyd and Schroedl. *American Antiquity* 52(4):845–856.

Hudson, Charles and C. C. Tesser, eds., 1994, *The Forgotten Centuries: Indians and Europeans in the American South, 1521–1704*. Athens: University of Georgia Press.

Humpf, Dorothy A., 1992, Health and demography in a 16th-century Southeastern chiefdom. In Barbara A. Little, ed., *Text-Aided Archaeology*, pp. 123–132. Boca Raton, FL: CRC Press.

Hunt, George T., 1940, *The Wars of the Iroquois: A Study in Intertribal Trade Relations*. Madison: University of Wisconsin Press. [reissued in paperback, 1960]

Hutchins, Thomas, 1784, *An Historical Narrative and Topographical Description of Louisiana, and West-Florida, Comprehending the River Mississippi with its Principal branches and Settlements, and the Rivers Pearl, Pascagoula, Mobille, Perdido, Escambia, Chacta-Hatcha, &c.: The Climate Soil, and Produce whether Animal, Vegetable, or Mineral; with Directions for Sailing into all the Bays, Lakes, Harbours and Rivers on the North Side of the Gulf of Mexico, and for Navigating between Islands situated along that Coast, and ascending the Mississippi River*. Philadelphia: Robert Aitken.

Ingram, J.K., 1885, Political economy. *Encyclopaedia Britannica*, 9th Ed., pp. 346–401. New York: Charles Scribner's Sons.

Isbell, William H., 1978, Environmental perturbations and the origin of the Andean state. In C. L. Redman et al., eds., *Social Archaeology: Beyond Subsistence and Dating*, pp. 303–313. New York: Academic Press.

Jackson, D. K., A. C. Fortier, and J. A. Williams, 1992, *The Sponemann Site 2: The Mississippian and Oneota Occupations*. American Bottom Archaeology. FAI-270 Site Report 24 for the Illinois Department of Transportation by the University of Illinois Press, Urbana.

Jackson, H. Edwin, 1991, The trade fair in hunter–gatherer interaction: The role of intersocietal trade in the evolution of poverty point culture. In S. A. Gregg, ed., *Between Bands and States*, pp. 265–86. Occasional Paper No. 9, Center for Archaeological Investigations, Southern Illinois University at Carbondale.

Jackson, H. Edwin and Susan L. Scott, 1995, The faunal record of the Southeastern elite: The implications of economy, social relations, and ideology. *Southeastern Archaeology* 14(2):103–119.

Jacobs, Jane, 1967, *The Economy of Cities*. New York: Random House.

Jacobs, Wilbur R., 1950, *Wilderness Politics and Indian Gifts: The Northern Colonial Frontier, 1748–1763*. Stanford, CA: Stanford University Press. [1967 reprint, Lincoln: University of Nebraska Press]

Jefferies, R. W., 1995, Late Middle Archaic exchange and interaction in the North American midcontinent. In M. Nassaney and K. Sassaman, eds., *Native American Interactions: Multiscalar Analyses and Interpretations in the Eastern Woodlands*, pp. 73–99. Knoxville: University of Tennessee Press.

Jefferies, R. W., and Brian Butler, eds., 1982, *The Carrier Mills Archaeological Project: Adaptation in the Saline Valley, Illinois*. Center for Archaeological Investigations, Research Paper No. 33, Southern Illinois University at Carbondale.

Jenkins, Ned. J. and R. A. Krause, 1986, *The Tombigbee Watershed in Southeastern Prehistory*. Tuscaloosa: University of Alabama Press.

Jennings, Frances, 1963, A vanishing Indian: Francis Parkman versus his sources. *Pennsylvania Magazine of History and Biography* 87:306–323.

Jennings, Frances, 1975, *The Invasion of America: Indians, Colonialism, and the Cant of Conquest*. Chapel Hill: University of North Carolina Press.

Jewell, Donald, 1961, *Archeology of the Oroville Dam Spillway*. Sacramento: Central California Archeological Foundation.

Jochim, Michael A., 1981, *Strategies for Survival: Cultural Behavior in an Ecological Context*. New York: Academic Press.

Johannessen, Sissel and C. A. Hastorf, eds., 1994, *Corn and Culture in the Prehistoric New World*. Boulder, CO: Westview Press.

Johnson, Allen W. and T. Earle, 1987, *The Evolution of Human Societies from Foraging Group to Agrarian State*. Stanford, CA: Stanford University Press.

Johnson, Gregory, 1977, Aspects of regional analysis in archaeology. *Annual Review of Anthropology* 6:479–508.

Johnson, Gregory, 1978, Information sources and the development of decision-making organizations. In C. L. Redman, et al, eds., *Social Archaeology: Beyond Subsistence and Dating*, pp. 87–112. New York: Academic Press.

Johnson, Gregory, 1982, Organizational structure and scalar stress. In C. Renfrew, M. Rowlands, and B. Seagraves, eds., *Theory and Explanation in Archaeology*, pp. 389–421. New York: Academic Press.

Johnson, Jay K., and F. L. Hayes, 1995, Shifting patterns of long-distance contact during the Middle Woodland Period in the Northern Yazoo Basin, Mississippi. In M. Nassaney and K. Sassaman, eds., *Native American Interactions: Multiscalar Analyses and Interpretations in the Eastern Woodlands*, pp. 100–121. Knoxville: University of Tennessee Press.

Jones, Joseph, 1880, Explorations of the aboriginal remains of Tennessee. Smithsonian Contributions to Knowledge 259. [Individual article dated October, 1876] *Smithsonian Contributions to Knowledge*, Volume 22, Article II.

Joutel, Henri, 1687, [1878] Relation de Henri Joutel. In Pierre Margry, ed., *Découvertes et Établissement des Français dans l'Ouest et dans le Sud de l'Amérique Septentrionale (1614–1754). Troisième Partie (1669–1698)*, pp. 91–534. Paris: Imprimerie D. Jouast. [translation of selections in 1962, *A Journal of La Salle's Last Voyage*, based on the English translation of 1714, as edited by Henry Reed Stiles. New York: Corinth Books]

Kahn, Joel, and Joseph Llobera, 1981, Towards a new Marxism or a new anthropology? In Joel Kahn and J. Llobera, eds., *The Anthropology of Pre-Capitalist Societies*, pp. 263–329. London: Macmillan.

Kauffman, Stuart A., 1992, *Origins of Order: Self-Organization and Selection in Evolution*. Oxford: Oxford University Press.

Keegan, William F., ed., 1987a, *Emergent Horticultural Economies of the Eastern Woodlands*. Center for Archaeological Investigations, Occasional Paper No. 7, Southern Illinois University at Carbondale.

Keegan, William F., 1987b, Diffusion of maize from South America: The Antillean connection reconstructed. In W. F. Keegan, ed., *Emergent Horticultural Economies of the Eastern Woodlands*, pp. 329–344. Occasional Paper No. 7, Center for Archaeological Investigations, Southern Illinois University at Carbondale.

Keegan, William F. and B. Butler, 1987, The microeconomic logic of horticultural intensification in the Eastern Woodlands. In W. Keegan, ed., *Emergent Horticultural Economies of the Eastern Woodlands*, pp. 109–127. Center for Archaeological Investigations, Occasional Paper No. 7, Southern Illinois University at Carbondale.

Keeley, Lawrence H., 1988, Hunter-gatherer economic complexity and "population pressure": A cross-cultural analysis. *Journal of Anthropological Archaeology* 7:373–411.

Kelly, J. Charles, 1952, Some geographical and cultural factors involved in Mexican–Southeastern contacts. In Sol Tax, ed., *Indian Tribes of Aboriginal America*, Selected Papers, 29th International Congress of Americanists, vol. 3, pp. 139–144, Chicago: University of Chicago Press.

Kelly, John E., 1990a, Range site community patterns and the Mississippian emergence. In B. Smith, ed., *The Mississippian Emergence*, pp. 67–112. Washington, DC: Smithsonian Institution Press.

Kelly, John E., 1990b, The emergence of Mississippian culture in the American Bottom Region. In B. Smith, ed., *The Mississippian Emergence*, pp. 113–152. Washington, DC: Smithsonian Institution Press.

Kelly, John E., 1991, Cahokia and its role as a gateway center in interregional exchange. In Thomas E. Emerson and R. B. Lewis, eds., *Cahokia and the Hinterlands: Middle Mississippian Cultures of the Midwest*, pp. 61–80. Urbana: University of Illinois Press.

Kelly, John E., 1992, The impact of maize on the development of nucleated settlements: An American Bottom example. In W. I. Woods, ed., *Late Prehistoric Agriculture: Observations from the Midwest*, pp. 167–197. Studies in Illinois Archaeology, No. 8, Illinois Historic Preservation Agency, Springfield.

Kelly, Robert L., 1991, Sedentism, sociopolitical inequality, and resource fluctuations. In S. A. Gregg, ed., *Between Bands and States*, pp. 135–58. Occasional Paper No. 9, Center for Archaeological Investigations, Southern Illinois University at Carbondale.

Kemp, W. B., 1971, The flow of energy in a hunting society. *Scientific American* 225:105–115.

Keslin, R. O., 1964, Archaeological implications on the role of salt and an element of cultural diffusion. *Missouri Archaeologist* 26.

Keynes, John Maynard, 1936, *The General Theory of Employment, Interest, and Money*. London: Macmillan.

King, Adam and J. A. Freer, 1995, The Mississippian Southeast: A world–systems perspective. In M. Nassaney and K. Sassaman, eds., *Native American Interactions: Multiscalar Analyses and Interpretations in the Eastern Woodlands*, pp. 266–288. Knoxville: University of Tennessee Press.

King, Frances B., 1987, The evolutionary effects of plant cultivation. In W. F. Keegan, ed., *Emergent Horticultural Economies of the Eastern Woodlands*, pp. 51–65. Occasional Paper No. 7, Center for Archaeological Investigations, Southern Illinois University at Carbondale.

Kleinmann, Dorothée, 1975, The salt springs of the Saale Valley. In K. W. de Brisay and K. A. Evans, eds., *Salt: The Study of an Ancient Industry*, pp. 45–46. Colchester, UK: Colchester Archaeological Group.

Kneberg, Madeline, 1952, The Tennessee area. In J. B. Griffin, ed., *Archeology of Eastern United States*, pp.190–198. Chicago: University of Chicago Press.

Knight, Vernon J. Jr., 1986, The institutional organization of Mississippian religion. *American Antiquity* 51:675–687.

Knight, Vernon J. Jr., 1990, Social organization and the evolution of hierarchy in Southeastern chiefdoms. *Journal of Anthropological Research* 46:1–23.

Knight, Vernon J. Jr., 1994, The formation of the Creeks. In C. Hudson and C. C. Tesser, eds., *The Forgotten Centuries: Indians and Europeans in the American South, 1521–1704*, pp. 373–392. Athens: University of Georgia Press.

Kohl, Philip L., 1985, Symbolic, cognitive archaeology: A new loss of innocence. *Dialectical Anthropology* 9:105–117.

Kohl, Philip L., 1987, State formation: Useful concept or Idée Fixe? In T. C. Patterson and C. W. Gailey, eds., *Power Relations and State Formation*, pp. 27–34. Washington, DC: Archeology Section, American Anthropological Association.

Kohler, Timothy A., 1991, The demise of Weeden Island, and post Weeden Island cultural stability, in non-Mississippianized Northern Florida. In M. S. Nassaney and C. R. Cobb,eds., *Stability, Transformation, and Variation: The Late Woodland Southeast*, pp. 91–110. New York: Plenum Press.

Krader, Lawrence, 1975, *The Asiatic Mode of Production: Sources, Development and Critique in the Writings of Karl Marx*. Assen, The Netherlands: Van Gorcum & Co.

Krause, Elliott A., 1982, *Division of Labor, A Political Perspective*. Contributions in Labor History No. 12. Westport, CT: Greenwood Press.

Kreisa, Paul P., 1991, *Mississippian Sites of the Lower Ohio River Valley in Kentucky*. Western Kentucky Project, Report No. 9. Department of Anthropology, University of Illinois, Urbana (submitted to Kentucky Heritage Council).

Kreisa, Paul P. and Charles Stout, 1991, Late Woodland adaptations in the Mississippi and Ohio Rivers confluence region. In M. S. Nassaney and C. R. Cobb, eds., *Stability, Transformation, and Variation: The Late Woodland Southeast*, pp. 121–147. New York: Plenum Press.

Krieger, Alex D., 1947, The eastward extension of Puebloan datings toward cultures of the Mississippi Valley. *American Antiquity* 12(3):141–148.

Kroeber, Alfred L., 1939, *Cultural and Natural Areas of Native North America*. University of California Publications in American Archaeology and Ethnology XXXVII. Berkeley: University of California Press.

Kroeber, Alfred L., 1944, *Configurations of Culture Growth*. Berkeley: University of California Press.

Kuttruff, Carl, 1991, Late Woodland settlement and subsistence in the Lower Kaskaskin River Valley, Illinois; A reconsideration. In M. S. Nassaney and C. R. Cobb, eds., *Stability, Transformation, and Variation: The Late Woodland Southeast*. pp. 47–68. New York: Plenum Press.

Kuttruff, Jenna T., 1988, Techniques and production complexity of Mississippian Period textiles from Spiro, Oklahoma. In *Textiles as Primary Sources: Proceedings of the First Symposium of the Textile Society of America*, by J. E. Volmer, compiler, pp. 145–150. Textile Society of America.

Kuusinen, O. V., Y. A. Arbatov, A. S. Belyakov, S. L. Vygodsky, A. G. Mileikovsky, and L. M. Sheidin, with the assistance of F. M. Burlatsky, N. I. Ivanov, B. M. Leibzon, A. A. Makarovsky, and Y. P. Sitkovsky, 1963, *Fundamentals of Marxism-Leninism Manual*, 2nd Rev. Ed. English Edition edited by Clemens Dutt. Moscow: Foreign Languages Publishing House.

Lafferty, Robert, 1977, *The evolution of the Mississippian settlement pattern and exploitative technology in the Black Bottom of southern Illinois*. Ph.D. dissertation, Department of Anthropology, Southern Illinois University at Carbondale.

Lafferty, Robert, 1994, Prehistoric exchange in the Lower Mississippi Valley. In Timothy G. Baugh and J. E. Ericson, eds., *Prehistoric Exchange Systems in North America*, pp. 177–213. New York: Plenum Press.

La Harpe, Bénard de, 1699, Voyage up the Mississippi in 1699–1700 by Mr. Le Sueur as given by Benard de la Harpe from Le Sueur's journal. In J. D. G. Shea, ed., [1861] *Early Voyages Up and Down the the Mississippi Valley, by Cavelier, St. Cosme, Le Sueur, Gravier, and Guignas*, pp. 89–111. Albany, NY: Joel Munsell.

La Harpe, Bénard de, 1719, Relation du voyage de Bénard de la Harpe. In Pierre Margry, ed., [1886], *Découvertes et Établissement des Français dans l'Ouest et dans le Sud de l'Amérique Septentrionale (1614–1754). Sixième Partie, Exploration des Affluents du Missisipi et Découverte des Mantagnes Rocheuses (1679–1754)*, pp. 243–306. Paris: Imprimerie Jouaust et Sigaux.

Lahren, C. H. and H. E. Berryman, 1984, Fracture patterns and status at Chucalissa [40SY1]: A biocultural approach. *Tennessee Anthropologist* 9:15–21.

Lallo, John, G., 1973, *The skeletal biology of three prehistoric American Indian societies from Dickson mounds*. Ph.D. dissertation, University of Massachusetts, Amherst.

Lallo, John G. and Jerome C. Rose, 1979, Patterns of stress, disease and mortality in two prehistoric populations from North America. *Journal of Human Evolution* 8:323–335.

Lancaster, Kelvin, 1973, *Modern Economics: Principles and Policy, Microeconomics*. Chicago: Rand McNally College Publishing.

Lane, Ralph, 1586, Account of the particularities of the imployments of the Englishmen left in Virginia, 1585–1586. As "Lane's account of the Englishmen left in Virginia, 1585–1586" in Henry S. Burrage, ed., 1932, *Early English and French Voyages, Chiefly from Hakluyt, 1534—1608*, pp. 246–271, Original Narratives of Early American History. New York: Charles Scribner's Sons.

Lankford, George E., 1984, Saying hello to the Timucua. *Mid-America Folklore* 12:73–23.

Lankford, George E., 1988, Saying hello in the Mississippi Valley. *Mid-America Folklore* 16:24–39.

Lankford, George E., 1992, Reysed after there manner. *Arkansas Archeologist* 31: 65–71.

Larsen, Clark S., 1982, The anthropology of St. Catherine's Island, 3. Prehistoric human biological adaptation. *Anthropological Papers of the American Museum of Natural History* 57(3):159–207.

Larsen, Clark S., 1984, Health and disease in prehistoric Georgia: The transition to agriculture. In M. Cohen and G. Armelagos, eds., *Paleopathology at the Origins of Agriculture*, pp. 367–392. New York: Academic Press.

Larson, Lewis H., 1971, Archaeological implications of social stratification at the Etowah Site, Georgia. In J. Brown, ed., *Approaches to the Social Dimensions of Mortuary Practices*, pp. 58–67. Society for American Archaeology, Memoir 25, Washington DC: Society for American Archaelogy.

Larson, Lewis H., 1972, Functional considerations of warfare in the Southeast during the Mississippi Period. *American Antiquity* 37:383–392.

Larson, Lewis H., 1980, *Aboriginal Subsistence Technology on the Southeastern Coastal Plain during the Late Prehistoric Period*. University of Florida Press, Gainesville.

La Salle, Réné Robert Cavelier, Sieur de, 1684, Memoir of the Sieur de la Salle reporting to the Monsiegneur de Seignelay the discoveries made by him under the order of his majesty. [1903] In *Collections of the Illinois State Historical Library* 1:115–125. [also 1903: In Isaac J. Cox, ed., *The Journeys of Rene Robert Cavelier, Sieur de LaSalle*, pp. 188–204. New York: Allerton Book Co.

La Source, Thaumur de, 1699, [1861] Letter of La Source. In J. D. G. Shea, ed., *Early Voyages Up and Down the Mississippi Valley, by Cavelier, St. Cosme, Le Sueur, Gravier, and Guignas*, pp. 79–86. Albany, NY: Joel Munsell.

Lathrap, Donald W., 1987, The introduction of maize in prehistoric Eastern North America: The view from Amazonia and the Santa Elena Peninsula. In W. F. Keegan, ed., *Emergent Horticultural Economies of the Eastern Woodlands*, pp. 345–371. Occasional Paper No. 7, Center for Archaeological Investigations, Southern Illinois University at Carbondale.

Laudonnière, Rene, 1586, L'Histoire notable de la Floride située ès Indes Occidentales, contenant les trois voyages faits en icelle par certains Capitaines et Pilotes françois, qui y a commandé l'espace d'un an trois moys: A laquelle a esté adjousté un quatriesme voyage fait par le Capitaine Gourgues, mise en lumière par M. Basnier. Paris: [see also The voyage of Rene Laudonniere to Florida. In Barnard Shipp, ed., (1881) *The History of Hernando de Soto and Florida*, pp. 510–543. Philadelphia: Robert M. Lindsay; facsimile reprint Kraus 1971. Also 1869, History of the first attempt of the French (the Huguenots) to colonize the newly discovered country of Florida. In B.F. French, ed., *Historical Collections of Louisiana, ...*, n.s., pp. 165–175, New York.

Lawson, John, 1709, *A New Voyage to Carolina; Containing the Exact Description and Natural History of that Country...* London.

Leach, Edmund R., 1954, *Political Systems of Highland Burma.* London: Bell. [Reprint 1965, Boston: Beacon Press]

Leach, Edmund R., 1963, *Rethinking Anthropology.* London: Athlone Press.

Le Clercq, Chrétien (based in part on Membré to whom it was attributed by Le Clercq), 1690, Narrative of La Salle's voyage down the Mississippi. In J. D. G. Shea, ed., [1903] *Discovery and Exploration of the Mississippi Valley,* 2nd ed., pp. 169–188. Albany, NY: Joseph McDonough. [See earlier parts 1680 - pp, pp. 86–101, 151–168] [Original in Chrétian Le Clercq, 1690, *Premier Établissement de la Foi dans la Nouvelle France,* 2:209–64. See note by Shea pp. 82–86] [Also in Isaac J. Cox, ed., *The Journeys of Rene Robert Cavelier, Sieur de LaSalle.* pp. 131–159. New York: Allerton Book Co.]

Lederer, John, 1672, *The Discoveries of John Lederer, in Three Several Marches from Virginia, to the West of Carolina, and Other Parts of the Continent: Begun in March 1669, and Ended in September 1670.* Collected and trans. by Sir William Talbot. London: Samuel Heyrick. [also in Alvord, Clarence W. and L. Bidgood, 1912, *The First Explorations of the Trans-Allegheny Region by the Virginians, 1650–1674,* pp. 133–171. Cleveland: Arthur H. Clark Co.].

Lee, R. B., 1968, What hunters do for a living, or how to make out on scarce resources. In R. B. Lee and I. DeVore, eds., *Man the Hunter,* pp. 30–48. Chicago: Aldine.

Lee, R. B., 1992, Art, science, or politics? The crisis in hunter–gatherer studies. *American Anthropologist* 94(1):31–54.

Lee, R. B. and I. DeVore, eds.,1968, *Man the Hunter,* Chicago: Aldine.

Lenski, Gerhard, 1966, *Power and Privilege: A Theory of Social Stratification.* New York: McGraw-Hill.

Leontief, Wassily W., 1936, Quantitative input–output relations in the economic system of the United States. *Review of Economics and Statistics* 18:105–125.

Leontief, Wassily W., 1986, *Input–Output Economics,* 2nd ed. New York: Oxford University Press.

Le Page du Pratz, Antoine S., 1758, *History of Louisiana or of the Western Parts of Virginia and Carolina: Containing a Description of the Countries that Lie on Both Sides of the River Missisippi: With an Account of the Settlements, Inhabitants, Soil, Climate, and Products. (Translated with some notes and observations relating to our colonies).* London: T. Becket. [Reprint of 1972, Baton Rouge, LA: Claitor's Publishing Division]

Levins, Richard and Richard Lewontin, 1985, *The Dialectical Biologist.* Cambridge, MA: Harvard University Press.

Lewis, Oscar, 1951, *Life in a Mexican Village: Tepotztlán Restudied.* Urbana: University of Illinois Press.

Lewis, R. Barry, ed., 1986, *Mississippian Towns of the Western Kentucky Border: The Adams, Wickliffe, and Sassafras Ridge Sites.* Frankfort: Kentucky Heritage Council.

Lexikon-Institut Bertelsmann, 1975, *Deutschland: Daten und Fakten zum Nachschlagen.* Berlin: Lexikon-Institut Bertelsmann.

Liette, Pierre, 1702, [1962] Memoir of Pierre Liette on the Illinois country. In Milo Milton Quaife, ed., *The Western Country in the 17th Century: The Memoirs of Antoine Lamothe Cadillac and Pierre Liette,* pp. 85–171. New York: Citadel Press.

Limp, W. Frederick and Van A. Reidhead, 1979, An economic evaluation of the potential of fish utilization in riverine environments. *American Antiquity* 44:70–78.

Little, Keith J. and Caleb Curren, 1990, Conquest archaeology of Alabama. In David H. Thomas, ed., *Archaeological and Historical Perspectives on the Spanish Borderlands East. Columbian Consequences,* vol. 2, pp. 169–195. Washington, DC: Smithsonian Institution Press.

Locke, John, 1674, A memorandum. In Alvord, Clarence W. and L. Bidgood, eds., [1912] *The First Explorations of the Trans-Allegheny Region by the Virginians, 1650–1674,* pp. 209–210. Cleveland: Arthur H. Clark Co. [Shaftesbury Papers Section 9, Bundle 48, No. 83, printed in *Calendar of State Papers, Colonial, America and the West Indies, 1669–1674,* no. 1428, original in Locke's mss.]

Lopinot, Neal H., 1992, Spatial and temporal variability in Mississippian subsistence: The archaeobotanical record. In W. I. Woods, ed., *Late Prehistoric Agriculture: Observations from the Midwest,* pp. 44–94. Studies in Illinois Archaeology, No. 8, Illinois Historic Preservation Agency, Springfield.

Lopinot, Neal H., 1994, A new crop of data on the Cahokian polity. In W. Green, ed., *Agricultural Origins and Development in the Midcontinent,* pp. 127–153. Report No. 19, Office of the State Archaeologist, University of Iowa, Iowa City.

Lowery, Woodbury, 1959, *The Spanish Settlements within the Present Limits of the United States*. [reprint of 1901, 1905 publications] New York: Russell & Russell.

Luhmann, Niklas, 1982, *The Differentiation of Society* (trans. by S. Holmes and C. Larmore). New York: Columbia University Press.

Lybyer, Albert H., 1931, Feudalism: Saracen and Ottoman. In E. Seligman, ed., *Encyclopaedia of the Social Sciences*, vol. 6, pp. 210–213. New York: Macmillan.

Lyon, Eugene, 1989, Pedro Menéndez's plan for settling La Florida. In J. T. Milanich and S. Milbrath, eds., *First Encounters: Spanish Explorations in the Caribbean and the United States, 1492–1570*, pp. 150–165. Gainesville: University of Florida Press.

MacCurdy, G. C., 1913, Shell gorgets from Missouri. *American Anthropologist* 15:395–414.

Malinowski, Bronislaw, 1922, *Argonauts of the Western Pacific*. Paperbound ed., 1961. New York: E. P. Dutton.

Malthus, Thomas R., 1798, *Essay on the Principle of Population as it Affects the Future Improvement of Society*. London. [1960, as *An Essay on Population*. New York: Dutton].

Mandel, Ernest, 1968, *Marxist Economic Theory*, (trans. by Brian Pearce). New York: Monthly Review Press.

Margry, Pierre, 1878–1888 *Découvertes et Établissements des Français dans l'Ouest et dans le Sud de l'Amérique Septentrionale (1614–1754): Memoires et Documents Originaux*, 6 vols. Paris: Imprimerie D. Jouaust.

Marshall, Alfred, 1890, *Principles of Economics* (vol.1, no more published). London: Macmillan. [1982, *Principles of Economics: An Introductory Volume* (originally published 1920, 8th ed. London: Macmillan and Co.) Philadelphia: Porcupine Press]

Martin, A. C., H. S. Zim, and A. L. Nelson, 1951, *American Wildlife and Plants: A Guide to Wildlife Food Habits*. New York: McGraw-Hill. [Dover reprint 1961]

Martin, Joel W., 1994, Southeastern Indians and the English trade in skins and slaves. In C. Hudson and C. C. Tesser, eds., *The Forgotten Centuries: Indians and Europeans in the American South, 1521–1704*, pp. 304–324. Athens: University of Georgia Press.

Martin, Paul S., G.I. Quimby, and D. Collier, 1947, *Indians before Columbus*. Chicago: University of Chicago Press.

Martin, William W., 1991, A functional analysis and comparison of three Mississippian-Period ceramic assemblages from the Black Bottom of Southern Illinois, Pope and Massac Counties. Unpublished M.S. thesis, Department of Anthropology, Southern Illinois University at Carbondale.

Martire d'Anghiera, Pietro [Martyr, Peter], 1533, *De rebus oceanicis et orbe novo decades tres*. Basle. [1555, *Decades of the Newe Worlde or West India*, trans. by Richard Eden, Guilhelmi Powell, London./facsimile reprint of latter, 1966, University Microfilms - Spanish trans. Joaquin Torres Asensio, Madrid 1892, repr. later]

Marx, Chico, G. Marx, H. Marx, and Z. Marx, 1929, *Cocoanuts*. Screenplay by Sam Harris, book by G. Kaufman. Paramount Pictures, Hollywood, CA.

Marx, Karl, 1844, Ökonomisch-philosophische Manuskripte aus dem Jahre 1844. First published 1932 in *Marx-Engels Gesamtausgabe* (of 1927–1935). [1968 *Marx/Engels Werke*, Ergänzungsband 1. S. 465–588. Berlin: Dietz Verlag]

Marx, Karl, 1846, Letter of December 28, 1846 to P.V. Annenkov in Paris. In 1965, *Selected Works* (3rd ed.), Karl Marx and Frederick Engels. Moscow: Progress Progress Publishers, pp, 659–669.

Marx, Karl, 1852, Der 18te Brumaire des Louis Napoleon. *Die Revolution* 1, Chapters published from January to March, New York: [= Der achtzehnte Brumaire des Louis Bonaparte. In 1975, *Selected Works* (3rd. ed.), Karl Marx and Frederick Engels. Moscow: Progress Publishers as "The Eighteenth Brumaire of Louis Bonaparte," pp. 94–179. Printed according to the 1869 ed. checked against the 1852 and 1885 eds.]

Marx, Karl, 1853, The British Rule in India. *New York Daily Tribune*, June 25. [In 1979, *Pre-Capitalist Socio-Economic Formations*, selections from K. Marx and F. Engels, pp. 69–76. Moscow: Progress Publishers]

Marx, Karl, 1857–1858 [1965] *Pre-Capitalist Economic Formations*. New York: International Publishers. [Sections entitled *Formen die der Kapitalistichen Produktion vorhergehen..* of 1857–8 mss. published in total in 1939–1941 as *Grundrisse der Kritik der Politischen Ökonomie*, Moscow: Also selections in 1979 *Pre-Capitalistic Socio-Economic Formations: A Collection* by K. Marx and F. Engels. Moscow: Progress Publishers]

Marx, Karl, 1859, *Zur Kritik der politischen Ökonomie*. Berlin: Duncker. [Many editions, 1964 *Marx/Engels Werke*, in Band 13. Berlin: Dietz Verlag. English trans. 1977: *A Contribution to the Critique of Political Economy*. Moscow: Progress Publishers]

Marx, Karl, 1867, *Das Kapital, Kritik der politischen Ökonomie. Buch I: Der Produktionsproseß des Kapitals.* Hamburg: Meissner. [In 1962 *Marx/Engels Werke*, Band 23 Berlin: Dietz Verlag, 1906 trans. S. Moore and E. Aveling, New York: Modern Library; 1965 Zusammenhang ausgewählt von B. Kautsky, Stuttgart: Alfred Kröner Verlag]

Marx, Karl and Friedrich Engels, 1846, *Die deutsche Ideologie. Kritik der neuesten deutschen Philosophie in ihrem Repräsentanten Feuerbach, B. Bauer und Stirner, und des deutschen Sozialismus in seinen verschiedenen Propheten.* Ms. [1959, *Marx/ Engels Werke*, Band 3:9–530. Berlin: Dietz Verlag]

Marx, Karl and Friedrich Engels, 1958–1968 *Karl Marx-Friedrich Engels Werke*. Berlin: Dietz Verlag.

Marx, Karl and Friedrich Engels, 1975, *Selected Works*. Moscow: Progress Publishers.

Marx, Karl and Friedrich Engels, 1979, *Pre-Capitalist Socio-Economic Formations: A Collection*. Moscow: Progress Publishers.

Mauss, Marcel, 1950, *Sociologie et Anthropologie*. Paris: Presses Universitaires de France.

McBride, Kevin A. and Robert E. Dewar, 1987, Agriculture and cultural evolution: Causes and effects in the Lower Connecticut River Valley. In W. F. Keegan, ed., *Emergent Horticultural Economies of the Eastern Woodlands*, pp. 305–328. Occasional Paper No. 7, Center for Archaeological Investigations, Southern Illinois University at Carbondale.

McGuire, Randall H., 1983, Breaking down cultural complexity: Inequality and heterogeneity. In M. Schiffer, ed., *Advances in Archaeological Method and Theory*, vol. 6, pp. 91–142. New York: Academic Press.

McGuire, Randall H., 1986, Economies and modes of production in the prehistoric Southwestern periphery. In F. Mathien and R. H. McGuire, eds., *Ripples in the Chichimec Sea: New Considerations of Southwestern–Mesoamerican Interactions*, pp. 243–269. Carbondale: Southern Illinois University Press.

McGuire, Randall H., 1992, *A Marxist Archaeology*. San Diego: Academic Press.

McGuire, Randall H., 1993, Archaeology and Marxism. In M. Schiffer, ed., *Archaeological Method and Theory*, vol. 5, pp. 101–157. Tucson: University of Arizona Press.

McKivergan, David A., Jr., 1995, Balanced reciprocity and peer polity interaction in the Late Prehistoric Southeastern United States. In M. Nassaney and K. Sassaman, eds., *Native American Interactions: Multiscalar Analyses and Interpretations in the Eastern Woodlands*, pp. 229–246. Knoxville: University of Tennessee Press.

McNaughton, S. J. and L. L. Wolf, 1973 *General Ecology*. New York: Holt, Rinehart, and Winston.

Mehrer, Mark W., 1995, *Cahokia's Countryside: Household Archaeology, Settlement Patterns and Social Power*. De Kalb: Northern Illinois University Press.

Meillassoux, Claude, 1964, *Anthropologie économique des Gouro de Côte d'Ivoire: De l'économie de subsistence à l'agriculture commerciale*. Le Monde d'Outre-mer Passé et Present, Première Serie, Études 27. Paris: Mouton.

Meillassoux, Claude, 1972, From reproduction to production: A Marxist approach to economic anthropology. *Economy and Society* 1:93–105.

Meillassoux, Claude, 1981, *Maidens, Meal and Money: Capitalism and the Domestic Economy*. Cambridge, UK: Cambridge University Press. [translation of 1977 *Femmes, grenier et capitaux*. Paris: Maspero]

Meillassoux, Claude, 1985, Past and future relevance of Marx and Engels's works to anthropology. *Dialectical Anthropology* 9:349–356.

Membré, Father Zenobius, Recollect., 1681, [1903] Narrative of La Salle's Voyage down the Mississippi. In J. D. G. Shea, ed., *Discovery and Exploration of the Mississippi Valley*, 2nd ed., pp. 169–188. Albany, NY: Joseph McDonough [original in LeClercq, 1690, *Établissement de Foi*]

Membré, Father Zenobius, Recollect., as "drawn up by Fr. Chretien Le Clerq," 1682a, [1903] Narrative of Adventures of La Salle's Party at Fort Crèvecœur, in Ilinois, from February, 1680, to June, 1681. In J. D. G. Shea, ed., *Discovery and Exploration of the Mississippi Valley*, 2nd ed., pp. 151–68. Albany, NY: Joseph McDonough. [original in LeClerq 1690 *Établissement de la Foi*]

Membré, Father Zenobius, Recollect., 1682b, Lettre du Père Zénobe Membré, 3 Juin 1682. In P. Margry, ed., 1878, *Découvertes et Établissements des Français dans l'Ouest et dans le Sud de l'Amérique Septentrionale (1614–1754): Memoires et Documents Originaux. Deuxième Partie (1678–1685)*, pp. 206–212.

Paris: Imprimerie D. Jouaust. [also in 1934, *The Franciscan Père Marquette: A Critical Biography of Father Zénobe Membré, O.F.M., La Salle's Chaplain and Missionary Companion 1645 (ca.)–1689*, by Marion A. Habig, Franciscan Studies 13, pp. 207–214. New York: Joseph F. Wagner]

Menéndez de Avilés, Pedro, 1565, Pedro Menéndez de Avilés. Memorial of Gonzalo Solís de Merás. Trans. Jeannette Thurber Connor, 1964 Facsmile of 1923 publication. Gainesville: University of Florida Press. [Original published in Spanish in Ruidíaz y Caravia, Eugenio, 1893 La Florida, su conquista y colonización por Pedro Menéndez de Avilés. Madrid] [some also in Barnard Shipp, ed., 1881, *The History of Hernando de Soto and Florida*, pp. 544–561. Philadelphia: Robert M. Lindsay] [facsimile reprint Kraus 1971]

Miernyk, William H., 1965, *The Elements of Input–Output Analysis*. Random House: New York.

Milanich, J. T., A. S. Cordell, V. J. Knight, Jr., T. A. Kohler, and B. J. Sigler-Lavelle, 1984, *McKeithen Weeden Island: The Culture of Northern Florida, A.D. 200–900*. Orlando, FL: Academic Press.

Milanich, J. T. and S. Milbrath, eds., 1989, *First Encounters: Spanish Explorations in the Caribbean and the United States, 1492–1570*. Gainesville: University of Florida Press.

Milfort, General (Louis LeClerc de), 1802, [1956] *Mémoire ou Coup-d'Œil Rapide Sur mes différens voyages et mon séjour dans la nation Crĕck*. Paris: Giguet et Michaud. [*Memoir or a Cursory Glance at My Different Travels & My Sojourn in the Creek Nation*, trans. G. de Courcey. Chicago: Lakeside Press]

Milner, Claire McHale, 1991, Localization in small-scale societies: Late Prehistoric social organization in the western Great Lakes. In S. A. Gregg, ed., *Between Bands and States*, pp. 35–57. Occasional Paper No. 9, Center for Archaeological Investigations, Southern Illinois University at Carbondale.

Milner, George R., 1980, Epidemic disease in the postcontact Southeast: A reappraisal. *Midcontinental Journal of Archaeology* 5:39–56.

Milner, George R., 1982, *Measuring prehistoric levels of health: A study of Mississippian Period skeletal remains from the American Bottom, Illinois*. Ph.D. dissertation, Department of Anthropology, University of Illinois at Urbana.

Milner, George R., 1983a, *The East St. Louis Stone Quarry Site Cemetery*. American Bottom Archaeology. FAI-270 Site Report No. 1 for the Illinois Department of Transportation, by the University of Illinois Press, Urbana.

Milner, George R., (Assisted by J. A. Williams), 1983b, *The Turner and DeMange Sites*. American Bottom Archaeology. FAI-270 Site Report No. 4 for the Illinois Department of Transportation by the University of Illinois Press, Urbana.

Milner, George R., 1984a, Social and temporal implications of variation among American Bottom Mississippian cemeteries. *American Antiquity* 49(3):468–488.

Milner, George R. (Assisted by J. A. Williams), 1984b, *The Julien Site*. American Bottom Archaeology. FAI-270 Site Report No. 7 for the Illinois Department of Transportation by the University of Illinois Press, Urbana.

Milner, George R. (Assisted by K. R. Cox and M. C. Meinkoth), 1984c, *The Robinson's Lake Site*. American Bottom Archaeology. FAI-270 Site Report No. 10 for the Illinois Department of Transportation by the University of Illinois Press, Urbana.

Milner, George R., 1986, Mississippian period population density in a segment of the Central Mississippi River Valley. *American Antiquity* 51(2):227–238.

Milner, George R., 1990, The Late Prehistoric Cahokia cultural system of the Mississippi River Valley: Foundations, fluorescence, and fragmentation. *Journal of World Prehistory* 4(1):1–43.

Milner, George R., 1991, American Bottom Mississippian cultures: Internal developments and external relations. In J. B. Stoltman, ed., *New Perspectives on Cahokia: Views from the Periphery*, pp. 29–47. Madison, WI: Prehistory Press.

Milner, George R., 1992, Morbidity, mortality, and the adaptive success of an Oneota population from west-central Illinois. In W. I. Woods, ed., *Late Prehistoric Agriculture: Observations from the Midwest*, pp. 136–166. Studies in Illinois Archaeology, No. 8. Illinois Historic Preservation Agency, Springfield.

Milner, George R., 1993, Settlements amidst swamps. *Illinois Archaeology* 5:374–380.

Milner, George R., 1995, An osteological perspective on warfare in prehistoric North America. In Beck, Lane A., ed., *Regional Approaches to Mortuary Analysis*, pp. 221–244. New York: Plenum Press.

Minet, 1685, Voyage made from Canada inland going southward during the year 1682. In Robert S. Weddle, ed., 1987, *La Salle, the Mississippi, and the Gulf*, pp. 29–68. College Station, Texas: Texas A&M University Press.

Mooney, James, 1928, The aboriginal population of America north of Mexico, edited by John R. Swanton. *Smithsonian Miscellaneous Collections* 80:1–40.

Moore, James A., A. C. Swedlund, and G. J. Armelagos, 1975, The use of life tables in paleodemography. In A.C. Swedlund, ed., *Population Studies in Archaeology and Biological Anthropology: A Symposium*, pp. 57–70. Memoir 30, Society of American Archaeology, Washington, DC.

Morgan, Lewis H., 1877, *Ancient Society*. New York: Holt.

Morgan, W. N., 1980, *Prehistoric Architecture in the Eastern United States*. Cambridge: MIT Press.

Morrow, Carol A., 1982, Analysis of Area A Middle-Archaic flaked stone technology. In R. W. Jefferies and B. Butler, eds., *The Carrier Mills Archaeological Project: Adaptation in the Saline Valley, Illinois*, pp. 1289–1322. Research Paper No. 33, Southern Illinois University, Center for Archaeological Investigations, Carbondale.

Morrow, Carol A. and M. McCorvie, 1993, *Layers of trail systems in the Midwestern U.S.: Archaeological, historical and modern environment*. Paper presented at the Society for American Archaeology 57th Annual Meeting, St, Louis, MO.

Morse, Dan F. and Phyllis A. Morse, 1983, *Archaeology of the Central Mississippi Valley*. New York: Academic Press.

Morse, Dan F. and Phyllis A. Morse, 1990, Emergent Mississippian in the Central Mississippi Valley. In B. Smith, ed., *The Mississippian Emergence*, pp. 53–173. Washington, DC: Smithsonian Institution Press.

Muller, Jon, 1966a, *An experimental theory of style*. Ph.D. dissertation, Department of Anthropology, Harvard University, Cambridge, MA.

Muller, Jon, 1966b, Archaeological analysis of art styles. *Tennessee Archaeologist* 22(1):25–39.

Muller, Jon, 1971, Review of *The Southeastern Ceremonial Complex and its Interpretation* by James H. Howard. *American Anthropologist* 72(1):182–183.

Muller, Jon, 1976, *Mississippian population and organization: Kincaid locality research, 1970–75*. Mss. on file, Center for Archaeological Investigations, Southern Illinois University at Carbondale.

Muller, Jon, 1978a, The Southeast. In Jesse D. Jennings, ed., *Ancient Native Americans*, pp. 280–325. San Francisco: W. H. Freeman.

Muller, Jon, 1978b, The Kincaid system: Mississippian settlement in the environs of a large site. In B. Smith, ed., *Mississippian Settlement Patterns*, pp. 269–292, New York: Academic Press.

Muller, Jon, 1979, Structural studies of art styles. In Justine Cordwell, ed., *The Visual Arts: Plastic and Graphic*, pp. 10–20, 139–211, The Hague, The Netherlands: Mouton.

Muller, Jon, 1983, The Southeast. In Jesse D. Jennings, ed., *Ancient North Americans*, pp. 372–419. San Francisco: W. H. Freeman.

Muller, Jon, 1984a, Mississippian specialization and salt. *American Antiquity* 49(3):489–507.

Muller, Jon, 1984b, Review of *Prehistoric Shell Engravings from Spiro*, by P. Phillips and J. Brown. *American Antiquity* 49(3):669–670.

Muller, Jon, 1985, *Archaeological survey of the Cave-in-Rock State Park*. Report submitted to the Illinois Department of Conservation. Also on file at the Center for Archaeological Investigations, Southern Illinois University, Carbondale.

Muller, Jon, 1986a, Pans and a grain of salt: Mississippian specialization revisited. *American Antiquity* 51(2):405–409.

Muller, Jon, 1986b, *Archaeology of the Lower Ohio River Valley*. New York: Academic Press.

Muller, Jon, 1987a, Salt, chert, and shell: Mississippian exchange and economy. In E. Brumfiel and T. Earle, eds., *Specialization, Exchange and Complex Societies*, pp. 10–21. Cambridge, UK: Cambridge University Press.

Muller, Jon, 1987b, Lower Ohio Valley emergent horticulture and Mississippian. In W. F. Keegan, ed., *Emergent Horticultural Economies of the Eastern Woodlands*, pp. 243–273. Occasional Paper No. 7, Center for Archaeological Investigations, Southern Illinois University at Carbondale.

Muller, Jon, 1988, Test for producer specialization: The Great Salt Spring. National Science Foundation Proposal, funded as BNS-89–07424.

Muller, Jon, 1989, The Southern cult. In P. Galloway, ed., *The Southeastern Ceremonial Complex: Artifacts and Analysis*, pp. 11–26. Lincoln: University of Nebraska Press.

Muller, Jon, 1991, The new holy family: A polemic on bourgeois idealism in archaeology. In R. Preucel, ed., *Processual and Postprocessual Archaeologies: Multiple Ways of Knowing the Past.*, pp. 251–261. Occasional Paper No. 10, Center for Archaeological Investigations, Southern Illinois University at Carbondale.

Muller, Jon, 1993a, Lower Ohio Valley Mississippian revisited: An autocritique of "The Kincaid System." In James B. Stoltman, ed., *Archaeology of Eastern North America: Papers in Honor of Stephen Williams*, pp. 128–142. Archaeological Report No. 25, Mississippi Department of Archives and History, Jackson.

Muller, Jon, 1993b, Eastern North American population dynamics. In T. Emerson, A. Fortier, and D. McElrath, eds., *Highways to the Past*, pp. 84–99. *Illinois Archaeology* 5(1-2).

Muller, Jon, 1994, Mississippian political economy with a grain of salt. In mss. J. Muller and C. Cobb, eds., *Production and Political Economies in the Mississippian Southeast* .

Muller, Jon, 1995a, Review of *Caddoan Saltmakers in the Quachita Valley*, edited by Ann Early. *Southeastern Archaeology* 14(1):95–96.

Muller, Jon, 1995b, Regional interaction in the Southeast. In M. Nassaney and K. Sassaman, eds., *Native American Interactions: Multiscalar Analyses and Interpretations in the Eastern Woodlands*, pp. 317–353. Knoxville: University of Tennessee Press.

Muller, Jon, in press, Native Eastern American population continuity and stability. In R. Paine, ed., *Integrating Archaeological Demography*, Occasional Papers, Center for Archaeological Investigations, Southern Illinois University.

Muller, Jon, and George Avery, 1982, *The Great Salt Spring: A preliminary report, 1981 season*. Report prepared for the National Forest Service and the Center for Archaeological Investigations, Southern Illinois University, Carbondale.

Muller, Jon, and Lisa Renken, 1989, Radiocarbon dates for the Great Salt Spring site: Dating saltpan variation. *Illinois Archaeology* 1(2):150–160.

Muller, Jon and Douglas Davy, 1977, *Cultural resources of the Ohio River floodplain in Illinois*. Huntington District Corps of Engineers Request No. DACW69–77-Q-0053.

Muller, Jon, ed., with contributions by L. Renken, J. Muller, and C. McGimsey, 1991, *Great Salt Spring structure*. Report Submitted to the Shawnee National Forest P.O. 43–51A8–1–0179.

Muller, Jon, ed., assisted by Lisa Renken, George Avery, and others, 1992, *The Great Salt Spring: Mississippian production and specialization*. Draft Report of March 1992, on file with the Shawnee National Forest, U. S. Forest Service, Harrisburg, ILL, and the Center for Archaeological Investigations, Southern Illinois University, Carbondale.

Muller, Jon, and Jeanette E. Stephens, 1983, *Mississippian and its frontiers*. Paper presented at the 48th Annual Meeting of the Society for American Archaeology, Pittsburgh, PA.

Muller, Jon, and Jeanette E. Stephens, 1991, Mississippian sociocultural adaptations. In B. Lewis and T. Emerson, eds., *Cahokia and the Hinterlands: Middle Mississippian Cultures of the Midwest*, pp. 297–310. Urbana: University of Illinois Press in cooperation with the Illinois Historic Preservation Agency.

Muller, Jon, Jeanette E. Stephens, and Terry Powell, 1981, Shawnee Unit (X). In M. Brown, ed., *Predictive Models in Illinois Archaeology: Report Summaries*, pp. 119–132. Springfield: Illinois Department of Conservation.

Munson, Cheryl, ed., 1984, *The Southwind Site: A Mississippian Village in Southwestern Indiana*. ms. report prepared for the Indiana Port Commission by the Glenn A. Black Laboratory, Indiana University.

Munson, Patrick, 1985, *Hickory silvaculture: A subsistence revolution in the prehistory of Eastern North America*. Paper presented at the Visiting Scholar Conference, Southern Illinois University, Carbondale.

Murdock, George P., 1949, *Social Structure*. New York: Macmillan.

Myer, W. E. (edited by John R. Swanton), 1928, Indian trails of the Southeast. *Bureau of American Ethnology, Annual Report* 42:727–857.

Nance, J. D., 1980, Non-site sampling in the Lower Cumberland River Valley. *Midcontinental Journal of Archaeology* 5(2):169–191.

Nance, J. D., 1984, Lithic exploitation studies in the Lower Tennessee–Cumberland Valleys, Western Kentucky. In B. Butler and E. May, eds., *Prehistoric Chert Exploitation: Studies from the Midcontinent*, pp. 101–127. Center for Archaeological Investigations, Occasional Paper No. 2, Southern Illinois University at Carbondale.

Naroll, R., 1962, Floor area and settlement population. *American Antiquity* 27:587–589.

Nassaney, Michael S., 1987, On the causes and consequences of subsistence intensification in the Missis-sippi Alluvial Valley. In W. F. Keegan, ed., *Emergent Horticultural Economies of the Eastern Woodlands*, pp. 129–151. Occasional Paper No. 7, Center for Archaeological Investigations, Southern Illinois University at Carbondale.

Nassaney, Michael S., 1991, Spatial–Temporal dimensions of social integration during the Coles Creek Pe-riod in central Arkansas. In *Stability, Transformation, and Variation: The Late Woodland Southeast*, M. S. Nassaney and C. R. Cobb, eds., pp. 177–220. New York: Plenum Press.

Nassaney, Michael S. and Charles R. Cobb, 1991a, Patterns and processes of Late Woodland development in the greater Southeastern United States. In *Stability, Transformation, and Variation: The Late Wood-land Southeast*, M. S. Nassaney and C. R. Cobb, eds., pp. 285–322. New York: Plenum Press.

Nassaney, Michael S. and Charles R. Cobb, editors, 1991b, *Stability, Transformation, and Variation: The Late Woodland Southeast*. New York: Plenum Press.

National Academy of Sciences (NAS), 1974, *Recommended Dietary Allowances*, 8th ed., Washington, DC.

Neitzel, Jill, ed., in press, *Great Towns and Regional Polities*, Amerind Foundation, Alberquerque: University of New Mexico Press.

Nenquin, Jacques, 1961, *Salt: A Study in Economic Prehistory*. Brugge, Belgium: De Tempel.

Neumann, Georg, 1952, Archeology and race in the American Indian. In J. B. Griffin, ed., *Archeology of Eastern United States*, pp. 13–34. Chicago: University of Chicago Press.

Nordhoff, Charles, 1875, *The Communistic Societies of the United States; from Personal Visit and Observation: Including Detailed Accounts of the Economists, Zoarites, Shakers, the Amana, Oneida, Bethel, Aurora, Icarian and Other Existing Societies; Their Religious Creeds, Social Practices, Numbers, Industries, and Present Condition*. New York: Harper & Brothers. [reprinted 1966, with a new introd. by Mark Hol-loway. New York: Dover Publications]

Noyes, John Humphrey, 1870, *History of American Socialisms*. Philadelphia: J. B. Lippincott & Co. [Reprint 1961, New York: Hillary House]

Nuñez Cabeça de Vaca, Alvar, 1542, *La relacion que dio Aluar nuñez cabeça de vaca de lo acaescido en las In-dias en la armada donde yua por gouernador Páphilo de narbáez, desde el año de veynte y siete hasta el año de teynta y seys que boluio a Seuilla con tres de su compañia:...* [translated, with related material, by Buckingham Smith, 1871, Relation of Alvar Nuñez Cabeça de Vaca. New York. Facsimile reprint, 1966, University Microfilms].

O'Brien, Patricia J., 1991, Early state economics: Cahokia, capital of the Ramey state. In Henri J.M. Claes-sen and Pieter van de Velde, eds., *Early State Economics*, pp. 143–175. London, UK: Transaction Publishers.

OED (Oxford English Dictionary) 1971, *The Compact Edition of the Oxford English Dictionary*. Oxford: Ox-ford University Press.

Ollman, Bertell, 1971, *Alienation: Marx's Conception of Man in Capitalist Society*. New York: Cambridge Uni-versity Press. [2nd ed. 1976]

Ostrovitianov, Iurri and Antonina Sterbalova, 1977, The social "genotype" of the East and the prospect of national states [Part I]. *Soviet Anthropology and Archeology* 16(1):27–48. [Original in Russian in *Novy Mir* 12:197–208, 1972]

Oviedo y Valdés, Gonzalo Fernandez de, 1547–1549 *Historia General y Natural de las Indias*. Originales autógrafos en la Real Academia de la Historia. [1959 in Biblioteca de Autores Españoles desde la Formacion del Lenguaje hasta Nuestros Dias. Tomos 117–121, Edición de Juan Perez de Tudela Bueso.] [Ranjel in Tomo 118 of series, Oviedo's Tomo II, Libro XVII, Capítulos XXI–XXX] [trans. by John E. Worth, 1993, in Clayton, et al.]

Page, John S., 1959, *Estimator's General Construction Man-Hour Manual*. Houston, TX: Gulf Publishing Co.

Park, Thomas K., 1992, Early trends toward class stratification: Chaos, common property, and flood reces-sion agriculture. *American Anthropologist* 94(1):90–117.

Patterson, Thomas C. and C. W. Gailey, 1987, *Power Relations and State Formation*. Washington, DC: Ar-cheology Section, American Anthropological Association.

Pauketat, Timothy R., 1986, *Predicting occupation span from ceramic refuse: A case study from the American Bottom*. M.A. Thesis, Department of Anthropology, Southern Illinois University at Carbondale.

Pauketat, Timothy R., 1987a, A functional consideration of a Mississippian domestic vessel assemblage. *Southeastern Archaeology* 6(1):1–15.

Pauketat, Timothy R., 1987b, Mississippian domestic economy and formation processes: A response to Prentice. *Midcontinental Journal of Archaeology* 12(1):77–88.

Pauketat, Timothy R., 1989, Monitoring Mississippian homestead occupation span and economy using ceramic refuse. *American Antiquity* 54(2):288–310.

Pauketat, Timothy R., 1992, The reign and ruin of the lords of Cahokia: A dialectic of dominance. In Alex W. Barker and T. R. Pauketat, eds., *Lords of the Southeast: Social Inequality and the Native Elites of Southeastern North America*, pp. 31–51. Archeological Papers of the American Anthropological Association, No. 3, Washington, DC: AAA.

Pauketat, Timothy R., 1993, *Temples for Cahokia Lords: Preston Holder's 1955–1956 Excavations of Kunnemann Mound*. Museum of Anthropology, Memoir 26, Ann Arbor: University of Michigan.

Pauketat, Timothy R., 1994, *The Ascent of Chiefs: Cahokia and Mississippian Politics in Native North America*. Tuscaloosa: University of Alabama Press.

Pauketat, Timothy R. and William I. Woods, 1986, Middle Mississippian structure analysis: The Lawrence Primas site (11-Ms-895) in the American Bottom. *Wisconsin Archaeologist* 67:104–127.

Peacock, D. P. S., 1982, *Pottery in the Roman World: An Ethnoarchaeological Approach*. London: Longman.

Pearson, H.W., 1957, The economy has no surplus: Critique of a theory of development. In K. Polanyi, C. Arensberg, and H. Pearson, eds., *Trade and Market in the Early Empires: Economics in History and Theory*, pp. 320–41. Glencoe, IL: Free Press.

Pearson, H. W., ed., 1977, *The Livelihood of Man/Karl Polanyi*. New York: Academic Press.

Peebles, Christopher S., 1971, Moundville and surrounding sites: Some structural considerations for mortuary practices II. *Memoirs of the Society for American Archaeology* 25:68–91.

Peebles, Christopher S., 1978, Determinants of settlement size and location in the Moundville phase. In B. Smith, ed., *Mississippian Settlement Patterns*, pp. 369–416. New York: Academic Press.

Peebles, Christopher S., 1983, Moundville: Late Prehistoric sociopolitical organization in the Southeastern United States. In Elisabeth Tooker, ed., *The Development of Political Organization in Native North America*, pp. 183–201. Proceedings, American Ethnological Society, Washington, DC.

Peebles, Christopher S., 1986, Paradise lost, strayed, and stolen: Prehistoric social devolution in the Southeast. In M. Richardson and M. C. Webb, eds., *The Burden of Being Civilized: An Anthropological Perspective on the Discontents of Civilization*, pp. 24–40. Proceedings 18, Southern Anthropological Society.

Peebles, Christopher S., 1987a, The rise and fall of the Mississippian in western Alabama: The Moundville and Summerville phases, A.D. 1000 to 1600. *Mississippi Archaeology* 22(1):1–31.

Peebles, Christopher S., 1987b, Moundville from A.D. 1000 to 1500 as seen from A.D. 1840 to 1985. In R. Drennan and C. Utribe, eds., *Chiefdoms in the Americas*, pp. 21–41. Lanham, MD: University Press of America.

Peebles, Christopher and Susan M. Kus, 1977, Some archaeological correlates of ranked societies. *American Antiquity* 42:421–448.

Peithman, Irvin, 1953, A preliminary report on salt-making and pottery manufacture at a prehistoric site in Gallatin County, Illinois. *Illinois State Archaeological Society Journal* 3(1):67–74.

Pennington, Campbell W., 1969, *The Tepehuan of Chihuahua; Their Material Culture*. Salt Lake City: University of Utah Press.

Penny, JoAnne, 1983, *The raw and the cooked: Nutritional evaluation of a prehistoric Mississippian diet*. M.A. thesis, Department of Anthropology, Southern Illinois University at Carbondale.

Peregrine, Peter, 1991, Prehistoric chiefdoms on the American midcontinent: A world-system based on prestige goods. In Christopher Chase-Dunn and T. D. Hall, eds., *Core/Periphery Relations in Precapitalist Worlds*. pp. 193–211. Boulder, CO: Westview Press.

Peregrine, Peter, 1995, Networks of power: The Mississippian world-system. In M. Nassaney and K. Sassaman, eds., *Native American Interactions: Multiscalar Analyses and Interpretations in the Eastern Woodlands*, pp. 247–265. Knoxville: University of Tennessee Press.

Perrine, Thomas M., 1873, Mounds near Anna, Union County, Illinois. In *Smithsonian Institution Annual Report for 1872*, pp. 418–420. Washington, DC.

Peterson, Lee Allen, 1977, *A Field Guide to Edible Wild Plants: Eastern/Central North America*. Boston: Houghton Mifflin Co.

Petty, William, 1690, [1st ed. 1631]*Political arithmetick, or A discourse concerning the extent and values of lands, people, buildings... As the same relates to every country in general, but more particularly to the territories of His Majesty of Great Britain, and his neighbours of Holland, Zealand, and France.* London: R. Clavel.

Petty, William, 1899, *The Economic Writings of Sir William Petty, Together with the Observations upon the Bills of Mortality, More Probably by Captain John Graunt, ed. by Charles Henry Hull...* Cambridge, UK: University Press.

Phillips, Philip and J. A. Brown, 1975–1983 *Pre-Columbian Shell Engravings from the Craig Mound at Spiro, Oklahoma* (6 vols.) Cambridge, MA: Peabody Museum Press.

Phillips, Philip and J.A. Brown, 1984, *Pre-Columbian Shell Engravings from the Craig Mound at Spiro, Oklahoma* (2-vol. softbound ed.) Cambridge, MA: Peabody Museum Press.

Phillips, William A., 1899, The aboriginal quarries and shops at Mill Creek, Union County, Illinois. *Proceedings of the American Association for the Advancement of Science* 48:361–363.

Phillips, William A., 1900, Aboriginal quarries and shops at Mill Creek, Illinois. *American Anthropologist* 2:37–52.

Pielou, E.C., 1977, *Mathematical Ecology* (2nd ed.). New York: John Wiley & Sons.

Pimental, David, W. Dritshilo, J. Krummel, J. Kutzman, 1975, Energy and land constraints in food protein production. *Science* 190:754–761.

Pinder, David, Izumi Shimada, and David Gregory, 1979, The nearest-neighbor statistic: archaeological application and new developments. *American Antiquity* 44(3):430–445.

Plog, Fred, 1977, Explaining change. In J. N. Hill, ed., *Explanation of Prehistoric Change*, pp. 17–58. Albuquerque: University of New Mexico Press.

Polanyi, Karl, 1944, *The Great Transformation.* New York: Toronto, Farrar & Rinehart.

Polanyi, Karl, 1957, The Economy as instituted process. In K. Polanyi, C. M. Armstrong, and H. W. Pearson, eds., *Trade and Market in the Early Empires*, pp. 243–270. Chicago: Henry Regnery.

Polanyi, Karl and Abraham Rotstein, 1966, *Dahomey and the Slave Trade; An Analysis of an Archaic Economy.* Monographs of the American Ethnological Society 42. Seattle: University of Washington Press.

Polanyi, Karl, Conrad M. Arensberg, and Harry W. Pearson eds., 1957, *Trade and Market in the Early Empires; Economies in History*, Glencoe, IL: Free Press.

Polhemus, Richard R., 1987, *The Toqua Site—40MR6: A Late Mississippian, Dallas phase town.* Publications in Anthropology 44, Nashville: Vanderbilt University.

Polhemus, Richard R., 1990, Dallas phase architecture and sociopolitical structure. In *Lamar Archaeology: Mississippian Chiefdoms in the Deep South*, Mark Williams and G. Shapiro, eds., pp. 125–138. Tuscaloosa: University of Alabama Press.

Porter, James W., 1969, The Mitchell site and prehistoric exchange systems at Cahokia A.D. 1000±300. In M. L. Fowler, ed., *Explorations into Cahokia Archaeology*, pp. 137–164. Illinois Archaeological Survey Bulletin 7, Urbana: Illinois Archaelogical Series.

Postan, M. M., 1975, *The Medieval Economy and Society: An Economic History of Britain in the Middle Ages.* New York: Penguin Books.

Potter, Stephen R., 1993, *Commoners, Tribute, and Chiefs: The Development of Algonquian Culture in the Potomac Valley.* Charlottesville: University Press of Virginia.

Powell, Mary Lucas, 1988, *Status and Health in Prehistory: A Case Study of the Moundville Chiefdom.* Washington, DC: Smithsonian Institution Press.

Powell, Mary Lucas, 1992a, Health and disease in the Late Prehistoric Southeast. In John W. Verrano and D. H. Ubelaker, eds., *Disease and Demography in the Americas*, pp. 41–53. Washington, DC: Smithsonian Institution Press.

Powell, Mary Lucas, 1992b, In the best of health? Disease and trauma among the Mississippian elite. In Alex W. Barker and T. R. Pauketat, eds., *Lords of the Southeast: Social Inequality and the Native Elites of Southeastern North America*, pp. 81–97. Archeological Paper No. 3 of the American Anthropological Association.

Powell, Mary Lucas, P. S. Bridges, A. M. W. Mires, eds., 1991, *What Mean These Bones? Studies in Southeastern Bioarchaeology.* Tuscaloosa: University of Alabama Press.

Prentice, Guy, 1983, Cottage industries: Concepts and implications. *Midcontinental Journal of Archaeology* 8(1):17–48.

Prentice, Guy, 1985, Economic differentiation among Mississippian farmsteads. *Midcontinental Journal of Archaeology* 10(1):77–122.

Prentice, Guy, 1986, An analysis of the symbolism expressed by the Birger figurine. *American Antiquity* 51(2):239–266.

Prentice, Guy, 1987, Marine shells as wealth items in Mississippian societies. *Midcontinental Journal of Archaeology* 12:193–223.

Preucel, Robert W., ed., 1991, *Processual and Postprocessual Archaeologies: Multiple Ways of Knowing the Past.*, Occasional Paper No. 10, Center for Archaeological Investigations, Southern Illinois University at Carbondale.

Priestley, Herbert Ingram, ed. and trans., 1928, *The Luna Papers: Documents Relating to the Expedition of Don Tristan de Luna y Arellano for the Conquest of la Florida in 1559–1561*, 2 volumes. Deland: Florida State Historical Society.

Priestley, Herbert Ingram, 1936, *Tristán de Luna: Conquistador of the Old South, A Study of Spanish Imperial Strategy.* Glendale, CA: Arthur H. Clark Co.

Pring, Martin, 1603, A Voyage Set Out from the Citie of Bristoll, 1603. In Henry S. Burrage, ed., [1932] *Early English and French Voyages, Chiefly from Hakluyt, 1534—1608*, pp. 345–352, Original Narratives of Early American History. New York: Charles Scribner's Sons.

Pulliam, Christopher B., 1987, Middle and Late Woodland horticultural practices in the western margin of the Mississippi River Valley. In W. F. Keegan, ed., *Emergent Horticultural Economies of the Eastern Woodlands*, pp. 185–199. Occasional Paper No. 7, Center for Archaeological Investigations, Southern Illinois University at Carbondale.

Quimby, George I., 1962, A year with a Chippewa family, 1763–1764. *Ethnohistory* 9(3):217–239.

Quitmyer, Irvy R., H. S. Hale, and D. S. Jones, 1985, Paleoseasonality determination based on incremental shell growth in the hard clam, *Mercenaria mercenaria*, and its implications for the analysis of three Georgia coastal shell middens. *Southeastern Archaeology* 4(1):27–40.

Rackerby, Frank, and Jon Muller, 1971, The Kincaid site and its environs. Unpublished Mss. prepared for *Mounds and Villages of Southern Illinois.*

Ramenofsky, Ann F., 1987, *Vectors of Death: The Archaeology of European Contact.* Albuquerque: University of New Mexico Press.

Ramenofsky, Ann F., 1990, Loss of innocence: Explanations of differential persistence in the sixteenth-century Southeast. In David H. Thomas, ed., *Archaeological and Historical Perspectives on the Spanish Borderlands East: Columbian Consequences*, Vol. 2 , pp. 31–48. Washington, DC: Smithsonian Institution Press.

Rankin, Robert L., 1993, Language affiliations of some de Soto Place names in Arkansas. In Gloria Young and Michael Hoffman, eds., *The Expedition of Hernando de Soto West of the Mississippi, 1541–1543. Proceedings of the De Soto Symposia, 1988 and 1990*, pp. 210–226. Fayetteville: University of Arkansas Press.

Rappaport, Roy, 1971, The flow of energy in an agricultural society. *Scientific American* 225:116–133.

Rappaport, Roy, 1984, *Pigs for the Ancestors: Ritual in the Ecology of a New Guinea People.* New, enlarged ed. [original 1968]. New Haven, CT: Yale University Press.

Redman, Charles R., 1977, The "analytical individual" and prehistoric style variability. In J. Hill and J. Gunn, eds., *The Individual in Prehistory: Studies of Variability in Style in Prehistoric Technologies*, pp. 41–53. New York: Academic Press.

Reidhead, Van A., 1981, *A Linear Programming Model of Prehistoric Subsistence Optimization: A Southeastern Indiana Example.* Prehistory Research Series 6(1). Indianapolis: Indiana Historical Society.

Renfrew, Colin, 1972, *The Emergence of Civilization: The Cyclades and the Aegean in the Third Millennium B.C.* London: Methuen.

Renfrew, Colin, 1975, Trade as action at a distance: Questions of integration and communication. In J. Sabloff and C. Lamberg-Karlovsky, eds., *Ancient Civilization and Trade*, pp. 3–59. School of American Research Advanced Seminar Series. Albuquerque: University of New Mexico Press.

Renfrew, Colin, 1982, Polity and power: Intensification and exploitation. In C. Renfrew and M. Wagstaff, eds., *An Island Polity: The Archaeology of Exploitation in Melos*, Cambridge, UK: Cambridge University Press.

Ribault, Jean, 1562, The true and last discoverie of Florida. In Hakluyt 1582:79–98 also in [1881] Barnard Shipp, ed., *The History of Hernando de Soto and Florida.* pp. 495–509. Philadelphia: Robert M. Lindsay. [Facsimile reprint Kraus 1971]

Ricardo, David, 1821, *On the Principles of Political Economy and Taxation,* 3rd ed. London: John Murray [Goldsmith's-Kress Library Of Economic Literature No. 23131]. [1st ed., 1817, Goldsmith's-Kress Library of Economic Literature No. 21734]

Rice, Prudence M., 1981, Evolution of specialized pottery production: A trial model. *Current Anthropology* 22(3):219–240.

Rice, Prudence M., 1989, Ceramic diversity, production and use. In R. D. Leonard and G. T. Jones, eds., *Quantifying Diversity in Archaeology,* pp. 109–117. Cambridge, UK: Cambridge University Press.

Richards, Audrey I., 1961, *Land, Labour and Diet in Northern Rhodesia: An Economic Study of the Bemba Tribe,* 2nd. ed. International African Institute. London: Oxford University Press.

Riley, Thomas J., 1987, Ridged-field agriculture and the Mississippian economic pattern. In W. F. Keegan, ed., *Emergent Horticultural Economies of the Eastern Woodlands,* pp. 295–304. Occasional Paper No. 7, Center for Archaeological Investigations, Southern Illinois University at Carbondale.

Rindos, David, 1984, *The Origins of Agriculture: An Evolutionary Perspective.* Orlando: Academic Press.

Riordan, Robert, 1975, *Ceramics and chronology: Mississippian settlement in the Black Bottom, Southern Illinois.* Ph.D. dissertation. Department of Anthropology, Southern Illinois University at Carbondale.

Robinson, R.K., 1976, *Social status, stature and pathology at Chucalissa (40SY1), Shelby County, Tennessee.* M.A. thesis, University of Tennessee, Knoxville.

Roemer, John E., 1981, *Analytical Foundations of Marxian Economic Theory.* Cambridge, UK: Cambridge University Press.

Rogers, J. Daniel, 1991, Patterns of change on the western margin of the Southeast, A.D. 600—900. In M. S. Nassaney and C. R. Cobb, eds., *Stability, Transformation, and Variation: The Late Woodland Southeast,* pp. 221–258. New York: Plenum Press.

Rogers, J. Daniel and B. Smith, eds., 1995, *Mississippian Communities and Households.* Tuscaloosa: University of Alabama Press.

Rolingson, Martha A., 1990, The Toltec Mounds site: A ceremonial center in the Arkansas River Lowland. In B. Smith, ed., *The Mississippian Emergence,* pp. 27–49. Washington, DC: Smithsonian Institution Press.

Romans, Bernard, 1775, *A Concise Natural History of East and West Florida.* New York: Author. [Facsimile ed., 1962, Gainesville: University of Florida Press]

Rose, J.C., 1973, *Analysis of dental micro-defects of prehistoric populations from Illinois.* Ph.D. dissertation, Amherst: University of Massachusetts.

Rose, J.C., 1977, Defective enamel histology of prehistoric teeth from Illinois. *American Journal of Physical Anthropology* 46:439–446.

Rosenberg, Michael, 1990, The mother of invention: Evolutionary theory, territoriality, and the origins of agriculture. *American Anthropologist* 92(2):399–415.

Rosenberg, Michael, 1994, Pattern, process, and hierarchy in the evolution of culture. *Journal of Anthropological Archaeology* 13:307–340.

Rosier, George, 1605, A True Relation of the most prosperous Voyage made this present yeere 1605, by Captaine George Waymouth... In Henry S. Burrage, ed., [1932] *Early English and French Voyages, Chiefly from Hakluyt, 1534—1608.* pp. 357–394, Original Narratives of Early American History. New York: Charles Scribner's Sons.

Rothschild, Nan A., 1979, Mortuary Behavior and Social Organization at Indian Knoll and Dickson Mounds. *American Antiquity* 44:658–675.

Rountree, Helen C., ed., 1993, *Powhatan Foreign Relations, 1500–1722.* Charlottesville: University Press of Virginia. [970.5P8881]

Rountree, Helen C. and E. R. Turner III, 1994, On the Fringe of the Southeast: The Powhatan paramount chiefdom in Virginia. In C. Hudson and C. C. Tesser, eds., *The Forgotten Centuries: Indians and Europeans in the American South, 1521–1704,* pp. 355–372. Athens: University of Georgia Press.

Rudolph, James L., 1984, Earth lodges and platform mounds: Changing public architecture in the Southeastern United States. *Southeastern Archaeology* 3(1):33–45.

Rudolph, Teresa Perry, 1981, *The distribution of Late Woodland sites in the Black Bottom area, Pope and Massac Counties, Illinois.* Unpublished M.A. Thesis, Department of Anthropology, Southern Illinois University at Carbondale.

Rudolph, Teresa, Perry, 1991, The Late Woodland "Problem" in North Georgia. In M. S. Nassaney and C. R. Cobb, eds., *Stability, Transformation, and Variation: The Late Woodland Southeast*, pp. 259–283. New York: Plenum Press.

Rudra, Ashok, 1988, Pre-capitalist modes of production in non-european societies. *Journal of Peasant Studies* 15(3):373–394.

Rue, Leonard Lee III, 1968, *Sportsman's Guide to Game Animals: A Field Book of North American Species.* New York: Harper & Row.

Rye, O. S., 1976, Keeping your temper under control: Materials and the manufacture of Papuan pottery. *Archaeology and Physical Anthropology in Oceania* 11(2):106–137.

Sahlins, Marshall, 1968, *Tribesmen.* Englewood Cliffs, NJ: Prentice-Hall.

Sahlins, Marshall, 1972, *Stone-Age Economics.* Chicago: Aldine.

Sahlins, Marshall, and Elman R. Service, eds., 1960, *Evolution and Culture.* Ann Arbor: University of Michigan Press.

Saitta, Dean J., 1988, Marxism, prehistory, and primitive communism. *Rethinking Marxism* 1:145–168.

Saitta, Dean J., 1991, Radical theory and the processual critique. In R. Preucel, ed., *Processual and Postprocessual Archaeologies: Multiple Ways of Knowing the Past*, pp. 54–59. Occasional Paper No. 10, Center for Archaeological Investigations, Southern Illinois University at Carbondale.

Saitta, Dean J., 1994, Agency, Class, and Archaeological Interpretation. *Journal of Anthropological Archaeology* 13:201–227.

Sanders, William T. and Barbara J. Price, 1968, *Mesoamerica: The Evolution of a Civilization.* New York: Random House.

Santeford, Lawrence, 1982, *Mississippian political organization and chipped stone artifacts: A typological model for the study of a prehistoric society in Southern Illinois.* Ph.D. dissertation, Department of Anthropology, Southern Illinois University at Carbondale.

Sattenspiel, Lisa and Henry Harpending, 1983, Stable populations and skeletal age. *American Antiquity* 48(3):489–498.

Sayer, Derek, 1987, *The Violence of Abstraction: The Analytic Foundations of Historical Materialism.* Oxford, UK: Basil Blackwell.

Scarry, C. Margaret, ed., 1993, *Foraging and Farming in the Eastern Woodlands.* Gainesville: University of Florida Press.

Scarry, C. Margaret and Lee Newsom, 1992, Archaeobotanical research in the Calusa homeland. In William Marquardt, ed., with the assistance of C. Payne, *Culture and Environment in the Domain of the Calusa*, pp. 375–401. Institute of Archaeology and Paleoenvironmental Studies, Monograph 1, Gainesville: University of Florida Press.

Scarry, John F., 1990, Mississippian emergence in the Fort Walton area: The evolution of the Cayson and Lake Jackson phases. In B. Smith, ed., *The Mississippian Emergence*, pp. 227–250. Washington, DC: Smithsonian Institution Press.

Scarry, John F., 1994, The Apalachee chiefdom: A Mississippian society on the fringe of the Mississippian world. In C. Hudson and C. C. Tesser, eds., *The Forgotten Centuries: Indians and Europeans in the American South, 1521–1704*, pp. 156–178. Athens: University of Georgia Press.

Scarry, John F. and B. G. McEwan, 1995, Domestic architecture in Apalachee Province: Apalachee and Spanish residential styles in the Late Prehistoric and Early Historic Period Southeast. *American Antiquity* 60(3):482–495.

Schnell, Frank T. V. Knight, Jr., and G. Schnell, 1981, *Cemochechobee: Archaeology of a Mississippian Ceremonial Center on the Chattachoochee River.* Gainesville: University of Florida Press.

Schoeninger, Margaret J. and C. S. Peebles, 1981, Notes on the relationship between social status and diet at Moundville. *Southeastern Archaeological Conference Bulletin* 24:96–97.

Schoeninger, Margaret J. and M. R. Schurr, 1994a, Interpreting carbon stable isotope ratios. In Sissel Johannessen and C.A. Hastorf, eds., *Corn and Culture in the Prehistoric New World*, pp. 55–66. Boulder, CO: Westview Press.

Schoeninger, Margaret J. and M. R. Schurr, 1994b, Human subsistence at Moundville: The stable isotope data. In V.J. Knight, Jr., and V. P. Steponaitis, eds., *Moundville Revisited.*

Schoolcraft, Henry R., 1851–1857 *Information Respecting the History, Condition and Prospects of the Indian Tribes of the United States: Collected and Prepared under the Direction of the Bureau of Indian Affairs, per Act of Congress of March 3d, 1847.* Parts I-VI. Philadelphia: Grambo & Co., Lippincott.

Schroedl, Gerald F. and C. Clifford Boyd, Jr., 1991, Late Woodland Period culture in east Tennessee. In M. S. Nassaney and C. R. Cobb, eds., *Stability, Transformation, and Variation: The Late Woodland Southeast*, pp. 69–90. New York: Plenum Press.

Schroedl, Gerald E., C. Clifford Boyd, Jr., and R. P. Stephen Davis, Jr., 1990, Explaining Mississippian origins in east Tennessee. In B. Smith, ed., *The Mississippian Emergence*, pp. 175–196. Washington, DC: Smithsonian Institution Press.

Schurr, Mark R. and Margaret J. Schoeninger, 1995, Associations between agricultural intensification and social complexity: An example from the Ohio Valley. *Journal of Anthropological Archaeology* 14(3):315–339.

Scudder, Thayer, 1962, *The Ecology of the Gwembe Tonga*. Kariba Studies, Vol. 2. Manchester, UK: Manchester University Press.

Sears, W. H., 1961, The study of social and religious systems in North American archaeology. *Current Anthropology* 12:223–246.

Sears, W. H., 1968, The state and settlement patterns in the New World. In K. C. Chang, ed., *Settlement Archaeology*, pp. 134–153, Palo Alto, CA: National Press Books.

Sebastian, Lynne, 1992, *The Chaco Anasazi: Sociopolitical Evolution in the Prehistoric Southwest*. Cambridge, UK: Cambridge University Press.

Seeman, Mark F., 1979, Feasting with the dead: Ohio charnel house ritual as a context for redistribution. In D. Brose and N. Greber, eds., *Hopewell Archaeology: The Chillicothe Conference*, pp. 39–46. Kent, OH: Kent State University Press.

Sellers, George Escol, 1877, Aboriginal pottery of the Salt-Springs, Illinois. *Popular Science Monthly* 11:573–585.

Service, Elman R., 1962, *Primitive Social Organization: An Evolutionary Perspective*. New York: Random House.

Service, Elman R., 1975, *Origins of the State and Civilization: The Process of Cultural Evolution*. New York: W. W. Norton.

Sherman, William T., 1891, *Memoirs of Gen. W. T. Sherman*, 4th ed. New York: Charles L. Webster & Co.

Shipman, Pat, 1981, *Life History of a Fossil: An Introduction to Taphonomy and Paleoecology*. Cambridge, MA: Harvard University Press.

Shipp, Barnard B., 1881, *The History of Hernando de Soto and Florida; or Record of the Events of Fifty-Six Years, from 1512 to 1568*. Philadelphia: Robert Lindsay.

Shott, Michael J., 1993, Spears, darts, and arrows: Late Woodland hunting techniques in the Upper Ohio Valley. *American Antiquity* 58(3):425–443.

Silverburg, Robert, 1968, *Mound Builders of Ancient America: The Archaeology of a Myth*. Greenwich, CT: New York Graphic Society.

Smith, Adam, 1776, *An Inquiry into the Nature and Causes of the Wealth of Nations*. London: for W. Strahan and T. Cadell.

Smith, Bruce D., 1974, Middle Mississippian exploitation of animal populations: A predictive model. *American Antiquity* 74:274–291.

Smith, Bruce D., 1975, *Middle Mississippian Exploitation of Animal Populations*. Anthropological Papers 57, Museum of Anthropology, University of Michigan.

Smith, Bruce D., ed., 1978a, *Mississippian Settlement Patterns*. New York: Academic Press.

Smith, Bruce D., 1978b, Variation in Mississippian settlement patterns. In B. D. Smith, ed., *Mississippian Settlement Patterns*, pp. 479–503. New York: Academic Press.

Smith, Bruce D., 1978c, *Prehistoric Patterns of Human Behavior: A Case Study in the Mississippi Valley*. New York: Academic Press.

Smith, Bruce D., 1981, The Division of Mound Exploration of the Bureau of (American) Ethnology and the birth of American archaeology. *Southeastern Archaeological Conference, Bulletin* 24:51–54.

Smith, Bruce D., 1984a, Mississippian expansion: Tracing the historical development of an explanatory model. *Southeastern Archaeology* 3(1):13–32.

Smith, Bruce D., 1984b, Chenopodium as a prehistoric domesticate in Eastern North America: Evidence from Russell Cave, Alabama. *Science* 226:165–167.

Smith, Bruce D., 1987, The independent domestication of indigenous seed-bearing plants in Eastern North America. In W. F. Keegan, ed., *Emergent Horticultural Economies of the Eastern Woodlands*, pp. 3–47.

Occasional Paper No. 7, Center for Archaeological Investigations, Southern Illinois University at Carbondale.

Smith, Bruce D., ed., 1990, *The Mississippian Emergence*. Washington, DC: Smithsonian Institution Press.

Smith, Bruce D., 1992, *Rivers of Change: Essays on Early Agriculture in Eastern North America*. Washington, DC: Smithsonian Institution Press.

Smith, Bruce D., 1995, The analysis of single household Mississippian settlements. In Rogers, J. D. and B. Smith, eds., *Mississippian Communities and Households*, pp. 224–249. Tuscaloosa: University of Alabama Press.

Smith, Bruce D., W. Cowan and M. Hoffman, 1992, Is it an indigene or a foreigner? In Bruce D. Smith, ed., *Rivers of Change: Essays on Early Agriculture in Eastern North America*, pp. 67–100. Washington, DC: Smithsonian Institution Press.

Smith, Buckingham (trans.), 1866, *Narratives of the Career of Hernando De Soto in the Conquest of Florida as Told by a Knight of Elvas and in a Relation by Luys Hernandez de Biedma, Factor of the Expedition*. New York: Bradford Club. [Translation of Gentleman of Elvas (Fidalgo Deluas), 1557, *Relaçam verdadeira dos trabalhos q ho gouernador dõ Fernãndo de souto e certos fidalgos portugueses passarom no descubriméto da prouincia da Frolida. Agora nouaméte feita per hú fidalgo Deluas.*]

Smith, John, 1612, *A Map of Virginia, with a Description of the Country, the Commodities, People, Government and Religion*. Oxford: Joseph Barnes. [Also 1969, in Philip L. Barbour, ed., *The Jamestown Voyages under the First Charter: 1606–1609*, Hakluyt Society Second Series 136, pp. 327–464. Cambridge, UK: Cambridge University Press]

Smith, John, 1624, *The Generall Historie of Virginia, New-England, and the Summer Isles...* London: Michael Sparkes. [Facsimile reprint 1966, Readex Microprint]

Smith, Maria O., 1986, Caries frequency and distribution in the Dallas skeletal remains from Toqua (40MR6), Monroe County, Tennessee. *Tennessee Anthropologist* 11(2):145–155.

Smith, Maria O., 1987, Pattern of antemortem tooth loss between selected aboriginal population of the Tennessee Valley Area. *Tennessee Anthropologist* 12(2):128–138.

Smith, Marvin T., 1987, *Archaeology of Aboriginal Culture Change in the Interior Southeast: Depopulation during the Early Historic Period*. Gainesville: University of Florida/Florida State Museum.

Smith, Marvin T., 1989, Indian responses to European contact: The Coosa example. In J. T. Milanich and S. Milbrath, eds., *First Encounters: Spanish Explorations in the Caribbean and the United States, 1492–1570*, pp. 135–149. Gainesville: University of Florida Press.

Smith, Marvin T., 1994, Aboriginal depopulation in the postcontact Southeast. In C. Hudson and C. C. Tesser, eds., *The Forgotten Centuries: Indians and Europeans in the American South, 1521–1704*, pp. 257–275. Athens: University of Georgia Press.

Smith, Marvin T. and David J. Hally, 1992, Chiefly behavior: Evidence from sixteenth-century Spanish accounts. In Alex W. Barker, and T. R. Pauketat, eds., *Lords of the Southeast: Social Inequality and the Native Elites of Southeastern North America*, Archeological Papers of the American Anthropological Association, No. 3, pp. 99–109.

Snow, Dean R., 1995, Microchronology and demographic evidence relating to the size of pre-Columbian North American Indian populations. *Science* 268:1601–1604.

Snow, Dean R. and Kim M. Lanphear, 1989, More methodological perspectives: A rejoinder of Dobyns. *Ethnohistory* 36:299–304.

Snyder, J. F., 1910, Prehistoric Illinois: The primitive flint industry. *Journal of the Illinois State Historical Society* 3(2):11–25.

Sobolik, Kirsten, ed., 1994, *Paleonutrition: The Diet and Health of Prehistoric Americans*. Occasional Paper No. 22, Center for Archaeological Investigations, Southern Illinois University at Carbondale.

Solo, Robert A., 1967, *Economic Organization and Social Systems*. Indianapolis: Bobbs-Merrill Co.

Southall, Aidan, 1965, Typology of states and political systems. In M. Banton, ed., *Political Systems and the Distribution of Power*, pp. 113–140. London: Frederick A. Praeger.

Southall, Aidan, 1988, On mode of production theory: The foraging mode of production and the kinship mode of production. *Dialectical Anthropology* 12:165–192.

Spencer, Charles, 1990, On the tempo and mode of state formation: Neoevolutionism reconsidered. *Journal of Anthropological Archaeology* 9:1–30.

Spielbauer, Ronald, 1976, *Chert resources and aboriginal chert utilization in western Union County, Illinois*. Ph.D. dissertation. Department of Anthropology, Southern Illinois University at Carbondale.

Stalin, Joseph, 1938, *Dialectical and Historical Materialism*. New York: International Publishers. [also in 1976, J. V. Stalin, *Problems of Leninism*, Peking: Foreign Languages Press]

Stark, Barbara L., 1986, Perspectives on the peripheries of Mesoamerica. In F. J. Mathien and R. H. McGuire, eds., *Ripples in the Chichimec Sea*, pp. 270–290. Carbondale: Southern Illinois University Press.

St. Cosme, Jean Francois Buisson de, 1699, Letter to the Bishop of Quebec. In J. D. G. Shea, ed., [1861] *Early Voyages Up and Down the the Mississippi Valley, by Cavelier, St. Cosme, Le Sueur, Gravier, and Guignas*, pp. 45–75. Albany, NY: Joel Munsell.

Ste. Croix, Geoffrey de, 1984, Class in Marx's conception of history, ancient and modern. *New Left Review* 146:94–111.

Stein, Gil J., 1995, *World systems theory and alternative modes of interaction in the archaeology of culture contact*. Paper presented at the Studies in Culture Contact: Interaction, Culture Change, and Archaeology Visiting Scholars Conference, Center for Archaeological Investigations, Carbondale, IL.

Steinbock, R. T., 1976, *Paleopathological Diagnosis and Interpretation*. Springfield, Illinois: Charles C. Thomas.

Stephens, Jeanette E., 1982, *The Mississippian household: Ethnohistorical and archaeological perspectives*. Paper presented at the 39th Annual Meeting of the Southeastern Archaeological Conference, Memphis, TN.

Stephens, Jeanette E., 1993, Settlement plans and community social interaction: An example from the Knoebel site in Southwestern Illinois. *Illinois Archaeology* 5:344–354.

Stephens, Jeanette E., 1995, *An Archaeological Survey of Dogtooth Bend on the Mississippi River in Alexander County, Illinois*. St. Louis District Historic Properties Management Report No. 45, U. S. Army Corps of Engineers, St. Louis District.

Steponaitis, Vincas P., 1981, Settlement hierarchies and political complexity in nonmarket societies: The formative period of the Valley of Mexico. *American Anthropologist* 83:320–363.

Steponaitis, Vincas P., 1983, *Ceramics, Chronology, and Community Patterns: An Archaeological Study at Moundville*. New York: Academic Press.

Steponaitis, Vincas P., 1991, Contrasting patterns of Mississippian development. In T. Earle, ed., *Chiefdoms: Power, Economy, and Ideology*, pp. 193–228. Cambridge, UK: Cambridge University Press.

Steponaitis, Vincas P., M. J. Blackman, and H. Neff, 1996, Large-scale patterns in the chemical composition of Mississippian pottery. *American Antiquity* 61:555–572.

Steward, Julian, 1955, *Theory of Culture Change: The Methodology of Multilinear Evolution*. Urbana: University of Illinois Press.

Steward, Julian H. and Louis C. Faron, 1959, *Native Peoples of South America*. New York: McGraw-Hill.

Stimmel, Carole, 1978, A preliminary report on the use of salt in shell tempered pottery of the Upper Mississippi Valley. *Wisconsin Archaeologist* 59(2):266–274.

Stoltman, James B., 1991a, Cahokia as seen from the peripheries. In James B. Stoltman, ed., *New Perspectives on Cahokia: Views from the Periphery*, pp. 349–354. Madison, WI: Prehistory Press.

Stoltman, James B., ed., 1991b, *New Perspectives on Cahokia: Views from the Periphery*. Madison, WI: Prehistory Press.

Strachey, William, 1612, *The Historie of Travell into Virginia Britania*. ms. in the Princeton University Library, published in 1953, Edited by Louis B. Wright and Virginia Freund. Hakluyt Society, Second Series, No. 103, London.

Sturtevant, William C., 1983, Tribe and state in the sixteenth and twentieth centuries. In Elisabeth Tooker, ed., *The Development of Political Organization in Native North America*, pp. 3–16. 1979 Proceedings of the American Ethnological Society. Washington, DC: American Ethnological Society.

Sullivan, Lynne P., 1987, The Mouse Creek household. *Southeastern Archaeology* 6:16–29.

Sullivan, Lynne P., 1995, Mississippian household and community organization in Eastern Tennessee. In J. D. Rogers and B. Smith, eds., *Mississippian Communities and Households*, pp. 99–123. Tuscaloosa: University of Alabama Press.

Swanton, John R., 1911, *Indian Tribes of the Lower Mississippi Valley and Adjacent Coast of the Gulf of Mexico*. Bureau of American Ethnology, Bulletin 43.

Swanton, John R., 1922, *Early History of the Creek Indians and Their Neighbors*. Bureau of American Ethnology, Bulletin 73.

Swanton, John R., 1928a, Social organization and social usages of the Indians of the Creek confederacy. *Bureau of American Ethnology, Annual Report* 42:23–472.

Swanton, John R., 1928b, Religious beliefs and medical practices of the Creek Indians. *Bureau of American Ethnology, Annual Report* 42:473–672.

Swanton, John R., 1928c, Aboriginal culture of the Southeast. *Bureau of American Ethnology, Annual Report* 42:673–726.

Swanton, John R., 1929, *Myths and Tales of the Southeastern Indians*. Bureau of American Ethnology, Bulletin 88.

Swanton, John R., 1939, *Final Report of the United States De Soto Expedition Commission*. Washington, DC: U.S. Government Printing Office. [Also 1985 reprint with new introductory material, Washington, DC: Smithsonian Institution Press]

Swanton, John R., 1942, *Source Material on the History and Ethnology of the Caddo Indians*. Bureau of American Ethnology, Bulletin 132.

Swanton, John R., 1946, *The Indians of the Southeastern United States*. Bureau of American Ethnology, Bulletin 137. [Reprint 1979, with some minor changes in illustrations, Washington, DC: Smithsonian Institution Press]

Swanton, John R., 1952, *The Indian Tribes of North America*. Bureau of American Ethnology, Bulletin 145. [Reprinted 1968, Washington, DC: Smithsonian Institution Press.]

Swedlund, Alan C., ed., 1975, *Population Studies in Archaeology and Biological Anthropology: A Symposium*. Memoir 30, Society of American Archaeology.

Tacitus, Cornelius, 98, *De origine et situ Germanorum*. Roma. [Latin and translation in 1970, Loeb Classical Library 35, Cambridge, MA: Harvard University Press; free translation in 1942, Moses Hadas, ed., *The Complete Works of Tacitus*. New York: The Modern Library.]

Taiz, Lincoln and Eduardo Zeiger, 1992, *Plant Physiology*. Redwood City, CA: Benjamin/Cummings.

Talon, Pierre and Jean-Baptiste Talon (Interrogations of), 1698, Interrogations faites à Pierre et Jean Talon, par ordre de M. le compte Pontchartrain, à leur arrivée de la Vera Cruz. In translation, 1987, as Voyage to the Mississippi throught the Gulf of Mexico in Robert S. Weddle, ed., *La Salle, the Mississippi, and the Gulf: Three Primary Documents*, pp. 225–258. College Station: Texas A&M University Press. [d'Iberville's extract (about 1/3 of original) 1878 in Pierre Margry, ed., *Découvertes et Établissement des Français dans l'Ouest et dans le Sud de l'Amérique Septentrionale (1614–1754). Troisième Partie (1669–1698)*, pp. 610–621. Paris: Imprimerie D. Jouast]

Thomas, Cyrus, 1894, *Report of the Mound Explorations of the Bureau of Ethnology*. Smithsonian Institution Bureau of Ethnology, 12th Annual Report, 1890–91, Washington, DC.

Thomas, David H., ed., 1990, *Columbian Consequences: Volume 2, Archaeological and Historical Perspectives on the Spanish Borderlands East*. Washington, DC: Smithsonian Institution Press.

Thomas, David H., ed., 1991, *Columbian Consequences: Volume 3, The Spanish Borderlands in Pan-American Perspective*. Washington, DC: Smithsonian Institution Press.

Thornton, Russell, 1987, *American Indian Holocaust and Survival*. Norman: University of Oklahoma Press.

Thornton, Russell with the assistance of C. W. Snipp and N. Breen, 1990, *The Cherokees: A Population History*. Lincoln: University of Nebraska Press.

Tonty, Henri de, 1682, Letter of Henri de Tonti, 23 Juillet 1682. In Marion A. Habig, [1934] *The Franciscan Père Marquette: A Critical Biography of Father Zénobe Membré, O. F. M., La Salle's Chaplain and Missionary Companion 1645 (ca.)–1689*, Franciscan Studies No. 13, pp. 215–229. New York: Joseph F. Wagner. [both French and English translation]

Tonty, Henri de, 1693, Memoir Sent in 1693, on the Discovery of the Mississippi and the Neighboring Nations by M. de la Salle from the Year 1678 to the Time of His Death, and by the Sieur de Tonty to the Year 1691. In *Collections of the Illinois State Historical Library* 1:128–164. [also in Isaac J. Cox, ed., *The Journeys of Rene Robert Cavelier, Sieur de LaSalle*, pp. 1–31. New York: Allerton]

Tonty, Henri de, 1702, Extract of a letter from M. de Tonti to M. d'Iberville, from the Chacta, March 14. (Extract by Claude de l'Isle). In Patricia K. Galloway, [1982], Henri de Tonti du village des Chacta, 1702: The beginning of the French alliance. In Patricia K. Galloway, ed., *La Salle and His Legacy: Frenchmen and Indians in the Lower Mississippi Valley*, pp. 168–172. Jackson: University Press of Mississippi.

Tosi, Maurizio, 1984, The notion of craft specialization and its representation in the archaeological record of early states in the Turanian Basin. In M. Spriggs, ed., *Marxist Perspectives in Archaeology*, pp. 22–52, Cambridge, UK: Cambridge University Press.

Trent, William, 1752, [1871] *Journal of Captain William Trent from Logstown to Pickawillany*, A.D. *1752..*, Alfred T. Goodman, editor. Cincinnati: Robt. Clarke & Co. [Facsimile reprint, Arno Press and *The New York Times* 1971]

Trigger, Bruce G., 1990, Monumental architecture: A thermodynamic explanation of symbolic behavior. *World Archaeology* 22:119–132.

Trigger, Bruce G., 1993, Marxism in contemporary Western archaeology. In M. Schiffer, ed., *Archaeological Method and Theory*, vol. 5, pp. 159–200. Tucson: University of Arizona Press.

Trotter, Mildred, and Goldine Gleser, 1958, A re-evaluation of estimation of stature based on measurements of stature taken during life and of long bones after death. *American Journal of Physical Anthropology* 16(1):79–123.

Turnbaugh, William A., 1979, Calumet ceremonialism as a nativistic response. *American Antiquity* 44(4):685–691.

Turner, Jonathan H., 1984, *Societal Stratification: A Theoretical Analysis*. New York: Columbia University Press.

Turner, Victor, 1957, *Schism and Continuity in an African Society*. Manchester, UK: Manchester University Press.

Tylor, E.B., 1865, *Researches into the Early History of Mankind and the Development of Civilization*. London: J. Murray.

Ubelaker, Douglas H., 1976, The sources and methodology for Mooney's estimates of North American Indian populations. In W. M. Deneven, ed., *The Native Population of the Americas in 1492*, pp. 243–288. Madison: University of Wisconsin Press.

Vander Leest, B. J., 1980, *The Ramey field, Cahokia surface collection: A functional analysis of spatial structure*. Ph.D. dissertation, Department of Anthropology, University of Wisconsin–Milwaukee.

van der Leeuw, Sander, 1981, Preliminary report on the analysis of Moundville phase ceramic technology. *Southeastern Archaeological Conference Bulletin* 24:105–108.

Varner, John G. and J. J. Varner, trans. and eds., 1951, *The Florida of the Inca...* Austin: University of Texas Press.

Verrano, John W. and D.H. Ubelaker, eds., 1992, *Disease and Demography in the Americas*. Washington, DC: Smithsonian Institution Press.

Verrazano, Giovanni [Verazzani, Juan], 1524, Letter to the King of France, July 8, 1524. Historical Society of New York, 1841, trans. J. Cogswell [excerpts in Shipp 1881, pp. 81–92]

Vogt, E. Z., 1965, Structural and conceptual replication in Zincantan culture. *American Anthropologist* 63:346–358.

Waldrop, M. Mitchell, 1992, *Complexity: The Emerging Science at the Edge of Order and Chaos*. New York: Simon & Schuster.

Wallace, Donald L. and J.B. Fehrenbacher, 1969, *Soil Survey of Gallatin County, Illinois*. Illinois Agricultural Experiment Station Soil Report No. 87. Soil Conservation Service, U.S. Department of Agriculture, Washington, DC.

Walliman, Isidor, 1981, *Estrangement: Marx's Conception of Human Nature and the Division of Labor*. Westport, CT: Greenwood Press.

Walthall, J., 1980, *Prehistoric Indians of the Southeast: Archaeology of Alabama and the Middle South*. University: University of Alabama Press.

Waselkov, Gregory A., 1978, Evolution of deer hunting in the Eastern Woodlands. *Midcontinental Journal of Archaeology* 3(1):15–34.

Waselkov, Gregory A., 1989a, Indian maps of the Colonial Southeast. In Peter H. Wood, G. A. Waselkov, and M. T. Hatley, eds., *Powhatan's Mantle: Indians in the Colonial Southeast*, pp. 292–343. Lincoln: University of Nebraska Press.

Waselkov, Gregory A., 1989b, Seventeenth-century trade in the Colonial Southeast. *Southeastern Archaeology* 8(2): 117–131.

Watt, Bernice K., and Annabel L. Merrill, 1975, *Composition of Foods: Raw, Processed, Prepared*. Agricultural Research Service, Consumer and Food Economics Institute, Washington, DC: U. S. Dept. of Agriculture, [1975 reprint of the 1963 rev. ed.]

Webb, William S., 1952, *The Jonathan Creek Village, Site 4, Marshall County, Kentucky*. Reports in Anthropology No. 8, University of Kentucky, Lexington.

Weddle, Robert S., ed., 1987, *La Salle, the Mississippi, and the Gulf*. College Station, TX: Texas A&M University Press.

Weigand, Phil C., 1976, The aboriginal use of coal at the Kincaid site in Illinois. ms. in possession of the author.

Weiner, Annette, 1976, *Women of Value, Men of Renown*. Austin: University of Texas Press.

Weiss, Kenneth M., 1973, *Demographic Models for Anthropology*. Memoirs No. 27, Society for American Archaeology.

Weiss, Kenneth M., 1975, Demographic disturbance and the use of life tables in anthropology. In A.C. Swedlund, ed., *Population Studies in Archaeology and Biological Anthropology: A Symposium*, pp. 46–56. Memoir 30, Society of American Archaeology.

Weiss, Kenneth M., 1976, Demographic theory and anthropological inference. *Annual Review of Anthropology* 5:351–381.

Welch, Paul Daniel, 1986, *Models of chiefdom economy: Prehistoric Moundville as a Case Study*. Ph.D. dissertation, Department of Anthropology, University of Michigan, Ann Arbor, MI.

Welch, Paul Daniel, 1990, Mississippian emergence in west-central Alabama In B. Smith, ed., *The Mississippian Emergence*, pp. 197–225. Washington, DC: Smithsonian Institution Press.

Welch, Paul Daniel, 1991, *Monopolistic control over goods and the political stability of the Moundville chiefdom*. Paper presented at the Society for American Archaeology 55th Annual Meeting, New Orleans, LA.

Welch, Paul Daniel, 1991, *Moundville's Economy*. Tuscaloosa: University of Alabama Press.

Welch, Paul Daniel, 1995, *Strategies for control of craft production in chiefdoms*. Paper presented at the 59th Annual Meeting of the Society for American Archaeology, Minneapolis, MN.

Welch, Paul Daniel and C. M. Scarry, 1995, Status-related variation in foodways in the Moundville chiefdom. *American Antiquity* 60(3):397–419.

Wentowski, Gloria J., 1970, *Salt as an ecological factor in the prehistory of the Southeastern United States*. M.A. thesis, Department of Anthropology, University of North Carolina, Chapel Hill.

Wesler, Kit W., 1991, Ceramics, chronology, and horizon markers at Wickliffe mounds. *American Antiquity* 56:278–290.

Whitaker, Thomas W. and G. N. Davis, 1962, *Cucurbits: Botany, Cultivation, and Utilization*. New York: Interscience Publishers.

White, Leslie, 1943, Energy and the evolution of culture. *American Anthropologist* 45:335–356.

White, Leslie, 1959, *The Evolution of Culture*. New York: McGraw-Hill.

Whitecotton, Joseph and Richard A. Pailes, 1986, New World Precolumbian world systems. In F. J. Mathien and R. H. McGuire, eds., *Ripples in the Chichimec Sea: New Considerations of Southwestern–Mesoamerican Interactions*, pp. 183–204. Carbondale: Southern Illinois University Press.

Wickham, Chris, 1984, The other transition: From the ancient world to feudalism. *Past and Present* 103:3–36.

Wickham, Chris, 1985, The uniqueness of the East. *Journal of Peasant Studies* 12(2&3):166–196.

Widmer, Randolph J., 1988, *The Evolution of the Calusa: A Nonagricultural Chiefdom on the Southwest Florida Coast*. Tuscaloosa: University of Alabama Press.

Widmer, Randolph J., 1994, The structure of Southeastern chiefdoms. In C. Hudson and C. C. Tesser, eds., *The Forgotten Centuries: Indians and Europeans in the American South, 1521–1704*, pp. 125–155. Athens: University of Georgia Press.

Wiessner, Polly, 1974, A functional estimator of population from floor area. *American Antiquity* 39:343–350.

Wilk, Richard R., ed., 1989, *The Household Economy: Reconsidering the Domestic Mode of Production*. Boulder, CO: Westview Press.

Will, G. F. and G. E. Hyde, 1917, *Corn Among the Indians of the Upper Missouri*. St. Louis, MO: William H. Miner Co. [reprint 1964, Lincoln: University of Nebraska Press]

Willey, Gordon R., 1949a, *Archaeology of the Florida Gulf Coast*. Smithsonian Miscellaneous Collections 113. Washington, DC: Smithsonian Institution Press.

Willey, Gordon R., 1949b, The Southeastern United States and South America: A comparative statement. In J. W. Griffin, ed., *The Florida Indian and His Neighbors*, pp. 101–116. Winter Park, FL: Rollins College.

Willey, G. R. and J. A. Sabloff, 1980, *A History of American Archaeology*, 2nd Edition. San Francisco: W.H. Freeman.

Williams, John L., 1837, *The Territory of Florida; or Sketches of the Topography, Civil and Natural History of the Country*. New York: A. T. Goodrich. [Facsmile, 1962, Gainesville: University of Florida Press]

Williams, J. R., 1974, The Baytown phases in the Cairo Lowland of Southeast Missouri. *Missouri Archaeologist 36* (whole issue).

Williams, Mark and G. Shapiro, eds., 1990, *Lamar Archaeology: Mississippian Chiefdoms in the Deep South*. Tuscaloosa: University of Alabama Press.

Williams, Stephen, 1991, *Fantastic Archaeology: The Wild Side of North American Prehistory*. Philadelphia: University of Pennsylvania Press.

Williams, Stephen and Jeffrey P. Brain, 1983, *Excavations at the Lake George Site, Yazoo County, Mississippi*. Paper No. 74 of the Peabody Museum of Archaeology and Ethnology. Cambridge, MA: Harvard University.

Williams, Stephen and John M. Goggin, 1956, The long-nosed god mask in Eastern United States. *Missouri Archaeologist 18*(3):4–72.

Wing, Elizabeth S. and A. B. Brown, 1979, *Paleonutrition: Method and Theory in Prehistoric Foodways*. New York: Academic Press.

Winterhalder, Bruce, 1986, Diet choice, risk, and food sharing in a stochastic environment. *Journal of Anthropological Archaeology* 5:369–392.

Winterhalder, Bruce, W. Baillargeon, F. Cappelletto, I. Daniel, and C, Prescott, 1988, The Population ecology of hunter-gatherers and their prey. *Journal of Anthropological Archaeology* 7:289–328.

Wittfogel, Karl A., 1963, *Oriental Despotism*. New Haven, CT: Yale University Press.

Witthoft, John, 1949, *Green Corn Ceremonialism in the Eastern Woodlands*. Occasional Paper, No. 113, Museum of Anthropology, University of Michigan.

Wobst, H. Martin, 1977, Stylistic behavior and information exchange. In Charles Cleland, ed., *For the Director: Research Essays in Honor of James B. Griffin*, pp. 317–342. Anthropological Papers 61, University of Michigan, Museum of Anthropology, Ann Arbor, MI.

Wolf, Eric R., 1966, *Peasants*. Englewood Cliffs, NJ: Prentice-Hall.

Wolf, Eric R., 1982, *Europe and the People without History*. Berkeley and Los Angeles: University of California Press.

Wolf, Eric R., 1982, Materialists and mentalists: A review article. *Comparative Studies in Society and History* 24(1):148–152.

Wolff, Richard D. and S. Resnick, 1987, *Economics: Marxian versus Neoclassical*. Baltimore, MD: Johns Hopkins University Press.

Wood, W. Raymond, 1968, Mississippian hunting and butchering patterns: Bone from the Vista Shelter, 23SR-20, Missouri. *American Antiquity* 33:170–179.

Woods, William I., 1987, Maize agriculture and the Late Prehistoric: A characterization of settlement location strategies. In W. F. Keegan, ed., *Emergent Horticultural Economies of the Eastern Woodlands*, pp. 275–294. Occasional Paper No. 7, Center for Archaeological Investigations, Southern Illinois University at Carbondale.

Woods, William I., ed., 1992, *Late Prehistoric Agriculture: Observations from the Midwest*. Studies in Illinois Archaeology, No. 8. Illinois Historic Preservation Agency, Springfield.

Woodward, Henry, 1674, A faithfull relation of my Westoe voiage. in Alexander S. Salley, Jr., ed., 1911, *Narratives of Early Carolina, 1650-1708*, pp. 130–134, New York. [reprint 1967, New York: Barnes & Noble, Inc.]

Worth, John E., 1994, Late Spanish military expeditions in the interior Southeast, 1597–1628. In C. Hudson and C. C. Tesser, eds., *The Forgotten Centuries: Indians and Europeans in the American South, 1521–1704*, pp. 104–122. Athens: University of Georgia Press.

Wright, Henry T., 1977, Recent research on the origin of the state. *Annual Review of Anthropology* 6:379–397.

Wright, Henry T., 1984, Prestate political formations. In T. Earle, ed., *On the Evolution of Complex Societies: Essays in Honor of Henry Hoijer, 1982*, pp. 41–78. Malibu, CA: Undena Publications.

Wymer, Dee Anne, 1987, The Middle Woodland–Late Woodland interface in central Ohio: Subsistence continuity amid cultural change. In W. F. Keegan, ed., *Emergent Horticultural Economies of the Eastern Woodlands*, pp. 201–216. Occasional Paper No. 7, Center for Archaeological Investigations, Southern Illinois University at Carbondale.

Yarnell, Richard A., 1976, Early plant husbandry in Eastern North America. In C. E. Cleland, ed., *Culture Change and Continuity: Essays in Honor of James Bennett Griffin*, pp. 265–273. New York: Academic Press.

Yarnell, Richard A., 1994, Investigations relevant to the native development of plant husbandry in Eastern North America: A brief and reasonably true account. In W. Green, ed., *Agricultural Origins and Development in the Midcontinent*, pp. 7–24. Report No. 19, Office of the State Archaeologist, Iowa City, IA.

Yerkes, Richard W., 1983, Microwear, microdrills, and Mississippian craft specialization. *American Antiquity* 48:499–518.

Yerkes, Richard W., 1986, Licks, pans and chiefs: A comment on "Mississippian Specialization and Salt." *American Antiquity* 51(2):402–404.

Yerkes, Richard W., 1987, *Prehistoric Life on the Mississippi Floodplain; Stone tool use, Settlement, organization, and subsistence practices at the Labras Lake site.* Chicago: University of Chicago Press.

Yerkes, Richard W., 1989, Mississippian craft specialization on the American Bottom. *Southeastern Archaeology* 8:93–106.

Yerkes, Richard W., 1991, Specialization in shell artifact production at Cahokia. In J. B. Stoltman, ed., *New Perspectives on Cahokia: Views from the Periphery*, pp. 49–64. Madison, WI: Prehistory Press.

Yoffee, Norman, 1979, The decline and rise of Mesopotamian civilization: An ethnoarchaeological perspective on the evolution of social complexity. *American Antiquity* 44(1):5–35.

Yoffee, Norman, 1993, Too many chiefs? (or, Safe texts for the '90s). In N. Yoffee and A. Sherratt, eds., *Archaeological Theory: Who Sets the Agendas*, pp. 60–78. Cambridge, UK: Cambridge University Press.

Yoffee, Norman and Andrew Sherratt, 1993a, Introduction: The sources of archaeological theory. In *Archaeological Theory: Who Sets the Agenda?*, pp. 1–9. Cambridge, UK: Cambridge University Press.

Yoffee, Norman and Andrew Sherratt, eds., 1993b, *Archaeological Theory: Who Sets the Agenda?* Cambridge, UK: Cambridge University Press.

Young, Gloria A. and Michael P. Hoffman, eds., 1993, *The Expedition of Hernando de Soto West of the Mississippi, 1541–1543.* Proceedings of the De Soto Symposia, 1988 and 1990. Fayetteville: University of Arkansas Press.

Zavialov, P. S. (Petr Stepanovich), 1974, *Nauchno-tekhnicheskaia revoliutsiia i mezhdunarodnaia spetsializatsiia proizvodstva pri kapitalizme.* Moskva: Mysl.

Zinsser, Hans, 1963, *Rats, Lice and History.* Boston: Little, Brown and Co.

Zipf, G. K., 1949, *Human Behavior and the Principle of Least Effort.* New York: Hafner.

Index

Ortiz, Juan, 77, 81, 88–89
Oviedo y Valdés, Gonzalo Fernandez de, 70
Owen, Robert, 4

Pacaha, 78, 80, 84, 86, 388
Palisades, 205, 195, 220
Paracoxi, 77
Parasites, 18–19, 400
Pardo, Juan, 103–104
Part-time specialization, 289, 342, 346, 350, 362,
        391
Pathology, 142, 153–156, 158–160
Patofa, 94
Patronage, 49–50, 279, 295, 347–348
Patterson, Thomas, 10, 39fn
Pauketat, Timothy, ix, 10, 39, 48, 55, 116, 156,
        190, 289, 299, 342, 344–345, 352
Pearls, 85, 101, 102, 105, 248, 275, 396
Peasant, comparison to, 223–224, 280
Pecan: *see Carya*
Peebles, Christopher, 40, 47
Penny, JoAnne, 144, 149, 150
Peregrine, Peter, 345–346, 365
Periods, 117–118, 366
Persimmon (*Diospyros virginiana*), 238, 241
Petty, William, 3
Phalaris Caroliniana: *see* Maygrass
Physical characteristics, 142
    health, 158–162
    stature, 142, 389
Piache, 77, 82
Plague (*Yersinia pestis*), 158fn
Plant domestication, 122, 143f
Plog, Fred, 122
Polhemus, Richard, 185
Police, 191
Political economy, vii–viii, 1–2, 41–42, 385, 387
    not just "politics," vii–viii, 2
    of Mississippian, 42–52
Polities, 202
    size, 64, 88–90, 202–206, 221, 271
Polygonum spp. (pokeweed, smartweed), 127,
        238
    Polygonum erectum (Erect knotweed), 127
    as a possible domesticate, 241
Ponce de León, 69
Population
    complexity and, 201–202
    density, 133, 206–221, 223
    estimates of, 218–219
    growth, 26, 34, 130–134, 162–170
    historical, 193–199, 206–207
    Mississippian, 199–201, 208–221
    "pressure," 130–133, 389
    profiles, 161–165

Population dynamics, 125fn, 130, 130–134,
        161–162, 166–171, 172–180
    historical, 171–178
    Mississippian, 178–180
    preMississippian 125fn, 130–134
Porter, James, 48
Postprocessual archaeology, 23
Potano (≈ Patanou), 101–102
Poverty Point, 121, 122
Powell, Mary Lucas, 142, 153, 156, 158, 159, 161
Power, viii, 10, 13, 39, 55–56, 64, 68, 76, 77, 106,
        156–157, 275–276, 278, 346, 362, 381,
        383, 384, 395, 396
    and "voting with one's feet," 381
Powers Fort (Towasaghy) site, 229
Powhatan, 106, 268
Precapitalist systems, 10
Precedence, 78, 80, 102, 110
Prentice, Guy, 48, 289, 299, 342
Prestations, 14, 47, 49, 70, 78, 84–86, 86–87, 96,
        103–104, 263–264, 283, 362, 381, 384,
        396
    of food, 86–87, 96, 97, 101, 102, 103–104
    of "prestige goods," 96, 101, 102, 114
    of skins, 84, 87, 96, 100, 101, 102, 104, 114,
        248–249
Prestige goods, 17, 46, 85–86, 279, 290, 305, 340,
        346–347, 358, 380, 390, 391; *see also* Dis-
        play goods
Price, 5, 6
Primitive accumulation, 18, 259
Principales, 76, 79, 81–82, 102, 103, 112, 113,
        395, 397
    authority, 83, 103
    service, 82
Process, 22–24
Processual archaeology, viii, 23
Production
    agency, 286
    consumption and, 299–300, 318, 358
    continuity, 298
    cycles, 143, 394
    differentiation, 299
    dimensions of specialization in, 292–296,
        297–300
    domestic, 12, 33, 35, 37, 48, 61, 191, 286, 390,
        394–396, 400, 402
    elites, 125, 269, 270–271, 286, 395, 396, 400
    exchange, 300
    extent, 297
    intensity, 298
    leadership, 279–280
    level of effort, 265–267, 298
    local and dispersed, 281
    location, 286–287, 297–298

INTERDISCIPLINARY CONTRIBUTIONS TO ARCHAEOLOGY
Chronological Listing of Volumes

PREHISTORIC EXCHANGE SYSTEMS IN NORTH AMERICA
Edited by Timothy G. Baugh and Jonathon E. Ericson

STYLE, SOCIETY, AND PERSON
Archaeological and Ethnological Perspectives
Edited by Christopher Carr and Jill E. Neitzel

REGIONAL APPROACHES TO MORTUARY ANALYSIS
Edited by Lane Anderson Beck

DIVERSITY AND COMPLEXITY IN PREHISTORIC MARITIME SOCIETIES
A Gulf of Maine Perspective
Bruce J. Bourque

CHESAPEAKE PREHISTORY
Old Traditions, New Directions
Richard J. Dent, Jr.

PREHISTORIC CULTURAL ECOLOGY AND EVOLUTION
Insights from Southern Jordan
Donald O. Henry

STONE TOOLS
Theoretical Insights into Human Prehistory
Edited by George H. Odell

THE ARCHAEOLOGY OF WEALTH
Consumer Behavior in English America
James G. Gibb

STATISTICS FOR ARCHAEOLOGISTS
A Commonsense Approach
Robert D. Drennan

DARWINIAN ARCHAEOLOGIES
Edited by Herbert Donald Graham Maschner

CASE STUDIES IN ENVIRONMENTAL ARCHAEOLOGY
Edited by Elizabeth J. Reitz, Lee A. Newsom, and Sylvia J. Scudder

HUMANS AT THE END OF THE ICE AGE
The Archaeology of the Pleistocene–Holocene Transition
Edited by Lawrence Guy Straus, Berit Valentin Eriksen, Jon M. Erlandson,
and David R. Yesner

VILLAGERS OF THE MAROS
A Portrait of an Early Bronze Age Society
John M. O'Shea

HUNTERS BETWEEN EAST AND WEST
The Paleolithic of Moravia
Jiří Svoboda, Vojen Ložek, and Emanuel Vlček

MISSISSIPPIAN POLITICAL ECONOMY
Jon Muller